THE THEORY OF CRITICISM

THE THEORY OF CRITICISM

From Plato to the Present
A Reader

edited and introduced by
RAMAN SELDEN

LONGMAN
LONDON AND NEW YORK

Longman Group UK Limited,
Longman House, Burnt Mill, Harlow,
Essex CM20 2JE, England
and Associated Companies throughout the world.

Published in the United States of America
by Longman Inc., New York

First published 1988
Fifth impression 1992

British Library Cataloguing in Publication Data
The Theory of Criticism From Plato to the Present
A Reader
1. Criticism – History
I. Selden, Raman
801′.95′09   PN86

ISBN 0-582-01723-8   CSD
ISBN 0-582-00328-8   PPR

Library of Congress Cataloging in Publication Data
The Theory of criticism from Plato to the present.
    Bibliography: p.
    Includes index.
    1. Criticism.   I. Selden, Raman.
PN81.T43   1988   801′.95   87–16889
ISBN 0-582-01723-8
ISBN 0-582-00328-8 (pbk.)

Set in Linotron 202 10/12pt Baskerville

Produced by Longman Singapore Publishers (Pte) Ltd.
Printed in Singapore

CONTENTS

Preface		x
Acknowledgements		xi
INTRODUCTION		1
PART I:	REPRESENTATION	7
CHAPTER 1.	IMAGINATIVE REPRESENTATION	9
	(A) Plato	12
	(B) Plotinus	18
	(C) C. W. F. von Schlegel	21
	(D) Samuel Taylor Coleridge	24
	(E) Percy Bysshe Shelley	28
	(F) W. B. Yeats	31
	(G) R. G. Collingwood	35
	(H) Wallace Stevens	36
CHAPTER 2.	MIMESIS AND REALISM	40
	(A) Aristotle	45
	(B) Emile Zola	51
	(C) Erich Auerbach	56
	(D) Georg Lukács	59
	(E) Bertholt Brecht	66
	(F) Alain Robbe-Grillet	73
	(G) Roland Barthes	76
CHAPTER 3.	NATURE AND TRUTH	78
	(A) John Dryden	81
	(B) Alexander Pope	85
	(C) William Wordsworth	86
	(D) Samuel Johnson	89
	(E) William Blake	91

CHAPTER 4.   LANGUAGE AND REPRESENTATION   95

    (A)   Ben Jonson   99
    (B)   Francis Bacon   101
    (C)   Thomas Sprat   105
    (D)   John Locke   106
    (E)   Ernst Cassirer   111
    (F)   Ferdinand de Saussure   113
    (G)   Ludwig Wittgenstein   115
    (H)   J. L. Austin   120

PART II: SUBJECTIVITY   123

CHAPTER 1.   WIT, JUDGEMENT, FANCY AND IMAGINATION   125

    (A)   Thomas Hobbes   129
    (B)   Joseph Addison   133
    (C)   Alexander Pope   139
    (D)   Alexander Gerard   139
    (E)   Samuel Taylor Coleridge   142
    (F)   T. E. Hulme   146
    (G)   I. A. Richards   146

CHAPTER 2.   GENIUS: NATURE VS ART   150

    (A)   Longinus   153
    (B)   Joseph Addison   155
    (C)   Alexander Pope   157
    (D)   Edward Young   158
    (E)   William Hazlitt   161

CHAPTER 3.   EMOTIVE THEORIES   164

    (A)   Longinus   167
    (B)   John Dennis   169
    (C)   Joseph Warton   173
    (D)   William Wordsworth   175
    (E)   J. S. Mill   178
    (F)   I. A. Richards   182

CHAPTER 4.   SUBJECTIVE CRITICISM AND THE READER'S
           RESPONSE   186

    (A)   Aristotle   191
    (B)   John Dryden   191
    (C)   René Rapin   193
    (D)   G. E. Lessing   194
    (E)   I. A. Richards   195
    (F)   William Empson   196
    (G)   Leo Spitzer   197
    (H)   Georges Poulet   200
    (I)   E. D. Hirsch Jr   203

(J)	H. R. Jauss	205
(K)	Paul Ricoeur	211
(L)	Wolfgang Iser	214
(M)	Norman Holland	218
(N)	David Bleich	219

CHAPTER 5. UNCONSCIOUS PROCESSES   222

(A)	Sigmund Freud	225
(B)	Carl Jung	227
(C)	Maud Bodkin	231
(D)	Ernest Jones	235
(E)	Jacques Lacan	236
(F)	Julia Kristeva	238

PART III: FORM, SYSTEM AND STRUCTURE   243

CHAPTER 1. THE AESTHETIC DIMENSION   245

(A)	Immanuel Kant	247
(B)	Walter Pater	249
(C)	K. J. Huysmans	251
(D)	Oscar Wilde	252
(E)	Benedetto Croce	254
(F)	A. C. Bradley	256
(G)	Clive Bell	259
(H)	Jan Mukařovský	261
(I)	Fredric Jameson	265

CHAPTER 2. UNITY AND LITERARINESS   268

(A)	Aristotle	271
(B)	Samuel Taylor Coleridge	273
(C)	Viktor Shklovsky	274
(D)	T. E. Hulme	277
(E)	John Crowe Ransom	279
(F)	Allen Tate	283
(G)	Cleanth Brooks	285
(H)	Mark Schorer	286

CHAPTER 3. AMBIGUITY AND POLYSEMY   289

(A)	Dante	292
(B)	Mikhail Bakhtin	293
(C)	William Empson	295
(D)	Cleanth Brooks	297
(E)	Roland Barthes	299

CHAPTER 4. IMPERSONALITY AND THE 'DEATH' OF THE
AUTHOR   303

(A)	John Keats	306
(B)	Ezra Pound	307

(C)	T. S. Eliot	310
(D)	W. K. Wimsatt	314
(E)	Susanne Langer	316
(F)	Roland Barthes	318

CHAPTER 5. RHETORIC: STYLE AND POINT OF VIEW   321

(A)	Cicero	324
(B)	George Puttenham	327
(C)	Erich Auerbach	328
(D)	Richard Ohmann	333
(E)	Henry James	335
(F)	Wayne C. Booth	337

CHAPTER 6. STRUCTURE AND SYSTEM   343

(A)	Plato	348
(B)	Aristotle	350
(C)	Ferdinand de Saussure	351
(D)	Vladimir Propp	353
(E)	Northrop Frye	355
(F)	A.-J. Greimas	359
(G)	Gérard Genette	364
(H)	Roman Jakobson	367
(I)	David Lodge	371
(J)	Jonathan Culler	375

CHAPTER 7. STRUCTURE AND INDETERMINACY   380

(A)	Friedrich Nietzsche	383
(B)	Jacques Derrida	385
(C)	Paul de Man	390
(D)	Geoffrey H. Hartman	394
(E)	Barbara Johnson	397

PART IV: HISTORY AND SOCIETY   401

CHAPTER 1. TRADITION AND INTERTEXTUALITY   405

(A)	T. S. Eliot	408
(B)	E. R. Curtius	410
(C)	Raymond Williams	414
(D)	Harold Bloom	415
(E)	Julia Kristeva	417

CHAPTER 2. HISTORY   419

(A)	H. A. Taine	423
(B)	Arthur O. Lovejoy	426
(C)	E. M. W. Tillyard	428
(D)	Raymond Williams	431
(E)	Lucien Goldmann	434
(F)	Michel Foucault	437
(G)	Claudio Guillén	438

CHAPTER 3.   SOCIETY   441

    (A)   John Dennis   444
    (B)   Karl Marx   446
    (C)   Walter Benjamin   447
    (D)   Malcolm Bradbury   452

CHAPTER 4.   IDEOLOGY   455

    (A)   William Blake   457
    (B)   Friedrich Engels   458
    (C)   Louis Althusser   459
    (D)   Pierre Macherey   463
    (E)   Terry Eagleton   466

PART V: MORALITY, CLASS AND GENDER   469

CHAPTER 1.   MORALISM   473

    (A)   Plato   476
    (B)   Sir Philip Sidney   478
    (C)   Samuel Johnson   481
    (D)   Percy Bysshe Shelley   483
    (E)   John Ruskin   485
    (F)   A. A. Zhdanov   487
    (G)   David Holbrook   488

CHAPTER 2.   LITERATURE AND 'LIFE'   490

    (A)   Matthew Arnold   494
    (B)   Henry James   501
    (C)   D. H. Lawrence   505
    (D)   F. R. Leavis   509
    (E)   Lionel Trilling   516

CHAPTER 3.   CLASS AND GENDER   519

    (A)   Richard Hoggart   522
    (B)   Raymond Williams   526
    (C)   Francis Mulhern   530
    (D)   Virginia Woolf   532
    (E)   Simone de Beauvoir   533
    (F)   Elaine Showalter   537
    (G)   Hélène Cixous   541

INDEX   544

PREFACE

The original inspirer of my interest in literary theory was John Oakley of Portsmouth Polytechnic. My debt to him is incalculable, though I do not associate him in any way with the shortcomings of this book. The earliest version of the anthology was produced for the uncomplaining students of English at the University of Durham in 1972. I am grateful to those students who expressed interest in the material during the 1970s and gave me the motivation to develop it and bring it up to date in later years. Jonathan Culler and MacDonald Emslie wrote generously about the anthology in 1974 and it was not their fault that no publisher saw a market for it then. I would like to thank them belatedly for their efforts on my behalf. I am grateful too to the publishers, Longman UK, for easing the book's passage through the laborious process of publication with such efficiency and good humour. Finally, I would like to thank David Carroll, Simon Parker, and Michael Wheeler for their assistance in checking the proofs and Phil Payne for assisting with translation.

Lancaster, September 1987

The Publishers regret to record that Raman Selden died after a short illness in May 1991 at the age of fifty-three. Ray Selden was a fine scholar and a lovely man. All those he has worked with will remember him with much affection and respect.

ACKNOWLEDGEMENTS

We are grateful to the following for permission to reproduce copyright material:

Edward Arnold (Publishers) Ltd for an abridged extract from *The Modes of Modern Writing: Metaphor, Metonymy, and the Typology of Modern Literature* by David Lodge; Associated Book Publishers (U.K.) Ltd for abridged extracts from 'The Genetic Structuralist Method in History of Literature' by Lucien Goldman, trans. A. Sheridan in *Towards a Sociology of the Novel*, Tavistock Publications 1985, and for *Theory of Literary Production* by Pierre Macherey, trans. G. Wall, Routledge & Kegan Paul plc 1978; Associated Book Publishers (U.K.) Ltd/Farrar Straus & Giroux Inc. for abridged extracts from 'Alienation in Chinese Acting' and 'The Popular and the Realistic' in *Brecht on Theatre* by Berthold Brecht, trans. John Willett, Methuen, London 1964, copyright © 1957, 1963 and 1964 by Suhrkamp Verlag, trans. copyright © 1964 by John Willett; Associated Book Publishers (U.K.) Ltd/Cornell University Press for abridged extracts from *Structuralist Poetics: Structuralism, Linguistics and the Study of Literature* by Jonathan Culler, Routledge & Kegan Paul plc, © Jonathan Culler 1975; Associated Book Publishers (U.K.) Ltd/Princeton University Press for abridged extracts from pp. 15,19, 79–80, & 82 of *European Literature and The Latin Middle Ages* by Ernst Robert Curtius, trans. Willard R. Trask, Routledge & Kegan Paul plc/Bollingen Series XXXVI, copyright 1953, © 1981 renewed by Princeton University Press; Associated Book Publishers (U.K.) Ltd/Johns Hopkins University Press for abridged extracts from *The Act of Reading* by Wolfgang Iser, Routledge & Kegan Paul plc; Associated Book Publishers/W. W. Norton Co. Inc. for abridged extracts from *Science and Poetry* by I. A. Richards, Routledge & Kegan Paul plc 1926; Basil Blackwell Ltd for an extract from *Language, Counter-Memory*

Practice: Selected Essays and Interviews by Michel Foucault, 1977;
Associated Book Publishers (U.K.) Ltd/Harcourt Brace
Jovanovich Inc. for abridged extracts from *Modern Man In Search
of a Soul* by C. G. Jung and from *Principles of Literary Criticism* by
I. A. Richards, Routledge & Kegan Paul plc/Harcourt Brace
Jovanovich Inc.; Basil Blackwell Ltd and the Translator,
Professor G. M. Anscombe, for abridged extracts from
Philosophical Investigations by Ludwig Wittgenstein; Basil Blackwell
Ltd/the Author, Julia Kristeva, for an abridged extract from
'The Speaking Subject' in *On Signs: A Semiotics Reader*, ed.
Marshall Blonsky; Basil Blackwell Ltd/Columbia University
Press for an abridged extract from 'Frontiers of Narrative' in
Figures in Literary Discourse by Gérard Genette, trans. Sheridan
1982, copyright © 1982 Columbia University Press; Authors'
Agents for an abridged extract from *The Social Context of Modern
English Literature* by Malcolm Bradbury, copyright Malcolm
Bradbury 1971; the Editor, Seymour Chatman, for abridged
extracts from 'Speech, Action and Style' by Richard Ohmann in
Literary Style: A Symposium ed. S. Chatman, Oxford University
Press Inc. 1971; Dobson Books Ltd/Harcourt Brace Jovanovich
Inc./the Author, Cleanth Brooks, for abridged extracts from *The
Well Wrought Urn*, copyright 1947, 1975 by Cleanth Brooks;
Cambridge University Press for abridged extracts from *A Selection
from Scrutiny* by F. R. Leavis, and from *Hermeneutics and the Human
Sciences* by P. Ricoeur; Jonathan Cape Ltd on behalf of Richard
Miller/Hill & Wang (a division of Farrar Straus & Giroux
Inc.)/Editions de Seuil for abridged extracts from *S/Z* by Roland
Barthes, trans. H. Miller, English trans. copyright 1974 by
Farrar Straus & Giroux Inc.; Jonathan Cape Ltd on behalf of
the Estate of Simone de Beauvoir/Alfred A. Knopf Inc. for
abridged extracts from *The Second Sex* by Simone de Beauvoir,
trans. and ed. H. M. Parshley, copyright 1952 by Alfred A.
Knopf Inc.; Jonathan Cape Ltd on behalf of Walter
Benjamin/Harcourt Brace Jovanovich Inc. for an abridged
extract from *Illuminations* by Walter Benjamin, copyright © 1955
by Suhrkamp Verlag, Frankfurt a.M., trans. Harry Zohn, ed.
Hannah Arendt, English trans. copyright © 1968 by Harcourt
Brace Jovanovich Inc.; Chatto & Windus: The Hogarth
Press/Harcourt Brace Jovanovich Inc. for an abridged
extract from *A Room of One's Own* by Virginia Woolf, copyright
1929 by Harcourt Brace Jovanovich Inc., renewed 1957 by
Leonard Woolf; Chatto & Windus: The Hogarth Press on behalf
of Sigmund Freud Copyrights Ltd, The Institute of Psycho-
Analysis, for an extract from 'Psychopathic Characters on the

Stage' in *The Complete Psychological Works of Sigmund Freud*, trans. and ed. James Strachey; Chatto & Windus Ltd on behalf of the Author's Literary Estate for an extract from *The Elizabethan World Picture* by E. M. W. Tillyard; Chatto & Windus Ltd/Lady Empson for two extracts from *Seven Types of Ambiguity* by William Empson; Chatto &Windus Ltd: The Hogarth Press/Oxford University Press Inc. for an extract from *The Uses of Literacy* by Richard Hoggart; Chatto & Windus Ltd and the Author, Raymond Williams, for extracts from *The Long Revolution* by Raymond Williams; William Collins Sons & Co. Ltd for abridged extracts from 'Introduction to the Structural Analysis of Narratives' and 'The Death of the Author' in *Image – Music – Text* by Roland Barthes, Fontana; Columbia University Press for an abridged extract from *The Revolution in Poetic Language* by Julia Kristeva; Faber & Faber Ltd/Harcourt Brace Jovanovich Inc. for abridged extracts from 'Tradition and the Individual Talent' and 'Hamlet' in *Selected Essays* by T. S. Eliot, copyright 1950 by Harcourt Brace Jovanovich Inc., renewed 1978 by Esme Valerie Eliot; Faber & Faber Ltd/Alfred A. Knopf Inc. for abridged extracts from *The Necessary Angel* by Wallace Stevens, copyright 1951 by Wallace Stevens; Faber & Faber Ltd/New Directions Inc. for abridged extracts from 'A Retrospect' and 'The Serious Artist' in *Literary Essays* by Ezra Pound, copyright 1935 by Ezra Pound; Grove Press Inc. for an abridged extract from 'A Future for the Novel' in *For a New Novel: Essays in Fiction* by Alain Robbe-Grillet, trans. R. Howard 1965; Harcourt Brace Jovanovich Inc. for abridged extracts from *A Gathering of Fugitives* by Lionel Trilling, copyright © 1956 by Lionel Trilling, renewed 1984 by Diana Trilling and from *Beyond Culture* by Lionel Trilling, copyright © 1965 by Lionel Trilling; Harvard University Press for abridged extracts from *The Great Chain of Being* by Arthur O. Lovejoy, copyright © 1936, 1964 by the President and Fellows of Harvard College; The Harvester Press/Wheatsheaf Books/University of Minnesota Press for abridged extracts from *Towards an Aesthetic of Reception* by Hans Robert Jauss, trans. T. Bahti 1982; the Author, David Holbrook, for abridged extracts from his *The Quest for Love*, Methuen 1964; Johns Hopkins University Press for abridged extracts from the following: 'Semiology and Rhetoric' by Paul de Man, trans. J. Harari in *Diacritics* 3, Fall 1973, 'The Critical Difference: Balzac's *Sarrasine* and Barthes' *S/Z* by Barbara Johnson in *Untying the Text* by Robert Young, *Diacritics VIII* (2), 1978, *Of Grammatology* by Jacques Derrida, trans. G. C. Spivak, 1976, 'The Cultural Importance of Art' by Susanne Langer in

Philosophical Sketches, 1962, 'Criticism and the Experience of Interiority' by Georges Poulet in *The Structuralist Controversy*, ed. Macksey and Donato, 1972, and *Subjective Criticism* by David Bleich, 1978; Mervyn Jones as Executor of Mrs. K. Jones/W. W. Norton & Co. Inc. for an abridged extract from *Hamlet and Oedipus* by Ernest Jones; Lawrence & Wishart Ltd for abridged extracts from 'Soviet Literature' by A. A. Zhdanov in *Problems of Soviet Literature*, ed. H. G. Scott, London 1977; The Merlin Press Ltd for an abridged extract from 'Art and Objective Truth' by George Lukács, trans. A. Kahn in *Writer and Critic*; Mouton de Gruyter for abridged extracts from 'Two Aspects of Language and Two Types of Aphasic Disturbances' by Roman Jakobson in *Fundamentals of Language*, 2nd edition, Mouton, The Hague, 1971; Peter Owen Ltd for abridged extracts from *A Course in General Linguistics* by Ferdinand de Saussure, trans. W. Baskin; Oxford University Press for abridged extracts from the following: *How to do Things with Words* by J. L. Austin, 2nd ed. 1975, *The Principles of Art* by R. G. Collingwood, 1938, and *Archetypal Patterns in Poetry* by Maud Bodkin, 1934; Oxford University Press Inc. for abridged extracts from *The Anxiety of Influence: A Theory of Poetry* by Harold Bloom, 1973; Princeton University Press for abridged extracts from *A Literature of Their Own: British Women Novelists from Brontë to Lessing* by Elaine Showalter, copyright 1977 by Princeton University Press; Progress Publishers for an abridged extract from 'Letter to Margaret Harkness, April 1888' in *On Art and Literature* by Friedrich Engels, 1976; Random House Inc. for abridged extracts from *The Will to Power* by Friedrich Nietzsche, ed. with commentary by Walter Kaufman and trans. Walter Kaufman & R. J. Hollingdale, copyright © 1967 by Walter Kaufman; Authors' Agents on behalf of the Author, Mark Schorer, for abridged extracts from his 'Technique as Discovery' in *The World We Imagine: Selected Essays*, Chatto & Windus Ltd 1969; Mrs. Helen H. Tate for an abridged extract from 'Tension in Poetry' in *Collected Essays* by Allan Tate, Allan Swallow 1959; University of Chicago Press for abridged extracts from the following: 'The Laugh of the Medusa' by Hélène Cixous, trans. Keith Cohen & Paula Bassoff, pp. 875–94, *Signs: Journal of Woman in Culture and Society* Vol. 1 No. 4, 1976, © 1976 by the University of Chicago Press, pp. 85–91 of *The Aims of Interpretation* by E. D. Hirsch, 1976, pp. 13–17, 22–3, 66–7, 81 of *The Rhetoric of Fiction* by Wayne Booth, 1961; University of Michigan/Prof. L. Matejka for abridged extracts from 'Aesthetic Function, Norm and Value as Social Facts' by Jan Mukařovský, trans. E. Suino in *Michigan Slavic Contributions No. 3;* University of

Minnesota Press for abridged extracts from pp. 4–5, 9 of *Problems of Dostoevsky's Poetics* by Mikhail Bakhtin, trans R. W. Rotsel; University of North Carolina Press for abridged extracts from *Modern Poetry and Tradition* by Cleanth Brooks, copyright 1939 the University of North Carolina Press; University of Nebraska Press for abridged extracts from 'Art as Technique' by Viktor Shklovsky in *Russian Formalist Criticism: Four Essays*, trans. and with an Introduction by Lee T. Lemon and Marion J. Reis, © 1965 by the University of Nebraska Press, and *Structural Semantics: An Attempt at a Method* by A. J. Greimas, trans. Daniele McDowell, Ronald Schleiffer and Alan Verlie, © Libraire Larousse 1966, Introduction and trans. copyright 1983 by the University of Nebraska Press; University of Texas Press for an abridged extract from pp. 19–22 of *Morphology of the Folktale* by V. Propp, trans. L. Scott, Austin & London: University of Texas Press 1968; the University Press of Kentucky for abridged extracts from 'The Intentional Fallacy' by W. K. Wimsatt in *The Verbal Icon*, © 1954 University Press of Kentucky, copyright renewed 1982 by Margaret H. Wimsatt; Verso Editions for abridged extracts from the following: *Charles Baudelaire: A Lyric Poet in the Era of High Capitalism* by Walter Benjamin, trans. H. Zohn, New Left Books 1973, 'A Letter on Art in reply to André Daspre' and 'Ideology and Ideological State Apparatuses' in *Lenin and Philosophy* by Louis Althusser, New Left Books 1966, *Criticism and Objectivity* by Terry Eagleton, New Left Books 1976, and *The Moment of Scrutiny* by Francis Mulhern, New Left Books 1979; Yale University Press for abridged extracts from pp. 265, 269–272 of *Criticism in the Wilderness* by Geoffrey H. Hartman, pp. 57, 60, 209–10 of *5 Readers Reading* by Norman N. Holland; Authors' Agents on behalf of Michael B. Yeats and Macmillan London Ltd/Macmillan Publishing Co. Inc. for an abridged extract from pp. 153–164 of 'The Symbolism of Poetry' in *Essays and Introductions* by W. B. Yeats, © Mrs. W. B. Yeats 1961.

We have unfortunately been unable to trace the copyright holders of 'Desire and the Interpretation of Desire in *Hamlet*' by Jacques Lacan, *Criticism Inc* by John Crowe Ransom, *Mimesis: The Representation of Reality in Western Literature* by Erich Auerbach, trans. Willard Trask, *Linguistics and Literary History* by Leo Spitzer, *Literature as System* by Claudio Guillén, *Anatomy of Criticism: Four Essays* by Northrop Frye, *Marxism and Form* by Fredric Jameson, *Language and Myth* by Earnst Cassirer, trans. Susanne Langer, and would appreciate any information which would enable us to do so.

To JOHN OAKLEY

*His hearers could not cough, or look aside
from him, without loss . . . . The fear of
every man that heard him, was, lest he
should make an end.*

INTRODUCTION

A new version of the Battle of the Books between the Ancients
and the Moderns has been raging in recent years: the former
complain that the Moderns behave as if literary theory never
existed before Barthes and Derrida reared their brazen heads.
The Moderns appear to regard traditional critics (even New
Critics) as prehistoric moles working in the dark before the
dawn of structuralism, semiotics and deconstruction. As is often
the case with ideological battles there is something to be said on
both sides of the argument. The rise of Theory in the 1960s did
mark a definite break with a predominantly humanistic and
often moralistic tradition in criticism. Even the self-proclaimed
'objectivity' of New Criticism, which reigned during the 1940s
and 1950s, was founded upon an inherited 'Romantic' poetics.
However, many proponents of deconstruction or Lacanian
criticism write as though all critics before 1968 were naively
'logocentric' and are therefore completely superseded by the new
vision of post-structuralism. This collection of critical extracts is
an attempt to place modern theories in some sort of historical
perspective.

The division of the volume into five parts owes something to
Roman Jakobson's celebrated diagram of linguistic
communication (omitting one feature):

CONTEXT (history)

ADDRESSER – MESSAGE (writing) – ADDRESSEE

(writer)   CODE (structure)   (reader)

For our purposes we interpret addresser as writer, message as
writing, addressee as reader, code as structure, and context as
history. Some critical discourses adopt the point of view of the
writer. Others explore the contribution of the reader or audience

to the meaning of a work. Others again are concerned with the work itself – the words on the page conceived as a self-sufficient entity. Structuralists attempt to discover the code or codes underlying particular kinds of 'message'. Finally, some consider that the primary focus of criticism should be the historical context of the work.

It would be tempting to suggest that a comprehensive and adequate critical discourse would be a synthesis of these approaches. However, in practice it is evident that the most powerful critics often have a clear commitment to one element in the circuit of communication, although they also have the ability to include the other dimensions within their theory in a subordinate role. For example, Wolfgang Iser's *The Implied Reader* and *The Act of Reading* privilege the reader's role in the literary process. His interest in phenomenology commits him to a set of assumptions centred around a complex notion of a reader's consciousness. He begins by asking the question 'What happens when we read?' So, a powerful critical practice seems to begin by committing itself to certain basic assumptions which involve the privileging of one dimension of the writing/reading process.

This one-sidedness of critical theories suggests that there can never be a complete, all-embracing mode of criticism which would satisfy all the requirements of every type of critical practice. Are we therefore compelled to adopt a *relativistic* view of critical theory and practice? Are students of literature faced with a number of paths, each of which has an equal claim to their attention? Do the problems of criticism reduce themselves to a question of *taste* or *predisposition*? There are two answers to this question. One suggests that the methods and assumptions adopted by critics merely reflect their *interests* or their 'will to power'. The other regards different critical methods as competing systems of *knowledge*. The first view is relativistic, but does not believe that critical views are just a matter of taste; the second is not relativistic, and presupposes that it is worth trying to refine critical theories and techniques in order to improve our knowledge of the processes of writing and reading.

It is possible to use this collection of extracts from either perspective. We may interpret the existence of different critical traditions as either an endlessly fascinating struggle for supremacy or a series of attempts to establish a knowledge of the literary process. It would even be possible to adopt both perspectives. Some critics certainly make their ideological motivation more apparent than others. Plato, for example, is explicitly concerned to police literature from a distinctly political point of view, and in this his arguments in the *Republic* sometimes resemble the Soviet doctrines on art and literature. Ideology sometimes hides its head more cleverly. On the other hand, to reduce all literary theory to mere ideology has its own dangers. Some critics embrace a more boldly 'objective' approach. For example, Aristotle's *Poetics* attempts in part to provide a scientific account of tragedy. Many modern critics, especially the disciples of Derrida and Lacan, are sceptical about the possibility of such knowledge, arguing that the very nature of language prevents us from using it to master any field; the devious and unpredictable nature of discourse always betrays us into self-contradiction.

These preliminary remarks make it clear that the whole field of critical theory is a veritable minefield for the unwary student of literature. However, those who believe it possible and desirable to circumvent the entire universe of 'theory' cannot deny the fact that no critical approach, no interpretation, and no way of reading a text can avoid implicit theory. When we fall back on familiar and apparently unproblematic terms such as 'realism', 'life', 'naturalness', 'imagination', 'emotion', 'organic unity', 'style', 'moral vision', 'myth', and 'tradition', we are drawing upon concepts which were once problematic and unfamiliar. We are, in effect, using old theories. However, some argue that implicit theory will do no harm so long as it remains invisible. F. R. Leavis accepted that others of a more philosophical bent might be capable of discovering the concepts underpinning particular critical writings, but he believed that such methodological self-consciousness could only damage a critic's own abilty to read and comment with a proper sensitivity to 'felt life'. A great deal of the scepticism about theory stems from the long-standing romantic suspicion of the intellect, epitomised in Wordsworth's well-known dictum:

> Our meddling intellect
> Misshapes the beauteous forms of things:-
> We murder to dissect.

There is also a long tradition in British thought of anti-theoretical and 'down-to-earth' 'common sense'. However, we should distinguish between the healthy scepticism of a Dr Johnson and the blind philistinism of chauvinistic critics who regard French or German or Italian theories as alien cultural forces which must be resisted by all true Englishmen.

The insularity of British criticism was disturbed in the late 1960s when there began a steady influx of continental theory through translations in journals and books. At first the impact was limited to a small élite of intellectuals who were easily isolated and regarded as modish playboys whose new-fangled toys would soon lose their fascination. However, the interest in theory spread, even as the ground shifted through various theoretical phases without settling on any definite favoured method. New journals sprang up, including *New Literary History*, *Critical Inquiry*, *Diacritics*, and *Literature and History*. New courses and new conferences were established in institutions of higher education.

Many older literary critics, who are naturally anxious to keep up with recent developments, complain with some justice of the arrogance of the new theorists, who dismiss or ignore the earlier phases of critical history, and appear unwilling to learn from the classical, neoclassical, romantic and modernist phases of literary criticism and poetics. These critics do not all share the attitudes of the hard-line anti-theorists, but they are being prevented from entering into dialogue with deconstruction or semiotics because theory seems to be insisting upon a total *discontinuity* with the past. This theme is very prominent in discussions of 'postmodernism', which often emphasize the profound cultural break even from the 'modernist' era associated with recent developments in our social and economic environment (electronics, nuclear physics, corporatism). If indeed we now live in a nuclear and post-humanist period, are we doomed to abandon all cultural roots and all *continuities*? This collection of extracts is in part an attempt to provide the reader with materials which suggest links and continuities at least as much as breaks and discontinuities.

A glance at the contents of each part of the Reader will make it clear that there are stronger continuities linking theories of 'representation' and 'morality' than those connecting theories of 'subjectivity' and 'form, system and structure'. There are obvious historical reasons for these discrepancies: the Romantics placed subjective experience at the centre of the literary stage; while the systematic and formalistic study of literature was present in classical and Renaissance poetics and rhetoric, it took on a different aspect in the twentieth century. These areas of relative discontinuity are, nevertheless, best understood by a comparative and historical method of study. The Russian Formalists' distinction between 'plot' and 'story' is clearly different from Aristotle's, but the difference can be interpreted as a critical dialogue rather than as a radical discontinuity. Not all such differences are so amenable to a dialogic understanding. The critical theories deriving from Marxist, psychoanalytic and post-structuralist thought are often so challenging in their implications that they threaten to cut off more traditional readers from all familiar moorings. These more radical discontinuities call for careful evaluation and not cries of despair or moral crusades.

The five parts of this book each raise fundamental questions about literature and its contexts. These may be summarized as follows:

i.   Does literature refer to or correspond to something outside texts? What sort of 'truth' does literature aim at?
ii. What mental processes, whether the writer's or the reader's, contribute to the production of literary texts?
iii. To what extent are texts 'autonomous'? What are the formal and structural properties of texts? Is a text's structure determinate or indeterminate?
iv. Is literature a part of history? Can we know what social, economic, geographical and other historical processes determine or condition the production of literary texts?
v.   Is literature primarily a form of moral experience? Do the moral ideas or the ideologies (conscious or unconscious) of writers determine the nature of their writings?

The five kinds of question do not exhaust those that might be put, but come near to comprehending most of the long-standing debates within criticism since Plato. Inevitably the thematic arrangement of the material involves some fragmentation of some critics' work and a concentration on particular aspects of others'. The approach is uncompromisingly *problem-centred* and not *author-centred*. It is important to anchor the extracts and their concerns in their historical contexts and not to be misled into a belief that the history of criticism can be scanned for the universally truthful answers to certain eternally valid questions. The questions and the answers change as the historical conditions change. Nevertheless, continuities exist as much as contrasts. Particular traditions survive or are strengthened, while others disappear for long periods, perhaps to be revived later as new thinking makes them re-usable.

General books on the history and theory of criticism

M. H. Abrams, *The Mirror and the Lamp: Romantic Theory and the Critical Tradition* (New York: Oxford UP, 1953).

J. W. H. Atkins, *English Literary Criticism: 17th and 18th Centuries* (London: Methuen, 1951).

Walter Jackson Bate, *From Classic to Romantic: Premises of Taste in Eighteenth Century England* (Cambridge, Mass.: Harvard UP, 1946).

Terry Eagleton, *Literary Theory: An Introduction* (Oxford: Blackwell, 1983).

D. W. Fokkema and E. Kunne-Ibsch, *The Theories of Literature in the Twentieth Century: Structuralism, Marxism, Aesthetics of Reception, Semiotics* (London: C. Hurst, 1977).

K. E. Gilbert and H. Kohn, *A History of Esthetics* (2nd edn, Bloomington: Indiana UP, 1953).

Ann Jefferson and David Robey (eds), *Modern Literary Theory: A Comparative Introduction* (2nd edn, London: Batsford, 1986).

J. W. Johnson, *The Formation of English Neoclassical Thought* (Princeton, NJ: Princeton UP, 1967).

Jerome J. McGann, *The Romantic Ideology: A Critical Investigation* (Chicago and London: Chicago UP, 1983).

Raman Selden, *A Reader's Guide to Contemporary Literary Theory* (Brighton: Harvester Press, 1985).

J. E. Spingarn, *History of Literary Criticism in the Renaissance* (New York: Columbia UP, 1898).

P. W. K. Stone, *The Art of Poetry 1750–1820: Theories of Poetic Composition and Style . . .* (London: Routledge & Kegan Paul, 1967).

Tzvetan Todorov, *Theories of the Symbol*, trans. Catherine Porter (Ithaca: Cornell UP, 1982).

René Wellek, *A History of Modern Criticism*, 6 vols (London: Jonathan Cape, 1955–86). Vols 5 and 6, on American Criticism 1900–50 and English Criticism 1900–50, were published in 1986.

René Wellek and Austin Warren, *Theory of Literature* (3rd edn, Harmondsworth: Penguin, 1963).

Raymond Williams, *Culture and Society 1780–1950* (London: Chatto & Windus, 1958).

W. K. Wimsatt and Cleanth Brooks, *Literary Criticism: A Short History* (New York: Alfred A. Knopf, 1957).

PART I:

REPRESENTATION

The idea that literary texts 'represent' something – the physical,
spiritual, mental, or social worlds – seems self-evident.
Structuralists and their successors have questioned this basic
assumption, arguing that discourse never represents because
language is a system which works not by symbolizing objects but
by producing 'differences' (for example, between one sound and
another). Despite this limitation we *believe* that words can represent – can give us back the 'presence' of – the things or ideas
we wish to regard as 'real'. The arguments of Derrida and his
followers, which develop this strong anti-representational
argument, are included in Part III, but the writings of
Wittgenstein, extracted in Part I, have similar implications
which will be discussed in the appropriate sectional introduction.

Before the recent period most literary critics worked on the
assumption that literature is a representation of life in some
sense. 'Represent' could mean to give a pictorial rendering or
symbolization of external objects, or to reveal the general and
universal features of human nature, or to present the ideal forms
which lie behind the external objects of the natural world.

Such theories involved the consideration of fundamental
philosophical questions about the nature of human knowledge
(epistemology), about the ultimate nature of reality
(metaphysics) and particularly about cognition. What do we
mean by 'reality'? What sort of reality can literature represent?
What might be called the 'materialist' view is that literature is
most truthful when it represents objects 'as they are' ('things in
themselves') outside the human mind. Such a view presupposes
that the process of knowing makes no difference to what is
known. Related to this is the view that literature should
represent not simply objects but the material causes of human

life with scientific precision. This approach is what Zola called 'naturalism'. At the other end of the spectrum is the mythopoeic view that literature creates its own reality. An extreme form of this idea is Art for Art's Sake, which sees literature as another world (a heterocosm). The following is a fuller tabulation of modes of representation:

i. Literal or scientific representation of natural objects and social life (Naturalism).

ii. Generalized representation of nature or the human passions (Classicism).

iii. Generalized representation of nature or the human passions, subjectively viewed (pre-romantic criticism).

iv. Representation of ideal forms inherent in nature and the mind (German Romanticism).

v. Representation of transcendental ideal forms (Neoplatonic idealism).

vi. Representation of art's own world (Art for Art's Sake).

In simple terms, the first three views may be called 'mimetic' and can be traced back to Aristotle. The second group may be called 'idealist' and can be traced back to Plato.

Terms such as 'reflection', 'imitation', 'realism', 'naturalness', 'objective truth' and 'imaginative truth' are bandied about by critics and students of literature alike. However, the same term may be used with all the different implications indicated in the above tabulation. Whether or not a student decides to adopt a particular weighting of a concept, it is worth trying to understand the trickiness of the terms we so readily employ in the hope that, in so doing, we will be able to produce more effective critical discourses.

CHAPTER 1

IMAGINATIVE REPRESENTATION

A large group of critics have shared a view of literary representation which is largely derived from their allegiance to philosophical idealism, most versions of which regard external objects as a world of mere appearances, of dead matter, to be brought to life only by the mythopoeic power of the philosopher poet.

Despite his expulsion of the poets from the well-run republic, Plato is the natural starting-point for a discussion of this approach. Plato regards the artist as an imitator of imitations: the painter's work is three times removed from 'the essential nature' of a thing: the artist imitates the physical object which is in turn a faint 'copy' of the Idea (or Form) of the thing. Plato's famous allegory of the Line, illustrating the four stages of cognition, represents a hierarchy of knowledge ranging from the lowest (*eikasia*), a mode limited to the perception of only the external appearances of things, to the highest (*noesis*), a mode affording access to the underlying principles of reality – the Ideas themselves upon which all the lower modes of cognition depend. The essential principles of the moral and physical world order are incorporated in what Plato calls 'the essential Form of Goodness'. The artist's products are relegated to the lowest level in the Line.

Succeeding Platonists defy Plato's rejection of the poets in the *Republic* by elevating art from the bottom to the top of the cognitive ladder. The poet no longer languishes in the world of appearances, but has direct access to the world of intelligible Forms. Art becomes an expression of the essential Form of the Good and the Beautiful. Plotinus, founder of the neoplatonic school of philosophy in Rome (third century AD) adopts a Platonic model of the cosmos according to which a world of appearances is subordinated to a world of reality somewhere beyond. All aspects of reality are ultimately emanations of the Divine One, the first being, to which they aspire to return. All Plotinus' aesthetic statements are by-products of this general theory of being.

He inverts the position of art in the cognitive ladder: it is actually identified with Beauty (the essential Form). However, the *products* of art are imperfect expressions of the ideas of Beauty in so far as the matter upon which Beauty is impressed resists the impression. The Platonist demands a correspondence between poetic matter and ideal Beauty perceived by the poet's superior intellect (*nous*). The external world is an apparition of lifeless objects which only the poet's vitalizing intellect can bring to life by endowing it with what Coleridge called 'the depth and height of the ideal world'.

Modern idealist criticism is usually associated with the word 'imagination', the faculty which corresponds to the Platonic *nous* (for the psychological aspects of imagination see Part II). At the end of the eighteenth century German Romanticism provided the vital philosophical impetus to the developments in other European countries. Kant's philosophy, and the critical writings of Schelling and the two Schlegels were major influences on English Romanticism. Friedrich Schlegel follows the Platonic tradition of representation, but insists that 'things of commonplace, and every day occurrence' should be presented as having as high a significance and as deep a purpose as the stories of kings and legendary heroes. Wordsworth's early poetry embodies this theory in practical form.

Coleridge's philosophy and criticism transmit German theories into British culture. He refuses to grant absolute priority in the process of cognition either to mind or to nature. He argues that all the principles of intelligence are inherent in nature *before* the act of consciousness arises, and that the act of intellectual apprehension involves the *focusing* of the images which impinge upon our consciousness. These images are full of *potential* intellectual meaning, but without the act of mental organization, the images remain inert and dissociated in nature. The mind does not simply impose an order upon nature, but rather discovers an order in nature, an order which he recognizes as an approximation ('fitted to the limits of the human mind'): the order is at once a mental construct and 'that which is within the thing'. The poet's task is to effect a reconciliation between a thought and a thing. He argues further that the ultimate source of those rays of intellect mirrored in natural objects and focused in the human mind is the Divine Mind itself. This philosophical (and theological) background lies behind his theory of the organic vitality of the poetic imagination which gives life to otherwise lifeless natural objects.

In contrast, Shelley's *Defence of Poetry* (1821) is built upon an otherworldly view of representation, according to which natural objects are unreal phantoms obscuring the eternal forms which are the true objects of poetic vision. So remote are questions of literary form or linguistic creativity in Shelley's work that for modern readers Shelley is hardly a literary critic at all.

Yeats, Wallace Stevens and R. G. Collingwood, like Coleridge, reacted against the common-sense tradition of empiricism. Yeats absorbed mystical thought, Collingwood attacked the narrow positivism of the dominant English philosophy of the 1920s, and Stevens attacked the modern 'obsession' with scientific 'truth'. Unlike the Romantics they connected a poet's imaginative powers with linguistic creativity: 'Poetry is a revelation in words by means of the words' (Stevens). Both Stevens and Yeats were influenced by the Art-for-Art's-Sake movement. Stevens followed the aesthete's doctrine that the poet has no social, moral or political *obligations*, but rejected the separation of art and reality. He argued that the artist's highest function is the creation of the social consciousness of reality itself. The poet creates the world in which we live and breathe as conscious beings and 'gives to life the supreme fictions without which we are unable to conceive of it'. The poet's creation of 'fictions' is an act of consciousness, a creative act of resistance to the pressure of convention (compare and contrast Shklovsky and Hulme, III, 2, c and d). The poet's world is not a literal representation of the external world ('things as they are') or even a generalized representation. Nor is it an esape from reality into an ideal world of transcendent forms. It is a fresh vision of reality, a reconstruction of a human consciousness of 'things as they are'.

Background reading

M. H. Abrams, *The Mirror and the Lamp* (New York: Oxford UP, 1953).
A. C. Bradley, *Oxford Lectures on Poetry* (London: Macmillan, 1909), see 'Shelley's View of Poetry'.
John Clubbe and Ernest J. Lovell Jr, *English Romanticism: the Grounds of Belief* (London: Macmillan, 1983).
John B. Halsted (ed.), *Romanticism* (New York: Harper & Row, 1967).

Paul Hamilton, *Coleridge's Poetics* (Oxford: Blackwell, 1983).

J. R. de J. Jackson, *Method and Imagination in Coleridge's Criticism* (London: Routledge & Kegan Paul, 1969).

Frank Lentricchia, *The Gaiety of Language: An Essay on the Radical Poetics of W. B. Yeats and Wallace Stevens* (Berkeley and Los Angeles: University of California Press, 1968).

Rupert C. Lodge, *Plato's Theory of Art* (London: Routledge & Kegan Paul, 1953).

Adalaide K. Morris, *Wallace Stevens: Imagination and Faith* (Princeton, NJ: Princeton UP, 1974).

G. N. G. Orsini, *Coleridge and German Idealism* (Carbondale and Edwardsville: Southern Illinois UP, 1969).

Joseph N. Riddel, *The Clairvoyant Eye: the Poetry and Poetics of Wallace Stevens* (Baton Rouge: Louisiana State UP, 1965).

Earl J. Schulze, *Shelley's Theory of Poetry: A Reappraisal* (The Hague and Paris: Mouton, 1966).

R. Wellek, *A History of Modern Criticism: 1750–1950*, vol. 2, 'The Romantic Age' (London: Jonathan Cape, 1955).

(A) PLATO

The Republic

[BOOK 6]

You have to imagine, then, that there are two ruling powers, and that one of them is set over the intellectual world, the other over the visible. I do not say heaven, lest you should fancy that I am playing upon the name (*ouranos, horatos*). May I suppose that you have this distinction of the visible and intelligible fixed in your mind?

I have.

Now take a line which has been cut into two unequal parts, and divide each of them again in the same proportion, and suppose the two main divisions to answer, one to the visible and the other to the intelligible, and then compare the subdivisions in respect of their clearness and want of clearness, and you will find that the first section in the sphere of the visible consists of images. And by images I mean, in the first place, shadows, and in the second place, reflections in water and in solid, smooth and polished bodies and the like: Do you understand?

Yes, I understand.

Imagine, now, the other section, of which this is only the

resemblance, to include the animals which we see, and everything that grows or is made.

Very good.

Would you not admit that both the sections of this division
have different degrees of truth, and that the copy is to the
original as the sphere of opinion is to the sphere of knowledge?

Most undoubtedly.

Next proceed to consider the manner in which the sphere of
the intellectual is to be divided.

In what manner?

Thus: – There are two subdivisions, in the lower of which the
soul uses the figures given by the former division as images; the
enquiry can only be hypothetical, and instead of going upwards
to a principle descends to the other end; in the higher of the
two, the soul passes out of hypotheses, and goes up to a
principle which is above hypotheses, making no use of images as
in the former case, but proceeding only in and through the ideas
themselves.

I do not quite understand your meaning, he said.

Then I will try again; you will understand me better when I
have made some preliminary remarks. You are aware that
students of geometry, arithmetic, and the kindred sciences
assume the odd and the even and the figures and three kinds of
angles and the like in their several branches of science; these are
their hypotheses, which they and everybody are supposed to
know, and therefore they do not deign to give any account of
them either to themselves or others; but they begin with them,
and go on until they arrive at last, and in a consistent manner,
at their conclusion?

Yes, he said, I know.

And do you not know also that although they make use of the
visible forms and reason about them, they are thinking not of
these, but of the ideals which they resemble; not of the figures
which they draw, but of the absolute square and the absolute
diameter, and so on – the forms which they draw or make, and
which have shadows and reflections in water of their own, are
converted by them into images, but they are really seeking to
behold the things themselves, which can only be seen with the
eye of the mind?

That is true.

And of this kind I spoke as the intelligible, although in the
search after it the soul is compelled to use hypotheses; not

ascending to a first principle, because she is unable to rise above
the region of hypothesis, but employing the objects of which the
shadows below are resemblances in their turn as images, they
having in relation to the shadows and reflections of them a
greater distinctness, and therefore a higher value.

I understand, he said, that you are speaking of the province of
geometry and the sister arts.

And when I speak of the other division of the intelligible, you
will understand me to speak of that other sort of knowledge
which reason herself attains by the power of dialectic, using the
hypotheses not as first principles, but only as hypotheses – that
is to say, as steps and points of departure into a world which is
above hypotheses, in order that she may soar beyond them to
the first principle of the whole; and clinging to this and then to
that which depends on this, by successive steps she descends
again without the aid of any sensible object, from ideas, through
ideas, and in ideas she ends.

I understand you, he replied; not perfectly, for you seem to
me to be describing a task which is really tremendous; but, at
any rate, I understand you to say that knowledge and being,
which the science of dialectic contemplates, are clearer than the
notions of the arts, as they are termed, which proceed from
hypotheses only: these are also contemplated by the
understanding, and not by the senses: yet, because they start
from hypotheses and do not ascend to a principle, those who
contemplate them appear to you not to exercise the higher
reason upon them, although when a first principle is added to
them they are cognizable by the higher reason. And the habit
which is concerned with geometry and the cognate sciences I
suppose that you would term understanding and not reason, as
being intermediate between opinion and reason.

You have quite conceived my meaning, I said; and now,
corresponding to these four divisions, let there be four faculties
in the soul – reason answering to the highest, understanding to
the second, faith (or conviction) to the third, and perception of
shadows to the last – and let there be a scale of them, and let
us suppose that the several faculties have clearness in the same
degree that their objects have truth.

I understand, he replied, and give my assent, and accept your
arrangement.

(Plato, *The Republic*, Book 6, translated by B. Jowett (3rd edn, Oxford:
Clarendon Press, 1888), pp. 210–13.)

[BOOK 10]

Of the many excellences which I perceive in the order of our
State, there is none which upon reflection pleases me better than
the rule about poetry.

To what do you refer?

To the rejection of imitative poetry, which certainly ought not
to be received; as I see far more clearly now that the parts of
the soul have been distinguished.

What do you mean?

Speaking in confidence, for I should not like to have my
words repeated to the tragedians and the rest of the imitative
tribe – but I do not mind saying to you, that all poetical
imitations are ruinous to the understanding of the hearers, and
that the knowledge of their true nature is the only antidote to
them.

Explain the purport of your remark.

Well, I will tell you, although I have always from my earliest
youth had an awe and love of Homer, which even now makes
the words falter on my lips, for he is the great captain and
teacher of the whole of that charming tragic company; but a
man is not to be reverenced more than the truth, and therefore I
will speak out.

Very good, he said.

Listen to me then, or rather, answer me.

Put your question.

Can you tell me what imitation is? for I really do not know.

A likely thing, then, that I should know.

Why not? for the duller eye may often see a thing sooner than
the keener.

Very true, he said; but in your presence, even if I had any
faint notion, I could not muster courage to utter it. Will you
enquire yourself?

Well then, shall we begin the enquiry in our usual manner:
Whenever a number of individuals have a common name, we
assume them to have also a corresponding idea or form: – do
you understand me?

I do.

Let us take any common instance; there are beds and tables
in the world – plenty of them, are there not?

Yes.

But there are only two ideas or forms of them – one the idea
of a bed, the other of a table.

True.

And the maker of either of them makes a bed or he makes a table for our use, in accordance with the idea – that is our way of speaking in this and similar instances – but no artificer makes the ideas themselves: how could he?

Impossible.

And there is another artist, – I should like to know what you would say of him.

Who is he?

One who is the maker of all the works of all other workmen.

What an extraordinary man!

Wait a little, and there will be more reason for your saying so. For this is he who is able to make not only vessels of every kind, but plants and animals, himself and all other things – the earth and heaven, and the things which are in heaven or under the earth; he makes the gods also.

He must be a wizard and no mistake.

Oh! you are incredulous, are you? Do you mean that there is no such maker or creator, or that in one sense there might be a maker of all these things but in another not? Do you see that there is a way in which you could make them all yourself?

What way?

An easy way enough; or rather, there are many ways in which the feat might be quickly and easily accomplished, none quicker than that of turning a mirror round and round – you would soon enough make the sun and the heavens, and the earth and yourself, and other animals and plants, and all the other things of which we were just now speaking, in the mirror.

Yes, he said; but they would be appearances only.

Very good, I said, you are coming to the point now. And the painter too is, as I conceive, just such another – a creator of appearances, is he not?

Of course.

But then I suppose you will say that what he creates is untrue. And yet there is a sense in which the painter also creates a bed?

Yes, he said, but not a real bed.

And what of the maker of the bed? were you not saying that he too makes, not the idea which, according to our view, is the essence of the bed, but only a particular bed?

Yes, I did.

Then if he does not make that which exists he cannot make true existence, but only some semblance of existence; and if any one were to say that the work of the maker of the bed, or of any other workman, has real existence, he could hardly be supposed to be speaking the truth.

At any rate, he replied, philosophers would say that he was not speaking the truth.

No wonder, then, that his work too is an indistinct expression of truth.

No wonder.

Suppose now that by the light of the examples just offered we enquire who this imitator is?

If you please.

Well then, here are three beds: one existing in nature, which is made by God, as I think that we may say – for no one else can be the maker?

No.

There is another which is the work of the carpenter?

Yes.

And the work of the painter is a third?

Yes.

Beds, then, are of three kinds, and there are three artists who superintend them: God, the maker of the bed, and the painter?

Yes, there are three of them. [. . .]

Then the imitator, I said, is a long way off the truth, and can do all things because he lightly touches on a small part of them, and that part an image. For example: a painter will paint a cobbler, carpenter, or any other artist, though he knows nothing of their arts; and, if he is a good artist, he may deceive children or simple persons, when he shows them his picture of a carpenter from a distance, and they will fancy that they are looking at a real carpenter.

Certainly.

And whenever any one informs us that he has found a man who knows all the arts, and all things else that anybody knows, and every single thing with a higher degree of accuracy than any other man – whoever tells us this, I think that we can only imagine him to be a simple creature who is likely to have been deceived by some wizard or actor whom he met, and whom he thought all-knowing, because he himself was unable to analyse the nature of knowledge and ignorance and imitation.

Most true.

And so, when we hear persons saying that the tragedians, and Homer, who is at their head, know all the arts and all things human, virtue as well as vice, and divine things too, for that the good poet cannot compose well unless he knows his subject, and that he who has not this knowledge can never be a poet, we ought to consider whether here also there may not be a similar illusion. Perhaps they may have come across imitators and been deceived by them; they may not have remembered when they saw their works that these were but imitations thrice removed from the truth, and could easily be made without any knowledge of the truth, because they are appearances only and not realities? Or, after all, they may be in the right, and poets do really know the things about which they seem to the many to speak so well?

The question, he said, should by all means be considered.

(Plato, *The Republic*, Book 10, translated by B. Jowett (3rd edn, Oxford: Clarendon Press, 1888), pp. 307–9, 311–12.)

(B) PLOTINUS

Enneads

[1.6.2–3, 'BEAUTY']

Let us, then, go back to the source, and indicate at once the Principle that bestows beauty on material things.

Undoubtedly this Principle exists; it is something that is perceived at the first glance, something which the soul names as from an ancient knowledge and, recognizing, welcomes it, enters into unison with it.

But let the soul fall in with the Ugly and at once it shrinks within itself, denies the thing, turns away from it, not accordant, resenting it.

Our interpretation is that the soul – by the very truth of its nature, by its affiliation to the noblest Existents in the hierarchy of Being – when it sees anything of that kin, or any trace of that kinship, thrills with an immediate delight, takes its own to itself, and thus stirs anew to the sense of its nature and of all its affinity.

But, is there any such likeness between the loveliness of this world and the splendours in the Supreme? Such a likeness in the particulars would make the two orders alike: but what is there in common between beauty here and beauty There?

We hold that all the loveliness of this world comes by communion in Ideal-Form.

All shapelessness whose kind admits of pattern and form, as long as it remains outside of Reason and Idea, is ugly by that very isolation from the Divine-Thought. And this is the Absolute Ugly: an ugly thing is something that has not been entirely mastered by pattern, that is by Reason, the Matter not yielding at all points and in all respects to Ideal-Form.

But where the Ideal-Form has entered, it has grouped and coordinated what from a diversity of parts was to become a unity: it has rallied confusion into co-operation: it has made the sum one harmonious coherence: for the Idea is a unity and what it moulds must come to unity as far as multiplicity may.

And on what has thus been compacted to unity, Beauty enthrones itself, giving itself to the parts as to the sum: when it lights on some natural unity, a thing of like parts, then it gives itself to that whole. Thus, for an illustration, there is the beauty, conferred by craftsmanship, of all a house with all its parts, and the beauty which some natural quality may give to a single stone.

This, then, is how the material thing becomes beautiful – by communicating in the thought that flows from the Divine.

And the soul includes a faculty peculiarly addressed to Beauty – one incomparably sure in the appreciation of its own, never in doubt whenever any lovely thing presents itself for judgement.

Or perhaps the soul itself acts immediately, affirming the Beautiful where it finds something accordant with the Ideal-Form within itself, using this Idea as a canon of accuracy in its decision.

But what accordance is there between the material and that which antedates all Matter?

On what principle does the architect, when he finds the house standing before him correspondent with his inner ideal of a house, pronounce it beautiful? Is it not that the house before him, the stones apart, is the inner idea stamped upon the mass of exterior matter, the indivisible exhibited in diversity?

(Plotinus, *Enneads: The Ethical Treatises, Being the Treatises of the First Ennead*, translated by S. Mackenna (London: Philip Lee Warner, for the Medici Society, 1917), pp. 79–81.)

[V.8.1, 'ON INTELLECTUAL BEAUTY']

It is a principle with us that one who has attained to the vision of the Intellectual Beauty and grasped the beauty of the

Authentic Intellect will be able also to come to understand the
Father and Transcendent of that Divine Being. It concerns us,
then, to try to see and say, for ourselves and as far as such
matters may be told, how the Beauty of the divine Intellect and
of the Intellectual Kosmos may be revealed to contemplation.

Let us go to the realm of magnitudes: – Suppose two blocks of
stone lying side by side: one is unpatterned, quite untouched by
art; the other has been minutely wrought by the craftsman's
hands into some statue of god or man, a Grace or a Muse, or if
a human being, not a portrait but a creation in which the
sculptor's art has concentrated all loveliness.

Now it must be seen that the stone thus brought under the
artist's hand to the beauty of form is beautiful not as stone – for
so the crude block would be as pleasant – but in virtue of the
form or idea introduced by the art. This form is not in the
material; it is in the designer before ever it enters the stone; and
the artificer holds it not by his equipment of eyes and hands but
by his participation in his art. The beauty, therefore, exists in a
far higher state in the art; for it does not come over integrally
into the work; that orginal beauty is not transferred; what comes
over is a derivative and a minor: and even that shows itself
upon the statue not integrally and with entire realization of
intention but only in so far as it has subdued the resistance of
the material.

Art, then, creating in the image of its own nature and content,
and working by the Idea or Reason-Principle of the beautiful
object it is to produce, must itself be beautiful in a far higher
and purer degree since it is the seat and source of that beauty,
indwelling in the art, which must naturally be more complete
than any comeliness of the external. In the degree in which the
beauty is diffused by entering into matter, it is so much the
weaker than that concentrated in unity; everything that reaches
outwards is the less for it, strength less stong, heat less hot,
every power less potent, and so beauty less beautiful.

Then again every prime cause must be, within itself, more
powerful than its effect can be: the musical does not derive from
an unmusical source but from music; and so the art exhibited in
the material work derives from an art yet higher.

Still the arts are not to be slighted on the ground that they
create by imitation of natural objects; for, to begin with, these
natural objects are themselves imitations; then, we must
recognise that they give no bare reproduction of the thing seen
but go back to the Ideas from which Nature itself derives, and,

furthermore, that much of their work is all their own; they are holders of beauty and add where nature is lacking. Thus Pheidias wrought the Zeus upon no model among things of sense but by apprehending what form Zeus must take if he chose to become manifest to sight.

(Plotinus, *The Divine Mind, Being the Treatises of the Fifth Ennead*, translated by S. Mackenna (London and Boston: Medici Society, 1926), pp. 73–4.)

(C) C. W. F. VON SCHLEGEL

Lectures on the History of Literature, Lecture 12

To determine the true and proper relation between poetry, and the past or the present, involves the investigation of the whole depth and essence of the art. In general, in our theories, with the exception of some very general, meaningless, and most commonly false definitions of the art itself, and of the beautiful, the chief subjects of attention are always the mere forms of poetry, things necessary without doubt, but by no means sufficient, to be known. As yet there has scarcely been any theory with regard to the proper subject of poetry, although such a theory would evidently be far the most useful in regard to the effect which poetry is to have upon life. In the preceding discourses I have endeavoured to supply this defect, and to give some glimpses of such a theory, wherever the nature of my topics has furnished me with an opportunity.

With regard to the representation of actual life in poetry, we must, about all things, remember that it is by no means certain that the actual and present are intractable or unworthy subjects of poetical representation, merely because in themselves they appear less noble and uncommon than the past. It is true that in what is near and present, the common and unpoetical come at all times more strongly and more conspicuously into view; while in the remote and the past, they occupy the distance, and leave the foreground to be filled with forms of greatness and sublimity alone. But this difficulty is one which the true poet can easily conquer; his art has no more favourite mode of displaying itself than in lending to things of common-place, and every day occurrence, the brilliancy of a poetic illumination, by extracting from them higher signification, and deeper purpose, and more refined feeling, than we had before suspected them of concealing, or dreamed them to be capable of exciting. Still the precision of the present is at all times binding and confining for the fancy, and when we, by our subject, impose so many fetters upon her, there is always reason to fear, that she will be inclined to make up for this restraint, by an excess of liberty in regard to language and description.

To make my views upon this point intelligible to you in the shortest way, I need only recall to your recollection what I said some time ago, with regard to subjects of a religious or Christian import. The invisible world, the Deity, and pure intellects, can never, upon the whole, be with propriety represented by us; nature and human beings are the proper and immediate subjects of poetry. But the higher and spiritual world can be everywhere embodied and shadowed forth in our terrestrial materials. In like manner the indirect representation of the actual and the present is the best and most appropriate. The bloom of young life, and the high ecstasies of passion, as well as the maturity of wise reflection, may all be combined with the old traditions of our nation; they will there have more room for exertion, and be displayed in a purer light than the present can command. The oldest poet of the past, Homer, is at the same time to us a describer of the present in its utmost liveliness and freshness. Every true poet carries into the past his own age, and, in a certain sense, himself. The following appears to me to be the true account of the proper relation between poetry and time. The proper business of poetry is to represent only the eternal, that which is, at all places, and in all times, significant and beautiful; but this cannot be accomplished without the intervention of a veil. Poetry requires to have a corporeal habitation, and this she finds in her best sphere, the traditions of a nation, the recollections and past of a people. In her representations of these, however, she introduces the whole wealth of the present, so far as that is susceptible of poetical ornament; she plunges also into the future, because she explains the apparent mysteries of earthly existence, accompanies individual life through all its development, down to its period of termination, and sheds from her magic mirror the light of a higher interpretation upon all things; she embraces all the tenses, the past, the present, and the future, in order to make a truly sensible representation of the eternal or the perfect time. Even in a philosophical sense, eternity is no nonentity, no mere negation of time, but rather its entire and undivided fullness, wherein all its elements are united, where the past becomes new and present, and with the present itself, is mingled the abundance of hope, and all the richness of futurity. . . .

It is only in the first and lowest scale of the drama, that I can place those pieces in which we are presented with the visible surface of life alone, the fleeting appearance of the rich picture of the world. It is thus that I view them, even although they display the highest sway of passion in tragedy, or the perfection of all social refinements and absurdities in comedy, so long as the whole business of the play is limited to external appearances, and these things are brought before us merely in perspective, and as pictures for the purposes of drawing our attention, and awakening the sympathy of our passions. The second order of the art is that, where in dramatic representations, together with passion and the pictoric appearance of things, a spirit of more profound sense and thought is predominate over the scene, wherein there is displayed a deep knowledge, not of individuals and their affairs alone, but of our whole species, of the world and of life, in all their manifold shapes, contradictions, and catastrophies, of man and of his being, that darkest of riddles – as such – as a riddle. Were this profound knowledge of us and our nature the only end of dramatic poetry, Shakespeare would not merely deserve to be called the first in his art, but there could scarcely be found a single poet, either among the ancients or the moderns, worthy for a moment to be compared with him. But in my opinion the art of the dramatic poet has, besides all this, yet another and a higher end. The enigma of life should not barely be expressed but solved; the perplexities of the present should indeed be represented, but from them our view should be led to the last development and the final issue. The poet should entwine the future with the present, and lay before our eyes the mysteries of the internal man. This is indeed something quite different from what we commonly demand in a tragedy by the name of catastrophe. There are many celebrated dramatic works wherein that sort of denouement, to which I here allude, is altogether wanting, or which, at least, have only the outward form, but are quite destitute of the internal being and spirit of it. . . .

(Carl Wilhelm Friedrich von Schlegel, *Lectures on the History of Literature, Ancient and Modern*, trans. J. G. Lockhart (1818; new edn, 1846), pp. 300–2, 308–9.)

(D) SAMUEL TAYLOR COLERIDGE

From 'On Poesy or Art' (1818)

As soon as the human mind is intelligibly addressed by an outward image exclusively of articulate speech, so soon does art commence. But please to observe that I have laid particular stress on the words 'human mind,' – meaning to exclude thereby all results common to man and all other sentient creatures, and consequently confining myself to the effect produced by the congruity of the animal impression with the reflective powers of the mind; so that not the thing presented, but that which is re-presented by the thing, shall be the source of the pleasure. In this sense nature itself is to a religious observer the art of God; and for the same cause art itself might be defined as of a middle quality between a thought and a thing, or as I said before, the union and reconciliation of that which is nature with that which is exclusively human. It is the figured language of thought, and is distinguished from nature by the unity of all the parts in one thought or idea. Hence nature itself would give us the impression of a work of art, if we could see the thought which is present at once in the whole and in every part; and a work of art will be just in proportion as it adequately conveys the thought, and rich in proportion to the variety of parts which it holds in unity.

If, therefore, the term 'mute' be taken as opposed not to sound but to articulate speech, the old definition of painting will in fact be the true and best definition of the Fine Arts in general, that is, *muta poesis*, mute poesy, and so of course poesy. And, as all languages perfect themselves by a gradual process of desynonymizing words originally equivalent, I have cherished the wish to use the word 'poesy' as the generic or common term, and to distinguish that species of poesy which is not *muta poesis* by its usual name 'poetry'; while of all the other species which collectively form the Fine Arts, there would remain this as the common definition, – that they all, like poetry, are to express intellectual purposes, thoughts, conceptions, and sentiments which have their origin in the human mind, – not, however, as poetry does, by means of articulate speech, but as nature or the divine art does, by form, color, magnitude, proportion, or by sound, that is, silently or musically.

Well! it may be said – but who has ever thought otherwise? We all know that art is the imitatress of nature. And, doubtless,

the truths which I hope to convey would be barren truisms, if
all men meant the same by the words 'imitate' and 'nature.' But
it would be flattering mankind at large, to presume that such is
the fact. First, to imitate. The impression on the wax is not an
imitation, but a copy, of the seal; the seal itself is an imitation.
But, further, in order to form a philosophic conception, we must
seek for the kind, as the heat in ice, invisible light, &c., whilst,
for practical purposes, we must have reference to the degree. It
is sufficient that philosophically we understand that in all
imitation two elements must coexist, and not only coexist, but
must be perceived as coexisting. These two constituent elements
are likeness and unlikeness, or sameness and difference, and in
all genuine creations of art there must be a union of these
disparates. The artist may take his point of view where he
pleases, provided that the desired effect be perceptibly produced,
– that there be likeness in the difference, difference in the
likeness, and a reconcilement of both in one. If there be likeness
to nature without any check of difference, the result is
disgusting, and the more complete the delusion, the more
loathsome the effect. Why are such simulations of nature, as
waxwork figures of men and women, so disagreeable? Because,
not finding the motion and the life which we expected, we are
shocked as by a falsehood, every circumstance of detail, which
before induced us to be interested, making the distance from
truth more palpable. You set out with a supposed reality and
are disappointed and disgusted with the deception; whilst, in
respect to a work of genuine imitation, you begin with an
acknowledged total difference, and then every touch of nature
gives you the pleasure of an approximation to truth. The
fundamental principle of all this is undoubtedly the horror of
falsehood and the love of truth inherent in the human breast.
The Greek tragic dance rested on these principles, and I can
deeply sympathize in imagination with the Greeks in this
favourite part of their theatrical exhibitions, when I call to mind
the pleasure I felt in beholding the combat of the Horatii and
Curiatii most exquisitely danced in Italy to the music of
Cimarosa.

Secondly, as to nature. We must imitate nature! yes, but what
in nature, – all and everything? No, the beautiful in nature. And
what then is the beautiful? What is beauty? It is, in the abstract,
the unity of the manifold, the coalescence of the diverse; in the
concrete, it is the union of the shapely (*formosum*) with the vital.
In the dead organic it depends on regularity of form, the first

and lowest species of which is the triangle with all its
modifications as in crystals, architecture, &c.; in the living
organic it is not mere regularity of form, which would produce a
sense of formality; neither is it subservient to any thing beside
itself. It may be present in a disagreeable object, in which the
proportion of the parts constitutes a whole; it does not arise
from association, as the agreeable does, but sometimes lies in the
rupture of association; it is not different to different individuals
and nations, as has been said, nor is it connected with the ideas
of the good, or the fit, or the useful. The sense of beauty is
intuitive, and beauty itself is all that inspires pleasure without,
and aloof from, and even contrarily to, interest.

If the artist copies the mere nature, the *natura naturata*, what
idle rivalry! If he proceeds only from a given form, which is
supposed to answer to the notion of beauty, what an emptiness,
what an unreality there always is in his productions, as in
Cipriani's pictures! Believe me, you must master the essence, the
natura naturans, which presupposes a bond between nature in the
higher sense and the soul of man.

The wisdom in nature is distinguished from that in man by
the co-instantaneity of the plan and the execution; the thought
and the product are one, or are given at once; but there is no
reflex act, and hence there is no moral responsibility. In man
there is reflexion, freedom, and choice; he is, therefore, the head
of the visible creation. In the objects of nature are presented, as
in a mirror, all the possible elements, steps, and processes of
intellect antecedent to consciousness, and therefore to the full
development of the intelligential act; and man's mind is the very
focus of all the rays of intellect which are scattered throughout
the images of nature. Now so to place these images, totalized,
and fitted to the limits of the human mind, as to elicit from, and
to superinduce upon, the forms themselves the moral reflexions
to which they approximate, to make the external internal, the
internal external, to make nature thought, and thought nature, –
this is the mystery of genius in the Fine Arts. Dare I add that
the genius must act on the feeling, that body is but a striving to
become mind, – that it is mind in its essence!

In every work of art there is a reconcilement of the external
with the internal; the conscious is so impressed on the
unconscious as to appear in it; as compare mere letters inscribed
on a tomb with figures themselves constituting the tomb. He
who combines the two is the man of genius; and for that reason
he must partake of both. Hence there is in genius itself an

unconscious activity; nay, that is the genius in the man of genius. And this is the true exposition of the rule that the artist must first eloign himself from nature in order to return to her with full effect. Why this? Because if he were to begin by mere painful copying, he would produce masks only, not forms breathing life. He must out of his own mind create forms according to the severe laws of the intellect, in order to generate in himself that co-ordination of freedom and law, that involution of obedience in the prescript, and of the prescript in the impulse to obey, which assimilates him to nature, and enables him to understand her. He merely absents himself for a season from her, that his own spirit, which has the same ground with nature, may learn her unspoken language in its main radicals, before he approaches to her endless compositions of them. Yes, not to acquire cold notions – lifeless technical rules – but living and life-producing ideas, which shall contain their own evidence, the certainty that they are essentially one with the germinal causes in nature, – his consciousness being the focus and mirror of both, – for this does the artist for a time abandon the external real in order to return to it with a complete sympathy with its internal and actual. For of all we see, hear, feel and touch the substance is and must be in ourselves; and therefore there is no alternative in reason between the dreary (and thank heaven! almost impossible) belief that every thing around us is but a phantom, or that the life which is in us is in them likewise; and that to know is to resemble, when we speak of objects out of ourselves, even as within ourselves to learn is, according to Plato, only to recollect; – the only effective answer to which, that I have been fortunate to meet with, is that which Pope has consecrated for future use in the line –

And coxcombs vanquish Berkeley with a grin!

The artist must imitate that which is within the thing, that which is active through form and figure, and discourses to us by symbols – the *Natur-geist*, or spirit of nature, as we unconsciously imitate those whom we love; for so only can he hope to produce any work truly natural in the object and truly human in the effect. The idea which puts the form together cannot itself be the form. It is above form, and is its essence, the universal in the individual, or the individuality itself – the glance and the exponent of the indwelling power.

Each thing that lives has its moment of self-exposition, and so has each period of each thing, if we remove the disturbing forces of accident. To do this is the business of ideal art, whether in images of childhood, youth, or age, in man or in woman. Hence in a good portrait is the abstract of the personal; it is not the likeness for actual comparison, but for recollection. This explains why the likeness of a very good portrait is not always recognized; because some persons never abstract, and amongst these are especially to be numbered the near relations and friends of the subject, in consequence of the constant pressure and check exercised on their minds by the actual presence of the original. And each thing that only appears to live has also its possible position of relation to life, as nature herself testifies, who, where she cannot be, prophesies her being in the crystallized metal, or the inhaling plant.

(Samuel Taylor Coleridge, 'On Poesy or Art' (1818), in *Miscellanies*, ed. T. Ashe, 1885, pp. 43–9.)

(E) PERCY BYSSHE SHELLEY

A Defence of Poetry (1821)

But poets, or those who imagine and express this indestructible order, are not only the authors of language and of music, of the dance, and architecture, and statuary, and painting; they are the institutors of laws, and the founders of civil society, and the inventors of the arts of life, and the teachers, who draw into a certain propinquity with the beautiful and the true, that partial apprehension of the agencies of the invisible world which is called religion. Hence all original religions are allegorical, or susceptible of allegory, and, like Janus, have a double face of false and true. Poets, according to the circumstances of the age and nation in which they appeared, were called, in the earlier epochs of the world, legislators, or prophets: a poet essentially comprises and unites both these characters. For he not only beholds intensely the present as it is, and discovers those laws according to which present things ought to be ordered, but he beholds the future in the present, and his thoughts are the germs of the flower and the fruit of latest time. Not that I assert poets to be prophets in the gross sense of the word, or that they can foretell the form as surely as they foreknow the spirit of events: such is the pretence of superstition, which would make poetry an attribute of prophecy, rather than prophecy an attribute of poetry. A poet participates in the eternal, the infinite, and the one; as far as relates to his conceptions, time and place and number are not. [. . .]

Lord Bacon was a poet. His language has a sweet and majestic rhythm, which satisfies the sense, no less than the almost super-human wisdom of his philosophy satisfies the intellect; it is a strain which distends, and then bursts the circumference of the reader's mind, and pours itself forth together with it into the universal element with which it has perpetual sympathy. All the authors of revolutions in opinion are not only necessarily poets as they are inventors, nor even as their words unveil the permanent analogy of things by images which participate in the life of truth; but as their periods are harmonious and rhythmical, and contain in themselves the elements of verse; being the echo of the eternal music. [. . .]

Dante was the first awakener of entranced Europe; he created a language, in itself music and persuasion, out of a chaos of inharmonious barbarisms. He was the congregator of those great spirits who presided over the resurrection of learning; the Lucifer of that starry flock which in the thirteenth century shone forth from republican Italy, as from a heaven, into the darkness of the benighted world. His very words are instinct with spirit; each is as a spark, a burning atom of inextinguishable thought; and many yet lie covered in the ashes of their birth, and pregnant with the lightning which has yet found no conductor. All high poetry is infinite; it is as the first acorn, which contained all oaks potentially. Veil after veil may be undrawn, and the inmost naked beauty of the meaning never exposed. A great poem is a fountain for ever overflowing with the waters of wisdom and delight; and after one person and one age has exhausted all its divine effluence which their peculiar relations enable them to share, another and yet another succeeds, and new relations are ever developed, the source of an unforeseen and an unconceived delight. [. . .]

Poetry is not like reasoning, a power to be exerted according to the determination of the will. A man cannot say, 'I will compose poetry.' The greatest poet even cannot say it; for the mind in creation is as a fading coal, which some invisible influence, like an inconstant wind, awakens to transitory brightness; this power arises from within, like the colour of a flower which fades and changes as it is developed, and the conscious portions of our natures are unprophetic either of its approach or its departure. [. . .]

Poetry is the record of the best and happiest moments of the happiest and best minds. We are aware of evanescent visitations of thought and feeling sometimes associated with place or person, sometimes regarding our own mind alone, and always arising unforeseen and departing unbidden, but elevating and delightful beyond all expression: so that even in the desire and the regret they leave, there cannot but be pleasure, participating as it does in the nature of its object. It is as it were the interpenetration of a diviner nature through our own; but its footsteps are like those of a wind over the sea, which the coming calm erases, and whose traces remain only as on the wrinkled sands which pave it. These and corresponding conditions of being are experienced principally by those of the most delicate sensibility and the most enlarged imagination; and the state of mind produced by them is at war with every base desire. The enthusiasm of virtue, love, patriotism, and friendship is essentially linked with such emotions; and whilst they last, self appears as what it is, an atom to a universe. Poets are not only subject to these experiences as spirits of the most refined organisation, but they can colour all that they combine with the evanescent hues of this ethereal world; a word, a trait in the representation of a scene or a passion will touch the enchanted chord, and reanimate, in those who have ever experienced these emotions, the sleeping, the cold, the buried image of the past. Poetry thus makes immortal all that is best and most beautiful in the world; it arrests the vanishing apparitions which haunt the interlunations of life, and veiling them, or in language or in form, sends them forth among mankind, bearing sweet news of kindred joy to those with whom their sisters abide – abide, because there is no portal of expression from the caverns of the spirit which they inhabit into the universe of things. Poetry redeems from decay the visitations of the divinity in man.

Poetry turns all things to loveliness; it exalts the beauty of that which is most beautiful, and it adds beauty to that which is most deformed; it marries exultation and horror, grief and pleasure, eternity and change; it subdues to union under its light yoke all irreconcilable things. It transmutes all that it touches, and every form moving within the radiance of its presence is changed by wondrous sympathy to an incarnation of the spirit which it breathes: its secret alchemy turns to potable gold the poisonous waters which flow from death through life; it strips the veil of familiarity from the world, and lays bare the naked and sleeping beauty, which is the spirit of its forms.

(Percy Bysshe Shelley, *A Defence of Poetry* (1821), *The Prose Works*, ed. R. H. Shepherd, 2 vols (London: Chatto & Windus, 1888), II. 4–5, 8, 27, 32–4.)

(F) W. B. YEATS

'The Symbolism of Poetry' (1900)

Symbolism, as seen in the writers of our day, would have no value if it were not seen also, under one 'disguise or another, in every great imaginative writer', writes Mr Arthur Symons in *The Symbolist Movement in Literature*, a subtle book which I cannot praise as I would, because it has been dedicated to me; and he goes on to show how many profound writers have in the last few years sought for a philosophy of poetry in the doctrine of symbolism, and how even in countries where it is almost scandalous to seek for any philosophy of poetry, new writers are following them in their search. [. . .]

All writers, all artists of any kind, in so far as they have had any philosophical or critical power, perhaps just in so far as they have been delicate artists at all, have had some philosophy, some criticism of their art; and it has often been this philosophy, or this criticism, that has evoked their most startling inspiration, calling into outer life some portion of the divine life, or of the buried reality, which could alone extinguish in the emotions what their philosophy or their criticism would extinguish in the intellect. They had sought for no new thing it may be, but only to understand and to copy the pure inspiration of early times, but because the divine life wars upon our outer life, and must needs change its weapons and its movements as we change ours, inspiration has come to them in beautiful startling shapes. The scientific movement brought with it a literature which was always tending to lose itself in externalities of all kinds, in opinion, in declamation, in picturesque writing, in word-painting, or in what Mr Symons has called an attempt 'to build in brick and mortar inside the covers of a book'; and now writers have begun to dwell upon the element of evocation, of suggestion, upon what we call the symbolism in great writers.

In 'Symbolism in painting', I tried to describe the element of symbolism that is in pictures and sculpture, and described a little the symbolism in poetry, but did not describe at all the continuous indefinable symbolism which is the substance of all style.

There are no lines with more melancholy beauty than these by Burns:

> The white moon is setting behind the white wave,
> And Time is setting with me, O!

and these lines are perfectly symbolical. Take from them the whiteness of the moon and of the wave, whose relation to the setting of Time is too subtle for the intellect, and you take from them their beauty. But, when all are together, moon and wave and whiteness and setting Time and the last melancholy cry, they evoke an emotion which cannot be evoked by any other arrangement of colours and sounds and forms. We may call this metaphorical writing, but it is better to call it symbolical writing, because metaphors are not profound enough to be moving, when they are not symbols, and when they are symbols they are the most perfect of all, because the most subtle, outside of pure sound, and through them one can best find out what symbols are. If one begins the reverie with any beautiful lines that one can remember, one finds they are like those by Burns. Begin with this line by Blake:

> The gay fishes on the wave when the moon sucks up the
>   dew;

or these lines by Nash:

> Brightness falls from the air,
> Queens have died young and fair,
> Dust hath closed Helen's eye;

or these lines by Shakespeare:

> Timon hath made his everlasting mansion
> Upon the beached verge of the salt flood;
> Who once a day with his embossed froth
> The turbulent surge shall cover;

or take some line that is quite simple, that gets its beauty from its place in a story, and see how it flickers with the light of the many symbols that have given the story its beauty, as a sword-blade may flicker with the light of burning towers.

All sounds, all colours, all forms, either because of their preordained energies or because of long association, evoke indefinable and yet precise emotions, or, as I prefer to think, call

down among us certain disembodied powers, whose footsteps
over our hearts we call emotions; and when sound, and colour,
and form are in a musical relation, a beautiful relation to one
another, they become, as it were, one sound, one colour, one
form, and evoke an emotion that is made out of their distinct
evocations and yet is one emotion. The same relation exists
between all portions of every work of art, whether it be an epic
or a song, and the more perfect it is, and the more various and
numerous the elements that have flowed into its perfection, the
more powerful will be the emotion, the power, the god it calls
among us. Because an emotion does not exist, or does not
become perceptible and active among us, till it has found its
expression, in colour or in sound or in form, or in all of these,
and because no two modulations or arrangements of these evoke
the same emotion, poets and painters and musicians, and in a
less degree because their effects are momentary, day and night
and cloud and shadow, are continually making and unmaking
mankind. It is indeed only those things which seem useless or
very feeble that have any power, and all those things that seem
useful or strong, armies, moving wheels, modes of architecture,
modes of government, speculations of the reason, would have
been a little different if some mind long ago had not given itself
to some emotion, as a woman gives herself to her lover, and
shaped sounds or colours or forms, or all of these, into a musical
relation, that their emotion might live in other minds. A little
lyric evokes an emotion, and this emotion gathers others about it
and melts into their being in the making of some great epic; and
at last, needing an always less delicate body, or symbol, as it
grows more powerful, it flows out, with all it has gathered,
among the blind instincts of daily life, where it moves a power
within powers, as one sees ring within ring in the stem of an old
tree. This is maybe what Arthur O'Shaughnessy meant when he
made his poets say they had built Nineveh with their sighing;
and I am certainly never sure, when I hear of some war, or of
some religious excitement, or of some new manufacture, or of
anything else that fills the ear of the world, that it has not all
happened because of something that a boy piped in Thessaly. I
remember once telling a seeress to ask one among the gods who,
as she believed, were standing about her in their symbolic
bodies, what would come of a charming but seeming trivial
labour of a friend, and the form answering, 'the devastation of
peoples and the overwhelming of cities'. I doubt indeed if the
crude circumstance of the world, which seems to create all our

emotions, does more than reflect, as in multiplying mirrors, the
emotions that have come to solitary men in moments of poetical
contemplation; or that love itself would be more than an animal
hunger but for the poet and his shadow the priest, for unless we
believe that outer things are the reality, we must believe that the
gross is the shadow of the subtle, that things are wise before
they become foolish, and secret before they cry out in the
market-place. Solitary men in moments of contemplation receive,
as I think, the creative impulse from the lowest of the Nine
Hierarchies [of angels?], and so make and unmake mankind, and
even the world itself, for does not 'the eye altering alter all'?

> Our towns are copied fragments from our breast;
> And all man's Babylons strive but to impart
> The grandeurs of his Babylonian heart.

If people were to accept the theory that poetry moves us because
of its symbolism, what change should one look for in the manner
of our poetry? A return to the way of our fathers, a casting out
of descriptions of nature for the sake of nature, of the moral law
for the sake of the moral law, a casting out of all anecdotes and
of that brooding over scientific opinion that so often extinguished
the central flame in Tennyson, and of that vehemence that
would make us do or not do certain things; or, in other words,
we should come to understand that the beryl stone was
enchanted by our fathers that it might unfold the pictures in its
heart, and not to mirror our own excited faces, or the boughs
waving outside the window. With this change of substance, this
return to imagination, this understanding that the laws of art,
which are the hidden laws of the world, can alone bind the
imagination, would come a change of style, and we would cast
out of serious poetry those energetic rhythms, as of a man
running, which are the invention of the will with its eyes always
on something to be done or undone; and we would seek out
those wavering, meditative, organic rhythms, which are the
embodiment of the imagination, that neither desires nor hates,
because it has done with time, and only wishes to gaze upon
some reality, some beauty; nor would it be any longer possible
for anybody to deny the importance of form, in all its kinds, for
although you can expound an opinion, or describe a thing, when
your words are not quite well chosen, you cannot give a body to
something that moves beyond the senses, unless your words are
as subtle, as complex, as full of mysterious life, as the body of a
flower or of a woman. The form of sincere poetry, unlike the

form of 'popular poetry', may indeed be sometimes obscure, or ungrammatical as in some of the best of the *Songs of Innocence and Experience*, but it must have the perfections that escape analysis, the subtleties that have a new meaning every day, and it must have all this whether it be but a little song made out of a moment of dreamy indolence, or some great epic made out of the dreams of one poet and of a hundred generations whose hands were never weary of the sword.

(W. B. Yeats, 'The Symbolism of Poetry' (1900), *Essays and Introductions* (London: Macmillan, 1961), pp. 153, 154–9, 163–4.)

(G) R. G. COLLINGWOOD

The Principles of Art (1938)

Theoretically, the artist is a person who comes to know himself, to know his own emotion. This is also knowing his world, that is, the sights and sounds and so forth which together make up his total imaginative experience. The two knowledges are to him one knowledge, because these sights and sounds are to him steeped in the emotion with which he contemplates them: they are the language in which that emotion utters itself to his consciousness. His world is his language. What it says to him it says about himself; his imaginative vision of it is his self-knowledge.

But this knowing of himself is a making of himself. At first he is mere psyche, the possessor of merely psychical experiences or impressions. The act of coming to know himself is the act of converting his impressions into ideas, and so of converting himself from mere psyche into consciousness. The coming to know his emotions is the coming to dominate them, to assert himself as their master. He has not yet, it is true, entered upon the life of morality; but he has taken an indispensable step forward towards it. He has learnt to acquire by his own efforts a new set of mental endowments. That is an accomplishment which must be learnt first, if later he is to acquire by his own effort mental endowments whose possession will bring him nearer to his moral ideal.

Moreover, his knowing of this new world is also the making of the new world which he is coming to know. The world he has come to know is a world consisting of language; a world where everything has the property of expressing emotion. In so far as this world is thus expressive or significant, it is he that has made it so. He has not, of course, made it 'out of nothing'. He is not God, but a finite mind still at a very elementary stage in the development of its powers. He has made it 'out of' what is presented to him in the still more elementary stage of purely psychical experience: colours, sounds, and so forth. I know that many readers, in loyalty to certain brands of metaphysic now popular, will wish to deny this. It might seem advisable for me to consider their denials, which are very familiar, and refute them, which would be very easy. But I will not do this. I am writing not to make converts, but to say what I think. If any reader thinks he knows better, I would rather he went on working out his own lines of thought than tried to adopt mine.

To return. The aesthetic experience, as we look back at it from a point of view where we distinguish theoretical from practical activity, thus presents characteristics of both kinds. It is a knowing of oneself and of one's world, these two knowns and knowings being not yet distinguished, so that the self is expressed in the world, the world consisting of language whose meaning is that emotional experience which constitutes the self, and the self consisting of emotions which are known only as expressed in the language which is the world. It is also a making of oneself and of one's world, the self which was psyche being remade in the shape of consciousness, and the world, which was crude sensa, being remade in the shape of language, or sensa converted into imagery and charged with emotional significance.

(R. G. Collingwood, *The Principles of Art* (1938; London: Oxford UP, 1963), pp. 291–2.)

(H) WALLACE STEVENS

The Necessary Angel (1951)

I am interested in the nature of poetry and I have stated its nature, from one of the many points of view from which it is possible to state it. It is an interdependence of the imagination and reality as equals. This is not a definition, since it is incomplete. But it states the nature of poetry. Then I am interested in the role of the poet and this is paramount. In this

area of my subject I might be expected to speak of the social,
that is to say sociological or political, obligation of the poet. He
has none. [. . .]

Dante in Purgatory and Paradise was still the voice of the
Middle Ages but not through fulfilling any social obligation.
Since that is the role most frequently urged, if that role is
eliminated, and if a possible poet is left facing life without any
categorical exactions upon him, what then? What is his function?
Certainly it is not to lead people out of the confusion in which
they find themselves. Nor is it, I think, to comfort them while
they follow their readers to and fro. I think that his function is
to make his imagination theirs and that he fulfills himself only
as he sees his imagination become the light in the minds of
others. His role, in short, is to help people to live their lives.
Time and time again it has been said that he may not address
himself to an élite. I think he may. There is not a poet whom
we prize living today that does not address himself to an élite.
The poet will continue to do this: to address himself to an élite
even in a classless society, unless, perhaps, this exposes him to
imprisonment or exile. In that event he is likely not to address
himself to anyone at all. He may, like Shostakovich, content
himself with pretence. He will, nevertheless, still be addressing
himself to an élite, for all poets address themselves to someone
and it is of the essence of that instinct, and it seems to amount
to an instinct, that it should be to an élite, not to a drab but to
a woman with the hair of a pythoness, not to a chamber of
commerce but to a gallery of one's own, if there are enough of
one's own to fill a gallery. And that élite, if it responds, not out
of complaisance, but because the poet has quickened it, because
he has educed from it that for which it was searching in itself
and in the life around it and which it had not yet quite found,
will thereafter do for the poet what he cannot do for himself,
that is to say, receive his poetry.

   I repeat that his role is to help people to live their lives. He
has had immensely to do with giving life whatever savor it
possesses. He has had to do with whatever the imagination and
the senses have made of the world. He has, in fact, had to do
with life except as the intellect has had to do with it and, as to
that, no one is needed to tell us that poetry and philosophy are
akin. I want to repeat for two reasons a number of observations
made by Charles Mauron. The first reason is that these
observations tell us what it is that a poet does to help people to

live their lives and the second is that they prepare the way for a word concerning escapism. They are: that the artist transforms us into epicures; that he has to discover the possible work of art in the real world, then to extract it, when he does not himself compose it entirely; that he is *un amoureux perpétuel* of the world that he contemplates and thereby enriches; that art sets out to express the human soul; and finally that everything like a firm grasp of reality is eliminated from the aesthetic field. With these aphorisms in mind, how is it possible to condemn escapism? The poetic process is psychologically an escapist process. The chatter about escapism is, to my way of thinking, merely common cant. My own remarks about resisting or evading the pressure of reality mean escapism, if analyzed. Escapism has a pejorative sense, which it cannot be supposed that I include in the sense in which I use the word. The pejorative sense applies where the poet is not attached to reality, where the imagination does not adhere to reality, which, for my part, I regard as fundamental. If we go back to the collection of solid, static objects extended in space, which Dr. Joad posited, and if we say that the space is blank space, nowhere, without color, and that the objects, though solid, have no shadows and, though static, exert a mournful power, and without elaborating this complete poverty, if suddenly we hear a different and familiar description of the place:

> This City now doth, like a garment, wear
> The beauty of the morning, silent, bare,
> Ships, towers, domes, theatres, and temples lie
> Open unto the fields, and to the sky;
> All bright and glittering in the smokeless air;

if we have this experience, we know how poets help people to live their lives. This illustration must serve for all the rest. There is, in fact, a world of poetry indistinguishable from the world in which we live, or, I ought to say, no doubt, from the world in which we shall come to live, since what makes the poet the potent figure that he is, or was, or ought to be, is that he creates the world to which we turn incessantly and without knowing it and that he gives to life the supreme fictions without which we are unable to conceive of it.

And what about the sound of words? What about nobility, of which the fortunes were to be a kind of test of the value of the poet? I do not know of anything that will appear to have suffered more from the passage of time than the music of poetry

and that has suffered less. The deepening need for words to
express our thoughts and feelings which, we are sure, are all the
truth that we shall ever experience, having no illusions, makes
us listen to words when we hear them, loving them and feeling
them, makes us search the sound of them, for a finality, a
perfection, an unalterable vibration, which it is only within the
power of the acutest poet to give them. Those of us who may
have been thinking of the path of poetry, those who understand
that words are thoughts and not only our own thoughts but the
thoughts of men and women ignorant of what it is that they are
thinking, must be conscious of this: that, above everything else,
poetry is words; and that words, above everything else, are, in
poetry, sounds. This being so, my time and yours might have
been better spent if I had been less interested in trying to give
our possible poet an identity and less interested in trying to
appoint him to his place. But unless I had done these things, it
might have been thought that I was rhetorical, when I was
speaking in the simplest way about things of such importance
that nothing is more so. A poet's words are of things that do not
exist without the words. Thus, the image of the charioteer and
of the winged horses, which has been held to be precious for all
of time that matters, was created by words of things that never
existed without the words. A description of Verrocchio's statue
could be the integration of an illusion equal to the statue itself.
Poetry is a revelation in words by means of the words. Croce
was not speaking of poetry in particular when he said that
language is perpetual creation. About nobility I cannot be sure
that the decline, not to say the disappearance of nobility is
anything more than a maladjustment between the imagination
and reality. We have been a little insane about the truth. We
have had an obsession. In its ultimate extension, the truth about
which we have been insane will lead us to look beyond the truth
to something in which the imagination will be the dominant
complement. It is not only that the imagination adheres to
reality, but, also, that reality adheres to the imagination and
that the interdependence is essential. We may emerge from our
bassesse and, if we do, how would it happen if not by the
intervention of some fortune of the mind? And what would that
fortune of the mind happen to be? It might be only
commonsense but even that, a commonsense beyond the truth,
would be a nobility of long descent.

(Wallace Stevens, *The Necessary Angel* (New York: Vintage Books, Knopf
and Random House, 1951), pp. 27–33.)

CHAPTER 2

MIMESIS AND REALISM

The most influential theory of representation is descended from Aristotle's *Poetics*. His work was often little known at first hand during the Renaissance, but the concept of 'mimesis' was widely used. The arguments of the *Poetics* also anticipate and resemble those put forward in the nineteenth and twentieth centuries by writers such as Emile Zola and Georg Lukács.

In Plato's *Republic* the term 'imitation' (*mimesis*) always carried a negative connotation: to imitate is to produce a secondary copy, a version which is less pure than the original. Aristotle, in contrast, treats imitation as a basic human faculty which expresses itself in a wide range of arts. He does not use the term 'mimesis' in a narrow sense. To imitate is not to produce a copy or mirror reflection of something, but involves a complex mediation of reality. This is evident from his division of mimesis into three aspects: 'means', 'objects' and 'manner'. One can imitate not only by 'means' of words or paint but with flute-playing and dancing. Secondly he recognizes that imitation always involves a rigorous *selection* of those objects which are deemed appropriate for imitation. For example, Aristotle considers that in tragedy the writer imitates people's actions rather than their characters. Developing Plato's notions he also sketches out what we would now call fictional modes ('manner') – the range of possible modes of presentation including authorial presence, absence, or purely dramatic presentation (see also Wayne Booth, III, 5, F).

Not only does Aristotle avoid a literal notion of representation but he preserves a subtle tension between the requirements of mimesis and those of aesthetic structure (see also Aristotle, III, 6, B). Art must correspond to life *and* achieve a certain structural order. As to correspondence, he contrasts the poet and the historian: the latter reflects the particular and the factual, the former the universal and the general. The poet is concerned with the 'probable', not merely the 'possible': 'A likely impossibility is always preferable to an unconvincing possibility.' There may be probability in a fairy story: the connection between one incident and another may conform to a sense of the probable; on the other hand, a plot which is full of coincidences, none of which is impossible, may seem improbable. Interestingly, that which makes for probability also makes for aesthetic coherence and harmony. A probable action in a play is not only an action which convinces an audience that it possesses a general truthfulness, but also an action which fits convincingly into a chain of actions (a plot) and contributes to a unified poetic whole. The same argument applies to universality. A writer's ability to present universal truths about human life depends upon his skill in constructing a plot which consists of a series of actions evolving with convincingness and inevitability. The writer does not merely imitate particular objects or events, but reveals the logical coherence underlying events in human life.

The next section (Nature and Truth) examines the way in which seventeenth– and eighteenth–century writers developed or rejected the Aristotelian notion of artistic truth. The modern proponents of 'naturalism' and 'realism' are not derived from Aristotle in any direct line, but, in a general sense, adopt the Aristotelian view of representation and not the Platonic view. There is also a theory of realism descended from classical commentaries on comedy (notably Donatus on Terence), which describe comedy as a 'mirror of life' (see Auerbach, III, 5, C). There are many difficulties and confusions associated with the term 'realism' of which four stand out:

i. Failure to distinguish between 'objective' (documentary) and 'subjective' (psychological) realisms.

ii. Application of the term to subject matter (low life, middle-class life, etc.) rather than to modes of presentation.

iii. Association of the term with neutrality and objectivity (Defoe and Truman Capote are realistic, but not Richardson and Virginia Woolf).

iv. The general assumption that language can represent the 'real'.

Many of these attitudes can be found in Emile Zola who used the term 'naturalism' to describe the kind of novel he wrote. Naturalistic writers have a 'scientific' attitude which leads them

to dwell upon the physical, biological and mechanical causes of
human life. Zola himself tried to apply the experimental methods
recommended in Claude Bernard's medical theories. The novel
must use 'observation' and 'experiment' to establish the
physiological causes of social relations. Zola sees no further need
for the imagination: novelists equipped with a modern scientific
method may now dispense with the old-fashioned imaginative
fictions which have propped up the art of the novel hitherto.
Zola contradicts Aristotle in arguing that the novelist represents
the concrete and the individual rather than the abstract and the
general.

Not surprisingly Marxist criticism has been deeply interested
in the concept of 'realism'. The so-called Brecht–Lukács debate
was a fascinating disagreement between a major critic of the
novel and a major dramatist. Lukács' theories are a development
of and an influence upon Soviet Socialist realism. His essay 'Art
and Objective Truth' is a useful survey of his thinking about
representation and the novel. He concentrates on four ideas:
reflection, idealism, materialism and objectivity.

To 'reflect' is 'to frame a mental structure' in words. Like
Aristotle Lukács believes that the writer does not simply register
individual objects or events, but gives us 'the full process of life'.
Art is a special way of reflecting reality, not to be confused with
reality itself. The notion of the novel's separation from reality
links Lukács with German idealist philosophy (Marx himself had
been profoundly influenced by Hegel) and distinguishes his
approach very clearly from Zola's. The novelist, he argues,
refuses to see reality as mechanical causation or random flux,
but tries to assist the reader to experience the process of reality
as an ordered and significantly shaped world. This 'idealist'
element means that Lukács' 'materialism' is not the pseudo-
scientific materialism of Zola but a materialism which seeks to
reveal the deep structural process of historical change. The
objectivity of realism, according to Lukács, is not a dispassionate
non-involvement but a commitment to a particular reading of
human society – 'the partisanship of objectivity'.

According to Lukács the nineteenth-century realist novel is a
model of literary form, because it achieves the adequate
reflection of human society, as is required by socialist realism.
Bertholt Brecht's profound disagreement with Lukács centres on
this question of form. Brecht believed that throughout history
'new problems loom up and demand new techniques. Reality
alters; to represent it the means of representation must alter

too.' Unlike Lukács he is profoundly anti-Aristotelian, not so much over the question of mimesis but on the issue of 'catharsis' (see II, 4, A). 'Aristotelian' theatre at the end of the nineteenth century, typified in Strindberg's plays, aimed at a maximum of dramatic illusion in order to involve the audience subjectively in an empathic identification with the characters. According to Brecht the whole pretence that what was going on on the stage was 'real' interfered with the effective communication between dramatist and audience. Only by recognizing that actors are acting can the audience begin seriously to involve themselves in the dramatist's *critical* presentation of reality. Every effort must be made to break down the illusion of reality and to resist the audience's tendency to 'empathize' by the use of masks, placards, back-projection, direct address to the audience, unnaturalistic scenery, and so on. This theory of the 'alienation effect' (*Verfremdung*) is a complete break with the late nineteenth-century theories of naturalism. Brecht rejects the idea that a particular literary form (the novel) is *the* ideal one for reflecting reality. He also rejects Lukács' contempt for literary modernism. Far from finding the techniques of Kafka, Proust and Joyce decadent in their subjectivity and pessimism, he believed that the same techniques could be used by socialists to reflect the social world powerfully.

Erich Auerbach's *Mimesis* made an important innovation in the concept of realism by linking it with stylistic development over long historical periods. He argues that in the classical period the 'separation of styles', which was the literary expression of social hierarchy, prevented the development of realism in the modern sense, because only characters of the highest social standing could be treated as truly serious. Ordinary human existence could be treated only in an unserious (comic or satiric) manner. The story of Christ, however, violates the principle of stylistic separation: the lowliest man (a carpenter) is identified with the highest being. What prevents medieval Christian literature from attaining the full seriousness of realism is its otherworldliness: full significance exists not on earth but in a heavenly dimension. Only in the modern novel does the writer present mundane reality in its historical particularity and with full seriousness.

The French 'new novel' threw into question many of the classic assumptions about realism. In his earlier writings Alain Robbe-Grillet appeared to achieve the ultimate realism. It was called '*chosisme*' (thingism) because it attempted to exclude all

human interference in the act of representation. He argued that
the 'descriptive adjective', which merely measures, defines and
delimits, must be perfected if the novel is to achieve a pure
representation. Humanism, Marxism, classicism, romanticism,
liberalism – all Western 'isms' – have systematically
appropriated the visual to the human. A chair is reduced from
its pure thingness (a configuration of lines and planes) to a
human artefact (something to sit on). This attempt to exclude
completely the human perception is of course absurdly
impractical, but this very absurdity is intended to suggest a
radical critique of the very concept of realism. The next step in
his work was a move toward absolute subjectivity: there are no
things but only *perceptions* of things – everything is a mental
image. The third and final move in his work (in a way all three
phases are simultaneous) was the obliteration of both things and
perception; we are left with only language.

Robbe-Grillet's final position is structuralist (see III, 6) in its
rejection of the entire representational view of language.
Narrative refers to nothing in reality, but, as Barthes put it,
'"what happens" is language alone, the adventure of language'.

Background reading

Hazard Adams, *The Interests of Criticism: An Introduction to Literary Theory*
(New York: Harcourt, Brace and World, 1969), ch. 2: 'Imitation
and Creation'.

Aristotle, *Poetics*, trans. Leon Golden, commentary O. B. Hardison
(Englewood Cliffs, NJ: Prentice-Hall, 1968), esp. 'Epilogue: On
Aristotelian Imitation'.

Aristotle, *Poetics*, ed. D. W. Lucas (Oxford: Clarendon Press, 1968).
Appendix on 'Imitation'.

G. J. Becker (ed.), *Documents of Modern Literary Realism* (Princeton, NJ:
Princeton UP, 1963).

Walter Benjamin, *Understanding Brecht*, trans. Anna Bostock (London:
New Left Books, 1973).

G. M. C. Brandes, *Main Currents in Nineteenth-Century Literature*, 6 vols
(London: Heinemann, 1901–5), vol. 4: *Naturalism in England*.

Bertold Brecht, 'Against Georg Lukács', *New Left Review*, 84 (1974),
39–54.

S. H. Butcher, *Aristotle's Theory of Poetry and Fine Art* (1895, 3rd edn,
London: Macmillan, 1902).

Lane Cooper, *The Poetics of Aristotle: Its Meaning and Influence* (London:
Harrap, 1923).

G. F. Else, *Aristotle's Poetics: The Argument* (Cambridge, Mass.: Harvard
UP, 1957).

A. H. House, *Aristotle's Poetics: A Course of Eight Lectures* (London: Rupert Hart-Davis, 1956).

Fredric Jameson, *Marxism and Form* (Princeton, NJ: Princeton UP, 1971), ch. 3: 'The Case for Georg Lukács'.

W. Mittenzwei, 'The Brecht–Lukács Debate', in *Preserve and Create: Essays in Marxist Literary Criticism*, ed. Gaylord C. LeRoy and Ursula Beitz (New York: Humanities Press, 1973).

Stefan Morawski, *Inquiries into the Fundamentals of Aesthetics* (Cambridge, Mass., and London: MIT Press, 1974), ch. 6: 'Mimesis and Realism'.

J. P. Stern, *On Realism* (London: Routledge & Kegan Paul, 1973).

René Wellek, *Concepts of Criticism* (New Haven and London: Yale UP, 1963), 'The Concept of Realism in Literary Scholarship'.

Raymond Williams, *The Long Revolution* (London: Chatto & Windus, 1961), ch. 7: 'Realism and the Contemporary English Novel'.

(A) ARISTOTLE

Poetics

[1]

Our subject being Poetry, I propose to speak not only of the art in general but also of its species and their respective capacities; of the structure of plot required for a good poem; of the number and nature of the constituent parts of a poem; and likewise of any other matters in the same line of inquiry. Let us follow the natural order and begin with the primary facts.

Epic poetry and Tragedy, as also Comedy, Dithyrambic poetry, and most flute-playing and lyre-playing, are all, viewed as a whole, modes of imitation. But at the same time they differ from one another in three ways, either by a difference of kind in their means, or by differences in the objects, or in the manner of their imitations.

I. Just as form and colour are used as means by some, who (whether by art or constant practice) imitate and portray many things by their aid, and the voice is used by others; so also in the above-mentioned group of arts, the means with them as a whole are rhythm, language, and harmony – used, however, either singly or in certain combinations. A combination of rhythm and harmony alone is the means in flute-playing and lyre-playing, and any other arts there may be of the same description, e.g. imitative piping. Rhythm alone, without harmony, is the means in the dancer's imitations; for even he, by the rhythms of his attitudes, may represent men's characters, as well as what they do and suffer. There is further an art which imitates by language alone, without harmony, in prose or in verse, and if in verse, either in some one or in a plurality of metres. This form of imitation is to this day without a name. We have no common name for a mime of Sophron or Xenarchus and a Socratic Conversation; and we should still be without one even if the imitation in the two instances were in trimeters or elegiacs or some other kind of verse – though it is the way with people to tack on 'poet' to the name of a metre, and talk of elegiac-poets and epic-poets, thinking that they call them poets not by reason of the imitative nature of their work, but indiscriminately by reason of the metre they write in. Even if a theory of medicine or physical philosophy be put forth in a metrical form, it is usual to describe the writer in this way; Homer and Empedocles, however, have really nothing in common apart from their metre; so that, if the one is to be called a poet, the other should be termed a physicist rather than a poet. [. . .] So much, then, as to these arts. There are, lastly, certain other arts, which combine all the means enumerated, rhythm, melody, and verse, e.g. Dithyrambic and Nomic poetry, Tragedy and Comedy; with this difference, however, that the three kinds of means are in some of them all employed together, and in others brought in separately, one after the other. These elements of difference in the above arts I term the means of their imitation.

[2]

II. The objects the imitator represents are actions, with agents who are necessarily either good men or bad – the diversities of human character being nearly always derivative from this primary distinction, since the line between virtue and vice is one dividing the whole of mankind. It follows, therefore, that the agents represented must be either above our own level of goodness, or beneath it, or just such as we are; in the same way as, with the painters, the personages of Polygnotus are better than we are, those of Pauson worse, and those of Dionysius just like ourselves. It is clear that each of the above-mentioned arts will admit of these differences, and that it will become a separate art by representing objects with this point of difference.

Even in dancing, flute-playing, and lyre-playing such diversities
are possible; and they are also possible in the nameless art that
uses language, prose or verse without harmony, as its means;
Homer's personages, for instance, are better than we are;
Cleophon's are on our own level; and those of Hegemon of
Thasos, the first writer of parodies, and Nicochares, the author
of the *Diliad*, are beneath it. [. . .] This difference it is that
distinguishes Tragedy and Comedy also; the one would make its
personages worse, and the other better, than the men of the
present day.

[3]

A third difference in these arts is in the manner in which each
kind of object is represented. Given both the same means and
the same kind of object for imitation, one may either (1) speak
at one moment in narrative and at another in an assumed
character, as Homer does; or (2) one may remain the same
throughout, without any such change; or (3) the imitators may
represent the whole story dramatically, as though they were
actually doing the things described.

As we said at the beginning, therefore, the differences in the
imitation of these arts come under three heads, their means,
their objects, and their manner. [. . .]

[4]

It is clear that the general origin of poetry was due to two
causes, each of them part of human nature. Imitation is natural
to man from childhood, one of his advantages over the lower
animals being this, that he is the most imitative creature in the
world, and learns at first by imitation. And it is also natural for
all to delight in works of imitation. The truth of this second
point is shown by experience: though the objects themselves may
be painful to see, we delight to view the most realistic
representations of them in art, the forms for example of the
lowest animals and of dead bodies. The explanation is to be
found in a further fact: to be learning something is the greatest
of pleasures not only to the philosopher but also to the rest of
mankind, however small their capacity for it; the reason of the
delight in seeing the picture is that one is at the same time
learning – gathering the meaning of things, e.g. that the man

there is so-and-so; for if one has not seen the thing before, one's pleasure will not be in the picture as an imitation of it, but will be due to the execution or colouring or some similar cause. Imitation, then, being natural to us – as also the sense of harmony and rhythm, the metres being obviously species of rhythms – it was through their original aptitude, and by a series of improvements for the most part gradual on their first efforts, that they created poetry out of their improvisations. [. . .]

[6]

I. As they act the stories, it follows that in the first place the Spectacle (or stage-appearance of the actors) must be some part of the whole; and in the second Melody and Diction, these two being the means of their imitation. Here by 'Diction' I mean merely this, the composition of the verses; and by 'Melody', what is too completely understood to require explanation. But further: the subject represented also is an action; and the action involves agents, who must necessarily have their distinctive qualities both of character and thought, since it is from these that we ascribe certain qualities to their actions. There are in the natural order of things, therefore, two causes, Character and Thought, of their actions, and consequently of their success or failure in their lives. Now the action (that which was done) is represented in the play by the Fable or Plot. The Fable, in our present sense of the term, is simply this, the combination of the incidents, or things done in the story; whereas Character is what makes us ascribe certain moral qualities to the agents; and Thought is shown in all they say when proving a particular point or, it may be, enunciating a general truth. There are six parts consequently of every tragedy, as a whole, that is, of such or such quality, viz. a Fable or Plot, Characters, Diction, Thought, Spectacle and Melody; two of them arising from the means, one from the manner, and three from the objects of the dramatic imitation; and there is nothing else besides these six. Of these, its formative elements, then, not a few of the dramatists have made due use, as every play, one may say, admits of Spectacle, Character, Fable, Diction, Melody, and Thought.

The most important of the six is the combination of the incidents of the story. Tragedy is essentially an imitation not of

persons but of action and life, of happiness and misery. All
human happiness or misery takes the form of action; the end for
which we live is a certain kind of activity, not a quality.
Character gives us qualities, but it is in our actions – what we
do – that we are happy or the reverse. In a play accordingly
they do not act in order to portray the Characters; they include
the Characters for the sake of the action. So that it is the action
in it, i.e. its Fable or Plot, that is the end and purpose of the
tragedy; and the end is everywhere the chief thing. Besides this,
a tragedy is impossible without action, but there may be one
without Character. The tragedies of most of the moderns are
characterless – a defect common among poets of all kinds, and
with its counterpart in painting in Zeuxis as compared with
Polygnotus; for whereas the latter is strong in character, the
work of Zeuxis is devoid of it. And again: one may string
together a series of characteristic speeches of the utmost finish as
regards Diction and Thought, and yet fail to produce the true
tragic effect; but one will have much better success with a
tragedy which, however inferior in these respects, has a Plot, a
combination of incidents, in it. And again: the most powerful
elements of attraction in Tragedy, the Peripeties and Discoveries,
are parts of the Plot. A further proof is in the fact that beginners
succeed earlier with the Diction and Characters than with the
construction of a story; and the same may be said of nearly all
the early dramatists. We maintain, therefore, that the first
essential, the life and soul, so to speak, of Tragedy is the Plot;
and that the Characters come second – compare the parallel in
painting, where the most beautiful colours laid on without order
will not give one the same pleasure as a simple black-and-white
sketch of a portrait. We maintain that Tragedy is primarily an
imitation of action, and that it is mainly for the sake of the
action that it imitates the personal agents. [. . .]

[9]

From what we have said it will be seen that the poet's function
is to describe, not the thing that has happened, but a kind of
thing that might happen, i.e. what is possible as being probable
or necessary. The distinction between historian and poet is not
in the one writing prose and the other verse – you might put the
work of Herodotus into verse, and it would still be a species of
history; it consists really in this, that the one describes the thing

that has been, and the other a kind of thing that might be. Hence poetry is something more philosophic and of graver import than history, since its statements are of the nature rather of universals, whereas those of history are singulars. By a universal statement I mean one as to what such or such a kind of man will probably or necessarily say or do – which is the aim of poetry, though it affixes proper names to the characters; by a singular statement, one as to what, say, Alcibiades did or had done to him. [. . .]

It is evident from the above that the poet must be more the poet of his stories or Plots than of his verses, inasmuch as he is a poet by virtue of the imitative element in his work, and it is actions that he imitates. And if he should come to take a subject from actual history, he is none the less a poet for that; since some historic occurrences may very well be in the probable and possible order of things; and it is in that aspect of them that he is their poet.

[24]

[. . .]

A likely impossibility is always preferable to an unconvincing possibility.

[25]

[. . .]

(1) The poet being an imitator just like the painter or other maker of likenesses, he must necessarily in all instances represent things in one or other of three aspects, either as they were or are, or as they are said or thought to be or to have been, or as they ought to be.   (2) All this he does in language, with an admixture, it may be, of strange words and metaphors, as also of the various modified forms of words, since the use of these is conceded in poetry.   (3) It is to be remembered, too, that there is not the same kind of correctness in poetry as in politics, or indeed any other art. [. . .]

Speaking generally, one has to justify (1) the Impossible by reference to the requirements of poetry, or to the better, or to opinion. For the purposes of poetry a convincing impossibility is preferable to an unconvincing possibility; and if men such as Zeuxis depicted be impossible, the answer is that it is

better they should be like that, as the artist ought to improve on
his model.

(Aristotle, *Poetics*, ed. Ingram Bywater (*On the Art of Poetry*) (Oxford:
Clarendon Press, 1920), pp. 23–7, 28–30, 35–8, 43, 44–5, 84, 85–6, 91.)

(B) EMILE ZOLA

'The Experimental Novel' (1880)

Now, to return to the novel, we can easily see that the novelist
is equally an observer and an experimentalist. The observer in
him gives the facts as he has observed them, suggests the point
of departure, displays the solid earth on which his characters are
to tread and the phenomena to develop. Then the
experimentalist appears and introduces an experiment, that is to
say, sets his characters going in a certain story so as to show
that the succession of facts will be such as the requirements of
the determinism of the phenomena under examination call for.
Here it is nearly always an experiment '*pour voir*,' as Claude
Bernard calls it. The novelist starts out in search of a truth. I
will take as an example the character of the *Baron Hulot*, in
'Cousine Bette,' by Balzac. The general fact observed by Balzac
is the ravages that the amorous temperament of a man makes in
his home, in his family, and in society. As soon as he has chosen
his subject he starts from known facts; then he makes his
experiment, and exposes *Hulot* to a series of trials, placing him
amid certain surroundings in order to exhibit how the
complicated machinery of his passions works. It is then evident
that there is not only observation there, but that there is also
experiment; as Balzac does not remain satisfied with
photographing the facts collected by him, but interferes in a
direct way to place his character in certain conditions, and of
these he remains the master. The problem is to know what such
a passion, acting in such a surrounding and under such
circumstances, would produce from the point of view of an
individual and of society; and an experimental novel, 'Cousine
Bette,' for example, is simply the report of the experiment that
the novelist conducts before the eyes of the public. In fact, the
whole operation consists in taking facts in nature, then in
studying the mechanism of these facts, acting upon them, by the
modification of circumstances and surroundings, without

deviating from the laws of nature. Finally, you possess knowledge of the man, scientific knowledge of him, in both his individual and social relations.

Doubtless we are still far from certainties in chemistry and even physiology. Nor do we know any more the reagents which decompose the passions, rendering them susceptible of analysis. Often, in this essay, I shall recall in similar fashion this fact, that the experimental novel is still younger than experimental medicine, and the latter is but just born. But I do not intend to exhibit the acquired results, I simply desire to clearly expose a method. If the experimental novelist is still groping in the most obscure and complex of all the sciences, this does not prevent this science from existing. It is undeniable that the naturalistic novel, such as we understand it to-day, is a real experiment that a novelist makes on man by the help of observation.

Besides, this opinion is not only mine, it is Claude Bernard's as well. He says in one place: 'In practical life men but make experiments on one another.' And again, in a more conclusive way, he expresses the whole theory of the experimental novel: 'When we reason on our own acts we have a certain guide, for we are conscious of what we think and how we feel. But if we wish to judge of the acts of another man, and know the motives which make him act, that is altogether a different thing. Without doubt we have before our eyes the movements of this man and his different acts, which are, we are sure, the modes of expression of his sensibility and his will. Further, we even admit that there is a necessary connection between the acts and their cause; but what is this cause? We do not feel it, we are not conscious of it, as we are when it acts in ourselves; we are therefore obliged to interpret it, and to guess at it, from the movements which we see and the words which we hear. We are obliged to check off this man's actions one by the other; we consider how he acted in such a circumstance, and, in a word, we have recourse to the experimental method.' All that I have spoken of further back is summed up in this last phrase, which is written by a savant.

I shall still call your attention to another illustration of Claude Bernard, which struck me as very forcible: 'The experimentalist is the examining magistrate of nature.' We novelists are the examining magistrates of men and their passions.

But see what splendid clearness breaks forth when this conception of the application of the experimental method to the novel is adequately grasped and is carried out with all the

scientific rigor which the matter permits to-day. A contemptible
reproach which they heap upon us naturalistic writers is the
desire to be solely photographers. We have in vain declared that
we admit the necessity of an artist's possessing an individual
temperament and a personal expression; they continue to reply
to us with these imbecile arguments, about the impossibility of
being strictly true, about the necessity of arranging facts to
produce a work of art of any kind. Well, with the application of
the experimental method to the novel that quarrel dies out. The
idea of experiment carries with it the idea of modification. We
start, indeed, from the true facts, which are our indestructible
basis; but to show the mechanism of these facts it is necessary
for us to produce and direct the phenomena; this is our share of
invention, here is the genius in the book. Thus without having
recourse to the questions of form and of style, which I shall
examine later, I maintain even at this point that we must
modify nature, without departing from nature, when we employ
the experimental method in our novels. If we bear in mind this
definition, that 'observation indicates and experiment teaches,'
we can even now claim for our books this great lesson of
experiment. [. . .]

The object of the experimental method in physiology and in
medicine is to study phenomena in order to become their
master. Claude Bernard in each page of 'L'Introduction' comes
back to this idea. He declares: 'All natural philosophy is
summed up in this: To know the laws which govern phenomena.
The experimental problem reduces itself to this: To foresee and
direct phenomena.' [. . .] If I were to define the experimental
novel I should not say, as Claude Bernard says, that a literary
work lies entirely in the personal feeling, for the reason that in
my opinion the personal feeling is but the first impulse. Later
nature, being there, makes itself felt, or at least that part of
nature of which science has given us the secret, and about which
we have no longer any right to romance. The experimental
novelist is therefore the one who accepts proven facts, who
points out in man and in society the mechanism of the
phenomena over which science is mistress, and who does not
interpose his personal sentiments, except in the phenomena
whose determinism is not yet settled, and who tries to test, as
much as he can, this personal sentiment, this idea *a priori*, by
observation and experiment.

(Emile Zola, 'The Experimental Novel', in *The Experimental Novel and
Other Essays*, trans. Belle M. Sherman (New York: Cassell, 1893),

pp. 8–11, 24, 53–4. The original French appeared in *Le roman
expérimental* (Paris, 1880).)

'Naturalism on the Stage' (1880)

Naturalism in letters is equally the return to nature and to man,
direct observation, exact anatomy, the acceptance and depicting
of what is. The task was the same for the writer as for the
savant. One and the other replaced abstractions by realities,
empirical formulas by rigorous analysis. Thus, no more abstract
characters in books, no more lying inventions, no more of the
absolute; but real characters, the true history of each one, the
story of daily life. It was a question of commencing all over
again; of knowing man down to the sources of his being before
coming to such conclusions as the idealists reached, who
invented types of character out of the whole cloth; and writers
had only to start the edifice at the foundation, bringing together
the greatest number of human data arranged in their logical
order. This is naturalism; starting in the first thinking brain, if
you wish; but whose greatest evolution, the definite evolution,
without doubt took place in the last century. [. . .]

I have said that the naturalistic novel is simply an inquiry
into nature, beings, and things. It no longer interests itself in the
ingenuity of a well-invented story, developed according to certain
rules. Imagination no longer has a place; plot matters little to the
novelist, who bothers himself with neither development, mystery,
nor *dénouement*; I mean that he does not intervene to take away
from or add to reality; he does not construct a framework out of
the whole cloth, according to the needs of a preconceived idea.
You start from the point that nature is sufficient, that you must
accept it as it is, without modification or pruning; it is grand
enough, beautiful enough to supply its own beginning, its
middle, and its end. Instead of imagining an adventure, of
complicating it, of arranging stage effects, which scene by scene
will lead to a final conclusion, you simply take the life study of a
person or a group of persons, whose actions you faithfully depict.
The work becomes a report, nothing more; it has but the merit
of exact observation, of more or less profound penetration and
analysis, of the logical connection of facts. [. . .] Entire nature is
its domain. It adopts the form which pleases it, taking the tone
which seems best, feeling no longer bounded by any limit. In
this we are far distant from the novel that our fathers were
acquainted with. It was a purely imaginative work, whose sole

end was to charm and distract its readers. [. . .] As to the acts [in plays], they are consistent with analysis in action, which is the most striking form of action one can make. When we have gotten rid of the child's play of a plot, the infantile game of tying up complicated threads in order to have the pleasure of untying them again; when a play shall be nothing more than a real and logical story – we shall then enter into perfect analysis; we shall analyze necessarily the double influence of characters over facts, of facts over characters. This is what has led me to say so often that the naturalistic formula carries us back to the source of our national stage, the classical formula. We find this continuous analysis of character, which I consider so necessary, in Corneille's tragedies and Molière's comedies; plot takes a secondary place, the work is a long dissertation in dialogue on man. Only instead of an abstract man I would make a natural man, put him in his proper surroundings, and analyze all the physical and social causes which make him what he is. In a word, the classical formula is to me a good one, on condition that the scientific method is employed in the study of actual society, in the same way that the chemist studies minerals and their properties. [. . .]

I now come to the language. They pretend to say that there is a special style for the stage. They want it to be a style altogether different from the ordinary style of speaking, more sonorous, more nervous, written in a higher key, cut in facets, no doubt to make the chandelier jets sparkle. In our time, for example, M. Dumas, *fils*, has the reputation of being a great dramatic author. His 'mots' are famous. They go off like sky rockets, falling again in showers to the applause of the spectators. Besides, all his characters speak the same language, the language of witty Paris, cutting in its pardoxes, having a good hit always in view, and sharp and hard. I do not deny the sparkle of this language – not a very solid sparkle, it is true – but I deny its truth. Nothing is so fatiguing as these continual sneering sentences. I would rather see more elasticity, greater naturalness. They are at one and the same time too well and not well enough written. The true style-setters of the epoch are the novelists; to find the infallible, living, original style you must turn to M. Gustave Flaubert and to MM. de Goncourt. When you compare M. Dumas' style to that of these great prose writers you find it is no longer correct – it has no color, no movement. What I want to hear on the stage is the language as it is spoken every day; if we cannot produce on the stage a conversation with its repetitions, its length, and its useless words, at least the movement and the tone of the conversation could be kept; the particular turn of mind of each talker, the reality, in a word, reproduced to the necessary extent. MM. Goncourt have made a curious attempt at this in 'Henriette Maréchal,' that play which no one would listen to, and which no one knows anything about. The Grecian actors spoke through a brass tube; under Louis XIV the comedians sang their rôles in a chanting tone to give them more pomp; to-day we are content to say that there is a particular language belonging to the stage, more sonorous and explosive. You can see by this that we are progressing. One day they will perceive that the best style on the stage is that which best sets forth the spoken conversation, which puts the proper word in the right place, giving it its just value.

(Emile Zola, 'Naturalism on the Stage', *The Experimental Novel and Other Essays*, trans. Belle M. Sherman (New York: Cassell, 1893), pp. 114–15, 123–4, 150–1, 153–4. The original French appeared in *Le roman expérimental* (Paris, 1880).)

(C) ERICH AUERBACH

Mimesis (1946)

EPILOGUE

The subject of this book, the interpretation of reality through literary representation or 'imitation,' has occupied me for a long time. My original starting point was Plato's discussion in Book 10 of the *Republic* – mimesis ranking third after truth – in conjunction with Dante's assertion that in the *Commedia* he presented true reality. As I studied the various methods of interpreting human events in the literature of Europe, I found my interest becoming more precise and focused. Some guiding ideas began to crystallize, and these I sought to pursue.

The first of these ideas concerns the doctrine of the ancients regarding the several levels of literary representation – a doctrine which was taken up again by every later classicistic movement. I came to understand that modern realism in the form it reached in France in the early nineteenth century is, as an aesthetic phenomenon, characterized by complete emancipation from that doctrine. This emancipation is more complete, and more

significant for later literary forms of the imitation of life, than
the mixture of *le sublime* with *le grotesque* proclaimed by the
contemporary romanticists. When Stendhal and Balzac took
random individuals from daily life in their dependence upon
current historical circumstances and made them the subjects of
serious, problematic, and even tragic representation, they broke
with the classical rule of distinct levels of style, for according to
this rule, everyday practical reality could find a place in
literature only within the frame of a low or intermediate kind of
style, that is to say, as either grotesquely comic or pleasant,
light, colorful, and elegant entertainment. They thus completed a
development which had long been in preparation (since the time
of the novel of manners and the *comédie larmoyante* of the
eighteenth century, and more pronouncedly since the *Sturm und
Drang* and early romanticism). And they opened the way for
modern realism, which has ever since developed in increasingly
rich forms, in keeping with the constantly changing and
expanding reality of modern life.

Looking at the problem in this fashion, I came to realize that
the revolution early in the nineteenth century against the
classical doctrine of levels of style could not possibly have been
the first of its kind. The barriers which the romanticists and the
contemporary realists tore down had been erected only toward
the end of the sixteenth century and during the seventeenth by
the advocates of a rigorous imitation of antique literature. Before
that time, both during the Middle Ages and on through the
Renaissance, a serious realism had existed. It had been possible
in literature as well as in the visual arts to represent the most
everyday phenomena of reality in a serious and significant
context. The doctrine of the levels of style had no absolute
validity. However different medieval and modern realism may
be, they are at one in this basic attitude. And it had long been
clear to me how this medieval conception of art had evolved,
and when and how the first break with the classical theory had
come about. It was the story of Christ, with its ruthless mixture
of everyday reality and the highest and most sublime tragedy,
which had conquered the classical rule of styles.

But if one compares the two breaks with the doctrine of
stylistic levels, one cannot but see at once that they come about
under completely different conditions and yielded completely
different results. The view of reality expressed in the Christian
works of late antiquity and the Middle Ages differs completely
from that of modern realism. It is very difficult to formulate the

specific character of the older Christian view in such a way that
the essential points are brought out and all of the pertinent
phenomena are included. A solution which struck me as on the
whole satisfactory resulted from an investigation of the semantic
history of the word *figura*. For this reason I use the term figural
to identify the conception of reality in late antiquity and the
Christian Middle Ages. What I mean by it is repeatedly
explained in this book (for example, pp. 63ff.); a detailed
presentation is to be found in my essay on *figura* (which has
been reprinted in my *Neue Dante-Studien, Istanbuler Schriften* No. 5,
Istanbul 1944, now Berne). In this conception, an occurrence on
earth signifies not only itself but at the same time another,
which it predicts or confirms, without prejudice to the power of
its concrete reality here and now. The connection between
occurrences is not regarded as primarily a chronological or
causal development but as a oneness within the divine plan, of
which all occurrences are parts and reflections. Their direct
earthly connection is of secondary importance, and often their
interpretation can altogether dispense with any knowledge of it.

These three closely related ideas, which gave the original
problem form, though at the same time they narrowed its scope,
are the base upon which the entire study is built. Naturally it
involves a variety of other motifs and problems inherent in the
abundance of historical phenomena which had to be treated. But
most of these are in some way related to the ideas mentioned,
and at any rate those ideas form the constant point of reference.

As for the methods employed, they have been discussed in an
earlier context (p. 484). A systematic and complete history of
realism would not only have been impossible, it would not have
served my purpose. For the guiding ideas had delimited the
subject matter in a very specific way. I was no longer concerned
with realism in general, the question was to what degree and in
what manner realistic subjects were treated seriously,
problematically, or tragically. As a result, merely comic works,
works which indubitably remained within the realm of the low
style, were excluded. They could at most be referred to
occasionally as contrasting illustrations, in the same sense in
which completely unrealistic works in the elevated style were to
be mentioned from time to time. The category of 'realistic works
of serious style and character' has never been treated or even
conceived as such. I have not seen fit to analyze it theoretically
and to describe it systematically. To do that would have
necessitated an arduous and, from the reader's point of view, a

tiresome search for definitions at the very beginning of my study. (Not even the term 'realistic' is unambiguous.) And it is most probable that I could not have managed without an unusual and clumsy terminology. The procedure I have employed – that of citing for every epoch a number of texts and using ese as test cases for my ideas – takes the reader directly into the subject and makes him sense what is at issue long before he is expected to cope with anything theoretical.

(Erich Auerbach, *Mimesis: The Representation of Reality in Western Literature*, trans. Willard Trask (Princeton, NJ: Princeton UP, 1953), pp. 554–6. Original German was published by A. Francke (Berne, 1946).)

(D) GEORG LUKÁCS

'Art and Objective Truth', from *Writer and Critic* (1965, 1970)

The artistic reflection of reality rests on the same contradiction as any other reflection of reality. What is specific to it is that it pursues another resolution of these contradictions than science. We can best define the specific character of the artistic reflection of reality by examining first in the abstract the goal it sets itself, in order then to illuminate the preconditions for attaining this goal. The goal for all great art is to provide a picture of reality in which the contradiction between appearance and reality, the particular and the general, the immediate and the conceptual, etc., is so resolved that the two converge into a spontaneous integrity in the direct impression of the work of art and provide a sense of an inseparable integrity. The universal appears as a quality of the individual and the particular, reality becomes manifest and can be experienced within appearance, the general principle is exposed as the specific impelling cause for the individual case being specially depicted. Engels characterized this essential mode of artistic creation clearly in a comment about characterization in a novel: 'Each is simultaneously a type and a particular individual, a "this one" (*Dieser*), as old Hegel expressed it, and so it must be.'

It follows then that every work of art must present a circumscribed, self-contained and complete context with its own *immediately* self-evident movement and structure. The necessity for

the immediate obviousness of the special context is clearest in
literature. The true, fundamental interrelationships in any novel
or drama can be disclosed only at the end. Because of the very
nature of their construction and effect, only the conclusion
provides full clarification of the beginning. Furthermore, the
composition would fail utterly and have no impact if the path to
this culmination were not clearly demarcated at every stage. The
motivating factors in the world depicted in a literary work of art
are revealed in an artistic sequence and climaxing. But this
climaxing must be accomplished within a direct unity of
appearance and reality present from the very beginning; in the
intensifying concretizing of both aspects, it must make their
unity ever more integral and self-evident.

This self-contained immediacy in the work of art presupposes
that every work of art evolve within itself all the preconditions
for its characters, situations, events, etc. The unity of appearance
and reality can become direct experience only if the reader
experiences every important aspect of the growth or change with
all their primary determining factors, if the outcome is never
simply handed to him but he is conducted to the outcome and
directly experiences the process leading to the outcome. The
basic materialism of all great artists (no matter whether their
ostensible philosophy is partly or completely idealistic) appears
in their clear depiction of the pertinent preconditions and
motivations out of which the consciousness of their characters
arises and develops.

Thus every significant work of art creates its 'own world'.
Characters, situations, actions, etc., in each have a unique
quality unlike that in any other work of art and entirely distinct
from anything in everyday reality. The greater the artist, the
more intensely his creative power permeates all aspects of his
work of art and the more pregnantly his fictional 'world' emerges
through all the details of the work. Balzac said of his *Comédie
Humaine*: 'My work has its own geography as well as its own
genealogy and its own families, its places and its objects, its
people and its facts; even as it possesses its heraldry, its
aristocracy and its bourgeoisie, its workmen and its peasants, its
politicians and its dandies and its army – in short, its world.'

Does not the establishment of such particularity in a work of
art preclude the fulfilment of its function as a reflection of
reality? By no means! It merely affirms the special character, the
peculiar kind of reflection of reality there is in art. The
apparently circumscribed world in the work of art and its

apparent non-correspondence with reality are founded on this peculiar character of the artistic reflection of reality. For this non-correspondence is merely an illusion, though a necessary one, essential and intrinsic to art. The effect of art, the immersion of the receptant in the action of the work of art, his complete penetration into the special 'world' of the work of art, results from the fact that the work by its very nature offers a truer, more complete, more vivid and more dynamic reflection of reality than the receptant otherwise possesses, that it conducts him on the basis of his own experiences and on the basis of the organization and generalization of his previous reproduction of reality beyond the bounds of his experiences toward a more concrete insight into reality. It is therefore only an illusion – as though the work itself were not a reflection of reality, as though the reader did not conceive of the special 'world' as a reflection of reality and did not compare it with his own experiences. He acts consistently in accordance with this pretence, and the effect of the work of art ceases once the reader becomes aware of a contradiction, once he senses that the work of art is not an accurate reflection of reality. But this illusion is in any case necessary. For the reader does not consciously compare an individual experience with an isolated event of the work of art but surrenders himself to the general effect of the work of art on the basis of his own assembled general experience. And the comparison between both reflections of reality remains unconscious so long as the reader is engrossed, that is, so long as his experiences regarding reality are broadened and deepened by the fiction of the work of art. Thus Balzac is not contradicting his statement about his 'own world' when he says, 'To be productive one needs only to study. French society should be the historian, I only its amanuensis.' [. . .]

The work of art must [. . .] reflect correctly and in proper proportion all important factors objectively determining the area of life it represents. It must so reflect these that this area of life becomes comprehensible from within and from without, re-experiencable, that it appears as a totality of life. This does not mean that every work of art must strive to reflect the objective, extensive totality of life. On the contrary, the extensive totality of reality necessarily is beyond the possible scope of any artistic creation; the totality of reality can only be reproduced intellectually in ever-increasing approximation through the infinite process of science. The totality of the work of art is rather intensive: the circumscribed and self-contained ordering of

those factors which objectively are of decisive significance for the
portion of life depicted, which determine its existence and
motion, its specific quality and its place in the total life process.
In this sense the briefest song is as much an intensive totality as
the mightiest epic. The objective character of the area of life
represented determines the quantity, quality, proportion, etc., of
the factors that emerge in interaction with the specific laws of
the literary form appropriate for the representation of this
portion of life.

[. . .] No matter whether the intention in the work of art is
the depiction of the whole of society or only an artificially
isolated incident, the aim will still be to depict the intensive
inexhaustibility of the subject. This means that it will aim at
involving creatively in its fiction all important factors which in
objective reality provide the basis for a particular event or
complex of events. And artistic involvement means that all these
factors will appear as personal attributes of the persons in the
action, as the specific qualities of the situations depicted, etc.;
thus in a directly perceptible unity of the individual and the
universal. Very few people are capable of such an experience of
reality. They achieve knowledge of general determinants in life
only through the abandonment of the immediate, only through
abstraction, only through generalized comparison of experiences.
(In this connection, the artist himself is no exception. His work
consists rather in elevating the experiences he obtains ordinarily
to artistic form, to a representation of the unity of the immediate
and the universal.) In representing individual men and
situations, the artist awakens the illusion of life. In depicting
them as exemplary men and situations (the unity of the
individual and the typical), in bringing to life the greatest
possible richness of the objective conditions of life as the
particular attributes of individual people and situations, he
makes his 'own world' emerge as the reflection of life in its total
motion, as process and totality, in that it intensifies and
surpasses in its totality and in its particulars the common
reflection of the events of life.

This depiction of the subtlety of life, of a richness beyond
ordinary experience, is only one side in the special mode of the
artistic representation of reality. If a work of art depicted only
the overflowing abundance of new concepts, only those aspects
which provide new insights, only the subtlety beyond the
common generalization about ordinary experience, then the
reader would merely be confused instead of being involved, for

the appearance of such aspects in life generally confuses people and leaves them at a loss. It is therefore necessary that *within* this richness and subtlety the artist introduce a new order of things which displaces or modifies the old abstractions. This is also a reflection of objective reality. For such a new order is never simply imposed on life but is derived from the new phenomena of life through reflection, comparison, etc. But in life itself it is always a question of two steps; in the first place, one is surprised by the new facts and sometimes even overwhelmed by them and then only does one need to deal with them intellectually by applying the dialectical method. In art these two steps coincide, not in the sense of a mechanical unity (for then the newness of the individual phenomena would again be annihilated) but in the sense of a process in which from the outset the order within the new phenomena manifesting the sublety of life is sensed and emerges in the course of the artistic climaxing ever more sharply and clearly.

This representation of life, structured and ordered more richly and strictly than ordinary life experience, is in intimate relation to the active social function, the propaganda effect of the genuine work of art. Such a depiction cannot possibly exhibit the lifeless and false objectivity of an 'impartial' imitation which takes no stand or provides no call to action. From Lenin, however, we know that this partisanship is not introduced into the external world arbitrarily by the individual but is a motive force inherent in reality which is made conscious through the correct dialectical reflection of reality and introduced into practice. This partisanship of objectivity must therefore be found intensified in the work of art – intensified in clarity and distinctness, for the subject matter of a work of art is consciously arranged and ordered by the artist toward this goal, in the sense of this partisanship; intensified, however, in objectivity too, for a genuine work of art is directed specifically toward depicting this partisanship as a quality in the subject matter, presenting it as a motive force inherent in it and growing organically out of it. When Engels approves of tendentiousness in literature he always means, as does Lenin after him, this 'partisanship of objectivity' and emphatically rejects any subjective superimposed tendentiousness: 'But I mean that the tendentiousness must spring out of the situation and action without being expressly pointed out.'

All bourgeois theories treating the problem of the aesthetic illusion allude to this dialectic in the artistic reflection of reality.

The paradox in the effect of a work of art is that we surrender ourselves to the work as though it presented reality to us, accept it as reality and immerse ourselves in it although we are always aware that it is not reality but simply a special form of reflecting reality. Lenin correctly observes: 'Art does not demand recognition as *reality*.' The illusion in art, the aesthetic illusion, depends therefore on the self-containment we have examined in the work of art and on the fact that the work of art in its totality reflects the full process of life and does not represent in its details reflections of particular phenomena of life which can be related individually to aspects of actual life on which they are modelled. Non-correspondence in this respect is the precondition of the artistic illusion, an illusion absolutely divorced from any such correspondence. On the other hand and inseparable from it is the fact that the aesthetic illusion is only possible when the work of art reflects the total objective process of life with *objective accuracy*.

This objective dialectic in the artistic reflection of reality is beyond the ken of bourgeois theory, and bourgeois theory always degenerates into subjectivism at least in specific points, if not in totality. Philosophic idealism must, as we have seen, isolate this characteristic of self-containment in a work of art and its elevation above ordinary reality, from material and objective reality; it must oppose the self-containment, the perfection of form in the work of art, to the theory of reflection. When objective idealism seeks to rescue and establish the objectivity of art abstractly, it inevitably falls into mysticism. It is by no means accidental that the Platonic theory of art as the reflection of 'ideas' exerts such a powerful historical influence right up to Schelling and Schopenhauer. And when the mechanical materialists fall into idealism because of the inadequacy of their philosophic conception of social phenomena, they usually go from a mechanical photographic theory of imitation to Platonism, to a theory of the artistic imitation of 'ideas'. (This is especially apparent with Shaftesbury and at times evident with Diderot.) But this mystical objectivism is always and inevitably transformed into subjectivism. The more the aspects of the self-containment of a work and of the dynamic character of the artistic elaboration and reshaping of reality are opposed to the theory of reflection instead of being derived from it dialectically, the more the principle of form, beauty and artistry is divorced from life; the more it becomes an unclear, subjective and mystical principle. The Platonic 'ideas' occasionally inflated and attenuated in the idealism of the period of bourgeois ascendancy, though artificially isolated from social reality, were reflections of decisive social problems and thus for all their idealistic distortion were full of content and were not without relevance; but with the decline of the class they more and more lose content. The social isolation of the personally dedicated artist in a declining society is mirrored in this mystical, subjective inflation of the principle of form divorced from any connection with life. The original despair of genuine artists over this situation passes to parasitic resignation and the self-complacency of 'art for art's sake' and its theory of art. Baudelaire sings of beauty in a tone of despondent subjective mysticism: 'Je trône dans l'azure comme un sphinx incompris.' In the later art for art's sake of the imperialist period such subjectivism evolves into a theory of a contemptuous, parasitic divorce of art from life, into a denial of any objectivity in art, a glorification of the 'sovereignty' of the creative individual and a theory of indifference to content and arbitrariness in form.

We have already seen that mechanical materialism tends toward an opposite direction. Sticking to the mechanical imitation of life as it is immediately perceived in all its superficial detail, it must deny the special character of the artistic reflection of reality or fall into idealism with all its distortions and subjectivism. The pseudo-objectivity of mechanical materialism, of the mechanical, direct imitation of the immediate world or phenomena, is thus inevitably transformed into idealistic subjectivism since it does not acknowledge the objectivity of the underlying laws and relationships that cannot immediately be perceived and since it sees in these laws and relationships no reflection of objective reality but simply technical means for superficial groupings of sense data. The weakness of the direct imitation of life in its particularity must intensify and develop further into subjective idealism without content as the general ideological development of the bourgeoisie transforms the philosophic materialist basis of this sort of artistic imitation of reality into agnostic idealism (the theory of empathy).

The objectivity of the artistic reflection of reality depends on the correct reflection of the totality. The artistic correctness of a detail thus has nothing to do with whether the detail corresponds to any similar detail in reality. The detail in a work of art is an accurate reflection of life when it is a necessary aspect of the accurate reflection of the total process of objective reality, no matter whether it was observed by the artist in life or created through imagination out of direct or indirect experience. On the other hand, the artistic truth of a detail which corresponds photographically to life is purely accidental, arbitrary and subjective. When, for example, the detail is not directly and obviously necessary to the context, then it is incidental to a work of art, its inclusion is arbitrary and subjective. It is therefore entirely possible that a collage of photographic material may provide an incorrect, subjective and arbitrary reflection of reality. For merely arranging thousands of chance details in a row never results in artistic necessity. In order to discipline accident into a proper context with artistic necessity, the necessity must be latent within the accidental and must appear as an inner motivation within the details themselves. The detail must be so selected and so depicted from the outset that its relationship with the totality may be organic and dynamic. Such selection and ordering of details depends solely on the artistic, objective reflection of reality. The isolation of details from the general context and their selection on the basis of a photographic correspondence with reality imply a rejection of the more profound problem of objective necessity, even a denial of the existence of this necessity. Artists who create thus, choose and organize material not out of the objective necessity in the subject matter but out of pure subjectivity, a fact which is manifested in the work as an objective anarchy in the selection and arrangement of their material.

(Georg Lukács, 'Art and Objective Truth', *Writer and Critic and Other Essays*, ed. and trans. Arthur Kahn (London. Merlin Press, 1970), pp. 34–43.)

(E) BERTHOLT BRECHT

'Alienation Effects in Chinese Acting' (1957)

The following is intended to refer briefly to the use of the alienation effect in traditional Chinese acting. This method was most recently used in Germany for plays of a non-aristotelian (not dependent on empathy) type as part of the attempts being made to evolve an epic theatre. The efforts in question were directed to playing in such a way that the audience was hindered from simply identifying itself with the characters in the play. Acceptance or rejection of their actions and utterances was meant to take place on a conscious plane, instead of, as hitherto, in the audience's subconscious. [. . .] The alienation effect is achieved in the Chinese theatre in the following way.

Above all, the Chinese artist never acts as if there were a fourth wall besides the three surrounding him. He expresses his awareness of being watched. This immediately removes one of the European stage's characteristic illusions. The audience can no longer have the illusion of being the unseen spectator at an event which is really taking place. A whole elaborate European stage technique, which helps to conceal the fact that the scenes are so arranged that the audience can view them in the easiest way, is thereby made unnecessary. The actors openly choose those positions which will best show them off to the audience, just as if they were *acrobats*. A further means is that the artist observes himself. Thus if he is representing a cloud, perhaps, showing its unexpected appearance, its soft and strong growth, its rapid yet gradual transformation, he will occasionally look at the audience as if to say: isn't it just like that? At the same time he also observes his own arms and legs, adducing them, testing them and perhaps finally approving them. An obvious glance at the floor, so as to judge the space available to him for his act, does not strike him as liable to break the illusion. In this way the artist separates mime (showing observation) from gesture (showing a cloud), but without detracting from the latter, since the body's attitude is reflected in the face and is wholly responsible for its expression. At one moment the expression is of well-managed restraint; at another, of utter triumph. The artist has been using his countenance as a blank sheet, to be inscribed by the gest of the body. [. . .]

The Chinese artist's performance often strikes the Western actor as cold. That does not mean that the Chinese theatre rejects all representation of feelings. The performer portrays incidents of utmost passion, but without his delivery becoming heated. At those points where the character portrayed is deeply excited the performer takes a lock of hair between his lips and chews it. But this is like a ritual, there is nothing eruptive about it. It is quite clearly somebody else's repetition of the incident: a representation, even though an artistic one. The performer shows that this man is not in control of himself, and he points to the outward signs. And so lack of control is decorously expressed, or if not decorously at any rate decorously for the stage. Among all the possible signs certain particular ones are picked out, with careful and visible consideration. Anger is naturally different from sulkiness, hatred from distaste, love from liking; but the corresponding fluctuations of feeling are portrayed economically. The coldness comes from the actor's holding himself remote from the character portrayed, along the lines described. He is careful not to make its sensations into those of the spectator. Nobody gets raped by the individual he portrays; this individual is not the spectator himself but his neighbour.

The Western actor does all he can to bring his spectator into the closest proximity to the events and the character he has to portray. To this end he persuades him to identify himself with him (the actor) and uses every energy to convert himself as completely as possible into a different type, that of the character in question. If this complete conversion succeeds then his art has been more or less expended. Once he has become the bank-clerk, doctor or general concerned he will need no more art than any of these people need 'in real life'.

This complete conversion operation is extremely exhausting. Stanislavsky puts forward a series of means – a complete system – by which what he calls 'creative mood' can repeatedly be manufactured afresh at every performance. For the actor cannot usually manage to feel for very long on end that he really is the other person; he soon gets exhausted and begins just to copy various superficialities of the other person's speech and hearing, whereupon the effect on the public drops off alarmingly. This is certainly due to the fact that the other person has been created by an 'intuitive' and accordingly murky process which takes place in the subconscious. The subconscious is not at all responsive to guidance; it has as it were a bad memory. [. . .]

The A-effect was achieved in the German epic theatre not only by the actor, but also by the music (choruses, songs) and the setting (placards, film etc.). It was principally designed to historicize the incidents portrayed. By this is meant the following:

The bourgeois theatre emphasized the timelessness of its objects. Its representation of people is bound by the alleged 'eternally human'. Its story is arranged in such a way as to create 'universal' situations that allow man with a capital M to express himself: man of every period and every colour. All its incidents are just one enormous cue, and this cue is followed by the 'eternal' response: the inevitable, usual, natural, purely human response. An example: a black man falls in love in the

same way as a white man; the story forces him to react with the
same expression as the white man (in theory this formula works
as well the other way round); and with that the sphere of art is
attained. The cue can take account of what is special, different;
the response is shared, there is no element of difference in it.
This notion may allow that such a thing as history exists, but it
is none the less unhistorical. A few circumstances vary, the
environments are altered, but Man remains unchanged. History
applies to the environment, not to Man. The environment is
remarkably unimportant, is treated simply as a pretext; it is a
variable quantity and something remarkably inhuman; it exists
in fact apart from Man, confronting him as a coherent whole,
whereas he is a fixed quantity, eternally unchanged. The idea of
man as a function of the environment and the environment as a
function of man, i.e. the breaking up of the environment into
relationships between men, corresponds to a new way of
thinking, the historical way. Rather than be sidetracked into the
philosophy of history, let us give an example. Suppose the
following is to be shown on the stage: a girl leaves home in
order to take a job in a fair-sized city (Piscator's *American
Tragedy*). For the bourgeois theatre this is an insignificant affair,
clearly the beginning of a story; it is what one has to have been
told in order to understand what comes after, or to be keyed up
for it. The actor's imagination will hardly be greatly fired by it.
In a sense the incident is universal: girls take jobs (in the case
in question one can be keyed up to see what in particular is
going to happen to her). Only in one way is it particular: this
girl goes away (if she had remained what comes after would not
have happened). The fact that her family lets her go is not the
object of the inquiry; it is understandable (the motives are
understandable). But for the historicizing theatre everything is
different. The theatre concentrates entirely on whatever in this
perfectly everyday event is remarkable, particular and
demanding inquiry. What! A family letting one of its members
leave the nest to earn her future living independently and
without help? Is she up to it? Will what she has learnt here as a
member of the family help her to earn her living? Can't families
keep a grip on their children any longer? Have they become (or
remained) a burden? Is it like that with every family? Was it
always like that? Is this the way of the world, something that
can't be affected? The fruit falls off the tree when ripe: does this
sentence apply here? Do children always make themselves
independent? Did they do so in every age? If so, and if it's

something biological, does it always happen in the same way, for
the same reasons and with the same results? These are the
questions (or a few of them) that the actors must answer if they
want to show the incident as a unique, historical one: if they
want to demonstrate a custom which leads to conclusions about
the entire structure of a society at a particular (transient) time.
But how is such an incident to be represented if its historic
character is to be brought out? How can the confusion of our
unfortunate epoch be striking? When the mother, in between
warnings and moral injunctions, packs her daughter's case – a
very small one – how is the following to be shown: So many
injunctions and so few clothes? Moral injunctions for a lifetime
and bread for five hours? How is the actress to speak the
mother's sentence as she hands over such a very small case –
'There, I guess that ought to do you' – in such way that it is
understood as a historic dictum? This can only be achieved if
the A-effect is brought out. The actress must not make the
sentence her own affair, she must hand it over for criticism, she
must help us to understand its causes and protest. [. . .]

In setting up new artistic principles and working out new
methods of representation we must start with the compelling
demands of a changing epoch; the necessity and the possibility
of remodelling society loom ahead. All incidents between men
must be noted, and everything must be seen from a social point
of view. Among other effects that a new theatre will need for its
social criticism and its historical reporting of completed
transformations is the A-effect.

(Bertholt Brecht, 'Alienation Effects in Chinese Acting', in *Brecht on
Theatre*, ed. and trans. John Willett (New York: Hill and Wang, 1964),
pp. 91, 91–2, 93–4, 96–8, 98–9.)

'The Popular and the Realistic' (1958)

We now come to the concept of 'Realism'. It is an old concept
which has been much used by many men and for many
purposes, and before it can be applied we must spring-clean it
too. This is necessary because when the people takes over its
inheritance there has to be a process of expropriation. Literary
works cannot be taken over like factories, or literary forms of
expression like industrial methods. Realist writing, of which
history offers many widely varying examples, is likewise

conditioned by the question of how, when and for what class it is made use of: conditioned down to the last small detail. As we have in mind a fighting people that is changing the real world we must not cling to 'well-tried' rules for telling a story, worthy models set up by literary history, eternal aesthetic laws. We must not abstract the one and only realism from certain given works, but shall make a lively use of all means, old and new, tried and untried, deriving from art and deriving from other sources, in order to put living reality in the hands of living people in such a way that it can be mastered. We shall take care not to ascribe realism to a particular historical form of novel belonging to a particular period, Balzac's or Tolstoy's, for instance, so as to set up purely formal and literary criteria of realism. We shall not restrict ourselves to speaking of realism in cases where one can (e.g.) smell, look, feel whatever is depicted, where 'atmosphere' is created and stories develop in such a way that the characters are psychologically stripped down. Our conception of *realism* needs to be broad and political, free from aesthetic restrictions and independent of convention. *Realist* means: laying bare society's causal network/showing up the dominant viewpoint as the viewpoint of the dominators/writing from the standpoint of the class which has prepared the broadest solutions for the most pressing problems afflicting human society/emphasizing the dynamics of development/concrete and so as to encourage abstraction.

It is a tall order, and it can be made taller. And we shall let the artist apply all his imagination, all his originality, his sense of humour and power of invention to its fulfilment. We will not stick to unduly detailed literary models or force the artist to follow over-precise rules for telling a story.

We shall establish that so-called sensuous writing (in which everything can be smelt, tasted, felt) is not to be identified automatically with realist writing, for we shall see that there are sensuously written works which are not realist, and realist works which are not sensuously written. We shall have to go carefully into the question whether the story is best developed by aiming at an eventual psychological stripping-down of the charaters. Our readers may quite well feel that they have not been given the key to what is happening if they are simply induced by a combination of arts to take part in the inner emotions of our books' heroes. By taking over the forms of Balzac and Tolstoy without a thorough inspection we might perhaps exhaust our readers, the people, just as these writers often do. Realism is not a pure question of form. Copying the methods of these realists, we should cease to be realists ourselves.

For time flows on, and if it did not it would be a poor look-out for those who have no golden tables to sit at. Methods wear out, stimuli fail. New problems loom up and demand new techniques. Reality alters; to represent it the means of representation must alter too. Nothing arises from nothing; the new springs from the old, but that is just what makes it new.

The oppressors do not always appear in the same mask. The masks cannot always be stripped off in the same way. There are so many tricks for dodging the mirror that is held out. Their military roads are termed motor roads. Their tanks are painted to look like Macduff's bushes. Their agents can show horny hands as if they were workers. Yes: it takes ingenuity to change the hunter into the quarry. What was popular yesterday is no longer so today, for the people of yesterday were not the people as it is today.

Anybody who is not bound by formal prejudices knows that there are many ways of suppressing truth and many ways of stating it: that indignation at inhuman conditions can be stimulated in many ways, by direct description of a pathetic or matter-of-fact kind, by narrating stories and parables, by jokes, by over- and understatement. In the theatre reality can be represented in a factual or a fantastic form. The actors can do without (or with the minimum of) makeup, appearing 'natural', and the whole thing can be a fake; they can wear grotesque masks and represent the truth. There is not much to argue about here: the means must be asked what the end is. The people knows how to ask this. Piscator's great experiments in the theatre (and my own), which repeatedly involved the exploding of conventional forms, found their chief support in the most progressive cadres of the working class. The workers judged everything by the amount of truth contained in it; they welcomed any innovation which helped the representation of truth, of the real mechanism of society; they rejected whatever seemed like playing, like machinery working for its own sake, i.e. no longer, or not yet, fulfilling a purpose. The workers' arguments were never literary or purely theatrical. 'You can't mix theatre and film': that sort of thing was never said. If the film was not properly used the most one heard was: 'that bit of film is unnecessary, it's distracting'. [. . .] The workers were not afraid to teach us, nor were they afraid to learn.

I speak from experience when I say that one need never be

frightened of putting bold and unaccustomed things before the proletariat, so long as they have to do with reality. [. . .]

So the criteria for the popular and the realistic need to be chosen not only with great care but also with an open mind. They must not be deduced from existing realist works and existing popular works, as is often the case. Such an approach would lead to purely formalistic criteria, and questions of popularity and realism would be decided by form.

One cannot decide if a work is realist or not by finding out whether it resembles existing, reputedly realist works which must be counted realist for their time. In each individual case the picture given of life must be compared, not with another picture, but with the actual life portrayed. And likewise where popularity is concerned there is a wholly formalistic procedure that has to be guarded against. The intelligibility of a work of literature is not ensured exclusively by its being written in exactly the same way as other works which people have understood. These other works too were not invariably written just like the works before them. Something was done towards their understanding. In the same way we must do something for the understanding of the new works. Besides *being popular* there is such a thing as *becoming popular*.

(Bertholt Brecht, 'The Popular and the Realistic', in *Brecht on Theatre*, ed. and trans. John Willett (New York: Hill & Wang, 1964), pp. 108–10, 111, 112.)

(F) ALAIN ROBBE-GRILLET

'A Future for the Novel' (1956)

It seems hardly reasonable at first glance to suppose that an entirely *new* literature might one day – now, for instance – be possible. The many attempts made these last thirty years to drag fiction out of its ruts have resulted, at best, in no more than isolated works. And – we are often told – none of these works, whatever its interest, has gained the adherence of a public comparable to that of the bourgeois novel. The only conception of the novel to have currency today is, in fact, that of Balzac.

Or that of Mme. de La Fayette. Already sacrosanct in her day, psychological analysis constituted the basis of all prose: it governed the conception of the book, the description of its

characters, the development of its plot. A 'good' novel, ever
since, has remained the study of a passion – or of a conflict of
passions, or of an absence of passion – in a given milieu. [. . .]

Even the least conditioned observer is unable to see the world
around him through entirely unprejudiced eyes. Not, of course,
that I have in mind the naive concern for objectivity which the
analysts of the (subjective) soul find it so easy to smile at.
Objectivity in the ordinary sense of the word – total
impersonality of observation – is all too obviously an illusion.
But *freedom* of observation should be possible, and yet it is not.
At every moment, a continuous fringe of culture (psychology,
ethics, metaphysics, etc.) is added to things, giving them a less
alien aspect, one that is more comprehensible, more reassuring.
Sometimes the camouflage is complete: a gesture vanishes from
our mind, supplanted by the emotions which supposedly
produced it, and we remember a landscape as *austere* or *calm*
without being able to evoke a single outline, a single,
determining element. Even if we immediately think, 'That's
literary,' we don't try to react against the thought. We accept
the fact that what is *literary* (the word has become pejorative)
functions like a grid or screen set with bits of different colored
glass that fracture our field of vision into tiny assimilable facets.

And if something resists this systematic appropriation of the
visual, if an element of the world breaks the glass, without
finding any place in the interpretative screen, we can always
make use of our convenient category of 'the absurd' in order to
absorb this awkward residue.

But the world is neither significant nor absurd. It *is*, quite
simply. That, in any case, is the most remarkable thing about it.
And suddenly the obviousness of this strikes us with irresistible
force. All at once the whole splendid construction collapses;
opening our eyes unexpectedly, we have experienced, once too
often, the shock of this stubborn reality we were pretending to
have mastered. Around us, defying the noisy pack of our
animistic or protective adjectives, things *are there*. Their surfaces
are distinct and smooth, *intact*, neither suspiciously brilliant nor
transparent. All our literature has not yet succeeded in eroding
their smallest corner, in flattening their slightest curve.

The countless movie versions of novels that encumber our
screens provide an occasion for repeating this curious experiment
as often as we like. The cinema, another heir of the
psychological and naturalistic tradition, generally has as its sole
purpose the transposition of a story into images: it aims

exclusively at imposing on the spectator, through the intermediary of some well-chosen scenes, the same meaning the written sentences communicated in their own fashion to the reader. But at any given moment the filmed narrative can drag us out of our interior comfort and into this proffered world with a violence not to be found in the corresponding text, whether novel or scenario.

Anyone can perceive the nature of the change that has occurred. In the initial novel, the objects and gestures forming the very fabric of the plot disappeared completely, leaving behind only their *significations*: the empty chair became only absence or expectation, the hand placed on a shoulder became a sign of friendliness, the bars on the window became only the impossibility of leaving . . . But in the cinema, one *sees* the chair, the movement of the hand, the shape of the bars. What they signify remains obvious, but instead of monopolizing our attention, it becomes something added, even something in excess, because what affects us, what persists in our memory, what appears as essential and irreducible to vague intellectual concepts are the gestures themselves, the objects, the movements, and the outlines, to which the image has suddenly (and unintentionally) restored their *reality*.

It may seem peculiar that such fragments of crude reality, which the filmed narrative cannot help presenting, strike us so vividly, whereas identical scenes in real life do not suffice to free us of our blindness. As a matter of fact, it is as if the very conventions of the photographic medium (the two dimensions, the black-and-white images, the frame of the screen, the difference of scale between scenes) help free us from our own conventions. The slightly 'unaccustomed' aspect of this reproduced world reveals, at the same time, the unaccustomed character of the world that surrounds us: it, too, is unaccustomed insofar as it refuses to conform to our habits of apprehension and to our classification.

Instead of this universe of 'signification' (psychological, social, functional), we must try, then, to construct a world both more solid and more immediate. Let it be first of all by their *presence* that objects and gestures establish themselves, and let this presence continue to prevail over whatever explanatory theory that may try to enclose them in a system of references, whether emotional, sociological, Freudian or metaphysical.

In this future universe of the novel, gestures and objects will be *there* before being *something*; and they will still be there afterwards, hard, unalterable, eternally present, mocking their own 'meaning,' that meaning which vainly tries to reduce them to the role of precarious tools, of a temporary and shameful fabric woven exclusively – and deliberately – by the superior human truth expressed in it, only to cast out this awkward auxiliary into immediate oblivion and darkness.

Henceforth, on the contrary, objects will gradually lose their instability and their secrets, will renounce their pseudo-mystery, that suspect interiority which Roland Barthes has called 'the romantic heart of things.' No longer will objects be merely the vague reflection of the hero's vague soul, the image of his torments, the shadow of his desires. Or rather, if objects still afford a momentary prop to human passions, they will do so only provisionally, and will accept the tyranny of significations only in appearance – derisively, one might say – the better to show how alien they remain to man. [. . .]

The revolution which has occurred is in kind: not only do we no longer consider the world as our own, our private property, designed according to our needs and readily domesticated, but we no longer even believe in its 'depth.' While essentialist conceptions of man met their destruction, the notion of 'condition' henceforth replacing that of 'nature,' the *surface* of things has ceased to be for us the mask of their heart, a sentiment that led to every kind of metaphysical transcendence.

Thus it is the entire literary language that must change, that is changing already. From day to day, we witness the growing repugnance felt by people of greater awareness for words of a visceral, analogical, or incantatory character. On the other hand, the visual or descriptive adjective, the word that contents itself with measuring, locating, limiting, defining, indicates a difficult but most likely direction for a new art of the novel.

(Alain Robbe–Grillet, 'A Future for the Novel', in *For a New Novel: Essays in Fiction*, trans. Richard Howard (New York: Grove Press, 1965), pp. 15, 18–22, 24. Original French was published by Editions de Minuit as *Pour un nouveau roman* (Paris, 1963).)

(G) ROLAND BARTHES

'Introduction to the Structural Analysis of Narratives' (1966)

Claims concerning the 'realism' of narrative are to be discounted. When a telephone call comes through in the office where he is on duty, Bond, so the author tells us, reflects that 'Communications with Hong Kong are as bad as they always were and just as difficult to obtain.' Neither Bond's 'reflection' nor the poor quality of the telephone call is the real piece of information; this contingency perhaps gives things more 'life' but the true information, which will come to fruition later, is the localization of the telephone call, Hong Kong. In all narrative imitation remains contingent. The function of narrative is not to 'represent,' it is to constitute a spectacle still very enigmatic for us but in any case not of a mimetic order. The 'reality' of a sequence lies not in the 'natural' succession of the actions composing it but in the logic there exposed, risked, and satisfied. Putting it another way, one could say that the origin of a sequence is not the observation of reality, but the need to vary and transcend the first *form* given man, namely repetition: a sequence is essentially a whole within which nothing is repeated. Logic has here an emancipatory value – and with it the entire narrative. It may be that men ceaselessly reinject into narrative what they have known, what they have experienced; but if they do, at least it is in a form which has vanquished repetition and instituted the model of a process of becoming. Narrative does not show, does not imitate; the passion which may excite us in reading a novel is not that of a 'vision' (in actual fact, we do not 'see' anything). Rather, it is that of meaning, that of a higher order of relation which also has its emotions, its hopes, its dangers, its triumphs. 'What takes place' in a narrative is from the referential (reality) point of view literally *nothing*; 'what happens' is language alone, the adventure of language, the unceasing celebration of its coming. Although we know scarcely more about the origins of narrative than we do about the origins of language, it can reasonably be suggested that narrative is contemporaneous with monologue, a creation seemingly posterior to that of dialogue. At all events, without wanting to strain the phylogenetic hypothesis, it may be significant that it is at the same moment (around the age of three) that the little human 'invents' at once sentence, narrative, and the Oedipus.

(Roland Barthes, 'Introduction to the Structural Analysis of Narratives', *Image-Music-Text*, trans. Stephen Heath (London: Fontana, 1977), pp. 123–4. Original French was 'Introduction à l'analyse structurale des récits', *Communications*, no. 8 (1966).)

CHAPTER 3

NATURE AND TRUTH

One of the major transitions in the history of criticism occurred between the late seventeenth century and the late eighteenth century and is associated with the gradual shift from a dominant Classicism to an ascendant Romanticism. The classical idea that literature imitates nature and truth took on a radically different meaning during this change.

By the seventeenth century the reputation and meaning of Aristotle had undergone a sea-change: the influential Italian commentaries by Robortello and Castelvetro turned Aristotle's scientifically framed poetics into a prescriptive set of rules for the ideal play or poem. In French criticism of the seventeenth century the rules became both an expression of social values and a symbol of classical orthodoxy. 'Correctness' in art was an aspect of correctness of moral and social behaviour. In England Thomas Rymer adopted the severe Aristotelianism of René Rapin and castigated the Elizabethan playwrights for failing to observe the unities and rules of probability. Earlier English Classicism was much less authoritarian and allowed scope for native taste and a variety of dramatic forms. These dry debates about the unities are surprisingly significant for literary theory and especially for the theory of imitation.

Dryden's *Essay on Dramatic Poesy* examines the conflict between French orthodoxy and English heterodoxy on the issue of dramatic representation and the rules. The protagonists ask 'What kind of correspondence between nature and art is to be desired?' Crites adopts a 'literal' theory requiring strict observance of the unities of time, place and action. Eugenius shows that even the ancients failed to observe them (indeed Aristotle scarcely mentions the unities of time or place). Eugenius proceeds to support a different and un-Aristotelian view of imitation: poets should imitate the passions of the soul, not actions. Classical writers (with the exception of Ovid) are criticized for neglecting the psychological side of representation. Neander (Dryden) defends the liberties taken by English drama (double plots, the mixed form of tragicomedy, and so on) and criticizes the tedious studies of passions in French drama.

Oddly enough the most interesting aspect of the debate centres on the subject of rhyme. Crites applies a crudely literal argument: people do not talk in rhyme and therefore rhyme is unnatural. Neander's reply, in support of rhyme, raises fundamental questions about the representation of nature in art. First the principle of *decorum* demands that in tragedy, in which the minds and fortunes of the most noble persons are presented, heroic rhyme 'is nearest nature, as being the noblest kind of modern verse' (the heroic couplet was conventionally used in heroic poetry). Later it emerges that the nobility of language is to be preferred even when we leave aside the requirements of decorum. In *A Defence of an Essay of Dramatic Poesy* Dryden openly declares that artistic effectiveness counts more than mere imitation. 'A bare imitation' will not 'excite the passions' or 'move admiration' in the audience. Therefore what is imitated must be 'heightened with all the arts and ornaments of poesy', even though people do not speak in rhyme. To imitate or represent is to go beyond a direct transcription from life. Art must elevate nature.

Pope's *An Essay on Criticism* includes an elusive and subtle account of the relation between art and nature. Nature is 'At once the source, and end, and test of art'. This line contains a complex tissue of assumptions in its tripartite definition: nature denotes (1) the objects of the external world imitated by art; (2) an order (divine?) embodying universal truth to which art aspires; (3) a set of permanent principles to which art tries to conform. Pope also examines the relationship between nature, the rules and the 'Ancients'. In Aristotle the principles governing poetry are derived from a study of actual plays (especially *Oedipus Tyrannus*), while in Dryden the 'rules' are tested against standards of social and psychological naturalness. According to Pope the poet imitates nature (the *source* of art) and at the same time imposes order upon nature ('nature methodiz'd'). The principles of nature have to be distilled from those inherent in nature. This complexity of formulation is possible only in poetry; a prose formulation would be cruder. A similar density of thought lies in the recommendation that the poet both goes directly to nature and relies upon the models of classical poetry. Virgil discovered that 'Nature and Homer were . . . the same'.

Aristotle's distinction between the universality of poetry and the particularity of history remained central to neoclassical poetics in the eighteenth century. Most agreed that literature addresses itself to general truth, but there were at least four variations of this tenet:

i.   A 'rhetorical' claim that the depiction of generality is always associated with grandness and elevation, while particularity goes with smallness and meanness.
ii. An aesthetic claim that generality is an effect of unity and simplicity, while particularity is one of confusion and chaos.
iii. An intuitive claim that generality goes with vagueness and excessive abstraction, while particularity promotes liveliness and concreteness.
iv. A moral view that general truths will move our minds by their universal truth, while what is transient and particular has no value.

Dr Johnson's belief in 'the grandeur of generality' is often expressed as a subtle combination of these attitudes: the best poetry is the representation of the 'individualized type' and the 'circumstantially general' (M. H. Abrams).

The early Romantic poets reacted strongly against the still prevailing 'common-sense' attitudes to poetry. They believed that observation and experience were not enough to make a poet; the poet was also a visionary. William Blake's *Marginalia* on Joshua Reynolds' *Discourses* are a violent attack on neoclassical theories about the derivation of rules from general nature: 'What is General Nature? is there Such a Thing? Strictly speaking all Knowledge is Particular.' He denied that the particular objects of nature are the poet's objects, and insisted that the imagination was the only source of truth and that natural objects tend to narrow and confine the imagination. Blake's poetic myths tell of an original unfallen Man who existed in androgynous form before the creation of nature, which came about in the process of the fall. The poet's imaginative faculty is capable of reaching back to this unfallen world and perceiving its traces in the lineaments of fallen nature. His visionary perceptions are highly particular and have none of the vague and abstract generality Blake associated with eighteenth-century philosophy (Locke) and art (Reynolds).

Wordsworth did not share Blake's visionary particularity, but developed a theory of poetry which owed much to eighteenth-century aesthetics. The object of poetry is 'truth, not individual and local, but general, and operative.' Poetry is the 'image of man and nature'. However, Wordsworth, unlike his eighteenth-century predecessors also emphasizes the subjective emotions of the poet: general truth is 'carried alive into the heart by passion'. The modifying power of subjective feeling becomes the central idea of romantic criticism. Like the German Romantics he believed that ordinary life is worthy of representation and adds his own distinctive emphasis by focusing on *rustic* existence which embodies 'the essential passions of the heart'. His views on language are well known: he aimed to adopt 'the very language of men' in his poetry. However, classical decorum oddly survives in his concern to remove 'what would otherwise be painful or disgusting in the passion'. Wordsworth's theory was often either inconsistent with his practice or simply inadequate to it. He needed the concepts of Coleridge to do it justice.

Background reading

W. J. Bate, *From Classic to Romantic* (Cambridge, Mass.: Harvard UP, 1946). See especially on Johnson and Reynolds.

Scott Elledge, 'The Background and Development in English Criticism of the Theories of Generality and Particularity', *PMLA*, 62 (1947).

Northrop Frye, *Fearful Symmetry* (Princeton, NJ: Princeton UP, 1947), ch. 1.

J. H. Hagstrum, *Samuel Johnson's Criticism* (Minneapolis: University of Minnesota Press, 1952), chs 5 and 6.

R. D. Hume, *Dryden's Criticism* (Ithaca: Cornell UP, 1970), chs 1 and 6.

W. J. B. Owen, *Wordsworth as Critic* (Toronto and Buffalo: Toronto UP, 1971).

E. Pechter, *Dryden's Classical Theory of Literature* (London etc.: Cambridge UP, 1975).

(A) JOHN DRYDEN

An Essay of Dramatic Poesy (1668)

I grant the French have performed what was possible on the ground-work of the Spanish plays; what was pleasant before, they have made regular: but there is not above one good play to be writ on all those plots; they are too much alike to please

often; which we need not the experience of our own stage to
justify. As for their new way of mingling mirth with serious plot,
I do not, with Lisideius, condemn the thing, though I cannot
approve their manner of doing it. He tells us, we cannot so
speedily recollect ourselves after a scene of great passion and
concernment, as to pass to another of mirth and humour, and to
enjoy it with any relish: but why should heimagine the soul of
man more heavy than his senses? Does not the eye pass from an
unpleasant object to a pleasant in a much shorter time than is
required to this? and does not the unpleasantness of the first
commend the beauty of the latter? The old rule of logic might
have convinced him, that contraries, when placed near, set off
each other. A continued gravity keeps the spirit too much bent;
we must refresh it sometimes, as we bait in a journey, that we
may go on with greater ease. A scene of mirth, mixed with
tragedy, has the same effect upon us which our music has
betwixt the acts; and that we find a relief to us from the best
plots and language of the stage, if the discourses have been long.
I must therefore have stronger arguments, ere I am convinced
that compassion and mirth in the same subject destroy each
other; and in the mean time cannot but conclude, to the honour
of our nation, that we have invented, increased, and perfected a
more pleasant way of writing for the stage, than was ever known
to the ancients or moderns of any nation, which is tragi-comedy.

And this leads me to wonder why Lisideius and many others
should cry up the barrenness of the French plots, above the
variety and copiousness of the English. Their plots are single;
they carry on one design, which is pushed forward by all the
actors, every scene in the play contributing and moving towards
it. Our plays, besides the main design, have underplots or by-
concernments, of less considerable persons and intrigues, which
are carried on with the motion of the main plot: just as they say
the orb of the fixed stars, and those of the planets, though they
have motions of their own, are whirled about by the motion of
the *Primum Mobile*, in which they are contained. That similitude
expresses much of the English stage; for if contrary motions may
be found in nature to agree; if a planet can go east and west at
the same time, one way by virtue of his own motion, the other
by the force of the First Mover, it will not be difficult to imagine
how the under-plot, which is only different, not contrary to the
great design, may naturally be conducted along with it.

Eugenius has already shown us, from the confession of the
French poets, that the Unity of Action is sufficiently preserved, if

all the imperfect actions of the play are conducing to the main design; but when those petty intrigues of a play are so ill ordered, that they have no coherence with the other, I must grant that Lisideius has reason to tax that want of due connexion; for co-ordination in a play is as dangerous and unnatural as in a state. In the mean time he must acknowledge, our variety, if well ordered, will afford a greater pleasure to the audience.

As for his other argument, that by pursuing one single theme they gain an advantage to express and work up the passions, I wish any example he could bring from them would make it good; for I confess their verses are to me the coldest I have ever read. Neither, indeed, is it possible for them, in the way they take, so to express passion, as that the effects of it should appear in the concernment of an audience, their speeches being so many declamations, which tire us with the length; so that instead of persuading us to grieve for their imaginary heroes, we are concerned for our own trouble, as we are in the tedious visits of bad company; we are in pain till they are gone. When the French stage came to be reformed by Cardinal Richelieu, those long harangues were introduced, to comply with the gravity of a churchman. Look upon the *Cinna* and the *Pompey*; they are not so properly to be called plays, as long discourses of reason of state; and *Polieucte* in matters of religion is as solemn as the long stops upon our organs. Since that time it is grown into a custom, and their actors speak by the hour-glass, as our parsons do; nay, they account it the grace of their parts, and think themselves disparaged by the poet, if they may not twice or thrice in a play entertain the audience with a speech of an hundred or two hundred lines. I deny not but this may suit well enough with the French; for as we, who are a more sullen people, come to be diverted at our plays, so they, who are of an airy and gay temper, come thither to make themselves more serious: and this I conceive to be one reason why comedy is more pleasing to us, and tragedies to them. But to speak generally: it cannot be denied that short speeches and replies are more apt to move the passions and beget concernment in us, than the other; for it is unnatural for any one in a gust of passion to speak long together, or for another in the same condition to suffer him, without interruption. Grief and passion are like floods raised in little brooks by a sudden rain; they are quickly up; and if the concernment be poured unexpectedly in upon us, it overflows us: but a long sober shower gives them leisure to run out as they came in, without troubling the ordinary current. As for Comedy, repartee is one of its chiefest graces; the greatest pleasure of the audience is a chace of wit, kept up on both sides, and swiftly managed. [. . .]

But I come now to the inference of your first argument. You said the dialogue of plays is presented as the effect of sudden thought, but no man speaks suddenly, or *ex tempore*, in rhyme; and you inferred from thence, that rhyme, which you acknowledge to be proper to epic poesy, cannot equally be proper to dramatic, unless we could suppose all men born so much more than poets, that verses should be made in them, not by them.

It has been formerly urged by you, and confessed by me, that since no man spoke any kind of verse *ex tempore*, that which was nearest Nature was to be preferred. I answer you, therefore, by distinguishing betwixt what is nearest to the nature of Comedy, which is the imitation of common persons and ordinary speaking, and what is nearest the nature of a serious play: this last is indeed the representation of Nature, but 'tis Nature wrought up to an higher pitch. The plot, the characters, the wit, the passions, the descriptions, are all exalted above the level of common converse, as high as the imagination of the poet can carry them, with proportion to verisimility. Tragedy, we know, is wont to image to us the minds and fortunes of noble persons, and to portray these exactly; heroic rhyme is nearest Nature, as being the noblest kind of modern verse.

A Defence of an Essay of Dramatic Poesy (1668)

But to return to verse; whether it be natural or not in plays, is a problem which is not demonstrable of either side: 'tis enough for me, that he acknowledges he had rather read good verse than prose: for if all the enemies of verse will confess as much, I shall not need to prove that it is natural. I am satisfied if it cause delight; for delight is the chief, if not the only, end of poesy: instruction can be admitted but in the second place, for poesy only instructs as it delights. 'Tis true, that to imitate well is a poet's work; but to affect the soul, and excite the passions, and, above all, to move admiration (which is the delight of serious plays), a bare imitation will not serve. The converse, therefore, which a poet is to imitate, must be heightened with all the arts and ornaments of poesy; and must be such as, strictly considered, could never be supposed spoken by any without premeditation.

As for what he urges, that *a play will still be supposed to be a composition of several persons speaking* ex tempore, *and that good verses are the hardest things which can be imagined to be so spoken*; I must crave leave to dissent from his opinion, as to the former part of it: for, if I am not deceived, a play is supposed to be the work of the poet, imitating or representing the conversation of several persons: and this I think to be as clear, as he thinks the contrary.

(John Dryden, *Of Dramatic Poesy: An Essay* (1668), *Essays*, ed. W. P. Ker, 2 vols (Oxford: Clarendon Press, 1900), I. 69–72, 100–1.)

(B) ALEXANDER POPE

An Essay on Criticism (1711)

First follow Nature, and your judgement frame
By her just standard, which is still the same;
Unerring Nature, still divinely bright,   70
One clear, unchang'd, and universal light,
Life, force, and beauty must to all impart,
At once the source, and end, and test of art.
Art from that fund each just supply provides,
Works without show, and without pomp presides: 75
In some fair body thus th' informing soul
With spirits feeds, with vigour fills the whole;
Each motion guides, and ev'ry nerve sustains,
It self unseen, but in th' effects, remains.
Some, to whom Heaven in wit has been profuse,   80
Want as much more to turn it to its use;
For wit and judgment often are at strife,
Though meant each other's aid, like man and wife.
'Tis more to guide than spur the Muse's steed;
Restrain his fury, than provoke his speed: 85
The winged courser, like a generous horse,
Shows most true mettle when you check his course.
   Those Rules of old discover'd, not devis'd,
Are nature still, but nature methodiz'd:
Nature, like liberty, is but restrain'd   90

By the same laws which first herself ordain'd [. . .]
Be Homer's works your study, and delight,
Read them by day, and meditate by night;   125
Thence form your judgment, thence your maxims bring,
And trace the Muses upward to their spring;
Still with itself compar'd, his text peruse;
And let your comment be the Mantuan Muse.
    When first young Maro in his boundless mind   130
A work t' outlast immortal Rome design'd,
Perhaps he seem'd above the Critick's law,
And but from Nature's fountains scorn'd to draw:
But when t'examine ev'ry part he came,
Nature and Homer were, he found, the same: 135
Convinc'd, amaz'd, he checks the bold design, ⎫
And rules as strict his labour'd work confine, ⎬
As if the Stagyrite o'erlook'd each line.   ⎭
Learn hence for ancient rules a just esteem;
To copy Nature is to copy them.   140

(Alexander Pope, *An Essay on Criticism* (1711), *Poetical Works*, Aldine edn,
3 vols (London: Bell, 1878), II.6, 7–8.)

(C) WILLIAM WORDSWORTH

Preface to *Lyrical Ballads,* 2nd ed. (1800)

The principal object, then, proposed in these Poems was to
choose incidents and situations from common life, and to relate
or describe them, throughout, as far as was possible in a
selection of language really used by men, and, at the same time,
to throw over them a certain colouring of imagination, whereby
ordinary things should be presented to the mind in an unusual
aspect; and, further, and above all, to make these incidents and
situations interesting by tracing in them, truly though not
ostentatiously, the primary laws of our nature: chiefly, as far as
regards the manner in which we associate ideas in a state of
excitement. Humble and rustic life was generally chosen,
because, in that condition, the essential passions of the heart find
a better soil in which they can attain their maturity, are less
under restraint, and speak a plainer and more emphatic
language; because in that condition of life our elementary
feelings coexist in a state of greater simplicity, and,

consequently, may be more accurately contemplated, and more
forcibly communicated; because the manners of rural life
germinate from those elementary feelings, and, from the
necessary character of rural occupations, are more easily
comprehended, and are more durable; and, lastly, because in
that condition the passions of men are incorporated with the
beautiful and permanent forms of nature. The language, too, of
these men has been adopted (purified indeed from what appear
to be its real defects, from all lasting and rational causes of
dislike or disgust) because such men hourly communicate with
the best objects from which the best part of language is
originally derived; and because, from their rank in society and
the sameness and narrow circle of their intercourse, being less
under the influence of social vanity, they convey their feelings
and notions in simple and unelaborated expressions.
Accordingly, such a language, arising out of repeated experience
and regular feelings, is a more permanent, and a far more
philosophical language, than that which is frequently substituted
for it by Poets, who think that they are conferring honour upon
themselves and their art, in proportion as they separate
themselves from the sympathies of men, and indulge in arbitrary
and capricious habits of expression, in order to furnish food for
fickle tastes, and fickle appetites, of their own creation.

But whatever portion of this faculty we may suppose even the
greatest Poet to possess, there cannot be a doubt that the
language which it will suggest to him, must often, in liveliness
and truth, fall short of that which is uttered by men in real life,
under the actual pressure of those passions, certain shadows of
which the Poet thus produces, or feels to be produced, in
himself.

However exalted a notion we would wish to cherish of the
character of a Poet, it is obvious, that while he describes and
imitates passions, his employment is in some degree mechanical,
compared with the freedom and power of real and substantial
action and suffering. So that it will be the wish of the Poet to
bring his feelings near to those of the persons whose feelings he
describes, nay, for short spaces of time, perhaps, to let himself
slip into an entire delusion, and even confound and identify his
own feelings with theirs; modifying only the language which is
thus suggested to him by a consideration that he describes for a
particular purpose, that of giving pleasure. Here, then, he will
apply the principle of selection which has been already insisted
upon. He will depend upon this for removing what would

otherwise be painful or disgusting in the passion; he will feel
that there is no necessity to trick out or to elevate nature: and,
the more industriously he applies this principle, the deeper will
be his faith that no words, which *his* fancy or imagination can
suggest, will be to be compared with those which are the
emanations of reality and truth.

But it may be said by those who do not object to the general
spirit of these remarks, that, as it is impossible for the Poet to
produce upon all occasions language as exquisitely fitted for the
passion as that which the real passion itself suggests, it is proper
that he should consider himself as in the situation of a
translator, who does not scruple to substitute excellencies of
another kind for those which are unattainable by him; and
endeavours occasionally to surpass his original, in order to make
some amends for the general inferiority to which he feels that he
must submit. But this would be to encourage idleness and
unmanly despair. Further, it is the language of men who speak
of what they do not understand; who talk of Poetry as of a
matter of amusement and idle pleasure; who will converse with
us as gravely about a *taste* for Poetry, as they express it, as if it
were a thing as indifferent as a taste for rope-dancing, or
Frontiniac or Sherry. Aristotle, I have been told, has said, that
Poetry is the most philosophic of all writing: it is so: its object is
truth, not individual and local, but general, and operative; not
standing upon external testimony, but carried alive into the
heart by passion: truth which is its own testimony, which gives
competence and confidence to the tribunal to which it appeals,
and receives them from the same tribunal. Poetry is the image of
man and nature. The obstacles which stand in the way of the
fidelity of the Biographer and Historian, and of their consequent
utility, are incalculably greater than those which are to be
encountered by the Poet who comprehends the dignity of his art.
The Poet writes under one restriction only, namely, the necessity
of giving immediate pleasure to a human Being possessed of that
information which may be expected from him, not as a lawyer, a
physician, a mariner, an astronomer, or a natural philosopher,
but as a Man. Except this one restriction, there is no object
standing between the Poet and the image of things; between this,
and the Biographer and Historian, there are a thousand.

(William Wordsworth, Preface to *Lyrical Ballads* (2nd edn, 1800), *Poetical
Works*, ed. Thomas Hutchinson (London: Henry Frowde, Oxford UP,
1895), pp. 935, 937–8.)

(D) SAMUEL JOHNSON

The History of Rasselas (1759)

CHAPTER X

Imlac's history continued. A dissertation upon poetry [. . .]

'The business of a poet, said Imlac, is to examine, not the individual, but the species; to remark general properties and large appearances: he does not number the streaks of the tulip, or describe the different shades in the verdure of the forest. He is to exhibit in his portraits of nature such prominent and striking features, as recall the original to every mind; and must neglect the minuter discriminations, which one may have remarked, and another have neglected, for those characteristics which are alike obvious to vigilance and carelessness.

'But the knowledge of nature is only half the task of a poet; he must be acquainted likewise with all the modes of life. His character requires that he estimate the happiness and misery of every condition; observe the power of all the passions in all their combinations, and trace the changes of the human mind as they are modified by various institutions and accidental influences of climate or custom, from the spriteliness of infancy to the despondence of decrepitude. He must divest himself of the prejudices of his age and country; he must consider right and wrong in their abstracted and invariable state; he must disregard present laws and opinions, and rise to general and transcendental truths, which will always be the same: he must therefore content himself with the slow progress of his name; contemn the applause of his own time, and commit his claims to the justice of posterity. He must write as the interpreter of nature, and the legislator of mankind, and consider himself as presiding over the thoughts and manners of future generations; as a being superiour to time and place. [. . .]'

(Samuel Johnson, *The History of Rasselas, Prince of Abissinia* (1759), *Works*, 12 vols (London, 1796), III. 329–30.)

'Preface to Shakespeare' (1765)

Nothing can please many, and please long, but just representations of general nature. Particular manners can be known to few, and therefore few only can judge how nearly they are copied. The irregular combinations of fanciful invention may delight a-while, by that novelty of which the common satiety of life sends us all in quest; but the pleasures of sudden wonder are soon exhausted, and the mind can only repose on the stability of truth.

Shakespeare is above all writers, at least above all modern writers, the poet of nature; the poet that holds up to his readers a faithful mirrour of manners and of life. His characters are not modified by the customs of particular places, unpractised by the rest of the world; by the peculiarities of studies or professions, which can operate but upon small numbers; or by the accidents of transient fashions or temporary opinions: they are the genuine progeny of common humanity, such as the world will always supply, and observation will always find. His persons act and speak by the influence of those general passions and principles by which all minds are agitated, and the whole system of life is continued in motion. In the writings of other poets a character is too often an individual; in those of *Shakespeare* it is commonly a species.

(Samuel Johnson, 'Preface to Shakespeare', *Johnson on Shakespeare*, ed. Sir Walter Raleigh (Oxford: Henry Frowde, 1908), pp. 11–12.)

Lives of the Poets (Cowley) (1783)

From this account of their compositions it will be readily inferred, that they [the Metaphysical poets] were not successful in representing or moving the affections. As they were wholly employed on something unexpected and surprising, they had no regard to that uniformity of sentiment which enables us to conceive and to excite the pains and the pleasure of other minds: they never enquired what, on any occasion, they should have said or done; but wrote rather as beholders than partakers of human nature; as Beings looking upon good and evil, impassive and at leisure; as Epicurean deities making remarks on the actions of men, and the vicissitudes of life, without interest and without emotion. Their courtship was void of fondness, and their lamentation of sorrow. Their wish was only to say what they hoped had been never said before.

Nor was the sublime more within their reach than the pathetick; for they never attempted that comprehension and expanse of thought which at once fills the whole mind, and of which the first effect is sudden astonishment, and the second rational admiration. Sublimity is produced by aggregation, and littleness by dispersion. Great thoughts are always general, and consist in positions not limited by exceptions, and in descriptions not descending to minuteness. It is with great propriety that Subtlety, which in its original import means exility of particles, is taken in its metaphorical meaning for nicety of distinction. Those writers who lay on the watch for novelty could have little hope of greatness; for great things cannot have escaped former observation. Their attempts were always analytick; they broke every image into fragments; and could no more represent, by their slender conceits and laboured particularities, the prospects of nature, or the scenes of life, than he, who dissects a sun-beam with a prism, can exhibit the wide effulgence of a summer noon.

(Samuel Johnson, *Lives of the English Poets*, Cowley (1783), ed. George Birkbeck Hill, 3 vols (Oxford: Clarendon, 1905), I. pp. 20–1.)

(E) WILLIAM BLAKE

Marginalia (Annotations to Reynold's *Discourses* written c.1808)

[Reynolds]   [*footnote*] He was a great generalizer. . . But this disposition to abstractions, to generalizing and classification, is the great glory of the human mind. . .

[Blake]   To Generalize is to be an Idiot. To Particularize is the Alone Distinction of Merit. General Knowledges are those Knowledges that Idiots possess. [. . .]

[Reynolds]   Following these rules, and using these precautions, when you have clearly and distinctly learned in what good colouring consists, you cannot do better than have recourse to nature herself, who is always at hand, and in comparison of whose true splendour the best coloured pictures are but faint and feeble.

[Blake]   Nonsense – Every Eye sees differently. As the Eye, Such the Object.

[Reynolds]   Instead of copying the touches of those great

masters, copy only their conceptions . . . Labour to invent on their general principles and way of thinking.

[Blake] General Principles Again! Unless you Consult Particulars you Cannot even Know or See Mich. Ang." or Rafael or any Thing Else. [. . .]

[Reynolds] The wish of the genuine painter must be more extensive: instead of endeavouring to amuse mankind with the minute neatness of his imitations, he must endeavour to improve them by the grandeur of his ideas.

[Blake] Without Minute Neatness of Execution The Sublime cannot Exist! Grandeur of Ideas is founded on Precision of Ideas. [. . .]

[Reynolds] . . . and the whole beauty and grandeur of the art consist, in my opinion, in being able to get above all singular forms, local customs, particularities, and details of every kind.

[Blake] A Folly. Singular & Particular Detail is the Foundation of the Sublime.

[Reynolds] All the objects which are exhibited to our view by nature, upon close examination will be found to have their blemishes and defects. The most beautiful forms have something about them like weakness, minuteness, or imperfection.

[Blake] Minuteness is their whole Beauty.

[Reynolds] This long laborious comparison should be the first study of the painter, who aims at the greatest style . . . he corrects nature by herself . . . This idea of the perfect state of nature, which the Artist calls the Ideal Beauty, is the great leading principle by which works of genius are conducted.

[Blake] Knowledge of Ideal Beauty is Not to be Acquired. It is Born with us. Innate Ideas are in Every Man Born with him; they are truly Himself. The Man who says that we have No Innate Ideas

must be a Fool & Knave, Having No Con-Science
or Innate Science. [. . .]

[Reynolds]   Thus it is from a reiterated experience, and a
close comparison of the objects in nature, that an
artist becomes possessed of the idea of that central
form . . . from which every deviation is deformity.

[Blake]   One Central Form Composed of all other Forms
being Granted, it does not therefore follow that all
other Forms are Deformity.

All Forms are Perfect in the Poets Mind, but
these are not Abstracted nor compounded from
Nature, but are from Imagination [. . .]

[Reynolds]   There is a rule, obtained out of general nature,
to contradict which is to fall into deformity.

[Blake]   What is General Nature? is there Such a Thing?
what is General Knowledge? is there such a Thing?
All Knowledge is Particular.

[Reynolds]   To the principle I have laid down, that the idea
of beauty in each species of beings is an invariable
one, it may be objected, that in every particular
species there are various central forms, which are
separate and distinct from each other, and yet are
each undeniably beautiful.

[Blake]   Here he loses sight of A Central Form & Gets
into Many Central Forms.

[Reynolds]   It is true, indeed, that these figures are each
perfect in their kind, though of different characters
and proportions; but still none of them is the
representation of an individual, but of a class.

[Blake]   Every Class is Individual. [. . .]

[Reynolds]   I should be sorry, if what is here recommended,
should be at all understood to countenance a
careless or indetermined manner of painting. For
though the painter is to overlook the accidental
discriminations of nature, he is to exhibit distinctly,
and with precision, the general forms of things.

[Blake]   Here he is for Determinate & yet for
                 Indeterminate.
                 Distinct General Form Cannot Exist.
                 Distinctness is Particular, Not General.

[Reynolds]   An History-painter paints man in general; a
                 Portrait-painter, a particular man, and
                 consequently a defective model.

[Blake]   A History Painter Paints The Hero, & not Man
                 in General, but most minutely in Particular.

[Reynolds]   . . . if a portrait-painter is desirous to raise and
                 improve his subject . . . he leaves out all the
                 minute breaks and peculiarities in the face, and
                 changes the dress from a temporary fashion to one
                 more permanent.

[Blake]   Folly! Of what consequence is it to the Arts
                 what a Portrait Painter does?

(William Blake, 'Annotations' (c.1808) in Sir Joshua Reynolds,
Discourses, Works (2nd edn, London: Cadell and Davies, 1798), pp. xcviii,
34, 35, 52, 58, 60, 61, 62, 63, 74, 106, 109.)

CHAPTER 4

LANGUAGE AND REPRESENTATION

Ludwig Wittgenstein's *Philosophical Investigations* opened an important debate in modern philosophy about the way in which thoughts and ideas are mediated by language. Citing a passage from Augustine's *Confessions* which describes the process of learning the meanings of words, he points to Augustine's assumption of a 'picture view' of language, according to which 'Every word has a meaning. This meaning is correlated with the word. It is the object for which the word stands.' Wittgenstein makes the obvious but often ignored point that certain words (conjunctions, for example) cannot 'picture' anything. The picture view supposes that a stable order of things is reflected in a stable order of words; new words arise only to describe new things. Wittgenstein proposes as an alternative view that the whole language system is made up of a series of discontinuous 'games', the rules for which are determined not absolutely by a uniform code but by the specific context in which the language usage occurs.

J. L. Austin's theory of 'speech acts' is related to Wittgenstein's view of language. Austin too rejects the old logical positivist view of language as description of a state of affairs in the world. He shows that while some statements may be 'constative' (referential), many others are 'performative' – they actually perform the actions they describe ('I declare this meeting open'). A speech act must have a context for it to have meaning. In other words we decide on meaning once we have decided whether or not a particular locution is an appropriate speech act within a particular conventional situation. 'I declare this meeting open' would not possess a performative function in an informal gathering such as a party, unless it were construed as a joke.

The question arises what status do statements in literary texts possess? Here are two of the answers that have been given: (1) fiction always involves a parasitic and essentially unserious use of performatives: a court-room oath in a film or novel is parasitic upon a real oath in a real court room; (2) rules of context and conventionality are determined according to a fictive text's genre. The second answer gives literary criticism something to do.

Ferdinand de Saussure, writing much earlier in the century, had already produced a theory of linguistics which departed radically from the picture view and which was to be the major impetus behind structuralism (see III,6). He insisted that not only does language not reflect things but that our thoughts have no shape before language comes along. Language arises when we divide the 'vague plane of sounds' into significant segments. The linking of thought and sound in the sign is described in III,6,C. The study of language is not about the connection between words and things but between sound and thought. This connection is entirely arbitrary: sounds do not represent anything; they are simply part of a signifying system. 'Red' is a piece of sound phonemically distinguishable from 'bed', while 'green' is phonemically distinct from 'greed'. A language system is something which permits us to make these distinctions. At another level 'red' and 'green' may be used as elements in a different system (traffic lights).

Both Wittgenstein and de Saussure have contributed to the undermining of a picture view of language and its accompanying common-sense philosophy. In order to appreciate the revolution in thinking which has occurred and which has deeply affected critical theory it is helpful to retrace the origins of the earlier view.

The sixteenth-century 'Anti-Ciceronian' movement culminated in Gabriel Harvey's *Ciceronianus* (1577). It was a reaction against the slavish imitation of Cicero's Latin prose style and especially against indulgence in the 'grand style' of rhetoric (e.g. the prose of John Lyly). The 'Attic' style favoured plainness and philosophical truth. Related to this movement was the demand, which arose at the end of the sixteenth century, for a 'neutral' language, appropriate to the new scientific and literary values of the period. Bacon's *Advancement of Learning* (1605) assumes the universality and permanence of nature, and the stability of the objects of perception. It therefore seemed natural to him to condemn the unreliability of the human mind and especially the misuse of language. Since nature could be understood through rational enquiry, there was no mystery preventing discovery. If scientists avoided the bad linguistic habits encouraged by medieval philosophers under the influence of Aristotle, they were capable of discovering the principles of nature for the benefit of humanity. Words must subserve things and not things words. Medieval 'schoolmen' wove cobwebs of learning from words and failed to develop a use of language which reflected nature as in a mirror. The mind itself, he argued, is like 'an uneven mirror on which the rays of objects fall and which mixes up its own nature with that of the object'. So, ideally the mind should passively reflect things and these images of things should be reflected without distortion in a clear langauge.

In the same period Ben Jonson's classicism also favoured a purity and simplicity of language use, but for rather different reasons. The poet should mirror *human nature* without distortion for the moral benefit of humanity. 'Language most shewes a man', argued Jonson, and believed that the classical stylistic values of brevity, clarity, and balance expressed the best qualities of human nature. He therefore attacked all inflated or grotesque uses of language as distortions of a true human nature. Interestingly, his comedies, which satirize the follies and vices of the human mind as they are expressed in language, are full of such distorted and puffed-up discourse.

Jonson's and Bacon's theory and practice were developed after 1660 by the advocates of 'rational' and classical values. John Locke's philosophical and political writings are a codification of the dominant 'common sense' ideology of the period. He enlarged Bacon's empirical view by introducing the concept of mathematical certainty (from Descartes). Descartes' focus upon *psychological* certainties was more in harmony with classical assumptions about the mind than Bacon's.

Locke's account of the development of language and ideas in infancy departs from Bacon's formula that 'words are but the images of matter'. General ideas are formed by reflection upon things and the general ideas give rise to language in the form of general names of things. The approach remains empirical because the ideas are derived from direct sense perception. However, he recognizes that some ideas exist independent of experience, such as mathemetical ideas. In addition, he makes an important and influential distinction between primary and secondary qualities of things, the latter (colour, taste, smell, etc.) existing only in the mind of the perceiver. This psychological aspect of Locke's theory was especially important for eighteenth-century literature and thought, when poetry and fiction were becoming more and more concerned with the subjective experience of reality (see II, 1–3). Empiricism itself remained strong, as did the picture view of language.

We have already discussed the displacement of the picture view of language in the work of Wittgenstein and de Saussure. This scepticism about language's power to represent reality produced a counter-reaction in the writings of certain 'post-Kantian' philosophers, notably Ernst Cassirer. Philosophers announced that language can only reflect the shape of the human mind and not the shape of the universe. Cassirer replied that this would apply to all uses of language, including science itself. Language's inability to copy the world was no discredit; we should instead celebrate the fact that the various uses of language are *symbolic forms* (cf. Langer, III,4,E) and not imitations. They create a spiritual reality which perhaps shapes and organizes our experience of that flux of time and space we call 'reality'. Cassirer's anti-empiricism, like Wallace Stevens' (see I,1,H), is as radical a rejection of the picture view as anything we find in the more fashionable structuralist tradition.

Background reading

R. Adolph, *The Rise of Modern Prose Style* (Cambridge, Mass.: Harvard UP, 1968).

John Casey, *The Language of Criticism* (London: Methuen, 1960), ch. 1 on Wittgenstein and criticism.

Morris W. Croll, *'Attic' and Baroque Prose Style: the Anti-Ciceronian Movement* (Princeton, NJ: Princeton UP, 1966).

A. C. Howell, *'Res et verba*: Words and Things', *ELH*, 13 (1946), 131–42.

L. C Knights, 'Bacon and the Dissociation of Sensibility', in *Explorations* (London: Chatto & Windus, 1947).

Mary Louise Pratt, *Toward a Speech Act Theory of Literary Discourse* (Bloomington: Indiana UP, 1977).

Wesley Trimpi, *Ben Jonson's Poems: A Study of the Plain Style* (Stanford, Cal.: Stanford UP, 1962).

Brian Vickers, *Francis Bacon and Renaissance Prose* (Cambridge: Cambridge UP, 1968).

Basil Willey, 'Bacon and the Rehabilitation of Nature', in *The Seventeenth Century Background* (New York: Columbia UP, 1935).

George Williamson, *The Senecan Amble: Prose Form from Bacon to Collier* (London: Faber & Faber, 1951).

(A) BEN JONSON

Timber, or Discoveries (1640)

Poetry and *Picture* are Arts of a like nature, and both are busie about imitation. It was excellently said of *Plutarch*, *Poetry* was a speaking Picture, and *Picture* a mute Poesie. For they both invent, faine, and devise many things, and accommodate all they invent to the use and service of nature. [. . .]

Language most shewes a man: speake, that I may see thee. It springs out of the most retired and inmost parts of us, and is the Image of the Parent of it, the mind. No glasse renders a mans forme or likenesse so true as his speech. Nay, it is likened to a man; and as we consider feature and composition in a man, so words in Language, in the greatnesse, aptnesse, sound, structure, and harmony of it. Some men are tall and bigge, so some Language is high and great. Then the words are chosen, their sound ample, the composition full, the absolution plenteous, and powr'd out, all grave, sinnewye, and strong. Some are little and Dwarfes; so of speech, it is humble and low, the words poore and flat, the members and *Periods* thinne and weake, without knitting or number. The middle are of a just stature. There the Language is plaine and pleasing: even without stopping, round without swelling; all well-torn'd, compos'd, elegant, and accurate. The vitious Language is vast and gaping, swelling and irregular; when it contends to be high, full of Rocke, Mountaine, and pointednesse: As it affects to be low, it is abject, and creeps, full of bogs and holes. And according to their Subject these stiles vary, and lose their names: For that which is high and lofty, declaring excellent matter, becomes vast and tumorous, Speaking of petty and inferiour things: so that which was even and apt in a meane and plaine subject, will appeare most poore and humble in a high Argument. Would you not laugh to meet a great Counsellor of state in a flat cap, with his trunck hose, and a hobby-horse Cloake, his Gloves under his girdle, and yond Haberdasher in a velvet Gowne, furr'd with sables?

Nothing is more ridiculous then to make an Author a *Dictator*, as the schooles have done *Aristotle*. The dammage is infinite knowledge receives by it. [. . .] Let *Aristotle* and others have their dues; but if wee can make farther Discoveries of truth and fitnesse then they, why are we envied? [. . .] Wee must not goe about like men anguish'd and perplex'd for vitious affectation of praise, but calmely study the separation of opinions, find the

errours have intervened, awake Antiquity, call former times into
question; but make no parties with the present, nor follow any
fierce undertakers, mingle no matter of doubtfull credit with the
simplicity of truth, but gently stirre the mould about the root of
the Question, and avoid all digladiations, facility of credit, or
superstitious simplicity; seeke the consonancy and concatenation
of Truth; stoope only to point of necessity, and what leads to
convenience. Then make exact animadversion where style hath
degenerated, where flourish'd and thriv'd in choisenesse of
Phrase, round and cleane composition of sentence, sweet falling
of the clause, varying an illustration by tropes and figures,
weight of Matter, worth of Subject, soundnesse of Argument, life
of Invention, and depth of Judgement. This is *Monte potiri*, to get
the hill: For no perfect Discovery can bee made upon a flat or a
levell.

Now that I have informed you in the knowing these things, let
mee leade you by the hand a little farther, in the direction of the
use, and make you an able Writer by practice. The conceits of
the mind are Pictures of things, and the tongue is the
Interpreter of those Pictures. The order of Gods creatures in
themselves is not only admirable and glorious, but eloquent;
Then he who could apprehend the consequence of things in their
truth, and utter his apprehensions as truly, were the best Writer
or Speaker. Therefore *Cicero* said much, when hee said, *Dicere
rectè nemo potest, nisi qui prudenter intelligit*. The shame of speaking
unskilfully were small if the tongue onely thereby were disgrac'd:
But as the Image of a *King* in his Seale ill-represented is not so
much a blemish to the waxe, or the Signet that seal'd it, as to
the Prince it representeth, so disordered speech is not so much
injury to the lips that give it forth, as to the disproportion and
incoherence of things in themselves, so negligently expressed.
Neither can his mind be thought to be in tune, whose words doe
jarre; nor his reason in frame, whose sentence is preposterous;
nor his Elocution cleare and perfect, whose utterance breakes it
selfe into fragments and uncertainties. Were it not a dishonour
to a mighty Prince, to have the Majesty of his embassage
spoyled by a carelesse Ambassadour? and is it not as great an
Indignity, that an excellent conceit and capacity, by the
indiligence of an idle tongue, should be disgrac'd? Negligent
speech doth not onely discredit the person of the Speaker, but it
discrediteth the opinion of his reason and judgement; it
discrediteth the force and uniformity of the matter and
substance. If it be so then in words, which fly and escape

censure, and where one good *Phrase* begs pardon for many
incongruities and faults, how shall he then be thought wise
whose penning is thin and shallow? How shall you looke for wit
from him whose leasure and head, assisted with the examination
of his eyes, yeeld you no life or sharpenesse in his writing?

(Ben Jonson, *Timber, or Discoveries* (1640), *Critical Essays of the 17th
Century*, ed. J. E. Spingarn, 3 vols (Oxford: Clarendon Press, 1908), I.
29, 41, 43–4.)

(B) FRANCIS BACON

Advancement of Learning (1605)

And thereof grew againe a delight in their manner of Stile and
Phrase, and an admiration of that kinde of writing; which was
much furthered & precipitated by the enmity & opposition that
the propounders of those primitive but seeming new opinions
had against the Schoole-men, who were generally of the
contrarie part, and whose Writings were altogether in a differing
Stile and fourme, taking libertie to coyne and frame new tearms
of Art to expresse their own sence, and to avoide circuite of
speech without regard to the purenesse, pleasantnesse, and (as I
may call it) lawfulnesse of the Phrase or word: And againe,
because the great labour that then was with the people [. . .] for
the winning and perswading of them there grewe of necessitie in
cheefe price and request eloquence and varietie of discourse, as
the fittest and forciblest accesse into the capacitie of the vulgar
sort; so that these foure causes concurring, the admiration of
ancient Authors, the hate of the Schoole-men, the exact studie of
Languages, and the efficacie of Preaching did bring in an
affectionate studie of eloquence and copie of speech, which then
began to flourish. This grew speedily to an excesse; for men
began to hunt more after wordes than matter, and more after
the choisenesse of the Phrase, and the round and cleane
composition of the sentence, and the sweet falling of the clauses,
and the varying and illustration of their workes with tropes and
figures, then after the weight of matter, worth of subject,
soundnesse of argument, life of invention, or depth of
judgement. [. . .]

Here, therefore, is the first distemper of learning, when men
studie words and not matter; whereof though I have represented

an example of late times, yet it hath beene and will be [. . .] in all time. And how is it possible but this should have an operation to discredite learning, even with vulgar capacities, when they see learned mens workes like the first Letter of a Patent or limmed Booke, which, though it hath large flourishes, yet it is but a Letter. It seemes to me that *Pigmalions* frenzie is a good embleme or portraiture of this vanitie; for wordes are but the Images of matter, and except they have life of reason and invention, to fall in love with them is all one as to fall in love with a Picture [. . .] Poesie is a part of Learning in measure of words for the most part restrained, but in all other points extreamely licensed, and doth truly referre to the Imagination, which, beeing not tyed to the Lawes of Matter, may at pleasure joyne that which Nature hath severed, & sever that which Nature hath joyned, and so make unlawfull Matches & divorses of things: [. . .] It is taken in two senses in respect of Wordes or Matter. In the first sense it is but a *Character* of stile, and belongeth to Arts of speeche, and is not pertinent for the present. In the later, it is, as hath beene saide, one of the principall Portions of learning, and is nothing else but FAINED HISTORY, which may be stiled as well in Prose as in Verse.

The use of this FAINED HISTORIE hath beene to give some shadowe of satisfaction to the minde of Man in those points wherein the Nature of things doth denie it, the world being in proportion inferiour to the soule; by reason whereof there is agreeable to the spirit of Man a more ample Greatnesse, a more exact Goodnesse, and a more absolute varietie then can bee found in the Nature of things. Therefore, because the Acts or Events of *true Historie* have not that Magnitude which satisfieth the minde of Man, *Poesie* faineth Acts and Events Greater and more Heroicall; because *true Historie* propoundeth the successes and issues of actions not so agreable to the merits of Vertue and Vice, therefore *Poesie* faines them more just in Retribution and more according to Revealed Providence; because *true Historie* representeth Actions and Events more ordinarie and lesse interchanged, therefore *Poesie* endueth them with more Rarenesse and more unexpected and alternative Variations: So as it appeareth that *Poesie* serveth and conferreth to Magnanimitie, Moralitie, and to delectation. And therefore it was ever thought to have some participation of divinesse, because it doth raise and erect the Minde, by submitting the shewes of things to the desires

of the Mind, whereas reason doth buckle and bowe the Mind
unto the Nature of things.

(Francis Bacon, *Advancement of Learning* (1605), *Critical Essays of the 17th
Century*, ed. J. E. Spingarn, 3 vols (Oxford: Clarendon Press, 1908), I. 2,
3, 5–6.)

Novum Organum (1620)

XXXVIII.

The idols and false notions which are now in possession of the
human understanding, and have taken deep root therein, not
only so beset men's minds that truth can hardly find entrance,
but even after entrance obtained, they will again in the very
instauration of the sciences meet and trouble us, unless men
being forewarned of the danger fortify themselves as far as may
be against their assaults.

XXXIX.

There are four classes of Idols which beset men's minds. To
these for distinction's sake I have assigned names, – calling the
first class *Idols of the Tribe*; the second, *Idols of the Cave*; the third,
Idols of the Market-place; the fourth, *Idols of the Theatre*. [. . .]

XLI.

The Idols of the Tribe have their foundation in human nature
itself, and in the tribe or race of men. For it is a false assertion
that the sense of man is the measure of things. On the contrary,
all perceptions as well of the sense as of the mind are according
to the measure of the individual and not according to the
measure of the universe. And the human understanding is like a
false mirror, which, receiving rays irregularly, distorts and
discolours the nature of things by mingling its own nature with
it.

XLII.

The Idols of the Cave are the idols of the individual man. For
every one (besides the errors common to human nature in

general) has a cave or den of his own, which refracts and
discolours the light of nature; owing either to his own proper
and peculiar nature; or to his education and conversation with
others; or to the reading of books, and the authority of those
whom he esteems and admires; or to the differences of
impressions, accordingly as they take place in a mind
preoccupied and predisposed or in a mind indifferent and
settled; or the like. So that the spirit of man (according as it is
meted out to different individuals) is in fact a thing variable and
full of perturbation, and governed as it were by chance. Whence
it was well observed by Heraclitus that men look for sciences in
their own lesser worlds, and not in the greater or common
world.

XLIII.

There are also Idols formed by the intercourse and association of
men with each other, which I call Idols of the Market-place, on
account of the commerce and consort of men there. For it is by
discourse that men associate; and words are imposed according
to the apprehension of the vulgar. And therefore the ill and unfit
choice of words wonderfully obstructs the understanding. Nor do
the definitions or explanations wherewith in some things learned
men are wont to guard and defend themselves, by any means set
the matter right. But words plainly force and overrule the
understanding, and throw all into confusion, and lead men away
into numberless empty controversies and idle fancies.

XLIV.

Lastly, there are Idols which have immigrated into men's minds
from the various dogmas of philosophies, and also from wrong
laws of demonstration. These I call Idols of the Theatre; because
in my judgment all the received systems are but so many stage-
plays, representing worlds of their own creation after an unreal
and scenic fashion. Nor is it only of the systems now in vogue,
or only of the ancient sects and philosophies, that I speak; for
many more plays of the same kind may yet be composed and in
like artificial manner set forth; seeing that errors the most widely
different have nevertheless causes for the most part alike. Neither
again do I mean this only of entire systems, but also of many

principles and axioms in science, which by tradition, credulity, and negligence have come to be received.

(Francis Bacon, *Novum Organum, Works*, ed. J. Spedding and R. L. Ellis, 14 vols (1857–74), IV. 53–5.)

(C) THOMAS SPRAT

History of the Royal Society (1667)

Who can behold without indignation how many mists and uncertainties these specious *Tropes* and *Figures* have brought on our knowledg? How many rewards which are due to more profitable and difficult *Arts* have been still snatch'd away by the easie vanity of *fine speaking*? For now I am warm'd with this just Anger, I cannot with-hold my self from betraying the shallowness of all these seeming Mysteries upon which *we Writers* and *Speakers* look so bigg. And, in few words, I dare say that, of all the Studies of men, nothing may be sooner obtain'd than this vicious abundance of *Phrase*, this trick of *Metaphors*, this volubility of *Tongue*, which makes so great a noise in the World. But I spend words in vain, for the evil is now so inveterate that it is hard to know whom to *blame*, or where to begin to *reform*. We all value one another so much upon this beautiful deceipt, and labour so long after it in the years of our education, that we cannot but ever after think kinder of it than it deserves. And indeed, in most other parts of Learning, I look on it to be a thing almost utterly desperate in its cure, and I think I may be plac'd amongst those *general mischiefs*, such as the *dissention* of Christian Princes, the *want of practice* in Religion, and the like, which have been so long spoken against that men are become insensible about them, every one shifting off the fault from himself to others, and so they are only made bare common places of complaint. It will suffice my present purpose to point out what has been done by the *Royal Society* towards the correcting of its excesses in *Natural Philosophy*, to which it is, of all others, a most profest enemy.

They have therefore been most rigorous in putting in execution the only Remedy that can be found for this *extravagance*, and that has been a constant Resolution to reject all amplifications, digressions, and swellings of style; to return back to the primitive purity and shortness, when men deliver'd so many *things* almost in an equal number of *words*. They have exacted from all their members a close, naked, natural way of speaking, positive expressions, clear senses, a native easiness, bringing all things as near the Mathematical plainness as they can, and preferring the language of Artizans, Countrymen, and Merchants, before that of Wits or Scholars.

(Thomas Sprat, *History of the Royal Society* (1667), *Critical Essays of the 17th Century*, ed. J. E. Spingarn, 3 vols (Oxford: Clarendon Press, 1908), II. 117–18.)

(D) JOHN LOCKE

Essay Concerning Human Understanding (1690)

[BOOK 2 CHAPTER II]

1. The better to understand the nature, manner, and extent of our knowledge, one thing is carefully to be observed concerning the ideas we have, and that is that some of them are simple and some complex.

Though the qualities that affect our senses are, in the things themselves, so united and blended that there is no separation, no distance between them, yet it is plain the ideas they produce in the mind enter by the senses simple and unmixed. For, though the sight and touch often take in from the same object, at the same time, different ideas, as a man sees at once motion and colour, the hand feels softness and warmth in the same piece of wax: yet the simple ideas thus united in the same subject are as perfectly distinct as those that come in by different senses. The coldness and hardness which a man feels in a piece of ice being as distinct ideas in the mind as the smell and whiteness of a lily, or as the taste of sugar, and smell of a rose; and there is nothing can be plainer to a man than the clear and distinct perception he has of those simple ideas; which, being each in itself uncompounded, contains in it nothing but one uniform appearance or conception in the mind, and is not distinguishable into different ideas.

2. These simple ideas, the materials of all our knowledge, are suggested and furnished to the mind only by those two ways above mentioned, viz. sensation and reflection. When the understanding is once stored with these simple ideas, it has the power to repeat, compare, and unite them, even to an almost

infinite variety, and so can make at pleasure new complex ideas. But it is not in the power of the most exalted wit or enlarged understanding, by any quickness or variety of thought, to invent or frame one new simple idea in the mind, not taken in by the ways before mentioned; nor can any force of the understanding destroy those that are there, the dominion of man in this little world of his own understanding being much what the same as it is in the great world of visible things; wherein his power, however managed by art and skill, reaches no further than to compound and divide the materials that are made to his hand, but can do nothing towards the making the least particle of new matter, or destroying one atom of what is already in being. The same inability will everyone find in himself, who shall go about to fashion in his understanding any simple idea, not received in by his senses from external objects, or by reflection from the operations of his own mind about them. I would have anyone try to fancy any taste which had never affected his palate, or frame the idea of a scent he had never smelt; and when he can do this, I will also conclude that a blind man hath ideas of colours and a deaf man true distinct notions of sounds.
3.   This is the reason why, though we cannot believe it impossible to God to make a creature with other organs and more ways to convey into the understanding the notice of corporeal things than those five, as they are usually counted, which he has given to man; yet I think it is not possible for anyone to imagine any other qualities in bodies, howsoever constituted, whereby they can be taken notice of besides sounds, tastes, smells, visible and tangible qualities. And had mankind been made with but four senses, the qualities then which are the object of the fifth sense had been as far from our notice, imagination, and conception as now any belonging to a sixth, seventh, or eighth sense can possibly be; which, whether yet some other creatures in some other parts of this vast and stupendous universe may not have, will be a great presumption to deny. [. . .]

[BOOK 3 CHAPTER II]

1.   Man, though he have great variety of thoughts, and such from which others as well as himself might receive profit and delight, yet they are all within his own breast, invisible and hidden from others, nor can of themselves be made to appear.

The comfort and advantage of society not being to be had
without communication of thoughts, it was necessary that man
should find out some external sensible signs whereby those
invisible ideas, which his thoughts are made up of, might be
made known to others. For this purpose nothing was so fit,
either for plenty or quickness, as those articulate sounds which
with so much ease and variety he found himself able to make.
Thus we may conceive how words, which were by nature so well
adapted to that purpose, came to be made use of by men as the
signs of their ideas: not by any natural connexion that there is
between particular articulate sounds and certain ideas, for then
there would be but one language amongst all men; but by a
voluntary imposition whereby such a word is made arbitrarily
the mark of such an idea. The use, then, of words is to be
sensible marks of ideas, and the ideas they stand for are their
proper and immediate signification.

2.   The use men have of these marks being either to record
their own thoughts for the assistance of their own memory or, as
it were, to bring out their ideas and lay them before the view of
others: words, in their primary or immediate signification, stand
for nothing but the ideas in the mind of him that uses them,
how imperfectly soever or carelessly those ideas are collected
from the things which they are supposed to represent. When a
man speaks to another, it is that he may be understood; and the
end of speech is that those sounds, as marks, may make known
his ideas to the hearer. That then which words are the marks of
are the ideas of the speaker; nor can anyone apply them as
marks, immediately, to anything else but the ideas that he
himself hath, for this would be to make them signs of his own
conceptions and yet apply them to other ideas, which would be
to make them signs and not signs of his ideas at the same time,
and so in effect to have no signification at all. Words being
voluntary signs, they cannot be voluntary signs imposed by him
on things he knows not. That would be to make them signs of
nothing, sounds without signification. A man cannot make his
words the signs either of qualities in things or of conceptions in
the mind of another, whereof he has none in his own. Till he
has some ideas of his own, he cannot suppose them to
correspond with the conceptions of another man; nor can he use
any signs for them: for thus they would be the signs of he knows
not what, which is in truth to be the signs of nothing. But when
he represents to himself other men's ideas by some of his own, if

he consent to give them the same names that other men do, it is still to his own ideas: to ideas that he has, and not to ideas that he has not.

3.   This is so necessary in the use of language that in this respect the knowing and the ignorant, the learned and unlearned, use the words they speak (with any meaning) all alike. They, in every man's mouth, stand for the ideas he has, and which he would express by them. A child having taken notice of nothing in the metal he hears called gold but the bright shining yellow colour, he applies the word gold only to his own idea of that colour and nothing else, and therefore calls the same colour in a peacock's tail gold. Another that hath better observed adds to shining yellow great weight, and then the sound gold, when he uses it, stands for a complex idea of a shining yellow and very weighty substance. Another adds to those qualities fusibility, and then the word gold to him signifies a body, bright, yellow, fusible, and very heavy. Another adds malleability. Each of these uses equally the word gold, when they have occasion to express the idea which they have applied it to; but it is evident that each can apply it only to his own idea, nor can he make it stand as a sign of such a complex idea as he has not.

4.   But though words, as they are used by men, can properly and immediately signify nothing but the ideas that are in the mind of the speaker, yet they in their thoughts give them a secret reference to two other things.

First, they suppose their words to be marks of the ideas in the minds also of other men, with whom they communicate: for else they should talk in vain and could not be understood, if the sounds they applied to one idea were such as by the hearer were applied to another, which is to speak two languages. But in this, men stand not usually to examine whether the idea they and those they discourse with have in their minds be the same, but think it enough that they use the word as they imagine in the common acceptation of that language, in which they suppose that the idea they make it a sign of is precisely the same to which the understanding men of that country apply that name.

5.   Secondly, because men would not be thought to talk barely of their own imaginations, but of things as really they are, therefore they often suppose their words to stand also for the reality of things. But this relating more particularly to

substances and their names, as perhaps the former does to simple ideas and modes, we shall speak of these two different ways of applying words more at large, when we come to treat of the names of mixed modes and substances in particular: though give me leave here to say that it is a perverting the use of words, and brings unavoidable obscurity and confusion into their signification, whenever we make them stand for anything but those ideas we have in our own minds. [. . .]

6.   The next thing to be considered is how general words come to be made. For since all things that exist are only particulars, how come we by general terms, or where find we those general natures they are supposed to stand for? Words become general by being made the signs of general ideas; and ideas become general by separating from them the circumstances of time and place and any other ideas that may determine them to this or that particular existence. By this way of abstraction they are made capable of representing more individuals than one: each of which, having in it a conformity to that abstract idea, is (as we call it) of that sort.

7.   But to deduce this a little more distinctly, it will not perhaps be amiss to trace our notions and names from their beginning and observe by what degrees we proceed and by what steps we enlarge our ideas from our first infancy. There is nothing more evident than that the ideas of the persons children converse with (to instance in them alone) are, like the persons themselves, only particular. The ideas of the nurse and the mother are well framed in their minds and, like pictures of them there, represent only those individuals. The names they first gave to them are confined to these individuals, and the names of nurse and mamma the child uses determine themselves to those persons. Afterwards, when time and a larger acquaintance have made them observe that there are a great many other things in the world that, in some common agreements of shape and several other qualities, resemble their father and mother and those persons they have been used to, they frame an idea which they find those many particulars do partake in, and to that they give, with others, the name man, for example. And thus they come to have a general name, and a general idea. Wherein they make nothing new, but only leave out of the complex idea they had of Peter and James, Mary and Jane that which is peculiar to each, and retain only what is common to them all.

[BOOK 3, CHAP. X]

1. Besides the imperfection that is naturally in language, and the obscurity and confusion that is so hard to be avoided in the use of words, there are several wilful faults and neglects which men are guilty of in this way of communication, whereby they render these signs less clear and distinct in their signification than naturally they need to be.

2. First, in this kind, the first and most palpable abuse is the using of words without clear and distinct ideas, or, which is worse, signs without anything signified. [. . .]

One may observe, in all languages, certains words that, if they be examined, will be found, in their first original and their appropriated use, not to stand for any clear and distinct ideas. These, for the most part, the several sects of philosophy and religion have introduced. For their authors or promoters, either affecting something singular and out of the way of common apprehensions, or to support some strange opinions or cover some weakness of their hypothesis, seldom fail to coin new words and such as, when they come to be examined, may justly be called insignificant terms. For having either had no determinate collection of ideas annexed to them when they were first invented or at least such as, if well examined, will be found inconsistent, it is no wonder if afterwards, in the vulgar use of the same party, they remain empty sounds with little or no signification amongst those who think it enough to have them often in their mouths, as the distinguishing characters of their church or school, without much troubling their heads to examine what are the precise ideas they stand for.

(John Locke, *Essay Concerning Human Understanding* (1690), *Philosophical Works* (London: G. Virtue, 1843), pp. 132–3, 312–14, 316–17, 363.)

(E) ERNST CASSIRER

Language and Myth (1946)

From this point of view [a naive realism which regards the reality of objects as something directly and unequivocally given, literally something tangible] all artistic creation becomes a mere imitation, which must always fall short of the original. Not only simple imitation of a sensibly presented model, but also what is known as idealization, manner, or style, must finally succumb to this verdict; for measured by the naked 'truth' of the object to be depicted, idealization itself is nothing but subjective misconception and falsification. And it seems that all other processes of mental gestation involve the same sort of outrageous distortion, the same departure from objective reality and the immediate data of experience. For all mental processes fail to grasp reality itself, and in order to represent it, to hold it at all, they are driven to the use of symbols. But all symbolism harbors the curse of mediacy; it is bound to obscure what it seeks to reveal. Thus the sound of *speech* strives to 'express' subjective and objective happening, the 'inner' and the 'outer' world; but what of this it can retain is not the life and individual fullness of existence, but only a dead abbreviation of it. All that 'denotation' to which the spoken word lays claim is really nothing more than mere suggestion; a 'suggestion' which, in face of the concrete variegation and totality of actual experience, must always appear a poor and empty shell. That is true of the external as well as the inner world: 'When *speaks* the soul, alas, the *soul* no longer speaks!'

From this point it is but a single step to the conclusion which the modern skeptical critics of language have drawn: the complete dissolution of any alleged truth content of language, and the realization that this content is nothing but a sort of phantasmagoria of the spirit. Moreover, from this standpoint, not only myth, art, and language, but even theoretical knowledge itself becomes a phantasmagoria; for even knowledge can never reproduce the true nature of things as they are, but must frame their essence in 'concepts.' But what are concepts save formulations and creations of thought, which, instead of giving us the true forms of objects, show us rather the forms of thought itself? Consequently all schemata which science evolves in order to classify, organize, and summarize the phenomena of the real world turn out to be nothing but arbitrary schemes – airy fabrics of the mind, which express not the nature of things, but the nature of mind. So knowledge, as well as myth, language, and art, has been reduced to a kind of fiction – to a fiction that recommends itself by its usefulness, but must not be measured by any strict standard of truth, if it is not to melt away into nothingness.

Against this self-dissolution of the spirit there is only one remedy: to accept in all seriousness what Kant calls his

'Copernican revolution.' Instead of measuring the content, meaning, and truth of intellectual forms by something extraneous which is supposed to be reproduced in them, we must find in these forms themselves the measure and criterion for their truth and intrinsic meaning. Instead of taking them as mere copies of something else, we must see in each of these spiritual forms a spontaneous law of generation; an original way and tendency of expression which is more than a mere record of something initially given in fixed categories of real existence. From this point of view, myth, art, language and science appear as symbols; not in the sense of mere figures which refer to some given reality by means of suggestion and allegorical renderings, but in the sense of forces each of which produces and posits a world of its own. In these realms the spirit exhibits itself in that inwardly determined dialectic by virtue of which alone there is any reality, any organized and definite Being at all. Thus the special symbolic forms are not imitations, but *organs* of reality, since it is solely by their agency that anything real becomes an object for intellectual apprehension, and as such is made visible to us. The question as to what reality is apart from these forms, and what are its independent attributes, becomes irrelevant here. For the mind, only that can be visible which has some definite form; but every form of existence has its source in some peculiar way of seeing, some intellectual formulation and intuition of meaning. Once language myth, art and science are recognized as such ideational forms, the basic philosophical question is no longer that of their relation to an absolute reality which forms, so to speak, their solid and substantial substratum; the central problem now is that of their mutual limitation and supplementation. Though they all function organically together in the construction of spiritual reality, yet each of these organs has its individual assignment.

(Ernst Cassirer, *Language and Myth*, trans. Susanne Langer (New York: Harper, 1946), pp. 6–9.)

(F) FERDINAND DE SAUSSURE

Course in General Linguistics (1915)

Psychologically our thought – apart from its expression in words – is only a shapeless and indistinct mass. Philosophers and linguists have always agreed in recognizing that without the help of signs we would be unable to make a clear-cut, consistent distinction between two ideas. Without language, thought is a vague, uncharted nebula. There are no pre-existing ideas, and nothing is distinct before the appearance of language.

Against the floating realm of thought, would sounds by themselves yield predelimited entities? No more so than ideas. Phonic substance is neither more fixed nor more rigid than thought; it is not a mold into which thought must of necessity fit but a plastic substance divided in turn into distinct parts to furnish the signifiers needed by thought. The linguistic fact can therefore be pictured in its totality – i.e. language – as a series of contiguous subdivisions marked off on both the indefinite plane of jumbled ideas (*A*) and the equally vague plane of sounds (*B*). The following diagram gives a rough idea of it:

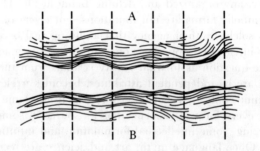

The characteristic role of language with respect to thought is not to create a material phonic means for expressing ideas but to serve as a link between thought and sound, under conditions that of necessity bring about the reciprocal delimitations of units. Thought, chaotic by nature, has to become ordered in the process of its decomposition. Neither are thoughts given material form nor are sounds transformed into mental entities; the somewhat mysterious fact is rather that 'thought-sound' implies division, and that language works out its units while taking shape between two shapeless masses. Visualize the air in contact with a sheet of water; if the atmospheric pressure changes, the surface of the water will be broken up into a series of divisions, waves; the waves resemble the union or coupling of thought with phonic substance. [. . .]

Language can also be compared with a sheet of paper: thought is the front and the sound the back; one cannot cut the front without cutting the back at the same time; likewise in language, one can neither divide sound from thought nor thought from sound; the division could be accomplished only abstractedly, and the result would be either pure psychology or pure phonology.

Linguistics then works in the borderland where the elements of sound and thought combine; *their combination produces a form, not a substance.*

These views give a better understanding of what was said before [. . . .] about the arbitrariness of signs. Not only are the two domains that are linked by the linguistic fact shapeless and confused, but the choice of a given slice of sound to name a given idea is completely arbitrary. If this were not true, the notion of value would be compromised, for it would include an externally imposed element. But actually values remain entirely relative, and that is why the bond between the sound and the idea is radically arbitrary.

The arbitrary nature of the sign explains in turn why the social fact alone can create a linguistic system. The community is necessary if values that owe their existence solely to usage and general acceptance are to be set up; by himself the individual is incapable of fixing a single value.

In addition, the idea of value, as defined, shows that to consider a term as simply the union of a certain sound with a certain concept is grossly misleading. To define it in this way would isolate the term from its system; it would mean assuming that one can start from the terms and construct the system by adding them together when, on the contrary, it is from the interdependent whole that one must start and through analysis obtain its elements.

(Ferdinand de Saussure, *Course in General Linguistics*, trans. Wade Baskin (rev. edn, Fontana, 1974), pp. 111–12. Original French, *Cours de linguistique générale*, was publ. 1915.)

(G) LUDWIG WITTGENSTEIN

Philosophical Investigations (1958)

22.   But how many kinds of sentence are there? Say assertion, question, and command? – There are *countless* kinds: countless different kinds of use of what we call 'symbols', 'words', 'sentences'. And this multiplicity is not something fixed, given once for all; but new types of language, new language-games, as

we may say, come into existence, and others become obsolete
and get forgotten. (We can get a *rough picture* of this from the
changes in mathematics.)

Here the term 'language-*game*' is meant to bring into
prominence the fact that the *speaking* of language is part of an
activity, or of a form of life.

Review the multiplicity of language-games in the following
examples, and in others:

> Giving orders, and obeying them –
> Describing the appearance of an object, or giving its
> > measurements –
> Constructing an object from a description (a
> > drawing) –
> Reporting an event –
> Speculating about an event –
> Forming and testing a hypothesis –
> Presenting the results of an experiment in tables and
> > diagrams –
> Making up a story; and reading it –
> Play-acting –
> Singing catches –
> Guessing riddles –
> Making a joke; telling it –
> Solving a problem in practical arithmetic –
> Translating from one language into another –
> Asking, thanking, cursing, greeting, praying.

– It is interesting to compare the multiplicity of the tools in
language and of the ways they are used, the multiplicity of kinds
of word and sentence, with what logicians have said about the
structure of language. (Including the author of the *Tractatus
Logico-Philosophicus*.)

24.   If you do not keep the multiplicity of language-games in
view you will perhaps be inclined to ask questions like: 'What is
a question?' – Is it the statement that I do not know such-and-
such, or the statement that I wish the other person would tell
me . . .? Or is it the description of my mental state of
uncertainty? – And is the cry 'Help?' such a description?

Think how many different kinds of thing are called
'description': description of a body's position by means of its co-
ordinates; description of a facial expression; description of a
sensation of touch; of a mood.

Of course it is possible to substitute the form of statement or description for the usual form of question: 'I want to know whether . . .' or 'I am in doubt whether . . .' – but this does not bring the different language-games any closer together. [. . .]

Someone might object against me: 'You take the easy way out! You talk about all sorts of language-games, but have nowhere said what the essence of a language-game, and hence of language, is: what is common to all these activities, and what makes them into language or parts of language. So you let yourself off the very part of the investigation that once gave you yourself most headache, the part about the *general form of propositions* and of language.'

And this is true. – Instead of producing something common to all that we call language, I am saying that these phenomena have no one thing in common which makes us use the same word for all, – but that they are *related* to one another in many different ways. And it is because of this relationship, or these relationships, that we call them all 'language'. I will try to explain this.

Consider for example the proceedings that we call 'games'. I mean board-games, card-games, ball-games, Olympic games, and so on. What is common to them all? – Don't say: 'There *must* be something common, or they would not be called "games"' – but *look and see* whether there is anything common to all. – For if you look at them you will not see something that is common to *all*, but similarities, relationships, and a whole series of them at that. To repeat: don't think, but look! – Look for example at board-games, with their multifarious relationships. Now pass to card-games; here you find many correspondences with the first group, but many common features drop out, and others appear. When we pass next to ball-games, much that is common is retained, but much is lost. – Are they all 'amusing'? Compare chess with noughts and crosses. Or is there always winning and losing, or competition between players? Think of patience. In ball games there is winning and losing; but when a child throws his ball at the wall and catches it again, this feature has disappeared. Look at the parts played by skill and luck; and at the difference between skill in chess and skill in tennis. Think now of games like ring-a-ring-a-roses; here is the element of amusement, but how many other characteristic features have disappeared! And we can go through the many, many other groups of games in the same way; can see how similarities crop up and disappear.

And the result of this examination is: we see a complicated network of similarities overlapping and criss-crossing: sometimes overall similarities, sometimes similarities of detail.

67.   I can think of no better expression to characterize these similarities than 'family resemblances'; for the various resemblances between members of a family: build, features, colour of eyes, gait, temperament, etc. etc. overlap and criss-cross in the same way. – And I shall say: 'games' form a family.

And for instance the kinds of number form a family in the same way. Why do we call something a 'number'? Well, perhaps because it has a – direct – relationship with several things that have hitherto been called number; and this can be said to give it an indirect relationship to other things we call the same name. And we extend our concept of number as in spinning a thread we twist fibre on fibre. And the strength of the thread does not reside in the fact that some one fibre runs through its whole length, but in the overlapping of many fibres.

But if someone wished to say: 'There is something common to all these constructions – namely the disjunction of all their common properties' – I should reply: Now you are only playing with words. One might as well say: 'Something runs through the whole thread – namely the continuous overlapping of those fibres'. [. . .]

At bottom, giving 'This is how things are' as the general form of propositions is the same as giving the definition: a proposition is whatever can be true or false. For instead of 'This is how things are' I could have said 'This is true'. (Or again 'This is false'.) But we have

> 'p' is true = p
> 'p' is false = not-p.

And to say that a proposition is whatever can be true or false amounts to saying: we call something a proposition when *in our language* we apply the calculus of truth functions to it.

Now it looks as if the definition – a proposition is whatever can be true or false – determined what a proposition was, by saying: what fits the concept 'true', or what the concept 'true' fits, is a proposition. So it is as if we had a concept of true and false, which we could use to determine what is and what is not a proposition. What *engages* with the concept of truth (as with a cogwheel), is a proposition.

But this is a bad picture. It is as if one were to say 'The king in chess in *the* piece that one can check.' But this can mean no more than that in our game of chess we only check the king. Just as the proposition that only a *proposition* can be true or false can say no more than that we only predicate 'true' and 'false' of what we call a proposition. And what a proposition is is in one sense determined by the rules of sentence formation (in English for example), and in another sense by the use of the sign in the language-game. And the use of the words 'true' and 'false' may be among the constituent parts of this game; and if so it *belongs* to our concept 'proposition' but does not '*fit*' it. As we might also say, check *belongs* to our concept of the king in chess (as so to speak a constituent part of it). To say that check did not *fit* our concept of the pawns, would mean that a game in which pawns were checked, in which, say, the players who lost their pawns lost, would be uninteresting or stupid or too complicated or something of the kind. [. . .]

Disputes do not break out (among mathematicians, say) over the question whether a rule has been obeyed or not. People don't come to blows over it, for example. That is part of the framework on which the working of our language is based (for example, in giving descriptions).

'So you are saying that human agreement decides what is true and what is false?' – It is what human beings *say* that is true and false; and they agree in the *language* they use. That is not agreement in opinions but in form of life. [. . .]

272.   The essential thing about private experience is really not that each person possesses his own exemplar, but that nobody knows whether other people also have *this* or something else. The assumption would thus be possible – though unverifiable – that one section of mankind had one sensation of red and another section another.

273.   What am I to say about the word 'red'? – that it means something 'confronting us all' and that everyone should really have another word, besides this one, to mean his *own* sensation of red? Or is it like this: the word 'red' means something known to everyone; and in addition, for each person, it means something known only to him? (Or perhaps rather: it *refers* to something known only to him.)

(Ludwig Wittgenstein, *Philosophical Investigations* trans. G. E. M. Anscombe (3rd edn, Oxford: Blackwell, 1967), Sections 22–3, 65–7, 136, 240–1, 272–3.)

(H) J. L. AUSTIN

How to Do Things with Words (1962)

And we began by distinguishing a whole group of senses of 'doing something' which are all included together when we say, what is obvious, that to say something is in the full normal sense to do something – which includes the utterance of certain noises, the utterance of certain words in a certain construction, and the utterance of them with a certain 'meaning' in the favourite, philosophical sense of that word, i.e. with a certain sense and with a certain reference.

The act of 'saying something' in this full normal sense I call, i.e. dub, the performance of a locutionary act and the study of utterances thus far and in these respects the study of locutions, or of the full units of speech. Our interest in the locutionary act is, of course, principally to make quite plain what it is, in order to distinguish it from other acts with which we are going to be primarily concerned. [. . .]

[Consider] our problem of the constative as opposed to the performative utterance. For example, it might be perfectly possible, with regard to an utterance, say 'It is going to charge', to make entirely plain 'what we were saying' in issuing the utterance, in all the senses so far distinguished, and yet not at all to have cleared up whether or not in issuing the utterance I was performing the act of *warning* or not. It may be perfectly clear what I mean by 'It is going to charge' or 'Shut the door', but not clear whether it is meant as a statement or warning, &c.

To perform a locutionary act is in general, we may say, also and *eo ipso* to perform an *illocutionary* act, as I propose to call it. To determine what illocutionary act is so performed we must determine in what way we are using the locution:

asking or answering a question,

giving some information or an assurance or a warning,

announcing a verdict or an intention,

pronouncing sentence,

making an appointment or an appeal or a criticism,

making an identification or giving a description,

and the numerous like. [. . .]

I explained the performance of an act in this new and second sense as the performance of an 'illocutionary' act, i.e. performance of an act *in* saying something as opposed to performance of an act *of* saying something; and I shall refer to the doctrine of the different types of function of language here in question as the doctrine of 'illocutionary forces'. [. . .]

It may be said that for too long philosophers have neglected this study, treating all problems as problems of 'locutionary usage', and indeed that the 'descriptive fallacy' mentioned in Lecture I commonly arises through mistaking a problem of the former kind for a problem of the latter kind. True, we are now getting out of this; for some years we have been realizing more and more clearly that the occasion of an utterance matters seriously, and that the words used are to some extent to be 'explained' by the 'context' in which they are designed to be or have actually been spoken in a linguistic interchange. [. . .]

There is yet a further sense in which to perform a locutionary act, and therein an illocutionary act, may also be to perform an act of another kind. Saying something will often, or even normally, produce certain consequential effects upon the feelings, thoughts, or actions of the audience, or of the speaker, or of other persons: and it may be done with the design, intention, or purpose of producing them; and we may then say, thinking of this, that the speaker has performed an act in the nomenclature of which reference is made either, only obliquely, or even, not at all, to the performance of the locutionary or illocutionary act. We shall call the performance of an act of this kind the performance of a *perlocutionary* act or *perlocution*. [. . .]

To take this farther, let us be quite clear that the expression 'use of language' can cover other matters even more diverse than the illocutionary and perlocutionary acts. For example, we may speak of the 'use of language' *for* something, e.g. for joking; and we may use 'in' in a way different from the illocutionary 'in', as when we say 'in saying "p" I was joking' or 'acting a part' or 'writing poetry'; or again we may speak of 'a poetical use of language' as distinct from 'the use of language in poetry'. These references to 'use of language' have nothing to do with the illocutionary act. For example, if I say 'Go and catch a falling star', it may be quite clear what both the meaning and the force of my utterance is, but still wholly unresolved which of these other kinds of things I may be doing. There are parasitic uses of language, which are 'not serious', not the 'full normal use'. The normal conditions of reference may be suspended, or no attempt made at a standard perlocutionary act, no attempt to make you do anything, as Walt Whitman does not seriously incite the eagle of liberty to soar.

We first distinguished a group of things we do in saying something, which together we summed up by saying we perform a *locutionary act*, which is roughly equivalent to uttering a certain sentence with a certain sense and reference, which again is roughly equivalent to 'meaning' in the traditional sense. Second, we said that we also perform *illocutionary acts* such as informing, ordering, warning, undertaking, &c., i.e. utterances which have a certain (conventional) force. Thirdly, we may also perform *perlocutionary acts*: what we bring about or achieve *by* saying something, such as convincing, persuading, deterring, and even, say, surprising or misleading.

(J. L. Austin, *How to Do Things with Words* (Oxford: Clarendon Press, 1962), pp. 94–5, 98, 99–100, 101, 104, 108.)

PART II:

SUBJECTIVITY

The twentieth century ha seen a remarkable growth of philosophical and psychological theories which take as their starting points the nature and processes of the human mind. The status of 'facts' or 'objects' and of the fixity of 'things' has dwindled under the brilliant light of psychoanalysis and phenomenology, which have highlighted the roles of unconscious processes and of our existential condition in determining our knowledge of the world. 'Subjective' kinds of critical theory have recently given prominence to (1) the reader's role in critical practice, and (2) the subjective processes which are at work in literary texts. If we follow these approaches we can no longer treat texts as self-contained verbal structures with definite meanings which the reader can process with accuracy. The texts themselves are fraught with unconscious movement, and their meanings are dependent on the reader's *active* engagement with textual structures.

Before the modern literary student can come to grips with the problems of subjective criticism it is essential to recognize that this subjective trajectory in criticism has a long history. Evidently the most powerful impetus in critical thought was the Romantic movement, which has deeply affected our modern consciousness and specifically the 'common-sense' discourse of literary commentary. At school we are still imbued with an essentially romantic approach to reading. The first three sections of Part II consider three familiar and fundamental concepts associated with this tradition:

i.   Imagination. This term has passed through many stages and significations between the seventeenth and twentieth centuries. However, the romantic meaning still

predominates in popular usage. The extracts place
Coleridge's influential statements about imagination and
fancy in the context of the previous two centuries'
development of these primarily psychological categories.

ii.   Genius. We need only think of Peter Shaffer's *Amadeus* to
recognize that we still use this romantic concept to define
the highest achievements in the arts. The extracts trace its
development from 'Longinus'.

iii. Emotion. Wordsworth's definition of poetry as 'emotion
recollected in tranquillity' remains the 'common-sense'
attitude. T. S. Eliot's efforts to reintroduce the idea that
intellect should be equally prominent in poetry have hardly
affected this popular view.

I have used the terms 'popular' and 'common sense', not in
order to promote a superior and élitist attitude towards
spontaneous kinds of literary response, but to draw attention to
the history of our cultural assumptions. Such assumptions about
the nature of literature and art are not necessarily value-free,
neutral or universal. New ways of understanding mental
processes, for example, come into conflict with common sense,
and when this happens we either suppress the conflict or resolve
it one way or another. One should add that some modern
theories ('phenomenological' ones, for example) are not in
conflict with the romantic tradition, at least in so far as they
continue to emphasize subjective experience as the source and
test of art.

CHAPTER 1

WIT, JUDGEMENT, FANCY AND IMAGINATION

The main classical authorities in literary criticism argued that literature imitated life. Plato's *Ion*, it is true, regards the poet as a divinely inspired being, but most Greek and Roman writers believed that the great author exercises a rational control over composition. Horace's advice became standard classical doctrine: 'I would advise one who has learned the imitative art to look to life and manners for a model, and draw from thence living words' (*Ars Poetica*, 317–18). The term 'rhetoric' (see III, 5) sums up the main classical legacy in criticism. The rhetorically trained poet begins by discovering his subject-matter (*inventio*) and disposing it in certain preordained forms (*dispositio*) and finally expressing it in appropriate words (*elocutio*). The classical writer's art is a *discipline*, involving the imitation of models, the observance of stylistic rules, and the use of pre-established figures of speech and rhythms.

Certain religious and scientific developments challenged classical authority during the Renaissance, but it was not until the seventeenth century that the beginnings of a modern psychology of art were established. During the 'Augustan' period (c. 1660–1780) these new ideas were blended with classicism with only occasionally anti-classical effects. However, during the following period the dominant classicism was finally displaced.

Thomas Hobbes (1588–1679), the philosopher, was both a contributor to English classical doctrines and the first English writer to explore in depth the subjective aspect of writing. His views were summed up in the following apothegm: 'Time and Education begets experience; Experience begets memory; Memory begets Judgment and Fancy: Judgment begets the strength and structure, and Fancy begets the ornaments of a Poem' (*Answer to Davenant*, 1650). Two important ideas are

contained in this brief quotation: (1) the poet's personal
experience is the source of poetry, and (2) the mental faculties of
the poet (judgement and fancy) have different functions in the
act of composition. Hobbes follows the classical tradition in
treating judgement as the superior faculty which controls fancy.
The transition from Hobbes' mechanistic psychology of the
imagination to Coleridge's organic and holistic conception is a
long and remarkable one.

Hobbes' psychology was founded upon the recently established
findings of Galileo and especially his theory of *mechanical motion*.
Ideas, for Hobbes, are no more than the residual motions in the
brain of sense impressions. 'Fancy' and 'imagination' are
synonymous terms for the image traces left in the brain, like
ripples in water which gradually fade under the weight of new
waves. The images are assembled in two ways: (1) by random
association, or (2) by 'regulated' succession. Poetry makes use of
the former to a large extent: fancy (or wit) resists the guidance
of judgement, preferring to associate experiences freely. Science
and law, for example, control fancy by directing thought along a
particular channel for a particular end. According to Hobbes the
best classical poetry combines fancy and judgement. The mind
would be a helpless mechanism of associations if it were not kept
in order by judgement.

Joseph Addison (1672–1719) adopted Locke's version of this
psychological model which retained the distinction between wit
(the assemblage of ideas) and judgement (the separation of
ideas). As a writer Addison was naturally concerned to justify
and dignify poetry's use of association. He argues that
discovering a resemblance between two ideas or images is not
enough; a poet must add 'delight' and 'surprise' by discovering
unusual likenesses. The subjective tendency of Addison's thought
is especially evident in his famous *Spectator* essays 'On the
Pleasures of the Imagination', which are probably the first
attempts to develop a full aesthetic theory. He adopts Locke's
distinction between primary and secondary qualities of matter.
Primary qualities are those mathematical and geometric
properties (extension, form, density) which are objectively certain
and outside the mind. Secondary qualities (colour, texture,
smell) have no existence in matter but only in the mind.
Addison founds his aesthetic theory on the mind's subjective
experience of the external world. When we look at a mountain
we see a structure of a certain bulk, but our imaginative
experience consists of the pleasurable sensations we experience

internally from its secondary qualities. Poets have a special ability to produce a description of things which 'often gives us more lively ideas than the sight of things themselves'. Notice how this completely reverses Hobbes' notion of poetry as an assemblage of fading images salvaged by the poet from an overcrowded memory. The poet actually 'gets the better of Nature'. Addison goes on to anticipate reader-response criticism (see II, 4) by addressing the problem of variation in response: some readers have a less developed imaginative power, which means that even the greatest poetry leaves them cold.

In the mid-eighteenth century associationism became a dominant position in philosophy. The Scottish common-sense school (Francis Hutcheson, Adam Smith, Thomas Reid, Dugald Stewart), as its name implies, believed that reason is able to control the powerful processes of association. However, the school of David Hartley, who was followed by Archibald Alison, Alexander Gerard and Abraham Tucker, took associationism to its limits.

Gerard's *Essay on Genius* (1774), an expansion of his *Essay on Taste* (1759), argues that the mind can neither control nor resist the flood of images and connections between images that arise in the mind. He takes to its logical conclusion Hobbes' account of 'unregulated' mental discourse, but unlike Hobbes regards the true poet as capable of new and numerous associations of images: the poet's 'boundless fertility' of imagination is to an extraordinary degree an automatic function, in Gerard's view.

Coleridge's theory of the imagination is both a development of associationist ideas and a strong reaction against them. He shows that Hartley's theories reduce the human mind to a passive victim of a mechanical process. He also rejected the Addisonian view of imaginative experience: beauty is not simply an effect in the mind of an external stimulus. In describing Wordsworth's poetry he assumes that the poet's mind is more *active* and *creative*. The imaginative faculty actually adds its own 'tone' and 'atmosphere' to the observations of sense experience. Coleridge's distinction between imagination and fancy enables him to argue the god-like creativity of imagination. By combining English associationism with German 'organic' philosophy (especially Schelling) he heightened the imagination's vital and shaping function. He reserved the term 'fancy' for the older, mechanical, associationist account: fancy is just a version of memory and like memory 'it must receive all its materials ready made from the law of association'. The art of rearranging these materials is a poetic function but is not enough to account for genius. Imagination does not simply reshuffle the cards of experience; it 'dissolves, diffuses, dissipates, in order to recreate'. Coleridge seems to have in mind God's dissolution of chaos and creation of the universe. By way of demonstration Coleridge can do no more than quote passages of great writing which the reader is assumed to acknowledge as truly imaginative.

Coleridge's notions of organic unity and imaginative power strongly influenced the New Criticism (see III, 2 and 3) and the intuitive approach of much modern criticism. I. A. Richards' work, which itself deeply influenced the New Criticism, combined an updated (but now obsolete) mechanical psychology with Coleridge's stress upon unification and the imagination's harmonizing power. Richards' theory of poetry may be summarized under the following points:

i.   A good poem transfers to the reader the beneficial psychological effects of the poet's original experience of the world.
ii. A good poem presupposes a good experience which allows the satisfaction of the greatest possible number of impulses and promotes a greater general balance of impulses.
iii. The poet is able to accommodate a greater number of impulses compared with the ordinary person who is forced to suppress many, since the dispositions to action which result from the stimuli are often in conflict. In tragedy, for example, the impulses of pity and fear are reconciled.

If we remove the neuro-psychology we are left with a Coleridgean organic theory: the imagination has the power to organize and unify the 'welter of disconnected impulses' which assail us. He accepts Coleridge's distinction between imagination and fancy, but reinterprets it as one between degrees of complexity: imaginative complexity is greater, but not necessarily more valuable. This shift is part of a modernist rejection of the Romantics' elevation of the sublime and spiritual levels of experience. Eliot and Pound held that poetry should combine the lofty and the mundane, emotion and intellect.

Much modern criticism has rejected the spiritual and organicist inheritance of Romanticism. Structuralist and psychoanalytic theories reject the notion of an individual imaginative experience and replace it with a linguistically based account of the 'signifying process' (see II, 5, E–F, III, 6, C).

Background reading

[On Coleridge see I, 1, D]

John Spencer Hill (ed.), *The Romantic Imagination: A Casebook* (London: Macmillan, 1977).

M. Kallich, 'The Association of Ideas and Critical Theory: Hobbes, Locke and Addison', *ELH*, 12 (1945), 290–315.

John Crowe Ransom, 'I. A. Richards: the Psychological Critic', in *The New Critics* (New York: New Directions, 1941).

I. A. Richards, *Coleridge on Imagination* (London: Kegan Paul, Trench, Trubner, 1934).

C. D. Thorpe, *The Aesthetic Theory of Thomas Hobbes* (University of Michigan Publications, 1940).

C. D. Thorpe, 'Addison's Contribution to Criticism', in *The Seventeenth Century*, ed. R. F. Jones *et al.* (Stanford, Cal.: Stanford UP, 1951).

Austin Warren, *Alexander Pope as Critic and Humanist* (Princeton NJ: Princeton UP, 1929, 1963).

(A) THOMAS HOBBES

Leviathan (1651)

[CHAPTER 2]

When a body is once in motion, it moveth, unless something else hinder it, eternally; and whatsoever hindreth it, cannot in an instant, but in time, and by degrees, quite extinguish it; and as we see in the water, though the wind cease, the waves give not over rolling for a long time after: so also it happeneth in that motion, which is made in the internal parts of a man, then, when he sees, dreams, &c. For after the object is removed, or the eye shut, we still retain an image of the thing seen, though more obscure than when we see it. And this is it, the Latins call *imagination*, from the image made in seeing; and apply the same, though improperly, to all the other senses. But the Greeks call it *fancy*; which signifies *appearance*, and is as proper to one sense, as to another. IMAGINATION therefore is nothing but *decaying sense*; and is found in men, and many other living creatures, as well sleeping, as waking.

The decay of sense in men waking, is not the decay of the

motion made in sense; but an obscuring of it, in such manner as the light of the sun obscureth the light of the stars; which stars do no less exercise their virtue, by which they are visible, in the day than in the night. But because amongst many strokes, which our eyes, ears, and other organs receive from external bodies, the predominant only is sensible; therefore, the light of the sun being predominant, we are not affected with the action of the stars. And any object being removed from our eyes, though the impression it made in us remain, yet other objects more present succeeding, and working on us, the imagination of the past is obscured, and made weak, as the voice of a man is in the noise of the day. From whence it followeth, that the longer the time is, after the sight or sense of any object, the weaker is the imagination. For the continual change of man's body destroys in time the parts which in sense were moved: so that distance of time, and of place, hath one and the same effect in us. For as at a great distance of place, that which we look at appears dim, and without distinction of the smaller parts; and as voices grow weak, and inarticulate; so also, after great distance of time, our imagination of the past is weak; and we lose, for example, of cities we have seen, many particular streets, and of actions, many particular circumstances. This *decaying sense*, when we would express the thing itself, I mean *fancy* itself, we call *imagination*, as I said before: but when we would express the decay, and signify that the sense is fading, old, and past, it is called *memory*. So that imagination and memory are but one thing, which for divers considerations hath divers names. [. . .]

[CHAPTER 3]

By *Consequence*, or TRAIN of thoughts, I understand that succession of one thought to another, which is called, to distinguish it from discourse in words, *mental discourse*.

When a man thinketh on any thing whatsoever, his next thought after, is not altogether so casual as it seems to be. Not every thought to every thought succeeds indifferently. But as we have no imagination, whereof we have not formerly had sense, in whole, or in parts; so we have no transition from one imagination to another, whereof we never had the like before in our senses. The reason whereof is this. All fancies are motions within us, relics of those made in the sense: and those motions that immediately succeeded one another in the sense, continue also together after sense: insomuch as the former coming again to take place, and be predominant, the latter followeth, by coherence of the matter moved, in such manner, as water upon a plane table is drawn which way any one part of it is guided by the finger. But because in sense, to one and the same thing perceived, sometimes one thing, sometimes another succeedeth, it comes to pass in time, that in the imagining of any thing, there is no certainty what we shall imagine next; only this is certain, it shall be something that succeeded the same before, at one time or another.

This train of thoughts, or mental discourse, is of two sorts. The first is *unguided, without design*, and inconstant; wherein there is no passionate thought, to govern and direct those that follow, to itself, as the end and scope of some desire, or other passion: in which case the thoughts are said to wander, and seem impertinent one to another, as in a dream. [. . .]

And yet in this wild ranging of the mind, a man may oft-times perceive the way of it, and the dependance of one thought upon another. For in a discourse of our present civil war, what could seem more impertinent, than to ask, as one did, what was the value of a Roman penny? Yet the coherence to me was manifest enough. For the thought of the war, introduced the thought of the delivering up the king to his enemies; the thought of that, brought in the thought of the delivering up of Christ; and that again the thought of the thirty pence, which was the price of that treason; and thence easily followed that malicious question, and all this in a moment of time; for thought is quick.

The second is more constant; as being *regulated* by some desire, and design. [. . .] In sum, the discourse of the mind, when it is governed by design, is nothing but *seeking*, or the faculty of invention, which the Latins called *sagacitas*, and *solertia*; a hunting out of the causes, of some effect, present or past; or of the effects, of some present or past cause. Sometimes a man seeks what he hath lost; and from that place, and time, wherein he misses it, his mind runs back, from place to place, and time to time, to find where, and when he had it; that is to say, to find some certain, and limited time and place, in which to begin a method of seeking. Again, from thence, his thoughts run over the same places and times, to find what action, or other occasion might make him lose it. This we call *remembrance*, or calling to mind: the Latins call it *reminiscentia*, as it were a *re-conning* of our former actions.

Sometimes a man knows a place determinate, within the

compass whereof he is to seek; and then his thoughts run over
all the parts thereof, in the same manner as one would sweep a
room, to find a jewel; or as a spaniel ranges the field, till he find
a scent; or as a man should run over the alphabet, to start a
rhyme. [. . .]

[CHAPTER 8]

[. . .] And by *virtues intellectual*, are always understood such
abilities of the mind, as men praise, value, and desire should be
in themselves; and go commonly under the name of a *good wit*;
though the same word *wit*, be used also, to distinguish one
certain ability from the rest.

These *virtues* are of two sorts; *natural*, and *acquired*. By natural,
I mean not, that which a man hath from his birth: for that is
nothing else but sense; wherein men differ so little one from
another, and from brute beasts, as it is not to be reckoned
amongst virtues. But I mean, that *wit*, which is gotten by use
only, and experience; without method, culture, or instruction.
This NATURAL WIT, consisteth principally in two things; *celerity
of imagining*, that is, swift succesion of one thought to another;
and *steady direction* to some approved end. On the contrary a
slow imagination, maketh that defect, or fault of the mind,
which is commonly called DULLNESS, *stupidity*, and sometimes
by other names that signify slowness of motion, or difficulty to
be moved.

And this difference of quickness, is caused by the difference of
men's passions; that love and dislike, some one thing, some
another: and therefore some men's thoughts run one way, some
another; and are held to, and observe differently the things that
pass through their imagination. And where as in this succession
of men's thoughts, there is nothing to observe in the things they
think on, but either in what they be *like one another*, or in what
they be *unlike*, or *what they serve for*, or *how they serve to such a
purpose*; those that observe their similitudes, in case they be such
as are but rarely observed by others, are said to have a *good wit*;
by which, in this occasion, is meant a *good fancy*. But they that
observe their differences, and dissimilitudes; which is called
distinguishing, and *discerning*, and *judging* between thing and thing;
in case, such discerning be not easy, are said to have a *good
judgment*: and particularly in matter of conversation and business;
wherein, times, places, and persons are to be discerned, this
virtue is called DISCRETION. The former, that is, fancy, without

the help of judgment, is not commended as a virtue: but the latter which is judgment, and discretion, is commended for itself, without the help of fancy. Besides the discretion of times, places, and persons, necessary to a good fancy, there is required also an often application of his thoughts to their end; that is to say, to some use to be made of them. This done; he that hath this virtue, will be easily fitted with similitudes, that will please, not only by illustrations of his discourse, and adorning it with new and apt metaphors; but also, by the rarity of their invention. But without steadiness, and direction to some end, a great fancy is one kind of madness; such as they have, that entering into any discourse, are snatched from their purpose, by every thing that comes in their thought, into so many, and so long digressions, and parentheses, that they utterly lose themselves: which kind of folly, I know no particular name for: but the cause of it is, sometimes want of experience; whereby that seemeth to a man new and rare, which doth not so to others: sometimes pusillanimity; by which that seems great to him, which other men think a trifle: and whatsoever is new, or great, and therefore thought fit to be told, withdraws a man by degrees from the intended way of his discourse.

In a good poem, whether it be *epic*, or *dramatic*; as also in *sonnets*, *epigrams*, and other pieces, both judgment and fancy are required: but the fancy must be more eminent; because they please for the extravagancy; but ought not to displease by indiscretion.

(Thomas Hobbes, *Leviathan* (1651), *English Works*, ed. W. Molesworth, 11 vols (London: Bohn, 1839–45), III. 4–6, 11–13, 14, 56–8.)

(B) JOSEPH ADDISON

The Spectator

[NO. 62. FRIDAY, MAY 11. 1711.]

Scribendi rectè sapere est et principium et fons. *Hor. Ars Poet.* ver. 309.

Sound judgment is the ground of writing well. *Roscommon.*

Mr. Locke has an admirable reflection upon the difference of wit and judgment, whereby he endeavours to show the reason why

they are not always the talents of the same person. His words
are as follow: 'And hence, perhaps, may be given some reason of
that common observation, "That men who have a great deal of
wit, and prompt memories, have not always the clearest
judgment, or deepest reason." For wit lying most in the
assemblage of ideas, and putting those together with quickness
and variety, wherein can be found any resemblance or congruity,
thereby to make up pleasant pictures, and agreeable visions in
the fancy; judgment, on the contrary, lies quite on the other
side, in separating carefully one from another, ideas wherein can
be found the least difference, thereby to avoid being misled by
similitude, and by affinity to take one thing for another. This is
a way of proceeding quite contrary to metaphor and allusion;
wherein, for the most part, lies that entertainment and
pleasantry of wit, which strikes so lively on the fancy, and is
therefore so acceptable to all people.'

This is, I think, the best and most philosophical account that
I have ever met with of wit, which generally, though not always,
consists in such a resemblance and congruity of ideas as this
author mentions. I shall only add to it, by way of explanation,
that every resemblance of ideas is not that which we call wit,
unless it be such an one that gives delight and surprise to the
reader. These two properties seem essential to wit, more
particularly the last of them. In order therefore that the
resemblance in the ideas be wit, it is necessary that the ideas
should not lie too near one another in the nature of things; for
where the likeness is obvious, it gives no surprise. To compare
one man's singing to that of another, or to represent the
whiteness of any object by that of milk and snow, or the variety
of its colours by those of the rainbow, cannot be called wit,
unless besides this obvious resemblance, there be some further
congruity discovered in the two ideas, that is capable of giving
the reader some surprise. Thus when a poet tells us the bosom
of his mistress is as white as snow, there is no wit in the
comparison; but when he adds with a sigh, it is as cold too, it
then grows into wit. Every reader's memory may supply him
with innumerable instances of the same nature. For this reason,
the similitudes in heroic poets, who endeavour rather to fill the
mind with great conceptions, than to divert it with such as are
new and surprising, have seldom any thing in them that can be
called wit. Mr. Locke's account of wit, with this short
explanation, comprehends most of the species of wit, as

metaphors, similitudes, allegories, enigmas, mottos, parables, fables, dreams, visions, dramatic writings, burlesque, and all the methods of allusion. There are many other pieces of wit (how remote soever they may appear at first sight from the foregoing description) which upon examination will be found to agree with it.

As true wit generally consists in this resemblance and congruity of ideas, false wit chiefly consists in the resemblance and congruity sometimes of single letters, as in anagrams, chronograms, lipograms, and acrostics: sometimes of syllables, as in echoes and doggerel rhymes: sometimes of words, as in puns and quibbles; and sometimes of whole sentences or poems, cast into the figures of eggs, axes, or altars: nay, some carry the notion of wit so far, as to ascribe it even to external mimickry; and to look upon a man as an ingenious person, that can resemble the tone, posture, or face of another.

As true wit consists in the resemblance of ideas, and false wit in the resemblance of words, according to the foregoing instances; there is another kind of wit which consists partly in the resemblance of ideas, and partly in the resemblance of words, which for distinction sake I shall call mixt wit. This kind of wit is that which abounds in Cowley, more than in any author that ever wrote. Mr. Waller has likewise a great deal of it. Mr. Dryden is very sparing in it. Milton had a genius much above it. Spenser is in the same class with Milton.

[NO. 413. TUESDAY, JUNE 24, 1712]

Things would make but a poor appearance to the eye, if we saw them only in their proper figures and motions: and what reason can we assign for their exciting in us many of those ideas which are different from any thing that exists in the objects themselves (for such are light and colours), were it not to add supernumerary ornaments to the universe, and make it more agreeable to the imagination? we are every where entertained with pleasing shows and apparitions; we discover imaginary glories in the heavens, and in the earth, and see some of this visionary beauty poured out upon the whole creation: but what a rough unsightly sketch of nature should we be entertained with, did all her colouring disappear, and the several distinctions of light and shade vanish? In short, our souls are at present delightfully lost and bewildered in a pleasing delusion, and we

walk about like the enchanted hero in a romance, who sees
beautiful castles, woods, and meadows; and, at the same time,
hears the warbling of birds, and the purling of streams; but,
upon the finishing of some secret spell, the fantastic scene breaks
up, and the disconsolate knight finds himself on a barren heath,
or in a solitary desert. It is not improbable that something like
this may be the state of the soul after its first separation, in
respect of the images it will receive from matter; though indeed
the ideas of colours are so pleasing and beautiful in the
imagination, that it is possible the soul will not be deprived of
them, but perhaps find them excited by some other occasional
cause, as they are at present by the different impressions of the
subtle matter on the organ of sight.

I have here supposed that my reader is acquainted with that
great modern discovery, which is at present universally
acknowledged by all the inquirers into natural philosophy:
namely, that light and colours, as apprehended by the
imagination, are only ideas in the mind, and not qualities that
have any existence in matter. As this is a truth which has been
proved incontestably by many modern philosophers, and is
indeed one of the finest speculations in that science, if the
English reader would see the notion explained at large, he may
find it in the eighth chapter of the second book of Mr. Locke's
Essay on Human Understanding.

[NO. 416. FRIDAY, JUNE 27, 1712]

Words, when well chosen, have so great a force in them, that a
description often gives us more lively ideas than the sight of
things themselves. The reader finds a scene drawn in stronger
colours, and painted more to the life in his imagination, by the
help of words, than by an actual survey of the scene which they
describe. In this case, the poet seems to get the better of nature:
he takes, indeed, the landscape after her, but gives it more
vigorous touches, heightens its beauty, and so enlivens the whole
piece, that the images which flow from the object themselves
appear weak and faint, in comparison of those that come from
the expressions. The reason, probably, may be, because, in the
survey of any object, we have only so much of it painted on the
imagination as comes in at the eye; but in its description, the
poet gives us as free a view of it as he pleases, and discovers to

us several parts, that either we did not attend to, or that lay out of our sight when we first beheld it. As we look on any object, our idea of it is, perhaps, made up of two or three simple ideas; but when the poet represents it, he may either give us a more complex idea of it, or only raise in us such ideas as are most apt to affect the imagination.

It may here be worth our while to examine how it comes to pass that several readers, who are all acquainted with the same language, and know the meaning of the words they read, should nevertheless have a different relish of the same descriptions. We find one transported with a passage, which another runs over with coldness and indifference; or finding the representation extremely natural, where another can perceive nothing of likeness and conformity. This different taste must proceed either from the perfection of imagination in one more than in another, or from the different ideas that several readers affix to the same words. For to have a true relish, and form a right judgment of a description, a man should be born with a good imagination, and must have well weighed the force and energy that lie in the several words of a language, so as to be able to distinguish which are most significant and expressive of their proper ideas, and what additional strength and beauty they are capable of receiving from conjunction with others. The fancy must be warm, to retain the print of those images it hath received from outward objects, and the judgment discerning, to know what expressions are most proper to clothe and adorn them to the best advantage. A man who is deficient in either of these respects, though he may receive the general notion of a description, can never see distinctly all its particular beauties; as a person with a weak sight may have the confused prospect of a place that lies before him without entering into its several parts, or discerning the variety of its colours in their full glory and perfection.

[NO. 417. SATURDAY, JUNE 28, 1712]

We may observe, that any single circumstance of what we have formerly seen often raises up a whole scene of imagery, and awakens numberless ideas that before slept in the imagination; such a particular smell or colour is able to fill the mind, on a sudden, with the picture of the fields or gardens where we first met with it, and to bring up into view all the variety of images

that once attended it. Our imagination takes the hint, and leads
us unexpectedly into cities or theatres, plains or meadows. We
may further observe, when the fancy thus reflects on the scenes
that have passed in it formerly, those which were at first
pleasant to behold appear more so upon reflection, and that
the memory heightens the delightfulness of the original. A
Cartesian would account for both these instances in the
following manner:

The set of ideas which we received from such a prospect or
garden, having entered the mind at the same time, have a set of
traces belonging to them in the brain, bordering very near upon
one another: when, therefore, any one of these ideas arises in the
imagination, and consequently despatches a flow of animal
spirits to its proper trace, these spirits, in the violence of their
motion, run not only into the trace to which they were more
particularly directed, but into several of those that lie about it.
By this means they awaken other ideas of the same set, which
immediately determine a new despatch of spirits, that in the
same manner open other neighbouring traces, till at last the
whole set of them is blown up, and the whole prospect or
garden flourishes in the imagination. But because the pleasure
we receive from these places far surmounted, and overcame the
little disagreeableness we found in them, for this reason there
was at first a wider passage worn in the pleasure traces, and, on
the contrary, so narrow a one in those which belonged to the
disagreeable ideas, that they were quickly stopt up, and rendered
incapable of receiving any animal spirits, and consequently of
exciting any unpleasant ideas in the memory.

It would be in vain to inquire whether the power of imagining
things strongly proceeds from any greater perfection in the soul,
or from any nicer texture in the brain of one man than another.
But this is certain, that a noble writer should be born with this
faculty in its full strength and vigour, so as to be able to receive
lively ideas from outward objects, to retain them long, and to
range them together, upon occasion, in such figures and
representations, as are most likely to hit the fancy of the reader.
A poet should take as much pains in forming his imagination, as
a philosopher in cultivating his understanding. He must gain a
due relish of the works of nature, and be thoroughly conversant
in the various scenery of a country life.

(Joseph Addison, *The Spectator*, nos 62 (11 May 1711), 413 (24 June
1712), 416 (27 June 1712), 417 (28 June 1712) one-volume edn
(London: Jones & Co., 1823), pp. 89–90, 596–7, 602–3.)

(C) ALEXANDER POPE

An Essay on Criticism (1711)

Some to conceit alone their taste confine,
And glittering thoughts struck out at every line; 290
Pleas'd with a work where nothing's just or fit,
One glaring chaos and wild heap of wit:
Poets, like painters, thus unskill'd to trace
The naked nature and the living grace,
With gold and jewels cover every part, 295
And hide with ornaments their want of art.
True wit is nature to advantage dress'd,
What oft was thought, but ne'er so well express'd;
Something whose truth convinc'd at sight we find, ·
That gives us back the image of our mind. 300
As shades more sweetly recommend the light,
So modest plainness sets off sprightly wit;
For works may have more wit than does them good,
As bodies perish through excess of blood.

   Others for language all their care express, 305
And value books, as women men, for dress:
Their Praise is still – The Stile is excellent:
The sense they humbly take upon content.
Words are like leaves; and where they most abound,
Much fruit of sense beneath is rarely found. 310
False eloquence, like the prismatic glass,
Its gawdy colours spreads on every place;
The face of nature we no more survey,
All glares alike, without distinction gay;
But true expression, like th' unchanging sun, ⎫ 315
Clears and improves whate'er it shines upon; ⎬
It gilds all objects, but it alters none. ⎭

(Alexander Pope, *An Essay on Criticism* (1711), Aldine edn of Pope, 3 vols
(London: Bell, 1878), II. 14–15.)

(D) ALEXANDER GERARD

An Essay on Genius (1774)

[PART I, SECTION III]

When memory presents ideas, it annexes to them a conviction
that the ideas themselves, or the objects from which they are

copied, were formerly perceived; and it exhibits the ideas in the same form and order in which the things themselves appeared. In time remembrance fails, ideas are perceived without being referred to any prior sensations of their originals, the order of the parts is forgotten. But even then, ideas do not lie in the mind without any connection or dependence. Imagination can connect them by new relations. It knits them together by other ties than what connected the real things from which they are derived, and often bestows a union upon ideas whose archetypes had no relation. In this operation it is far from being capricious or irregular, but for the most part observes general and established rules. There are certain qualities which either really belong, or at least are supposed to belong, to all the ideas that are associated by the imagination. These qualities must be considered as, by the constitution of our nature, rendering ideas fit to be associated. It is impossible to give a reason why these qualities unite ideas; it is not necessary at present to explain particularly what they are. Experience informs us that the influence of association is very great. By means of it multitudes of ideas originally distinct and unconnected rise always in company, so that one of them cannot make its appearance without introducing all the rest. On this account, human thought is perfectly restless. It requires no labor to run from one idea to others. We have so great a propensity to do it that no resolution has force enough to restrain us from it, nor will the strongest efforts be able to confine us long to the contemplation of a single idea. We are incessantly looking round to every side without intending it; we employ ourselves about many objects, almost at the same instant. Nay, association is often so strong that it bestows a sort of cohesion on several separate ideas, and makes them start up in numberless combinations, many of them different from every form which the senses have perceived, and thus produces a new creation. In this operation of the imagination, its associating power, we shall, on a careful examination, discover the origin of genius.

Association being an operation of fancy common to all men, some of its effects are universal. In every individual it displays itself in many instances. Not to mention such cases as are totally unconnected with our present subject, scarce any person is so stupid as not to have sometime in his life produced a bright flash of imagination, though surrounded, it may be, with a wide extent of darkness. But such transient blazes do not necessarily imply real genius. It is something more permanent and uniform.

It requires a peculiar vigor of association. In order to produce it, the imagination must be comprehensive, regular, and active.

Genius implies such *comprehensiveness* of imagination as enables a man on every occasion to call in the conceptions that are necessary for executing the designs or completing the works in which he engages. This takes place when the associating principles are strong and fit for acting in an extensive sphere. If they be weak, they will call in memory to their aid. Unable to guide our steps in an unknown country, they keep in the roads to which we have been accustomed, and are directed in suggesting ideas by the connections which we remember. Every production of a man who labors under this debility of mind bears evident marks of barrenness, a quality more opposite to true genius than any other. [. . .] But when the associating principles are vigorous, imagination, conscious as it were of its own strength, sallies forth, without needing support or asking assistance, into regions hitherto unexplored, and penetrates into their remotest corners, unfatigued with the length of the way. In a man of genius, the power of association is so great that when any idea is present to his mind, it immediately leads him to the conception of those that are connected with it. No sooner almost is a design formed, or the hint of a subject started, than all the ideas which are requisite for completing it rush into his view as if they were conjured up by the force of magic. His daring imagination traverses all nature and collects materials fit for his purpose from all the most distant corners of the universe and presents them at the very instant when they become useful or necessary. In consequence of this, he takes in a comprehensive view of every subject to which his genius is adapted.

Thus, when the associating principles are strong and have an extensive influence, they naturally form, in proportion to the degree of their strength, that boundless fertility, that inexhaustible copiousness of invention, which is not only one necessary ingredient in true genius but the first and most essential constituent of it. The smallest production will in some measure discover in what extent this power is possessed. A work of real genius always proclaims in the clearest manner that immense quantities of materials have been collected by fancy and subjected to the author's choice. There is no particular, perhaps, in the works of Homer that has been more universally remarked and admired than the prodigious compass of imagination which they show. His penetration has gained him access to all the magazines of ideas and enabled him to draw materials from every part of nature and from the whole circle of human arts. Knowledge of them was prerequisite, but could have been of no service after it was obtained, without the liveliest fancy, suggesting them readily and applying them on suitable occasions.

(Alexander Gerard, *An Essay on Genius* (London and Edinburgh, 1774), pp. 39–42, 43–4.)

(E) SAMUEL TAYLOR COLERIDGE

Biographia Literaria (1817)

[CHAPTER 4]

It was not however the freedom from false taste, whether as to common defects, or to those more properly his [Wordsworth's] own, which made so unusual an impression on my feelings immediately, and subsequently on my judgement. It was the union of deep feeling with profound thought; the fine balance of truth in observing, with the imaginative faculty in modifying the objects observed; and above all the original gift of spreading the tone, the *atmosphere*, and with it the depth and height of the ideal world around forms, incidents, and situations, of which, for the common view, custom had bedimmed all the lustre, had dried up the sparkle and the dewdrops. 'To find no contradiction in the union of old and new; to contemplate the Ancient of Days and all his works with feelings as fresh, as if all had then sprang forth at the first creative fiat, characterizes the mind that feels the riddle of the world, and may help to unravel it. To carry on the feelings of childhood into the powers of manhood; to combine the child's sense of wonder and novelty with the appearances, which every day for perhaps forty years had rendered familiar:

> With sun and moon and stars throughout the year
> And man and woman;

this is the character and privilege of genius, and one of the marks which distinguish genius from talents. And therefore it is the prime merit of genius and its most unequivocal mode of manifestation, so to represent familiar objects as to awaken in the minds of others a kindred feeling concerning them and that freshness of sensation which is the constant accompaniment of mental, no less than of bodily, convalescence. Who has not a thousand times seen snow fall on water? Who has not watched it with a new feeling, from the time that he has read Burns' comparison of sensual pleasure:

> To snow that falls upon a river
> A moment white – then gone for ever!

In poems, equally as in philosophic disquisitions, genius produces the strongest impressions of novelty, while it rescues the most admitted truths from the impotence caused by the very circumstance of their universal admission. Truths of all others the most awful and mysterious, yet being at the same time of universal interest, are too often considered as *so* true, that they lose all the life and efficiency of truth, and lie bed-ridden in the dormitory of the soul, side by side with the most despised and exploded errors.' *The Friend*, p. 76, No. 5.

This excellence, which in all Mr Wordsworth's writings is more or less predominant, and which constitutes the character of his mind, I no sooner felt, than I sought to understand. Repeated meditations led me first to suspect (and a more intimate analysis of the human faculties, their appropriate marks, functions and effects, matured my conjecture into full conviction), that fancy and imagination were two distinct and widely different faculties, instead of being, according to the general belief, either two names with one meaning, or, at furthest, the lower and higher degree of one and the same power. It is not, I own, easy to conceive a more apposite translation of the Greek *Phantasia* than the Latin *Imaginatio*; but it is equally true that in all societies there exists an instinct of growth, a certain collective, unconscious good sense working progressively to desynonymize those words originally of the same meaning, which the conflux of dialects had supplied to the more homogeneous languages, as the Greek and German, and which the same cause, joined with accidents of translation from original works of different countries, occasion in mixt languages like our own. The first and most important point to be proved is that two conceptions perfectly distinct are confused under one and the same word, and (this done) to appropriate that word exclusively to one meaning, and the synonyme (should there be one) to the other. But if (as will be often the case in the arts and sciences) no synonyme exists, we must either invent or borrow a word. In the present instance the appropriation had already begun and been legitimated in the derivative adjective:

Milton had a highly *imaginative*, Cowley a very *fanciful*, mind. If therefore I should succeed in establishing the actual existence of two faculties generally different, the nomenclature would be at once determined. To the faculty by which I had characterized Milton we should confine the term *imagination*; while the other would be contra-distinguished as *fancy*. Now were it once fully ascertained that this division is no less grounded in nature than that of delirium from mania, or Otway's

> Lutes, laurels, seas of milk and ships of amber,

from Shakespeare's

> What! have his daughters brought him to this pass?

or from the preceding apostrophe to the elements, the theory of the fine arts and of poetry in particular could not, I thought, but derive some additional and important light [. . .] it was Mr Wordsworth's purpose to consider the influences of fancy and imagination as they are manifested in poetry, and from the different effects to conclude their diversity in kind; while it is my object to investigate the seminal principle, and then from the kind to deduce the degree. My friend has drawn a masterly sketch of the branches with their *poetic* fruitage. I wish to add the trunk, and even the roots, as far as they lift themselves above ground, and are visible to the naked eye of our common consciousness. [. . .]

[CHAPTER 6]

Conceive, [. . .] a broad stream, winding through a mountainous country with an indefinite number of currents, varying and running into each other according as the gusts chance to blow from the opening of the mountains. The temporary union of several currents in one, so as to form the main current of the moment, would present an accurate image of Hartley's theory of the will.

Had this been really the case, the consequence would have been that our whole life would be divided between the despotism of outward impressions, and that of senseless and passive memory. Take his law in its highest abstraction and most philosophical form, viz. that every partial representation recalls the total representation of which it was a part; and the law becomes nugatory, were it only from its universality. In practice it would indeed be mere lawlessness. Consider how immense must be the sphere of a total impression from the top of St Paul's church; and how rapid and continuous the series of such total impressions. If therefore we suppose the absence of all interference of the will, reason and judgement, one or other of two consequences must result. Either the ideas (or relicts of such impression) will exactly imitate the order of the impression itself, which would be absolute *delirium*: or any one part of that impression might recall any other part, and (as from the law of continuity, there must exist in every total impression some one or more parts which are components of some other following total impression, and so on *ad infinitum*) *any* part of *any* impression might recall *any* part of any *other*, without a cause present to determine *what* it should be. For to bring in the will, or reason, as causes of their own cause, that is, as at once causes and effects, can satisfy those only who, in their pretended evidences of a God, having first demanded organization as the sole cause and ground of intellect, will then coolly demand the pre-existence of intellect as the cause and ground-work of organization. There is in truth but one state to which this theory applies at all, namely that of complete light-headedness; and even to this it applies but partially, because the will and reason are perhaps never wholly suspended. [. . .]

[CHAPTER 13]

The IMAGINATION then I consider either as primary, or secondary. The primary Imagination I hold to be the living power and prime Agent of all human Perception, and as a repetition in the finite mind of the eternal act of creation in the infinite I AM. The secondary Imagination I consider as an echo of the former, co-existing with the conscious will, yet still as identical with the primary in the *kind* of its agency, and differing only in *degree*, and in the *mode* of its operation. It dissolves, diffuses, dissipates, in order to re-create; or where this process is rendered impossible, yet still, at all events, it struggles to idealize and to unify. It is essentially *vital*, even as all objects (*as* objects) are essentially fixed and dead.

Fancy, on the contrary, has no other counters to play with but fixities and definites. The Fancy is indeed no other than a mode of Memory emancipated from the order of time and space; while it is blended with, and modified by that empirical phaenomenon of the will which we express by the word CHOICE. But equally

with the ordinary memory the Fancy must receive all its
materials ready made from the law of association.

(Samuel Taylor Coleridge, *Biographia Literaria* (1817), ed. J. Shawcross,
2 vols (London: Oxford UP, 1907), I. 59–62, 64, 76–7, 202.)

(F) T. E. HULME

Speculations (1924)

I have still to show that in the verse which is to come, fancy
will be the necessary weapon of the classical school. The positive
quality I have talked about can be manifested in ballad verse by
extreme directness and simplicity, such as you get in 'On Fair
Kirkconnel Lea.' But the particular verse we are going to get
will be cheerful, dry and sophisticated, and here the necessary
weapon of the positive quality must be fancy.

Subject doesn't matter; the quality in it is the same as you get
in the more romantic people.

It isn't the scale or kind of emotion produced that decides,
but this one fact: Is there any real zest in it? Did the poet have
an actually realised visual object before him in which he
delighted? It doesn't matter if it were a lady's shoe or the starry
heavens.

Fancy is not mere decoration added on to plain speech. Plain
speech is essentially inaccurate. It is only by new metaphors,
that is, by fancy, that it can be made precise.

When the analogy has not enough connection with the thing
described to be quite parallel with it, where it overlays the thing
it described and there is a certain excess, there you have the
play of fancy – that I grant is inferior to imagination.

But where the analogy is every bit of it necessary for accurate
description in the sense of the word accurate I have previously
described and your only objection to this kind of fancy is that it
is not serious in the effect it produces, then I think the objection
to be entirely invalid.

(T. E. Hulme, *Speculations* (London: Routledge & Kegan Paul, 1924),
pp. 137–8.)

(G) I. A. RICHARDS

Science and Poetry (1926)

Why does the poet use these words and no others? Not because
they stand for a series of thoughts which in themselves are what

he is concerned to communicate. It is never what a poem *says* which matters, but what it *is*. The poet is not writing as a scientist. He uses these words because the interests whose movement is the growth of the poem combine to bring them, just in this form, into his consciousness *as a means of ordering, controlling and consolidating* the uttered experience of which they are themselves a main part. The experience itself, the tide of impulses sweeping through the mind, is the source and the sanction of the words. They represent this experience itself, not any set of perceptions or reflections, though often to a reader who approaches the poem wrongly they will seem to be only a series of remarks about other things. But to a suitable reader the words – if they actually spring from experience and are not due to verbal habits, to the desire to be effective, to factitious excogitation, to imitation, to irrelevant contrivances, or to any other of the failings which prevent most people from writing poetry – the words will reproduce in his mind a similar play of interests putting him for the while into a similar situation and leading to the same response.

(I. A. Richards, *Science and Poetry* (London: Kegan Paul, Trench, Trubner, 1926), pp. 13, 14, 58–61.)

Principles of Literary Criticism (1924)

[CHAPTER 32]

In describing the poet we laid stress upon the availability of his experience, upon the width of the field of stimulation which he can accept, and the completeness of the response which he can make. Compared with him the ordinary man suppresses nine-tenths of his impulses, because he is incapable of managing them without confusion. He goes about in blinkers because what he would otherwise see would upset him. But the poet through his superior power of ordering experience is freed from this necessity. Impulses which commonly interfere with one another and are conflicting, independent, and mutually distractive, in him combine into a stable poise. He selects, of course, but the range of suppression which is necessary for him is diminished, and for this very reason such suppressions as he makes are more rigorously carried out. Hence the curious local callousness of the artist which so often strikes the observer.

But these impulses active in the artist become mutually modified and thereby ordered to an extent which only occurs in the ordinary man at rare moments, under the shock of, for

example, a great bereavement or an undreamt-of happiness; at
instants when the 'film of familiarity and selfish solicitude',
which commonly hides nine-tenths of life from him, seems to be
lifted and he feels strangely alive and aware of the actuality of
existence. In these moments his myriad inhibitions are weakened;
his responses, canalized – to use an inappropriate metaphor – by
routine and by practical but restricted convenience, break
loose and make up a new order with one another; he feels as
though everything were beginning anew. But for most men after
their early years such experiences are infrequent; a time comes
when they are incapable of them unaided, and they receive
them only through the arts. For great art has this effect,
and owes thereto its supreme place in human life.

The poet makes unconsciously a selection which outwits the
force of habit; the impulses he awakens are freed, through the
very means by which they are aroused, from the inhibitions that
ordinary circumstances encourage; the irrelevant and the
extraneous is excluded; and upon the resulting simplified but
widened field of impulses he imposes an order which their
greater plasticity allows them to accept. Almost always too the
chief part of his work is done through those impulses which we
have seen to be most uniform and regular, those which are
aroused by what are called the 'formal elements'. They are also
the most primitive, and for that reason commonly among those
which are most inhibited, most curtailed and subordinated to
super-imposed purposes. We rarely let a colour affect us purely
as a colour, we use it as a sign by which we recognize some
coloured object. Thus our responses to colours in themselves
become so abbreviated that many people come to think that the
pigments painters use are in some way more colourful than
Nature. What happens is that inhibitions are released, and at
the same time mutual interactions between impulses take place
which only sunsets seem to evoke in everyday experience. We
have seen in discussing communication one reason for the pre-
eminence of 'formal elements' in art, the uniformity of the
responses which they can be depended upon to produce. In their
primitiveness we find another. The sense that the accidental and
adventitious aspect of life has receded, that we are beginning
again, that our contact with actuality is increased, is largely due
to this restoration of their full natural powers to sensations.

But this restoration is not enough; merely looking at a
landscape in a mirror, or standing on one's head will do it.
What is much more essential is the increased organization, the
heightened power of combining all the several effects of formal

elements into a single response, which the poet bestows. To point out that 'the sense of musical delight is a gift of the imagination' was one of Coleridge's most brilliant feats. It is in such resolution of a welter of disconnected impulses into a single ordered response that in all the arts imagination is most shown, but for the reason that here its operation is most intricate and most inaccessible to observation, we shall study it more profitably in its other manifestations.

We have suggested, but only by accident, that imagination characteristically produces effects similar to those which accompany great and sudden crises in experience. This would be misleading. What is true is that those imaginative syntheses which most nearly approach to these climaxes, Tragedy for example, are the most easy to analyse. What clearer instance of the 'balance or reconciliation of opposite and discordant qualities' can be found than Tragedy. Pity, the impulse to approach, and Terror, the impulse to retreat, are brought in Tragedy to a reconciliation which they find nowhere else, and with them who knows what other allied groups of equally discordant impulses. Their union in an ordered single response is the *catharsis* by which Tragedy is recognized, whether Aristotle meant anything of this kind or not. This is the explanation of that sense of release, of repose in the midst of stress, of balance and composure, given by Tragedy, for there is no other way in which such impulses, once awakened, can be set at rest without suppression.

It is essential to recognize that in the full tragic experience there is no suppression. The mind does not shy away from anything, it does not protect itself with any illusion, it stands uncomforted, unintimidated, alone and self-reliant. The test of its success is whether it can face what is before it and respond to it without any of the innumerable subterfuges by which it ordinarily dodges the full development of experience. Suppressions and sublimations alike are devices by which we endeavour to avoid issues which might bewilder us. The essence of Tragedy is that it forces us to live for a moment without them. When we succeed we find, as usual, that there is no difficulty; the difficulty came from the suppressions and sublimations. The joy which is so strangely the heart of the experience is not an indication that 'all's right with the world' or that 'somewhere, somehow, there is Justice'; it is an indication that all is right here and now in the nervous system.

(I. A. Richards, *Principles of Literary Criticism* (2nd edn, London: Routledge & Kegan Paul, 1926; reset, 1967), pp. 101, 211–12.)

CHAPTER 2

GENIUS: NATURE VS ART

It is easy to assume that the classical critics were concerned about only technical knowledge in art and literature. However, not only did Plato, in the *Ion*, describe the poet's possession by 'divine frenzy', but the author known as 'Longinus' wrote a treatise 'On Sublimity' and introduced ideas of natural ability in writers which go beyond mere technical skill. 'Longinus' probably lived in the first century AD and was in touch with Roman and Jewish traditions of thought. The quality he describes as 'sublimity' (*hypsos*) is based on writers' mental characteristics – their 'greatness of soul' (*megalopsychia*). Such naturally gifted writers have the power of conceiving impressive thoughts, and of making a strong emotional impact on the reader. 'Sublimity' is also characterized by its irresistible effect on readers.

The Romantics transmitted to modern thought the notion of 'originality', which for many decades of this century was tacitly accepted as a self-evident value in all the arts. However, it was always evident that no discourse could be self-originating, and that all discourse is social rather than individual. We all draw upon what Ferdinand de Saussure called 'langue' – the system which makes all utterance possible. Nevertheless, it is also obvious that new styles and genres sometimes arise and that individuals contribute to this 'origination'. The Romantics played up the uniqueness and individuality of genius and played down the collective nature of all art and literature. The theories of structuralism, Marxism and post-structuralism reject this order of priority by focusing upon the structures and processes which define and produce the very possibilities of individuality and subjectivity.

'Longinus' anticipates many themes and assumptions developed in the eighteenth and nineteenth centuries. He distinguishes between mere 'rhetoric' (the command of verbal techniques) and 'genuine' poetic power. Genius is not restrained by rules and conventions, and can attain to what Alexander Pope called 'a grace beyond the reach of art'. Longinus believed that the skills of art can offer no more than a supporting role in the fostering of natural talent. Pope actually modifies this emphasis somewhat, largely because he took his version of Longinus from the great French neoclassical poet Boileau, who believed that the rules of art should not be ignored without strong reasons (see II,2,C). True genius can express sublime ideas which are associated with large scenes and aspects of nature, not small and intimate realities. Longinus preserves a certain rhetorical attitude towards the idea of sublimity which was significantly changed in the writings of Boileau and Pope. He associated grand ideas with grand words, and recommended certain literary devices to achieve this effect of sublimity. One exceptional passage in which he discusses the sublimity of *Genesis* was to be taken up by Boileau. 'Let there be light' is an example of great thoughts, capable of striking the reader with wonder, but which does not involve grand words. Here we have an example of simple grandeur.

Like Plato, Longinus talks of the poet's divine frenzy, the inspired poetic trance. While this may appear to undermine the idea of originality, his emphasis on the mysterious nature of inspiration preserves the sense of the sublime poet's special gifts. This belief in the poet's divine inspiration was easily assimilated into a Christian form in the Renaissance. However, such claims, except in the case of the loftiest writings, were considered absurd by the rationally inclined poets of the later seventeenth century. The notions of inspiration and 'enthusiasm' were discarded because of their associations with the 'crazy' Puritanism of the Civil Wars, until new ways were found to restore their dignity.

What some call the 'pre-Romantic' phase of critical theory began very early in the eighteenth century. Samuel Cobb, for example, argued in 'Discourse on Criticism' (1707) for the importance of original genius over classical training and imitation. Edward Young's *Conjectures on Original Composition* (1759) is the most celebrated version of this influential argument. His fascinating text weaves a series of contrasts between originality and imitation, using metaphors and analogies each of which carries a slightly different weight and emphasis. At one point he considers that an imitation of a classical original is a mere duplication. Later, he switches to a different image: the imitation is a transplantation of the original to a foreign soil. The original is a new plant, which grows naturally. A further switch denies the imitation its plantlike status: only the original is organic; the imitation is mechanical, since it is derived from 'pre-existent materials' mechanically 'wrought up' by art and labour. This anticipates Coleridge's linking of imagination with organic creation, and fancy with mechanical reworking of existing objects. Young does not manage to preserve a clear demarcation between original and imitative forms of writing and is forced to make awkward qualifications. Imitation of the classical is acceptable if it is imitation of the spirit and taste of the originals, or if it is done in the spirit of 'emulation'. Like Pope he accepts that the classics established a mastery hardly to be excelled; we cannot expect to do more than to compete as equals.

William Hazlitt wrote on genius in the high period of Romanticism. He follows Coleridge in treating imaginative genius as belonging to *a different order* from ordinary 'capacity'. He preserves the idea that one cannot define or intellectually grasp the nature of the productions of genius. However, he introduces an emphasis on the profundity of genius which is not found in the eighteenth century. 'Originality' actually achieves 'new and valuable knowledge'. He follows Wordsworth in believing that insights of imagination are achieved by receptivity or what Wordsworth called a 'wise passiveness'. A further modern note is struck in Hazlitt's account of the distinctive and individual quality of original achievements.

Background reading

W. P. Albrecht, *Hazlitt and the Creative Imagination* (Lawrence: University of Kansas Press, 1965).

David Bromwich, *Hazlitt: The Mind of a Critic* (New York and Oxford: Oxford UP, 1983).

T. R. Henn, *Longinus and English Criticism* (Cambridge: Cambridge UP, 1934).

W. J. Hipple Jr, *The Beautiful, the Sublime and the Picturesque in Eighteenth-Century British Aesthetic Theory* (Carbondale: Southern Illinois UP, 1957).

John Kinnaird, *William Hazlitt: Critic of Power* (New York: Columbia UP, 1978).

S. Monk, *The Sublime: A Study of Critical Theories in XVIII-Century England* (1935; Ann Arbor: University of Michigan Press, 1960).

M. Nicolson, *Mountain Gloom and Mountain Glory: The Development of the Aesthetics of the Infinite* (Ithaca: Cornell UP, 1959).

D. A. Russell (ed.), *'Longinus' On the Sublime* (Oxford: Clarendon Press, 1964), introduction.

W. K. Wimsatt and Cleanth Brooks, *Literary Criticism: A Short History* (New York: Alfred A. Knopf, 1957), ch. 6 (Longinus).

(A) 'LONGINUS'

On the Sublime (3rd C. AD)

[CHAPTER 7]

The true sublime, by some virtue of its nature, elevates us: uplifted with a sense of proud possession, we are filled with joyful pride, as if we had ourselves produced the very thing we heard. If, then, a man of sense, well-versed in literature, after hearing a passage several times finds that it does not affect him with a sense of sublimity, and does not leave behind in his mind more food for thought than the mere words at first suggest, but rather that on careful consideration it sinks in his esteem, then it cannot really be the true sublime, if its effect does not outlast the moment of utterance. For what is truly great gives abundant food for thought: it is irksome, nay, impossible, to resist its effect: the memory of it is stubborn and indelible. To speak generally, you should consider that to be truly beautiful and sublime which pleases all people at all times. For when men who differ in their habits, their lives, their tastes, their ages, their dates, all agree together in holding one and the same view about the same writings, then the unanimous verdict, as it were, of such discordant judges makes our faith in the admired passage strong and indisputable.

[CHAPTER 35]

What then was in the mind of those demigods who aimed only at what is greatest in writing and scorned detailed accuracy? Among many other things this, that Nature has distinguished man, as a creature of no mean or ignoble quality. As if she were inviting us rather to some great gathering, she has called us into life, into the whole universe, there to be spectators of all that she has made and eager competitors for honour; and she therefore from the first breathed into our hearts an unconquerable passion for whatever is great and more divine than ourselves. Thus within the scope of human enterprise there lie such powers of contemplation and thought that even the whole universe cannot satisfy them, but our ideas often pass beyond the limits that enring us. Look at life from all sides and see how in all things the extraordinary, the great, the beautiful stand supreme, and you will soon realize the object of our creation. So it is by some natural instinct that we admire, surely not the small streams, clear and useful as they are, but the Nile, the Danube, the Rhine, and far above all, the sea. The little fire we kindle for ourselves keeps clear and steady, yet we do not therefore regard it with more amazement than the fires of Heaven, which are often darkened, or think it more wonderful than the craters of Etna in eruption, hurling up rocks and whole hills from their depths and sometimes shooting forth rivers of that pure Titanic fire. But on all such matters I would only say this, that what is useful and indeed necessary is cheap enough; it is always the unusual which wins our wonder.

[CHAPTER 36]

In dealing, then, with writers of genius, whose grandeur is of a kind that comes within the limits of use and profit, we must at the outset form the conclusion that, while they are far from unerring, yet they are all more than human. Other qualities prove their possessors men, sublimity lifts them near the mighty mind of God. Correctness escapes censure: greatness earns admiration as well. We need hardly add that each of these great men again and again redeems all his mistakes by a single touch of sublimity and true excellence; and, what is finally decisive, if we were to pick out all the faults in Homer, Demosthenes, Plato and all the other greatest authors and put them together, we should find them a tiny fraction, not the ten-thousandth part, of the true excellence to be found on every page of these demi-gods.

(*Longinus On the Sublime* (Greek title: *Peri Hupsous,*) trans. A. O. Prickard (Oxford: Clarendon Press, 1906), pp. 11–12, 65–7.)

(B) JOSEPH ADDISON

The Spectator

[NO. 160. MONDAY, SEPTEMBER 3, 1711]

——Cui mens divinior, atque os
Magna sonaturum, des nominis hujus honorem.
                                        Hor. Lib. 1. Sat. iv. 43.

On him confer the Poet's sacred name,
Whose lofty voice declares the heav'nly flame.

There is no character more frequently given to a writer, than that of being a genius. I have heard many a little sonneteer called a fine genius. There is not an heroic scribbler in the nation, that has not his admirers who think him a great genius; and as for your smatterers in tragedy, there is scarce a man among them who is not cried up by one or other for a prodigious genius.

My design in this paper is to consider what is properly a great genius, and to throw some thoughts together on so uncommon a subject.

Among great geniuses those few draw the admiration of all the world upon them, and stand up as the prodigies of mankind, who by the mere strength of natural parts, and without any assistance of art or learning, have produced works that were the delight of their own times, and the wonder of posterity. There appears something nobly wild and extravagant in these great natural geniuses that is infinitely more beautiful than all the turn and polishing of what the French call a *bel esprit*, by which they would express a genius refined by conversation, reflection, and the reading of the most polite authors. The greatest genius which runs through the arts and sciences, takes a kind of tincture from them, and falls unavoidably into imitation.

Many of these great natural geniuses that were never disciplined and broken by rules of art, are to be found among the ancients, and in particular among those of the more eastern parts of the world. Homer has innumerable flights that Virgil was not able to reach, and in the Old Testament we find several passages more elevated and sublime than any in Homer. At the same time that we allow a greater and more daring genius to the ancients, we must own that the greatest of them very much failed in, or, if you will, that they were much above the nicety and correctness of the moderns. In their similitudes and allusions, provided there was a likeness, they did not much trouble themselves about the decency of the comparison: thus Solomon resembles the nose of his beloved to the tower of Lebanon which looketh towards Damascus; as the coming of a thief in the night, is a similitude of the same kind in the New Testament. It would be endless to make collections of this nature; Homer illustrates one of his heroes encompassed with the enemy, by an ass in a fiel of corn that has his sides belaboured by all the boys of the village without stirring a foot for it; and another of them tossing to and fro in his bed and burning with resentment, to a piece of flesh broiled on the coals. This particular failure in the ancients, opens a large field of raillery to the little wits, who can laugh at an indecency, but not relish the sublime in these sorts of writings. [. . .]

[W]e are to consider that the rule of observing what the French call the *bienseance* in an allusion, has been found out of later years, and in the colder regions of the world; where we would make some amends for our want of force and spirit, by a scrupulous nicety and exactness in our compositions. Our countryman Shakspeare was a remarkable instance of this first kind of great geniuses.

I cannot quit this head without observing that Pindar was a great genius of the first class, who was hurried on by a natural fire and impetuosity to vast conceptions of things and noble sallies of imagination. At the same time, can any thing be more ridiculous than for men of a sober and moderate fancy to imitate this poet's way of writing in those monstrous compositions which go among us under the name of Pindarics? When I see people copying works, which, as Horace has represented them, are singular in their kind, and inimitable; when I see men following irregularities by rule, and by the little tricks of art straining after the most unbounded flights of nature, I cannot but apply to them that passage in Terence:

——Incerta hæc si tu postules
Ratione certâ facere, nihilo plus agas,
Quàm si des operam, ut cum ratione insanias.

Eun. Act. 1. Sc. 1.

You may as well pretend to be mad and in your senses at the same time, as to think of reducing these uncertain things to any certainty by reason.

In short, a modern Pindaric writer compared with Pindar, is like a sister among the Camisars [Calvinist insurgents] compared with Virgil's Sibyl: there is the distortion, grimace, and outward figure, but nothing of that divine impulse which raises the mind above itself, and makes the sounds more than human.

There is another kind of great geniuses which I shall place in a second class, not as I think them inferior to the first, but only for distinction's sake, as they are of a different kind. This second class of great geniuses are those that have formed themselves by rules, and submitted the greatness of their natural talents to the corrections and restraints of art. Such among the Greeks were Plato and Aristotle; among the Romans Virgil and Tully; among the English, Milton and Sir Francis Bacon.

The genius in both these classes of authors may be equally great, but shows itself after a different manner. In the first it is like a rich soil in a happy climate, that produces a whole wilderness of noble plants rising in a thousand beautiful landscapes, without any certain order or regularity. In the other it is the same rich soil under the same happy climate, that has been laid out in walks and parterres, and cut into shape and beauty by the skill of the gardener.

The great danger in these latter kind of geniuses, is lest they cramp their own abilities too much by imitation, and form themselves altogether upon models, without giving the full play to their own natural parts. An imitation of the best authors is not to compare with a good original; and I believe we may observe that very few writers make an extraordinary figure in the world, who have not something in their way of thinking or expressing themselves, that is peculiar to them, and entirely their own.

(Joseph Addison, *The Spectator*, no. 160 (3 September 1711), one volume edn (London: Jones & Co., 1823), pp. 228–9.)

(C) ALEXANDER POPE

An Essay on Criticism (1711)

Some beauties yet, no precepts can declare,
For there's a happiness as well as care.
Musick resembles poetry, in each

Are nameless graces which no methods teach,
And which a master-hand alone can reach.   145
If, where the rules not far enough extend,
(Since rules were made but to promote their end)
Some lucky licence answers to the full
Th' intent propos'd, that licence is a rule.
Thus Pegasus, a nearer way to take,   150
May boldly deviate from the common track.
Great wits sometimes may gloriously offend,
And rise to faults true criticks dare not mend;
From vulgar bounds with brave disorder part,
And snatch a grace beyond the reach of art,   155
Which, without passing thro' the judgment, gains
The heart, and all its end at once attains.
In prospects, thus, some objects please our eyes, ⎫
Which out of nature's common order rise,   ⎬
The shapeless rock, or hanging precipice.   ⎭   160
But tho' the ancients thus their rules invade,
(As kings dispense with laws themselves have made)
Moderns, beware! Or if you must offend
Against the precept, ne'er transgress its end,
Let it be seldom, and compell'd by need,   165
And have, at least, their precedent to plead.
The critick else proceeds without remorse,
Seizes your fame, and puts his laws in force.

(Alexander Pope, *An Essay on Criticism* (1711), Aldine edn of Pope, 3 vols
(London: Bell, 1878), II, 15–16.)

(D) EDWARD YOUNG

Conjectures on Original Composition (1759)

But there are, who write with vigor, and success, to the world's
Delight, and their own Renown. These are the glorious fruits
where Genius prevails. The mind of a man of Genius is a fertile
and pleasant field, pleasant as *Elysium*, and fertile as *Tempe*; it
enjoys a perpetual Spring. Of that Spring, *Originals* are the
fairest Flowers: *Imitations* are of quicker growth, but fainter
bloom. *Imitations* are of two kinds; one of Nature, one of Authors:
The first we call *Originals*, and confine the term *Imitation* to the
second. I shall not enter into the curious enquiry of what is, or

is not, strictly speaking, *Original*, content with what all must allow, that some Compositions are more so than others; and the more they are so, I say, the better. *Originals* are, and ought to be, great Favourites, for they are great Benefactors; they extend the Republic of Letters, and add a new province to its dominion: *Imitators* only give us a sort of Duplicates of what we had, possibly much better, before; increasing the mere Drug of books, while all that makes them valuable, *Knowlege* and *Genius*, are at a stand. The pen of an *Original* Writer, like *Armida's* wand, out of a barren waste calls a blooming spring: Out of that blooming spring an *Imitator* is a transplanter of Laurels, which sometimes die on removal, always languish in a foreign soil.

But suppose an *Imitator* to be most excellent (and such there are), yet still he but nobly builds on another's foundation; his Debt is, at least, equal to his Glory; which therefore, on the ballance, cannot be very great. On the contrary, an *Original*, tho' but indifferent (its *Originality* being set aside,) yet has something to boast. [. . .]

Still farther: An *Imitator* shares his crown, if he has one, with the chosen Object of his Imitation; an *Original* enjoys an undivided applause. An *Original* may be said to be of a *vegetable* nature; it rises spontaneously from the vital root of Genius; it *grows*, it is not *made*: *Imitations* are often a sort of *Manufacture* wrought up by those *Mechanics*, *Art*, and *Labour*, out of pre-existent materials not their own.

Must we then, you say, not imitate antient Authors? Imitate them, by all means; but imitate aright. He that imitates the divine *Iliad*, does not imitate *Homer*; but he who takes the same method, which *Homer* took, for arriving at a capacity of accomplishing a work so great. Tread in his steps to the sole Fountain of Immortality; drink where he drank, at the true *Helicon*, that is, at the breast of Nature: Imitate; but imitate not the *Composition*, but the *Man*. For may not his Paradox pass into a Maxim? *viz.* 'The less we copy the renowned Antients, we shall resemble them the more.'

But possibly you may reply, that you must either imitate *Homer*, or depart from Nature. Not so: For suppose You was to change place, in time, with *Homer*; then, if you write naturally, you might as well charge *Homer* with an imitation of You. Can you be said to imitate *Homer* for writing so, as you would have written, if *Homer* had never been? As far as a regard to Nature, and sound Sense, will permit a Departure from your great Predecessors; so far, ambitiously, depart from them; the farther from them in *Similitude*, the nearer are you to them in *Excellence*; you rise by it into an *Original*; become a noble Collateral, not an humble Descendant from them. Let us build our Compositions with the Spirit, and in the Taste, of the Antients; but not with their Materials.

[. . .] what, for the most part, mean we by Genius, but the Power of accomplishing great things without the means generally reputed necessary to that end? A *Genius* differs from a *good Understanding*, as a Magician from a good Architect; *That* raises his structure by means invisible; *This* by the skilful use of common tools. Hence Genius has ever been supposed to partake of something Divine. [. . .]

Learning, destitute of this superior Aid, is fond, and proud, of what has cost it much pains; is a great Lover of Rules, and Boaster of famed Examples: As Beauties less perfect, who owe half their Charms to cautious Art, she inveighs against natural unstudied Graces, and small harmless Indecorums, and sets rigid Bounds to that Liberty, to which Genius often owes its supreme Glory; but the No-Genius its Frequent Ruin. For unprescribed Beauties, and unexampled Excellence, which are Characteristics of *Genius*, lie without the Pale of *Learning*'s Authorities, and Laws; which Pale, Genius must leap to come at them: But by that leap, if Genius is wanting, we break our Necks; we lose that little credit, which possibly we might have enjoyed before. For Rules, like Crutches, are a needful Aid to the Lame, tho' an Impediment to the Strong. [. . .] There is something in Poetry beyond Prose-reason; there are Mysteries in it not to be explained, but admired; which render mere Prose-men Infidels to their Divinity.

This is the difference between those two Luminaries in Literature, the well-accomplished Scholar, and the divinely-inspired Enthusiast; the *First* is, as the bright morning star; the *Second*, as the rising sun. The writer who neglects those two rules above will never stand alone; he makes one of a group and thinks in wretched unanimity with the throng: Incumbered with the notions of others, and impoverished by their abundance, he conceives not the least embryo of new thought; opens not the least vista thro' the gloom of ordinary writers, into the bright walks of rare Imagination, and singular Design; while the true Genius is crossing all publick roads into fresh untrodden ground; he, up to the knees in Antiquity, is treading the sacred footsteps of great examples, with the blind veneration of a bigot saluting the papal toe; comfortably hoping full absolution for the sins of his own understanding, from the powerful charm of touching his idol's Infallibility.

(Edward Young, *Conjectures on Original Composition* (1759), pp. 9–12, 20–2, 26–8, 54–5.)

(E) WILLIAM HAZLITT

Table Talk (1821), 'On Genius and Common Sense'

Genius in ordinary is a more obstinate and less versatile thing. It is sufficiently exclusive and self-willed, quaint and peculiar. It does some one thing by virtue of doing nothing else: it excels in some one pursuit by being blind to all excellence but its own. It is just the reverse of the cameleon; for it does not borrow, but lend its colour to all about it: or like the glow-worm, discloses a little circle of gorgeous light in the twilight of obscurity, in the night of intellect, that surrounds it. So did Rembrandt. If ever there was a man of genius, he was one, in the proper sense of the term. He lived in and revealed to others a world of his own, and might be said to have invented a new view of nature. He did not discover things *out of* nature, in fiction or fairy land, or make a voyage to the moon 'to descry new lands, rivers, or mountains in her spotty globe,' but saw things *in* nature that every one had missed before him, and gave others eyes to see them with. This is the test and triumph of originality, not to shew us what has never been, and what we may therefore very easily never have dreamt of, but to point out to us what is before our eyes and under our feet, though we have had no suspicion of its existence, for want of sufficient strength of intuition, of determined grasp of mind to seize and retain it. Rembrandt's conquests were not over the *ideal*, but the real. He did not contrive a new story or character, but we nearly owe to him a fifth part of painting, the knowledge of *chiaroscuro* – a distinct power and element in art and nature. [. . .] He was led to adopt this style of broad and startling contrast from its congeniality to his own feelings: his mind grappled with that which afforded the best exercise to its master-powers: he was bold in act, because he was urged on by a strong native impulse. Originality is then nothing but nature and feeling working in the mind. A man does not affect to be original: he is so, because he cannot help it, and often without knowing it. This extraordinary artist indeed might be said to have had a particular organ for colour. His eye seemed to come in contact with it as a feeling, to lay hold of it as a substance, rather than to contemplate it as a visual object. The texture of his landscapes is 'of the earth, earthy' – his clouds are humid, heavy, slow; his shadows are 'darkness that may be felt,' a 'palpable obscure;' his lights are lumps of liquid splendour! There is something more in this than can be accounted for from design or accident: Rembrandt was not a man made up of two or three rules and directions for acquiring genius. [. . .]

Capacity is not the same thing as genius. Capacity may be described to relate to the quantity of knowledge, however acquired; genius to its quality and the mode of acquiring it. Capacity is a power over given ideas or combinations of ideas; genius is the power over those which are not given, and for which no obvious or precise rule can be laid down. Or capacity is power of any sort: genius is power of a different sort from what has yet been shown. A retentive memory, a clear understanding is capacity, but it is not genius. [. . .]

There is no place for genius but in the indefinite and unknown. The discovery of the binomial theorem was an effort of genius; but there was none shown in Jedediah Buxton's being able to multiply 9 figures by 9 in his head. If he could have multiplied 90 figures by 90 instead of 9, it would have been equally useless toil and trouble. He is a man of capacity who possesses considerable intellectual riches: he is a man of genius who finds out a vein of new ore. Originality is the seeing nature differently from others, and yet as it is in itself. It is not singularity or affectation, but the discovery of new and valuable truth. All the world do not see the whole meaning of any object they have been looking at. Habit blinds them to some things: short-sightedness to others. Every mind is not a gauge and measure of truth. Nature has her surface and her dark recesses. She is deep, obscure, and infinite. It is only minds on whom she makes her fullest impressions that can penetrate her shrine or unveil her *Holy of Holies*. It is only those whom she has filled with her spirit that have the boldness or the power to reveal her mysteries to others. But nature has a thousand aspects, and one man can only draw out one of them. Whoever does this, is a man of genius. One displays her force, another her refinement, one her power of harmony, another her suddenness of contrast, one her beauty of form, another her splendour of colour. Each does that for which he is best fitted by his particular genius,

that is to say, by some quality of mind in which the quality of
the object sinks deepest, where it finds the most cordial
welcome, is perceived to its utmost extent, and where again it
forces its way out from the fulness with which it has taken
possession of the mind of the student. The imagination gives out
what it has first absorbed by congeniality of temperament, what
it has attracted and moulded into itself by elective affinity, as
the loadstone draws and impregnates iron. A little originality is
more esteemed and sought for than the greatest acquired talent,
because it throws a new light upon things, and is peculiar to the
individual. The other is common; and may be had for the
asking, to any amount.

(William Hazlitt, 'On Genius and Common Sense', *Table-Talk*,
1821; London, Edinburgh, Glasgow, New York and Toronto, 1901,
pp. 54–5, 58, 59–60).

CHAPTER 3

EMOTIVE THEORIES

The Romantic inheritance has been remarkably persistent in shaping 'common-sense' attitudes towards poetry. Late Victorian and Georgian criticism promoted an indulgent 'Longinian' form of affective criticism which regarded great poetry as a pure expression of emotion. Sublime poetry has direct physiological effects: when we read it, we shiver, weep, and experience exaltation. Logan Pearsal Smith's comments on Milton are an example of this Longinian mode of criticism:

> Meaning, as Housman has said, is of the intellect, poetry isn't . . . . Housman quotes Milton's line: 'Nymphs and Shepherds, dance no more'. 'What is it in those six simple words', he asks, 'that can draw tears, as I know it can, to eyes of more readers than one?' It is an essence, a spirit that escapes all analysis (*Milton and his Modern Critics*, 1940, pp. 48–9).

The idea that poetry is a mysterious and inexplicable communication between an inspired poet and a receptive reader goes back to 'Longinus'. He believed that sublime poetry contained either great ideas or great emotion. The poet's great thoughts are often conveyed through words directly expressing an emotion which guarantees the sublimity of the poetry. The dangers of failure are great: if no genuine and sincere emotional power is communicated to the reader the poem will look ridiculously pompous and grandiose. The presence of lofty emotion is the mysterious quintessence which turns earthly words to spiritual gold.

There is also a rhetorical strand in Longinus' theory, which treats grand emotions as the *appropriate* concomitant of great thoughts. Some emotions are petty and demeaning (jealousy, timidity), and therefore unsuitable in sublime poetry. He recommends certain stylistic devices for producing emotional effects – for example, piling up phrase upon phrase. However, he at times appears to abandon the rhetorical view when he refers to the silent or plain sublime, in which simple words (the Biblical 'Let there be light') or even total silence (the silent ghost of Ajax in Homer's *Odyssey*) can stir the deepest emotions in the reader.

After the seventeenth century the terms 'emotion', 'passion' and 'feeling' become gradually more complex in their connotations and usage as they are moulded by different psychological theories. 'Emotion' usually conveys either the poet's *expression* of an inner state of mind and body, or the reader's *re-experiencing* of the original expression. 'Feeling', in Romantic usage, often alludes to the organic state of bodily sensation, pleasing or painful, which accompanies perception. It may also stand for an intuitive form of knowledge as distinct from scientific reason.

John Dennis, in his *Grounds of Criticism* (1704), introduced into English criticism an emphasis upon the importance of strong 'passion' in the best poetry. He observed classical precedent and followed Dryden's example by naming 'instruction' and 'pleasure' as the two ends of poetry. However, he breaks with the classical approach by stating that both ends are achieved 'by exciting passion'. While Plato had banned poets from his republic because he feared that the powerful emotions aroused by poetry would be a dangerous influence on the young, Dennis argues the reverse: the more violent the passions aroused the greater the possibility of the reader's moral reformation. Dennis remains within the rhetorical tradition in his careful distinctions between greater and lesser types of poetry which are to be accompanied by greater and lesser expressions of passion. Nevertheless, his insistence on the necessity of passion in all great poetry is prophetic.

Joseph Warton's study (1756) of Alexander Pope also links emotion and sublimity. He follows the Roman poet Horace in distinguishing between the 'poetic' and the 'prosaic'. Horace had regarded genuine poetry, such as tragic drama or epic, as more elevated than the modest muse of satire who walks on the ground and uses ordinary prose accents. Warton transforms this essentially rhetorical scheme into a fundamental dichotomy between the poetry of reason and 'genuine' poetry. Pope is a poet of reason and writes 'from and to the head rather than the heart'. His poetry does not 'ravish and transport' his reader or stir 'strong emotions'.

Wordsworth's famous definition of poetry as 'the spontaneous overflow of powerful feelings' is often quoted out of context. First, Wordsworth makes it clear that the poet's words conjure up passions which only approximate to the real passions originally experienced. More importantly, he qualifies the stress upon the emotional purity of poetry by adding that the poet 'had also thought long and deeply. For our continued influxes of feeling are modified and directed by our thoughts.' A poet expresses 'what he thinks and feels'. When he comes to talk of scientific knowledge as an alternative to poetic knowledge it is surprising to discover that Wordsworth resists the temptation to establish a clear-cut dichotomy between poetry as emotional knowledge and science as intellectual knowledge. He even imagines the possibility of the poet ultimately working alongside the scientist, 'carrying sensation into the midst of the objects of science itself'.

J. S. Mill's restatement of Wordsworth's arguments produces a much more rigid antithesis. His own personal problems as the precocious son of James Mill drove him to seek solace in poetry, which for him had 'no connection with struggle or imperfection'. Subtly the complex of thought and feeling in Wordsworth's theory of poetry became an emotive theory. Imaginative writing will always possess 'some dominant *feeling*'. The 'poetry of a poet is Feeling itself', and any thoughts which the feelings suggest are carried along irresistibly by the current of feeling. Mill's theory of poetry involves a 'fact/value' dichotomy which became deep-rooted in critical discourse for a hundred years.

The poetics of I. A. Richards is founded on a similar opposition between the emotive and the referential functions of language. While scientific language produces statements, poetry produces 'pseudo-statements'. This downgrading of poetic language is only apparent, since the delicate organization of the mind can be achieved only by freeing our sources of knowledge from the narrow confines of verifiable and factual statement. The psychological benefits of poetry are sufficient justification for the high valuation of emotive language: 'the acceptance which a pseudo-statement receives is entirely governed by its effects upon our feelings and attitudes'. Richards valued, not the immediate sensations of aesthetic experience (see Pater, III,1,B), but the permanent and lasting 'modifications in the structure of the mind' which the reading of poetry could effect. Poetry 'is the supreme form of *emotive* language'. The element which all true aesthetic experiences share is 'synaesthesis' – a balance and harmony within our 'impulses'.

Richards' psychological theory, with its strange neurological diagrams and pseudo-scientific underpinning, soon seemed outmoded. However, his account of poetry's power to harmonize 'impulses' by the use of non-referential (emotive) language was taken up and developed in New Criticism (III,2 and 3). The New Critics also preserved his rather crude poetry/prose distinction in more subtle forms (see Ransom and Tate, III,2,E and F). In many respects the New Critics rejected the whole emotive view of literature. W. K. Wimsatt's essay on 'The Affective Fallacy' (1949) argued that the reader's emotional response is not the object of critical study. On the other hand he found much of value in Richards' interest in the harmonizing power of poetry. Abandoning the amateur psychology, Wimsatt prefers to adopt T. S. Eliot's 'impersonal' view of poetry's reworking of emotional material (see III,4,C). A great poem or play gives us an 'objective correlative' for an emotion, not a direct expression of emotion. Eliot argued that we must separate 'the man who suffers and the mind which creates'. It is not the intensity of emotions that matters but the 'intensity of the artistic process'. For him poetry is not 'a turning loose of emotion, but an escape from emotion'.

Background reading

John Jones, *The Egotistical Sublime: A History of Wordsworth's Imagination* (London: Chatto & Windus, 1970).

John Needham, *The Completest Mode: I. A. Richards and the Continuity of English Literary Criticism* (Edinburgh: Edinburgh UP, 1982).

A. H. Warren, *English Poetic Theory, 1825–1865* (Princeton, NJ: Princeton UP, 1950), ch. 4 on Mill.

W. K. Wimsatt, 'The Affective Fallacy', in *The Verbal Icon* (Lexington: University of Kentucky Press, 1954).

(A) 'LONGINUS'

On the Sublime (3rd C. AD)

[CHAPTER 8]

There are, one may say, some five genuine sources of the sublime in literature, the common groundwork, as it were, of all

five being a natural faculty of expression, without which nothing
can be done. The first and most powerful is the command of
full-blooded ideas – I have defined this in my book on
Xenophon – and the second is the inspiration of vehement
emotion. These two constituents of the sublime are for the most
part congenital. But the other three come partly of art, namely
the proper construction of figures – these being probably of two
kinds, figures of thought and figures of speech – and, over and
above these, nobility of phrase, which again may be resolved
into choice of words and the use of metaphor and elaborated
diction. The fifth cause of grandeur, which embraces all those
already mentioned, is the general effect of dignity and elevation.[1]
Let us then consider all that is involved under each of these
heads, merely prefacing this, that Cecilius has omitted some of
these five classes, one obvious omission being that of emotion.
Now if he thought that sublimity and emotion were the same
thing, and that one always essentially involved the other, he is
wrong. For one can find emotion that is mean and devoid of
sublimity, for instance feelings of commiseration, annoyance, and
fear. On the other hand, many sublime passages are quite apart
from emotion. There are thousands of examples, for instance, the
poet's daring lines about the Aloadae:

> Ossa then up on Olympus they strove to set, then upon
>   Ossa
> Pelion, ashiver with leaves, to build them a ladder to
>   Heaven;

and the still greater conception that follows,

> Yea and indeed they had done it.

[. . .] I would confidently lay it down that nothing makes so
much for grandeur as genuine emotion in the right place. It
inspires the words as it were with a fine frenzy and fills them
with divine afflatus.

[CHAPTER 39]

Of those factors of sublimity which we specified at the
beginning, one still remains, good friend – I mean the

|1. The five 'sources' are (1) the command of full-blooded ideas; (2) emotion;
(3) the proper use of 'figures'; (4) nobility of phrase; (5) general effect. In chapter
xxxix. σύνθεσις means the arrangement of words. Here the phrase seems to mean
the putting together of the words and clauses into a total effect of grandeur,
making a *whole* of them.

arrangement of the words themselves in a certain order. On this question I have in two treatises given a sufficient account of such conclusions as I could reach, and for our present purpose I need only add this, that men find in melody not only a natural instrument of persuasion and pleasure, but also a marvellous instrument of grandeur and emotion. [. . .]

We hold, then, that composition, which is a kind of melody in words – words which are part of man's nature and reach not his ears only but his very soul – stirring as it does myriad ideas of words, thoughts, things, beauty, musical charm, all of which are born and bred in us; while, moreover, by the blending of its own manifold tones it brings into the hearts of the bystanders the speaker's actual emotion so that all who hear him share in it, and by piling phrase on phrase builds up one majestic whole – we hold, I say, that by these very means it casts a spell on us and always turns *our* thoughts towards what is majestic and dignified and sublime and all else that it embraces, winning a complete mastery over our minds.

(*Longinus On the Sublime*, trans. A. O. Prickard (Oxford: Clarendon Press, 1906), pp. 12–13, 14, 70, 71.)

(B) JOHN DENNIS

Grounds of Criticism (1704)

[CHAPTER 3]

We have said above, that as Poetry is an Art, it must have a certain end, and that there must be means that are proper for the attaining that end, which means are otherwise called the Rules; but that we may make this appear the more plainly, let us declare what Poetry is. Poetry, then, is an Art by which a Poet excites Passion (and for that very cause entertains sense) in order to satisfy and improve, to delight and reform, the Mind, and so to make Mankind happier and better; from which it appears that Poetry has two Ends, a subordinate, and a final one: the subordinate one is Pleasure, and the final one is Instruction.

First, the subordinate end of Poetry is to please, for that Pleasure is the business and design of Poetry is evident, because Poetry, unless it pleases, nay and pleases to a height, is the most contemptible thing in the World. Other things may be borne with if they are indifferent, but Poetry, unless it is transporting, is abominable – nay, it has only the Name of Poetry, so inseparable is Pleasure from the very nature of the thing.

But, secondly, the final End of Poetry is to reform the Manners. [. . .]

Now the proper Means for Poetry to attain both its subordinate and final End is by exciting Passion. First, the subordinate End of Poetry, which is to please, is attained by exciting Passion, because everyone who is pleased is moved, and either desires, or rejoices, or admires, or hopes, or the like. As we are moved by Pleasure, which is Happiness, to do everything we do, we may find upon a little Reflection that every Man is incited by some Passion or other either to Action or to Contemplation; and Passion is the result either of Action or of Contemplation, as long as either of them please; and the more either of them pleases, the more they are attended with Passion. The satisfaction that we receive from Geometry itself comes from the joy of having found out Truth, and the desire of finding more. And the satiety that seizes us upon too long a Lecture proceeds from nothing but from the weariness of our Spirits, and consequently from the cessation or the decay of those two pleasing Passions.

But, secondly, Poetry attains its final end, which is the reforming the Minds of Men, by exciting of Passion. And here I dare be bold to affirm that all Instruction whatever depends upon Passion. The Moral Philosophers themselves, even the driest of them, can never instruct and reform, unless they move, for either they make Vice odious and Virtue lovely, or they deter you from one by the Apprehension of Misery, or they incite you to the other by the Happiness they make you expect from it; or they work upon your Shame, or upon your Pride, or upon your Indignation. And therefore Poetry instructs and reforms more powerfully than Philosophy can do because it moves more powerfully; And therefore it instructs more easily, too. For whereas all Men have Passions, and great Passions of one sort or another, and whereas those Passions will be employed, and whatever way they move, they that way draw the Man, it follows that Philosophy can instruct but hardly, because it moves but gently, for the violent Passions, not finding their Account in those faint emotions, begin to rebel and fly to their old Objects; whereas Poetry, at the same time that it instructs us powerfully, must reform us easily, because it makes the very Violence of the Passions contribute to our Reformation. For the generality of

Mankind are apparently swayed by their Passions, nay, and perhaps the very best and wisest of them. The greatest Philosophers and the greatest Princes are influenced by their Favourites, and so are the wisest Magistrates. And 'tis for this reason that not only the Devil, who must be supposed to understand human nature, corrupts mankind by their Passions [: . .] but God himself, who made the Soul, and best understands its nature, converts it by its Passions. For whereas Philosophy pretends to correct human Passions by human Reason (that is, things that are strong and ungovernable by something that is feeble and weak) Poetry by the force of the Passion instructs and reforms the Reason, which is the Design of the true Religion, as we have shown in another place. So that we have here already laid down one great Rule necessary for the succeeding in Poetry, for since it can attain neither its subordinate nor its final End without exciting of Passion, it follows that, where there is nothing which directly tends to the moving of that, there can be no Poetry, and that consequently a Poet ought to contrive everything in order to the moving of Passion – that not only the Fable, the Incidents and Characters, but the very Sentiments and the Expressions, ought all to be designed for that. For since Poetry pleases and instructs us more even than Philosophy itself, only because it moves us more, it follows that the more Poetry moves, the more it pleases and instructs; and it is for this reason that Tragedy, to those who have a Taste of it, is both more pleasing and more instructing than Comedy. And this naturally brings us to the dividing Poetry into the greater and the less.

1. The greater Poetry is an Art by which a Poet justly and reasonably excites great Passion that he may please and instruct, and comprehends Epic, Tragic, and the greater Lyric Poetry.

2. The less Poetry is an Art by which a Poet excites less Passion for the forementioned Ends, and includes in it Comedy and Satire, and the little Ode, and Elegiac and Pastoral poems. [. . .]

Though *Longinus* did by long Study and habitude know the Sublime when he saw it, as well as any man, yet he had not so clear a knowledge of the Nature of it as to explain it clearly to others. For if he had done that . . ., he would have defined it, but he has been so far from defining it that in one place he has given an account of it that is contrary to the true nature of it. For he tells us in that chapter which treats of the Fountains of Sublimity that Loftiness is often without any Passion at all, which is contrary to the true nature of it. The Sublime is indeed often without Common Passion, as ordinary Passion is often without that. But then it is never without Enthusiastic Passion, for the Sublime is nothing else but a great Thought, or great Thoughts, moving the Soul from its ordinary situation by the Enthusiasm which naturally attends them. Now *Longinus* had a notion of Enthusiastic Passion, for he establishes it in that very chapter for the second source of Sublimity. Now *Longinus*, by affirming that the sublime may be without not only that, but ordinary Passion, says a thing that is not only contrary to the true nature of it, but contradictory to himself. For he tells us in the beginning of the Treatise that the Sublime does not so properly persuade us as it ravishes and transports us, and produces in us a certain Admiration mingled with astonishment and with surprise, which is quite another thing than the barely pleasing, or the barely persuading; that it gives a noble Vigour to a Discourse, an invincible force, which commits a pleasing Rape upon the very Soul of the reader; that whenever it breaks out where it ought to do, like the Artillery of *Jove* it thunders, blazes, and strikes at once, and shows all the united force of a Writer. Now I leave the Reader to judge whether *Longinus* has not been saying here all along that Sublimity is never without Passion. . . .

[CHAPTER 5]

We shall show [. . . .] in the Sequel of this Discourse that not only the remaining Enthusiastic Passions, Horror, Sadness, Joy, and Desire, but that even the ordinary Passions which contribute most to the greatness of Poetry, as Admiration, Terror, and Pity, are chiefly to be derived from Religion; but that the Passions of both sorts must, for the most part, flow greater from Revelation than from natural Religion, because all revealed Religion, whether true or pretended, speaks to the senses, brings the Wonders of another World more home to us, and so makes the Passions which it raises the greater.

The fundamental Rule then that we pretend to lay down for the succeeding or excelling in the greater Poetry is that the constitution of the Poem be religious that it may be throughout pathetic.

(John Dennis, *The Grounds of Criticism in Poetry* (London: Strahan and Lintot, 1704), pp. 8–9, 10–14, 77–9.)

(C) JOSEPH WARTON

An Essay on the Genius and Writings of Pope (1756, 1782)

We do not, it should seem, sufficiently attend to the difference there is betwixt a *man of wit*, a *man of sense*, and a *true poet*. Donne and Swift were undoubtedly men of wit and men of sense: but what traces have they left of pure poetry? It is remarkable that Dryden says of Donne, 'He was the greatest wit, though not the greatest poet, of this nation.' [. . .] Which of these characters is the most valuable and useful is entirely out of the question: all I plead for is to have their several provinces kept distinct from each other; and to impress on the reader that a clear head and acute understanding are not sufficient alone to make a *poet*; that the most solid observations on human life, expressed with the utmost elegance and brevity, are *morality*, and not *poetry*; that the *Epistles* of Boileau in rhyme are no more poetical than the *Characters* of La Bruyère in prose; and that it is a creative and glowing *imagination* [. . . .] and that alone, that can stamp a writer with this exalted and very uncommon character which so few possess and of which so few can properly judge.

Thus have I endeavored to give a critical account, with freedom, but it is hoped, with impartiality, of each of Pope's works, by which review it will appear that the *largest* portion of them is of the *didactic, moral,* and *satiric* kind, and consequently not of the most *poetic* species *of poetry*: whence it is manifest that *good sense* and *judgment* were his characteristical excellencies rather than *fancy* and *invention*: not that the author of *The Rape of the Lock* and *Eloisa* can be thought to want *imagination*; but because his *imagination* was not his predominant talent, because he indulged it not, and because he gave not so many proofs of *this* talent as of the *other*. This turn of mind led him to admire French models; he studied Boileau attentively, formed himself upon him as Milton formed himself upon the Grecian and Italian sons of *fancy*. He stuck to describing *modern manners*, but those *manners* because they are *familiar, uniform, artificial,* and *polished*, are, in their very nature, unfit for any lofty effort of the Muse. He gradually became one of the most correct, even, and exact poets that ever wrote, polishing his pieces with a care and assiduity that no business or avocation ever interrupted; so that if he does not frequently ravish and transport his reader, yet he does not disgust him with unexpected inequalities and absurd improprieties. Whatever poetical enthusiasm he actually possessed, he withheld and stifled. The perusal of him affects not our minds with such strong emotions as we feel from Homer and Milton, so that no man of a true poetical spirit is *master of himself while he reads* them. Hence, he is a writer fit for universal perusal, adapted to all ages and stations, for the old and for the young, the man of business and the scholar. He who would think *The Fairy Queen, Palamon and Arcite, The Tempest,* or *Comus* childish and romantic might relish Pope. Surely it is no narrow and niggardly encomium to say he is the great Poet of Reason, the *first* of *ethical* authors in verse. And this species of writing is, after all, the surest road to an extensive reputation. It lies more level to the general capacities of men than the higher flights of more genuine poetry.

I conclude these reflections with a remarkable fact. In no polished nation, after criticism has been much studied and the rules of writing established, has any very extraordinary work ever appeared. This has visibly been the case in Greece, in Rome, and in France after Aristotle, Horace, and Boileau had written their *Arts of Poetry.* In our own country, the rules of the drama, for instance, were never more completely understood than at present; yet what *uninteresting*, though *faultless*, tragedies have we lately seen! So much better is our judgement than our execution. How to account for the fact here mentioned, adequately and justly, would be attended with all those difficulties that await discussions relative to the productions of the human mind and to the delicate and secret causes that influence them. Whether or no the natural powers be not confined and debilitated by that timidity and caution which is occasioned by a rigid regard to the dictates of art; or whether that philosophical, that geometrical and systematical spirit so much in vogue, which has spread itself from the sciences even into polite literature by consulting only *reason*, has not diminished and destroyed *sentiment* and made our poets write from and to the *head* rather than the *heart*; or whether, lastly, when just models, from which the rules have necessarily been drawn, have once appeared, succeeding writers, by vainly and ambitiously striving to surpass those just models, and to shine and surprise, do not become stiff, and forced, and affected in their thoughts and diction.

(Joseph Warton, *An Essay on the Genius and Writings of Pope* (1756, 1782), 2 vols (5th edn, London: 1806), I. ii–iii, 198–9; II. 401–2.)

(D) WILLIAM WORDSWORTH

Preface to *Lyrical Ballads* (2nd edition, 1800)

For all good poetry is the spontaneous overflow of powerful feelings: and though this be true, Poems to which any value can be attached were never produced on any variety of subjects but by a man who, being possessed of more than usual organic sensibility, had also thought long and deeply. For our continued influxes of feeling are modified and directed by our thoughts, which are indeed the representatives of all our past feelings; and, as by contemplating the relation of these general representatives to each other, we discover what is really important to men, so, by the repetition and continuance of this act, our feelings will be connected with important subjects, till at length, if we be originally possessed of much sensibility, such habits of mind will be produced, that, by obeying blindly and mechanically the impulses of those habits, we shall describe objects, and utter sentiments, of such a nature, and in such connection with each other, that the understanding of the Reader must necessarily be in some degree enlightened, and his affections strengthened and purified.

Taking up the subject, then, upon general grounds, let me ask, what is meant by the word Poet? What is a Poet? To whom does he address himself? And what language is to be expected from him? He is a man speaking to men: a man, it is true, endowed with more lively sensibility, more enthusiasm and tenderness, who has a greater knowledge of human nature, and a more comprehensive soul, than are supposed to be common among mankind; a man pleased with his own passions and volitions, and who rejoices more than other men in the spirit of life that is in him; delighting to contemplate similar volitions and passions as manifested in the goings-on of the Universe, and habitually impelled to create them where he does not find them. To these qualities he has added a disposition to be affected more than other men by absent things as if they were present; an ability of conjuring up in himself passions, which are indeed far from being the same as those produced by real events, yet (especially in those parts of the general sympathy which are pleasing and delightful) do more nearly resemble the passions produced by real events, than anything which, from the motions of their own minds merely, other men are accustomed to feel in themselves: – whence, and from practice, he has acquired a greater readiness and power in expressing what he thinks and feels, and especially those thoughts and feelings which, by his own choice, or from the structure of his own mind, arise in him without immediate external excitement. [. . .]

He [The Poet] considers man and nature as essentially adapted to each other, and the mind of man as naturally the mirror of the fairest and most interesting properties of nature. And thus the Poet, prompted by this feeling of pleasure, which accompanies him through the whole course of his studies, converses with general nature, which affections akin to those, which, through labour and length of time, the Man of science has raised up in himself, by conversing with those particular parts of nature which are the objects of his studies. The knowledge both of the Poet and the Man of science is pleasure; but the knowledge of the one cleaves to us as a necessary part of our existence, our natural and unalienable inheritance; the other is a personal and individual acquisition, slow to come to us, and by no habitual and direct sympathy connecting us with our fellow-beings. The Man of science seeks truth as a remote and unknown benefactor; he cherishes and loves it in his solitude: the Poet, singing a song in which all human beings join with him, rejoices in the presence of truth as our visible friend and hourly companion. Poetry is the breath and finer spirit of all knowledge; it is the impassioned expression which is in the countenance of all Science. Emphatically may it be said of the Poet, as Shakespeare hath said of man, 'that he looks before and after.' He is the rock of defence for human nature; an upholder and preserver, carrying everywhere with him relationship and love. In spite of difference of soil and climate, of language and manners, of laws and customs: in spite of things silently gone out of mind, and things violently destroyed; the Poet binds together by passion and knowledge the vast empire of human society, as it is spread over the whole earth, and over all time. The objects of the Poet's thoughts are everywhere; though the eyes and senses of man are, it is true, his favourite guides, yet he will follow wheresoever he can find an atmosphere of sensation in which to move his wings. Poetry is the first and last of all knowledge – it is as immortal as the heart of man. If the labours of Men of science should ever create any material revolution, direct or indirect, in our condition, and in the impressions which we habitually receive, the Poet will sleep then no more than at present; he will be ready to follow the steps of the Man of science, not only in those general indirect effects, but he will be at his side, carrying sensation into the midst of the objects of the science itself. The remotest discoveries of the Chemist, the Botanist, or Mineralogist, will be as proper objects of the Poet's art as any upon which it can be employed, if the time should ever come when these things shall be familiar to us, and the relations under which they are contemplated by the followers of these respective sciences shall be manifestly and palpably material to us as enjoying and suffering beings. If the time should ever come when what is now called science, thus familiarised to men, shall be ready to put on, as it were, a form of flesh and blood, the Poet will lend his divine spirit to aid the transfiguration, and will welcome the Being thus produced, as a dear and genuine inmate of the household of man.

  I have said that poetry is the spontaneous overflow of powerful feelings: it takes its origin from emotion recollected in tranquillity: the emotion is contemplated till, by a species of reaction, the tranquillity gradually disappears, and an emotion, kindred to that which was before the subject of contemplation, is gradually produced, and does itself actually exist in the mind. In this mood successful composition generally begins, and in a mood similar to this it is carried on; but the emotion, of whatever kind, and in whatever degree, from various causes, is qualified by various pleasures, so that in describing any passions whatsoever, which are voluntarily described, the mind will, upon the whole, be in a state of enjoyment. If Nature be thus cautious to preserve in a state of enjoyment a being so employed, the Poet ought to profit by the lesson held forth to him, and ought especially to take care, that, whatever passions he communicates to his Reader, those passions, if his Reader's mind be sound and vigorous, should always be accompanied with an overbalance of pleasure. Now the music of harmonious metrical language, the sense of difficulty overcome, and the blind association of pleasure which has been previously received from works of rhyme or metre of the same or similar construction, an indistinct perception perpetually renewed of language closely resembling that of real life, and yet, in the circumstance of metre, differing from it so widely – all these imperceptibly make up a complex feeling of delight, which is of the most important use in tempering the painful feeling always found intermingled with powerful descriptions of the deeper passions. This effect is always produced in pathetic and impassioned poetry; while, in lighter

compositions, the ease and gracefulness with which the Poet
manages his numbers are themselves confessedly a principal
source of the gratification of the Reader.

(William Wordsworth, Preface to *Lyrical Ballads* (2nd edn, 1800), *Poetical
Works*, ed. Thomas Hutchinson (London: Henry Frowde, Oxford UP,
1895), pp. 935, 937, 938–9, 940–1.)

(E) JOHN STUART MILL

Autobiography (1875)

The other important change which my opinions at this time
underwent, was that I, for the first time, gave its proper place,
among the prime necessities of human well-being, to the internal
culture of the individual. I ceased to attach almost exclusive
importance to the ordering of outward circumstances, and the
training of the human being for speculation and for action.

I had now learnt by experience that the passive susceptibilities
needed to be cultivated as well as the active capacities, and
required to be nourished and enriched as well as guided. I did
not, for an instant, lose sight of, or undervalue, that part of the
truth which I had seen before; I never turned recreant to
intellectual culture, or ceased to consider the power and practice
of analysis as an essential condition both of individual and of
social improvement. But I thought that it had consequences
which required to be corrected, by joining other kinds of
cultivation with it. The maintenance of a due balance among the
faculties, now seemed to me of primary importance. The
cultivation of the feelings became one of the cardinal points in
my ethical and philosophical creed. And my thoughts and
inclinations turned in an increasing degree towards whatever
seemed capable of being instrumental to that object. [. . .]

What made Wordsworth's poems a medicine for my state of
mind, was that they expressed, not mere outward beauty, but
states of feeling, and of thought coloured by feeling, under the
excitement of beauty. They seemed to be the very culture of the
feelings, which I was in quest of. In them I seemed to draw
from a source of inward joy, of sympathetic and imaginative
pleasure, which could be shared in by all human beings; which
had no connexion with struggle or imperfection, but would be
made richer by every improvement in the physical or social

condition of mankind. From them I seemed to learn what would be the perennial sources of happiness, when all the greater evils of life shall have been removed. And I felt myself at once better and happier as I came under their influence. There have certainly been, even in our own age, greater poets than Wordsworth; but poetry of deeper and loftier feeling could not have done for me at that time what his did. I needed to be made to feel that there was real, permanent happiness in tranquil contemplation. Wordsworth taught me this, not only without turning away from, but with a greatly increased interest in, the common feelings and common destiny of human beings. And the delight which these poems gave me, proved that with culture of this sort, there was nothing to dread from the most confirmed habit of analysis. At the conclusion of the Poems came the famous Ode, falsely called Platonic, 'Intimations of Immortality' in which, along with more than his usual sweetness of melody and rhythm, and along with the two passages of grand imagery but bad philosophy so often quoted, I found that he too had had similar experience to mine; that he also had felt that the first freshness of youthful enjoyment of life was not lasting; but that he had sought for compensation, and found it, in the way in which he was now teaching me to find it. The result was that I gradually, but completely, emerged from my habitual depression, and was never again subject to it. I long continued to value Wordsworth less according to his intrinsic merits, than by the measure of what he had done for me. Compared with the greatest poets, he may be said to be the poet of unpoetical natures, possessed of quiet and contemplative tastes. But unpoetical natures are precisely those which require poetic cultivation. This cultivation Wordsworth is much more fitted to give, than poets who are intrinsically far more poets than he.

(J. S. Mill, *Autobiography* (London: Longmans, 1873), pp. 143–4, 148–9.)

'What Is Poetry?' (1833)

The object of poetry is confessedly to act upon the emotions; and therein is poetry sufficiently distinguished from what Wordsworth affirms to be its logical opposite, namely, not prose, but matter of fact or science. The one addresses itself to the belief, the other to the feelings. The one does its work by convincing or persuading, the other by moving. The one acts by presenting a proposition to the understanding, the other by offering interesting objects of contemplation to the sensibilities.

This, however, leaves us very far from a definition of poetry. We have distinguished it from one thing, but we are bound to distinguish it from everything. To bring thoughts or images to the mind for the purpose of acting upon the emotions, does not belong to poetry alone. It is equally the province (for example) of the novelist: and yet the faculty of the poet and that of the novelist are as distinct as any other two faculties; and the faculty of the novelist and of the orator, or of the poet and the metaphysician. The two characters may be united, as characters the most disparate may; but they have no natural connection.

Many of the finest poems are in the form of fictitious narratives, and in almost all good serious fictions there is true poetry. But there is a radical distinction between the interest felt in a story as such, and the interest excited by poetry; for the one is derived from incident, the other from the representation of feeling. In one, the source of the emotion excited is the exhibition of a state or states of human sensibility; in the other, of a series of states of mere outward circumstances. Now, all minds are capable of being affected more or less by representations of the latter kind, and all, or almost all, by those of the former; yet the two sources of interest correspond to two distinct, and (as respects their greatest development) mutually exclusive, characters of mind.

(J. S. Mill, 'What Is Poetry?' (1833), reprinted in *Dissertations and Discussions*, 2 vols (London: J. W. Parker & Son, 1859), I. 64–5.)

'Two Kinds of Poetry' (1833)

To the man of science or of business, objects group themselves according to the artifical classifications which the understanding has voluntarily made for the convenience of thought or of practice. But where any of the impressions are vivid and intense, the associations into which these enter are the ruling ones: it being a well-known law of association, that the stronger a feeling is, the more quickly and strongly it associates itself with any other object or feeling. Where, therefore, nature has given strong feelings, and education has not created factitious tendencies stronger than the natural ones, the prevailing associations will be those which connect objects and ideas with emotions, and with each other through the intervention of emotions. Thoughts and images will be linked together, according to the similarity of the feelings which cling to them. A thought will introduce a thought by first introducing a feeling which is allied with it. At the centre of each group of thoughts or images will be found a feeling; and the thoughts or images are only there because the feeling was there. All the combinations which the mind puts together, all the pictures which it paints, the wholes which Imagination constructs out of the materials supplied by Fancy, will be indebted to some dominant *feeling*, not as in other natures to a dominant *thought*, for their unity and consistency of character – for that distinguishes them from incoherences.

The difference, then, between the poetry of a poet, and the poetry of a cultivated but not naturally poetic mind, is, that in the latter, with however bright a halo of feeling the thought may be surrounded and glorified, the thought itself is still the conspicuous object; while the poetry of a poet is Feeling itself, employing Thought only as the medium of its utterance. In the one, feeling waits upon thought; in the other, thought upon feeling. The one writer has a distinct aim, common to him with any other didactic author; he desires to convey the thought, and he conveys it clothed in the feelings which it excites in himself, or which he deems most appropriate to it. The other merely pours forth the overflowing of his feelings; and all the thoughts which those feelings suggest are floated promiscuously along the stream.

And nevertheless, there *is* poetry which could not emanate but from a mental and physical constitution peculiar, not in the kind, but in the degree of its susceptibility: a constitution which makes its possessor capable of greater happiness than mankind in general, and also of greater unhappiness; and because greater, so also more various. And such poetry, to all who know enough of nature to own it as being in nature, is much more poetry, is poetry in a far higher sense, than any other; since the common element of all poetry, that which constitutes poetry, human feeling, enters far more largely into this than into the poetry of culture. Not only because the natures which we have called poetical, really feel more, and consequently have more feeling to express; but because, the capacity of feeling being so great, feeling, when excited and not voluntarily resisted, seizes the helm of their thoughts, and the succession of ideas and images becomes the mere utterance of an emotion; not, as in other natures, the emotion a mere ornamental colouring of the thought.

Ordinary education and the ordinary course of life are constantly at work counteracting this quality of mind, and substituting habits more suitable to their own end: if instead of substituting, they were content to superadd, there were nothing to complain of. But when will education consist, not in repressing any mental faculty or power, from the uncontrolled action of which danger is apprehended, but in training up to its proper strength the corrective and antagonist power?

In whomsoever the quality which we have described exists, and is not stifled, that person is a poet. Doubtless he is a greater poet in proportion as the fineness of his perceptions, whether of sense or of internal consciousness, furnishes him with an ampler supply of lovely images – the vigour and richness of his intellect with a greater abundance of moving thoughts. For it is through these thoughts and images that the feeling speaks, and through their impressiveness that it impresses itself, and finds response in other hearts; and from these media of transmitting it (contrary to the laws of physical nature) increase of intensity is reflected back upon the feeling itself. But all these it is possible to have, and not be a poet; they are mere materials, which the poet shares in common with other people. What constitutes the poet is not the imagery nor the thoughts, nor even the feelings, but the law according to which they are called up. He is a poet, not because he has ideas of any particular kind, but because the succession of his ideas is subordinate to the course of his emotions.

(J. S. Mill, 'Two Kinds of Poetry' (1833), ibid., I. 82–3, 88–90.)

(F) I. A. RICHARDS

Science and Poetry (1926)

[. . .] the agitation which is the experience [of reading a poem by Wordsworth] divides into a major and a minor branch, though the two streams have innumerable interconnections and influence one another intimately. Indeed, it is only as an expositor's artifice that we may speak of them as two streams.

The minor branch we may call the intellectual stream; the other, which we may call the active, or emotional, stream, is made up of the play of our interests.

The intellectual stream is comparatively easy to follow; it

follows itself, so to speak; but it is the less important of the two. In poetry it matters only *as a means*; it directs and excites the active stream. It is made up of thoughts, which are not static little entities that bob up into consciousness and down again out of it, but fluent happenings, events, which refer or point to the things the thoughts are 'of.' [. . .]

This pointing to things is all that thoughts do. They appear to do much more – to copy or to create – which are our chief illusions. The realm of pure thought is not an autonomous state. Our thoughts are the servants of our interests, and even when they seem to rebel it is some among our interests which are in insurrection. Our thoughts are pointers and it is the other, the active, stream which deals with the things which thoughts point to.

Some people who read verse (they do not often read much of it), are so constituted that very little more happens than this intellectual stream of thoughts. It is perhaps superfluous to point out that they miss the real poem. [. . .]

We must look further. In the poetic approach the relevant consequences are not logical or to be arrived at by a partial relaxation of logic. Except occasionally and by accident logic does not enter at all. The relevant consequences are those which arise through our emotional organization. The acceptance which a pseudo-statement receives is entirely governed by its effects upon our feelings and attitudes. Logic only comes in, if at all, in subordination, as a servant to our emotional response. It is an unruly servant, however, as poets and readers are constantly discovering. A pseudo-statement is 'true' if it suits and serves some attitude or links together attitudes which on other grounds are desirable. This kind of 'truth' is so opposed to scientific 'truth' that it is a pity to use so similar a word, but at present it is difficult to avoid the malpractice.

This brief analysis may be sufficient to indicate the fundamental disparity and opposition between pseudo-statements as they occur in poetry and statements as they occur in science. A pseudo-statement is a form of words which is justified entirely by its effect in releasing or organizing our impulses and attitudes [. . .]; a statement, on the other hand, is justified by its truth, *i.e.*, its correspondence, in a highly technical sense, with the fact to which it points.

Statements true and false alike do, of course, constantly touch off attitudes and action. Our daily practical existence is largely guided by them. On the whole true statements are of more service to us than false ones. None the less we do not and, at present, cannot order our emotions and attitudes by true statements alone. Nor is there any probability that we ever shall contrive to do so. This is one of the great new dangers to which civilization is exposed. Countless pseudo-statements – about God, about the universe, about human nature, the relations of mind to mind, about the soul, its rank and destiny – pseudo-statements which are pivotal points in the organization of the mind, vital to its well-being, have suddenly become, for sincere, honest and informed minds, impossible to believe as for centuries they have been believed. The accustomed incidences of the modes of believing are changed irrecoverably; and the knowledge which has displaced them is not of a kind upon which an equally fine organization of the mind can be based.

This is the contemporary situation. The remedy, since there is no prospect of our gaining adequate knowledge, and since indeed it is fairly clear that scientific knowledge cannot meet this need, is to cut our pseudo-statements free from that kind of belief which is appropriate to verified statements. So released they will be changed, of course, but they can still be the main instruments by which we order our attitudes to one another and to the world.

(I. A. Richards, *Science and Poetry* (London: Kegan Paul, Trench, Trubner, 1926), pp. 13, 14, 58–61.)

Principles of Literary Criticism (1924)

Words, when used symbolically or scientifically, not figuratively and emotively, are only capable of directing thought to a comparatively few features of the more common situations. But feeling is sometimes a more subtle way of referring, more dangerous also, because more difficult to corroborate and to control, and more liable to confusion. There is no inherent superiority, however, in feeling as opposed to thought, there is merely a difference in applicability; nor is there any opposition or clash between them except for those who are mistaken either in their thinking or in their feeling, or in both. [. . .]

A statement may be used for the sake of the *reference*, true or false, which it causes. This is the *scientific* use of language. But it may also be used for the sake of the effects in emotion and attitude produced by the reference it occasions. This is the *emotive* use of language. The distinction once clearly grasped is simple. We may either use words for the sake of the references they promote, or we may use them for the sake of the attitudes and emotions which ensue. Many arrangements of words evoke attitudes without any reference being required *en route*. They operate like musical phrases. But usually references are involved *as conditions* for, or *stages in*, the ensuing development of attitudes, yet it is still the attitudes not the references which are important. It matters not at all in such cases whether the references are true or false. Their sole function is to bring about and support the attitudes which are the further response. The questioning, verificatory way of handling them is irrelevant, and in a competent reader it is not allowed to interfere. 'Better a plausible impossibility than an improbable possibility' said Aristotle very wisely; there is less danger of an inappropriate reaction.

The differences between the mental processes involved in the two cases are very great, though easily overlooked. Consider what failure for each use amounts to. For scientific language a difference in the references is itself failure: the end has not been attained. But for emotive language the widest differences in reference are of no importance if the further effects in attitude and emotion are of the required kind.

Further, in the scientific use of language not only must the references be correct for success, but the connections and relations of references to one another must be of the kind which we call logical. They must not get in one another's way, and must be so organized as not to impede further reference. But for emotive purposes logical arrangement is not necessary. It may be and often is an obstacle. For what matters is that the series of attitudes due to the references should have their own proper organization, their own emotional interconnection, and this often has no dependence upon the logical relations of such references as may be concerned in bringing the attitudes into being.

(I. A. Richards, *Principles of Literary Criticism* (2nd edn, London: Routledge & Kegan Paul, 1926; reset, 1967), pp. 101, 211–12.)

CHAPTER 4

SUBJECTIVE CRITICISM AND THE READER'S RESPONSE

There are several competing interpretations of Aristotle's famous but brief discussion of 'catharsis' in tragedy. The term in Greek can mean 'purgation', 'purification' or 'clarification'. The first two versions focus upon the audience's psychological processes, while the third treats catharsis as something occurring in the play. 'Purgation' involves the driving out of unwanted emotions (pity and fear), while 'purification' assumes that the emotions are not expelled but moderated or contained. The first view is based on the model of a medical cure, the second on the idea of moral refinement. The extract from René Rapin is a variation on the 'purification' view of catharsis. Rapin believed that the dramatist aimed to move the soul of the audience to 'tender sentiments' by depicting powerful passions. G. E. Lessing's later interpretation concentrates the 'purification' in the transcendent emotion of pity, since 'the best man is the man who pities most'. The third view, which appealed strongly to the New Critics, is that catharsis is a clarification of the pitiable and fearful incidents of the play: the artistic organization of incidents produces a clarification of their relationship with universal truths. The audience learns something from this clarification.

The various interpretations of Aristotle point to differences in critics' conceptions of the reader's or audience's role in the artistic process. However, all of them treat the text as the sole determinant of meaning. Whether catharsis takes place in the text or in the reader, the text remains the active cause and the only authority for its meaning. Of course, the very fact that interpreters of Aristotle disagree tends to support the modern view that the text alone cannot authorize an interpretation, since the reader also *contributes* something to the process of interpretation. If we assume that the reader's contribution is important, we cease to be surprised by the fact of disagreement and/or by the plurality of interpretations.

A central question raised by modern criticism is 'Does the text or the reader determine the process of interpretation?' At one extreme, we might imagine that the text completely controls the reader's response, and, at the other, that the reader's activity is primary. A great deal of modern 'subjective' criticism emphasizes the shaping activity of the reader. I. A. Richards and William Empson, both key figures in the development of New Criticism, were interested in the psychology of reading. Richards believed that poetry could effect 'permanent modifications in the structure of the [reader's] mind'. Empson was fascinated by the uncanny ways in which readers learn how to make sense of complex texts. Jonathan Culler's notion of the reader's 'literary competence' (see III,6,J) owes something to Empson's approach.

The social world in which a work is produced and received evidently has a shaping effect on interpretation. Dryden argued that the standards of literature are greatly affected by the prevailing standards of 'conversation'. The King's restoration in 1660 brought back refinement to the stage which, according to many, had passed through a barbarous period under the Roundheads. Writers and audiences once again had before them fine examples of 'wit and conversation' provided by the court. The Augustans, culturally dominant between about 1660 and 1780, ridiculed 'middle-class' writing for its lack of refinement and civilized values. Pope, in *The Dunciad*, treated the urban culture of London as a threat to the received wisdom of Greece and Rome. In his 'Epistle to Augustus' even the monarch (the Hanoverian George II) is an enemy of the arts. In this period social and literary values are closely and explicitly connected. According to the Prague theorist Mukařovský (see III,1,H) aesthetic ideas are always socially determined.

Recently, Hans Robert Jauss has argued that the literary work exists only as the collective interpretation of successive generations of readers. Every audience or readership responds to a literary work through the lenses of a particular 'horizon of expectations' (set of conventions or rules). A major influence on Jauss is the tradition of hermeneutical philosophy and especially the work of Hans-Georg Gadamer who developed an aesthetic theory based on Heidegger's philosophical ideas. Heidegger had emphasized the *givenness* of human existence: we cannot escape the *historical* nature of the human condition. Gadamer believes that reading is an attempt to bridge a gap between past and present. Reading in the present we cannot escape the preconceptions of our culture, but we can try within this historical limitation to attempt an understanding which may after all bring new light to an old text. The 'horizon of expectations' in which we do our thinking may somehow fuse with the horizons of past writing and reading. There is a mutual benefit to be gained from this process. Jauss developed a new kind of literary history based on Gadamer's theories, focusing not upon the text, the author, or literary influences, but upon the *reception* of the text from the time of its composition to the present. A text is not an objective monument surrounded by a chaotic penumbra of interpretations; its identity is determined by the horizons within which it is received. The hermeneutical writings of Paul Ricoeur are a subtle fusion of Heidegger, Freud and Marx. Like Gadamer and Jauss he sees a positive gain in self-understanding for the reader arising from the hermeneutic struggle to understand another's text.

E. D. Hirsch is critical of the historicism of the Heideggerian school, and he uses the arguments of Edmund Husserl, whose 'phenomenology' aimed to establish a knowledge of reality, not in terms of objects but in terms of the mind's structure. For Husserl the meaning of a literary text is bound up with the writer's 'mental' object: it consists of whatever he or she had 'in mind' when the work was composed. Meaning is thus an 'intentional' object (not a physical object). Hirsch seized upon this argument to counter the relativism of much modern literary criticism. His distinction between 'meaning' and 'significance' is an attempt to overcome the age-old problem of multiple interpretation. 'Meaning' is fixed and is identical with the author's 'intention', while 'significance' is a term used for an historically conditioned interpretation of a given work. A work's meaning is the author's and should not be appropriated by the reader; this would amount to theft or moral interference. Hirsch tries to protect the author from what he considers the moral bullying of interpretation. However, it is not clear whether any critic can establish with certainty the mental object which coincided with the text at the moment(s) of composition.

Husserl believed that if we concentrate on the pure contents of our minds, 'putting in brackets' everything which is outside our minds, we will be able to grasp the essential nature of reality. A phenomenological criticism involves an 'immanent' reading of a text, placing in parentheses everything outside the text, and reducing it to a pure manifestation of the writer's consciousness.

The phenomenological relations between the world and the writer's mind are given expression in the text: the structures of the writer's mind, and especially the ways in which he or she conceives relations between subjects and objects, are communicated to the reader directly through the language of the work. In order to achieve this absolute understanding of the work the reader must become a perfectly objective and totally receptive mind. The so-called Geneva School of critics, which includes Georges Poulet, follows this method.

Wolfgang Iser is the most eclectic of the 'reception' theorists, borrowing concepts not only from phenomenology but also from formalism, semiotics, and gestalt psychology, and so on. He concentrates rigorously on the act of reading itself – on the gradually unfolding process by which a reader assimilates and incorporates the various facets and levels of a text. The major influence on his approach is the disciple of Husserl, Roman Ingarden, whose *The Literary Work of Art* (1931) depicted the text as a totality made up of several strata, from the level of the word to that of the 'schematized aspects'. The latter arise because, unlike real objects, fictional entities contain 'spots of indeterminacy' which the reader must fill or 'concretize'. However, this does not mean that the reader can make the text mean what s/he likes, because the schematized aspects of the text provide a skeleton of determinate meanings (a 'network of response-inviting structures') which prompts the reader to respond in certain ways. According to Iser the literary work does not simply represent objects, but refers to the world by presenting norms or value systems, several of which may be included in a single novel and embodied in particular characters. The text suspends the validity of these norms within its fictional world, and forces the reader to relate them to one another and to 'actualize' a final valuation, and to fill the 'gaps' between the various aspects of the text. This somewhat uneasy division between passive and active reading roles is expressed by Iser in terms of a split reader: the 'actual reader' brings a stock of experience to the images which pass through his or her mind; the 'implied reader' is created by the text's skeleton, which impels the reader towards solutions. Finally, Iser offers a useful model of the reading process which has much in common with the work of Stanley Fish. The reader's journey through a book is a continuous process of adjustments of viewpoint. We hold in our minds certain expectations, based on our memory of characters and events, but the expectations are continually modified as the text advances.

We grasp a series of changing viewpoints, each one establishing a new total perpective.

Reader-response criticism in the United States has sometimes adopted a more individualistic focus. Norman Holland and David Bleich use psychology as their starting point. Holland believes that we all possess an 'identity theme' which, like a musical theme, is capable of variation, but which remains a stable strand of identity. When we read, we process the text in terms of this theme: we 'use the literary work to symbolize and finally replicate ourselves'. Bleich believes that all knowledge is 'made by people and not found', because the objects of our enquiry are changed by our acts of observation. Secondly, all knowledge serves the needs of the community. Faced with creative works we should ask 'What are the individual and communal occasions for these symbolic renderings of experience?' 'Subjective criticism' assumes that our main motivation in reading is to understand ourselves. This assumption leads Bleich to distinguish between the reader's *spontaneous* response to a text and his or her *objective* statement of its meaning. We can only understand a particular reading or interpretation if we also understand the reader's personal response and the history of the reader's psychological growth and development.

The range of approaches within reader-response criticism is so great that it is difficult to make generalizations about its overall significance. Even so, one can at least say that it has made it difficult to talk about the 'meaning' of a text without taking into account the reader's contribution to it.

Background reading

R. C. Holub, *Reception Theory: A Critical Introduction* (London and New York: Methuen, 1984).

David Couzens Hoy, *The Critical Circle: Literature, History, and Philosophical Hermeneutics* (Berkeley, Los Angeles, London: University of California Press, 1978).

Elder Olson (ed.), *Aristotle's Poetics and English Literature* (Chicago and London: University of Chicago Press, 1965), chs 4, 6, and 7 (Catharsis).

Susan R. Suleiman and Inge Crosman (eds), *The Reader in the Text: Essays on Audience and Interpretation* (Princeton, NJ: Princeton UP, 1980).

Jane P. Tompkins, *Reader-Response Criticism: From Formalism to Post-Structuralism* (Baltimore: Johns Hopkins UP, 1980).

Mario J. Valdés and Owen Miller (eds), *Identity of the Literary Text* (Toronto, Buffalo, London: University of Toronto Press, 1985).

(A) ARISTOTLE

Poetics

The tragic fear and pity may be aroused by the Spectacle; but they may also be aroused by the very structure and incidents of the play – which is the better way and shows the better poet. The Plot in fact should be so framed that, even without seeing the things take place, he who simply hears the account of them shall be filled with horror and pity at the incidents; which is just the effect that the mere recital of the story in *Oedipus* would have on one. To produce this same effect by means of the Spectacle is less artistic, and requires extraneous aid. Those, however, who make use of the Spectacle to put before us that which is merely monstrous and not productive of fear, are wholly out of touch with Tragedy; not every kind of pleasure should be required of a tragedy, but only its own proper pleasure.

The tragic pleasure is that of pity and fear, and the poet has to produce it by a work of imitation; it is clear, therefore, that the causes should be included in the incidents of his story. Let us see, then, what kinds of incident strike one as horrible, or rather as piteous. In a deed of this description the parties must necessarily be either friends, or enemies, or indifferent to one another. Now when enemy does it on enemy, there is nothing to move us to pity either in his doing or in his meditating the deed, except so far as the actual pain of the sufferer is concerned; and the same is true when the parties are indifferent to one another. Whenever the tragic deed, however, is done within the family – when murder or the like is done or meditated by brother on brother, by son on father, by mother on son, or son on mother – these are the situations the poet should seek after.

(Aristotle, *Poetics*, trans. Ingram Bywater, *On the Art of Poetry* (Oxford: Clarendon Press, 1920), pp. 52–3).

(B) JOHN DRYDEN

Defence of the Epilogue (1672)

And this leads me to the last and greatest advantage of our writing, which proceeds from *conversation*. In the age wherein those poets lived, there was less of gallantry than in ours;

neither did they keep the best company of theirs. Their fortune
has been much like that of Epicurus, in the retirement of his
gardens; to live almost unknown, and to be celebrated after their
decease. I cannot find that any of them had been conversant in
courts, except Ben Johnson; and his genius lay not so much that
way, as to make an improvement by it. Greatness was not then
so easy of access, nor conversation so free, as now it is. I
cannot, therefore, conceive it any insolence to affirm, that, by
the knowledge and pattern of their wit who writ before us, and
by the advantage of our own conversation, the discourse and
raillery of our comedies excel what has been written by them.
And this will be denied by none, but some few old fellows who
value themselves on their acquaintance with the *Black Friars*;
who, because they saw their plays, would pretend a right to
judge ours. The memory of these grave gentlemen is their only
plea for being wits. They can tell a story of Ben Johnson, and,
perhaps, have had fancy enough to give a supper in the *Apollo*,
that they might be called his sons; and, because they were
drawn in to be laughed at in those times, they think themselves
now sufficiently entitled to laugh at ours. Learning I never saw
in any of them; and wit no more than they could remember. In
short, they were unlucky to have been bred in an unpolished
age, and more unlucky to live to a refined one. They have lasted
beyond their own, and are cast behind ours; and, not contented
to have known little at the age of twenty, they boast of their
ignorance at threescore.

Now, if they ask me, whence it is that our conversation is so
much refined? I must freely, and without flattery, ascribe it to
the court; and, in it, particularly to the King, whose example
gives a law to it. His own misfortunes, and the nation's, afforded
him an opportunity, which is rarely allowed to sovereign princes,
I mean of travelling, and being conversant in the most polished
courts of Europe; and, thereby, of cultivating a spirit which was
formed by nature to receive the impressions of a gallant and
generous education. At his return, he found a nation lost as
much in barbarism as in rebellion; and, as the excellency of his
nature forgave the one, so the excellency of his manners
reformed the other. The desire of imitating so great a pattern
first awakened the dull and heavy spirits of the English from
their natural reservedness; loosened them from their stiff forms of
conversation, and made them easy and pliant to each other in
discourse. Thus, insensibly, our way of living became more free;
and the fire of the English wit, which was before stifled under a

constrained, melancholy way of breeding, began first to display its force, by mixing the solidity of our nation with the air and gaiety of our neighbours. This being granted to be true, it would be a wonder if the poets, whose work is imitation, should be the only persons in three kingdoms who should not receive advantage by it; or, if they should not more easily imitate the wit and conversation of the present age than of the past.

(Dryden, *Defence of the Epilogue* (1672), *Essays* ed. W. P. Ker, 2 vols (Oxford: Clarendon Press, 1900), I. 175–6.)

(C) RENÉ RAPIN

Reflections on Aristotle's Treatise of Poesie, trans. Thomas Rymer (1674)

But it is not enough the *Tragedy* be furnished with all the most moving and terrible Adventures that *History* can afford to stir in the heart those motions it pretends, to the end it may cure the mind of those *vain fears* that may annoy it, and those *childish compassions* that may soften it. 'Tis also necessary, says the Philosopher, that every Poet employ these great objects of terror and pity as the two most powerful springs in art, to produce that pleasure which *Tragedy* may yield. And this pleasure, which is properly of the mind, consists in the agitation of the Soul moved by the passions. *Tragedy* cannot be delightful to the Spectator unless he become sensible to all that is represented; he must *enter* into all the different thoughts of the Actors, *interest* himself in the Adventures, *fear*, *hope*, *afflict* himself, and *rejoice* with them. The Theatre is dull and languid when it ceases to produce these motions in the Soul of those that stand by. But as of all passions, *fear* and *pity* are those that make strongest impressions on the heart of man, by the natural disposition he has of being afraid, and of being mollified, *Aristotle* has chosen these amongst the rest to move more powerfully the Soul by the tender *sentiments* they cause, when the heart admits and is pierced by them. In effect, when the Soul is shaken by motions so natural and so humane, all the impressions it feels become delightful; its trouble pleases, and the emotion it finds is a kind of charm to it, which does cast it into a sweet and profound meditation, and which insensibly does engage it in all the interests that are managed on the Theatre. 'Tis then that the heart yields itself over to all the objects that are proposed, that all images strike it, that it espouses the sentiments of all those that speak, and becomes susceptible of all the passions that are presented because 'tis moved. And in this *agitation* consists all the pleasure that one is capable to receive from *Tragedy*; for the spirit of man does please itself with the different *situations* caused by the different objects and the various passions that are represented.

(René Rapin, *Reflections on Aristotle's Treatise of Poesie*, trans. Thomas Rymer (London: Herringman, 1674) pp. 105–6. French original also 1674.)

(D) GOTTHOLD EPHRAIM LESSING

Letter to Nicolai (on tragedy), 13 Nov. 1756

Terror in tragedy is nothing more than being taken by surprise by pity, whether I know the object of my pity or not. For example, the priest at last exclaims: 'You, Oedipus, are the murderer of Laius'; I am terrified, for all at once I see the righteous Oedipus unfortunate, and immediately my pity is aroused. Another example: a ghost appears; I am terrified; my pity is taken by surprise by the thought that he would not appear if he were not bringing misfortune to someone or other, and also by the dark image of this misfortune whether or not I know the person whom it is to assail. Pity, thus taken by surprise, is called terror. Correct me if I am wrong.

Now for admiration! Admiration! Oh in tragedy, to express myself in oracular fashion, we meet a transformed kind of pity. The hero is unfortunate but he is raised so high above his misfortune and is even so proud of it that, in my thoughts too, it starts to lose its terror and I tend rather to envy than pity him.

The steps are thus as follows: terror, pity, admiration. The whole ladder, however, is to be called pity; and terror and admiration are only the first rungs, the beginning and the end of pity. For instance, I hear suddenly: 'Cato is on the point of being killed by Caesar.' Terror! But then I become acquainted with the noble character of the former and after that with his unfortunate state. Terror dissolves into pity. But now I hear him say: 'The world that serves Caesar is no longer worthy of me.' Admiration sets limits to pity. The poet uses terror to announce pity and admiration, as it were, as relief from it. The road to pity would be too long for the spectator if his attention were not held by the first shock of terror, and pity wears thin if it is not strengthened in admiration. So, if it is true that the whole art of the tragic poet rests precisely on the evoking and sustaining of pity alone, then I can merely add that the purpose of tragedy is this: it should increase our capacity to feel pity. It should not merely teach us to feel pity towards this or that unfortunate man, but it should intensify our powers of empathy to the point that we are touched by misfortune at whatever time or in whatever form it may appear, experiencing it directly ourselves. And now I refer to a principle, the truth of which Herr Moses may demonstrate to you if, in direct conflict with your own feelings, you choose to doubt it. The man who pities most is the best of men, the one who is most open to social virtues and to all forms of generosity. So, whoever makes us feel pity makes us better and more virtuous, and tragedy, which has the former effect, also has the latter or – it has the former effect *in order to* have the latter one. Apologise to Aristotle [whose theory of catharis Lessing is contesting] for this, or show me where I am wrong.

(Gotthold Ephraim Lessing, *Correspondence*, To Nicolai, 13 November 1756 (trans. J. P. Payne).)

(E) I. A RICHARDS

Principles of Literary Criticism (1924)

Emotions are primarily signs of attitudes and owe their great prominence in the theory of art to this. For it is the attitudes evoked which are the all-important part of any experience. Upon the texture and form of the attitudes involved its value depends. It is not the intensity of the conscious experience, its thrill, its pleasure or its poignancy which gives it value, but the organization of its impulses for freedom and fullness of life. There are plenty of ecstatic instants which are valueless; the character of consciousness at any moment is no certain sign of the excellence of the impulses from which it arises. It is the most convenient sign that is available, but it is very ambiguous and may be very misleading. A more reliable but less accessible set of signs can be found in the readiness for this or that kind of behaviour in which we find ourselves after the experience. Too great insistence upon the quality of the momentary *consciousness* which the arts occasion has in recent times been a prevalent critical blunder. The Epilogue to Pater's *Renaissance* is the *locus classicus*. The after-effects, the permanent modifications in the structure of the mind, which works of art can produce, have been overlooked. No one is ever quite the same again after any experience; his possibilities have altered in some degree. And among all the agents by which 'the widening of the sphere of human sensibility' may be brought about, the arts are the most powerful, since it is through them that men may most co-operate and in these experiences that the mind most easily and with least interference organizes itself.

(I. A. Richards, *Principles of Literary Criticism* (2nd edn, London: Routledge & Kegan Paul, 1926; reset, 1967), pp. 101–2.)

(F) WILLIAM EMPSON

Seven Types of Ambiguity (1930)

I am not sure that I have been approaching this matter with an adequate skeleton of metaphysics. For instance, Mr. Richards distinguishes a poem into Sense, Feeling, Tone, and Intention; you may say an interpretation is not being done properly (if the analyst has conquered the country, still he is not ruling it) unless these four are separated out into sub-headings and the shades of grammar that convey the contents of each sub-heading are then listed in turn. But the process of apprehension, both of the poem and of its analysis, is not at all like reading a list; one wants as far as clarity will allow to say things in the form in which they will be remembered when properly digested. People remember a complex notion as a sort of feeling that involves facts and judgments; one cannot give or state the feeling directly, any more than the feeling of being able to ride a bicycle; it is the result of a capacity, though it might be acquired perhaps by reading a list. But to state the fact and the judgment (the thought and the feeling) separately, as two different relevant matters, is a bad way of suggesting how they are combined; it makes the reader apprehend as two things what he must, in fact, apprehend as one thing. Detailed analysis of this kind might be excellent as psychology, but it would hardly be literary criticism; it would start much further back; and a mere reader of the poem would have to read a great deal of it to get the information he wanted.

This notion of unity is of peculiar importance; not only, though chiefly, in poetry, but in all literature and most conversation. One may remember, rather as a comparison than as an explanation, what Pavlov found in the brains of his dogs; that stimulation of a particular region produced inhibition, almost immediately, over regions in the neighbourhood, and at the region itself a moment later. Thus to say a thing in two parts is different in incalculable ways from saying it as a unit; Coleridge says somewhere that the mind insists on having a single word for a single mental operation, and will use an inadequate word rather than two adequate ones. When you are holding a variety of things in your mind, or using for a single matter a variety of intellectual machinery, the only way of applying all your criteria is to apply them simultaneously; the only way of forcing the reader to grasp your total meaning is to arrange that he can only feel satisfied if he is bearing all the elements in mind at the moment of conviction; the only way of not giving something heterogeneous is to give something which is at every point a compound.

(William Empson, *Seven Types of Ambiguity* (1930; London: Penguin, 1961), pp. 238–9.)

(G) LEO SPITZER

Linguistics and Literary History (1948)

Thus, what has been disclosed by the study of Rabelais' language, the literary study would corroborate; it could not be otherwise, since language is only one outward crystallization of the 'inward form,' or, to use another metaphor: the life-blood of the poetic creation is everywhere the same, whether we tap the organism at 'language' or 'ideas,' at 'plot' or at 'composition.' As regards the last, I could as well have begun with a study of the rather loose literary composition of Rabelais' writings and only later have gone over to his ideas, his plot, his language. Because I happened to be a linguist it was from the linguistic angle that I started, to fight my way to his unity. Obviously, no fellow scholar must be required to do the same. What he must be asked to do, however, is, I believe, to work from the surface

to the 'inward life-center' of the work of art: first observing
details about the superficial appearance of the particular work
(and the 'ideas' expressed by a poet are, also, only one of the
superficial traits in a work of art); then, grouping these details
and seeking to integrate them into a creative principle which
may have been present in the soul of the artist; and, finally,
making the return trip to all the other groups of observations in
order to find whether the 'inward form' one has tentatively
constructed gives an account of the whole. The scholar will
surely be able to state, after three or four of these 'fro voyages,'
whether he has found the life-giving center, the sun of the solar
system (by then he will know whether he is really permanently
installed in the center, or whether he finds himself in an
'excentric' or peripheric position). There is no shadow of truth
in the objection raised not long ago by one of the representatives
of the mechanist Yale school of linguists against the 'circularity
of arguments' of the mentalists: against the 'explanation of a
linguistic fact by an assumed psychological process for which the
only evidence is the fact to be explained.' I could immediately
reply that my school is not satisfied with psychologizing one trait
but bases its assumptions on several traits carefully grouped and
integrated; one should, in fact, embrace *all* the linguistic traits
observable with a given author. [. . .] And the circle of which
the adversary just quoted speaks is not a vicious one; on the
contrary, it is the basic operation in the humanities, the *Zirkel im
Verstehen* as Dilthey has termed the discovery, made by the
Romantic scholar and theologian Schleiermacher, that
cognizance in philology is reached not only by the gradual
progression from one detail to another detail, but by the
anticipation or divination of the whole – because 'the detail can
be understood only by the whole and any explanation of detail
presupposes the understanding of the whole.' Our to-and-fro
voyage from certain outward details to the inner center and back
again to other series of details is only an application of the
principle of the 'philological circle'. [. . .] My personal way has
been from the observed detail to ever broadening units which
rest, to an increasing degree, on speculation. It is, I think, the
philological, the inductive way, which seeks to show significance
in the apparently futile, in contrast to the deductive procedure
which begins with units assumed as given – and which is rather
the way followed by the theologians who start from on high, to
take the downward path toward the earthly maze of detail, or by
the mathematicians, who treat their axioms as if these were

God-given. In philology, which deals with the all-too-human, with the interrelated and the intertwined aspects of human affairs, the deductive method has its place only as a verification of the principle found by induction – which rests on observation.

But, of course, the attempt to discover significance in the detail, the habit of taking a detail of language as seriously as the meaning of a work of art – or, in other words, the attitude which sees all manifestations of man as equally serious – this is an outgrowth of the preestablished firm conviction, the 'axiom,' of the philologian, that details are not an inchoate chance aggregation of dispersed material through which no light shines. The philologian must believe in the existence of some light from on high, of some *post nubila Phoebus*. If he did not know that at the end of his journey there would be awaiting him a life-giving draught from some *dive bouteille*, he would not have commenced it: 'Tu ne me chercherais pas si tu ne m'avais pas déjà trouvé,' says Pascal's God. Thus, humanistic thought, in spite of the methodological distinction just made, is not so completely divorced from that of the theologian as is generally believed; it is not by chance that the 'philological circle' was discovered by a theologian, who was wont to harmonize the discordant, to retrace the beauty of God in this world. This attitude is reflected in the word coined by Schleiermacher: *Weltanschauung*: 'die Welt anschauen': 'to see, to cognize the universe *in its sensuous detail*. [. . .]

Why do I insist that it is impossible to offer the reader a step-by-step rationale to be applied to a work of art? For one reason, that the first step, on which all may hinge, can never be planned: it must already have taken place. This first step is the awareness of having been struck by a detail, followed by a conviction that this detail is connected basically with the work of art; it means that one has made an 'observation,' – which is the starting point of a theory, that one has been prompted to raise a question – which must find an answer. To begin by omitting this first step must doom any attempt at interpretation – as was the case with the dissertation [. . . .] devoted to the 'imagery' of Diderot, in which the concept 'imagery' was based on no preliminary observation but on a ready-made category applied from without to the work of art.

Unfortunately, I know of no way to guarantee either the 'impression' or the conviction just described: they are the results of talent, experience, and faith. And, even then, the first step is not to be taken at our own volition: how often, with all the theoretical experience of method accumulated in me over the years, have I stared blankly, quite similar to one of my beginning students, at a page that would not yield its magic. The only way leading out of this state of unproductivity is to read and reread, patiently and confidently, in an endeavor to become, as it were, soaked through and through with the atmosphere of the work. And suddenly, one word, one line, stands out, and we realize that, now, a relationship has been established between the poem and us. From this point on, I have usually found that, what with other observations adding themselves to the first, and with previous experiences of the circle intervening, and with associations given by previous education building up before me (all of this quickened, in my own case, by a quasi-metaphysical urge toward solution) it does not seem long until the characteristic 'click' occurs, which is the indication that detail and whole have found a common denominator – which gives the etymology of the writing. [. . .] For every poem the critic needs a separate inspiration, a separate light from above (it is this constant need which makes for humility, and it is the accumulation of past enlightenments that encourages a sort of pious confidence). Indeed, a Protean mutability is required of the critic, for the device which has proved successful for one work of art cannot be applied mechanically to another. [. . .] The mutability required of the critic can be gained only by repeated experiences with totally different writers; the 'click' will come oftener and more quickly after several experiences of 'clicks' have been realized by the critic. And, even then, it is not a foregone conclusion that it will inevitably come; nor can one ever foretell just when and where it will materialize ('The Spirit bloweth . . .').

(Leo Spitzer, *Linguistics and Literary History* (Princeton, NJ: Princeton UP, 1948), pp. 18–20, 23–4, 26–7, 28.)

(H) GEORGES POULET

'Criticism and the Experience of Interiority' (1966)

Now what happens when I read a book? Am I then the subject of a series of predications which are not *my* predications? That is impossible, perhaps even a contradiction in terms. I feel sure that as soon as I think something, that something becomes in some indefinable way my own. Whatever I think is a part of *my* mental world. And yet here I am thinking a thought which manifestly belongs to another mental world, which is being thought in me just as though I did not exist. Already the notion is inconceivable and seems even more so if I reflect that, since every thought must have a subject to think it, this *thought* which is alien to me and yet in me, must also have in me a *subject* which is alien to me. It all happens, then, as though reading were the act by which a thought managed to bestow itself within me with a subject not myself. Whenever I read, I mentally pronounce an *I*, and yet the *I* which I pronounce is not myself. This is true even when the hero of a novel is presented in the third person, and even when there is no hero and nothing but reflections or propositions: for as soon as something is presented as *thought*, there has to be a thinking subject with whom, at least for the time being, I identify, forgetting myself, alienated from myself. 'Je est un autre,' said Rimbaud. Another *I*, who has replaced my own, and who will continue to do so as long as I read. Reading is just that: a way of giving way not only to a host of alien words, images, ideas, but also to the very alien principle which utters them and shelters them.

The phenomenon is indeed hard to explain, even to conceive, and yet, once admitted, it explains to me what might otherwise seem even more inexplicable. For how could I explain, without such take-over of my innermost subjective being, the astonishing facility with which I not only understand but even *feel* what I read. When I read as I ought – that is without mental reservation, without any desire to preserve my independence of judgement, and with the total commitment required of any reader – my comprehension becomes intuitive and any feeling proposed to me is immediately assumed by me. In other words, the kind of comprehension in question here is not a movement from the unknown to the known, from the strange to the familiar, from outside to inside. It might rather be called a phenomenon by which mental objects rise up from the depths of consciousness into the light of recognition. On the other hand – and without contradiction – reading implies something resembling the apperception I have of myself, the action by which I grasp straightway what I think as being thought by a subject (who, in this case, is not I). Whatever sort of alienation I may endure, reading does not interrupt my activity as subject.

Reading, then, is the act in which the subjective principle which I call *I*, is modified in such a way that I no longer have the right, strictly speaking, to consider it as my *I*. I am on loan to another, and this other thinks, feels, suffers, and acts within me. The phenomenon appears in its most obvious and even naïvest form in the sort of spell brought about by certain cheap kinds of reading, such as thrillers, of which I say, 'It gripped me.' Now it is important to note that this possession of myself by another takes place not only on the level of objective thought, that is with regard to images, sensations, ideas which reading affords me, but also on the level of my very subjectivity.

When I am absorbed in reading, a second self takes over, a self which thinks and feels for me. Withdrawn in some recess of myself, do I then silently witness this dispossession? Do I derive from it some comfort, or, on the contrary, a kind of anguish? However that may be, someone else holds the center of the stage, and the question which imposes itself, which I am absolutely obliged to ask myself, is this: 'Who is the usurper who occupies the forefront? Who is this mind who alone all by himself fills my consciousness and who, when I say *I*, is indeed that *I*?'

There is an immediate answer to this question, perhaps too easy an answer. This *I* who 'thinks in me' when I read a book, is the *I* of the one who writes the book. When I read Baudelaire or Racine, it is really Baudelaire or Racine who thinks, feels, allows himself to be read within me. Thus a book is not only a book, it is the means by which an author actually preserves his ideas, his feelings, his modes of dreaming and living. It is his means of saving his identity from death. Such an interpretation of reading is not false. It seems to justify what is commonly called the biographical explication of literary texts. Indeed every word of literature is impregnated with the mind of the one who wrote it. As he makes us read it, he awakens in us the analogue of what he thought or felt. To understand a literary work, then, is to let the individual who wrote it reveal himself to us *in* us. It is not the biography which explicates the work, but rather the work which sometimes enables us to understand the biography.

(Georges Poulet, 'Criticism and the Experience of Interiority', *The Structuralist Controversy*, ed. Richard Macksey and Eugenio Donato (Chicago and London: Chicago UP, 1972), pp. 59–61.)

(I) E. D. HIRSCH, JR

The Aims of Interpretation (1976)

In resisting some claims of current 'metaphysical hermeneutics' I must admit to at least one metaphysical assertion: an interpreter is not necessarily so trapped in historicity that he loses his freedom; he is free to choose his aims, and within the context of those aims and the broad conventions of language, he is free to choose his meanings. I therefore understand the current controversy over historicity as a conflict not of abstract theories, but of values. When we are urged to adopt present relevance rather than original meaning as the 'best meaning,' we find ourselves repeating the old pattern of controversy between the medieval allegorists (the Heideggerians of an earlier day) and the later humanists. While this conflict cannot be resolved by mere analysis, its issues can be clarified, and clarification may bring unforeseen agreement.

Sometimes, for instance, the conflict between proponents of original and of anachronistic meaning is shown by analysis to be no conflict at all. These arguments about meaning sometimes originate in a failure to notice that meaning and significance – two different things – are being given the same name. [. . .]

For some time now literary theorists, particularly the New Critics, have attempted to preserve this distinction under a different guise, and have deplored the use of biographical or historical information for restricting textual meaning to its original historical or biographical circumstances. Even if Shakespeare had written *Richard II* to support the rebellion of Essex (which of course he didn't) that wouldn't limit the meaning of the play to its original application. When the followers of Essex brought out the play's significance to their political aims, however, no great violence was done to its original meaning. Nor would any important distortion result from documents that showed autobiographical impulses in Shakespeare's portrayal of Richard. Modern applications of Shakespeare's original meaning could be equally innocent of distortive influence. For a self-identical meaning (original or anachronistic, simple or complex) has the great advantage of flexibility; being very sure of itself, of its self-identity, it can enter new worlds and play new roles with confidence.

If one resists confusing meaning and significance, one gets the impression that most controversies in interpretation do not really involve a conflict over original meaning versus anachronistic meaning. Usually the debates can be readily transposed into disagreement over the proper *emphases* of an interpretation, over whether it is better to explain original meaning or to bring out some aspect of the significance of meaning, for the interpreter or for present-day readers. The followers of Essex took the second course, without necessarily distorting Shakespeare's meaning. [. . .] In examples like these, original meaning is tacitly assumed even while original significance is ignored. Whenever interpretive conflicts are concerned only with emphasis in the conduct of a commentary, then they are conflicts about immediate aims and not about meanings. Most interpreters retain a respect for original meaning, and recognition of this might mollify some of our disagreements.

No doubt, what I am saying could never bring together certain extreme controversialists like Roland Barthes and Raymond Picard who have recently acted out the old dilemmas of original versus anachronistic meaning in their polemics over Racine. What can one say by way of reconciliation if Barthes claims to be uninterested in Racine's original meaning, and Picard argues that Racine could not have meant what Barthes construes from the texts? It is difficult for a non-specialist to judge the true facts of this noted case, but I have the impression that the controversy provides an unusually pure modern example of the rival claims between original and anachronistic meaning. Most recent conflicts between ancients like Picard and moderns like Barthes are not so clearly drawn, since most of us would be chagrined to learn that we had made elementary mistakes in construing the language of an early period, and our very embarrassment would indicate that we recognized the co-equal and harmonious claims of original meaning and modern significance, even if Barthes does not. At the same time, most interpreters would reject the opposite excess (even if Picard does not) of ignoring the difference between original meaning and original significance, an oversight that is the occupational vice of antiquarians.

[. . .] [L]et me state what I consider to be a fundamental ethical maxim for interpretation, a maxim that claims no privileged sanction from metaphysics or analysis, but only from general ethical tenets, generally shared. *Unless there is a powerful overriding value in disregarding an author's intention (i.e., original meaning), we who interpret as a vocation should not disregard it.* Mere individual preference would not be such an overriding value, nor would be the mere preferences of many persons. [. . .]

I am not impressed with the view that this ethical imperative of speech, to which we all submit in ordinary discourse, is not applicable to written speech or, in particular, to literary texts. No literary theorist from Coleridge to the present has succeeded in formulating a viable distinction between the nature of ordinary written speech and the nature of literary written speech. For reasons I shall not pause to detail in this place, I believe the distinction can never be successfully formulated, and the futility of attempting the distinction will come to be generally recognized. Moreover, if it is seen that there is no viable distinction between 'literature' and other classifications of written speech, it will also come to be recognized that the ethics of language hold good in all uses of language, oral and written, in poetry as well as in philosophy. All are ethically governed by the intentions of the author. To treat an author's words merely as grist for one's own mill is ethically analogous to using another man merely for one's own purposes. I do not say such ruthlessness of interpretation is never justifiable in principle, but I cannot imagine an occasion where it would be justifiable in the professional practice of interpretation. The peculiarly modern anarchy of every man for himself in matters of interpretation may sound like the ultimate victory of the Protestant spirit. Actually, such anarchy is the direct consequence of transgressing the fundamental ethical norms of speech and its interpretation.

(E. D. Hirsch, *The Aims of Interpretation* (Chicago and London: Chicago UP, 1976), pp. 85, 87–9, 90–1.)

(J) HANS ROBERT JAUSS

'Literary History as a Challenge to Literary Theory' (1970)

Thesis 1. A renewal of literary history demands the removal of the prejudices of historical objectivism and the grounding of the traditional aesthetics of production and representation in an aesthetics of reception and influence. The historicity of literature rests not on an organization of 'literary facts' that is established *post festum*, but rather on the preceding experience of the literary work by its readers.

R. G. Collingwood's postulate, posed in his critique of the prevailing ideology of objectivity in history – 'History is nothing but the re-enactment of past thought in the historian's mind' – is even more valid for literary history. For the positivistic view of history as the 'objective' description of a series of events in an isolated past neglects the artistic character as well as the specific historicity of literature. A literary work is not an object that stands by itself and that offers the same view to each reader in each period. It is not a monument that monologically reveals its timeless essence. It is much more like an orchestration that strikes ever new resonances among its readers and that frees the text from the material of the words and brings it to a contemporary existence: 'words that must, at the same tim that they speak to him, create an interlocutor capable of understanding them.' This dialogical character of the literary work also establishes why philological understanding can exist only in a perpetual confrontation with the text, and cannot be allowed to be reduced to a knowledge of facts. Philological understanding always remains related to interpretation that must set as its goal, along with learning about the object, the reflection on and description of the completion of this knowledge as a moment of new understanding.

History of literature is a process of aesthetic reception and production that takes place in the realization of literary texts on the part of the receptive reader, the reflective critic, and the author in his continuing productivity. The endlessly growing sum of literary 'facts' that winds up in the conventional literary histories is merely left over from this process; it is only the collected and classified past and therefore not history at all, but pseudo-history. Anyone who considers a series of such literary facts as a piece of the history of literature confuses the eventful character of a work of art with that of historical matter-of-factness. The *Perceval* of Chrétien de Troyes, as a literary event, is not 'historical' in the same sense as, for example, the Third Crusade, which was occurring at about the same time. It is not a 'fact' that could be explained as caused by a series of situational preconditions and motives, by the intent of a historical action as it can be reconstructed, and by the necessary and secondary consequences of this deed. The historical context in which a literary work appears is not a factical, independent series of events that exists apart from an observer. *Perceval* becomes a literary event only for its reader, who reads this last work of Chrétien with a memory of his earlier works and who recognizes its individuality in comparison with these and other works that he already knows, so that he gains a new criterion for evaluating future works. In contrast to a political event, a literary event has no unavoidable consequences subsisting on their own that no succeeding generation can ever escape. A literary event can continue to have an effect only if those who come after it still or once again respond to it – if there are readers who again appropriate the past work or authors who want to imitate, outdo, or refute it. The coherence of literature as an event is primarily mediated in the horizon of expectations of the literary experience of contemporary and later readers, critics, and authors. Whether it is possible to comprehend and represent the history of literature in its unique historicity depends on whether this horizon of expectations can be objectified.

Thesis 2. The analysis of the literary experience of the reader avoids the threatening pitfalls of psychology if it describes the reception and the influence of a work within the objectifiable system of expectations that arises for each work in the historical moment of its appearance, from a pre-understanding of the genre, from the form and themes of already familiar works, and from the opposition between poetic and practical language [. . .]

A literary work, even when it appears to be new, does not present itself as something absolutely new in an informational vacuum, but predisposes its audience to a very specific kind of reception by announcements, overt and covert signals, familiar characteristics, or implicit allusions. It awakens memories of that which was already read, brings the reader to a specific emotional attitude, and with its beginning arouses expectations for the 'middle and end,' which can then be maintained intact or altered, reoriented, or even fulfilled ironically in the course of the reading according to specific rules of the genre or type of text. The psychic process in the reception of a text is, in the primary horizon of aesthetic experience, by no means only an arbitrary series of merely subjective impressions, but rather the carrying out of specific instructions in a process of directed perception, which can be comprehended according to its constitutive motivations and triggering signals, and which also can be described by a textual linguistics. [. . .]

A corresponding process of the continuous establishing and altering of horizons also determines the relationship of the individual text to the succession of texts that forms the genre.

The new text evokes for the reader (listener) the horizon of expectations and rules familiar from earlier texts, which are then varied, corrected, altered, or even just reproduced. Variation and correction determine the scope, whereas alteration and reproduction determine the borders of a genre-structure. The interpretative reception of a text always presupposes the context of experience of aesthetic perception: the question of the subjectivity of the interpretation and of the taste of different readers or levels of readers can be asked meaningfully only when one has first clarified which transsubjective horizon of understanding conditions the influence of the text. [. . .]

Thesis 3. Reconstructed in this way, the horizon of expectations of a work allows one to determine its artistic character by the kind and the degree of its influence on a presupposed audience. If one characterizes as aesthetic distance the disparity between the given horizon of expectations and the appearance of a new work, whose reception can result in a 'change of horizons' through negation of familiar experiences or through raising newly articulated experiences to the level of consciousness, then this aesthetic distance can be objectified historically along the spectrum of the audience's reactions and criticism's judgment (spontaneous success, rejection or shock, scattered approval, gradual or belated understanding).

The way in which a literary work, at the historical moment of its appearance, satisfies, surpasses, disappoints, or refutes the expectations of its first audience obviously provides a criterion for the determination of its aesthetic value. The distance between the horizon of expectations and the work, between the familiarity of previous aesthetic experience and the 'horizonal change' demanded by the reception of the new work, determines the artistic character of a literary work, according to an aesthetics of reception: to the degree that this distance decreases, and no turn toward the horizon of yet-unknown experience is demanded of the receiving consciousness, the closer the work comes to the sphere of 'culinary' or entertainment art [*Unterhaltungskunst*]. This latter work can be characterized by an aesthetics of reception as not demanding any horizonal change, but rather as precisely fulfilling the expectations prescribed by a ruling standard of taste, in that it satisfies the desire for the reproduction of the familiarly beautiful; confirms familiar sentiments; sanctions wishful notions; makes unusual experiences enjoyable as 'sensations'; or even raises moral problems, but only to 'solve them in an edifying manner as predecided questions. If, conversely, the artistic character of a work is to be measured by the aesthetic distance with which it opposes the expectations of its first audience, then it follows that this distance, at first experienced as a pleasing or alienating new perspective, can disappear for later readers, to the extent that the original negativity of the work has become self-evident and has itself entered into the horizon of future aesthetic experience, as a henceforth familiar expectation. The classical character of the so-called masterworks especially belongs to this second horizonal change; their beautiful form that has become self-evident, and their seemingly unquestionable 'eternal meaning' bring them, according to an aesthetics of reception, dangerously close to the irresistibly convincing and enjoyable 'culinary' art, so that it requires a special effort to read them 'against the grain' of the accustomed experience to catch sight of their artistic character once again.

The relationship between literature and audience includes more than the facts that every work has its own specific, historically and sociologically determinable audience, that every writer is dependent on the milieu, views, and ideology of his audience, and that literary success presupposes a book 'which expresses what the group expects, a book which presents the group with its own image.' This objectivist determination of literary success according to the congruence of the work's intention with the expectations of a social group always leads literary sociology into a dilemma whenever later or ongoing influence is to be explained. Thus R. Escarpit wants to presuppose a 'collective basis in space or time' for the 'illusion of the lasting quality' of a writer, which in the case of Molière leads to an astonishing prognosis: 'Molière is still young for the Frenchman of the twentieth century because his world still lives, and a sphere of culture, views, and language still binds us to him . . . But the sphere becomes even smaller, and Molière will age and die when the things which our culture still has in common with the France of Molière die' (p. 117). As if Molière had only mirrored the 'mores of his time' and had only remained successful through this supposed intention! Where the congruence between work and social group does not exist, or no longer exists, as for example with the reception of a work in a foreign language, Escarpit is able to help himself by inserting a 'myth' in between: 'myths that are invented by a later world for which the reality that they substitute for has become alien'

(p. 111). As if all reception beyond the first, socially determined audience for a work were only a 'distorted echo,' only a result of 'subjective myths,' and did not itself have its objective a priori once again in the received work as the limit and possibility of later understanding! The sociology of literature does not view its object dialectically enough when it determines the circle of author, work, and audience so one-sidedly. The determination is reversible: there are works that at the moment of their appearance are not yet directed at any specific audience, but that break through the familiar horizon of literary expectations so completely that an audience can only gradually develop for them. When, then, the new horizon of expectations has achieved more general currency, the power of the altered aesthetic norm can be demonstrated in that the audience experiences formerly successful works as outmoded, and withdraws its appreciation. Only in view of such horizonal change does the analysis of literary influence achieve the dimension of a literary history of readers, and do the statistical curves of the bestsellers provide historical knowledge. [. . .]

Thesis 4. The reconstruction of the horizon of expectations, in the face of which a work was created and received in the past, enables one on the other hand to pose questions that the text gave an answer to, and thereby to discover how the contemporary reader could have viewed and understood the work. This approach corrects the mostly unrecognized norms of a classicist or modernizing understanding of art, and avoids the circular recourse to a general 'spirit of the age'. It brings to view the hermeneutic difference between the former and the current understanding of a work; it raises to consciousness the history of its reception, which mediates both positions; and it thereby calls into question as a platonizing dogma of philological metaphysics the apparently self-evident claims that in the literary text, literature [Dichtung] is eternally present, and that its objective meaning, determined once and for all, is at all times immediately accessible to the interpreter. [. . .]

In *Truth and Method* Hans-Georg Gadamer, whose critique of historical objectivism I am assuming here, described the principle of the history of influence, which seeks to present the reality of history in understanding itself, as an application of the logic of question and answer to the historical tradition. In a continuation of Collingwood's thesis that 'one can understand a text only when one has understood the question to which it is an answer,' Gadamer demonstrates that the reconstructed question can no longer stand within its original horizon because this historical horizon is always already enveloped within the horizon of the present: 'Understanding is always the process of the fusion of these horizons that we suppose to exist by themselves.' The historical question cannot exist for itself; it must merge with the question 'that the tradition is for us.' One thereby solves the question with which René Wellek described the aporia of literary judgment: should the philologist evaluate a literary work according to the perspective of the past, the standpoint of the present, or the 'verdict of the ages'? The actual standards of a past could be so narrow that their use would only make poorer a work that in the history of its influence had unfolded a rich semantic potential. The aesthetic judgment of the present would favor a canon of works that correspond to modern taste, but would unjustly evaluate all other works only because their function in their time is no longer evident. And the history of influence itself, as instructive as it might be, is as 'authority open to the same objections as the authority of the author's contemporaries.' Wellek's conclusion – that there is no possibility of avoiding our own judgment; one must only make this judgment as objective as possible in that one does what every scholar does, namely, 'isolate the object' – is no solution to the aporia, but rather a relapse into objectivism. The 'verdict of the ages' on a literary work is more than merely 'the accumulated judgment of other readers, critics, viewers, and even professors'; it is the successive unfolding of the potential for meaning that is embedded in a work and actualized in the stages of its historical reception as it discloses itself to understanding judgment, so long as this faculty achieves in a controlled fashion the 'fusion of horizons' in the encounter with the tradition.

(Hans Robert Jauss, *Toward an Aesthetic of Reception*, trans. Timothy Bahti (Brighton: Harvester Press, 1982), pp. 20–2, 23, 25–7, 28, 29–30, 34–6. Original German: Suhrkamp Verlag, 1970.)

(K) PAUL RICOEUR

Hermeneutics and the Human Sciences (1981)

Here I shall say that the notion of subject must be submitted to critique parallel to that which the theory of metaphor

exercises on the notion of object. In fact, it is the same
philosophical error which must be taken by its two extremities:
objectivity as confronting the subject, the subject as
reigning over objectivity.

At this stage, everything gained from the critique of the
illusions of the subject must be integrated into hermeneutics.
This critique, which I see conducted in either a Freudian or a
Marxist tradition, constitutes the modern form of the critique of
'prejudice'.

According to the Marxist tradition, the critique of the subject
is one aspect of the general theory of ideology. Our
understanding is based on prejudices which are linked to our
position in the power relations of society, a position which is
partially unknown to us. Moreover, we are propelled to act by
hidden interests. Whence the falsification of reality. Thus the
critique of 'false consciousness' becomes an integral part of
hermeneutics. Here I see the place for a necessary dialogue
between hermeneutics and the theory of ideology as developed,
for instance, by Habermas.

According to the Freudian tradition, the critique of the subject
is one part of the critique of 'illusions'. Here I am interested in
psychoanalysis, not as a grid for reading a text, but as the self-
criticism of the reader, as the purification of the act of
appropriation. In *Freud and Philosophy*, I spoke of an effect of self-
analysis which I called the relinquishment of the subject. As
Freud said, the subject is not master in his own house. This
critique is addressed to what could be called the 'narcissism of
the reader': to find only oneself in a text, to impose and
rediscover onself.

Relinquishment is a fundamental moment of appropriation
and distinguishes it from any form of 'taking possession'.
Appropriation is also and primarily a 'letting-go'. Reading is an
appropriation-divestiture. How can this letting-go, this
relinquishment, be incorporated into appropriation? Essentially
by linking appropriation to the revelatory power of the text
which we have described as its referential dimension. It is in
allowing itself to be carried off towards the reference of the text
that the *ego* divests itself of itself. [. . .]

The link between appropriation and revelation is, in my view,
the cornerstone of a hermeneutics which seeks both to overcome
the failures of historicism and to remain faithful to the original
intention of Schleiermacher's hermeneutics. To understand an
author better than he understood himself is to unfold the

revelatory power implicit in his discourse, beyond the limited horizon of his own existential situation.

On this basis, it is possible to refute fallacious views about the concept of interpretation. In the first place, appropriation does not imply any direct congeniality of one soul with another. Nothing is less intersubjective or dialogical than the encounter with a text; what Gadamer calls the 'fusion of horizons' expresses the convergence of the *world* horizons of the writer and the reader. The ideality of the text remains the mediator in this process of the fusion of horizons.

According to another fallacious view, the hermeneutical task would be governed by the original audience's understanding of the text. As Gadamer has firmly demonstrated, this is a complete mistake: the Letters of Saint Paul are no less addressed to me than to the Romans, the Galatians, the Corinthians, etc. Only dialogue has a 'you', whose identification proceeds from the dialogue itself. If the meaning of a text is open to anyone who can read, then it is the omni-temporality of meaning which opens it to unknown readers; and the historicity of reading is the counterpart of this specific omni-temporality. From the moment that the text escapes from its author and from his situation, it also escapes from its original audience. Hence it can procure new readers for itself.

According to a third fallacious view, the appropriation of the meaning of a text would subsume interpretation to the finite capacities of understanding of a present reader. The English and French translation of *Aneignung* by 'appropriation' reinforces this suspicion. Do we not place the meaning of the text under the domination of the subject who interprets? This objection can be dismissed by observing that what is 'made our own' is not something mental, not the intention of another subject, nor some design supposedly hidden behind the text; rather, it is the projection of a world, the proposal of a mode of being-in-the-world, which the text discloses in front of itself by means of its non-ostensive references. Far from saying that a subject, who already masters his own being-in-the-world, projects the *a priori* of his own understanding and interpolates this *a priori* in the text, I shall say that appropriation is the process by which the revelation of new modes of being – or, if you prefer Wittgenstein to Heidegger, new 'forms of life' – *gives* the subject new capacities for knowing himself. If the reference of a text is the projection of a world, then it is not in the first instance the reader who projects himself. The reader is rather broadened in his capacity to project himself by receiving a new mode of being from the text itself.

Thus appropriation ceases to appear as a kind of possession, as a way of taking hold of . . . It implies instead a moment of dispossession of the narcissistic *ego*. This process of dispossession is the work of the sort of universality and atemporality implied by the explanatory procedures. Only the interpretation which satisfies the injunction of the text, which follows the 'arrow' of meaning and endeavours to 'think in accordance with' it, engenders a new *self*-understanding. By the expression '*self*-understanding', I should like to contrast the *self* which emerges from the understanding of the text to the *ego* which claims to precede this understanding. It is the text, with its universal power of unveiling, which gives a *self* to the *ego*.

(Paul Ricoeur, *Hermeneutics and the Human Sciences* (1981), ed. and trans. John B. Thompson (Cambridge, London, New York: Cambridge UP, 1981), pp. 190–3.)

(L) WOLFGANG ISER

The Act of Reading (1976)

Although it is clear that acts of comprehension are guided by the structures of the text, the latter can never exercise complete control, and this is where one might sense a touch of arbitrariness. However, it must be borne in mind that fictional texts constitute their own objects and do not copy something already in existence. For this reason they cannot have the total determinacy of real objects, and, indeed, it is the elements of indeterminacy that enable the text to 'communicate' with the reader, in the sense that they induce him to participate both in the production and the comprehension of the work's intention. [. . .]

It is generally recognized that literary texts take on their reality by being read, and this in turn means that texts must already contain certain conditions of actualization that will allow their meaning to be assembled in the responsive mind of the recipient. The concept of the implied reader is therefore a textual structure anticipating the presence of a recipient without necessarily defining him: this concept prestructures the role to be assumed by each recipient, and this holds true even when texts deliberately appear to ignore their possible recipient or actively exclude him. Thus the concept of the implied reader designates a network of response-inviting structures, which impel the reader to grasp the text. [. . .]

If we view the relation between text and reader as a kind of self-regulating system, we can define the text itself as an array of sign impulses (signifiers) which are received by the reader. As he reads, there is a constant 'feedback' of 'information' already received, so that he himself is bound to insert his own ideas into the process of communication. This can again be illustrated by the Fielding example. Scarcely has Allworthy made the acquaintance of Captain Blifil, when he is deceived by him. The very fact that he lets himself be duped then has to be fed back into the text as follows: the linguistically denoted perfection lacks certain essential attributes that prevent it from being 'really' perfect. Thus events which were originally unpredictable, in the light of information denoted by the language signs (the name Allworthy, his virtues, his residence in Paradise Hall), now become acceptable, but this process involves two important factors: (1) the reader has constructed a signified which was not denoted by the signifiers, and (2) by doing so, he creates a basic condition of comprehension that enables him to grasp the peculiar nature of the 'perfection' intended by the text. But these signifieds, which the reader himself produces, are constantly changing in the course of his reading. If we stay with the Fielding example, we will find that after the reader has corrected his initial signified, as regards Allworthy's perfection, the latter has to pass judgment on an ambivalent action of Tom's. Instead of judging by appearances – as we would now expect him to do – Allworthy recognizes the hidden motive. This information again has to be fed back into the reader's signified, which must be corrected to the extent that evidently Allworthy is not lacking in judgment when good motives are being thwarted by bad circumstances. Once more, then, an unpredictable event has to be fitted into the overall picture, and in this case the adjustment is all the finer because the reader has had to modify the signified, which he himself had produced. Thus the reader's communication with the text is a dynamic process of self-correction, as he formulates signifieds which he must then continually modify. It is cybernetic in nature as it involves a feedback of effects and information throughout a sequence of changing situational frames; smaller units progressively merge into bigger ones, so that meaning gathers meaning in a kind of snowballing process.

In our attempts to describe the intersubjective structure of the process through which a text is transferred and translated, our first problem is the fact that the whole text can never be perceived at any one time. In this respect it differs from given objects, which can generally be viewed or at least conceived as a whole. The object of the text can only be imagined by way of different consecutive phases of reading. We always stand outside the given object, whereas we are situated inside the literary text. The relation between text and reader is therefore quite different from that between object and observer: instead of a subject-object relationship, there is a moving viewpoint which travels along *inside* that which it has to apprehend. This mode of grasping an object is unique to literature.

In describing the inner consciousness of time, Husserl once wrote: 'Every originally constitutent process is inspired by protensions, which construct and collect the seed of what is to come, as such, and bring it to fruition.' This remark draws attention to an elementary factor which plays a central part in the reading process. The semantic pointers of individual sentences always imply an expectation of some kind – Husserl calls these expectations 'protensions.' As this structure is inherent in *all* intentional sentence correlates, it follows that their interplay will lead not so much to the fulfillment of expectations as to their continual modification. Now herein lies a basic structure of the wandering viewpoint. The reader's position in the text is at the point of intersection between retention and protension. Each individual sentence correlate prefigures a particular horizon, but this is immediately transformed into the background for the next correlate and must therefore necessarily be modified. Since each sentence correlate aims at things to come, the prefigured horizon will offer a view which – however concrete it may be – must contain indeterminacies, and so arouse expectations as to the manner in which these are to be resolved. Each new correlate, then, will answer expectations (either positively or negatively) and, at the same time, will arouse new expectations. As far as the sequence of sentences is concerned, there are two fundamentally different possibilities. If the new correlate begins to confirm the expectations aroused by its predecessor, the range of possible semantic horizons will be correspondingly narrowed. This is normally the case with texts that are to describe a particular object, for their concern is to narrow the range in order to bring out the individuality of that object. In most literary texts, however, the sequence of sentences is so structured that the correlates serve to modify and even frustrate the expectations they have aroused. In so doing, they automatically have a retroactive effect on what has already been read, which now appears quite different. Furthermore, what has been read shrinks in the memory to a foreshortened background, but it is being constantly evoked in a new context and so modified by new correlates that instigate a restructuring of past syntheses. This does not mean that the past returns in full to the present, for then memory and perception would become indistinguishable, but it does mean that memory undergoes a transformation. That which is remembered becomes open to new connections, and these in turn influence the expectations aroused by the individual correlates in the sequence of sentences.

It is clear, then, that throughout the reading process there is a continual interplay between modified expectations and transformed memories. However, the text itself does not formulate expectations or their modification; nor does it specify how the connectability of memories is to be implemented. This is the province of the reader himself, and so here we have a first insight into how the synthetizing activity of the reader enables the text to be translated and transferred to his own mind. This process of translation also shows up the basic hermeneutic structure of reading. Each sentence correlate contains what one might call a hollow section, which looks forward to the next correlate, and a retrospective section, which answers the expectations of the preceding sentence (now part of the remembered background). Thus every moment of reading is a dialectic of protension and retention, conveying a future horizon yet to be occupied, along with a past (and continually fading) horizon already filled, the wandering viewpoint carves its passage through both at the same time and leaves them to merge together in its wake. There is no escaping this process, for – as has already been pointed out – the text cannot at any one moment be grasped as a whole. But what may at first sight have seemed like a disadvantage, in comparison with our normal modes of perception, may now be seen to offer distinct advantages, in so far as it permits a process through which the aesthetic object is constantly being structured and restructured. As there is no definite frame of reference to regulate this process, successful communication must ultimately depend on the reader's creative activity.

(Wolfgang Iser, *The Act of Reading* (London and Henley: Routledge & Kegan Paul, 1978), pp. 24, 34, 67, 108–9, 110–12. Original German: *Der Akt des Lesens* (Munich, 1976).

(M) NORMAN HOLLAND

5 Readers Reading (1975)

'The *perception* of the "whole person,"' says Lichtenstein, summing up his own conception of this kind of interpretation of a personality, 'means the process of abstracting an invariant from the multitude of [bodily and behavioral transformations during the whole life of the individual]. This invariant, when perceived in our encounter with another individual, we describe as the individual's "personality"' – or 'myth' or 'humour' or 'character' or 'ego identity' or 'lifestyle' or *'mythe personnel'* or 'identity theme'. [. . .]

Once a person's identity theme is established it never changes, however. (Lichtenstein goes so far as to argue the 'identity principle' is prior even to man's drive for pleasure. To give up identity one would have to become a thing – die.) At the same time, the individual can grow and change infinitely within that style. Similarly, the individual's theme is (probably) not in and of itself healthy or unhealthy – only what he does with it. [. . .] To analyze the five readers' readings, I brought to bear four principles, each of which is really only an aspect of one basic principle: *a reader responds to a literary work by assimilating it to his own psychological processes, that is, to his search for successful solutions within his identity theme to the multiple demands, both inner and outer, on his ego.* Now, I can accent different facets of this one basic principle to talk about four different phases of reading. I can consider the identity theme as a kind of mime to think about the way a reader has to make what he reads match his defensive and adaptive capacities, shaping it until it will fit. Alternatively, I can accent the reader's characteristic kinds of pleasure in considering the way, once in, he uses the literary work as a source of pleasure, projecting into it the particular kind of fantasy that unconsciously gratifies him. When he transforms that fantasy to themes that are of particular concern to him, I can use his identity theme to define his characteristic transformations. Then, in considering his moment-by-moment reading, I can speak of the reader's characteristic expectations, again in terms of his identity theme.

One can also think of these four principles in terms of two broad modalities: taking external reality into and then using it within the ongoing psychological life of the organism. Taking in outside realities, we have seen, involves the ability to give up imaginary satisfactions and really act on one's environment. Hence, it calls for problem-solving thought and a defensive attention to danger. Using what has been taken in, however, is much more primitive, much more a matter of fantasy, immediate gratification, and feelings of omnipotence uncorrected by the external world. One mode is alert and wary, the other relaxed and open to gratification, although both are variations on the basic identity theme through which we take in all external realities.

If we absorb literature like the rest of the outer world, through adaptations that protect gratification in terms of one particular identity theme, then we respond to statements about literature the same way.

(Norman Holland, *5 Readers Reading* (New Haven and London: Yale UP, 1975), pp. 57, 60, 209–10.)

(N) DAVID BLEICH

Subjective Criticism (1978)

The idea of resymbolization is both an explanation of language use and an explanation of explanation. It explains the linguistic report of facts in terms of the motives of the reporter, and it explains the accepted explanation of acts in terms of the motives of those seeking the explanation. The many linguistic functions, in all disciplines and among all people, may be understood as originating in different motives which eventuate in the same mental act of resymbolization. But following the formulation of Cassirer and Langer, symbolic activity other than language may be conceived as similarly motivated. The symbolic formalism of the arts, the humanities, and the quantitative sciences can be most fruitfully understood in terms of the motives of those who create and use it, with special regard for individual and communal occasions of creation and response.

When scientific explanation follows from the acceptance of a paradigm, this paradigm is constituted by a communal motive; mathematical formalism is an instrument of this motive. Mathematical systems resymbolize those experiences which the original belief in the paradigm has deemed 'presently adaptive to understand.' Artistic expression and historical explanation likewise proceed from communal motives, represented by styles or schools, but the local formalism is color or words rather than mathematics. My linguistically articulated response to a work of art is just as much a symbolic explanation of experience as are Newton's laws of motion. The structure of motivation in each case is different, but both explanations are motivated resymbolizations.

The distinction between symbolization and resymbolization corresponds, respectively, to the use of language as simple denotation and as complex explanation. Symbolization involves ordinary acts of naming and predication of the elementary sort first learned by infants. Resymbolization refers to the mentation performed in conscious response to rudimentary symbolizations. When we become aware that a symbolic objectification system is unsatisfactory, we try to resymbolize or explain it. As Kuhn discusses, such explanation can actually change the object of attention from, say (to use his examples), a swinging stone into a pendulum or Euclidian space into Riemannian space. The motive for such important changes grows from personal and communal subjectivity. Resymbolization rewords (or reworks) established symbols in a direction more adaptive to present needs. [. . .] The subjective paradigm, in emphasizing the distinction between real objects, symbolic objects, and subjects (i.e., people), holds that only subjects are capable of initiating action and that the most fundamental form of that action is the motivated division of experience into those three classes. The distinction a subject feels between himself and the symbols he uses is the basis of sanity and conscious functioning. Symbols are the subjective correlatives of experience, just as the name *myself* is the symbol of the feeling and awareness of self. Because the reader is actually dealing with his symbolization of the text, knowledge of the reading experience has to begin with that subjective dialectic. The most that a reader can do with the real object, the text, is to see it. Readers of the same text will agree that their sensorimotor experience of the text is the same. They may also agree that the nominal meaning of the words is the same for each of them. Beyond these agreements, the only consensus about a text is on its role as a symbolic object, which means that further discussion of this text is predicated on each reader's symbolization and resymbolization of it. These two actions by the reader convert the text into a literary work. Therefore, discussion of the work must refer to the subjective syntheses of the reader and not to the reader's interaction with the text.

(David Bleich, *Subjective Criticism* (Baltimore and London: Johns Hopkins UP, 1978), pp. 65–6, 110–11.)

CHAPTER 5

UNCONSCIOUS PROCESSES

Western thought has often recognized that the human mind is a divided kingdom, and that the rational part is in contention with passion, imagination or even divine inspiration. The non-rational forces can be regarded as threatening or beneficent: a dream may be a gift from the gods or an easy opening for Satan. The theories of Freud and Jung not only attempt a systematic study of these non-rational processes, but they assert their primacy in the development of a human life. If our adult selves are determined by unconscious processes, then this clearly has major implications for the study of literature, since in this discursive field above all the unconscious is freely expressed.

Freud argued that the unconscious is a system of 'drives', especially childhood wishes, which is suppressed in the normal course of maturation when the child becomes socialized and accepts the constraints of civilization (especially the sexual constraints). The drives try to assert themselves, but can only express themselves in indirect forms: symptoms, jokes, dreams, when the censorship of the superego is relaxed. Classic psychoanalysis regarded literary texts as symptoms or dreams. That is, they treated the text as if it were the direct expression of the author's psyche. Jacques Lacan's reinterpretation of Freud links the unconscious directly with language: the unconscious arises from the mismatch between language (the symbolic system we enter after infancy) and desire. He uses Saussure's model of language as a system of signs in which signifiers are linked arbitrarily to signifieds (see III,6,C). He adopts Jakobson's ingenious distinction between metaphoric and metonymic dimensions of language (see III,6,H) and shows that dreams are structured by these linguistic processes (paralleled by Freud's 'condensation' and 'displacement').

Julia Kristeva uses psychoanalytic theory in order to privilege poetry in the general order of discourse. She argues that Western thought has persisted in assuming the necessity of a unified 'subject', which is guaranteed and facilitated by the stabilizing medium of *syntax*: an orderly syntax makes for an orderly mind. However, reason has never had things all its own way: pleasure and desire continue to disrupt the clear lines of rationality. A human being is a space across which an indefinite flux of physical and psychic impulses flows and reflows. This flux is gradually regulated from childhood by the constraints of family and society. Beneath the mature adult's controlled linguistic and social performances remains the activity of the prelinguistic flux. Kristeva calls this material 'semiotic', because it works like an unorganized signifying process. The regulation of the semiotic flux produces logic, syntax, and rationality, which she calls 'the symbolic'. Poetry and especially modernist poetry allows the impulses of semiotic desire to emerge and threaten the symbolic. The avant-garde artist and poet challenge tendencies to impose order through repressive structures. Kristeva also notices, disturbingly, that fascism fascinated many of these artists (one thinks of Lawrence and Ezra Pound).

The example of *Hamlet* usefully illustrates the different kinds of Freudian interpretation which are possible. Freud treats Hamlet as a subject for psychoanalysis. He finds in him a conflict between impulse and repression. While Hamlet's instincts (his Oedipal feelings) are repressed he remains 'normal', but once his drives are forced into consciousness he is flung into a state of neurosis. It is not clear whether Freud believes that Shakespeare possessed psychoanalytic insights, or that the play projects the dramatist's own psyche. However, his main interest is in the audience's psychic reactions to the play. In this respect he anticipates Holland's reader-oriented psychological studies (see II,4,M). Ernest Jones' classic psychoanalytic study of *Hamlet* extends Freud's arguments somewhat by highlighting the Oedipus complex: Hamlet cannot contemplate the 'thought of incest and parricide combined' (Claudius is in the place of the father).

Lacan's slippery essay on *Hamlet* centres on the insubstantiality of Hamlet's image of the father. Lacan's theory of the individual's entry into the social world involves our adopting a 'subject' position. We achieve this situatedness on entering the symbolic system of language which gives us a place in the chain of discourse – an 'I' and a gender orientation

within the family (he/she, daughter/son). Lacan's account of the
Oedipus Complex cannot be summarized here, but the role of
the 'phallus' is crucial in it. The phallus is at once the physical
penis and also a symbol or signifier of potency. The Complex
develops around the question of the absence or lack of the
phallus in the mother. The male child goes through various
phases of identification with the phallus. Essentially the phallus
is an *imaginary object of desire* which may be attached to a real or
imaginary phallus. Hamlet wishes to strike the king because he
possesses the phallus, but, since the phallus is ultimately a
signifier, it lacks substance and is a mere 'nothing'. Hence the
endless deferments and frustrations in Hamlet's struggle to take
revenge on the 'king'.

While Freud treated literature as the expression of the
author's unconscious mind, Jung refused to treat literature as a
mere pathological symptom. The poet's vision, according to
Jung, is not the product of a 'poetic mood' or 'rich fantasy', but
is drawn directly from 'primordial experience', transmitted
through the 'collective unconscious'. This collective unconscious
is 'a certain psychological disposition shaped by the forces of
heredity'. Myths, legends and fairy tales transmit in purest form
certain archetypal images which inevitably reappear in all great
literature. The images express aspects of humanity's universal
experience (birth, life, death, the seasons). Maud Bodkin treats
the archetypal symbols as images shared by the minds of all
human beings. The regularity of nature is taken as grounds for
assuming the regularity of the appearance of the symbols in
literature. Northrop Frye tried to establish a complex and
systematic theory of literature upon these apparent certainties
(see III,6,E).

Background reading

M. Bowie, 'Jacques Lacan', in *Structuralism and Since: from Lévi-Strauss to
    Derrida*, ed. John Sturrock (Oxford: Oxford UP, 1979).
Robert Con Davis (ed.), *The Fictional Father: Lacanian Readings of the Text*
    (Amherst: University of Massachusetts Press, 1981).
Shoshana Felman (ed.), *Literature and Psychoanalysis: the Question of
    Reading – Otherwise* (Baltimore: Johns Hopkins UP, 1982).
Frederick J. Hoffman, *Freudianism and the Literary Mind* (2nd edn, Baton
    Rouge: Lousiana State UP, 1957).
Edith Kurzweil and William Phillips (eds), *Literature and Psychoanalysis*
    (New York: Columbia UP, 1983).

Simon Lesser, *Fiction and the Unconscious* (Boston: Beacon Press, 1957).

Janet F. MacCannell, *Figuring Lacan: Criticism and the Cultural Unconscious* (London and Sydney: Croom Helm, 1986).

Colin McCabe (ed.), *The Talking Cure: Essays in Psychoanalysis and Language* (London and Basingstoke: Macmillan, 1981).

William Phillips (ed.), *Art and Psychoanalysis* (New York: Criterion Books, 1957).

Alan Roland (ed.), *Psychoanalysis, Creativity and Literature* (New York: Columbia UP, 1978).

Joseph H. Smith (ed.), *The Literary Freud* (New Haven and London: Yale UP, 1980).

Elizabeth Wright, *Psychoanalytic Criticism: Theory in Practice* (London and New York: Methuen, 1984).

(A) SIGMUND FREUD

'Psychopathic Characters on the Stage' (c. 1905)

If, as has been assumed since the time of Aristotle, the purpose of drama is to arouse 'terror and pity' and so 'to purge the emotions', we can describe that purpose in rather more detail by saying that it is a question of opening up sources of pleasure or enjoyment in our emotional life, just as, in the case of intellectual activity, joking or fun open up similar sources, many of which that activity had made inaccessible. In this connection the prime factor is unquestionably the process of getting rid of one's own emotions by 'blowing off steam'; and the consequent enjoyment corresponds on the one hand to the relief produced by a thorough discharge and on the other hand, no doubt, to an accompanying sexual excitation; for the latter, as we may suppose, appears as a by-product whenever an affect is aroused, and gives people the sense, which they so much desire, of a raising of the potential of their psychical state. Being present as an interested spectator at a spectacle or play does for adults what play does for children, whose hesitant hopes of being able to do what grown-up people do are in that way gratified. [. . .]

[P]sychological drama turns into psychopathological drama when the source of the suffering in which we take part and from which we are meant to derive pleasure is no longer a conflict between two almost equally conscious impulses but between a conscious impulse and a repressed one. Here the precondition of enjoyment is that the spectator should himself be a neurotic, for it is only such people who can derive pleasure instead of simple aversion from the revelation and the more or less conscious recognition of a repressed impulse. In anyone who is not neurotic this recognition will meet only with aversion and will call up a readiness to repeat the act of repression which has earlier been successfully brought to bear on the impulse: for in such people a single expenditure of repression has been enough to hold the repressed impulse completely in check. But in neurotics the repression is on the brink of failing; it is unstable and needs a constant renewal of expenditure, and this expenditure is spared if recognition of the impulse is brought about. Thus it is only in neurotics that a struggle can occur of a kind which can be made the subject of a drama; but even in them the dramatist will provoke not merely an *enjoyment* of the liberation but a *resistance* to it as well. [. . .]

The first of these modern dramas is *Hamlet*. It has as its subject the way in which a man who has so far been normal becomes neurotic owing to the peculiar nature of the task by which he is faced, a man, that is, in whom an impulse that has hitherto been successfully repressed endeavours to make its way into action. *Hamlet* is distinguished by three characteristics which seem important in connection with our present discussion.
(1) The hero is not psychopathic, but only becomes psychopathic in the course of the action of the play. (2) The repressed impulse is one of those which are similarly repressed in all of us, and the repression of which is part and parcel of the foundations of our personal evolution. It is this repression which is shaken up by the situation in the play. As a result of these two characteristics it is easy for us to recognize ourselves in the hero: we are susceptible to the same conflict as he is, since 'a person who does not lose his reason under certain conditions can have no reason to lose'. (3) It appears as a necessary precondition of this form of art that the impulse that is struggling into consciousness, however clearly it is recognizable, is never given a definite name; so that in the spectator too the process is carried through with his attention averted, and he is in the grip of his emotions instead of taking stock of what is happening. A certain amount of resistance is no doubt saved in this way, just as, in an analytic treatment, we find derivatives of the repressed material reaching consciousness, owing to a lower resistance, while the repressed material itself is unable to do so. After all, the conflict in *Hamlet* is so effectively concealed that it was left to me to unearth it.

(Sigmund Freud, 'Psychopathic Characters on the Stage' (c. 1905), *Art and Literature*, translation from the Strachey edn, Penguin Freud Library, vol. 14 (Harmondsworth: Penguin, 1985), pp. 121, 125–6.)

(B) CARL JUNG

Psychology and Literature (1930)

The profound difference between the first and second parts of *Faust* marks the difference between the psychological and the visionary modes of artistic creation. The latter reverses all the conditions of the former. The experience that furnishes the material for artistic expression is no longer familiar. It is a strange something that derives its existence from the hinterland of man's mind – that suggests the abyss of time separating us from pre-human ages, or evokes a super-human world of contrasting light and darkness. It is a primordial experience which surpasses man's understanding, and to which his is therefore in danger of succumbing. [. . .]

The obscurity as to the sources of the material in visionary creation is very strange, and the exact opposite of what we find in the psychological mode of creation. We are even led to suspect that this obscurity is not unintentional. We are naturally inclined to suppose – and Freudian psychology encourages us to do so – that some highly personal experience underlies this grotesque darkness. [. . .]

Although a discussion of the poet's personality and psychic disposition belongs strictly to the second part of my essay, I cannot avoid taking up in the present connection this Freudian view of the visionary work of art. For one thing, it has aroused considerable attention. And then it is the only well-known attempt that has been made to give a 'scientific' explanation of the sources of the visionary material or to formulate a theory of the psychic processes that underlie this curious mode of artistic creation. I assume that my own view of the question is not well known or generally understood. With this preliminary remark, I will now try to present it briefly.

If we insist on deriving the vision from a personal experience, we must treat the former as something secondary – as a mere substitute for reality. The result is that we strip the vision of its primordial quality and take it as nothing but a symptom. The pregnant chaos then shrinks to the proportions of a psychic disturbance. With this account of the matter we feel reassured and turn again to our picture of a well-ordered cosmos. Since we are practical and reasonable, we do not expect the cosmos to be perfect; we accept these unavoidable imperfections which we call abnormalities and diseases, and we take it for granted that human nature is not exempt from them. The frightening revelation of abysses that defy the human understanding is dismissed as illusion, and the poet is regarded as a victim and perpetrator of deception. Even to the poet, his primordial experience was 'human – all too human', to such a degree that he could not face its meaning but had to conceal it from himself.

We shall do well, I think, to make fully explicit all the implications of that way of accounting for artistic creation which consists in reducing it to personal factors. We should see clearly where it leads. The truth is that it takes us away from the psychological study of the work of art, and confronts us with the psychic disposition of the poet himself. That the latter presents an important problem is not to be denied, but the work of art is something in its own right, and may not be conjured away. The question of the significance to the poet of his own creative work – of his regarding it as a trifle, as a screen, as a source of suffering or as an achievement – does not concern us at the moment, our task being to interpret the work of art psychologically. For this undertaking it is essential that we give serious consideration to the basic experience that underlies it – namely, to the vision. We must take it at least as seriously as we do the experiences that underlie the psychological mode of artistic creation, and no one doubts that they are both real and serious. It looks, indeed, as if the visionary experience were something quite apart from the ordinary lot of man, and for this reason we have difficulty in believing that it is real. It has about it an unfortunate suggestion of obscure metaphysics and of occultism, so that we feel called upon to intervene in the name of a well-intentioned reasonableness. Our conclusion is that it would be better not to take such things too seriously, lest the world revert again to a benighted superstition. We may, of course, have a predilection for the occult; but ordinarily we dismiss the visionary experience as the outcome of a rich fantasy or of a poetic mood – that is to say, as a kind of poetic licence psychologically understood. Certain of the poets encourage this interpretation in order to put a wholesome distance between themselves and their work. Spitteler, for example, stoutly maintained that it was one and the same whether the poet sang of an Olympian Spring or to the theme: 'May is here!' The truth is that poets are human beings, and that what a poet has to say about his work is often far from being the most illuminating word on the subject. What is required of us, then, is nothing less than to defend the importance of the visionary experience against the poet himself. [. . .]

From the very first beginnings of human society onward man's efforts to give his vague intimations a binding form have left their traces. Even in the Rhodesian cliff-drawings of the Old Stone Age there appears, side by side with the most amazingly life-like representations of animals, an abstract pattern – a double cross contained in a circle. This design has turned up in every cultural region, more or less, and we find it today not only in Christian churches, but in Tibetan monasteries as well. It is the so-called sun-wheel, and as it dates from a time when no one had thought of wheels as a mechanical device, it cannot have had its source in any experience of the external world. It is rather a symbol that stands for a psychic happening; it covers an experience of the inner world, and is no doubt as lifelike a representation as the famous rhinoceros with the tick-birds on its back. There has never been a primitive culture that did not possess a system of secret teaching, and in many cultures this system is highly developed. The men's councils and the totem-clans preserve this teaching about hidden things that lie apart from man's daytime existence – things which, from primeval times, have always constituted his most vital experiences. Knowledge about them is handed on to younger men in the rites of initiation. The mysteries of the Graeco-Roman world performed the same office, and the rich mythology of antiquity is a relic of such experiences in the earliest stages of human development.

It is therefore to be expected of the poet that he will resort to mythology in order to give his experience its most fitting expression. It would be a serious mistake to suppose that he works with materials received at second-hand. The primordial experience is the source of his creativeness; it cannot be fathomed, and therefore requires mythological imagery to give it form. In itself it offers no words or images, for it is a vision seen 'as in a glass, darkly'. It is merely a deep presentiment that strives to find expression. It is like a whirlwind that seizes everything within reach and, by carrying it aloft, assumes a visible shape. Since the particular expression can never exhaust the possibilities of the vision, but falls far short of it in richness of content, the poet must have at his disposal a huge store of materials if he is to communicate even a few of his intimations. What is more, he must resort to an imagery that is difficult to handle and full of contradictions in order to express the weird paradoxicality of his vision. Dante's presentiments are clothed in images that run the gamut of Heaven and Hell; Goethe must bring in the Blocksberg and the infernal regions of Greek antiquity; Wagner needs the whole body of Nordic myth; Nietzsche returns to the hieratic style and recreates the legendary seer of prehistoric times; Blake invents for himself indescribable figures, and Spitteler borrows old names for new creatures of the imagination. And no intermediate step is missing in the whole range from the ineffably sublime to the perversely grotesque.

Psychology can do nothing towards the elucidation of this colourful imagery except bring together materials for comparison and offer a terminology for its discussion. According to this terminology, that which appears in the vision is the collective unconscious. We mean by collective unconscious, a certain psychic disposition shaped by the forces of heredity; from it consciousness has developed. In the physical structure of the body we find traces of earlier stages of evolution, and we may expect the human psyche also to conform in its make-up to the law of phylogeny. It is a fact that in eclipses of consciousness – in dreams, narcotic states, and cases of insanity – there come to the surface psychic products or contents that show all the traits of primitive levels of psychic development. The images themselves are sometimes of such a primitive character that we might suppose them derived from ancient, esoteric teaching. Mythological themes clothed in modern dress also frequently appear. What is of particular importance for the study of literature in these manifestations of the collective unconscious is that they are compensatory to the conscious attitude. This is to say that they can bring a one-sided, abnormal, or dangerous state of consciousness into equilibrium in an apparently purposive way. In dreams we can see this process very clearly in its positive aspect. In cases of insanity the compensatory process is often perfectly obvious, but takes a negative form. There are persons, for instance, who have anxiously shut themselves off from all the world only to discover one day that their most intimate secrets are known and talked about by everyone. [. . .]

It makes no difference whether the poet knows that his work is begotten, grows, and matures with him, or whether he supposes that by taking thought he produces it out of the void. His opinion of the matter does not change the fact that his own work outgrows him as a child its mother. The creative process has feminine quality, and the creative work arises from unconscious depths – we might say, from the realm of the mothers. Whenever the creative force predominates, human life is ruled and moulded by the unconscious as against the active will, and the conscious ego is swept along on a subterranean current, being nothing more than a helpless observer of events. The work in process becomes the poet's fate and determines his psychic development. It is not Goethe who creates *Faust*, but *Faust* which creates Goethe. And what is *Faust* but a symbol?. [. . .]

The secret of artistic creation and of the effectiveness of art is to be found in a return to the state of *participation mystique* – to that level of experience at which it is man who lives, and not the individual, and at which the weal or woe of the single human being does not count, but only human existence. This is why every great work of art is objective and impersonal, but none the less profoundly moves us each and all. And this is also why the personal life of the poet cannot be held essential to his art – but at most a help or a hindrance to his creative task. He may go the way of a Philistine, a good citizen, a neurotic, a fool or a criminal. His personal career may be inevitable and interesting, but it does not explain the poet.

(Carl Jung, *Psychology and Literature*, reprinted in *Modern Man in Search of a Soul*, trans. W. S. Dell and Cary F. Baynes (London: Routledge & Kegan Paul, 1933), pp. 180, 182–3, 184–6, 188–91, 196–7, 198–9.)

(C) MAUD BODKIN

Archetypal Patterns in Poetry (1934)

In an article, 'On the relation of analytical psychology to poetic art', Dr. C. G. Jung has set forth an hypothesis in regard to the psychological significance of poetry. The special emotional significance possessed by certain poems – a significance going beyond any definite meaning conveyed – he attributes to the stirring in the reader's mind, within or beneath his conscious response, of unconscious forces which he terms 'primordial images', or archetypes. These archetypes he describes as 'psychic residua of numberless experiences of the same type', experiences which have happened not to the individual but to his ancestors, and of which the results are inherited in the structure of the brain, *a priori* determinants of individual experience.

It is the aim of the present writer to examine this hypothesis, testing it in regard to examples where we can bring together the recorded experience and reflection of minds approaching the matter from different standpoints. It is hoped that, in this way, something may be done towards enriching the formulated theory of the systematic psychologist through the insight of more intuitive thinkers, while at the same time the intuitive thinker's results may receive somewhat more exact definition. [. . .]

It is within the general field of anthropology or social psychology that I conceive the inquiry to lie which I am here attempting to pursue. I shall use the term 'archetypal pattern' to refer to that within us which, in Gilbert Murray's phrase, leaps in response to the effective presentation in poetry of an ancient theme. The hypothesis to be examined is that in poetry – and here we are to consider in particular tragic poetry – we may identify themes having a particular form or pattern which persists amid variation from age to age, and which corresponds to a pattern or configuration of emotional tendencies in the minds of those who are stirred by the theme. [. . .]

When a great poet uses the stories that have taken shape in the fantasy of the community, it is not his individual sensibility alone that he objectifies. Responding with unusual sensitiveness to the words and images which already express the emotional experience of the community, the poet arranges these so as to utilize to the full their evocative power. Thus he attains for himself vision and possession of the experience engendered between his own soul and the life around him, and communicates that experience, at once individual and collective, to others, so far as they can respond adequately to the words and images he uses.

We see, then, why, if we wish to contemplate the emotional patterns hidden in our individual lives, we may study them in the mirror of our spontaneous actions, so far as we can recall them, or in dreams and in the flow of waking fantasy; but if we would contemplate the archetypal patterns that we have in common with men of past generations, we do well to study them in the experience communicated by the great poetry that has continued to stir emotional response from age to age. In studying such poetry here, we are not asking what was in the

mind of Aeschylus or of Shakespeare when he fashioned the
figure of Orestes or of Hamlet, nor do we ask how these figures
affected a Greek or an Elizabethan audience. The question is
between the writer and the reader of this book: what do the
figures of Orestes and Hamlet stand for in the experience
communicated to us, as we see, read, or vividly recall the Greek
or Shakespearian tragedy?. [. . .]

The method by which I suggest that the poem selected ['The
Ancient Mariner'] should be studied differs from that proposed
by Richards to his students, not only in being applied to poems
already known and valued, but also as demanding no attempt at
critical judgement. It is concerned with emotional response only,
not with opinion. It is akin to that method proposed by Keats –
that one should read a page of poetry, or distilled prose, and
wander with it, muse, reflect, and prophesy, and dream, upon it.
Some such element of absorbed musing, or reverie, must be
present if there is to be real contact between the poem and the
personality. So much is demanded by the nature of the matter to
be studied. For such absorption, moreover, a certain spontaneity
is necessary, incompatible with the methods of the laboratory.
One must choose a time when the mind is ready to respond,
which it will not do to order. On the other hand there is
needed, in addition to spontaneity of subjective response, a
sharply objective and precise observation of results, if the
knowledge sought is to be attained. It is no easy task to exercise
such observation upon the tangles of obscure imagery that rise
and fall like seaweed in the waves, as the currents of reverie
flow. The power to observe accurately may be in part a product
of training in introspection under ordinary laboratory conditions.
It may be aided also by such practice as Freudian and other
analysts require in cool recognition of elements within our minds
which clash with aesthetic or moral estimates of self. In the last
resort, however, this introspective power seems a gift of nature
rather than of training, dependent perhaps upon the depth of the
sense of need for knowledge of the inner life – whether the
personal life, or that life of impersonal feeling which is
communicated by poetry. [. . .]

In poetic vision, says Vivante, 'our whole being is stirred,
every fibre of it'; 'crude instincts and remote experiences' are
present; but these are 'approached and made intelligible by
actual values and forms (*actual*, that is, present and active,
realizing themselves anew).' It is this view which, as it seems to
me, is verified by the psychological student of literature, against

the view of those psychologists who believe that crude instincts and remote experiences maintain, even in highly conscious and developed minds, a subterranean existence, repressed but unchanged. [. . .]

Gathering up our results into the form of an answer to the question proposed in this section, concerning the function of poetry, and in particular of poetry in which we feel the pattern we have called the Rebirth archetype, we may say that all poetry, laying hold of the individual through the sensuous resources of language, communicates in some measure the experience of an emotional but supra-personal life; and that poetry in which we re-live, as such a suprapersonal experience though in terms of our own emotional resources, the tidal ebb toward death followed by life renewal, affords us a means of increased awareness, and of fuller expression and control, of our own lives in their secret and momentous obedience to universal rhythms. [. . .]

It is time to survey, in its main course, the argument of this book.

In its first pages an hypothesis was proposed for investigation, formulated in terms suggested by Dr. Jung, that archetypal patterns, or images, are present within the experience communicated through poetry, and may be discovered there by reflective analysis. These patterns were likened, in the first essay, to the culture-patterns studied by anthropologists. As corresponding to certain ancient and recurring themes of poetry – such as that of a usurping monarch overthrown by an heir of the king he has displaced – the patterns, viewed psychologically, may be described as organizations of emotional tendencies, determined partly through the distinctive experience of the race or community within whose history the theme has arisen. When, in later essays, the patterns studied were analysed to their most universal elements, the relation to particular culture-patterns, on the one side, was shown as balanced by a relation to the most general conceptions of philosophy. Thus, the patterns we have called the Rebirth and Paradise-Hades archetypes, while finding expression in myths and legends of particular communities, could also be felt as characterizing the flow, or texture, of universal experience. Similarly, the images studied of man, woman, god, devil, in any particular instance of their occurrence in poetry can be considered either as related to the sensibility of a certain poet, and a certain age and country, or as a mode of expressing something potentially realizable in human experience of any time or place.

(Maud Bodkin, *Archetypal Patterns in Poetry* (London: Oxford UP, 1934), pp. 1, 4, 8, 29–30, 66, 89, 314–15.)

(D) ERNEST JONES

Hamlet and Oedipus (1949)

Extensive studies of the past half century, inspired by Freud, have taught us that a psychoneurosis means a state of mirtd where the person is unduly, and often painfully, driven or thwarted by the 'unconscious' part of his mind, that buried part that was once the infant's mind and still lives on side by side with the adult mentality that has developed out of it and should have taken its place. It signifies *internal* mental conflict. We have here the reason why it is impossible to discuss intelligently the state of mind of anyone suffering from a psychoneurosis, whether the description is of a living person or an imagined one, without correlating the manifestations with what must have operated in his infancy and is *still operating*. That is what I propose to attempt here.

For some deep-seated reason, which is to him unacceptable, Hamlet is plunged into anguish at the thought of his father being replaced in his mother's affections by someone else. It is as if his devotion to his mother had made him so jealous for her affection that he had found it hard enough to share this even with his father and could not endure to share it with still another man. Against this thought, however, suggestive as it is, may be urged three objections. First, if it were in itself a full statement of the matter, Hamlet would have been aware of the jealousy, whereas we have concluded that the mental process we are seeking is hidden from him. Secondly, we see in it no evidence of the arousing of an old and forgotten memory. And, thirdly, Hamlet is being deprived by Claudius of no greater share in the Queen's affection than he had been by his own father, for the two brothers made exactly similar claims in this respect – namely, those of a loved husband. The last-named objection, however, leads us to the heart of the situation. How if, in fact, Hamlet had in years gone by, as a child, bitterly resented having had to share his mother's affection even with his own father, had regarded him as a rival, and had secretly wished him out of the way so that he might enjoy undisputed and undisturbed the monopoly of that affection? If such thoughts had been present in his mind in childhood days they evidently would have been 'repressed', and all traces of them obliterated, by filial piety and other educative influences. The actual realization of his early wish in the death of his father at the hands of a jealous rival would then have stimulated into activity these 'repressed' memories, which would have produced, in the form of depression and other suffering, an obscure aftermath of his childhood's conflict. This is at all events the mechanism that is actually found in the real Hamlets who are investigated psychologically.

The explanation, therefore, of the delay and self-frustration exhibited in the endeavour to fulfil his father's demand for vengeance is that to Hamlet the thought of incest and parricide combined is too intolerable to be borne. One part of him tries to carry out the task, the other flinches inexorably from the thought of it. How fain would he blot it out in that 'bestial oblivion' which unfortunately for him his conscience contemns. He is torn and tortured in an insoluble inner conflict.

(Ernest Jones, *Hamlet and Oedipus* (1949; New York and London: W. W. Norton, 1976), pp. 69–70.)

(E) JACQUES LACAN

'Desire and the Interpretation of Desire in *Hamlet*' (1959)

Indeed, the 'something rotten' with which poor Hamlet is confronted is most closely connected with the position of the subject with regard to the phallus. And the phallus is everywhere present in the disorder in which we find Hamlet each time he approaches one of the crucial moments of his action.

There's something very strange in the way Hamlet speaks about his dead father, an exaltation and idealization of his dead father which comes down to something like this: Hamlet has no voice with which to say whatever he may have to say about him. He actually chokes up and finally concludes by saying – in

a particular form of the signifier that is called 'pregnant' in
English, referring to something that has a meaning beyond its
meaning – that he can find nothing to say about his father
except that he was like anyone else. What he means is very
obviously the opposite. This is the first indication, the first trace,
of what I want to talk about here.

Another trace is that the rejection, deprecation, contempt that
he casts on Claudius has every appearance of *dénégation*
[negation: which may be interpreted as admiration]. The
torrent of insults that he unleashes on Claudius – in the
presence of his mother, namely – culminates in the phrase 'a
king of shreds and patches.' We surely cannot fail to relate this
to the fact that, in the tragedy of Hamlet, unlike that of
Oedipus, after the murder of the father, the phallus is still there.
It's there indeed, and it is precisely Claudius who is called upon
to embody it.

Claudius' real phallus is always somewhere in the picture.
What does Hamlet have to reproach his mother for, after all, if
not for having filled herself with it? And with dejected arm and
speech he sends her back to that fatal, fateful object, here real
indeed, around which the play revolves.

The question at hand is the enigmatic manifestation of the
signifier of power, of potency: the Oedipal situation, when it
appears in the particularly striking form in the real that we have
in *Hamlet*, with the criminal, the usurper, in place and
functioning *as* usurper. What stays Hamlet's arm? It's not fear –
he has nothing but contempt for the guy – it's because he knows
that he must strike something other than what's there. Indeed,
two minutes later, when he arrives at his mother's chamber and
is beginning to give her all holy hell, he hears a noise behind
the curtain, and he lunges out without looking first.

I don't recall now what astute commentator pointed out that
Hamlet cannot possibly believe that it's Claudius, because he's
just left him in the next room. Nevertheless, when he has
disemboweled poor Polonius, he remarks: 'Thou wretched, rash,
intruding fool . . . ./ I took thee for thy better.' Everyone thinks
that he meant to kill the king, but in the presence of Claudius,
the real king and the usurper as well, he did after all hold back:
he wanted something or someone better, wanted to cut him off,
too, in the blossoms of his sin. Claudius, as he knelt there before
him, wasn't quite what Hamlet was after – he wasn't the right
one.

It's a question of the phallus, and that's why he will never be able to strike it, until the moment when he has made the complete sacrifice – without wanting to, moreover – of all narcissistic attachments, i.e., when he is mortally wounded and knows it. The thing is strange and obvious, recorded in all sorts of little riddles in Hamlet's style.

Polonius for him is merely a 'calf,' one that he has in some sense sacrificed to the spirit of his father. When he's stashed him under the stairs and everyone asks him what's going on, he goes into a few of his jokes, which are always so disconcerting for his adversaries. Everyone wonders whether what he says is really what he means, because what says gets them all where they're the touchiest. But for him to say it, he must know so much that they can't believe it, and so on and so forth.

This is a position that must be quite familiar to us from the phenomenon of the avowal made by the subject. He speaks these words which up till now have remained as good as sealed to the commentators: 'The body is with the king' – he doesn't use the word 'corpse,' please notice – 'but the king is not with the body.' Replace the word 'king' with the word 'phallus,' and you'll see that that's exactly the point – the body is bound up [*engagé*] in this matter of the phallus – and how – but the phallus, on the contrary, is bound to nothing: it always slips through your fingers [. . .]

> Hamlet: The king is a thing –
> Guildenstern: A thing, my lord?
> Hamlet: Of nothing.

(Jacques Lacan, 'Desire and the Interpretation of Desire in *Hamlet*' (1959), from French text ed. Jacques-Alain Miller, trans. James Hulbert, *Yale French Studies*, no. 55/56 (1977), pp. 49–50, 51–2.)

(F) JULIA KRISTEVA

'The Speaking Subject' (1985)

It is poetic language (in the Russian Formalist sense of the term, that is, poetry and prose) which best effects the never-ending process of the *rapprochement* between the signifiable and the referent. Poetic language accomplishes this function through two essential procedures: first, rhythmic and stylistic markings [which replace] logic as the motivation of the signifier, i.e. the repletion of the distinguishing or arbitrary void which separates the signifier from the signified. Secondly, poetic language accomplishes this function by operations which are more infrequent, found in marginal texts, operations which disturb the syntactic chain by means of ellipses or indefinite embeddings of grammatical categories.

Given that the coherence of the sign and of the predicate synthesis are the guarantors of the unity of the speaking subject, any attack against the sign or syntax is the mark of a re-evaluation process *vis-à-vis* the speaking subject's unity. I say that the particularities of poetic language designate a subject, as we say in French, *en procès*, on trial and in process. [. . .]

I should like to develop here an attempt to describe the trial of sense and the subject in the infinite-indefinite contest between the referent and the signifiable. I distinguish two modalities of signification: the semiotic and the symbolic.

By *semiotic*, I mean the primary organization (in Freudian terms) of drives by rhythms, intonations and primary processes (displacement, slippage, condensation). Genetically, the semiotic is found in the first echolalias of infants. Logically, it functions in all adult discourses as a supplementary register to that of sign and predicate synthesis. Plato speaks of this in the *Timaeus*, in his invocation of a state of language anterior to the word, even to the syllable, and which, quite different from the paternal name, has a maternal connotation. Plato calls this the *chora*, the receptacle, the place before the space which is always already named, one, paternal, sign and predication.

By *symbolic*, I mean precisely the functioning of the sign and predications. The symbolic is constituted beginning with what psychoanalysis calls the mirror stage and the consequent capacities for absence, representation or abstraction. The symbolic is a matter, therefore, of language as a system of meaning (as structuralism and generative grammar study it) – a language with a foreclosed subject or with a transcendental subject-ego.

Sense as a trial and the speaking subject on trial articulate themselves precisely on the impetus of the interaction between these two modalities. The return, the emergence of the semiotic in the symbolic, is subservient to transformational conditions in the relation between subject and receiver: anguish, frustration, identification or projection all break down the unity of the transcendental ego and its system of homogeneous sense and give free rein to what is heterogeneous in sense, that is, to the drive. This heterogeneity (which is the materialistic postulate of the theory) manifests itself in the signifying chain only by the phenomena which I have just called semiotic.

In these circumstances, the speaking subject undergoes a transition to a void, to zero: loss of identity, afflux of drive and a return of symbolic capacities, but this time in order to take control of *drive* itself. This is precisely what expands the limits of the signifiable: a new aspect of the displacement between the referent/signifiable, a new aspect of the body, has thus found its signification. [. . .]

The present renewal of semiology considers sense as a signifying process and a heterogeneous dynamic, and challenges the logical imprisonment of the subject in order to open the subject towards the body and society. This seems to me to contribute to the elaboration of a more current conception of the subject in contemporary history: a subject precisely 'on trial' as this is manifested in certain marginal experiences (modern art, psychoses, drugs). But also as this reveals itself in current political situations of the twentieth century, beginning with fascism, among other such manifestations. This is a subject in a crisis of rationality, struggling with its drives, the most impulsive of which Freud said was the death drive.

I can add that a textual study of Céline, undertaken in the methodical manner which I have just outlined, seems to me to show that the speaking subject, i.e. the author and the receiver, attempts a dynamic organization of the mst profound crises of rationality. This dynamic organization is one which insures both social communication and the subject's pleasure or, as we say, *jouissance*, as characterized by the theories of catastrophe. This dynamic organization operates on two levels; first, on the level of fiction, i.e. as interrupted narrative structure, as thematic of death and of violence arising from the tradition of the apocalyptic genre, and also as thematic of laughter, the mask, nonsense and music, arising from the tradition of the carnival genre.

Secondly, and more importantly, this dynamic organization operates on a clearly definable linguistic level, effectuated by the usage of slang intended to introduce nonsense into the lexicon, and by frequent syntactical ellipses which cause the more primordial semiotic, rhythmic and intonational determination to appear beyond what I call the symbolic function.

These most profound crises of rationality, which are in this way dynamically organized, are accompanied by a rigid investiture of other archaic and repressive structures, when and if their attempts at becoming semiotic–symbolic fail. These archaic and repressive structures include order, the family, normalcy, normative classical psychological-tending discourse, all of which are just so many characteristics of fascist ideology. Consequently, we may conclude that texts on experiencing limits – this is modern art – constitute the most direct and risky approach to the fascist phenomenon. And parenthetically, we know how much the avant-garde artists have been tempted by fascism. At the same time, these texts constitute the fascist phenomenon's most radical opposition, that is, the defence which is most solidly anchored in the speaking being.

I conclude by indicating that, far from being simply a semiological preoccupation, the renewal of the conception of meaning and of the subject as practice and process concerns an entire socio-historical horizon.

(Julia Kristeva, 'The Speaking Subject' (1985), *On Signs: A Semiotics Reader*, ed. Marshall Blonsky (Oxford: Blackwell, 1985), pp. 215, 216–18, 219–20.)

FORM, SYSTEM AND STRUCTURE

Parts I and II examined (respectively) theories which foreground representation and theories which foreground subjectivity (in the text, author or reader). Part III concentrates on theories which treat a literary work as a self-contained or systematic entity, or as part of a larger 'textual' structure. These theories tend to be impersonal and a–historical in their approach. A concern for the formal, systematic and structural properties of literature are by no means absent from pre-twentieth-century poetics. Aristotle's *Poetics*, classical rhetoric and Renaissance genre theories are obvious examples of systematic approaches to literary and oratorical discourses. The study of rhetoric was revived in the Renaissance and was applied to literature rather than to oratory. In the modern period, Erich Auerbach and Ernst Robert Curtius have demonstrated the fruitfulness of the rhetorical approach when it is used as part of a historical study of literature (in this respect they also belong in Part IV – see IV,1,B). Modern philosophy and linguistics, which have given criticism a 'linguistic turn', have transformed the concepts of form and structure as understood in earlier periods. This development marks a return to some of the concerns of classical rhetoric, which focused on the linguistic means of expression. However, the Russian Formalists and the New Critics applied themselves to linguistic structure in order to discover the specific nature of literary language, while classical rhetoric had aimed to improve the *effectiveness* of all forms of discourse. Post-structuralist theories also refuse to recognize a specifically 'literary' discourse. Terry Eagleton has recently argued for a return to the classical focus on 'effectiveness', but construes it as 'political effectiveness' (see *Literary Theory: An Introduction*, 1983, pp. 205–7).

In the late eighteenth century the Kantian revolution in

philosophy permitted the separation of aesthetic experience from other mental processes. The aesthetic movement and the Art-for-Art's-Sake era explored the often perverse and subversive implications of such a separation. It was not until the twentieth century, in Russian Formalism, that the study of literature became systematic in its formalism. Significantly, the Russian theorists were deeply influenced by linguistics.

In Britain and America, New Criticism was the dominant critical tradition for several decades, and has only recently begun to retreat before the growth of theories following the rise of structuralism. New critics rejected the abstract spirituality of Romanticism and what they considered the vague aestheticism of Pater in favour of a more 'concrete' critical practice which treated the text as an autonomous entity whose organic unity required a careful analysis. The structuralist and post-structuralist criticisms have not yet produced the sort of consensus achieved by New Criticism. This may be because the extrinsic drives of the post-structuralist theories threaten to dissolve the literary academy, forcing critics to break down the disciplinary barriers between literature, linguistics, sociology, philosophy, theology, anthropology, and psychoanalysis. For some this is a welcome ecumenical trend, but for others it is a threatening and dehumanizing process. Literature loses its privileged status and is treated as just one form of 'textuality'. The entire field of Formalist, New Critical, structuralist and post-structuralist criticisms includes a number of common themes as well as a series of profound conflicts.

CHAPTER 1

THE AESTHETIC DIMENSION

Théophile Gautier coined the term 'Art for Art's sake' in the preface to *Mademoiselle de Maupin* (1835). He declared: 'Les choses sont belles en proportion inverse de leur utilité.' Baudelaire developed Gautier's concern for the formal and plastic qualities of poetry into a demonic religion of art. He regarded a poet with a moral intention as a cheap and degraded artist. The foundations of this anti-bourgeois view of art were the German writings on aesthetics by Hegel, Schelling and especially Kant. In his *Critique of Judgement* (1790) Kant argued that aesthetic judgements were made by the imagination, not by the understanding. Such judgements are purely subjective and answer the question 'Does this object please me?' However, aesthetic satisfaction is 'entirely disinterested' and therefore potentially *universal*. Later, Clive Bell followed this argument when explaining that we may differ about which objects we find beautiful but agree about the quality we find beautiful in objects, which he calls 'significant form'. The disinterestedness of aesthetic judgement means that we appreciate beauty for its own sake and not for its moral or other utility. However, while art is without extrinsic 'purpose', it is internally 'purposive': it obeys its own internal logic as art. Further, art creates a second (independent) nature from the material provided by real nature. These Kantian ideas shaped most of the aesthetic thought of the next one hundred years.

After Kant it became fashionable to mock the neoclassical idea that art imitates nature. Max Beerbohm, in the *Yellow Book*, celebrated a 'new epoch of artifice'. Oscar Wilde declared: 'The first duty of life is to be as artificial as possible. What the second duty is no one has as yet discovered.' Huysman's *À Rebours* (1884) describes the perverse life of Des Esseintes, a dedicated aesthete, who prefers artificial flowers and man-made scenery to living nature. Wilde formulated the anti-mimetic, anti-moralist view of art in its wittiest form in *The Decay of Lying* (1891). Another feature of British aestheticism was its subjective attitude. Walter Pater's Conclusion to his book on the Renaissance (1873) remained a touchstone of aestheticism for some time. He accepted Kant's idea that art was disinterested, but insisted on the purely subjective and individual nature of aesthetic experience. The purpose of art is to provide the individual with the intensest possible moments of aesthetic experience: 'To burn always with this hard, gemlike flame, to maintain this ecstasy, is success in life.' Pater contributed much to the Longinian strain in British criticism in the early twentieth century (Sir Walter Raleigh and George Saintsbury, for example). Even I. A. Richards (see II,3,F) adopts a Paterian focus on the reader's state of consciousness before the aesthetic object.

Art for Art's Sake, in its perverse fashion, raised the potentially serious question of art's 'autonomy'. There are two directions in which the concept can move: one towards an ivory tower, escapist, view of art, and the other towards the Kantian idea of art as a heterocosm (another world). The great Shakespearean critic A. C. Bradley, whose writings are in the Hegelian tradition, declared that poetry is 'a world by itself, independent, complete, autonomous', requiring us to conform to its laws. He qualifies this by reminding us that reality and poetry are connected by underground similarities. His approach (especially his insistence on the inseparability of form and content) has affinities with the subsequent New Critics, even though the latter rejected Bradley's Romantic spirituality. The New Critics transformed the idea of the aesthetic autonomy of poetry into a rigorous concept of literary form.

Finally, two modern critics are included in this section in order to show that even sociological approaches to theory find it necessary to redefine or accommodate the concept of the aesthetic. Jan Mukařovský, a member of the Prague Linguistic Circle (founded in 1926), developed a sociological theory of the 'aesthetic function' which questions the idea, put forward by Clive Bell, for example, that aesthetic qualities reside in the artistic object. He argues that the aesthetic function is an ever-shifting boundary and not a watertight category. The same object can possess several overlapping or discontinuous functions: a pile of bricks may be treated as building materials, a door stop, or an aesthetic object. Society determines whether or not a particular form of discourse is treated as an aesthetic object. From this perspective there is no eternal sphere of Beauty in which great works float in a permanent heaven of art. Definitions of art will depend upon the prevailing ideologies of particular societies.

Fredric Jameson's Hegelian–Marxist study, *Marxism and Form* (1971), contains arguments about the aesthetic dimension of literary texts. In his account of Hemingway he considers that the author's preoccupation with style is paradoxically an expression of Hemingway's inability to cope with the complexities of modern American life and his retreat into foreign, exotic societies. The 'inner form' of Hemingway's work is 'both disguise and revelation of the concrete'. The effect of Jameson's argument is to focus attention on the formal aspect of the works, but at the same time to question the autonomy of the work. He also suggests that a writer's retreat into style is never 'innocent': the real world is both repressed and revealed in the aesthetic gesture.

Background reading

John Casey, 'The Autonomy of Art', in *Philosophy and the Arts* (Royal Institute of Philosophy Lectures, vol. 6, 1973).

William Gaunt, *The Aesthetic Adventure* (Harmondsworth: Penguin Books, 1957; revised edn, 1975).

Graham Hough, *The Last Romantics* (London: Duckworth, 1947), chs 4 and 5 (Pater and Fin-de-Siècle).

Robert V. Johnson, *Aestheticism* (London: Methuen, 1969).

Enid M. Starkie, *From Gautier to Eliot* (London: Hutchinson, 1960).

René Wellek, *Immanuel Kant in England, 1793–1838* (Princeton, NJ: Princeton UP, 1931). Extract in *Discriminations: Further Concepts of Criticism* (New Haven and London: Yale UP, 1963).

Edmund Wilson, *Axel's Castle* (New York and London: Scribner's, 1931).

(A) IMMANUEL KANT

The Critique of Judgement (1790)

In order to decide whether anything is beautiful or not, we refer the representation, not by the Understanding to the Object for cognition but, by the Imagination (perhaps in conjunction with the Understanding) to the subject, and its feeling of pleasure or pain. The judgement of taste is therefore not a judgement of cognition, and is consequently not logical but aesthetical, by which we understand that whose determining ground can be *no other than subjective*. Every reference of representations, even that of sensations, may be objective (and then it signifies the real in an empirical representation); save only the reference to the feeling of pleasure and pain, by which nothing in the Object is signified, but through which there is a feeling in the subject, as it is affected by the representation. [. . .]

The beautiful is that which apart from concepts is represented as the object of a universal satisfaction.

This explanation of the beautiful can be derived from the preceding explanation of it as the object of an entirely disinterested satisfaction. For the fact of which every one is conscious, that the satisfaction is for him quite disinterested, implies in his judgement a ground of satisfaction for every one. For since it does not rest on any inclination of the subject (nor upon any other premeditated interest), but since he who judges feels himself quite *free* as regards the satisfaction which he attaches to the object, he cannot find the ground of this satisfaction in any private conditions connected with his own subject; and hence it must be regarded as grounded on what he can presuppose in every other man. Consequently he must believe that he has reason for attributing a similar satisfaction to every one. He will therefore speak of the beautiful, as if beauty were a characteristic of the object and the judgement logical (constituting a cognition of the Object by means of concepts of it); although it is only aesthetical and involves merely a reference of the representation of the object to the subject. For it has this similarity to a logical judgement that we can presuppose its validity for every one. But this universality cannot arise from concepts; for from concepts there is no transition to the feeling of pleasure or pain (except in pure practical laws, which bring an interest with them such as is not bound up with the pure judgement of taste). Consequently the judgement of taste, accompanied with the consciousness of separation from all interest, must claim validity for every one, without this universality depending on Objects. That is, there must be bound up with it a title to subjective universality. [. . .]

The Imagination (as a productive faculty of cognition) is very powerful in creating another nature, as it were, out of the material that actual nature gives it. We entertain ourselves with it when experience proves too commonplace, and by it we remould experience, always indeed in accordance with analogical laws, but yet also in accordance with principles which occupy a higher place in Reason (laws too which are just as natural to us as those by which Understanding comprehends empirical nature). Thus we feel our freedom from the law of association (which attaches to the empirical employment of Imagination), so that the material which we borrow from nature in accordance with this law can be worked up into something different which surpasses nature. [. . .]

In a word the aesthetical Idea is a representation of the Imagination associated with a given concept, which is bound up with such a multiplicity of partial representations in its free employment, that for it no expression marking a definite concept can be found; and such a representation, therefore, adds to a concept much ineffable thought, the feeling of which quickens the cognitive faculties, and with language, which is the mere letter, binds up spirit also.

(Immanuel Kant, *The Critique of Judgement* (1790), ed. and trans. J. H. Bernard (2nd edn, 1914), pp. 45–6, 53, 55–6, 198, 201.)

(B) WALTER PATER

'Conclusion', *The Renaissance* (1873)

Experience, already reduced to a group of impressions, is ringed round for each one of us by that thick wall of personality through which no real voice has ever pierced on its way to us, or from us to that which we can only conjecture to be without. Every one of those impressions is the impression of the individual in his isolation, each mind keeping as a solitary prisoner its own dream of a world. Analysis goes a step farther still, and assures us that those impressions of the individual mind to which, for each one of us, experience dwindles down, are in perpetual flight; that each of them is limited by time, and that as time is infinitely divisible, each of them is infinitely divisible also; all that is actual in it being a single moment, gone while we try to apprehend it, of which it may ever be more truly said that it has ceased to be than that it is. To such a tremulous wisp constantly re-forming itself on the stream, to a single sharp impression, with a sense in it, a relic more or less fleeting, of such moments gone by, what is real in our life fines itself down.

It is with this movement, with the passage and dissolution of impressions, images, sensations, that analysis leaves off – that continual vanishing away, that strange, perpetual weaving and unweaving of ourselves.

Philosophiren, says Novalis, *ist dephlegmatisiren vivificiren*. The service of philosophy, of speculative culture, towards the human spirit, is to rouse, to startle it to a life of constant and eager observation. Every moment some form grows perfect in hand or face; some tone on the hills or the sea is choicer than the rest; some mood of passion or insight or intellectual excitement is irresistibly real and attractive to us, – for that moment only. Not the fruit of experience, but experience itself, is the end. A counted number of pulses only is given to us of a variegated, dramatic life. How may we see in them all that is to be seen in them by the finest senses? How shall we pass most swiftly from point to point, and be present always at the focus where the greatest number of vital forces unite in their purest energy?

To burn always with this hard, gemlike flame, to maintain this ecstasy, is success in life. In a sense it might even be said that our failure is to form habits: for, after all, habit is relative to a stereotyped world, and meantime it is only the roughness of the eye that makes any two persons, things, situations, seem alike. While all melts under our feet, we may well grasp at any exquisite passion, or any contribution to knowledge that seems by a lifted horizon to set the spirit free for a moment, or any stirring of the senses, strange dyes, strange colours, and curious odours, or work of the artist's hands, or the face of one's friend. Not to discriminate every moment some passionate attitude in those about us, and in the very brilliancy of their gifts some tragic dividing of forces on their ways, is, on this short day of frost and sun, to sleep before evening. [. . .] Well! we are all *condamnés*, as Victor Hugo says: we are all under sentence of death but with a sort of indefinite reprieve – *les hommes sont tous condamnés à mort avec des sursis indéfinis*: we have an interval, and then our place knows us no more. Some spend this interval in listlessness, some in high passions, the wisest, at least among 'the children of this world,' in art and song. For our one chance lies in expanding that interval, in getting as many pulsations as possible into the given time. Great passions may give us this quickened sense of life, ecstasy and sorrow of love, the various forms of enthusiastic activity, disinterested or otherwise, which come naturally to many of us. Only be sure it is passion – that it does yield you this fruit of a quickened, multiplied consciousness. Of such wisdom, the poetic passion, the desire of beauty, the love of art for its own sake, has most. For art comes to you, proposing frankly to give nothing but the highest quality to your moments as they pass, and simply for those moments' sake.

(Walter Pater, *The Renaissance* (1873, 4th edn, London and New York: Macmillan, 1893), pp. 249–51, 252–3.)

(C) KARL JORIS HUYSMANS

Against the Grain [*À Rebours*] (1884)

To tell the truth, artifice was in Des Esseintes's philosophy the distinctive mark of human genius.

As he used to say, Nature has had her day; she has definitely and finally exhausted the patience of refined temperaments by the sickening monotony of her landscapes and skyscapes. When all is said and done, what a narrow, vulgar affair it all is, like a petty shopkeeper selling one article of goods to the exclusion of all others; what a tiresome store of green meadows and trees, what a wearisome, commonplace collection of mountains and seas!

In fact, there is not one of her inventions, deemed so subtle and so wonderful, which the ingenuity of mankind cannot create; no forest of Fontainebleau, no fairest moonlight landscape, but can be reproduced by stage scenery illuminated by floodlighting; no waterfall but can be imitated by the proper application of hydraulics, till there is no distinguishing the copy from the original; no mountain crag that papier-maché cannot counterfeit; no flower that well chosen silks and delicate shreds of paper cannot match!

Yes, there is no denying it, she is in her dotage and has long ago exhausted the simple-minded admiration of the true artist; the time is undoubtedly come when her productions must be superseded by art . . .

Of all the forms of literature that of the prose poem was Des Esseintes's favourite. Handled by the alchemist of genius, it should, according to him, contain in its small compass, like a meat extract, so to speak, the essence of the novel, while suppressing its long, tedious analytical passages and superfluous descriptions. Again and again Des Esseintes had pondered the fascinating problem of writing a novel concentrated in a few sentences, but which would contain the cohobated juice of the hundreds of pages always taken up in describing the setting, sketching the characters, gathering together the necessary incidental observations and minor details. In that case, so inevitable and unalterable would be the words selected that they must take the place of all others; in so ingenious and masterly a fashion would each adjective be chosen that it could not with any justice be robbed of its right to be there, and would open up such wide vistas that the reader must dream for weeks about its meaning, at once precise and manifold, and enable him to know the present, reconstruct the past, divine the future of the spiritual history of the characters, all revealed by the light of this one epithet.

The novel, thus conceived, thus condensed in a page or two, would become a communion, an interchange of thought between a hieratic author and an ideal reader, a spiritual collaboration by consent between half a dozen persons of superior intellect scattered across the globe, an aesthetic feast for epicures, to be enjoyed by them alone.

In a word, the prose poem represented in Des Esseintes's eyes the solid juice, the osmazone of literature, the essential oil of art.

(Karl Joris Huysmans, *A Rebours* (1884), trans. anon, as *Against the Grain* (Paris: Groves and Michaux, 1926), pp. 31–2, 268–9. Translation modified by editor.)

(D) OSCAR WILDE

'The Decay of Lying', *Intentions* (1891)

VIVIAN. My own experience is that the more we study Art, the less we care for Nature. What Art really reveals to us is Nature's lack of design, her curious crudities, her extraordinary monotony, her absolutely unfinishd condition. Nature has good intentions, of course, but, as Aristotle once said, she cannot carry them out. When I look at a landscape I cannot help seeing all its defects. It is fortunate for us, however, that Nature is so imperfect, as otherwise we should have no art at all. Art is our spirited protest, our gallant attempt to teach Nature her proper place. As for the infinite variety of Nature, that is a pure myth. It is not to be found in Nature herself. It resides in the imagination, or fancy, or cultivated blindness of the man who looks at her. [. . .] The public imagine that, because they are interested in their immediate surroundings, Art should be interested in them also, and should take them as her subject-matter. But the mere fact that they are interested in these things makes them unsuitable subjects for Art. The only beautiful things, as somebody once said, are the things that do not concern us. As long as a thing is useful or necessary to us, or affects us in any way, either for pain or for pleasure, or appeals strongly to our sympathies, or is a vital part of the environment in which we live, it is outside the proper sphere of art. To art's subject-matter we should be more or less indifferent. We should, at any rate, have no preferences, no prejudices, no partisan feeling of any kind. [. . .]

Paradox though it may seem – and paradoxes are always dangerous things – it is none the less true that Life imitates art far more than Art imitates life. We have all seen in our own day in England how a certain curious and fascinating type of beauty, invented and emphasised by two imaginative painters, has so influenced Life that whenever one goes to a private view or to an artistic salon one sees, here the mystic eyes of Rossetti's dream, the long ivory throat, the strange square-cut jaw, the loosened shadowy hair that he so ardently loved, there the sweet maidenhood of 'The Golden Stair,' the blossom-like mouth and weary loveliness of the 'Laus Amoris,' the passion-pale face of Andromeda, the thin hands and lithe beauty of the Vivian in 'Merlin's Dream.' And it has always been so. A great artist invents a type, and Life tries to copy it, to reproduce it in a popular form, like an enterprising publisher. [. . .]

CYRIL. The theory is certainly a very curious one, but to make it complete you must show that Nature, no less than Life, is an imitation of Art. Are you prepared to prove that?

VIVIAN. My dear fellow, I am prepared to prove anything.

CYRIL. Nature follows the landscape painter, then, and takes her effects from him?

VIVIAN. Certainly. Where, if not from the Impressionists, do we get those wonderful brown fogs that come creeping down our streets, blurring the gas-lamps and changing the houses into monstrous shadows? To whom, if not to them and their master, do we owe the lovely silver mists that brood over our river, and turn to faint forms of fading grace, curved bridge and swaying barge? The extraordinary change that has taken place in the climate of London during the last ten years is entirely due to a particular school of Art. You smile. Consider the matter from a scientific or a metaphysical point of view, and you will find that

I am right. For what is Nature? Nature is no great mother who
has borne us. She is our creation. It is in our brain that she
quickens to life. Things are because we see them, and what we
see, and how we see it, depends on the Arts that have influenced
us. To look at a thing is very different from seeing a thing. One
does not see anything until one sees its beauty. Then, and then
only, does it come into existence. At present, people see fogs, not
because there are fogs, but because poets and painters have
taught them the mysterious loveliness of such effects. There may
have been fogs for centuries in London. I dare say there were.
But no one saw them, and so we do not know anything about
them. They did not exist till Art had invented them.

(Oscar Wilde, 'The Decay of Lying', *Intentions* (1891, London: Methuen,
1908), pp. 1–2, 16–17, 30–1, 38–9.)

(E) BENEDETTO CROCE

Aesthetic (1902)

Knowledge has two forms: it is either *intuitive* knowledge or
logical knowledge; knowledge obtained through the *imagination* or
knowledge obtained through the *intellect*; knowledge of the
individual or knowledge of the *universal*; of *individual things* or of the
relations between them: it is, in fact, productive either of *images* or
of *concepts*. [. . .]

And yet there is a sure method of distinguishing true intuition,
true representation, from that which is inferior to it: the spiritual
fact from the mechanical, passive, natural fact. Every true
intuition or representation is also *expression*. That which does not
objectify itself in expression is not intuition or representation,
but sensation and mere natural fact. The spirit only intuites in
making, forming, expressing. He who separates intuition from
expression never succeeds in reuniting them.

Intuitive activity *possesses intuitions to the extent that it expresses
them* . . .

These distinctions established, we must condemn as erroneous
every theory which annexes the æsthetic activity to the practical,
or introduces the laws of the second into the first. That science
is theory and art practice has been many times affirmed. Those
who make this statement, and look upon the æsthetic fact as a
practical fact, do not do so capriciously or because they are

groping in the void; but because they have their eye on something which is really practical. But the practical which they aim is not Æsthetic, nor within Æsthetic; it is *outside and beside it*; and although often found united, they are not united necessarily or by the bond of identity of nature.

The æsthetic fact is altogether completed in the expressive elaboration of impressions. When we have achieved the word within us, conceived definitely and vividly a figure or a statue, or found a musical motive, expression is born and is complete; there is no need for anything else. If after this we should open our mouths – *will* to open them to speak, or our throats to sing, that is to say, utter by word of mouth and audible melody what we have completely said or sung to ourselves; or if we should stretch out – *will* to stretch out our hands to touch the notes of the piano, or to take up the brush and chisel, thus making on a large scale movements which we have already made in little and rapidly, in a material in which we leave more or less durable traces; this is all an addition, a fact which obeys quite different laws from the former, with which we are not concerned for the moment, although we recognize henceforth that this second movement is a production of things, a *practical* fact, or fact of *will*. It is usual to distinguish the internal from the external work of art: the terminology seems to us infelicitous, for the work of art (the æsthetic work) is always *internal*; and what is called *external* is no longer a work of art. [. . .]

For the same reasons the search for the *end of art* is ridiculous, when it is understood of art as art. And since to fix an end is to choose, the theory that the content of art must be *selected* is another form of the same error. A selection among impressions and sensations implies that these are already expressions, otherwise how could a selection be made among the continuous and indistinct? To choose is to will: to will this and not to will that: and this and that must be before us, expressed. Practice follows, it does not precede theory; expression is free insiration.

The true artist, in fact, finds himself big with his theme, he knows not how; he feels the moment of birth drawing near, but he cannot will it or not will it. If he were to wish to act in opposition to his inspiration, to make an arbitrary choice, if, born Anacreon, he should wish to sing of Atreus and of Alcides, his lyre would warn him of his mistake, sounding only of Venus and of Love, notwithstanding his efforts to the contrary.

The theme or content cannot, therefore, be practically or morally charged with epithets of praise or blame. When critics of art remark that a theme is *badly selected*, in cases where that observation has a just foundation, it is a question of blaming, not the selection of the theme (which would be absurd), but the manner in which the artist has treated it, the failure of the expression due to the contradictions which it contains. And when the same critics object to the theme or content of works which they proclaim to be artistically perfect as being unworthy of art and blameworthy; if these expressions really are perfect, there is nothing to be done but to advise the critics to leave the artists in peace, for they can only derive inspiration from what has moved their soul. They should rather direct their attention towards effecting changes in surrounding nature and society, that such impressions and states of soul should not recur. If ugliness were to vanish from the world, if universal virtue and felicity were established there, perhaps artists would no longer represent perverse or pessimistic feelings, but calm, innocent and joyous feelings, Arcadians of a real Arcady. But so long as ugliness and turpitude exist in nature and impose themselves upon the artist, to prevent the expression of these things also is impossible; and when it has arisen, *factum infectum fieri nequit*. We speak thus entirely from the æsthetic point of view, and of pure criticism of art. [. . .]

The impossibility of choice of content completes the theorem of the *independence of art*, and is also the only legitimate meaning of the expression: *art for art's sake*. Art is independent both of science and of the useful and the moral. There should be no fear lest frivolous or cold art should thus be justified, since what is truly frivolous or cold is so because it has not been raised to expression; or in other words, frivolity and frigidity come always from the form of the æsthetic treatment, from failure to grasp a content, not from the material qualities of the content itself.

(Benedetto Croce, *Aesthetic*, trans. Douglas Ainslie (2nd edn, London: Macmillan, 1902), pp. 1, 8, 50–2, 52–3.)

(F) A. C. BRADLEY

'Poetry for Poetry's Sake', *Oxford Lectures on Poetry* (1909)

What then does the formula 'Poetry for poetry's sake' tell us about this experience? It says, as I understand it, these things.

First, this [imaginative] experience [of reading] is an end in itself, is worth having on its own account, has an intrinsic value. Next, its *poetic* value is this intrinsic worth alone. Poetry may have also an ulterior value as a means to culture or religion; because it conveys instruction, or softens the passions, or furthers a good cause; because it brings the poet fame or money or a quiet conscience. So much the better: let it be valued for these reasons too. But its ulterior worth neither is nor can directly determine its poetic worth as a satisfying imaginative experience; and this is to be judged entirely from within. And to these two positions the formula would add, though not of necessity, a third. The consideration of ulterior ends, whether by the poet in the act of composing or by the reader in the act of experiencing, tends to lower poetic value. It does so because it tends to change the nature of poetry by taking it out of its own atmosphere. For its nature is to be not a part, nor yet a copy, of the real world (as we commonly understand that phrase), but to be a world by itself, independent, complete, autonomous; and to possess it fully you must enter that world, conform to its laws, and ignore for the time the beliefs, aims, and particular conditions which belong to you in the other world of reality. [. . .]

Again, our formula may be accused of cutting poetry away from its connection with life. And this accusation raises so huge a problem that I must ask leave to be dogmatic as well as brief. There is plenty of connection between life and poetry, but it is, so to say, a connection underground. The two may be called different forms of the same thing: one of them having (in the usual sense) reality, but seldom fully satisfying imagination; while the other offers something which satisfies imagination but has not full 'reality.' They are parallel developments which nowhere meet, or, if I may use loosely a word which will be serviceable later, they are analogues. Hence we understand one by help of the other, and even, in a sense, care for one because of the other; but hence also, poetry neither is life, nor, strictly speaking, a copy of it. They differ not only because one has more mass and the other a more perfect shape, but because they have different *kinds* of existence. The one touches us as beings occupying a given position in space and time, and having feelings, desires, and purposes due to that position: it appeals to imagination, but appeals to much besides. What meets us in poetry has not a position in the same series of time and space, or, if it has or had such a position, it is taken apart from much that belonged to it there; and therefore it makes no direct appeal to those feelings, desires, and purposes, but speaks only to contemplative imagination – imagination the reverse of empty or emotionless, imagination saturated with the results of 'real' experience, but still contemplative. [. . .]

Now I believe it will be found that a large part of the controversy we are dealing with arises from a confusion between these two distinctions of substance and form, and of subject and poem. The extreme formalist lays his whole weight on the form because he thinks its opposite is the mere subject. The general reader is angry, but makes the same mistake, and gives to the subject praises that rightly belong to the substance. I will read an example of what I mean. I can only explain the following words of a good critic by supposing that for the moment he has fallen into this confusion: 'The mere matter of all poetry – to wit, the appearances of nature and the thoughts and feelings of men – being unalterable, it follows that the difference between poet and poet will depend upon the manner of each in applying language, metre, rhyme, cadence, and what not, to this invariable material.' What has become here of the substance of *Paradise Lost* – the story, scenery, characters, sentiments, as they are in the poem? They have vanished clean away. Nothing is left but the form on one side, and on the other not even the subject, but a supposed invariable material, the appearances of nature and the thoughts and feelings of men. Is it surprising that the whole value should then be found in the form? [. . .]

In pure poetry it is otherwise. Pure poetry is not the decoration of a preconceived and clearly defined matter: it springs from the creative impulse of a vague imaginative mass pressing for development and definition. If the poet already knew exactly what he meant to say, why should he write the poem? The poem would in fact already be written. For only its completion can reveal, even to him, exactly what he wanted. When he began and while he was at work, he did not possess his meaning; it possessed him. It was not a fully formed soul asking for a body: it was an inchoate soul in the inchoate body of perhaps two or three vague ideas and a few scattered phrases. The growing of this body into its full stature and perfect shape was the same thing as the gradual self-definition of the meaning. And this is the reason why such poems strike us as creations, not manufactures, and have the magical effect which mere decoration cannot produce. This is also the reason why, if we insist on asking for the meaning of such a poem, we can only be answered 'It means itself.' [. . .] About the best poetry, and not only the best, there floats an atmosphere of infinite suggestion. The poet speaks to us of one thing, but in this one thing there seems to lurk the secret of all. He said what he meant, but his meaning seems to beckon away beyond itself, or rather to expand into something boundless which is only focused in it; something also which, we feel, would satisfy not only the imagination, but the whole of us. [. . .]

This all-embracing perfection cannot be expressed in poetic words or words of any kind, nor yet in music or in colour, but the suggestion of it is in much poetry, if not all, and poetry has in this suggestion, this 'meaning,' a great part of its value. We do it wrong, and we defeat our own purposes, when we try to bend it to them:

> We do it wrong, being so majestical,
> To offer it the show of violence;
> For it is as the air invulnerable,
> And our vain blows malicious mockery.

It is a spirit. It comes we know not whence. It will not speak at our bidding, nor answer in our language. It is not our servant; it is our master.

(A. C. Bradley, 'Poetry for Poetry's Sake', *Oxford Lectures on Poetry* (1909), (London and Basingstoke: Macmillan, 1965), pp. 4–5, 6–7, 13, 23–4, 26, 26–7.)

(G) CLIVE BELL

Art (1914)

All systems of aesthetics must be based on personal experience – that is to say, they must be subjective.

Yet, though all aesthetic theories must be based on aesthetic judgments, and ultimately all aesthetic judgments must be matters of personal taste, it would be rash to assert that no theory of aesthetics can have general validity. For, though A, B, C, D are the works that move me, and A, D, E, F the works that move you, it may well be that x is the only quality believed by either of us to be common to all the works in his list. We may all agree about aesthetics, and yet differ about particular works of art. We may differ as to the presence or absence of the quality *x*. My immediate object will be to show that significant form is the only quality common and peculiar to all the works of visual art that move me; and I will ask those whose aesthetic experience does not tally with mine to see whether this quality is not also, in their judgment, common to all works that move them, and whether they can discover any other quality of which the same can be said. [. . .]

In pure aesthetics we have only to consider our emotion and its object; for the purposes of aesthetics we have no right, neither is there any necessity, to pry behind the object into the state of mind of him who made it. [. . .] For a discussion of aesthetics, it need be agreed only that forms arranged and combined according to certain unknown and mysterious laws do move us in a particular way, and that it is the business of an artist so to combine and arrange them that they shall move us. These moving combinations and arrangements I have called, for the sake of convenience and for a reason that will appear later, 'Significant Form.' [. . .]

Art is above morals, or, rather, all art is moral because, as I hope to show presently, works of art are immediate means to good. Once we have judged a thing a work of art, we have judged it ethically of the first importance and put it beyond the reach of the moralist. [. . .]

Let no one imagine that representation is bad in itself; a realistic form may be as significant, in its place as part of the design, as an abstract. But if a representative form has value, it is as form, not as representation. The representative element in a work of art may or may not be harmful; always it is irrelevant. For, to appreciate a work of art we need bring with us nothing from life, no knowledge of its ideas and affairs, no familiarity with its emotions. Art transports us from the world of man's activity to a world of aesthetic exaltation. For a moment we are shut off from human interests; our anticipations and memories are arrested; we are lifted above the stream of life. [. . .] Significant form stands charged with the power to provoke aesthetic emotion in anyone capable of feeling it. The ideas of men go buzz and die like gnats; men change their institutions and their customs as they change their coats; the intellectual triumphs of one age are the follies of another; only great art remains stable and unobscure. Great art remains stable and unobscure because the feelings that it awakens are independent of time and place, because its kingdom is not of this world. [. . .]

Certainly, in those moments of exaltation, that art can give, it is easy to believe that we have been possessed by an emotion that comes from the world of reality. Those who take this view will have to say that there is in all things the stuff out of which art is made – reality; artists, even, can grasp it only when they have reduced things to their purest condition of being – to pure form – unless they be of those who come at it mysteriously unaided by externals; only in pure form can a sense of it be expressed. On this hypothesis the peculiarity of the artist would seem to be that he possesses the power of surely and frequently seizing reality (generally behind pure form), and the power of expressing his sense of it, in pure form always. [. . .]

Call it by what name you will, the thing that I am talking about is that which lies behind the appearance of all things – that which gives to all things their individual significance, the thing in itself, the ultimate reality. And if a more or less unconscious apprehension of this latent reality of material things be, indeed, the cause of that strange emotion, a passion to express which is the inspiration of many artists, it seems reasonable to suppose that those who, unaided by material objects, experience the same emotion have come by another road to the same country.

(Clive Bell, *Art* (London: Chatto & Windus, 1914), pp. 9–10, 11, 20, 25, 37, 56–7, 69–70.)

(H) JAN MUKAŘOVSKÝ

Aesthetic Function, Norm and Value as Social Facts (1936)

There are [. . .] – within art and outside of it – objects which, by virtue of their organization are meant to have an aesthetic effect. This is actually the essential property of art. But an active capacity for the aesthetic function is not a real property of an object, even if the object has been deliberately composed with the aesthetic function in mind. Rather, the aesthetic function manifests itself only under certain conditions, i.e. in a certain social context. A phenomenon which, in one time period, country, etc., was the privileged bearer of the aesthetic function may be incapable of bearing this function in a different time, country, etc. In the history of art there is no lack of cases in which the original aesthetic or artistic effect of a certain product was re-discovered only through scientific research. [. . .]

Summarizing our remarks on the distribution and influence of the aesthetic function, we may draw the following conclusions: 1. The aesthetic is, in itself, neither a real property of an object nor is it explicitly connected to some of its properties. 2. The aesthetic function of an object is likewise not totally under the control of an individual, although from a purely subjective standpoint the aesthetic function may be acquired (or, conversely, lost) by anything, regardless of its organization. 3. Stabilizing the aesthetic function is a matter for the collective and is a component in the relationship between the human collective and the world. Hence any given distribution of the aesthetic function in the material world is tied to a particular social entity. The manner in which this entity deals with the aesthetic function predetermines, in the final analysis, both the objective organization of objects intended to produce an aesthetic effect and the subjective aesthetic reaction to those objects. Thus, for example, in periods when the collective tends toward intensive application of the aesthetic function, the individual is more free to relate aesthetically to objects, either actively (in creating them) or passively (in perceiving them). The tendencies to widen or narrow the aesthetic realm, since they are social facts, always manifest a number of attendant symptoms. In this sense, poetic Symbolism and Decadence, with their panaestheticism, are parallel to and synonymous with modern decorative art, which is expanding the boundaries of art to excess. All of these phenomena are symptomatic of the extreme hypertrophy of the aesthetic function within a contemporaneous social context. A similar set of parallel phenomena may be observed today. Modern (Constructivist) architecture is tending, in theory and practice, to abandon artistic features and proclaims its ambition to become a science, or, more precisely, an application of scientific concepts, and of sociological concepts in particular. Surrealist poets and artists are approaching the problem from a different direction. They base their approach on scientific research into the subconscious. So-called Socialist Realism in literature, particularly in Russian literature, belongs in part to this category since it requires of art, first and foremost, the synthetic depiction and propagation of a new social order. The common denominator of these varied and sometimes partially inimical tendencies is the polemic versus 'artistry' which was so much emphasized in the recent past, i.e., a reaction to the realization of absolute supremacy of the aesthetic function in art – a reaction which is expressed by the current tendency of art to approach the realm of extra-aesthetic phenomena.

The aesthetic sphere develops as a whole and is, in addition, constantly related to those aspects of reality which, at a given point in time, do not exhibit the aesthetic function at all. Such unity and integrity are possible only if we assume a collective awareness which combines the ties among objects bearing the aesthetic function and which unifies mutually isolated individual states of awareness. We are not postulating collective awareness as a psychological reality, nor does this term indicate simply the total import of a group of social components to individual states of consciousness. Collective awareness is a social fact. It can be defined as the locus of existence of individual systems of cultural phenomena such as language, religion, science, politics, etc. These systems are realities even though they can not be perceived by the senses. They reveal their existence by exerting a normative influence on empirical reality. Thus, for example, any deviation from a linguistic system embedded in the collective awareness is spontaneously noted and is evaluated as a mistake. The aesthetic also appears in the collective awareness, primarily as a system of norms. [. . .]

Wherever in social intercourse it becomes necessary to emphasize any act, object or person, to focus on it, to free it from undesirable associations, the aesthetic function emerges as an accompanying factor; cp. the aesthetic function of any ceremonial (including religion) or the aesthetic coloration of public celebrations. Due to its isolating properties, the aesthetic function can also become a socially differentiating factor; cp. the greater sensitivity toward the aesthetic function, and its more intensive utilization, in the higher levels of society which attempt to distinguish themselves from the other social levels (the aesthetic function as a factor in 'prestige'), or the deliberate use of the aesthetic function to stress the importance of people in power, as well as to separate them from the rest of the collective (e.g., the clothing of the actual people in power or of their subordinates, their residences, etc.). The isolating power of the aesthetic function – or rather its ability to direct attention to an object or a person – makes it an important concomitant factor in the erotic function. Note, for example, clothing, especially women's clothing, in which these two functions often merge completely.

Another important feature of the aesthetic function is the pleasure which it evokes. Hence its ability to facilitate acts to which it belongs as a secondary function, as well as the ability to intensify the pleasure connected with them; cp. the use of the aesthetic function in child-rearing, dining, housing, etc. Finally we must mention a third, unique property of the aesthetic function, conditioned by the fact that this function attaches above all to the *form* of an object or act; it is the ability to supplant some other function which the item (object or act) has lost in the course of its development. Hence the frequent aesthetic coloration of relics, either material (e.g., ruins, folk dress in areas where its other functions – practical, magical, etc. – have vanished), or non-material (e.g., various rituals). It is appropriate here to mention the well-known fact that the same process often occurs with scientific works which, in the period of their origin, possessed both an intellectual and a concomitant aesthetic function. The works outlived their scientific validity and went on to function partially or entirely aesthetically – cf. *Dějiny* by Palacký or the works of Buffon. An aesthetic function which supplants other functions often causes cultural conservatism in the sense that is preserves for a future period human products and institutions which have lost their original, practical function, so that they can again be used, this time in a different practical function.

Thus the aesthetic function means much more than mere coating on the surface of an object or of the world, as some people would have us think. It significantly affects the lives of individuals and society, shares in the organization of contacts – active as well as passive – of individuals with that reality in which they find themselves. The remainder of this article will be devoted, as we noted above, to a more detailed examination of the social importance of aesthetic phenomena. This introduction was an attempt to delimit the aesthetic realm and to explore the nature of its developmental dynamics.

(Jan Mukařovský, *Aesthetic Function, Norm and Value as Social Facts*, trans. Mark E. Suino, Michigan Slavic Contributions, no. 3 (Ann Arbor: University of Michigan, 1970), pp. 3, 18–20, 21–3. Original Czech, 1936.)

(I) FREDRIC JAMESON

Marxism and Form (1971)

When we turn now from popular culture to the more sophisticated artifacts of official literature, we find that the fact of artistic *elaboration* adds a new complexity to the structure of the work. [. . .] In particular, art-literature can be said to reckon the whole value of its own creation itself into the process, so that the inner form of literary works, at least in modern times, can be said to have as their subject either production as such or *literary* production as well – both being in any case distinct from the ostensible or manifest content of the work.

Thus it is a mistake to think, for instance, that the books of Hemingway deal essentially with such things as courage, love, and death; in reality, their deepest subject is simply the writing of a certain type of sentence, the practice of a determinate style. This is indeed the most 'concrete' experience in Hemingway, yet to understand its relationship to the other, more dramatic experiences we must reformulate our notion of inner form after the more complex model of a *hierarchy of motivations*, in which the various elements of the work are ordered at various levels from the surface, and serve so to speak as pretexts each for the existence of a deeper one, so that in the long run everything in the work exists in order to bring to expression that deepest level of the work which is the concrete itself; or, reversing the model after the fashion of the Prague School, to *foreground* the work's most essential content.

Thus the enormous influence of Hemingway as a kind of life model would seem to derive first from a kind of ethical content, not a 'philosophy of life' so much as an instinctive and intransigent refusal of what suddenly turns out to have ceased to be real living. 'It isn't fun any more': such is the irrevocable boundary line between euphoria and ill humor, between real life and a kind of failure to live which exasperates and poisons the existence of the hero and everyone else around him. Such are the two poles of Hemingway's creation: those incomparable moments of plenitude in nature on the one hand, and on the other, bitching and sudden moods, sudden fits of envy or temper. [. . .]

Thus one is wrong to say that Hemingway began by wishing to express or convey certain basic experiences; rather, he began by wishing to write a certain type of sentence, a kind of neutral *compte rendu* of external displacements, and very quickly he found that such a sentence could do two kinds of things well: register movement in the external world, and suggest the tension and fitful resentment between people which is intermittently expressed in their spoken comment.

So we return to our initial contention that what really happens in a Hemingway novel, the most essential event, the dominant category of experience for both writer and reader alike, is the process of writing; and this is perhaps clearest in a simpler work like the *Green Hills of Africa*, where the shooting of the animal in the content is but the pretext for the *description* of the shooting in the form. The reader is not so much interested in observing the kill as he is in whether Hemingway's language will be able to rise to the occasion: 'A little beyond there a flock of guineas quick-legged across the road running steady-headed with the motion of trotters. As I jumped from the car and sprinted after them they rocketed up, their legs tucked close beneath them, heavy-bodied, short wings drumming, cackling, to go over the trees ahead. I dropped two that thumped hard when they fell and as they lay, wings beating, Abdullah cut their heads off so they would be legal eating.' The real 'pursuit' involved is thus the pursuit of the sentence itself.

From this central point in Hemingway's creation all the rest can be deduced: the experience of sentence-production is the form taken in Hemingway's world by nonalienated work. Writing, now conceived as a *skill*, is then assimilated to the other skills of hunting and bullfighting, of fishing and warfare, which project a total image of man's active and all-absorbing technical participation in the outside world. Such an ideology of technique clearly reflects the more general American work situation, where, in the context of the open frontier and the blurring of class structure, the American male is conventionally evaluated according to the number of different jobs he has had, and skills he possesses. The Hemingway cult of *machismo* is just this attempt to come to terms with the great industrial transformation of America after World War I: it satisfies the Protestant work ethic at the same time that it glorifies leisure; it reconciles the deepest and most life-giving impulses toward wholeness with a status quo in which only sports allow you to feel alive and undamaged.

As for the human environment of Hemingway's books, expatriation is itself a kind of device or pretext for them. For the immense and complex fabric of American social reality itself is clearly inaccessible to the careful and selective type of sentence which he practices: so it is useful to have to do with a reality thinned out, the reality of foreign cultures and of foreign languages, where the individual beings come before us not in the density of a concrete social situation in which we also are involved, but rather with the cleanness of objects which can be verbally circumscribed. And when at the end of his life the world began to change, and the Cuban Revolution made a retreat back within the borders of the United States in order, it does not seem too farfetched to speculate that it was the resistance of such American reality, which as a writer he had never practiced, that brought him to stylistic impotence and ultimate suicide.

If this suggests something of the way in which a Marxist criticism would reconstruct the inner form of a literary work, as both disguise and revelation of the concrete, it remains for us to say a word about the implications of such a theory for judgment or literary evaluations as they are currently practiced. For to claim that the task of the critic is to reveal this censored dimension of the work implies precisely that, at least in art as it is practiced today, in the society in which it is practiced, the surface of the work is a kind of mystification in its structure.

(Fredric Jameson, *Marxism and Form* (Princeton, NJ: Princeton UP, 1971), pp. 408–10, 411–13.)

CHAPTER 2

UNITY AND LITERARINESS

The concept of 'unity' in literary studies was once treated as axiomatic, but in recent years it has been made problematic by post-structuralists and others who have addressed those aspects of 'textuality' and subjectivity which introduce disruption and 'heterogeneity'. It still remains true, however, that we often bring to our reading an almost unconscious premise – that the finest literary texts will have no loose ends and no gaps, flaws, lapses, or unmanageable contradictions. This may be a hangover from our Romantic and New Critical inheritance. An emphasis on unity belongs with 'organicist' thought and with a specialist approach to literary study. Both tendencies are present in Aristotle's *Poetics*, according to which a tragedy is required to be a 'whole' by possessing a beginning, middle and end. The parts of a play must have an inevitability and necessity: nothing should be included which is inessential. A tragedy should have the unity of an organic form.

The Romantic belief in the 'vital' principle promoted this organicist conception of a literary work. Colderidge argued that a poem is not a sequence of purple patches linked by neutral passages acting as connective filling. Every element is a 'harmonising part'. The New Critics were anti-Romantic in many respects, but they also believed in the essential unity of literary texts. They had a less airy notion of a poem's ontology, and were fundamentally modern in their concern for the *linguistic specificity* of a work's unity.

An awareness that language is *constructed* and is not a transparent vehicle of thought is distinctive of modern criticism. Both Russian Formalism and New Criticism ask the question 'What is distinctive about the way literature uses language?' They both regard literature as a special use of language which is able to convey experience in a fresh or novel way. Shklovsky argues that the devices of literature deliberately roughen the surface of language in order to gain the reader's attention and to 'defamiliarize' perceptions which otherwise would remain automatic or habitual. Interestingly, T. E. Hulme, an important influence on New Criticism, developed the same theory in different terms when he wrote about poetry's special power of giving us the 'exact curve' of a thing. The poet's 'zest' in expressing a particular perception motivates this concern for precision in poetic language. The emphasis on the concreteness of poetry's apprehension of reality is central in New Criticism. Ransom's *The World's Body* (1938), as its title suggests, regards poetic language as more inclusive, more comprehensive, in its power to communicate the fullness of experience; 'prose statement' gives us only a thin apprehension of actuality. Literature was regarded as the preserver of sensibility and whole-mindedness, standing against the pressure of mass culture and industrial society. The American Southern Critics (Ransom, Tate, and others) grounded their theories in a conservative 'agrarian' politics which sought to preserve (or rather revive) what was felt to be a more truly human way of life. Literature was both an escape from modern life and an ideal realm of true humanity. The Russian Formalists, especially Shklovsky, were not really interested in experience itself. Attention is focused not upon the extra-literary dimension of a 'defamiliarized' perception but upon the literary process itself. In this respect 'defamiliarization' also differs from Brecht's 'alienation effect' (see I,2,E) which is concerned with altering the audience's perceptions in order to change their political attitudes and actions. The Formalists were criticized by Trotsky and others for being concerned purely with matters of technique and for ignoring the 'social command'.

Roman Jakobson asked the question 'What is literariness?' What makes literature literary? The Formalists believed that a true study of literature concentrates on the formal devices which are used to produce the effects of defamiliarization. Shklovsky's classic study of Laurence Sterne's *Tristram Shandy* draws attention to the extent of Sterne's literariness: the 'content' of the novel (the story of Tristram's birth, etc.) is subordinated to the elaboration of devices which dislocate the story, retard description, lengthen perceptions, and generally roughen the surface of the discourse. The most literary thing a writer can do is to draw attention to – 'to lay bare' – the devices themselves.

New Critics treated poetry as the norm of literary language.

Accepting the Romantic fact/value dichotomy (see II,3,intro.), as formulated in I. A. Richards' work (II,3,F), they contrasted poetic language with science and 'matter of fact'. Poetry is what is left over when you extract a mere prose paraphrase, or, in a more sophisticated version, it is a condensation of the whole gamut of meanings from the matter-of-fact to the most subjective connotation. They extended the Romantic notions of literature by offering a more inclusive definition of the poetic: poetry is not confined to the sublime, the infinite, and the noble; it embraces the mundane, the intellectual, and the ironic. As we shall see in the next section, this support of a 'unified sensibility', as T. S. Eliot called it, tended to encourage complexity, ambiguity, and polysemy. However, the insistence on *experience* and on *unity* prevented the idea of multiple meaning from getting out of hand (with the notable exception of the prophetic William Empson – see III,3,C).

Both the Formalists and the New Critics treat the literary text as an autonomous (or 'autotelic') object. Only by isolating the text from its author and its contexts can the critic, in their view, develop a properly rigorous and objective analysis. The establishment and development of literary criticism as a discipline depended on this missionary sense of possessing an autonomous object of study. The New Critics reacted strongly against old-fashioned biographical and historical interpretations of literature, because they failed to explain the *literary* process, and specifically the ways in which literary works absorb biography, history, language, and so on, into their structures. The New Critics were able to claim that literary study was at last a properly constituted academic practice with rigorous analytic procedures and a clearly defined object of study. This achievement was not seriously challenged until the 1970s.

Background reading

Stephen Bann and John E. Bowlt (eds), *Russian Formalism* (Edinburgh: Scottish Academic Press, 1973).

Tony Bennett, *Formalism and Marxism* (London and New York: Methuen, 1979).

Victor Erlich, *Russian Formalism: History-Doctrine* (3rd edn, New Haven: Yale UP, 1981).

John Fekete, *The Critical Twilight: Explorations in the Ideology of Anglo-American Literary Theory from Eliot to McLuhan* (London, Henley and Boston: Routledge & Kegan Paul, 1977), Part 2.

Gerald Graff, 'What was New Criticism?' in *Literature Against Itself* (Chicago and London: University of Chicago Press, 1979).

Murray Krieger, *The New Apologists for Poetry* (Minneapolis: University of Minnesota Press, 1956), chs 4, 5 and 7.

David Robey, 'Anglo-American New Criticism', in *Modern Literary Theory*, ed. Ann Jefferson and David Robey (2nd edn, London: Batsford, 1986).

Raman Selden, *Criticism and Objectivity* (London: Allen & Unwin, 1984), ch. 4 on Russian Formalism.

Lewis P. Simpson (ed.), *The Possibilities of Order: Cleanth Brooks and his Work* (Louisiana State UP, 1976).

Peter Steiner, *Russian Formalism: A Metapoetics* (Ithaca: Cornell UP, 1984).

E. M. Thompson, *Russian Formalism and Anglo-American New Criticism* (The Hague: Mouton, 1971).

René Wellek, 'J. C. Ransom's Theory of Poetry', in *Literary Theory and Structure*, ed. Frank Brady *et al.* (New Haven and London: Yale UP, 1973).

(A) ARISTOTLE

Poetics

[CHAPTERS 7,8,23]

. . . [L]et us now consider the proper construction of the Fable or Plot, as that is at once the first and the most important thing in Tragedy. We have laid it down that a tragedy is an imitation of an action that is complete in itself, as a whole of some magnitude; for a whole may be of no magnitude to speak of. Now a whole is that which has beginning, middle, and end. A beginning is that which is not itself necessarily after anything else, and which has naturally something else after it; an end is that which is naturally after something itself, either as its necessary or usual consequent, and with nothing else after it; and a middle, that which is by nature after one thing and has also another after it. A well-constructed Plot, therefore, cannot either begin or end at any point one likes; beginning and end in it must be of the forms just described. Again: to be beautiful, a living creature, and every whole made of parts, must not only present a certain order in its arrangement of parts, but also be of a certain definite magnitude. Beauty is a matter of size and order, and therefore impossible either (1) in a very minute creature, since our perception becomes indistinct as it approaches instantaneity; or (2) in a creature of vast size – one, say, 1,000 miles long – as in that case, instead of the object being seen all at once, the unity and wholeness of it is lost to the beholder. Just in the same way, then, as a beautiful whole made up of parts, or a beautiful living creature, must be of some size, a size to be taken in by the eye, so a story or Plot must be of some length, but of a length to be taken in by the memory. As for the limit of its length, so far as that is relative to public performances and spectators, it does not fall within the theory of poetry. If they had to perform a hundred tragedies, they would be timed by water-clocks, as they are said to have been at one period. The limit, however, set by the actual nature of the thing is this: the longer the story, consistently with its being comprehensible as a whole, the finer it is by reason of its magnitude. As a rough general formula, 'a length which allows of the hero passing by a series of probable or necessary stages from misfortune to happiness, or from happiness to misfortune', may suffice as a limit for the magnitude of the story.

The Unity of a Plot does not consist, as some suppose, in its having one man as its subject. An infinity of things befall that one man, some of which it is impossible to reduce to unity; and in like manner there are many actions of one man which cannot be made to form one action. One sees, therefore, the mistake of all the poets who have written a *Heracleid*, a *Theseid*, or similar poems; they suppose that, because Heracles was one man, the story also of Heracles must be one story. Homer, however, evidently understood this point quite well, whether by art or instinct, just in the same way as he excels the rest in every other respect. In writing an *Odyssey*, he did not make the poem cover all that ever befell his hero – it befell him, for instance, to get wounded on Parnassus and also to feign madness at the time of the call to arms, but the two incidents had no probable or necessary connexion with one another – instead of doing that, he took an action with a Unity of the kind we are describing as the subject of the *Odyssey*, as also of the *Iliad*. The truth is that, just as in the other imitative arts one imitation is always of one thing, so in poetry the story, as an imitation of action, must represent one action, a complete whole, with its several incidents so closely connected that the transposal or withdrawal of any one of them will disjoin and dislocate the whole. For that which makes no perceptible difference by its presence or absence is no real part of the whole. [. . .]

As for the poetry which merely narrates, or imitates by means of versified language (without action), it is evident that it has several points in common with Tragedy.

I. The construction of its stories should clearly be like that in a drama; they should be based on a single action, one that is a complete whole in itself, with a beginning, middle, and end, so as to enable the work to produce its own proper pleasure with all the organic unity of a living creature. Nor should one suppose that there is anything like them in our usual histories. A history has to deal not with one action, but with one period and all that happened in that to one or more persons, however disconnected the several events may have been.

(Aristotle, *Poetics*, trans. Ingram Bywater, *On the Art of Poetry* (Oxford: Clarendon Press, 1920), pp. 39–43, 79.)

(B) SAMUEL TAYLOR COLERIDGE

Biographia Literaria (1817)

[CHAPTER 14]

The final definition [of a poem . . .] may be thus worded. A poem is that species of composition, which is opposed to works of science, by proposing for its *immediate* object pleasure, not truth; and from all other species (having *this* object in common with it) it is discriminated by proposing to itself such delight from the *whole* as is compatible with a distinct gratification from each component *part*.

Controversy is not seldom excited in consequence of the disputants attaching each a different meaning to the same word; and in few instances has this been more striking than in disputes concerning the present subject. If a man chooses to call every composition a poem which is rhyme, or measure, or both, I must leave his opinion uncontroverted. The distinction is at least competent to characterize the writer's intention. If it were subjoined that the whole is likewise entertaining or affecting, as a tale, or as a series of interesting reflections, I of course admit this as another fit ingredient of a poem, and an additional merit. But if the definition sought for be that of a *legitimate* poem, I answer it must be one the parts of which mutually support and explain each other; all in their proportion harmonizing with, and supporting the purpose and known influences of metrical arrangement. The philosophic critics of all ages coincide with the ultimate judgment of all countries in equally denying the praises of a just poem, on the one hand, to a series of striking lines or

distiches, each of which absorbing the whole attention of the
reader to itself disjoins it from its context, and makes it a
separate whole, instead of a harmonizing part; and on the other
hand, to an unsustained composition, from which the reader
collects rapidly the general result, unattracted by the component
parts. The reader should be carried forward, not merely or
chiefly by the mechanical impulse of curiosity, or by a restless
desire to arrive at the final solution; but by the pleasureable
activity of mind excited by the attractions of the journey itself.

(Samuel Taylor Coleridge, *Biographia Literaria* (1817), ed. J. Shawcross,
2 vols (London: Oxford UP, 1907), II. 10–11.)

(C) VIKTOR SHKLOVSKY

'Art as Technique' (1917)

We must, then, speak about the laws of expenditure and
economy in poetic language not on the basis of an analogy with
prose, but on the basis of the laws of poetic language.

If we start to examine the general laws of perception, we see
that as perception becomes habitual, it becomes automatic.
Thus, for example, all of our habits retreat into the area of the
unconsciously automatic; if one remembers the sensations of
holding a pen or of speaking in a foreign language for the first
time and compares that with his feeling at performing the action
for the ten thousandth time, he will agree with us. [. . .]

And so life is reckoned as nothing. Habitualization devours
works, clothes, furniture, one's wife, and the fear of war. 'If the
whole complex lives of many people go on unconsciously, then
such lives are as if they had never been.' And art exists that one
may recover the sensation of life; it exists to make one feel
things, to make the stone *stony*. The purpose of art is to impart
the sensation of things as they are perceived and not as they are
known. The technique of art is to make objects 'unfamiliar,' to
make forms difficult, to increase the difficulty and length of
perception because the process of perception is an aesthetic end
in itself and must be prolonged. *Art is a way of experiencing the
artfulness of an object; the object is not important.* [. . .]

After we see an object several times, we begin to recognize it.
The object is in front of us and we know about it, but we do
not see it – hence we cannot say anything significant about it.
Art removes objects from the automatism of perception in

several ways. Here I want to illustrate a way used repeatedly by Leo Tolstoy, that writer who, for Merezhkovsky at least, seems to present things as if he himself saw them, saw them in their entirety, and did not alter them.

Tolstoy makes the familiar seem strange by not naming the familiar object. He describes an object as if he were seeing it for the first time, an event as if it were happening for the first time. In describing something he avoids the accepted names of its parts and instead names corresponding parts of other objects. For example, in 'Shame' Tolstoy 'defamiliarizes' the idea of flogging in this way: 'to strip people who have broken the law, to hurl them to the floor, and to rap on their bottoms with switches,' and, after a few lines, 'to lash about on the naked buttocks.' Then he remarks:

> Just why precisely this stupid, savage means of causing pain and not any other – why not prick the shoulders or any part of the body with needles, squeeze the hands or the feet in a vise, or anything like that?

I apologize for this harsh example, but it is typical of Tolstoy's way of pricking the conscience. The familiar act of flogging is made unfamiliar both by the description and by the proposal to change its form without changing its nature. Tolstoy uses this technique of 'defamiliarization' constantly. The narrator of 'Kholstomer,' for example, is a horse, and it is the horse's point of view (rather than a person's) that makes the content of the story seem unfamiliar. [. . .]

In studying poetic speech in its phonetic and lexical structure as well as in its characteristic distribution of words and in the characteristic thought structures compounded from the words, we find everywhere the artistic trademark – that is, we find material obviously created to remove the automatism of perception; the author's purpose is to create the vision which results from that deautomatized perception. A work is created 'artistically' so that its perception is impeded and the greatest possible effect is produced through the slowness of the perception. As a result of this lingering, the object is perceived not in its extension in space, but, so to speak, in its continuity. Thus 'poetic language' gives satisfaction. According to Aristotle, poetic language must appear strange and wonderful; and, in fact, it is often actually foreign: the Sumerian used by the Assyrians, the Latin of Europe during the Middle Ages, the Arabisms of the Persians, the Old Bulgarian of Russian literature, or the elevated, almost literary language of folk songs. The common archaisms of poetic language, the intricacy of the sweet new style [*dolce stil nuovo*], the obscure style of the language of Arnaut Daniel with the 'roughened' [*harte*] forms *which make pronunciation difficult* – these are used in much the same way. Leo Jakubinsky has demonstrated the principle of phonetic 'roughening' of poetic language in the particular case of the repetition of identical sounds. The language of poetry is, then, a difficult, roughened, impeded language.

(Viktor Shklovsky, 'Art as Technique' (1917), *Russian Formalist Criticism: Four Essays*, trans. Lee T. Lemon and Marion J. Reis (Lincoln and London: University of Nebraska Press, 1965), pp. 11, 12, 13–14, 21–2.)

'Sterne's *Tristram Shandy*' (1921)

In this essay to I do not propose to analyze Laurence Sterne's novel, but rather to illustrate general laws of plot. Formalistically, Sterne was an extreme revolutionary; it was characteristic of him to 'lay bare' his technique. [. . .]

Sterne even lays bare the technique of combining separate story lines to make up the novel. In general, he accentuates the very structure of the novel. By violating the form, he forces us to attend to it; and, for him, this awareness of the form through its violation constitutes the content of the novel. [. . .]

A few words about sentimentality in general are appropriate here. Sentimentality cannot serve as the mainstay of art, since art has no mainstay. The presentation of things from 'a sentimental point of view' is a special method of presentation, like the presentation of them from the point of view of a horse (as in Tolstoy's 'Kholstomer') or of a giant (as in Swift's *Gulliver's Travels*).

Art is essentially trans-emotional, as in stories told of persons rolled into the sea in a barrel spiked inside like an iron maiden. In the Russian version of 'Tom Thumb' children will not permit the omission even of the detail of the cannibal cutting off the heads of his daughters, not because children are cruel, but because the detail is part of the legend. Professor Anichkov's *Ceremonial Songs of Spring* includes vernal dancing songs which deal with ugly, quarrelsome husbands; maggots; and death. Although these are unpleasant, they are part of the songs. Gore in art is not necessarily gory; it rhymes with *amor* – it is either the substance of the tonal structure or material for the construction of figures of speech.

Art, then, is unsympathetic – or beyond sympathy – except where the feeling of compassion is evoked as material for the artistic structure. In discussing such emotion we have to examine it from the point of view of the composition itself, in exactly the same way that a mechanic must examine a driving belt to understand the details of a machine; he certainly would not study the driving belt as if he were a vegetarian.

(Viktor Shklovsky, 'Sterne's *Tristram Shandy*' (1921), *Russian Formalist Criticism: Four Essays*, trans. Lee T. Lemon and Marion J. Reis (Lincoln and London: University of Nebraska Press, 1965), pp. 27, 30–1, 43–4.)

(D) T. E. HULME

Speculations (1924)

The great aim is accurate, precise and definite description. [. . .] each man sees a little differently, and to get out clearly and exactly what he does see, he must have a terrific struggle with language, whether it be with words or the technique of other arts. Language has its own special nature, its own conventions and communal ideas. It is only by a concentrated effort of the mind that you can hold it fixed to your own purpose. I always think that the fundamental process at the back of all the arts might be represented by the following metaphor. You know what I call architect's curves – flat pieces of wood with all different kinds of curvature. By a suitable selection from these you can draw approximately any curve you like. The artist I take to be the man who simply can't bear the idea of that 'approximately.' He will get the exact curve of what he sees whether it be an object or an idea in the mind. I shall here have to change my metaphor a little to get the process in his mind. Suppose that instead of your curved pieces of wood you have a springy piece of steel of the same types of curvature as the wood. Now the state of tension or concentration of mind, if he is doing anything really good in this struggle against the ingrained habit of the technique, may be represented by a man employing all his fingers to bend the steel out of its own curve and into the exact curve which you want. Something different to what it would assume naturally.

There are then two things to distinguish, first the particular faculty of mind to see things as they really are, and apart from the conventional ways in which you have been trained to see them. This is itself rare enough in all consciousness. Second, the concentrated state of mind, the grip over oneself which is necessary in the actual expression of what one sees. To prevent one falling into the conventional curves of ingrained technique, to hold on through infinite detail and trouble to the exact curve you want. [. . .]

I can now get at that positive fundamental quality of verse which constitutes excellence, which has nothing to do with infinity, with mystery or with emotions.

This is the point I aim at, then, in my argument. I prophesy that a period of dry, hard, classical verse is coming. I have met the preliminary objection founded on the bad romantic æsthetic that in such verse, from which the infinite is excluded, you cannot have the essence of poetry at all.

After attempting to sketch out what this positive quality is, I can get on to the end of my paper in this way: That where you get this quality exhibited in the realm of the emotions you get imagination, and that where you get this quality exhibited in the contemplation of finite things you get fancy. [. . .]

I shall maintain that wherever you get an extraordinary interest in a thing, a great zest in its contemplation which carries on the contemplator to accurate description in the sense of the word accurate I have just analysed, there you have sufficient justification for poetry. It must be an intense zest which heightens a thing out of the level of prose. I am using contemplation here just in the same way that Plato used it, only applied to a different subject; it is a detached interest. 'The object of æsthetic contemplation is something framed apart by itself and regarded without memory or expectation, simply as being itself, as end not means, as individual not universal.'

To take a concrete example. I am taking an extreme case. If you are walking behind a woman in the street, you notice the curious way in which the skirt rebounds from her heels. If that peculiar kind of motion becomes of such interest to you that you will search about until you can get the exact epithet which hits it off, there you have a properly æsthetic emotion. But it is the zest with which you look at the thing which decides you to make the effort. In this sense the feeling that was in Herrick's mind when he wrote 'the tempestuous petticoat' was exactly the same as that which in bigger and vaguer matters makes the best romantic verse.

It doesn't matter an atom that the emotion produced is not of dignified vagueness, but on the contrary amusing; the point is

that exactly the same activity is at work as in the highest verse.
That is the avoidance of conventional language in order to get
the exact curve of the thing. [. . .]

If it is sincere in the accurate sense, when the whole of the
analogy is necessary to get out the exact curve of the feeling or
thing you want to express – there you seem to me to have the
highest verse, even though the subject be trivial and the
emotions of the infinite far away.

It is very difficult to use any terminology at all for this kind of
thing. For whatever word you use is at once sentimentalised.
Take Coleridge's word 'vital.' It is used loosely by all kinds of
people who talk about art, to mean something vaguely and
mysteriously significant. In fact, vital and mechanical is to them
exactly the same antithesis as between good and bad.

Nothing of the kind; Coleridge uses it in a perfectly definite
and what I call dry sense. It is just this: A mechanical
complexity is the sum of its parts. Put them side by side and
you get the whole. Now vital or organic is merely a convenient
metaphor for a complexity of a different kind, that in which the
parts cannot be said to be elements as each one is modified by
the other's presence, and each one to a certain extent is the
whole. The leg of a chair by itself is still a leg. My leg by itself
wouldn't be.

(T. E. Hulme, *Speculations* (London: Routledge & Kegan Paul, 1924),
pp. 132–4, 136–7, 138–9.)

(E) JOHN CROWE RANSOM

'Criticism, Inc.', *The World's Body* (1937)

What is criticism? Easier to ask, What is criticism not? It is an
act now notoriously arbitrary and undefined. We feel certain
that the critical act is not one of those which the professors of
literature habitually perform, and cause their students to
perform. And it is our melancholy impression that it is not often
cleanly performed in those loose compositions, by writers of
perfectly indeterminate qualifications, that appear in print as
reviews of books.

Professor Crane excludes from criticism works of historical
scholarship and of Neo-Humanism, but more exclusions are
possible than that. I should wish to exclude;

1. Personal registrations, which are declarations of the effect of the art-work upon the critic as reader. The first law to be prescribed to criticism, if we may assume such authority, is that it shall be objective, shall cite the nature of the object rather than its effects upon the subject. Therefore it is hardly criticism to assert that the proper literary work is one that we can read twice; or one that causes in us some remarkable physiological effect, such as oblivion of the outer world, the flowing of tears, visceral or laryngeal sensations, and such like; or one that induces perfect illusion, or brings us into a spiritual ecstasy; or even one that produces a catharsis of our emotions. Aristotle concerned himself with this last in making up his definition of tragedy – though he did not fail to make some acute analyses of the objective features of the work also. I have read that some modern Broadway producers of comedy require a reliable person to seat himself in a trial audience and count the laughs; their method of testing is not so subtle as Aristotle's, but both are concerned with the effects. Such concern seems to reflect the view that art comes into being because the artist, or the employer behind him, has designs upon the public, whether high moral designs or box-office ones. It is an odious view in either case, because it denies the autonomy of the artist as one who interests himself in the artistic object in his own right, and likewise the autonomy of the work itself as existing for its own sake. [. . .] Furthermore, we must regard as uncritical the use of an extensive vocabulary which ascribes to the object properties really discovered in the subject, as: *moving, exciting, entertaining, pitiful; great*, if I am not mistaken, and *admirable*, on a slightly different ground; and, in strictness, *beautiful* itself.

2. Synopsis and paraphrase. The high-school classes and the women's clubs delight in these procedures, which are easiest of all the systematic exercises possible in the discussion of literary objects. I do not mean that the critic never uses them in his analysis of fiction and poetry, but he does not consider plot or story as identical with the real content. Plot is an abstract from content.

3. Historical studies. These have a very wide range, and include studies of the general literary background; author's biography, of course with special reference to autobiographical evidences in the work itself; bibliographical items; the citation of literary originals and analogues, and therefore what, in general, is called comparative literature. Nothing can be more stimulating to critical analysis than comparative literature. But it may be

conducted only superficially, if the comparisons are perfunctory and mechanical, or if the scholar is content with merely making the parallel citations.

4. Linguistic studies. Under this head come those studies which define the meaning of unusual words and idioms, including the foreign and archaic ones, and identify the allusions. The total benefit of linguistics for criticism would be the assurance that the latter was based on perfect logical understanding of the content, or 'interpretation'. Acquaintance with all the languages and literatures in the world would not necessarily produce a critic, though it might save one from damaging errors.

5. Moral studies. The moral standard applied is the one appropriate to the reviewer; it may be the Christian ethic, or the Aristotelian one, or the new proletarian gospel. But the moral content is not the whole content, which should never be relinquished.

6. Any other special studies which deal with some abstract or prose content taken out of the work. Nearly all departments of knowledge may conceivably find their own materials in literature, and take them out. Studies have been made of Chaucer's command of medieval sciences, of Spenser's view of the Irish question, of Shakespeare's understanding of the law, of Milton's geography, of Hardy's place-names. The critic may well inform himself of these materials as possessed by the artist, but his business as critic is to discuss the literary assimilation of them. [. . .]

Studies in the technique of the art belong to criticism certainly. They cannot belong anywhere else, because the technique is not peculiar to any prose materials discoverable in the work of art, nor to anything else but the unique form of that art. A very large volume of studies is indicated by this classification. They would be technical studies of poetry, for instance, the art I am specifically discussing, if they treated its metrics; its inversions, solecisms, lapses from the prose norm of language, and from close prose logic; its tropes; its fictions, or inventions, by which it secures 'aesthetic distance' and removes itself from history; or any other devices, on the general understanding that any systematic usage which does not hold good for prose is a poetic device.

A device with a purpose: the superior critic is not content with the compilation of the separate devices; they suggest to him a much more general question. The critic speculates on why poetry, through its devices, is at such pains to dissociate itself from prose at all, and what it is trying to represent that cannot be represented by prose.

I intrude here with an idea of my own, which may serve as a starting-point of discussion. Poetry distinguishes itself from prose on the technical side by the devices which are, precisely, its means of escaping from prose. Something is continually being killed by prose which the poet wants to preserve. But this must be put philosophically. (Philosophy sounds hard, but it deals with natural and fundamental forms of experience.)

The critic should regard the poem as nothing short of a desperate ontological or metaphysical manoeuvre. The poet himself, in the agony of composition, has something like this sense of his labours. The poet perpetuates in his poem an order of existence which in actual life is constantly crumbling beneath his touch. His poem celebrates the object which is real, individual, and qualitatively infinite. He knows that his practical interests will reduce this living object to a mere utility, and that his sciences will disintegrate it for their convenience into their respective abstracts. The poet wishes to defend his object's existence against its enemies, and the critic wishes to know what he is doing, and how. The critic should find in the poem a total poetic or individual object which tends to be universalized, but is not permitted to suffer this fate. His identification of the poetic object is in terms of the universal or commonplace object to which it tends, and of the tissue, or totality of connotation, which holds it secure. How does he make out the universal object? It is the prose object, which any forthright prosy reader can discover to him by an immediate paraphrase; it is a kind of story, character, thing, scene, or moral principle. And where is the tissue that keeps it from coming out of the poetic object? That is, for the laws of the prose logic, its superfluity; and I think I would even say, its irrelevance.

A poet is said to be distinguishable in terms of his style. It is a comprehensive word, and probably means: the general character of his irrelevances, or tissues. All his technical devices contribute to it, elaborating or individualizing the universal, the core-object; likewise all his material detail. For each poem even, ideally, there is distinguishable a logical object or universal, but at the same time a tissue of irrelevance from which it does not really emerge. The critic has to take the poem apart, or analyse it, for the sake of uncovering these features. With all the finesse possible, it is rude and patchy business by comparison with the living integrity of the poem. But without it there could hardly be much understanding of the value of poetry, or of the natural history behind any adult poem.

The language I have used may sound too formidable, but I seem to find that a profound criticism generally works by some such considerations. However the critic may spell them, the two terms are in his mind: the prose core to which he can violently reduce the total object, and the differentia, residue, or tissue, which keeps the object poetical or entire. The character of the poem resides for the good critic in its way of exhibiting the residuary quality. The character of the poet is defined by the kind of prose object to which his interest evidently attaches, plus his way of involving it firmly in the residuary tissue. And doubtless, incidentally, the wise critic can often read behind the poet's public character his private history as a man with a weakness for lapsing into some special form of prosy or scientific bondage.

(John Crowe Ransom, 'Criticism, Inc.', *The World's Body* (New York and London: Scribner's, 1938), pp. 342–5, 346–9.)

(F) ALLEN TATE,

'Tension in Poetry' (1938)

[. . .] I am using the term [*tension*] not as a general metaphor, but as a special one, derived from lopping the prefixes off the logical terms *ex*tension and *in*tension. What I am saying, of course, is that the meaning of poetry is its 'tension,' the full organized body of all the extension and intension that we can find in it. The remotest figurative significance that we can derive does not invalidate the extensions of the literal statement. Or we may begin with the literal statement and by stages develop the complications of metaphor: at every stage we may pause to state the meaning so far apprehended, and at every stage the meaning will be coherent.

The meanings that we select at different points along the infinite line between extreme intension and extreme extension will vary with our personal 'drive,' or 'interest,' or 'approach': the Platonist will tend to stay pretty close to the end of the line where extension, and simple abstraction of the object into a universal, is easiest, for he will be a fanatic in morals or some

kind of works, and will insist upon the shortest way with what
will ever appear to him the dissenting ambiguities at the
intensive end of the scale. The Platonist (I do not say that his
opponent is the Aristotelian) might decide that Marvell's 'To
His Coy Mistress' recommends immoral behaviour to the young
men, in whose behalf he would try to suppress the poem. That,
of course, would be one 'true' meaning of 'To His Coy Mistress,'
but it is a meaning that the full tension of the poem will not
allow us to entertain exclusively. For we are compelled, since it
is there, to give equal weight to an intensive meaning so rich
that, without contradicting the literal statement of the
lover–mistress convention, it lifts that convention into an insight
into one phase of the human predicament – the conflict of
sensuality and asceticism.

I should like to quote now, not from Marvell, but a stanza
from Donne that I hope will reinforce a little what I have just
said and connect it with some earlier remarks.

> Our two soules therefore, which are one
> > Though I must goe, endure not yet
> A breach, but an expansion,
> > Like gold to aiery thinnesse beate.

Here Donne brings together the developing imagery of twenty
lines under the implicit proposition: the unity of two lovers'
souls is a nonspatial entity, and is therefore indivisible. That, I
believe, is what Mr. John Crowe Ransom would call the logic of
the passage; it is the abstract form of its extensive meaning.
Now the interesting feature here is the logical contradiction of
embodying the unitary, non-spatial soul in a spatial image: the
malleable gold is a plane whose surface can always be extended
mathematically by one-half towards infinity; the souls are this
infinity. The finite image of the gold, in extension, logically
contradicts the intensive meaning (infinity) which it conveys; but
it does not invalidate that meaning. We have seen that Cowley
compelled us to ignore the denoted diaper in order that we
might take seriously the violet which it pretended to swathe. But
in Donne's 'Valediction: forbidding mourning' the clear
denotation of the gold contains, by intension, the full meaning of
the passage. If we reject the gold, we reject the meaning, for
the meaning is wholly absorbed into the image of the gold.
Intension and extension are here one, and they enrich each
other. [. . .]

The metaphysical poet as a rationalist begins at or near the

extensive or denoting end of the line; the romantic or Symbolist
poet at the other, intensive end; and each by a straining feat of
the imagination tries to push his meanings as far as he can
towards the opposite end, so as to occupy the entire scale.

(Allen Tate, 'Tension in Poetry' (1938) *Collected Essays* (Denver: Alan
Swallow, 1959), pp. 82–4, 86.)

(G) CLEANTH BROOKS

'Metaphor and the Tradition', *Modern Poetry and the Tradition* (1939)

The significant relationship between the modernist poets and the
seventeenth-century poets of wit lies here – in their common
conception of the use of metaphor [. . .] the metaphysical poets
and the modernists stand opposed to both the neoclassic and
Romantic poets on the issue of metaphor. [. . .]

Coleridge [. . .] says that the true poet will know intuitively
'what differences of style it [the imagination] at once inspires
and justifies; what intermixture of conscious volition is natural to
that state.' And so he will. But the modern poet will probably
feel that a larger 'intermixture of conscious volition' is natural
than Coleridge felt was natural, and will probably regard as
truly imaginative the figures which Coleridge and his nineteenth-
century followers would dismiss as 'mere works of the will.'
Moreover, with the modern poet, the value of the figure must in
all cases be referred to its function in the context in which it
occurs, with the recognition that the range of possible functions
is wide; the figure may have a negative function as well as a
positive – may serve irony as well as ennoblement. Our only test
for the validity of any figure must be an appeal to the whole
context in which it occurs: Does it contribute to the total effect,
or not?

Most clearly of all, the metaphysical poets reveal the
essentially functional character of all metaphor. We cannot
remove the comparisons from their poems, as we might remove
ornaments or illustrations attached to a statement, without
demolishing the poems. The comparison *is* the poem in a
structural sense.

And now one may consider the fundamental fallacy which
underlies the Romantic and neoclassical account of the functions

of figurative language. In that account, metaphor is merely subsidiary. For 'to illustrate' is to illustrate something, and the illustration of a proposition implies that the proposition could be made without recourse to the illustration. Obviously, the phrase 'to decorate' assumes for the decoration merely a subsidiary function. Housman, as we have seen, gives the show away by frankly regarding metaphor and simile as 'accessories.'

Metaphor is not to be considered, then, as the alternative of the poet, which he may elect to use or not, since he may state the matter directly and straightforwardly if he chooses. It is frequently the only means available if he is to write at all. Consider the example [a comparison between the lovers and parallel lines, in 'Definition of Love'] quoted from Marvell. If we count as part of his statement, not only the proposition in its logical paraphrase, but the qualifications which it receives from the poet's emphasis and the poet's attitude – obviously the 'what' that is stated is stated by the metaphor, *and only by the metaphor.*

(Cleanth Brooks, *Modern Poetry and the Tradition* (University of North Carolina Press, 1939; New York: Oxford UP, 1965), pp. 11, 14–16.)

(H) MARK SCHORER

'Technique as Discovery' (1948)

Modern criticism, through its exacting scrutiny of literary texts, has demonstrated with finality that in art beauty and truth are indivisible and one. The Keatsian overtones of these terms are mitigated and an old dilemma solved if for beauty we substitute form, and for truth, content. We may, without risk of loss, narrow them even more, and speak of technique and subject matter. Modern criticism has shown us that to speak of content as such is not to speak of art at all, but of experience; and that it is only when we speak of the *achieved* content, the form, the work of art as a work of art, that we speak as critics. The difference between content, or experience, and achieved content, or art, is technique.

When we speak of technique, then, we speak of nearly everything. For technique is the means by which the writer's experience, which is his subject matter, compels him to attend to it; technique is the only means he has of discovering, exploring, developing his subject, of conveying its meaning, and, finally, of evaluating it. And surely it follows that certain techniques are sharper tools than others, and will discover more; that the writer capable of the most exacting technical scrutiny of his subject matter will produce works with the most satisfying content, works with thickness and resonance; works which reverberate, works with maximum meaning.

We are no longer able to regard as seriously intended criticism of poetry which does not assume these generalizations; but the case for fiction has not yet been established. The novel is still read as though its content has some value in itself, as though the subject matter of fiction has greater or lesser value in itself, and as though technique were not a primary but a supplementary element, capable perhaps of not unattractive embellishments upon the surface of the subject, but hardly of its essence. Or technique is thought of in blunter terms than those which one associates with poetry, as such relatively obvious matters as the arrangement of events to create plot; or, within plot, of suspense and climax; or as the means of revealing character motivation, relationship, and development; or as the use of point of view, but point of view as some nearly arbitrary device for the heightening of dramatic interest through the narrowing or broadening of perspective upon the material, rather than as a means towards the positive definition of theme. As for the resources of language, these, somehow, we almost never think of as a part of the technique of fiction – language as used to create a certain texture and tone which in themselves state and define themes and meanings; or language, the counters of our ordinary speech, as forced, through conscious manipulation, into all those larger meanings which our ordinary speech almost never intends. Technique in fiction, all this is a way of saying, we somehow continue to regard as merely a means to organizing material which is 'given' rather than as the means of exploring and defining the values in an area of experience which, for the first time *then*, are being given. [. . .]

Technique in fiction is, of course, all those obvious forms of it which are usually taken to be the whole of it, and many others; but for present purposes, let it be thought of in two respects particularly: the uses to which language, as language, is put to express the quality of the experience in question; and the uses of point of view not only as a mode of dramatic delimitation, but more particularly, of thematic definition. Technique is really what T. S. Eliot means by 'convention': any selection, structure, or distortion, any form or rhythm imposed upon the world of action; by means of which, it should be added, our apprehension of the world of action is enriched or renewed. In this sense, everything is technique which is not the lump of experience itself, and one cannot properly say that a writer has no technique, or that he eschews technique, for, being a writer, he cannot do so. We can speak of good and bad technique, of adequate and inadequate, of technique which serves the novel's purpose, or disserves.

(Mark Schorer, 'Technique as Discovery', *The World We Imagine: Selected Essays* (London: Chatto & Windus, 1969), pp. 3–4, 5.)

CHAPTER 3

AMBIGUITY AND POLYSEMY

Both the classical and the Christian traditions developed forms
of allegorical reading in order to preserve the status of ancient
texts. To discover a level of meaning beyond the 'literal' one was
to give a text a new lease of life. The pagan deities of Homer's
epics and Ovid's erotic poetry could be masked and given new
and more elevated meanings by the allegorizers. The moralizing
translator was trying to replace one meaning by another. At a
more general level, the Judaeo-Christian tradition developed two
solutions to the problem of meaning. The first is closely related
to what Derrida (see III, 7, B) calls 'phonocentrism'. Western
philosophy since Plato locates authoritative meaning in speech
(rather than writing): meaning is *present* in the Word (the Word
was made flesh). The Text is treated as having the authority of
divine utterance, and therefore can have only one true meaning;
no ambivalence or indeterminacy can exist in God's Word. If
God's Word is to be preserved in its purity it must be
interpreted unequivocally by God's undisputed spiritual leaders
on earth. A Church founded upon such principles will inevitably
spawn innumerable heresies. The second tradition, typified in
medieval biblical exegesis, allows a cleverly differentiated
layering of meaning. There remains a *literal* meaning, but it
lacks the full depth of spiritual and moral significance. The
familiar distinction between the letter and the spirit of the law
recognizes that whatever codified and agreed definitions of legal
meaning we may possess, there exists, in addition, a moral and
spiritual interpretation which transcends the literal one.
However, most disputes about meaning will be confined to the
letter of the law. Dante's well-known version of the fourfold
exegetical theory uses the term 'allegory' to embrace all the non-
literal versions of meaning. E. D. Hirsch's distinction between

'meaning' and 'significance' (see II, 4, I) corresponds roughly to Dante's. The 'meaning' is what the author had in mind, while what the interpreter may read into the text is a 'significance'. Hirsch's approach is legalistic in spirit: the author has a proprietary right to the text's meaning, and anyone who infringes that right by treating the text's significances as having as much validity as the author's meaning is doing something improper. The exegetical model of Dante appears more liberal but in the end is no less severe in its *limitation* of meaning: certain clearly denoted moral and spiritual 'significances' are recognized as valid.

After Nietzsche, Freud and Saussure, the circumscription of textual meaning has been harder to sustain. The relativizing of 'Truth', the fading of the Descartian 'subject' in the face of the 'Unconscious' (see II, 5, F), and the splitting of the sign and the arbitrary linkage of signifier and signified have all made it difficult to preserve univocal meaning or stable significance. The New Critics (see III, 2, D–H) tried to stabilize the polyvalence of texts, mainly by asserting the determinate structure of works (Wimsatt called poems 'verbal icons'): 'ambiguities', 'ironies' and 'tensions' in poems and plays are not considered disruptive or chaotic, because they are seen as being harmonized in the total order of the work. Cleanth Brooks considers that 'paradox' belongs to the 'very nature of poetic language'. A poem is 'a total pattern', able to incorporate the disparities and contradictions of experience. In this way the poet preserves both plurality and unity. To accept that the text's plurality might overflow the strict confines of the poem's structure was unthinkable to the New Critics.

Only William Empson anticipates the post-structuralist idea of the 'plural' text. By concerning himself with the problem of how the reader construes meaning rather than what goes on in the text Empson opens up the question of polysemy (multiple signification). More than any other New Critic he understood that language is always 'rich and dishevelled' and can only be kept within bounds by an effort of the mind to impose unity. The 'forces' which hold disparate meanings together are evidently reader intuitions not structural elements in the texts. The reader's productivity in the process of reading (cf. Empson, II, 4, F) inevitably disturbs the idea of stable meaning, except as *imposed* by the reader.

The Bakhtin school developed from the confluence of Russian Formalism and Marxism towards the end of the 1920s. There is uncertainty about the identities of its members (Bakhtin, Medvedev and Vološinov). Vološinov rejected Saussure's static view of language, and argued that all utterances must be seen in their dynamic social contexts. Words are always the arena of ideological struggle, and are never passive univocal counters. In times of social unrest the 'multi-accentual' nature of language comes to the fore. Bakhtin's writings on Rabelais and Dostoevsky use a similar approach to disrupt the notion of authorial omniscience and single vision. Dostoevsky, he says, permits a free play of value systems, rejecting the 'monologic' novel in which the author imposes his authority on the entire discourse. Dostoevsky evolved the 'polyphonic' (or dialogic) novel in which the consciousnesses of the various characters do not merge with the author's viewpoint. There are some interesting connections between Bakhtin's concept of 'dialogic' utterance and some kinds of deconstructive and psychoanalytic criticism.

At an early stage in the exposure of English-speaking readers to French structuralism it was argued that the *nouvelle critique* was merely New Criticism writ large. This is far from the truth. Barthes' *S/Z* (1970) is the culmination of his structuralist phase and the inauguration of his post-structuralist phase. He departs from New Criticism in several essential ways: (1) he believes that criticism is in the same order of discourse as literature. Both are part of the 'general text' ('the infinity of language'). The 'codes' which determine our reading are present as much in the reader as in the text; (2) the 'writerly' text is plural in a much more radical sense than the 'verbal icon'. The text's meanings can never be limited; new systems of meaning can always be brought to bear on it; (3) the subjectivity of the reader/critic is no less plural than the text. The New Critics had written as though their own discourse was perfectly pure and unproblematic.

Barthes' theory of codes differs drastically from the more familiar structuralist notion of system (see III, 6). The codes are not determinate in number; Barthes gives us five but there may be more. The structure which the codes produce is not a fixed one, but an ever-growing multiplicity of significations. They do not 'manifest a structure' but 'produce a structuration'. They are the systems which operate in all our interpretive activities, and they refer us back to the 'already' – the entire linguistic, psychic, and cultural matrix. There is no 'origin', only an 'already'. Derrida (see III, 7, B) gives us the philosophical version of this post-structuralist critique of language.

Background reading

Erich Auerbach, *Dante, Poet of the Secular World*, trans. R. Manheim (Chicago and London: Chicago UP, 1961).

Rosalind Coward and John Ellis, *Language and Materialism: Developments in Semiology and the Theory of the Subject* (London: Routledge & Kegan Paul, 1977).

R. Hollander, *Allegory in Dante's Commedia* (Princeton, NJ: Princeton UP, 1969), chs 1 and 2.

Annette Lavers, *Roland Barthes: Structuralism and After* (London: Methuen, 1982).

Christopher Norris, *William Empson and the Philosophy of Literary Criticism* (London: Athlone Press, 1978).

Philip Rollinson, *Classical Theories of Allegory and Christian Culture* (Pittsburgh: Duquesne UP, and Harvester: Brighton, 1981).

David Silverman and Brian Torode, *The Material World* (London, Boston and Henley: Routledge & Kegan Paul, 1980), ch. 11: 'The Significance of Barthes'.

(A) DANTE

'Letter to Can Grande' (1319)

For the clearness, therefore, of what I shall say, it must be understood that the meaning of this work is not simple, but rather can be said to be of many significations, that is, of several meanings; for there is one meaning that is derived from the letter, and another that is derived from the things indicated by the letter. The first is called *literal*, but the second *allegorical* or *mystical*. That this method of expounding may be more clearly set forth, we can consider it in these lines: 'When Israel went out of Egypt, the house of Jacob from a people of strange language; Judah was his sanctuary and Israel his dominion.' For if we consider the *letter* alone, the departure of the children of Israel from Egypt in the time of Moses is signified; if the *allegory*, our redemption accomplished in Christ is signified; if the *moral meaning*, the conversion of the soul from the sorrow and misery of sin to a state of grace is signified; if the *anagogical*, the departure of the sanctified soul from the slavery of this corruption to the liberty of everlasting glory is signified. And although these mystical meanings are called by various names, they can in general all be said to be allegorical, since they differ from the literal or historic; for the word *Allegoria* is derived from the Greek ἀλλοῖος, which in Latin is *alienum* or *diversum*.

Now that these things have been explained, it is evident that
the subject around which the alternate meanings revolve must be
double. And therefore the subject of this work must be
understood as taken according to the letter, and then as
interpreted according to the allegorical meaning. The subject,
then, of the whole work, taken according to the letter alone, is
simply a consideration of the state of souls after death; for from
and around this the action of the whole work turneth. But if the
work is considered according to its allegorical meaning, the
subject is man, liable to the reward or punishment of Justice,
according as through the freedom of the will he is deserving or
undeserving.

(Dante, *Eleven Letters*, trans. Charles Sterrett Latham (Boston and New
York: Houghton, Mifflin, 1892), pp. 193–5.)

(B) MIKHAIL BAKHTIN

Problems of Dostoevsky's Poetics (1929)

*The plurality of independent and unmerged voices and consciousnesses and
the genuine polyphony of full-valued voices are in fact characteristics of
Dostoevsky's novels.* It is not a multitude of characters and fates
within a unified objective world, illuminated by the author's
unified consciousness that unfolds in his works, but precisely the
plurality of equal consciousnesses and their worlds, which are combined
here into the unity of a given event, while at the same time
retaining their unmergedness. In the author's creative plan,
Dostoevsky's principal heroes are indeed *not only objects of the
author's word, but subjects of their own directly significant word*
(neposredstvenno znachashchee slovo) *as well.* Therefore the
hero's word is here by no means limited to its usual functions of
characterization and plot development, but neither does it serve
as the expression of the author's own ideological position (as in
Byron, for example). The hero's consciousness is given as a
separate, a *foreign* consciousness, but at the same time it is not
objectified, it does not become closed off, it is not made the
simple object of the author's consciousness. In this sense the
image of Dostoevsky's hero is not the same as the usual
objectivized image of the hero in the traditional novel.

Dostoevsky is the creator of the *polyphonic novel*. He originated
an essentially new novelistic genre. Therefore his work cannot be

confined within any boundaries and does not submit itself to any of the historical-literary schemata which we are accustomed to apply to manifestations of the European novel. In his works there appears a hero whose voice is constructed in the same way that the voice of the author himself is constructed in the usual novel. The hero's word about himself and about the world is every bit as valid as the usual authorial word; it is not subordinated to the objectivized image of the hero as one of his characteristics, nor does it serve as mouthpiece for the author's voice. It possesses an exceptional independence in the structure of the work, standing as if *alongside* the author's word and in a peculiar way combining with it and with the full-valued voices of the other heroes.

It follows therefrom that the usual material or psychological bonds necessary for the pragmatic development of the plot are insufficient for Dostoevsky's world: they presuppose the heroes' objectivization and materialization as integral to the author's plan and they connect and combine completed images of people in the unity of a monologically perceived and understood world. Dostoevsky's plan presupposes the plurality of consciousnesses of equal value, together with their worlds. In Dostoevsky's novels the usual plot pragmatics play a secondary role and fulfill special functions, different from their usual ones. The final bonds which create the unity of his novelistic world are of another sort; the basic event disclosed by his novel is not amenable to the usual plot-pragmatic (*siuzhetno-pragmaticheskoe*) interpretation.

Further, the very orientation of the narration – whether it is carried out by the author, a narrator, or one of the heroes – must be completely different than in novels of the monological type. The position from which the story is told, the image is constructed, or the information is given must be oriented in a new way to this new world, the world of full-fledged subjects, not objects. The narrational, representational, and informational word must work out some sort of new relationship to its object.

Thus, all of the elements of Dostoevsky's novelistic structure are profoundly original; they are all determined by that new artistic task which only he succeeded in setting and fulfilling in all its breadth and depth: the task of constructing a polyphonic world and destroying the established forms of the basically *monological* (homophonic) European novel. [. . .]

Dostoevsky's originality lies not in the fact that he monologically proclaimed the worth of the personality – others had done so before him, – but in the fact that he was able to see and to show it with artistic objectivity as another, a foreign, personality, without lyricizing it or merging it with his own voice, while at the same time not reducing it to materialized psychic reality. The high appraisal of the personality's worth did not appear for the first time in Dostoevsky's *Weltanschauung*, but the artistic image of a foreign personality (if we accept Askoldov's term) and of multiple unmerged personalities joined in the unity of a given spiritual event, was realized for the first time in his novels.

(Mikhail Bakhtin, *Problems of Dostoevsky's Poetics*, trans. R. W. Rotscl (Ann Arbor: Ardis, 1973), pp. 4–5, 9.)

(C) WILLIAM EMPSON

Seven Types of Ambiguity (1930)

[T]he preface to *Oxford Poetry*, 1927, stated [. . .] that there is a 'logical conflict, between the denotary and the connotatory sense of words; between, that is to say, an asceticism tending to kill language by stripping words of all association and a hedonism tending to kill language by dissipating their sense under a multiplicity of associations.' The methods I have been using seem to assume that all poetical language is debauched into associations to any required degree; I ought at this point to pay decent homage to the opposing power.

Evidently all the subsidiary meanings must be relevant, because anything (phrase, sentence, or poem) meant to be considered as a unit must be unitary, must stand for a single order of the mind. In complicated situations this unity is threatened; you are thinking of several things, or one thing as it is shown by several things, or one thing in several ways. A sort of unity may be given by the knowledge of a scheme on which all the things occur; so that the scheme itself becomes the one thing which is being considered. More generally one may say that if an ambiguity is to be unitary there must be 'forces' holding its elements together, and I ought then, in considering ambiguities, to have discussed what the forces were, whether they were adequate. But the situation here is like the situation in my first chapter, about rhythm; it is hard to show in detail how the rhythm acts, and one can arrive at the same result by showing the effects of the rhythm upon the meaning of the words.

Some sort of parallel may be found in the way logical connectives (the statement of logical form in addition to logical content) are usually unnecessary and often misleading, because too simple. Omitting an adjective one would need 'therefore,' stressing the adjective 'although'; both logical connections are implied if the sentences are just put one after another. In the same way, people are accustomed to judge automatically the forces that hold together a variety of ideas; they feel they know about the forces, if they have analysed the ideas; many forces, indeed, are covertly included within ideas; and so of the two elements, each of which defines the other, it is much easier to find words for the ideas than for the forces. Most of the ambiguities I have considered here seem to me beautiful; I consider, then, that I have shown by example, in showing the nature of the ambiguity, the nature of the forces which are adequate to hold it together. It would seem very artificial to do it the other way round, and very tedious to do it both ways at once. I wish only, then, to say here that such vaguely imagined 'forces' are essential to the totality of a poem, and that they cannot be discussed in terms of ambiguity, because they are complementary to it. But by discussing ambiguity, a great deal may be made clear about them. In particular, if there is contradiction, it must imply tension; the more prominent the contradiction, the greater the tension; in some way other than by the contradiction, the tension must be conveyed, and must be sustained.

An ambiguity, then, is not satisfying in itself, nor is it, considered as a device on its own, a thing to be attempted; it must in each case arise from, and be justified by, the peculiar requirements of the situation. On the other hand, it is a thing which the more interesting and valuable situations are more likely to justify. Thus the practice of 'trying not to be ambiguous' has a great deal to be said for it, and I suppose was followed by most of the poets I have considered. It is likely to lead to results more direct, more communicable, and hence more durable; it is a necessary safeguard against being ambiguous without proper occasion, and it leads to more serious ambiguities when such occasions arise. [. . .]

As for the immediate importance of the study of ambiguity, it would be easy enough to take up an alarmist attitude, and say that the English language needs nursing by the analyst very badly indeed. Always rich and dishevelled, it is fast becoming very rich and dishevelled; always without adequate devices for showing the syntax intended, it is fast throwing away the few devices it had; it is growing liable to mean more things, and less willing to stop and exclude the other possible meanings. A brief study of novels will show that English, as spoken by educated people, has simplified its grammar during the last century to an extraordinary degree. People sometimes say that words are now used as flat counters, in a way which ignores their delicacy; that English is coming to use fewer of its words, and those more crudely. But this journalist flatness does not mean that the words have simple meanings, only that the word is used, as at a distance, to stand for a vague and complicated mass of ideas and systems which the journalist has no time to apprehend. The sciences might be expected to diminish the ambiguity of the language, both because of their tradition of clarity and because much of their jargon has, if not only one meaning, at any rate only one setting and point of view. But such words are not in general use; they only act as a further disturbing influence on the words used already. English is becoming an aggregate of vocabularies only loosely in connection with one another, which yet have many words in common, so that there is much danger of accidental ambiguity, and you have to bear firmly in mind the small clique for whom the author is writing. It is to combat this that so much recent writing has been determinedly unintelligible from any but the precise point of view intended.

(William Empson, *Seven Types of Ambiguity* (1930; London: Penguin Books, 1961), pp. 234–5, 236.)

(D) CLEANTH BROOKS

The Well Wrought Urn: Studies in the Structure of Poetry (1947)

But I am not here interested in enumerating the possible variations; I am interested rather in our seeing that the paradoxes spring from the very nature of the poet's language: it is a language in which the connotations play as great a part as the denotations. And I do not mean that the connotations are important as supplying some sort of frill or trimming, something external to the real matter in hand. I mean that the poet does not use a notation at all – as the scientist may properly be said to do so. The poet, within limits, has to make up his language as he goes.

T. S. Eliot has commented upon 'that perpetual slight alteration of language, words perpetually juxtaposed in new and sudden combinations', which occurs in poetry. It *is* perpetual; it cannot be kept out of the poem; it can only be directed and controlled. The tendency of science is necessarily to stabilize terms, to freeze them into strict denotations; the poet's tendency is by contrast disruptive. The terms are continually modifying each other, and thus violating their dictionary meanings. To take a very simple example, consider the adjectives in the first lines of Wordsworth's evening sonnet: *beauteous, calm, free, holy, quiet, breathless*. The juxtapositions are hardly startling; and yet notice this: the evening is like a nun breathless with adoration. The adjective 'breathless' suggests tremendous excitement; and yet the evening is not only quiet but *calm*. There is no final contradiction, to be sure: it is *that* kind of calm and *that* kind of excitement, and the two states may well occur together. But the poet has no one term. Even if he had a polysyllabic technical term, the term would not provide the solution for his problem. He must work by contradiction and qualification.

We may approach the problem in this way: the poet has to work by analogies. All of the subtler states of emotion, as I. A. Richards has pointed out, necessarily demand metaphor for their expression. The poet must work by analogies, but the metaphors do not lie in the same plane or fit neatly edge to edge. There is a continual tilting of the planes; necessary overlappings, discrepancies, contradictions. Even the most direct and simple poet is forced into paradoxes far more often than we think, if we are sufficiently alive to what he is doing. [. . .]

[W]e must draw a sharp distinction between the attractiveness or beauty of any particular item taken as such and the 'beauty' of the poem considered as a whole. The latter is the effect of a total pattern, and of a kind of pattern which can incorporate within itself items intrinsically beautiful or ugly, attractive or repulsive. Unless one asserts the primacy of the pattern, a poem becomes merely a bouquet of intrinsically beautiful items.

But though it is in terms of structure that we must describe poetry, the term 'structure' is certainly not altogether satisfactory as a term. One means by it something far more internal than the metrical pattern, say, or than the sequence of images. The structure meant is certainly not 'form' in the conventional sense in which we think of form as a kind of envelope which 'contains' the 'content'. The structure obviously is everywhere conditioned by the nature of the material which goes into the poem. The nature of the material sets the problem to be solved, and the solution is the ordering of the material.

Pope's *Rape of the Lock* will illustrate: the structure is not the heroic couplet as such, or the canto arrangement; for, important as is Pope's use of the couplet as one means by which he secures the total effect, the heroic couplet can be used – has been used many times – as an instrument is securing very different effects. The structure of the poem, furthermore, is not that of the mock-epic convention, though here, since the term 'mock-epic' has implications of attitude, we approach a little nearer to the kind of structure of which we speak.

The structure meant is a structure of meanings, evaluations, and interpretations; and the principle of unity which informs it seems to be one of balancing and harmonizing connotations, attitudes, and meanings. But even here one needs to make important qualifications: the principle is not one which involves the arrangement of the various elements into homogeneous groupings, pairing like with like. It unites the like with the unlike. It does not unite them, however, by the simple process of allowing one connotation to cancel out another nor does it reduce the contradictory attitudes to harmony by a process of subtraction. The unity is not a unity of the sort to be achieved by the reduction and simplification appropriate to an algebraic formula. It is a positive unity, not a negative; it represents not a residue but an achieved harmony.

The attempt to deal with a structure such as this may account for the frequent occurrence in the preceding chapters of such terms as 'ambiguity', 'paradox', 'complex of attitudes', and – most frequent of all, and perhaps most annoying to the reader – 'irony'. I hasten to add that I hold no brief for these terms as such. Perhaps they are inadequate. Perhaps they are misleading. It is to be hoped in that case that we can eventually improve upon them.

(Cleanth Brooks, *The Well Wrought Urn* (1947; London: Methuen, 1968), pp. 5–6 158–60.)

(E) ROLAND BARTHES

S/Z (1970)

Let us first posit the image of a triumphant plural, unimpoverished by any constraint of representation (of imitation). In this ideal text, the networks are many and interact, without any one of them being able to surpass the rest; this text is a galaxy of signifiers, not a structure of signifieds; it has no beginning; it is reversible; we gain access to it by several entrances, none of which can be authoritatively declared to be the main one; the codes it mobilizes extend *as far as the eye can reach*, they are indeterminable (meaning here is never subject to a principle of determination, unless by throwing dice); the systems of meaning can take over this absolutely plural text, but their number is never closed, based as it is on the infinity of language. [. . .]

I read the text. This statement, consonant with the 'genius' of the language (subject, verb, complement), is not always true. The more plural the text, the less it is written before I read it; I do not make it undergo a predicative operation, consequent upon its being, an operation known as *reading*, and *I* is not an innocent subject, anterior to the text, one which will subsequently deal with the text as it would an object to dismantle or a site to occupy. This 'I' which approaches the text is already itself a plurality of other texts, of codes which are infinite or, more precisely, lost (whose origin is lost). [. . .]

As chance would have it (but what is chance?), the first three lexias – the title and the first sentence of the story – have already provided us with the five major codes under which all the textual signifiers can be grouped: without straining a point, there will e no other codes throughout the story but these five, and each and every lexia will fall under one of these five codes. Let us sum them up in order of their appearance, without trying to put them in any order of importance. Under the hermeneutic code, we list the various (formal) terms by which an enigma can be distinguished, suggested, formulated, held in suspense, and finally disclosed (these terms will not always occur, they will often be repeated; they will not appear in any fixed order). As for the semes, we merely indicate them – without, in other words, trying either to link them to a character (or a place or an object) or to arrange them in some order so that they form a single thematic grouping; we allow them the instability, the dispersion, characteristic of motes of dust, flickers of meaning. Moreover, we shall refrain from structuring the symbolic grouping; this is the place for multivalence and for reversibility; the main task is always to demonstrate that this field can be entered from any number of points, thereby making depth and secrecy problematic. Actions (terms of the proairetic code) can fall into various sequences which should be indicated merely by listing them, since the proairetic sequence is never more than the result of an artifice of reading: whoever reads the text amasses certain data under some generic titles for actions (*stroll, murder, rendezvous*), and this title embodies the sequence; the sequence exists when and because it can be given a name, it unfolds as this process of naming takes place, as a title is sought or confirmed; its basis is therefore more empirical than rational, and it is useless to attempt to force it into a statutory order; its only logic is that of the 'already-done' or 'already-read' – whence the variety of sequences (some trivial, some melodramatic) and the variety of terms (numerous or few); here again, we shall not attempt to put them into any order. Indicating them (externally and internally) will suffice to demonstrate the plural meaning entangled in them. Lastly, the cultural codes are references to a science or a body of knowledge; in drawing attention to them, we merely indicate the type of knowledge (physical, physiological, medical, psychological, literary, historical, etc.) referred to, without going so far as to construct (or reconstruct) the culture they express.

XII. THE WEAVING OF VOICES

The five codes create a kind of network, a *topos* through which the entire text passes (or rather, in passing, becomes text). Thus, if we make no effort to structure each code, or the five codes among themselves, we do so deliberately, in order to assume the multivalence of the text, its partial reversibility. We are, in fact, concerned not to manifest a structure but to produce a structuration. The blanks and loseness of the analysis will be like footprints marking the escape of the text; for if the text is subject to some form, this form is not unitary, architectonic, finite: it is the fragment, the shards, the broken or obliterated network – all the movements and inflections of a vast 'dissolve,' which permits both overlapping and loss of messages. Hence we use *Code* here not in the sense of a list, a paradigm that must be reconstituted. The code is a perspective of quotations, a mirage of structures; we know only its departures and returns; the units which have resulted from it (those we inventory) are themselves, always, ventures out of the text, the mark, the sign of a virtual digression toward the remainder of a catalogue (*The Kidnapping* refers to every kidnapping ever written); they are so many fragments of something that has always been *already* read, seen, done, experienced; the code is the wake of that *already*. Referring to what has been written, i.e., to the Book (of culture, of life, of life as culture), it makes the text into a prospectus of this Book. Or again: each code is one of the forces that can take over the text (of which the text is the network), one of the voices out of which the text is woven. Alongside each utterance, one might say that off-stage voices can be heard: they are the codes: in their interweaving, these voices (whose origin is 'lost' in the vast perspective of the *already-written*) de-originate the utterance: the convergence of the voices (of the codes) becomes *writing*, a stereographic space where the five codes, the five voices, intersect: the Voice of Empirics (the proairetisms), the Voice of the Person (the semes), the Voice of Science (the cultural codes), the Voice of Truth (the hermeneutisms), the Voice of Symbol.

(Roland Barthes, *S/Z*, trans. Richard Miller (London: Jonathan Cape, 1975), pp. 5–6, 10, 18–21. Original French: Editions du Seuil, Paris, 1970.)

CHAPTER 4

IMPERSONALITY AND THE 'DEATH' OF THE AUTHOR

It may be the case that the notion of a stable individual identity is a relatively modern one. Certainly the concept of the 'author' as the unique source of his or her works is not implied in much of early poetics and literary criticism. The word 'poet' means 'maker' – one who fashions material into a new form. Did God, the first 'maker', fashion the universe out of pre-existing matter or from His own Body? Does the poet make poems from the 'already-written' or from inner resources? Some critical traditions place the source of creativity beyond the author's conscious control. According to the common classical and Christian view of poetic inspiration, the poet does not originate the poem but is the inspired channel for a divine act of creation. Freudian theories suggest that creativity originates in the unconscious mind. Marxists have often argued that the modern notion of the author is historically determined: the rise of bourgeois individualism from the late seventeenth century was partly expressed in the ideological concept of the 'author' – the unique proprietor of his own thoughts.

Wordsworthian Romanticism, in fulfilment of the needs of industrial society, fostered the belief in the 'full presence' of authorial intention in its poetic expression. When we read a poem by Wordsworth the sense of a personality and an immediacy of utterance is compellingly communicated. Much modern literary theory questions this apparent presence. Interestingly, Keats objected to the Wordsworthian 'egotistical sublime', which seemed to him to lack that 'negative capability' which belonged to the 'poetical character'. The poet has no 'identity', argues Keats, but is capable of receiving or becoming other identities. Keats' thinking is partly governed by the fact/value dichotomy which has run through much literary criticism since the Romantics: poetic language is the language of the imagination and feelings, and should categorically be distinguished from the language of reason or science (see Mill and Richards, II,3,E–F). The scientific or practical mind cannot understand the poet's passivity, which refuses to seek definite conclusions.

The 'impersonality' associated with Modernism is rather different from, though not unrelated to, Keatsian 'negative capability'. The dramatic model of impersonality, present in both Keats and T. S. Eliot, is not unlike Bakhtin's concept of 'dialogic discourse' (see III,3,B): the author appears to allow the characters their own free consciousnesses. Ezra Pound and T. S. Eliot developed a new 'cool' poetic ideal: the poet rejects the Wordsworthian preoccupation with the self. For Pound the poet is like a sculptor shaping and paring down a verbal structure in order to make it perfectly correspond to an emotional state (not necessarily the poet's). This is not an expressive activity, but a technical one. As Eliot argued, the mind of the poet is an impersonal *medium* and not a personality. Poetry is not a 'turning loose of emotion, but an escape from emotion'. The feelings explored in the poem are not expressions of the poet's emotional state. According to his theory of the 'objective correlative' a bad work of art introduces an 'emotion' in excess of the objective structure of events represented in the work. In *Hamlet* Shakespeare had, presumably, not succeeded in working out in an impersonal fashion some cluster of emotions that troubled him. Hamlet's disgust does not have an adequate 'object' in the play's plot. Oddly, Eliot seems to ignore the obvious psychoanalytic explanation of this 'excessive' emotion.

The New Critics adopted Eliot's concept of impersonality and out of it Wimsatt formulated the influential essays on the 'intentional fallacy' and the 'affective fallacy'. Both assume that the poem is an autonomous artefact – the offspring of the poet's mind, but not finally governed by the author's intention or the reader's personal response. The poem's meaning can be derived only from the poem itself and not from a supposed 'intention' which preceded it. We can deduce a poet's intention only from the poem itself, which 'realizes' the intention. In other words, once it is written the poem is no longer the author's property.

The notion of 'symbolic form' became current in the 1940s in the work of Ernst Cassirer (see I,4,E) and Susanne Langer, who sought to rescue the discredited Romantic claims for poetry (and art in general). Langer's Neo-Kantian philosophy treats art as a privileged vehicle of human feelings, which are *objectively* embodied within the symbolic languages which art has evolved. For her, art is not self-expression but the symbolization of emotion (she carefully distinguishes between two meanings of 'express'). Aesthetic symbols are not mere personal registrations but actualizations of emotion which would not be achieved except in art: 'For, although a work of art reveals the character of subjectivity, it is itself objective; its purpose is to *objectify* the life of feeling' (*Feeling and Form*, 1953).

In post-structuralist critical theory the 'person' of the author is replaced by the 'subject'. This grammatical category (the subject of a sentence) is an open space, or place, within the structure of language, waiting to be filled in a particular context. In Barthes' famous essay 'The Death of the Author' the 'author' can only situate him/herself at the point of confluence of the 'already-written' (see above, III,3,E). The author is no longer a point of origin, and cannot 'express' anything but only mix the chains of discourse which constitute the 'general text'. The writer contains an 'immense dictionary' of discourses which interweave in the text. The 'author' like God is a mythical concept. We cannot explain the text by pointing to the author as its origin.

What Fredric Jameson called 'the prison-house of language' impels us to embrace a literary impersonality which is far more disturbing and radical in its implications than what we find in the Romantics or the Modernists. The author is not an empathic receptor or a catalyst or a craftsman, but is an 'empty subject' awaiting the moment of 'enunciation' in which the 'I' will receive its definition. The 'author' becomes 'the subject of the enunciation'.

Background reading

Ian F. A. Bell, *Critic as Scientist: The Modernist Poetics of Ezra Pound* (London: Methuen, 1981).

Murray Krieger, *The New Apologists for Poetry* (Minneapolis: University of Minnesota Press, 1956), ch. 2.

A. J. Minnis, *Medieval Theory of Authorship* (London: Scolar Press, 1984).

Allan Mowbray, *T. S. Eliot's Impersonal Theory of Poetry* (Lewisburg: Bucknell UP, 1974).

W. K. Wimsatt and Cleanth Brooks, *Literary Criticism: A Short History* (New York: Alfred A. Knopf, 1957), ch. 29: 'Eliot and Pound: An Impersonal Art'.

Janet Wolff, *The Social Production of Art* (London: Macmillan, 1981), ch. 6: 'The Death of the Author'.

(A) JOHN KEATS

Letters

[21 DEC. 1817, TO G. & T. KEATS]

I had not a dispute, but a disquisition with Dilke, on various subjects; several things dove-tailed in my mind, and at once it struck me what quality went to form a man of achievement, especially in literature, and which Shakespeare possessed so enormously – I mean *Negative Capability*, that is, when man is capable of being in uncertainties, mysteries, doubts, without any irritable reaching after fact and reason. Coleridge, for instance, would let go by a fine isolated verisimilitude caught from the Penetralium of mystery, from being incapable of remaining content with half-knowledge. This pursued through volumes would perhaps take us no further than this, that with a great poet the sense of Beauty overcomes every other consideration, or rather obliterates all consideration.

[19 FEB. 1818, TO J. H. REYNOLDS]

Man should not dispute or assert but whisper results to his neighbour and thus by every germ of spirit sucking the sap from mould ethereal every human might become great, and Humanity instead of being a wide heath of Furze and Briars with here and there a remote Oak or Pine, would become a grand democracy of Forest Trees! It has been an old comparison for our urging on – the Beehive; however, it seems to me that we should rather be the flower than the Bee – for it is a false notion that more is gained by receiving than giving – no, the receiver and the giver are equal in their benefits. The flower, I doubt not, receives a fair guerdon from the Bee – its leaves blush deeper in the next spring – and who shall say between Man and Woman which is the most delighted? Now it is more noble to sit like Jove than to fly like Mercury – let us not therefore go hurrying about and collecting honey, bee-like buzzing here and there impatiently from a knowledge of what is to be aimed at; but let us open our leaves like a flower and be passive and receptive – budding patiently under the eye of Apollo and taking hints from every noble insect that favours us with a visit – sap will be given us for meat and dew for drink.

[27 OCT. 1818, TO R. WOODHOUSE]

As to the poetical Character itself (I mean that sort of which, if I am any thing, I am a Member; that sort distinguished from the wordsworthian or egotistical sublime; which is a thing per se and stands alone) it is not itself – it has no self – it is every thing and nothing – It has no character – it enjoys light and shade; it lives in gusto, be it foul or fair, high or low, rich or poor, mean or elevated – It has as much delight in conceiving an Iago as an Imogen. What shocks the virtuous philosopher, delights the camelion Poet. It does no harm from its relish of the dark side of things any more than from its taste for the bright one; because they both end in speculation. A Poet is the most unpoetical of any thing in existence; because he has no Identity – he is continually in for [informing?] and filling some other Body – The Sun, the Moon, the Sea and Men and Women who are creatures of impulse are poetical and have about them an unchangeable attribute – the poet has none; no identity – he is certainly the most unpoetical of all God's Creatures. If then he has no self, and if I am a Poet, where is the Wonder that I should say I would write no more? Might I not at that very instant have been cogitating on the Characters of Saturn and Ops? It is a wretched thing to confess; but is a very fact that not one word I ever utter can be taken for granted as an opinion growing out of my identical nature – how can it, when I have no nature? When I am in a room with People if I ever am free from speculating on creations of my own brain, then not myself goes home to myself: but the identity of every one in the room begins to [so?] to press upon me that I am in a very little time an[ni]hilated – not only among Men; it would be the same in a Nursery of children: I know not whether I make myself wholly understood: I hope enough so to let you see that no dependence is to be placed on what I said that day.

(John Keats, *Letters*, ed. M. B. Forman (1895; London: Oxford University Press, 1931), 2 vols, I. 77, 112–13, 245–6.)

(B) EZRA POUND

'A Retrospect' (1918)

In the spring or early summer of 1912, 'H. D.', Richard Aldington and myself decided that we were agreed upon the three principles following:

1. Direct treatment of the 'thing' whether subjective or objective.
2. To use absolutely no word that does not contribute to the presentation.
3. As regarding rhythm: to compose in the sequence of the musical phrase, not in sequence of a metronome. [. . .]

A FEW DON'TS

An 'Image' is that which presents an intellectual and emotional complex in an instant of time. I use the term 'complex' rather in the technical sense employed by the newer psychologists, such as Hart, though we might not agree absolutely in our application.

It is the presentation of such a 'complex' instantaneously which gives that sense of sudden liberation; that sense of freedom from time limits and space limits; that sense of sudden growth, which we experience in the presence of the greatest works of art. [. . .]

LANGUAGE

Use no superfluous word, no adjective which does not reveal something.

Don't use such an expression as 'dim lands *of peace*'. It dulls the image. It mixes an abstraction with the concrete. It comes from the writer's not realizing that the natural object is always the *adequate* symbol. [. . .]

As for the nineteenth century, with all respect to its achievements, I think we shall look back upon it as a rather blurry, messy sort of period, a rather sentimentalistic, mannerish sort of a period. I say this without any self-righteousness, with no self-satisfaction. [. . .]

As to twentieth century poetry, and the poetry which I expect to see written during the next decade or so, it will, I think, move against poppy-cock, it will be harder and saner, it will be what Mr Hewlett calls 'nearer the bone'. It will be as much like granite as it can be, its force will lie in its truth, its interpretative power (of course, poetic force does always rest there); I mean it will not try to seem forcible by rhetorical din, and luxurious riot. We will have fewer painted adjectives impeding the shock and stroke of it. At least for myself, I want it so, austere, direct, free from emotional slither.

What is there now, in 1917, to be added?

(Ezra Pound, 'A Retrospect' (1918), *Literary Essays*, ed. T. S. Eliot (London: Faber & Faber, 1954), pp. 3, 4, 4–5, 6, 11, 12.)

'The Serious Artist' (1913)

Roughly then, Good writing is writing that is perfectly controlled, the writer says just what he means. He says it with complete clarity and simplicity. He uses the smallest possible number of words. I do not mean that he skimps paper, or that he screws about like Tacitus to get his thought crowded into the least possible space. But, granting that two sentences are at times easier to understand than one sentence containing the double meaning, the author tries to communicate with the reader with the greatest possible despatch, save where for any one of forty reasons he does not wish to do so.

You wish to communicate an idea and its concomitant emotions, or an emotion and its concomitant ideas, or a sensation and its derivative emotions, or an impression that is emotive, etc., etc., etc. You begin with the yeowl and the bark, and you develop into the dance and into music, and into music with words, and finally into words with music, and finally into words with a vague adumbration of music, words suggestive of music, words measured, or words in a rhythm that preserves some accurate trait of the emotive impression, or of the sheer character of the fostering or parental emotion.

When this rhythm, or when the vowel and consonantal melody or sequence seems truly to bear the trace of emotion which the poem (for we have come at last to the poem) is intended to communicate, we say that this part of the work is good. And 'this part of the work' is by now 'technique'. That 'dry, dull, pedantic' technique, that all bad artists rail against. It is only a part of technique, it is rhythm, cadence, and the arrangement of sounds.

Also the 'prose', the words and their sense must be such as fit the emotion. Or, from the other side, ideas, or fragments of ideas, the emotion and concomitant emotions of this 'Intellectual and Emotional Complex' (for we have come to the intellectual and emotional complex) must be in harmony, they must form an organism, they must be an oak sprung from an acorn. [. . .]

The prose author has shown the triumph of his intellect and one knows that such triumph is not without its sufferings by the way, but by the verses one is brought upon the passionate moment. This moment has brought with it nothing that violates the prose simplicities. The intellect has not found it but the intellect has been moved.

There is little but folly in seeking the lines of division, yet if the two arts must be divided we may as well use that line as any other. In the verse something has come upon the intelligence. In the prose the intelligence has found a subject for its observations. The poetic fact pre-exists.

(Ezra Pound, 'The Serious Artist' (1913), *Literary Essays*, ed. T. S. Eliot (London: Faber & Faber, 1954), pp. 50, 53–4.)

(C) T. S. ELIOT

'Tradition and the Individual Talent' (1919)

Honest criticism and sensitive appreciation is directed not upon the poet but upon the poetry. [. . .] I have tried to point out the importance of the relation of the poem to other poems by other authors, and suggested the conception of poetry as a living whole of all the poetry that has ever been written. The other aspect of this Impersonal theory of poetry is the relation of the poem to its author. And I hinted, by an analogy, that the mind of the mature poet differs from that of the immature one not precisely in any valuation of 'personality', not being necessarily more interesting, or having 'more to say', but rather by being a more finely perfected medium in which special, or very varied, feelings are at liberty to enter into new combinations.

The analogy was that of the catalyst. When the two gases previously mentioned are mixed in the presence of a filament of platinum, they form sulphurous acid. This combination takes place only if the platinum is present; nevertheless the newly formed acid contains no trace of platinum, and the platinum itself is apparently unaffected: has remained inert, neutral, and unchanged. The mind of the poet is the shred of platinum. It may partly or exclusively operate upon the experience of the man himself; but, the more perfect the artist, the more completely separate in him will be the man who suffers and the mind which creates; the more perfectly will the mind digest and transmute the passions which are its material.

The experience, you will notice, the elements which enter the presence of the transforming catalyst, are of two kinds: emotions and feelings. The effect of a work of art upon the person who enjoys it is an experience different in kind from any experience not of art. It may be formed out of one emotion, or may be a combination of several; and various feelings, inhering for the writer in particular words or phrases or images, may be added to compose the final result. Or great poetry may be made without the direct use of any emotion whatever: composed out of feelings solely. Canto XV of the *Inferno* (Brunetto Latini) is a working up of the emotion evident in the situation; but the effect, though single as that of any work of art, is obtained by considerable complexity of detail. The last quatrain gives an image, a feeling attaching to an image, which 'came', which did not develop simply out of what precedes, but which was probably in suspension in the poet's mind until the proper combination arrived for it to add itself to. The poet's mind is in fact a receptacle for seizing and storing up numberless feelings, phrases, images, which remain there until all the particles which can unite to form a new compound are present together.

If you compare several representative passages of the greatest poetry you see how great is the variety of types of combination, and also how completely any semi-ethical criterion of 'sublimity' misses the mark. For it is not the 'greatness', the intensity, of the emotions, the components, but the intensity of the artistic process, the pressure, so to speak, under which the fusion takes place, that counts. The episode of Paolo and Francesca employs a definite emotion, but the intensity of the poetry is something quite different from whatever intensity in the supposed experience it may give the impression of. It is no more intense, furthermore, than Canto XXVI, the voyage of Ulysses, which has not the direct dependence upon an emotion. Great variety is possible in the process of transmutation of emotion: the murder of Agamemnon, or the agony of Othello, gives an artistic effect apparently closer to a possible original than the scenes from Dante. In the *Agamemnon*, the artistic emotion approximates to the emotion of an actual spectator; in *Othello* to the emotion of the protagonist himself. But the difference between art and the event is always absolute; the combination which is the murder of Agamemnon is probably as complex as that which is the voyage of Ulysses. In either case there has been a fusion of elements. The ode of Keats contains a number of feelings which have nothing particular to do with the nightingale, but which the nightingale, partly perhaps because of its attractive name, and partly because of its reputation, served to bring together.

The point of view which I am struggling to attack is perhaps related to the metaphysical theory of the substantial unity of the soul: for my meaning is, that the poet has, not a 'personality' to express, but a particular medium, which is only a medium and not a personality, in which impressions and experiences combine in peculiar and unexpected ways. Impressions and experiences which are important for the man may take no place in the poetry, and those which become important in the poetry may play quite a negligible part in the man, the personality. [. . .]

It is not in his personal emotions, the emotions provoked by particular events in his life, that the poet is in any way remarkable or interesting. His particular emotions may be simple, or crude, or flat. The emotion in his poetry will be a very complex thing, but not with the complexity of the emotions of people who have very complex or unusual emotions in life. One error, in fact, of eccentricity in poetry is to seek for new human emotions to express; and in this search for novelty in the wrong place it discovers the perverse. The business of the poet is not to find new emotions, but to use the ordinary ones and, in working them up into poetry, to express feelings which are not in actual emotions at all. And emotions which he has never experienced will serve his turn as well as those familiar to him. Consequently, we must believe that 'emotion recollected in tranquillity' is an inexact formula. For it is neither emotion, nor recollection, nor, without distortion of meaning, tranquillity. It is a concentration, and a new thing resulting from the concentration, of a very great number of experiences which to the practical and active person would not seem to be experiences at all; it is a concentration which does not happen consciously or of deliberation. These experiences are not 'recollected', and they finally unite in an atmosphere which is 'tranquil' only in that it is a passive attending upon the event. Of course this is not quite the whole story. There is a great deal, in the writing of poetry, which must be conscious and deliberate. In fact, the bad poet is usually unconscious where he ought to be conscious, and conscious where he ought to be unconscious. Both errors tend to make him 'personal'. Poetry is not a turning loose of emotion, but an escape from emotion; it is not the expression of personality, but an escape from personality. But, of course, only those who have personality and emotions know what it means to want to escape from these things.

(T. S. Eliot, 'Tradition and the Individual Talent' (1919), *Selected Essays* (London: Faber & Faber, 1932), pp. 17–20, 20–1.)

'Hamlet' (1919)

The only way of expressing emotion in the form of art is by finding an 'objective correlative'; in other words, a set of objects, a situation, a chain of events which shall be the formula of that *particular* emotion; such that when the external facts, which must terminate in sensory experience, are given, the emotion is immediately evoked. If you examine any of Shakespeare's more successful tragedies, you will find this exact equivalence; you will find that the state of mind of Lady Macbeth walking in her sleep has been communicated to you by a skilful accumulation of imagined sensory impressions; the words of Macbeth on hearing of his wife's death strike us as if, given the sequence of events, these words were automatically released by the last event in the series. The artistic 'inevitability' lies in this complete adequacy of the external to the emotion; and this is precisely what is deficient in *Hamlet*. Hamlet (the man) is dominated by an emotion which is inexpressible, because it is in *excess* of the facts as they appear. And the supposed identity of Hamlet with his author is genuine to this point: that Hamlet's bafflement at the absence of objective equivalent to his feelings is a prolongation of the bafflement of his creator in the face of his artistic problem. Hamlet is up against the difficulty that his disgust is occasioned by his mother, but that his mother is not an adequate equivalent for it; his disgust envelops and exceeds her. It is thus a feeling which he cannot understand; he cannot objectify it, and it therefore remains to poison life and obstruct action. None of the possible actions can satisfy it; and nothing that Shakespeare can do with the plot can express Hamlet for him. And it must be noticed that the very nature of the *données* of the problem precludes objective equivalence. To have heightened the criminality of Gertrude would have been to provide the formula for a totally different emotion in Hamlet; it is just *because* her character is so negative and insignificant that she arouses in Hamlet the feeling which she is incapable of representing.

(T.S. Eliot, 'Hamlet' (1919) *Selected Essays* (London: Faber & Faber, 1932), pp. 145–6.)

(D) W. K. WIMSATT

'The Intentional Fallacy' (1946)

'Intention,' as we shall use the term, corresponds to *what he intended* in a formula which more or less explicitly has had wide acceptance. 'In order to judge the poet's performance, we must know *what he intended*.' Intention is design or plan in the author's mind. Intention has obvious affinities for the author's attitude toward his work, the way he felt, what made him write.

We begin our discussion with a series of propositions summarized and abstracted to a degree where they seem to us axiomatic.

1. A poem does not come into existence by accident. The words of a poem, as Professor Stoll has remarked, come out of a head, not out of a hat. Yet to insist on the designing intellect as a *cause* of a poem is not to grant the design or intention as a *standard* by which the critic is to judge the worth of the poet's performance.

2. One must ask how a critic expects to get an answer to the question about intention. How is he to find out what the poet tried to do? If the poet succeeded in doing it, then the poem itself shows what he was trying to do. And if the poet did not succeed, then the poem is not adequate evidence, and the critic must go outside the poem – for evidence of an intention that did not become effective in the poem. 'Only one *caveat* must be borne in mind,' says an eminent intentionalist in a moment when his theory repudiates itself; 'the poet's aim must be judged at the moment of the creative act, that is to say, by the art of the poem itself.'

3. Judging a poem is like judging a pudding or a machine. One demands that it work. It is only because an artifact works that we infer the intention of an artificer. 'A poem should not mean but be.' A poem can *be* only through its *meaning* – since its medium is words – yet it *is*, simply *is*, in the sense that we have no excuse for inquiring what part is intended or meant. Poetry is

a feat of style by which a complex of meaning is handled all at
once. Poetry succeeds because all or most of what is said or
implied is relevant; what is irrevelant has been excluded, like
lumps from pudding and 'bugs' from machinery. In this respect
poetry differs from practical messages, which are successful if
and only if we correctly infer the intention. They are more
abstract than poetry.

4. The meaning of a poem may certainly be a personal one,
in the sense that a poem expresses a personality or state of soul
rather than a physical object like an apple. But even a short
lyric poem is dramatic, the response of a speaker (no matter
how abstractly conceived) to a situation (no matter how
universalized). We ought to impute the thoughts and attitudes of
the poem immediately to the dramatic *speaker*, and if to the
author at all, only by an act of biographical inference.

5. There is a sense in which an author, by revision, may
better achieve his original intention. But it is a very abstract
sense. He intended to write a better work, or a better work of a
certain kind, and now has done it. But it follows that his former
concrete intention was not his intention. 'He's the man we were
in search of, that's true,' says Hardy's rustic constable, 'and yet
he's not the man we were in search of. For the man we were in
search of was not the man we wanted.'

Allusiveness in poetry is one of several critical issues by which
we have illustrated the more abstract issue of intentionalism, but
it may be for today the most important illustration. As a poetic
practice allusiveness would appear to be in some recent poems
an extreme corollary of the romantic intentionalist assumption,
and as a critical issue it challenges and brings to light in a
special way the basic premise of intentionalism. The following
instance from the poetry of Eliot may serve to epitomize the
practical implications of what we have been saying. In Eliot's
'Love Song of J. Alfred Prufrock,' toward the end, occurs the
line: 'I have heard the mermaids singing, each to each,' and this
bears a certain resemblance to a line in a Song by John Donne,
'Teach me to heare Mermaides singing', so that for the reader
acquainted to a certain degree with Donne's poetry, the critical
question arises: Is Eliot's line an allusion to Donne's? Is
Prufrock thinking about Donne? Is Eliot thinking about Donne?
We suggest that there are two radically different ways of looking
for an answer to this question. There is (1) the way of poetic
analysis and exegesis, which inquires whether it makes any sense

if Eliot-Prufrock *is* thinking about Donne. In an earlier part of
the poem, when Prufrock asks, 'Would it have been worth while,
. . . To have squeezed the universe into a ball,' his words take
half their sadness and irony from certain energetic and
passionate lines of Marvel 'To His Coy Mistress.' But the
exegetical inquirer may wonder whether mermaids considered as
'strange sights' (to hear them is in Donne's poem analogous to
getting with child a mandrake root) have much to do with
Prufrock's mermaids, which seem to be symbols of romance and
dynamism, and which incidentally have literary authentication, if
they need it, in a line of a sonnet by Gérard de Nerval. This
method of inquiry may lead to the conclusion that the given
resemblance between Eliot and Donne is without significance
and is better not thought of, or the method may have the
disadvantage of providing no certain conclusion. Nevertheless,
we submit that this is the true and objective way of criticism, as
contrasted to what the very uncertainty of exegesis might tempt
a second kind of critic to undertake: (2) the way of biographical
or genetic inquiry, in which, taking advantage of the fact that
Eliot is still alive, and in the spirit of a man who would settle a
bet, the critic writes to Eliot and asks what he meant, or if he
had Donne in mind. We shall not here weigh the probabilities –
whether Eliot would answer that he meant nothing at all, had
nothing at all in mind – a sufficiently good answer to such a
question – or in an unguarded moment might furnish a clear
and, within its limit, irrefutable answer. Our point is that such
an answer to such an inquiry would have nothing to do with the
poem 'Prufrock'; it would not be a critical inquiry. Critical
inquiries, unlike bets, are not settled in this way. Critical
inquiries are not settled by consulting the oracle.

(W. K. Wimsatt, 'The Intentional Fallacy' (written with Monroe
Beardsley), *The Verbal Icon* (University of Kentucky Press, 1954; London:
Methuen, 1970), pp. 4–5, 17–18.)

(E) SUSANNE LANGER

Philosophical Sketches (1962)

The word 'expression' has two principal meanings. In one sense
it means self-expression – giving vent to our feelings. In this
sense it refers to a symptom of what we feel. Self-expression is a

spontaneous reaction to an actual, present situation, an event, the company we are in, things people say, or what the weather does to us; it bespeaks the physical and mental state we are in and the emotions that stir us.

In another sense, however, 'expression' means the presentation of an idea, usually by the proper and apt use of words. But a device for presenting an idea is what we call a symbol, not a symptom. Thus a word is a symbol, and so is a meaningful combination of words. [. . .]

[T]he phenomena of feeling and emotion are usually treated by philosophers as irrational. The only pattern discursive thought can find in them is the pattern of outward events that occasion them. There are different degrees of fear, but they are thought of as so many degrees of the same simple feeling.

But human feeling is a fabric, not a vague mass. It has an intricate dynamic pattern, possible combinations and new emergent phenomena. It is a pattern of organically interdependent and interdetermined tensions and resolutions, a pattern of almost infinitely complex activation and cadence. [. . .]

It is, I think, this dynamic pattern that finds its formal expression in the arts. The expressiveness of art is like that of a symbol, not that of an emotional symptom; it is as a formulation of feeling for our conception that a work of art is properly said to be expressive. It may serve somebody's need of self-expression besides, but that is not what makes it good or bad art. In a special sense one may call a work of art a symbol of feeling, for, like a symbol, it formulates our ideas of inward experience, as discourse formulates our ideas of things and facts in the outside world. A work of art differs from a genuine symbol – that is, a symbol in the full and usual sense – in that it does not point beyond itself to something else. Its relation to feeling is a rather special one that we cannot undertake to analyze here; in effect, the feeling it expresses appears to be directly given with it – as the sense of a true metaphor, or the value of a religious myth – and is not separable from its expression. We speak of the feeling *of*, or the feeling *in*, a work of art, not the feeling it means. And we speak truly; a work of art presents something like a direct vision of vitality, emotion, subjective reality.

The primary function of art is to objectify feeling so that we can contemplate and understand it. It is the formulation of so-called 'inward experience,' the 'inner life,' that is impossible to achieve by discursive thought, because its forms are

incommensurable with the forms of language and all its
derivatives (e.g., mathematics, symbolic logic). Art objectifies the
sentience and desire, self-consciousness and world-consciousness,
emotions and moods, that are generally regarded as irrational
because words cannot give us clear ideas of them. But the
premise tacitly assumed in such a judgment – namely, that
anything language cannot express is formless and irrational –
seems to me to be an error. I believe the life of feeling is not
irrational; its logical forms are merely very different from the
structures of discourse. But they are so much like the dynamic
forms of art that art is their natural symbol. Through plastic
works, music, fiction, dance, or dramatic forms we can conceive
what vitality and emotion feel like.

(Susanne Langer, 'The Cultural Importance of Art', *Philosophical Sketches*
(The Johns Hopkins Press, 1962; New York: Mentor, 1964), pp. 78,
80–1.)

(F) ROLAND BARTHES

'The Death of the Author' (1968)

[L]inguistics has recently provided the destruction of the Author
with a valuable analytical tool by showing that the whole of the
enunciation is an empty process, functioning perfectly without
there being any need for it to be filled with the person of the
interlocutors. Linguistically, the author is never more than the
instance writing, just as *I* is nothing other than the instance
saying *I*: language knows a 'subject', not a 'person', and this
subject, empty outside of the very enunciation which defines it,
suffices to make language 'hold together', suffices, that is to say,
to exhaust it.

The removal of the Author (one could talk here with Brecht of
a veritable 'distancing', the Author diminishing like a figurine at
the far end of the literary stage) is not merely an historical fact
or an act of writing; it utterly transforms the modern text (or –
which is the same thing – the text is henceforth made and read
in such a way that at all its levels the author is absent). The
temporality is different. The Author, when believed in, is always
conceived of as the past of his own book: book and author stand
automatically on a single line divided into a *before* and an *after*.
The Author is thought to *nourish* the book, which is to say that

he exists before it, thinks, suffers, lives for it, is in the same
relation of antecedence to his work as a father to his child. In
complete contrast, the modern scriptor is born simultaneously
with the text, is in no way equipped with a being preceding or
exceeding the writing, is not the subject with the book as
predicate; there is no other time than that of the enunciation
and every text is eternally written *here and now*. The fact is (or, it
follows) that *writing* can no longer designate an operation of
recording, notation, representation, 'depiction' (as the Classics
would say); rather, it designates exactly what linguists, referring
to Oxford philosophy, call a performative, a rare verbal form
(exclusively given in the first person and in the present tense) in
which the enunciation has no other content (contains no other
proposition) than the act by which it is uttered – something like
the *I declare* of kings or the *I sing* of very ancient poets. Having
buried the Author, the modern scriptor can thus no longer
believe, as according to the pathetic view of his predecessors,
that this hand is too slow for his thought or passion and that
consequently, making a law of necessity, he must emphasize this
delay and indefinitely 'polish' his form. For him, on the
contrary, the hand, cut off from any voice, borne by a pure
gesture of inscription (and not of expression), traces a field
without origin – or which, at least, has no other origin than
language itself, language which ceaselessly calls into question all
origins.

We know now that a text is not a line of words releasing a
single 'theological' meaning (the 'message' of the Author-God)
but a multi-dimensional space in which a variety of writings,
none of them original, blend and clash. The text is a tissue of
quotations drawn from the innumerable centres of culture.
Similar to Bouvard and Pécuchet, those eternal copyists, at once
sublime and comic and whose profound ridiculousness indicates
precisely the truth of writing, the writer can only imitate a
gesture that is always anterior, never original. His only power is
to mix writings, to counter the ones with the others, in such a
way as never to rest on any one of them. Did he wish to *express
himself*, he ought at least to know that the inner 'thing' he thinks
to 'translate' is itself only a ready-formed dictionary, its words
only explainable through other words, and so on indefinitely;
something experienced in exemplary fashion by the young
Thomas de Quincey, he who was so good at Greek that in order
to translate absolutely modern ideas and images into that dead
language, he had, so Baudelaire tells us (in *Paradis Artificiels*),

'created for himself an unfailing dictionary, vastly more extensive and complex than those resulting from the ordinary patience of purely literary themes'. Succeeding the Author, the scriptor no longer bears within him passions, humours, feelings, impressions, but rather this immense dictionary from which he draws a writing that can know no halt: life never does more than imitate the book, and the book itself is only a tissue of signs, an imitation that is lost, infinitely deferred.

Once the Author is removed, the claim to decipher a text becomes quite futile. To give a text an Author is to impose a limit on that text, to furnish it with a final signified, to close the writing. Such a conception suits criticism very well, the latter then allotting itself the important task of discovering the Author (or its hypostases: society, history, psyché, liberty) beneath the work: when the Author has been found, the text is 'explained' – victory to the critic. Hence there is no surprise in the fact that, historically, the reign of the Author has also been that of the Critic, nor again in the fact that criticism (be it new) is today undermined along with the Author. In the multiplicity of writing, everything is to be *disentangled*, nothing *deciphered*; the structure can be followed, 'run' (like the thread of a stocking) at every point and at every level, but there is nothing beneath: the space of writing is to be ranged over, not pierced; writing ceaselessly posits meaning ceaselessly to evaporate it, carrying out a systematic exemption of meaning. In precisely this way literature (it would be better from now on to say *writing*), by refusing to assign a 'secret', an ultimate meaning, to the text (and to the world as text), liberates what may be called *an anti-theological activity*, an activity that is truly revolutionary since to refuse to fix meaning is, in the end, to refuse God and his hypostases – reason, science, law.

(Roland Barthes, 'The Death of the Author', *Image-Music-Text*, trans. Stephen Heath (London: Fontana, 1977), pp. 145–7.)

CHAPTER 5

RHETORIC: STYLE AND POINT OF VIEW

A theory of style was always prominent in classical rhetoric. The term 'rhetoric' describes the art of public speaking (especially political and forensic). Cicero's treatise on oratory (*Orator*) enunciates the classic principle of stylistic appropriateness: the grand style is best for swaying emotions, the plain style for conveying information, and the middle or 'tempered' style for giving pleasure. The principle of *decorum* – choosing words appropriate to the subject of one's discourse – has a much wider application. The classical tradition in literature is strongly associated with the principle of adherence to decorum:

> For different styles with different subjects sort,
> As several garbs with country, town, and court.
>   (Pope, *Essay on Criticism*, 323–3.)

Puttenham, in his *The Arte of English Poesie*, presents the rhetorical theory of style as part of his poetics. He also brings out very clearly the social dimension of the theory: the stylistic level of a poem should be appropriate to the class or status of its characters and the general level of society depicted. The 'Pyramus and Thisbe' entertainment at the end of Shakespeare's *A Midsummer Night's Dream* shows the incongruities arising from having a 'tragic' play performed by 'rude mechanicals' before the court. It is 'Merry and tragical'!

A great deal of debate in classical and neo-classical criticism centres on the question of which style is best in literature. One might describe the main traditions in seventeenth-century poetry in terms of style. The Spenserian and Miltonic line combines lofty subject and grand or elevated style, while the poetic tradition of Ben Jonson (the Sons of Ben) adopted a mainly plain-style verse, and associated plainness with honesty and truth. The values of what Cicero calls 'Attic' oratory predominate in classicism: a writer should use 'pure' (received) idiom, should avoid unnecessary metaphors or neologisms, and should be rational. The attacks on the Elizabethan tragedies of Marlowe and Kyd were often made by upholders of the plain style. The 'fustian' magniloquence of Marlowe's ranting heroes is ridiculous because stylistic grandeur is not matched (in their view) by spiritual or moral grandeur. Ben Jonson complained about 'the *scenicall* strutting, and furious vociferation' of these dramatic heroes. Cicero argued that 'the orator of grandiloquence, if he has no other quality, seems to be scarcely sane'.

In our century the rhetorical theory of style has been developed most impressively in the writings of Ernst Curtius (see IV, 1, B) and Erich Auerbach. The latter saw a continuing dialectical unfolding of 'realism' in Western literature from Homer to Virginia Woolf in terms of a tension between the classical 'separation of styles' and the Christian mixing of styles. In the Judaeo-Christian tradition the most 'ordinary' person or context can also be the most sublime. In his study of Shakespeare Auerbach shows that the great tragic figures have about them the smell of humanity; the 'everyday processes of life' are not excluded from the tragic world. On the other hand, the tragic figures are all princely and not of humble origin, with one possible exception (Shylock). The middle and lower classes are never rendered 'tragically'. Even so, the noble heroes are fully 'creatural': they suffer as ordinary human beings suffer. Auerbach is in effect arguing that Shakespeare's 'realism' marks a stage in the progressive deepening of literary realism, but there is still some way to go before the comprehensive realism of Balzac and Stendhal. Auerbach's ideal is a mixed style which is fully of this world.

Richard Ohmann's essay 'Speech, Action and Style' (1971) argues that J. L. Austin's speech-act theory (see I, 4, H) provides an important complement to the theory of style. The different literary kinds do not merely involve the appropriate (or shockingly inappropriate) use of words but they involve following or violating the rules for 'illocutionary acts' (such as 'performatives'). In one sense, literary uses of illocutionary acts always break the rules, because the conditions are not present for such acts to follow the rules. Ohmann solves this by accepting the orthodox view that literary speech acts are 'parasitic' on real ones. When people swear oaths in a play we do not treat them as real oaths, but merely hypothetical ones. Interestingly, he suggests that it would be possible to produce a typology of genres based upon the way in which each genre uses speech acts. Ohmann is sketching in a modern form of stylistics.

Though it has some things in common with the New Critics, Wayne Booth's celebrated *The Rhetoric of Fiction* (1961) belongs to the neo-Aristotelian tradition of criticism which was also known as the Chicago School. Like Aristotle, Booth is interested in rhetoric at the level of structures higher than the word. He believed that an adequate rhetoric of fiction would have to account for the different kinds of narrator and narration to be found in novels. He starts by offering a valuable criticism of Henry James' theories of 'point of view'. James had favoured the more indirect forms of narration, which removed the author from direct involvement with the telling of his story. The best novels 'show' characters, feeling, and events, rather than 'tell' them. The illusion of life will be created if the reader is not dominated by a single centre of consciousness. The day of the 'omniscient' narrator, who presents the characters as intimately known creations, is over. The ideal, for James and for the Modernists who followed, is the dramatic representation (c.f. Bakhtin's 'dialogic' discourse, III, 3, B, and T. S. Eliot, III, 4, C) in which the author is at a distance from his creations. In drama we have 'showing' rather than 'telling'. James describes various kinds of narrator whose lack of total knowledge ('bewilderment') makes for a greater sense of moral interest. Booth questions the assumption that 'telling' is always bad, and proposes to explore the entire rhetoric of authorial voices and narrative. He skilfully shows that 'telling' can be as 'objective' and as artistic as 'showing'.

Booth advocates a separation of 'author' from 'implied author'. The point he is making is that the sense of an authorial position which the reader picks up is always a fictional entity and never identical with an actual author. In this way we avoid all those foolish forms of criticism which consisted of attacking the author for the views of his narrator or for being insincere. However, Booth finds himself inevitably backtracking towards some notion of a moral centre or coherence – an equivalent to an artistic sincerity or moral vision. In this he differs from Bakhtin (III, 3, B) and the post-structuralists (see Barthes, III, 4, F) who theorise a more radically fissured or dispersed authorial identity.

Background reading

Howard S. Babb (ed.), *Essays in Stylistic Analysis* (New York: Harcourt
   Brace Jovanovich, 1972).
Peter Dixon, *Rhetoric* (London: Methuen, 1971).
George A. Kennedy, *Classical Rhetoric and Its Christian and Secular Tradition
   from Ancient to Modern Times* (Chapel Hill: University of North
   Carolina Press, 1980).
Susan S. Lanser, *The Narrative Act: Point of View in Prose Fiction*
   (Princeton, NJ: Princeton UP, 1981).
D. A. Russell, 'Rhetoric and Criticism', *Greece and Rome*, 14 (1967),
   130–44.
S. (Istvan) Ullman, *Style in the French Novel* (2nd impr., Oxford:
   Blackwell, 1964), introduction.

(A) CICERO

Orator (c. 46 BC)

There are in all three styles of oratory, in each of which certain
individuals have excelled, but very few have attained our ideal
by excelling in all three. Those employing the 'grandiloquent'
style, if I may use the term, possessed both the full weight of
thought and the grandeur of diction: they were forceful, versatile,
copious and solemn, trained and skilled in arousing and swaying
the emotions; some pursued this effect by a rough, severe and
bristling style without regular or rounded periods; others used a
smooth and ordered style with finished periods. At the other end
of the spectrum were those who were plain and concise in style,
explaining everything and emphasizing clarity rather than
impressiveness, using a refined, compressed style, devoid of
ornament. Within this group some were skilful but unpolished
and consciously resembled untrained and unskilled speakers;
others had the same dryness of style but were neater, and were
elegant, even brilliant and slightly ornate. In between these
extremes there was an intermediate and, so to speak, tempered
style, which does not possess the intellectual appeal of the latter
group nor the fireworks of the former; having affinities with both
but excelling in neither, it participates in both but has no skill
in either: it flows along in a single tenor, so to speak,
contributing nothing but ease and uniformity, and merely adding
a few blooms to the garland, and diversifying the whole speech
with modest ornaments of diction and thought. [. . .]
   The man of eloquence [. . .] will be one who can speak in

court or in deliberative councils so as to provide proof, pleasure and persuasion. The first necessity is to prove, to please is charming, and to sway gives victory (for it is of all things the one which most contributes to winning verdicts). For these three functions of the orator there are three styles: the plain style for proof, the middle style for pleasure, the grand style for persuasion. In this last lies the whole strength of the orator. [. . .] The orator must have an eye to propriety not only in thought but in words. For the same kinds of words or thoughts must not be used when portraying every condition of life, every rank, every position or every age (the same applies to place, time and audience). The rule in oratory as in life is always to observe propriety. This depends on the subject matter, and on the character of both the speakers and the audience. Philosophers are accustomed to treat this extensive subject under the heading of 'duties' (and not when they discuss the ideal, for that is unvaried and unchanging); the critics treat it in relation to poetry; orators in relation to every kind and aspect of speech. How lacking in decorum it would be [. . .] to speak meanly and meagrely about the majesty of the Roman people. [. . .]

First we must describe the one whom some call the only true 'Attic' orator. He is restrained and plain, he follows ordinary usage, and differs more than is supposed from those who lack eloquence. Consequently the audience, even if they are themselves no speakers, believe they can speak in that manner. For that simplicity of style seems easy to imitate at first thought, but nothing is more difficult in practice. For though it is not full-blooded, it should nevertheless have some sap in it, so that, though it lack great strength, it may still, so to speak, be in good health. [. . .] And so, the plain-style orator, while being elegant will not be daring in coining words and will be modest in metaphor, sparing in archaisms, and reserved in other adornments of language and thought. He may use metaphor a little more frequently because it is often found in the speech of both townspeople and countrypeople. The latter, for example, say that their vines are 'bejewelled', the fields 'thirsty', the crops 'happy', and the grain 'luxuriant'. These are all daring enough, but either there is a similarity to the source from which the word is borrowed, or, if the thing has no proper term, the borrowing is done to clarify meaning and not just as word-play. The restrained speaker may use this figure a little more freely than others, but not as daringly as if he were using the grandest style. Consequently, indecorum, the nature of which should be

evident from our account of decorum, also arises when a
metaphor is far-fetched or when one is used in the plain style
when it would be better suited in another style. [. . .]

To the [. . .] middle and tempered style belong all the figures
of words and many of thought. Middle-style orators will develop
their argument with breadth and erudition, and bring in
commonplaces without undue emphasis. Why say more? Such
orators often come from philosophical academies. [. . .] It is,
indeed, a brilliant and florid, an ornamented and polished style,
in which all the elegancies of language and thought are
intertwined [. . .] scorned by the plain speakers and rejected by
the grand, it found its home in the middle class of which I am
speaking.

The third type of orator is splendid, copious, stately and
ornate; he undoubtedly possesses the greatest power. This is the
person whose richness and fluency of speech have caused
admiring nations to allow eloquence the greatest power in the
state. I refer to the kind of eloquence which thunders like a
mighty torrent, which all look up to and admire, but despair of
emulating. This eloquence can sway minds and move in every
way. Now it overwhelms the emotions, now it enters
imperceptibly; now it implants new ideas and uproots the old.
But there is a great difference between this style and the above-
mentioned. The speaker who has mastered the plain and pointed
style so as to be able to speak cleverly and neatly, and has not
conceived anything higher, is certainly a great orator, if not the
greatest. [. . .] The orator of the middle style [. . .] once he has
marshalled his forces, will not dread the uncertainties and
pitfalls of speaking. Even if he is not completely successful, as is
often the case, he will not run a great risk, for he has not far to
fall. But this grandiloquent, impetuous and fiery orator of ours,
to whom we give the highest status, is little to be admired, if he
is naturally gifted in this alone or trains himself only in this
style, or devotes himself only to this without tempering his
eloquence with the other two styles. For the plain orator is
considered wise because he speaks clearly and cleverly; the
middle-style orator is pleasing; but the orator of grandiloquence,
if he has no other quality, seems to be scarcely sane. For if a
man who can say nothing calmly and moderately, nothing with
proper organization, precision clarity or wit [. . .]
if he begins to inflame emotions without preparing the ears
of his audience, he has all the appearance of being a raving

lunatic among the sane and a drunken reveller among the
sober.

(Cicero, *Orator* (46 BC), from sections V. 20–2, XXI. 69, 71–2, XXIII,
75–6, XXIV, 81–2, XXVII. 95–XXVIII. 99. Translation by editor.)

(B) [GEORGE] PUTTENHAM

The Arte of English Poesie (1589)

But generally, to have the stile decent & comely it behooveth
the maker or Poet to follow the nature of his subject, that is if
his matter be high and loftie that the stile be so to, if meane,
the stile also to be meane, if base, the stile humble and base
accordingly: and they that do otherwise use it, applying to
meane matter hie and loftie stile, and to hie matters stile eyther
meane or base, and to the base matters the meane or hie stile,
do utterly disgrace their poesie and shew themselves nothing
skilfull in their arte, nor having regard to the decencie, which is
the chiefe praise of any writer. Therefore to ridde all lovers of
learning from that errour, I will, as neere as I can, set downe
which matters be hie and loftie, which be but meane, and which
be low and base, to the intent the stiles may be fashioned to the
matters, and keepe their *decorum* and good proportion in every
respect. [. . .]
   The matters therefore that concerne the Gods and divine
things are highest of all other to be couched in writing; next to
them the noble gests and great fortunes of Princes, and the
notable accidents of time, as the greatest affaires of war &
peace: these be all high subjectes, and therefore are delivered
over to the Poets *Hymnick* & historicall who be occupied either in
divine laudes or in *heroicall* reports. The meane matters be those
that concerne meane men, their life the busines, as lawyers,
gentlemen, and marchants, good housholders and honest
Citizens, and which sound neither to matters of state nor of
warre, nor leagues, nor great alliances, but smatch all the
common conversation, as of the civiller and better sort of men.
The base and low matters be the doings of the common artificer,
servingman, yeoman, groome, husbandman, day-labourer, sailer,
shepheard, swynard, and such like of homely calling, degree, and
bringing up. So that in every of the sayd three degrees not the

selfe same vertues be egally to be praysed nor the same vices egally to be dispraised, nor their loves, mariages, quarels, contracts, and other behaviours be like high nor do require to be set fourth with the like stile, but every one in his degree and decencie, which made that all *hymnes* and histories and Tragedies were written in the high stile, all Comedies and Enterludes and other common Poesies of loves and such like in the meane stile, all *Eglogues* and pastorall poemes in the low and base stile; otherwise they had bene utterly disproporcioned.

As figures be the instruments of ornament in every language, so be they also in a sorte abuses or rather trespasses in speach, because they passe the ordinary limits of common utterance, and be occupied of purpose to deceive the eare and also the minde, drawing it from plainnesse and simplicitie to a certaine doublenesse, whereby our talke is the more guilefull & abusing. For what els is your *Metaphor* but an inversion of sense by transport; your *allegorie* by a duplicitie of meaning or dissimulation under covert and darke intendments. [. . .]

[Judges forbid figurative language because it distorts the truth.] This no doubt is true and was by them gravely considered; but in this case, because our maker or Poet is appointed not for a judge, but rather for a pleader, and that of pleasant & lovely causes and nothing perillous, such as be those for the triall of life, limme, or livelyhood, and before judges neither sower nor severe, but in the eare of princely dames, young ladies, gentlewomen, and courtiers, beyng all for the most part either meeke of nature, or of pleasant humour, and that all his abuses tende but to dispose the hearers to mirth and sollace by pleasant conveyance and efficacy of speach, they are not in truth to be accompted vices but for vertues in the poetical science very commendable.

([George] Puttenham, *The Arte of English Poesie* (1589), *Elizabethan Critical Essays*, ed. G. Gregory Smith, 2 vols (London: Oxford UP, 1904), pp. 154–5, 158–61.)

(C) ERICH AUERBACH

Mimesis (1946)

Prince Henry: Before God, I am exceeding weary.
Poins: Is it come to that? I had thought weariness durst not have attached one of so high blood.

Prince Henry: Faith, it does me; though it discolours the complexion of my greatness to acknowledge it. Does it not show vilely in me to desire small beer?

Poins: Why, a prince should not be so loosely studied as to remember so weak a composition.

Prince Henry: Belike, then, my appetite was not princely got; for, by my troth, I do now remember the poor creature, small beer. But, indeed, these humble considerations make me out of love with my greatness. What a disgrace is it to me to remember thy name? or to know thy face tomorrow? or to take note how many silk stockings thou hast; viz., these, and those that were thy peach-coloured ones? or to bear the inventory of thy shirts, as, one for superfluity, and one other for use? . . .

This is a conversation between Prince Henry (subsequently King Henry) and one of the boon companions of his youthful frolics. It occurs in Shakespeare's *Henry IV*, part 2, at the beginning of the second scene of act 2. The comic disapproval of the fact that a person of such high rank should be subject to weariness and the desire for small beer, that his mind should be obliged so much as to notice the existence of so lowly a creature as Poins and even to remember the inventory of his clothes, is a satire on the trend – no longer negligible in Shakespeare's day – toward a strict separation between the sublime and the realm of everyday realities. Attempts in this direction were inspired by the example of antiquity, especially by Seneca, and were spread by the humanist imitators of antique drama in Italy, France, and in England itself. But they had not yet met with complete success. However important the influence of antiquity may have been on Shakespeare, it could not mislead him, nor yet other dramatists of the Elizabethan period, into this separation of styles. The medieval-Christian and at the same time popular-English tradition which opposed such a development was still too strong. At a much later period, more than a century and a half after his death, Shakespeare's work became the ideal and the example for all movements of revolt against the strict separation of styles in French classicism. Let us try to determine what the mixture of styles in his work signifies. [. . .]

A large number of the elements of mixed style are mentioned or alluded to in these few lines: the element of physical creaturalness, that of lowly everyday objects, and that of the mixture of classes involving persons of high and low rank; there is also a marked mixture of high and low expressions in the diction, there is even use of one of the classical terms which characterize the low style, the word 'humble.' All this is abundantly represented in Shakespeare's tragic works. Examples of the portrayal of the physical-creatural are numerous: Hamlet is fat and short of breath (according to another reading he is not fat but hot); Caesar faints from the stench of the mob acclaiming him; Cassio in *Othello* is drunk; hunger and thirst, cold and heat affect tragic characters too; they suffer from the inclemencies of the weather and the ravages of illness: in Ophelia's case insanity is represented with such realistic psychology that the resulting stylistic effect is completely different from what we find in Euripides' *Herakles* for example; and death, which can be depicted on the level of the pure sublime, here often has its medieval and creatural appearance (skeletons, the smell of decomposition, etc.). Nowhere is there an attempt to avoid mentioning everyday utensils or, in general, to avoid the concrete portrayal of the everyday processes of life; these things have a much larger place than they do in antique tragedy, although there too, even before Euripides, they were not so completely taboo as with the classicists of the sixteenth and seventeenth centuries.

More important than this is the mixture of characters and the consequent mixture of tragic and comic elements. To be sure, all the characters whom Shakespeare treats in the sublime and tragic manner are of high rank. He does not, as the Middle Ages did, conceive of 'everyman' as tragic. He is also more consciously aristocratic than Montaigne. In his work the *humaine condition* is reflected very differently in the different classes, not only in practical terms but also from the point of view of aesthetic dignity. His tragic heroes are kings, princes, commanders, noblemen, and the great figures of Roman history. A borderline case is Shylock. [. . .]

For him Shylock, both in terms of class and aesthetically, is a low figure, unworthy of tragic treatment, whose tragic involvement is conjured up for a moment, but is only an added spice in the triumph of a higher, nobler, freer, and also more aristocratic humanity. Our Prince has the same views. Far be it from him to respect Poins as his equal, although he is the best among the characters in the Falstaff group, although he possesses both wit and valor. What arrogance there is in the words he addresses to him only a few lines before the passage quoted above: '. . . I could tell to thee — as to one it pleases me,

for fault of a better, to call my friend . . .' The manner in which
Shakespeare elsewhere treats the middle and lower classes we
shall take up in due course. In any case, he never renders them
tragically. His conception of the sublime and tragic is altogether
aristocratic.

But if we disregard this class restriction, Shakespeare's mixing
of styles in the portrayal of his characters is very pronounced. In
most of the plays which have a generally tragic tenor there is an
extremely close interweaving of the tragic and the comic, the
sublime and the low [. . .] not a few of Shakespeare's tragic
characters have their own innate tendency to break the stylistic
tenor in a humorous, realistic, or bitterly grotesque fashion. [. . .]

Even Romeo's sudden falling in love with Juliet, for example,
is almost fit for a comedy, and an almost unconscious
development takes the characters in this play of love from
childlike beginnings to a tragic climax. Gloucester's successful
wooing of Lady Anne at the bier of Henry VI (*King Richard III*,
I.ii), has something darkly grotesque; Cleopatra is childish and
moody; even Caesar is undecided, superstitious, and his
rhetorical pride is almost comically exaggerated. There is much
more of this nature. Hamlet and Lear especially furnish the most
significant examples. Hamlet's half real, half pretended insanity
rages, within a single scene and even a single speech, through all
levels of style. He jumps from the obscene to the lyrical or
sublime, from the ironically incongruous to dark and profound
meditation, from humiliating scorn leveled at others and himself
to the solemn assumption of the right to judge and proud self-
assertion. Lear's rich, forceful, and emotional arbitrariness has in
its incomparable sublimity elements that strike us as painfully
senile and theatrical. The speeches of his faithful fool themselves
tear at his mantle of sublimity; but more incisive are the stylistic
ruptures which lie in his own nature: his excesses of emotion, his
impotent and helpless outbursts of anger, his inclination to
indulge in bitterly grotesque histrionics. [. . .]

He is always ready to exaggerate; he wants to force heaven
and earth to witness the extremes of his humiliation and to hear
his complaints. Such gestures seem immeasurably shocking in an
old man of eighty, in a great king. And yet they do not in the
least detract from his dignity and greatness. His nature is so
unconditionally royal that humiliation only brings it out more
strongly. Shakespeare makes him speak the famous words 'aye,
every inch a king,' himself, from the depth of his insanity,

grotesquely accoutered, a madman playing the king for a moment. Yet we do not laugh, we weep, and not only in pity but at the same time in admiration for such greatness, which seems only the greater and more indestructible in its brittle creaturality. [. . .]

Shakespeare includes earthly reality, and even its most trivial forms, in a thousand refractions and mixtures, but [. . .] his purpose goes far beyond the representation of reality in its merely earthly coherence; he embraces reality but he transcends it. This is already apparent in the presence of ghosts and witches in his plays, and in the often unrealistic style in which the influences of Seneca, of Petrarchism, and of other fashions of the day are fused in a characteristically concrete but only erratically realistic manner. It is still more significantly revealed in the inner structure of the action which is often – and especially in the most important plays – only erratically and sporadically realistic and often shows a tendency to break through into the realm of the fairy tale, of playful fancy, or of the supernatural and demonic.

From another viewpoint too the tragic in Shakespeare is not completely realistic. We alluded to it at the beginning of this chapter. He does not take ordinary everyday reality seriously or tragically. He treats only noblemen, princes and kings, statesmen, commanders, and antique heroes tragically. When common people or soldiers or other representatives of the middle or lower classes appear, it is always in the low style, in one of the many variations of the comic which he commands. This separation of styles in accordance with class appears more consistently in him than in medieval works of literature and art, particularly those of Christian inspiration, and it is doubtless a reflection of the antique conception of the tragic. It is true, as we have said, that in him tragic personages of the higher classes exhibit frequent stylistic lapses into the corporeal-creatural, the grotesque, and the ambiguous; but the reverse is hardly so. Shylock would seem to be the only figure which might be cited as an exception, and we have seen that in his case too the tragic motifs are dropped at the end.

(Erich Auerbach, *Mimesis: The Representation of Reality in Western Literature*, trans. Willard Trask (Princeton, NJ: Princeton UP, 1953), pp. 312–13, 313–14, 315, 316–17, 327–8. Original German was published by A. Francke (Berne, 1946).)

(D) RICHARD OHMANN

'Speech, Action and Style' (1971)

In summary, and in schematic form, consider the utterance, 'Stop, or I'll shoot.'

Locutionary act:	Saying 'Stop, or I'll shoot.'
Illocutionary acts:	*Threatening, ordering,* . . .
Perlocutionary acts:	Frightening, enraging, . . .

Since I am speaking of a problem in literary theory, I should add that all three kinds of act may be performed in and through writing. The nature of the locutionary act is thereby altered in obvious ways, the illocutionary act is more or less attenuated, and the perlocutionary act is more or less delayed.

Of the three, illocutionary acts are the most elusive. Austin remarks that philosophers of language habitually slide away from illocutionary acts, toward either locutionary or perlocutionary acts, to the detriment of their study. The same holds, I believe, for us, although illocutionary acts offer rich expressive possibilities, and are deeply rooted in a system of rules quite close to the heart of our literary concerns. Let us consider, briefly, those rules. To this end, I quote Austin's criteria for the 'felicity' (successful functioning) of one class of illocutionary act, *performatives* such as 'I vote no,' 'I hereby dismiss the class,' and 'I bid three spades' – a particularly pure sort of speech act, since it asserts nothing true or false, but simply performs the act in question.

1) There must exist an accepted conventional procedure having a certain conventional effect, that procedure to include the uttering of certain words by certain persons in certain circumstances, and further,
2) the particular persons and circumstances in a given case must be appropriate for the invocation of the particular procedure invoked.
3) The procedure must be executed by all participants both correctly and
4) completely.
5) Where, as often, the procedure is designed for use by persons having certain thoughts or feelings, or for the inauguration of certain consequential conduct on the part of any participant, then a person participating in and so

> invoking the procedure must in fact have those thoughts or
> feelings, and the participants must intend so to conduct
> themselves, and further
> 6)   must actually so conduct themselves subsequently. [. . .]

A discourse is a set of grammatical structures with meanings. It
is also an attempt to influence the reader. I am suggesting that
these facts about the ontology of discourse have been well
recognized in theories of style, but that a third – that a
discourse is a series of illocutionary acts – has not, and ought to
be.

In written discourse, the conditions of action are altered in
obvious ways: the audience is dispersed and uncertain; there is
often nothing but internal evidence to tell us whether the writer
has beliefs and feelings appropriate to his acts, and nothing at
all to tell us whether he conducts himself appropriately
afterward. Nonetheless, writing is parasitic on speech in this, as
in all matters. [. . .]

The style of the book builds in part on acts that are defective
or incompatible. The social contract that exists between writer
and reader is repeatedly broken. And hence the validity of *all*
social contracts and *all* conventions is shaken. When a text
violates syntactic or semantic rules, cognitive or logical
dissonance ensues. Violating the rules for illocutionary acts also
produces a kind of chaos, but, predictably, a *social* one.

The absurdity of verbal conventions that have lost their power
to stabilize traffic among people, thus leaving speech unanchored
to that which makes it social action, has not been overlooked by
our writers. In a time when they have sought emblems of
isolation and expressions of the felt absurdity of things, many
have found their way to abuses of the illocutionary act similar to
those in *Watt*. The 'theater of the absurd,' in particular, has
created a medium of social exchange much like the flamingoes
and hedgehogs used as croquet mallets and balls in *Alice's
Adventures in Wonderland*, and with similar results. And prose
writers are fairly common, who, like Borges and Barthelme rend
the particular illocutionary conventions on which narrative is
based. This is to suggest that, just as some traits of locutionary
style may be discovered which a whole group of writers at a
given time have found cognitively and aesthetically valid,
peculiarities of illocutionary act may also figure importantly in
literary fashion. It is natural that writers should be specially
sensitive to the expressive potential of those acts that are done
with words. As Frye says, ritual, 'the content of action . . . is

something continuously latent in the order of words.'

I suspect, also – to gesture at just one more reach of this topic – that styles of illocutionary action help to determine the most fundamental literary types. Thus comedy, particularly as it approaches farce, is likely to establish its world through a repetitive or mechanical series of speech acts, as if in confirmation of Bergson's ideas about comedy and action. For instance, the first few pages of *The Importance of Being Earnest* consist almost entirely in an exchange of *questions* and *assertions*. [. . .]

Or recall the beginning of *The Alchemist*, which is a sustained sequence of *epithets* and *threats*, hurled by Face and Subtle at each other, with Doll Common intruding now and then a *plea* for temperance. [. . .]

By contrast, tragedies are often more varied in illocutionary acts, as if to establish at the start a fuller range of human emotion and action. *Hamlet* begins with a *question*, a *refusal*, two *commands*, a kind of *loyalty oath* ('long live the king'), a *question*, a *statement*, a *compliment*, a *statement*, an *order*, *thanks*, and a *complaint* – all this, of course, between two guardsmen.

Frye speaks of literature as 'a body of hypothetical verbal structures,' with the polemical emphasis on the word 'hypothetical.' For present purposes, I would shift the focus slightly, and say that a work of literature is also a series of hypothetical *acts*, grounded in the conventions for verbal action that we have all thoroughly learned. In fact I would go farther, and say that literature can be accurately *defined* as discourse in which the seeming acts are hypothetical. Around them, the reader, using his elaborate knowledge of the rules for illocutionary acts, constructs the hypothetical speakers and circumstances – the fictional world – that will make sense of the given acts. This performance is what we know as mimesis.

(Richard Ohmann, 'Speech, Action, and Style', *Literary Style: A Symposium*, ed. Seymour Chatman (London and New York: Oxford UP, 1971), pp. 246–7, 248, 252–4.)

(E) HENRY JAMES

Preface to *The Princess Casamassima* (1886)

I recognise at the same time, and in planning *The Princess Casamassima* felt it highly important to recognise, the danger of filling too full any supposed and above all any obviously limited vessel of consciousness. If persons either tragically or comically embroiled with life allow us the comic or tragic value of their embroilment in proportion as their struggle is a measured and directed one, it is strangely true, none the less, that beyond a certain point they are spoiled for us by this carrying of a due light. They may carry too much of it for our credence, for our compassion, for our derision. They may be shown as knowing too much and feeling too much – not certainly for their remaining remarkable, but for their remaining 'natural' and typical, for their having the needful communities with our own precious liability to fall into traps and be bewildered. It seems probable that if we were never bewildered there would never be a story to tell about us; we should partake of the superior nature of the all-knowing immortals whose annals are dreadfully dull so long as flurried humans are not, for the positive relief of bored Olympians, mixed up with them. Therefore it is that the wary reader for the most part warns the novelist against making his characters too *interpretative* of the muddle of fate, or in other words too divinely, too priggishly clever.

(Henry James, Preface to *The Princess Casamassima* (1886; London: Macmillan, 1921), 2 vols, I. x–xi.)

Preface to *The Golden Bowl* (1905)

Among many matters thrown into relief by a refreshed acquaintance with 'The Golden Bowl' what perhaps most stands out for me is the still marked inveteracy of a certain indirect and oblique view of my presented action; unless indeed I make up my mind to call this mode of treatment, on the contrary, any superficial appearance notwithstanding, the very straightest and closest possible. I have already betrayed, as an accepted habit, and even to extravagance commented on, my preference for dealing with my subject-matter, for 'seeing my story,' through the opportunity and the sensibility of some more or less detached, some not strictly involved, though thoroughly interested and intelligent, witness or reporter, some person who contributes to the case mainly a certain amount of criticism and interpretation of it. Again and again, on review, the shorter things in especial that I have gathered into this Series have ranged themselves not as my own impersonal account of the affair in hand, but as my account of somebody's impression of it – the terms of this person's access to it and estimate of it contributing thus by some fine little law to intensification of interest. The somebody is often, among my shorter tales I recognise, but an unnamed, unintroduced and (save by right of intrinsic wit) unwarranted participant, the impersonal author's concrete deputy or delegate, a convenient substitute or apologist for the creative power otherwise so veiled and disembodied. My instinct appears repeatedly to have been that to arrive at the facts retailed and the figures introduced by the given help of some other conscious and confessed agent is essentially to find the whole business – that is, as I say, its effective interest – enriched *by the way*. I have in other words constantly inclined to the idea of the particular attaching case *plus* some near individual view of it; that nearness quite having thus to become an imagined observer's, a projected, charmed painter's or poet's – however avowed the 'minor' quality in the latter – close and sensitive contact with it. Anything, in short, I now reflect, must always have seemed to me better – better for the process and the effect of representation, my irrepressible ideal – than the mere muffled majesty of irresponsible 'authorship.'

(Henry James, Preface to *The Golden Bowl* (1905; London: Macmillan, 1923), 2 vols, I. v–vi.)

(F) WAYNE BOOTH

The Rhetoric of Fiction (1961)

Since Flaubert, many authors and critics have been convinced that 'objective' or 'impersonal' or 'dramatic' modes of narration are naturally superior to any mode that allows for direct appearances by the author or his reliable spokesman. Sometimes, as we shall see in the next three chapters, the complex issues involved in this shift have been reduced to a convenient distinction between 'showing,' which is artistic, and 'telling,' which is inartistic. [. . .]

Why is it that an episode 'told' by Fielding can strike us as more fully realized than many of the scenes scrupulously 'shown' by imitators of James or Hemingway? Why does some authorial commentary ruin the work in which it occurs, while the

prolonged commentary of *Tristram Shandy* can still enthral us?
What, after all, does an author do when he 'intrudes' to 'tell' us
something about his story? Such questions force us to consider
closely what happens when an author engages a reader fully
with a work of fiction; they lead us to a view of fictional
technique which necessarily goes far beyond the reductions that
we have sometimes accepted under the concept of 'point of
view'. [. . .]

One cannot restore telling to critical respect simply by
jumping to its defense – not on this field of battle. Its opponents
would have most of the effective ammunition. Many novels *are*
seriously flawed by careless intrusions. What is more, it is easy
to prove that an episode shown is more effective than the same
episode told, so long as we must choose between two and only
two technical extremes. And, finally, the novelists and critics
who have deplored telling have won for fiction the kind of
standing as a major art form which, before Flaubert, was
generally denied to it, and they have often shown a seriousness
and devotion to their art that in itself carries conviction about
their doctrines. Nothing is gained – indeed, everything is lost – if
we say to James and Flaubert that we admire their experiments
in artistic seriousness, but that we prefer now to relax our
standards a little and encourage the novelist to go back to
concocting what James called 'great fluid puddings,' There may
be room, in the house of fiction, even for formless puddings – to
be read, presumably, in one's slack hours or declining years. But
I should not like to find myself defending them as art and on
the ground that they are formless.

But are we faced with such a simple and disconcerting choice
as the champions of showing have sometimes claimed? Does it,
after all, make sense to set up two ways of conveying a story,
one all good, the other all bad; one all art and form, the other
all clumsiness and irrelevancy; one all showing and rendering
and drama and objectivity, the other all telling and subjectivity
and preaching and inertness? Allen Tate seems to think hat it
does. 'The action,' he says of a passage from *Madame Bovary* –
and it is an excellent passage – 'the action is not stated from the
point of view of the author; it is rendered in terms of situation
and scene. To have made this the viable property of the art of
fiction was to have virtually made the art of fiction.' 'It has been
through Flaubert that the novel has at last caught up with
poetry.' This is dramatic, challenging – perhaps it is even the
sort of inspiriting program which might yield to a young novelist

enough conviction about the importance of what he is doing to get it done. But is it true?

I cannot prove that it is not – given Tate's definitions of 'art' and 'poetry.' But I hope to show that it has been at best misleading, and that the distinction on which it is based is inadequate, not only in dealing with early fiction like the *Decameron* but also in dealing with yesterday's *succès d'estime*.

It will be useful first to look at some of the reasons for the widespread acceptance of the distinction. If we are to conclude that there was after all an art of fiction before Flaubert, and that the art even in the most impersonal fiction does not reside exclusively in the moments of vivid dramatic rendering, why has there been such widespread suspicion of everything but the rendered scene? [. . .]

At this point in the mid-twentieth century we can see, after all, how easy it is to write a story that tells itself, freed of all authorial intrusion, shown with a consistent treatment of point of view. Even untalented writers can be taught to observe this fourth 'unity.' But we also know by now that in the process they have not necessarily learned to write good fiction. If they know only this, they know how to write fiction that will look modern – perhaps more 'early modern' than late, but still modern. What they have yet to learn, if they know only this, is the art of choosing what to dramatize fully and what to curtail, what to summarize and what to heighten. And like any art, this one cannot be learned from abstract rules. [. . .]

As he writes, he [the author] creates not simply an ideal, impersonal 'man in general' but an implied version of 'himself' that is different from the implied authors we meet in other men's works. To some novelists it has seemed, indeed, that they were discovering or creating themselves as they wrote. As Jessamyn West says, it is sometimes 'only by writing the story that the novelist can discover – not his story – but its writer, the official scribe, so to speak, for that narrative.' Whether we call this implied author an 'official scribe,' or adopt the term recently revived by Kathleen Tillotson – the author's 'second self' – it is clear that the picture the reader gets of this presence is one of the author's most important effects. However impersonal he may try to be, his reader will inevitably construct a picture of the official scribe who writes in this manner – and of course that official scribe will never be neutral toward all values. Our reactions to his various commitments, secret or overt, will help to determine our response to the work. The reader's role in this

relationship I must save for chapter v. Our present problem is
the intricate relationship of the so-called real author with his
various official versions of himself.

We must say various versions, for regardless of how sincere an
author may try to be, his different works will imply different
versions, different ideal combinations of norms. Just as one's
personal letters imply different versions of oneself, depending on
the differing relationships with each correspondent and the
purpose of each letter, so the writer sets himself out with a
different air depending on the needs of particular works. [. . .]

It is a curious fact that we have no terms either for this
created 'second self' or for our relationship with him. None of
our terms for various aspects of the narrator is quite accurate.
'Persona,' 'mask,' and 'narrator' are sometimes used, but they
more commonly refer to the speaker in the work who is after all
only one of the elements created by the implied author and who
may be separated from him by large ironies. 'Narrator' is
usually taken to mean the 'I' of a work, but the 'I' is seldom if
ever identical with the implied image of the artist.

'Theme,' 'meaning,' 'symbolic significance,' 'theology,' or even
'ontology' – all these have been used to described the norms
which the reader must apprehend in each work if he is to grasp
it adequately. Such terms are useful for some purposes, but they
can be misleading because they almost inevitably come to seem
like purposes for which the works exist. [. . .]

Our sense of the implied author includes not only the
extractable meanings but also the moral and emotional content
of each bit of action and suffering of all of the characters. It
includes, in short, the intuitive apprehension of a completed
artistic whole; the chief value to which *this* implied author is
committed, regardless of what party his creator belongs to in
real life, is that which is expressed by the total form.

Three other terms are sometimes used to name the core of
norms and choices which I am calling the implied author. 'Style'
is sometimes broadly used to cover whatever it is that gives us a
sense, from word to word and line to line, that the author sees
more deeply and judges more profoundly than his presented
characters. But, though style is one of our main sources of
insight into the author's norms, in carrying such strong
overtones of the merely verbal the word *style* excludes our sense
of the author's skill in his choice of character and episode and
scene and idea. 'Tone' is similarly used to refer to the implicit

evaluation which the author manages to convey behind his explicit presentation, but it almost inevitably suggests again something limited to the merely verbal; some aspects of the implied author may be inferred through tonal variations, but his major qualities will depend also on the hard facts of action and character in the tale that is told.

Similarly, 'technique' has at times been expanded to cover all discernible signs of the author's artistry. If everyone used 'technique' as Mark Schorer does, covering with it almost the entire range of choices made by the author, then it might very well serve our purposes. But it is usually taken for a much narrower matter, and consequently it will not do. We can be satisfied only with a term that is as broad as the work itself but still capable of calling attention to that work as the product of a choosing, evaluating person rather than as a self-existing thing. The 'implied author' chooses, consciously or unconsciously, what we read; we infer him as an ideal, literary, created version of the real man; he is the sum of his own choices.

It is only by distinguishing between the author and his implied image that we can avoid pointless and unverifiable talk about such qualities as 'sincerity' or 'seriousness' in the author. Because Ford Madox Ford thinks of Fielding and Defoe and Thackeray as the unmediated authors of their novels, he must end by condemning them as insincere, since there is every reason to believe that they write 'passages of virtuous aspirations that were in no way any aspirations of theirs.' Presumably he is relying on external evidences of Fielding's lack of virtuous aspirations. But we have only the work as evidence for the only kind of sincerity that concerns us: Is the implied author in harmony with himself – that is, are his other choices in harmony with his explicit narrative character? If a narrator who by every trustworthy sign is presented to us as a reliable spokesman for the author professes to believe in values which are never realized in the structure as a whole, we can then talk of an insincere work. A great work establishes the 'sincerity' of its implied author, regardless of how grossly the man who created that author may belie in his *other* forms of conduct the values embodied in his work. For all we know, the only sincere moments of his life may have been lived as he wrote his novel. [. . .]

We see, then, that none of the [. . .] claims to objectivity in the author has any necessary bearing on technical decisions.

Though it may be important at a given moment in the history of an art or in the development of a writer to stress the dangers of a misguided commitment, partiality, or emotional involvement, the tendency to connect the author's objectivity with a required impersonality of technique is quite indefensible.

(Wayne C. Booth, *The Rhetoric of Fiction* (Chicago and London: Chicago UP, 1961), pp. 8–9, 28–9, 64, 70–1, 73–5, 83.)

CHAPTER 6

STRUCTURE AND SYSTEM

Some literary critics dismiss new critical movements on the grounds that there are no new ideas under the sun. The word 'structure' is certainly not new, and there are many anticipations of 'structuralism' in earlier philosophy and poetics. However, history *does* affect the meaning and significance of words. The 'linguistic turn' of philosophy and criticism in the twentieth century has transformed the concept of 'structure'. Nevertheless, it is right to see a proto-structuralist dimension in, for example, Aristotle's *Poetics*. His account of the structure of dramatic plots reduces all possible plots to four:

> Simple plots
> Plots with Peripety
> Plots with Discovery
> Plots with Peripety and Discovery

In stating that the last type is the best, Aristotle is departing from a 'structuralist' approach in the modern sense. A structuralist would rest content with discovering the set of variables which is capable of generating all possible dramatic imitations. Another difference is that a structuralist model usually takes the form of 'binary oppositions'.

Ferdinand de Saussure's account of the system of language (*langue*) asserts that the object of study is *social* and not individual. He does not try to give an explanation of human utterances (*paroles*) but rather of 'language' (*langue*) – the system which underlies human speech (*parole*). Applied to literature this would mean that we study not individual poems and plays (*paroles*) but the system which produces them. In order to isolate a linguistic system it is necessary to cut a 'synchronic' slice from the 'diachronic' flow of language. Saussure makes a comparison with understanding chess. To grasp the system of chess and to discover the rules actually followed by players, we need to ignore any changes which have occurred in the game (e.g. alterations of the functions of pieces) over time. Similarly, if we wish to understand the system underlying a literary genre, we must treat the examples we study as belonging to a timeless synchronic order. History, in this perpective, can exist only as a sequence of synchronic moments or segments.

Saussure regards language as one among many 'semiotic' (sign) systems. The 'sign' is not what other linguistic theories called a 'symbol'. The latter is a linguistic item corresponding to a 'referent' (tree = 🌳). The sign has no necessary correspondence to any referent, but has a bipartite structure:

$$\text{SIGN} = \frac{\text{SIGNIFIER}}{\text{SIGNIFIED}} \quad [\text{Referent}]$$

The signifier is the graphic or acoustic image and the signified is the concept (what you think when you write or utter the signifier). The relation between the two is like that between two sides of a sheet of paper. However, this comparison implies a unity which is not necessarily the case. First, as Saussure notes, the relation between them is 'arbitrary', and secondly, one signifier can evidently have more than one signified. All that one can say is that in a particular and unambiguous context there *is* a unity. The proponents of 'deconstruction' dwell upon the instability which they argue is inherent in signification, whereas the structuralists treat signification as a stable and systematic process.

The concept of the 'binary opposition' is fundamental to much structuralist theory. One phoneme, the lowest-level linguistic unit, is distinguished from another by its *difference*. The difference between the two sybillants /s/ and /z/ is expressed in terms of a binary opposition – 'voiced' and 'unvoiced'. The whole phonetic system is a system of such differences. All sign systems are similarly identified in terms of binary patterns (on–off, presence–absence, sweet–sour, cooked–raw, etc.). Claude Lévi-Strauss, the French anthropologist, is the master exponent of this type of structural analysis. Literary systems too can be expressed in terms of binary oppositions.

Structuralist narrative theory (narratology) takes 'language' (*langue*) as its model. The structure of a sentence is seen as the model of the structure of narrative. At a simple level this can be seen in Propp's study of Russian fairytales: he identifies the 'subject' of the sentence with the typical characters, and the 'predicate' with the typical actions of such tales. He discovers thirty-one basic units of narrative (*'functions'*), and seven 'spheres of action' (*'actants'*). A. J. Greimas develops Propp's and other narratologists' models in an attempt to theorize not just a single genre but the universal 'grammar' of narrative, by constructing a semantic analysis of sentence structure. In place of Propp's seven *actants* he proposes three pairs of 'binary oppositions' which are built into semantic patterns. This 'phonemic' type of analysis is 'structuralist' in the Saussurean sense. The resulting matrix of *actants* is simple and yet capable of generating, under the pressure of 'supplementary investments', every conceivable narrative utterance (including non-literary narratives in philosophy, politics, religion, and so on).

Though not a 'structuralist' in the linguistic sense, Northrop Frye is structuralist in his scientific ambition to establish the principles of the entire literary system from Homer to the present day. A fundamental level of the structure (along with 'modes', 'archetypes' and genres) are 'myths'. Four narrative categories (comic, romantic, tragic and ironic) correspond to the four 'myths' of spring, summer, autumn and winter. The myths which inform all literature are expressed in two main symbolic patterns – the apocalyptic (Gods and Heaven) and the demonic (Devils and Hell). The myths are expressed in archetypal symbols (compare and contrast Jung and Bodkin, II, 5, B–C) which are directly or indirectly present in all literature. Frye solves the problem raised by the historical development of different genres and different content by introducing the Freudian concept of 'displacement'. In a realistic novel the archetypal symbols reappear but, in order to avoid implausibility, the author displaces the mythic content into less prominent details within the fiction. Frye's constant aim is to establish the universal structures of all literature.

Plato and Aristotle were interested in the distinction between (1) pure representation (*mimesis*) when speeches are presented without narrative (*diegesis*) intervention and (2) forms in which there is a mixture of narration and imitation. Typically, according to Plato, dramatic forms use pure imitation, and the epic mixes pure imitation and authorial interventions. Lyric forms involve purely authorial utterance with no 'imitation'.

Gérard Genette, in structuralist fashion, offers a universal theory of narrative in the form of three binary oppositions, two of which are discussed in our extract. He argues that the mimesis/diegesis distinction cannot be sustained, because there can be no unmediated representation; all representations are 'narrated'. To have pure representation would be like having bits of reality actually in a 'realistic' picture. Another distinction – between 'narrative' and 'discourse' – takes us onto a different plane. 'Narrative' is a sort of pure telling in which 'no one speaks', while 'discourse' draws attention to the speaking subject. In the nineteenth-century novel we appear to approach the perfect ideal of objective narration in which there is no discourse. However, as Genette shows, such purity is in practice always impossible: a judging mind is always insinuated into narration making it inevitably impure. He adds a significant linguistic dimension by showing that certain grammatical forms belong with narrative and others with discourse.

One particular binary opposition – metaphor and metonymy – has proved especially fruitful as a heuristic device in literary criticism. Jakobson's study of 'aphasia' (speech defect) starts by restating the fundamental distinction between the horizontal and the vertical dimensions of language, which are related to those between *langue* and *parole*. A sentence can be viewed from either perspective: (1) each element is *selected* on the basis of *similarity* from a set of possible elements (vertical, or paradigmatic); (2) the elements are *combined* in a particular sequence (horizontal, or syntagmatic). Jakobson discovered that the abnormal inability of aphasics to select or combine was directly related to normal linguistic functioning. All discourse tends to go towards one or other pole. This is expressed by the distinction between metaphor (which involves selection) and metonymy (which involves deletion from the sequence, as Lodge pointed out). Jakobson suggested that all the arts tend to gravitate toward one pole or the other. David Lodge, in *The Modes of Modern Writing* (1977), applied the theory to modern literature. He adds a number of important refinements to Jakobson's brief account. For example, he shows that 'context is all important': what is metaphoric in one context may be metonymic in another. In a geographical context the fog in Dickens' *Bleak House* is metonymic (fog = London); in a social context, it is metaphoric (fog = the legal system).

Jonathan Culler's *Structuralist Poetics* (1975) made a contribution to reader-response criticism (see II,4, J–N). He argued that a truly structuralist knowledge of the literary system would have as its object not the structure of literary texts but the structure of readers' interpretive acts. Using Noam Chomsky's terminology he used the term 'literary competence' to describe that institutionally acquired ability of readers to read texts as literature and to make judgements as to what constitutes an acceptable interpretation of a particular work. Culler emphasizes that structuralists are not concerned with interpretations as such but only with the competence which underlies interpretations. One of the things all readers do is to 'naturalize' the texts they read, even those texts which present challenges to competence. Poetics, according to Culler, should attempt to discover the rules which are followed by readers when they 'make sense' of texts. As is the case with most structuralist theories, it is essential to exclude the diachronic dimension. We are not supposed to ask which institutions produce what competences and whose power enforces a particular competence, any more than we should ask about the history of the chess pieces when we try to understand how the game is played.

Background reading

'A Survey of Semiotics', *Times Literary Supplement*, 5 and 12 Oct. 1973.

Jonathan Culler, *Ferdinand de Saussure* (London: Fontana/Collins, 1976).

Robert D. Denham, *Northrop Frye and Critical Method* (Pennsylvania State UP, 1978).

Jacques Ehrmann (ed.), *Structuralism* (Garden City, NY: Doubleday, 1970).

Terence Hawkes, *Structuralism and Semiotics* (London: Methuen, 1977).

Sándor Hervey, *Semiotic Perspectives* (London: Allen & Unwin, 1983).

Fredric Jameson, *The Prison-House of Language: A Critical Account of Structuralism and Russian Formalism* (Princeton, NJ: Princeton UP, 1972).

Murray Krieger (ed.) *Northrop Frye and Modern Criticism* (New York and London: Columbia UP, 1966).

Richard Macksey and Eugenio Donato, (eds), *The Structuralist Controversy* (Baltimore: Johns Hopkins Press, 1970).

S. Rimmon-Kenan, *Narrative Fiction: Contemporary Poetics* (London: Methuen, 1983).

David Robey (ed.), *Structuralism: an Introduction* (Oxford: Clarendon Press, 1973).

Robert Scholes, *Structuralism in Literature: An Introduction* (New Haven and London: Yale UP, 1974).

Tzvetan Todorov, *Introduction to Poetics*, trans. R. Howard (Brighton: Harvester Press, 1981).

Tzvetan Todorov (ed.), *French Literary Theory Today, A Reader*, trans. R. Carter (Cambridge: Cambridge UP, 1983).

(A) PLATO

The Republic

[BOOK 3]

And narration may be either simple narration, or imitation, or a union of the two?

That again, he said, I do not quite understand.

I fear that I must be a ridiculous teacher when I have so much difficulty in making myself apprehended. Like a bad speaker, therefore, I will not take the whole of the subject, but will break a piece off in illustration of my meaning. You know the first lines of the Iliad, in which the poet says that Chryses prayed Agamemnon to release his daughter, and that Agamemnon flew into a passion with him; whereupon Chryses, failing of his object, invoked the anger of the God against the Achaeans. Now as far as these lines,

> 'And he prayed all the Greeks, but especially the two sons
> of Atreus, the chiefs of the people,'

the poet is speaking in his own person; he never leads us to suppose that he is any one else. But in what follows he takes the person of Chryses, and then he does all that he can to make us believe that the speaker is not Homer, but the aged priest himself. And in this double form he has cast the entire narrative of the events which occurred at Troy and in Ithaca and throughout the Odyssey.

Yes.

And a narrative it remains both in the speeches which the poet recites from time to time and in the intermediate passages?

Quite true.

But when the poet speaks in the person of another, may we not say that he assimilates his style to that of the person who, as he informs you, is going to speak?

Certainly.

And this assimiliation of himself to another, either by the use of voice or gesture, is the imitation of the person whose character he assumes?

Of course.

Then in this case the narrative of the poet may be said to proceed by way of imitation?

Very true.

Or, if the poet everywhere appears and never conceals himself, then again the imitation is dropped, and his poetry becomes simple narration. However, in order that I may make my meaning quite clear, and that you may no more say, 'I don't understand,' I will show how the change might be effected. If Homer had said, 'The priest came, having his daughter's ransom in his hands, supplicating the Achaeans, and above all the kings;' and then if, instead of speaking in the person of Chryses, he had continued in his own person, the words would have been, not imitation, but simple narration. The passage would have run as follows (I am no poet, and therefore I drop the metre), 'The priest came and prayed the gods on behalf of the Greeks that they might capture Troy and return safely home, but begged that they would give him back his daughter, and take the ransom which he brought, and respect the God. Thus he spoke, and the other Greeks revered the priest and assented. But Agamemnon was wroth, and bade him depart and not come again, lest the staff and chaplets of the God should be of no avail to him – the daughter of Chryses should not be released, he said – she should grow old with him in Argos. And then he told him to go away and not to provoke him, if he intended to get home unscathed. And the old man went away in fear and silence, and, when he had left the camp, he called upon Apollo by his many names, reminding him of everything which he had done pleasing to him, whether in building his temples, or in offering sacrifice, and praying that his good deeds might be returned to him, and that the Achaeans might expiate his tears by the arrows of the god,' – and so on. In this way the whole becomes simple narrative.

I understand, he said.

Or you may suppose the opposite case – that the intermediate passages are omitted, and the dialogue only left.

That also, he said, I understand; you mean, for example, as in tragedy.

You have conceived my meaning perfectly; and if I mistake not, what you failed to apprehend before is now made clear to you, that poetry and mythology are, in some cases, wholly imitative – instances of this are supplied by tragedy and comedy; there is likewise the opposite style, in which the poet is the only speaker – of this the dithyramb affords the best example; and the combination of both is found in epic, and in several other styles of poetry.

(Plato, *The Republic*, trans. B. Jowett (3rd edn, Oxford: Clarendon Press, 1888), pp. 77–9.)

(B) ARISTOTLE

Poetics

[CHAPTERS 10 AND 11]

Plots are either simple or complex, since the actions they represent are naturally of this twofold description. The action, proceeding in the way defined, as one continuous whole, I call simple, when the change in the hero's fortunes takes place without Peripety or Discovery; and complex, when it involves one or the other, or both. These should each of them arise out of the structure of the Plot itself, so as to be the consequence, necessary or probable, of the antecedents. There is a great difference between a thing happening *propter hoc* and *post hoc*.

A Peripety is the change from one state of things within the play to its opposite of the kind described, and that too in the way we are saying, in the probable or necessary sequence of events; as it is for instance in *Oedipus*: here the opposite state of things is produced by the Messenger, who, coming to gladden Oedipus and to remove his fears as to his mother, reveals the secret of his birth. And in *Lynceus*: just as he is being led off for execution, with Danaus at his side to put him to death, the incidents preceding this bring it about that he is saved and Danaus put to death. A Discovery is, as the very word implies, a change from ignorance to knowledge, and thus to either love or hate, in the personages marked for good or evil fortune. The finest form of Discovery is one attended by Peripeties, like that which goes with the Discovery in *Oedipus*. There are no doubt other forms of it; what we have said may happen in a way in reference to inanimate things, even things of a very casual kind; and it is also possible to discover whether some one has done or not done something. But the form most directly connected with the Plot and the action of the piece is the first-mentioned. This, with a Peripety, will arouse either pity or fear – actions of that nature being what Tragedy is assumed to represent; and it will also serve to bring about the happy or unhappy ending. The Discovery, then, being of persons, it may be that of one party only to the other, the latter being already known; or both the parties may have to discover themselves. Iphigenia, for instance, was discovered to Orestes by sending the letter; and another Discovery was required to reveal him to Iphigenia.

(Aristotle, *Poetics*, ed. Ingram Bywater, *On the Art of Poetry* (Oxford: Clarendon Press, 1920), pp. 46–8.)

(C) FERDINAND DE SAUSSURE

Course in General Linguistics (1915)

If we could embrace the sum of word-images stored in the minds of all individuals, we could identify the social bond that constitutes language. It is a storehouse filled by the members of a given community through their active use of speaking, a grammatical system that has a potential existence in each brain, or, more specifically, in the brains of a group of individuals. For language is not complete in any speaker; it exists perfectly only within a collectivity.

In separating language from speaking we are at the same time separating: (1) what is social from what is individual; and (2) what is essential from what is accessory and more or less accidental.

Language is not a function of the speaker; it is a product that is passively assimilated by the individual. It never requires premeditation, and reflection enters in only for the purpose of classification, which we shall take up later.

Speaking, on the contrary, is an individual act. It is wilful and intellectual. Within the act, we should distinguish between: (1) the combinations by which the speaker uses the language code for expressing his own thought; and (2) the psychophysical mechanism that allows him to exteriorize those combinations. [. . .]

Language is a system of signs that express ideas, and is therefore comparable to a system of writing, the alphabet of deaf-mutes, symbolic rites, polite formulas, military signals, etc. But it is the most important of all these systems.

A science that studies the life of signs within society is conceivable; it would be a part of social psychology and consequently of general psychology; I shall call it *semiology* (from Greek *sēmeîon* 'sign'). Semiology would show what constitutes signs, what laws govern them. Since the science does not yet exist, no one can say what it would be; but it has a right to existence, a place staked out in advance. Linguistics is only a part of the general science of semiology; the laws discovered by semiology will be applicable to linguistics, and the latter will circumscribe a well-defined area within the mass of anthropological facts.

To determine the exact place of semiology is the task of the psychologist. The task of the linguist is to find out what makes language a special system within the mass of semiological data. This issue will be taken up again later; here I wish merely to call attention to one thing: if I have succeeded in assigning linguistics a place among the sciences, it is because I have related it to semiology.

Why has semiology not yet been recognized as an independent science with its own object like all the other sciences? Linguists have been going around in circles: language, better than anything else, offers a basis for understanding the semiological problem; but language must, to put it correctly, be studied in itself; heretofore language has almost always been studied in connection with something else, from other viewpoints. [. . .] By studying rites, customs, etc. as signs, I believe that we shall throw new light on the facts and point up the need for including them in a science of semiology and explaining them by its laws.

In internal linguistics the picture differs completely. Just any arrangement will not do. Language is a system that has its own arrangement. Comparison with chess will bring out the point. In chess, what is external can be separated relatively easily from what is internal. The fact that the game passed from Persia to Europe is external; against that, everything having to do with its system and rules is internal. If I use ivory chessmen instead of wooden ones, the change has no effect on the system; but if I decrease or increase the number of chessmen, this change has a profound effect on the 'grammar' of the game. One must always distinguish between what is internal and what is external. In each instance one can determine the nature of the phenomenon by applying this rule: everything that changes the system in any way is internal. [. . .]

The linguistic sign is then a two-sided psychological entity that can be represented by the drawing:

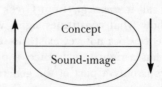

The two elements are intimately united, and each recalls the other. Whether we try to find the meaning of the Latin word *arbor* or the word that Latin uses to designate the concept 'tree,' it is clear that only the associations sanctioned by that language appear to us to conform to reality, and we disregard whatever others might be imagined.

Our definition of the linguistic sign poses an important question of terminology. I call the combination of a concept and a sound-image a *sign*, but in current usage the term generally designates only a sound-image, a word, for example (*arbor*, etc.). One tends to forget that *arbor* is called a sign only because it carries the concept 'tree,' with the result that the idea of the sensory part implies the idea of the whole.

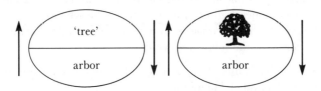

Ambiguity would disappear if the three notions involved here were designated by three names, each suggesting and opposing the others. I propose to retain the word *sign* [*signe*] to designate the whole and to replace *concept* and *sound-image* respectively by *signified* [*signifié*] and *signifier* [*signifiant*]; the last two terms have the advantage of indicating the opposition that separates them from each other and from the whole of which they are parts. [. . .]

But to indicate more clearly the opposition and crossing of two orders of phenomena that relate to the same object, I prefer to speak of *synchronic* and *diachronic* linguistics. Everything that relates to the static side of our science is synchronic; everything that has to do with evolution is diachronic. Similarly, *synchrony* and *diachrony* designate respectively a language-state and an evolutionary phase.

(Ferdinand de Saussure, *Course in General Linguistics*, trans. Wade Baskin (revised edn, Fontana, 1974), pp. 13–14, 16, 17, 22–3, 66–7, 81. Original French, *Cours de linguistique générale*, was published in 1915.)

(D) VLADIMIR PROPP

Morphology of the Folktale (1928)

Let us first of all attempt to formulate our task. As already stated in the foreword, this work is dedicated to the study of *fairy* tales. The existence of fairy tales as a special class is assumed as an essential working hypothesis. By 'fairy tales' are meant at present those tales classified by Aarne under numbers

300 to 749. This definition is artificial, but the occasion will subsequently arise to give a more precise determination on the basis of resultant conclusions. We are undertaking a comparison of the themes of these tales. For the sake of comparison we shall separate the component parts of fairy tales by special methods; and then, we shall make a comparison of tales according to their components. The result will be a morphology (i.e., a description of the tale according to its component parts and the relationship of these components to each other and to the whole).

What methods can achieve an accurate description of the tale? Let us compare the following events:

1. A tsar gives an eagle to a hero. The eagle carries the hero away to another kingdom.
2. An old man gives Súčenko a horse. The horse carries Súčenko away to another kingdom.
3. A sorcerer gives Iván a little boat. The boat takes Iván to another kingdom.
4. A princess gives Iván a ring. Young men appearing from out of the ring carry Iván away into another kingdom, and so forth.

Both constants and variables are present in the preceding instances. The names of the dramatis personae change (as well as the attributes of each), but neither their actions nor functions change. From this we can draw the inference that a tale often attributes identical actions to various personages. This makes possible the study of the tale *according to the functions of its dramatis personae.* [. . .]

The observations cited may be briefly formulated in the following manner:

1. *Functions of characters serve as stable, constant elements in a tale, independent of how and by whom they are fulfilled. They constitute the fundamental components of a tale.*
2. *The number of functions known to the fairy tale is limited.*

If functions are delineated, a second question arises: in what classification and in what sequence are these functions encountered? [. . .]

The sequence of events has its own laws. The short story too has similar laws, as do organic formations. Theft cannot take place before the door is forced. Insofar as the tale is concerned, it has its own entirely particular and specific laws. The sequence of elements, as we shall see later on, is strictly *uniform.* Freedom within this sequence is restricted by very narrow limits which can be exactly formulated. We thus obtain the third basic thesis of this work, subject to further development and verification:

The sequence of functions is always identical.

(Vladimir Propp, *Morphology of the Folktale*, trans, Laurence Scott (2nd edn, Austin and London: University of Texas Press, 1968), pp. 19–20, 21, 22.)

(E) NORTHROP FRYE

Anatomy of Criticism (1957)

The structural principles of painting are frequently described in terms of their analogues in plane geometry (or solid, by a further reach of analogy). A famous letter of Cézanne speaks of the approximation of pictorial form to the sphere and the cube, and the practice of abstract painters seems to confirm his point. Geometrical shapes are analogous only to pictorial forms, not by any means identical with them; the real structural principles of painting are to be derived, not from an external analogy with something else, but from the internal analogy of the art itself. The structural principles of literature, similarly, are to be derived from archetypal and anagogic criticism, the only kinds that assume a larger context of literature as a whole. But we saw in the first essay that, as the modes of fiction move from the mythical to the low mimetic and ironic, they approach a point of extreme 'realism' or representative likeness to life. It follows that the mythical mode, the stories about gods, in which characters have the greatest possibe power of action, is the most abstract and conventionalized of all literary modes, just as the corresponding modes in other arts – religious Byzantine painting, for example – show the highest degree of stylization in their structure. Hence the structural principles of literature are as closely related to mythology and comparative religion as those of painting are to geometry. In this essay we shall be using the symbolism of the Bible, and to a lesser extent Classical mythology, as a grammar of literary archetypes. [. . .]

We begin our study of archetypes, then, with a world of myth, an abstract or purely literary world of fictional and thematic design, unaffected by canons of plausible adaptation to familar experience. In terms of narrative, myth is the imitation of actions near or at the conceivable limits of desire. The gods enjoy beautiful women, fight one another with prodigious strength, comfort and assist man, or else watch his miseries from the height of their immortal freedom. The fact that myth operates at the top level of human desire does not mean that it necessarily presents its world as attained or attainable by human beings. In terms of meaning or *dianoia*, myth is the same world looked at as an area or field of activity, bearing in mind our principle that the meaning or pattern of poetry is a structure of imagery with conceptual implications. The world of mythical imagery is usually represented by the conception of heaven or Paradise in religion, and it is apocalyptic, in the sense of that word already explained, a world of total metaphor, in which everything is potentially identical with everything else, as though it were all inside a single infinite body.

Realism or the art of verisimilitude, evokes the response 'How like that is to what we know!' When what is written is *like* what is known, we have an art of extended or implied simile. And as realism is an art of implicit simile, myth is an art of implicit metaphorical identity. The word 'sun-god,' with a hyphen used instead of a predicate, is a pure ideogram, in Pound's terminology, or literal metaphor, in ours. In myth we see the structural principles of literature isolated; in realism we see the *same* structural principles (not similar ones) fitting into a context of plausibility. [. . .] The presence of a mythical structure in realistic fiction, however, poses certain technical problems for making it plausible, and the devices used in solving these problems may be given the general name of *displacement*.

Myth, then, is one extreme of literary design; naturalism is the other, and in between lies the whole area of romance, using that term to mean [. . .] the tendency [. . .] to displace myth in a human direction and yet, in contrast to 'realism', to conventionalize content in an idealized direction. The central principle of displacement is that what can be metaphorically identified in a myth can only be linked in romance by some form of simile: analogy, significant association, incidental accompanying imagery, and the like. In a myth we can have a sun-god or a tree-god; in a romance we may have a person who is significantly associated with the sun or trees. In more realistic modes the association becomes less significant and more a matter of incidental, even coincidental or accidental, imagery. In the dragon-killing legend of the St. George and Perseus family, of which more hereafter, a country under an old feeble king is terrorized by a dragon who eventually demands the king's daughter, but is slain by the hero. This seems to be a romantic analogy (perhaps also, in this case, a descendant) of a myth of a waste land restored to life by a fertility god. In the myth, then, the dragon and the old king would be identified. We can in fact concentrate the myth still further into an Oedipus fantasy in which the hero is not the old king's son-in-law but his son, and the rescued damsel the hero's mother. If the story were a private dream such identifications would be made as a matter of course. But to make it a plausible, symmetrical, and morally acceptable story a good deal of displacement is necessary, and it is only after a comparative study of the story type has been made that the metaphorical structure within it begins to emerge. [. . .]

[W]e have, in myth, the story of Proserpine, who disappears into the underworld for six months of every year. The pure myth is clearly one of death and revival; the story as we have it is slightly displaced, but the mythical pattern is easy to see. The same structural element often recurs in Shakespearean comedy, where it has to be adapted to a roughly high mimetic level of credibility. Hero in *Much Ado* is dead enough to have a funeral song, and plausible explanations are postponed until after the end of the play. Imogen in *Cymbeline* has an assumed name and an empty grave, but she too gets some funeral obsequies. But the story of Hermione and Perdita is so close to the Demeter and Proserpine myth that hardly any serious pretence of plausible explanations is made. Hermione, after her disappearance, returns once as a ghost in a dream, and her coming to life from a statue, a displacement of the Pygmalion myth, is said to require an awakening of faith, even though, on one level of plausibility, she has not been a statue at all, and nothing has taken place except a harmless deception. We notice how much more abstractly mythical a thematic writer can be than a fictional one: Spenser's Florimell, for instance, disappears under the sea for the winter with no questions asked, leaving a 'snowy lady' in her place and returning with a great outburst of spring floods at the end of the fourth book.

In the low mimetic, we recognize the same structural pattern of the death and revival of the heroine when Esther Summerson gets smallpox, or Lorna Doone is shot at her marriage altar. But we are getting closer to the conventions of realism, and although Lorna's eyes are 'dim with death,' we know that the author does not really mean death if he is planning to revive her. [. . .]

This affinity between the mythical and the abstractly literary illuminates many aspects of fiction, especially the more popular fiction which is realistic enough to be plausible in its incidents and yet romantic enough to be a 'good story,' which means a clearly designed one. The introduction of an omen or portent, or the device of making a whole story the fulfilment of a prophecy given at the beginning, is an example. Such a device suggests, in its existential projection, a conception of ineluctable fate or hidden omnipotent will. Actually, it is a piece of pure literary design, giving the beginning some symmetrical relationship with the end, and the only ineluctable will involved is that of the author. Hence we often find it even in writers not temperamentally much in sympathy with the portentous. In *Anna Karenina*, for instance, the death of the railway porter in the opening book is accepted by Anna as an omen for herself. Similarly, if we find portents and omens in Sophocles, they are there primarily because they fit the structure of his type of dramatic tragedy, and prove nothing about any clear-cut beliefs in fate held by either dramatist or audience.

We have, then, three organizations of myths and archetypal symbols in literature. First, there is undisplaced myth, generally concerned with gods or demons, and which takes the form of two contrasting worlds of total metaphorical identification, one desirable and the other undesirable. These worlds are often identified with the existential heavens and hells of the religions contemporary with such literature. These two forms of metaphorical organization we call the apocalyptic and the demonic respectively. Second, we have the general tendency we have called romantic, the tendency to suggest implicit mythical patterns in a world more closely associated with human experience. Third, we have the tendency of 'realism' (my distaste for this inept term is reflected in the quotation marks) to throw the emphasis on content and representation rather than on the shape of the story. Ironic literature begins with realism and tends toward myth, its mythical patterns being as a rule more suggestive of the demonic than of the apocalyptic, though sometimes it simply continues the romantic tradition of stylization. Hawthorne, Poe, Conrad, Hardy and Virginia Woolf all provide examples.

In looking at a picture, we may stand close to it and analyze the details of brush work and palette knife. This corresponds roughly to the rhetorical analysis of the new critics in literature. At a little distance back, the design comes into clearer view, and we study rather the content represented: this is the best distance for realistic Dutch pictures, for example, where we are in a sense reading the picture. The further back we go, the more conscious we are of the organizing design. At a great distance from, say, a Madonna, we can see nothing but the archetype of the Madonna, a large centripetal blue mass with a contrasting point of interest at its center. In the criticism of literature, too, we often have to 'stand back' from the poem to see its archetypal organization. If we 'stand back' from Spenser's *Mutabilitie Cantoes*, we see a background or ordered circular light and a sinister black mass thrusting up into the lower foreground – much the same archetypal shape that we see in the opening of the Book of Job. If we 'stand back' from the beginning of the fifth act of *Hamlet*, we see a grave opening on the stage, the hero, his enemy, and the heroine descending into it, followed by a fatal struggle in the upper world. If we 'stand back' from a realistic novel such as Tolstoy's *Resurrection* or Zola's *Germinal*, we can see the mythopoeic designs indicated by those titles.

(Northrop Frye, *Anatomy of Criticism: Four Essays* (Princeton, NJ: Princeton UP, 1957), pp. 134–5, 136–7, 138, 139–40.)

(F) A.-J. GREIMAS

Structural Semantics (1966)

After defining the folktale as a display on a temporal line of its thirty-one functions, Propp raises the question about the actants, or the dramatis personae, as he calls them. His conception of the actants is functional: the characters are defined, according to him, by the 'spheres of action' in which they participate, these spheres being constituted by the bundles of functions which are attributed to them. [. . .]

The result is that if the actors can be established within a tale-occurrence, the actants, which are classifications of actors, can be established only from the corpus of all the tales: an articulation of actors constitutes a particular *tale*; a structure of actants constitutes a *genre*. The actants therefore possess a metalinguistic status in relation to the actors. They presuppose, by the way, a functional analysis – that is to say, the achieved constitution of the spheres of action.

This double procedure – the establishment of the actors by the description of the functions and the reduction of the classifications of actors to actants of the genre – allows Propp to establish a definitive inventory of the actants, which are:

1. *The villain*
2. *The donor (provider)*
3. *The helper*
4. *The sought-for person (and her father)*
5. *The dispatcher*
6. *The hero*
7. *The false hero*

This inventory authorizes Propp to give an actantial definition of the Russian folktale as a story with seven characters. [. . .]

The interest in Souriau's thought lies in the fact that he has shown that the actantial interpretation can be applied to a kind of narrative – theatrical works – quite different from the folktale and that his results are comparable to Propp's. We find here, although expressed differently, the same distinction between the events of the story [*l'histoire événementielle*] (which is for him only a collection of 'dramatic subjects') and the level of the semantic description (which is made from the 'situations,' which can be decomposed into the action of actants). Finally, we find here a limited inventory of actants (which he calls, according to traditional syntactic terminology, *functions*). [. . .]

Souriau's inventory is presented in the following manner:

Lion . . . . the oriented thematic Force

Sun . . . . the Representative of the wished-for Good, of the orienting Value

Earth　　　　virtual Recipient of that Good (that for which . . . . the Lion is working)

Mars . . . . . . .the Opponent

Libra . . . . . . .the Arbiter, attributer of the Good

Moon　　　　the Rescue, the doubling of one of the . . . . preceding forces

We must not be discouraged by the energetic and astrological character of Souriau's terminology: it does not succeed in concealing reflections that are not without coherence. [. . .]

A first glance allows us to find and identify in the two inventories of Propp and Souriau the two syntactic actants which constitute the category 'Subject' vs. 'Object.' It is striking, we must note at this time, that the relationship between the subject and object which we had so much trouble defining precisely, and never succeeded in defining completely, appears here with a semantic investment identical in both inventories, that of 'desire.' It seems possible to conceive that the transitivity or the *teleological relationship*, as we suggested calling it, situated in the mythical dimension of the manifestation, appears following the semic combination as a sememe realizing the *effect of meaning* of 'desire.' If this is so, the two micro-universes, the genre 'folktale' and the genre 'drama', defined by a first actantial category articulated in relation to desire, are capable of producing narrative-occurrences where desire will be manifested under the simultaneously practical and mythical form of 'the quest.' [. . .]

The search for what could correspond, in Propp and Souriau's intentions, to that second actantial category cannot fail to raise some difficulties because of the frequent syncretic manifestation of actants (already encountered at the level of syntax), the often noticed plurality of two actants present under the form of a single actor. For instance, in a narrative that is only a common love story ending in marriage without the parents' intervention, the subject is also the receiver, while the object is at the same time the sender of love:

$$\frac{He}{She} \approx \frac{\text{Subject} + \text{Receiver}}{\text{Object} + \text{Sender}}$$

Four actants are there, symmetrical and inverted, but syncretized under the form of two actors. But we see also – Michel Legrand's couplet sung in the 'Umbrellas of Cherbourg' makes the point in an impressive synopsis:

a man, a woman,
an apple, a drama

– with what ease the disjunction of the object and the sender can produce a model with three actants.

In a narrative of the type of *The Quest for the Holy Grail*, on the contrary, four actants, quite distinct, are articulated in two categories:

$$\frac{\text{Subject}}{\text{Object}} \approx \frac{Hero}{Holy\ Grail}$$

$$\frac{\text{Sender}}{\text{Receiver}} \approx \frac{God}{Mankind}$$

[. . .]

It is much more difficult to be sure of the categorical articulation of the other actants if only because we lack a syntactic model. Two spheres of activity, however, and, inside those, two distinct kinds of functions are recognized without difficulty.

1. The first kinds bring the help by acting in the direction of the desire or by facilitating communication.

2. The others, on the contrary, create obstacles by opposing either the realization of the desire or the communication of the object.

These two bundles of functions can be attributed to two distinct actants that we will designate under the name of

Helper vs. Opponent

This distinction corresponds rather well to the distinction made by Souriau, from whom we borrow the term *opponent*: we prefer the term of *helper* introduced by Guy Michaud, to Souriau's 'rescue.' In Propp's formulation we find that opponent is pejoratively called *villain* (traitor), while *helper* takes in two characters, the *helper* and the *donor* (*provider*). At first sight, this elasticity of analysis may be surprising.

We must not forget, however, that the actants are established by Propp, not to mention Souriau, from their spheres of action, that is to say, with the help of the reduction of the single functions, and without taking into account an indispensable homologation. We do not intend to criticize Propp here, whose role as a precursor is considerable, but simply to register the progress made during the last thirty years by virtue of the general development of structuralist procedures. We should also consider that it is easier to operate when two comparable inventories are at our disposal, instead of simply one.

We can wonder what corresponds, in the mythical universe whose actantial structure we want to make explicit, to this opposition between the helper and the opponent. At first glance, everything takes place as if, besides the principal parties in question, there would appear now in the drama projected on an axiological screen actants representing in a schematic fashion the benevolent and malevolent forces in the world, incarnations of the guardian angel and the devil of medieval Christian drama. What is also striking is the secondary character of these two actants. In a little play on words, we could say, thinking of the participial form by which we designated them (for example, 'the opposing' [*opposant*]: i.e. the 'opponent']), that they are the circumstantial 'participants,' and not the true actants of the drama [*spectacle*]. Participles are in fact only adjectives which modify substantives in the same way that adverbs modify verbs. [. . .]

Inferred from inventories which remain, in spite of everything, provisional, constructed by considering the syntactic structure of natural languages, this model seems to possess, because of its simplicity and for the analysis of mythical manifestations only, a certain operational value. Its simplicity lies in the fact that it is entirely centered on the object of desire aimed at by the subject and situated, as object of communication, between the sender. and the receiver – the desire of the subject being, in its part, modulated in projections from the helper and opponent:

sender → | object | → receiver

helper → | subject | ← opponent

[. . .]

Therefore, we would say that the possible particularizations of the model should convey first the relationship between the actants 'subject' vs. 'object' and then be manifested as a class of variables constituted by supplementary investments.

Thus, with great simplification, it could be said that for a learned philosopher of the classical age the relationship of desire would be specified, by a semic investment, as the desire of knowing, and the actants of his drama of knowledge would be distributed more or less in the following manner:

Subject .... *philosopher*
Object .... *world*
Sender .... *God*
Receiver .... *mankind*
Opponent .... *matter*
Helper .... *mind*

In the same way, Marxist ideology as expressed by a militant could be distributed, thanks to its desire to help man, in a parallel fashion:

Subject .... *man*
Object .... *classless society*
Sender .... *history*

Receiver .... *mankind*
Opponent .... *bourgeois class*
Helper .... *working class*

(A.–J. Greimas, *Structural Semantics*, trans. Daniele McDowell *et al.*
(Lincoln and London: University of Nebraska Press, 1983), pp. 200,
200–1, 201, 202, 203–4, 205–6, 207, 207–8. French original was
Sémantique structurale (Paris: Larousse, 1966).)

(G) GÉRARD GENETTE

'Frontiers of Narrative' (1966)

We have here a new division, of very wide scope, since it divides
into two parts of roughly equal importance the whole of what we
now call literature.

This division corresponds more or less to the distinction
proposed by Émile Benveniste between *narrative* (or *story*) and
discourse, except that Benveniste includes in the category of
discourse everything that Aristotle called direct imitation, and
which actually consists, at least as far as its verbal part is
concerned, of discourse attributed by the poet or narrator to one
of his characters. Benveniste shows that certain grammatical
forms, like the pronoun 'I' (and its implicit reference 'you'), the
pronominal (certain demonstratives), or adverbial indicators (like
'here,' 'now,' 'yesterday,' 'today,' 'tomorrow,' etc.) and – at least
in French – certain tenses of the verb, like the present, the
present anterior, or the future, are confined to discourse, whereas
narrative in its strict form is marked by the exclusive use of the
third person and such forms as the aorist (past definite) and the
pluperfect. Whatever the details and variations from one idiom
to another, all these differences amount clearly to an opposition
between the objectivity of narrative and the subjectivity of
discourse; but it should be pointed out that such objectivity and
subjectivity are defined by criteria of a strictly linguistic order:
'subjective' discourse is that in which, explicitly or not, the
presence of (or reference to) *I* is marked, but this is not defined
in any other way except as the person who is speaking this
discourse, just as the present, which is the tense *par excellence* of
the discursive mode, is not defined other than as the moment
when the discourse is being spoken, its use marking 'the

coincidence of the event described with the instance of discourse that describes it.' Conversely, the objectivity of narrative is defined by the absence of any reference to the narrator: 'As a matter of fact, there is then no longer even a narrator. The events are set forth chronologically, as they occur. No one speaks here; the events seem to narrate themselves.' [. . .]

In discourse, someone speaks, and his situation in the very act of speaking is the focus of the most important significations; in narrative, as Benveniste forcefully puts it, *no one speaks*, in the sense that at no moment do we ask ourselves *who is speaking*, *where*, *when*, and so forth, in order to receive the full signification of the text.

But it should be added at once that these essences of narrative and discourse so defined are almost never to be found in their pure state in any text: there is almost always a certain proportion of narrative in discourse, a certain amount of discourse in narrative. In fact, the symmetry stops here, for it is as if both types of expression were very differently affected by the contamination: the insertion of narrative elements in the level of discourse is not enough to emancipate discourse, for they generally remain linked to the reference by the speaker, who remains implicitly present in the background, and who may intervene again at any moment without this return being experienced as an 'intrusion.' [. . .]

It is obvious that narrative does not integrate these discursive enclaves, rightly called by Georges Blin 'authorial intrusions,' as easily as discourse receives the narrative enclaves: narrative inserted into discourse is transformed into an element of discourse, discourse inserted into narrative remains discourse and forms a sort of cyst that is very easy to recognize and to locate. The purity of narrative, one might say, is more manifest than that of discourse.

Though the reason for this dissymmetry is very simple, it indicates for us a decisive character of narrative: in fact, discourse has no purity to preserve, for it is the broadest and most universal 'natural' mode of language, welcoming by definition all other forms; narrative, on the other hand, is a particular mode, marked, defined by a number of exclusions and restrictive conditions (refusal of the present, the first person, and so forth). Discourse can 'recount' without ceasing to be discourse, narrative cannot 'discourse' without emerging from itself. Nor can it abstain from it completely, however, without

falling into aridity and poverty: this is why narrative exists
nowhere, so to speak, in its strict form. The slightest general
observation, the slightest adjective that is [a] little more than
descriptive, the most discreet comparison, the most modest
'perhaps,' the most inoffensive of logical articulations introduces
into its web a type of speech that is alien to it, refractory as it
were. In order to study the detail of these sometimes microscopic
accidents, we would need innumerable, meticulous analyses of
texts. One of the objects of this study would be to list and
classify the means by which narrative literature (and in
particular the novel) has tried to organize in an acceptable way,
within its own *lexis*, the delicate relations maintained within it
between the requirements of narrative and the needs of
discourse. [. . .]

The only moment when the balance between narrative and
discourse seems to have been assumed with a perfectly good
conscience, without either scruple or ostentation, is obviously in
the nineteenth century, the classical age of objective narration,
from Balzac to Tolstoy; we see, on the contrary, how the
modern period has stressed awareness of difficulty to the extent
of making certain types of elocution almost physically impossible
for the most lucid and rigorous of writers. [. . .]

All the fluctuations of contemporary fictional writing could no
doubt be analyzed from this point of view, and particularly the
tendency today, perhaps the reverse of the earlier one, and quite
overt in a Phillipe Sollers or a Jean Thibaudeau, for example, to
absorb the narrative in the present discourse of the writer in the
process of writing, in what Michel Foucault calls 'discourse
bound up with the act of writing, contemporary with its
unfolding and enclosed within it.' It is as if literature had
exhausted or overflowed the resources of its representative mode,
and wanted to fold back into the indefinite murmur of its own
discourse. Perhaps the novel, after poetry, is about to emerge
definitively from the age of representation. Perhaps narrative, in
the negative singularity that we have just attributed to it, is
already for us, as art was for Hegel, *a thing of the past*, which we
must hurry to consider as it retreats, before it has completely
disappeared from our horizon.

(Gérard Genette, 'Frontiers of Narrative', *Figures of Literary Discourse*,
trans. Alan Sheridan (Oxford: Blackwell, 1982), pp. 138–9, 141–2,
142, 143. Original French was *Figures II* (Paris: Editions du Seuil,
1969).)

(H) ROMAN JAKOBSON

'Two Aspects of Language' (1956)

Any linguistic sign involves two modes of arrangement.

(1) COMBINATION. Any sign is made up of constituent signs and/or occurs only in combination with other signs. This means that any linguistic unit at one and the same time serves as a context for simpler units and/or finds its own context in a more complex linguistic unit. Hence any actual grouping of linguistic units binds them into a superior unit: combination and contexture are two faces of the same operation.

(2) SELECTION. A selection between alternatives implies the possibility of substituting one for the other, equivalent to the former in one respect and different from it in another. Actually, selection and substitution are two faces of the same operation. [. . .] It is clear that speech disturbances may affect in varying degrees the individual's capacity for combination and selection of linguistic units, and indeed the question of which of these two operations is chiefly impaired proves to be of far-reaching significance in describing, analyzing, and classifying the diverse forms of aphasia. [. . .]

For aphasics of the first type (selection deficiency), the context is the indispensable and decisive factor. When presented with scraps of words or sentences, such a patient readily completes them. His speech is merely reactive: he easily carries on conversation, but has difficulties in starting a dialogue; he is able to reply to a real or imaginary addresser when he is, or imagines himself to be, the addressee of the message. It is particularly hard for him to perform, or even to understand, such a closed discourse as the monologue. The more his utterances are dependent on the context, the better he copes with his verbal task. [. . .]

In the theory of language, since the early Middle Ages, it has repeatedly been asserted that the word out of context has no meaning. The validity of this statement is, however, confined to aphasia, or, more exactly, to one type of aphasia. In the pathological cases under discussion an isolated word means actually nothing but 'blab'. As numerous tests have disclosed, for such patients two occurrences of the same word in two different contexts are mere homonyms. Since distinctive vocables carry a higher amount of information than homonyms, some aphasics of this type tend to supplant the contextual variant of one word by different terms, each of them specific for the given environment. Thus Goldstein's patient never uttered the word *knife* alone, but, according to its use and surroundings, alternately called the knife *pencil-sharpener, apple-parer, bread-knife, knife-and-fork*; so that the word *knife* was changed from a free form, capable of occurring alone, into a bound form.

'I have a good apartment, entrance hall, bedroom, kitchen,' Goldstein's patient says. 'There are also big apartments, only in the rear live bachelors.' A more explicit form, the word-group *unmarried people*, could have been substituted for *bachelors*, but this univerbal term was selected by the speaker. When repeatedly asked what a bachelor was, the patient did not answer and was 'apparently in distress'. A reply like 'a bachelor is an unmarried man' or 'an unmarried man is a bachelor' would present an equational predication and thus a projection of a substitution set from the lexical code of the English language into the context of the given message. The equivalent terms become two correlated parts of the sentence and consequently are tied by contiguity. The patient was able to select the appropriate term *bachelor* when it was supported by the context of a customary conversation about 'bachelor apartments', but was incapable of utilizing the substitution set *bachelor = unmarried man* as the topic of a sentence, because the ability for autonomous selection and substitution had been affected. The equational sentence vainly demanded from the patient carries as its sole information: '"bachelor" means an unmarried man' or 'an unmarried man is called "a bachelor"'. [. . .]

When the selective capacity is strongly impaired and the gift for combination at least partly preserved, then CONTIGUITY determines the patient's whole verbal behavior, and we may designate this type of aphasia SIMILARITY DISORDER. [. . .] Impairment of the ability to PROPOSITIONIZE, or, generally speaking, to combine simpler linguistic entities into more complex units, is actually confined to one type of aphasia, the opposite of the type discussed in the preceding chapter. There is no WORDLESSNESS, since the entity preserved in most of such cases is the WORD, which can be defined as the highest among the linguistic units compulsorily coded, i.e., we compose our own sentences and utterances out of the word stock supplied by the code.

This contexture-deficient aphasia, which could be termed CONTIGUITY DISORDER, diminishes the extent and variety of sentences.

The type of aphasia affecting contexture tends to give rise to infantile one-sentence utterances and one-word sentences. Only a few longer, stereotyped, 'ready made' sentences manage to survive. In advanced cases of this disease, each utterance is reduced to a single one-word sentence. While contexture disintegrates, the selective operation goes on. 'To say what a thing is, is to say what it is like', Jackson notes. The patient confined to the substitution set (once contexture is deficient) deals with similarities, and his approximate identifications are of a metaphoric nature, contrary to the metonymic ones familiar to the opposite type of aphasics. *Spyglass* for *microscope*, or *fire* for *gaslight* are typical examples of such QUASI-METAPHORIC EXPRESSIONS, as Jackson termed them, since, in contradistinction to rhetoric or poetic metaphors, they present no deliberate transfer of meaning. [. . .]

The varieties of aphasia are numerous and diverse, but all of them lie between the two polar types just described. Every form of aphasic disturbance consists in some impairment, more or less severe, either of the faculty for selection and substitution or for combination and contexture. The former affliction involves a deterioration of metalinguistic operations, while the latter damages the capacity for maintaining the hierarchy of linguistic units. The relation of similarity is suppressed in the former, the relation of contiguity in the latter type of aphasia. Metaphor is alien to the similarity disorder, and metonymy to the contiguity disorder.

The development of a discourse may take place along two different semantic lines: one topic may lead to another either through their similarity or through their contiguity. The METAPHORIC way would be the most appropriate term for the first case and the METONYMIC way for the second, since they find their most condensed expression in metaphor and metonymy respectively. In aphasia one or the other of these two processes is restricted or totally blocked – an effect which makes the study of aphasia particularly illuminating for the linguist. In normal verbal behavior both processes are continually operative, but careful observation will reveal that under the influence of a cultural pattern, personality, and verbal style, preference is given to one of the two processes over the other.

In a well-known psychological test, children are confronted with some noun and told to utter the first verbal response that comes into their heads. In this experiment two opposite linguistic predilections are invariably exhibited: the response is intended either as a substitute for, or as a complement to, the stimulus. In the latter case the stimulus and the response together form a proper syntactic construction, most usually a sentence. These two types of reaction have been labeled SUBSTITUTIVE and PREDICATIVE.

To the stimulus *hut* one response was *burnt out*; another, *is a poor little house*. Both reactions are predicative; but the first creates a purely narrative context, while in the second there is a double connection with the subject *hut*: on the one hand, a positional (namely, syntactic) contiguity, and on the other a semantic similarity.

The same stimulus produced the following substitutive reactions: the tautology *hut*; the synonyms *cabin* and *hovel*; the antonym *palace*, and the metaphors *den* and *burrow*. The capacity of two words to replace one another is an instance of positional similarity, and, in addition, all these responses are linked to the stimulus by semantic similarity (or contrast). Metonymical responses to the same stimulus, such as *thatch litter*, or *poverty*, combine and contrast the positional similarity with semantic contiguity.

In manipulating these two kinds of connection (similarity and contiguity) in both their aspects (positional and semantic) – selecting, combining, and ranking them – an individual exhibits his personal style, his verbal predilections and preferences. [. . .]

In poetry there are various motives which determine the choice between these alternants. The primacy of the metaphoric process in the literary schools of romanticism and symbolism has been repeatedly acknowledged, but it is still insufficiently realized that it is the predominance of metonymy which underlies and actually predetermines the so-called 'realistic' trend, which belongs to an intermediary stage between the decline of romanticism and the rise of symbolism and is opposed to both. Following the path of contiguous relationships, the realist author metonymically digresses from the plot to the atmosphere and from the characters to the setting in space and time. He is fond of synecdochic details. In the scene of Anna Karenina's suicide Tolstoj's artistic attention is focused on the heroine's handbag; and in *War and Peace* the synecdoches 'hair on the upper lip' and 'bare shoulders' are used by the same writer to stand for the female characters to whom these features belong.

The alternative predominance of one or the other of these two processes is by no means confined to verbal art. The same oscillation occurs in sign systems other than language. A salient example from the history of painting is the manifestly metonymical orientation of cubism, where the object is transformed into a set of synecdoches; the surrealist painters responded with a patently metaphorical attitude. Ever since the productions of D. W. Griffith, the art of the cinema, with its highly developed capacity for changing the angle, perspective, and focus of 'shots', has broken with the tradition of the theater and ranged an unprecedented variety of synecdochic 'close-ups' and metonymic 'set-ups' in general. In such motion pictures as those of Charlie Chaplin and Eisenstein, these devices in turn were overlayed by a novel, metaphoric 'montage' with its 'lap dissolves' – the filmic similes.

(Roman Jakobson 'Two Aspects of Language and Two Types of Aphasic Disturbances', *Fundamentals of Language* (2nd edn, The Hague: Mouton, 1971), pp. 74, 77, 77–8, 79–80, 84, 85, 86, 90–1, 91–2.)

(I) DAVID LODGE

The Modes of Modern Writing (1977)

We tend to take the camera eye for granted, and to accept the 'truth' of what it shows us even though its perspective is never exactly the same as human vision.

This verisimilitude can be explained as a function of the metonymic character of the film medium. We move through time and space lineally and our sensory experience is a succession of contiguities. The basic units of the film, the shot and the scene, are composed along the same line of contiguity and combination, and the devices by which the one-damn-thing-after-another of experience is rendered more dramatic and meaningful are characteristically metonymic devices that operate along the same axis: the synecdochic close-up that represents the whole by the part, the slow-motion sequence that retards without rupturing the natural tempo of successiveness, the high or low angle shot that 'defamiliarizes', without departing from, the action it is focused on. Consciousness is not, of course, bound to the line of spatio-temporal contiguity, in the way that sensory experience is, but then film does not deal very much or very

effectively with consciousness except insofar as it is manifested
in behaviour and speech, or can be reflected in landscape
through the pathetic fallacy, or suggested by music on the
sound track.

This does not mean that film has no metaphoric devices, or
that it may not be pushed in the direction of metaphorical
structure. Jakobson categorizes montage as metaphoric,
presumably because it juxtaposes images on the basis of their
similarity (or contrast) rather than their contiguity in space-time.
However, the fact that the techniques of cutting and splicing by
which montage is achieved are also the techniques of all film
editing, by which any film of the least degree of sophistication is
composed, creates the possibility of confusion here. John
Harrington, for example, in his *The Rhetoric of Film*, defines
montage as

> a rhetorical arrangement of juxtaposed shots. The
> combination, or gestalt, produces an idea by combining the
> visual elements of two dissimilar images. A longing face, for
> instance, juxtaposed to a turkey dinner suggests hunger. Or
> the image of a fox following that of a man making a
> business deal would indicate slyness. Segments of film
> working together to create a single idea have no counterpart
> in nature; their juxtaposition occurs through the editor's
> imaginative yoke.

The main drift of this definition confirms Jakobson's
classification of montage as metaphorical, but the first of
Harrington's examples is in fact metonymic or synecdochic in
Jakobson's sense: longing faces and turkey dinners *are* found
together in nature (i.e. real contexts) and all that has been done
in this hypothetical montage is to delete some of the links (e.g. a
window) in a chain of contiguities that would link the face with
the turkey. The fox and the businessman, on the other hand, are
not contiguous in nature, but are connected in the montage
through a suggested similarity of behaviour, as in the verbal
metaphor 'a foxy businessman'. Context is all-important. If the
montage of longing face and turkey dinner described by
Harrington were in a film adaptation of *A Christmas Carol*, we
should interpret it metonymically; if it were interpolated in a
documentary about starving animals, it would be metaphoric.
Those favourite filmic metaphors for sexual intercourse in the
pre-permissive cinema, skyrockets and waves pounding on the
shore, could be disguised as metonymic background if the

consummation were taking place on a beach on Independence Day, but would be perceived as overtly metaphorical if it were taking place on Christmas Eve in a city penthouse. [. . .]

My suggestion is that we can best accomplish this task of defining the formal character of Larkin's verse by regarding him as a 'metonymic' poet.

Poetry, especially lyric poetry, is an inherently metaphoric mode, and to displace it towards the metonymic pole is (whether Larkin likes it or not) an 'experimental' literary gesture. Such poetry makes its impact by appearing daringly, even shockingly unpoetic, particularly when the accepted poetic mode is elaborately metaphoric. [. . .]

To call Larkin a metonymic poet does not imply that he uses no metaphors – of course he does. Some of his poems are based on extended analogies – 'Next, Please', 'No Road' and 'Toads', for instance. [S]uch poems become more rare in his later collections. [. . .]

Many of his poems have no metaphors at all – for example, 'Myxomatosis', 'Poetry of Departures', 'Days', 'As Bad as a Mile', 'Afternoons'. And in what are perhaps his finest and most characteristic poems, the metaphors are foregrounded against a predominantly metonymic background, which is in turn foregrounded against the background of the (metaphoric) poetic tradition. 'The Whitsun Weddings' is a classic example of this technique.

> That Whitsun, I was late getting away:
>   Not till about
> One-twenty on the sunlit Saturday
> Did my three-quarters-empty train pull out,
> All windows down, all cushions hot, all sense
> Of being in a hurry gone. We ran
> Behind the backs of houses, crossed a street
> Of blinding windscreens, smelt the fish-dock; thence
> The river's level drifting breadth began,
> Where sky and Lincolnshire and water meet.

This opening stanza has a characteristically casual, colloquial tone, and the near-redundant specificity ('One-twenty', 'three-quarters-empty') of a personal anecdote, a 'true story' (compare Wordsworth's 'I've measured it from side to side,/'Tis three feet long, and two feet wide'). The scenery is evoked by metonymic and synecdochic detail ('drifting breadth', 'blinding windscreens' etc.) as are the wedding parties that the poet observes at the

stations on the way to London, seeing off bridal couples on their
honeymoons. [. . .]

It is in the last stanza that the poem suddenly, powerfully,
'takes off', transcends the merely empirical, almost sociological
observation of its earlier stanzas and affirms the poet's sense of
sharing, vicariously, in the onward surge of life as represented
by the newly wedded couples collected together in the train
('this frail travelling coincidence') and the unpredictable but
fertile possibilities the future holds for them.

> We slowed again,
> And as the tightened brakes took hold, there swelled
> A sense of falling, like an arrow-shower
> Sent out of sight, somewhere becoming rain.

This metaphor, with its mythical, magical and archaic
resonances, is powerful partly because it is so different from
anything else in the poem (except for 'religious wounding', and
that has a tone of humorous overstatement quite absent from the
last stanza).

Something similar happens in Larkin's most famous poem,
'Church Going', where the last stanza has a dignity and
grandeur of diction –

> A serious house on serious earth it is,
> In whose blent air all our compulsions meet,
> Are recognized, and robed as destinies

which comes as a thrilling surprise after the downbeat, slightly
ironic tone of the preceding stanzas, a tone established in the
first stanza:

> Hatless, I take off
> My cycle-clips in awkward reverence.

That line-and-a-half must be the most often quoted fragment of
Larkin's poetry, and the way in which the homely 'cycle-clips'
damps down the metaphysical overtones of 'reverence' and
guarantees the trustworthy ordinariness of the poetic persona is
indeed deeply typical of Larkin. But if his poetry were limited to
merely avoiding the pitfalls of poetic pretentiousness and
insincerity it would not interest us for very long. Again and
again he surprises us, especially in the closing lines of his poems,
by his ability to transcend – or turn ironically upon – the severe
restraints he seems to have placed upon authentic expression of
feeling in poetry. Sometimes, as in 'The Whitsun Weddings' and

'Church Going', this is accomplished by allowing a current of metaphorical language to flow into the poem, with the effect of a river bursting through a dam.

(David Lodge, *The Modes of Modern Writing: Metaphor, Metonymy, and the Typology of Modern Literature* (London: Edward Arnold, 1977), pp. 84, 214, 216–17, 218–19.)

(J) JONATHAN CULLER

Structuralist Poetics (1975)

When a speaker of a language hears a phonetic sequence, he is able to give it meaning because he brings to the act of communication an amazing repertoire of conscious and unconscious knowledge. Mastery of the phonological, syntactic and semantic systems of his language enables him to convert the sounds into discrete units, to recognize words, and to assign a structural description and interpretation to the resulting sentence, even though it be quite new to him. Without this implicit knowledge, this internalized grammar, the sequence of sounds does not speak to him. We are nevertheless inclined to say that the phonological and grammatical structure and the meaning are *properties* of the utterance, and there is no harm in that way of speaking so long as we remember that they are properties of the utterance only with respect to a particular grammar. Another grammar would assign different properties to the sequence (according to the grammar of a different language, for example, it would be nonsense). To speak of the structure of a sentence is necessarily to imply an internalized grammar that gives it that structure.

We also tend to think of meaning and structure as properties of literary works, and from one point of view this is perfectly correct: when the sequence of words is treated *as a literary work* it has these properties. But that qualification suggests the relevance and importance of the linguistic analogy. The work has structure and meaning because it is read in a particular way, because these potential properties, latent in the object itself, are actualized by the theory of discourse applied in the act of reading. 'How can one discover structure without the help of a methodological model?' asks Barthes. To read a text as literature is not to make one's mind a *tabula rasa* and approach it without preconceptions; one must bring to it an implicit understanding of the operations of literary discourse which tells one what to look for.

Anyone lacking this knowledge, anyone wholly unacquainted with literature and unfamiliar with the conventions by which fictions are read, would, for example, be quite baffled if presented with a poem. His knowledge of the language would enable him to understand phrases and sentences, but he would not know, quite literally, what to *make* of this strange concatenation of phrases. He would be unable to read it *as* literature – as we say with emphasis to those who would use literary works for other purposes – because he lacks the complex 'literary competence' which enables others to proceed. He has not internalized the 'grammar' of literature which would permit him to convert linguistic sequences into literary structures and meanings.

If the analogy seems less than exact it is because in the case of language it is much more obvious that understanding depends on mastery of a system. But the time and energy devoted to literary training in schools and universities indicate that the understanding of literature also depends on experience and mastery. Since literature is a second-order semiotic system which has language as its basis, a knowledge of language will take one a certain distance in one's encounter with literary texts, and it may be difficult to specify precisely where understanding comes to depend on one's supplementary knowledge of literature. But the difficulty of drawing a line does not obscure the palpable difference between understanding the language of a poem, in the sense that one could provide a rough translation into another language, and understanding the poem. If one knows French, one can translate Mallarmé's 'Salut', but that translation is not a thematic synthesis – it is not what we would ordinarily call 'understanding the poem' – and in order to identify various levels of coherence and set them in relation to one another under the synoptic heading or theme of the 'literary quest' one must have considerable experience of the conventions for reading poetry.

The easiest way to grasp the importance of these conventions is to take a piece of journalistic prose or a sentence from a novel and set it down on the page as a poem. The properties assigned to the sentence by a grammar of English remain unchanged, and the different meanings which the text acquires cannot therefore be attributed to one's knowledge of the language but must be ascribed to the special conventions for reading poetry which lead one to look at the language in new ways, to make relevant properties of the language which were previously unexploited, to subject the text to a different series of interpretive operations. But one can also show the importance of these conventions by measuring the distance between the language of a poem and its critical interpretation – a distance bridged by the conventions of reading which comprise the institution of poetry.

Anyone who knows English understands the language of Blake's 'Ah! Sun-flower':

Ah, Sun-flower, weary of time,
Who countest the steps of the Sun,
Seeking after that sweet golden clime
Where the traveller's journey is done:

Where the Youth pined away with desire,
And the pale Virgin shrouded in snow
Arise from their graves, and aspire
Where my Sun-flower wishes to go.

But there is some distance between an understanding of the language and the thematic statement with which a critic concludes his discussion of the poem: 'Blake's dialectical thrust at asceticism is more than adroit. You do not surmount Nature by denying its prime claim of sexuality. Instead you fall utterly into the dull round of its cyclic aspirations.' How does one reach this reading? What are the operations which lead from the text to this representation of understanding? The primary convention is what might be called the rule of significance: read the poem as expressing a significant attitude to some problem concerning man and/or his relation to the universe. The sunflower is therefore given the value of an emblem and the metaphors of 'counting' and 'seeking' are taken not just as figurative indications of the flower's tendency to turn towards the sun but as metaphorical operators which make the sunflower an instance of the human aspirations compassed by these two lines. The conventions of metaphorical coherence – that one should attempt through semantic transformations to produce coherence on the levels of both tenor and vehicle – lead one to oppose time to eternity and to make 'that sweet golden clime' both the sunset which marks the closure of the daily temporal cycle and the eternity of death when 'the traveller's journey is done'. The identification of sunset and death is further justified by the convention which allows one to inscribe the poem in a poetic tradition. More important, however, is the convention of thematic unity, which forces one to give the youth and virgin of the second stanza a role which justifies choosing them as examples of aspiration; and since the semantic feature they share is a repression of sexuality, one must find a way of integrating that with the rest of the poem. [. . .]

[. . .] the claims of schools and universities to offer literary training cannot be lightly dismissed. To believe that the whole institution of literary education is but a gigantic confidence trick, would strain even a determined credulity, for it is, alas, only too clear that knowledge of a language and a certain experience of the world do not suffice to make someone a perceptive and competent reader. That achievement requires acquaintance with a range of literature and in many cases some form of guidance. The time and effort devoted to literary education by generations of students and teachers creates a strong presumption that there is something to be learned, and teachers do not hesitate to judge their pupils' progress towards a general literary competence. Most would claim, no doubt with good reason, that their examinations are designed not simply to determine whether their students have read various set works but to test their acquisition of an ability. [. . .]

To assimilate or interpret something is to bring it within the modes of order which culture makes available, and this is usually done by talking about it in a mode of discourse which a culture takes as natural. This process goes by various names in structuralist writing: recuperation, naturalization, motivation, *vraisemblablisation*. 'Recuperation' stresses the notion of recovery, of putting to use. It may be defined as the desire to leave no chaff, to make everything wheat, to let nothing escape the process of assimilation; it is thus a central component of studies which assert the organic unity of the text and the contribution of all its parts to its meanings or effects. 'Naturalization' emphasizes the fact that the strange or deviant is brought within a discursive order and thus made to seem natural. 'Motivation', which was the Russian formalists' term, is the process of justifying items within the work itself by showing that they are not arbitrary or incoherent but quite comprehensible in terms of functions which we can name. *Vraisemblablisation* stresses the importance of cultural models of the *vraisemblable* as sources of meaning and coherence.

Whatever one calls the process, it is one of the basic activities of the mind. We can, it seems, make anything signify. If a computer were programmed to produce random sequences of English sentences we could make sense of the texts it produced by imagining a variety of functions and contexts. If all else failed, we could read a sequence of words with no apparent order as signifying absurdity or chaos and then, by giving it an allegorical relation to the world, take it as a statement about the incoherence and absurdity of our own languages. As the example of Beckett shows, we can always make the meaningless meaningful by production of an appropriate context. And usually our contexts need not be so extreme. Much of Robbe-Grillet can be recuperated if we read it as the musings or speech of a pathological narrator, and that framework gives critics a hold so that they can go on to discuss the implications of the particular pathology in question. Certain dislocations in poetic texts can be read as signs of a prophetic or ecstatic state or as indications of a Rimbaudian 'dérèglement de tous les sens'. To place the text in such frameworks is to make it legible and intelligible. When Eliot says that modern poetry must be difficult because of the discontinuities of modern culture, when William Carlos Williams argues that his variable foot is necessary in a post-Einsteinian world where all order is questioned, when Humpty-Dumpty tells Alice that 'slithy' means 'lithe' and 'slimy', all are engaged in recuperation or naturalization.

(Jonathan Culler, *Structuralist Poetics* (London: Routledge & Kegan Paul, 1975), pp. 113–15, 121, 137–38.)

CHAPTER 7

STRUCTURE AND
INDETERMINACY

In everyday usage 'rhetoric' is a negative term. We tend to
share the Romantics' contempt for the rhetorical attitude to
writing. Orators and their literary counterparts, they argued,
lack 'sincerity', because their discourse is consciously tutored by
prescriptions and rules. Romantic poets claim that they speak
from the heart, and their discourse is 'original', not founded
upon the imitative training of the neoclassical poets. Twentieth-
century criticism has often abandoned this Romantic faith in the
possibility of 'authentic' and original utterance (see III, 4).
Nietzsche's belief that language is essentially figurative and not
referential or expressive was taken up by the key theorists of
'post-structuralism', notably Jacques Derrida, Michel Foucault,
Hayden White and Paul de Man. There is no original
unrhetorical language: discourse is always shaped by 'desire'
which in turn is communicated in tropes and figures. According
to Nietzsche there are no absolute truths. A theory is 'true' only
if it accords with prevailing institutional and political
expectations. Copernicus' theory that the universe was
heliocentric was not 'true' in the sixteenth century, and only
gradually entered the realm of 'truth'.

Paul de Man developed this argument about rhetoric to its
fullest extent. He takes the view that 'figures of speech' (tropes)
pervade language, exerting a force which destabilizes logic and
grammar. A trope or figure allows a writer to say one thing but
mean something else, by substituting one meaning for another
(metaphor) or displacing meaning from one sign in a chain to
another (metonymy). The disruptive effects of figural discourse
create momentary difficulties and breaks in communication. As
the Archie Bunker example in the de Man extract shows

(III,7,C), rhetoric often disrupts grammar and forces us to suppress its implications in order to preserve the rigour of 'meaning'. He believes that this vital indeterminacy of meaning is paramount in literature.

The major influence on de Man and other American critics belonging to the Yale School is Jacques Derrida whose 'Structure, Sign, and Play' paper, given at a symposium at Johns Hopkins University in 1966, inaugurated the deconstructive movement in the United States. The essay put in question the metaphysical assumptions of Western philosophy since Plato. The concepts of unity, centre, and presence have been fundamental in Western thought. Even structuralists treated the term 'structure' as an unproblematic and stable 'centre' of meaning. Derrida does not suggest that we can ever break free from the conceptual universe we inherit, but we *can* resist the attempts made by thinkers to impose upon us one pole in a particular binary opposition (e.g. body/soul, good/bad, nature/nurture) and to treat it as a guarantor of truth and 'presence'. For example, Western thinking often privileges 'speech' at the expense of 'writing'. Speech offers true 'presence', while writing is impure and supplementary. Derrida calls this privileging of speech 'phonocentrism', which is a particular example of what he calls 'logocentrism' (the belief that there is an ultimate word, truth, or reality which can be the foundation of our thoughts and experiences). Derrida shows that speech has the same semiotic characteristics (see Saussure, III,6,C) as writing, and that it is just as reasonable to regard speech as a form of writing as the reverse. Having reversed the 'violent hierarchy' speech/writing, a deconstructive reading proceeds to displace the new hierarchy which has been created, leaving us with a sense of the necessary *indeterminacy* of all signifying processes. Critics of Derrida have put the common-sense objection: 'If there is no determinate meaning or truth, what are you trying to achieve in your books?' Derrida tries to deal with this problem by avoiding determinate concepts in his own discourse. All his terms are overtly deconstructed . 'Différance', 'gram', 'supplement', 'trace', and so on, contain marks of indeterminacy. For example, 'différance' alludes both to the spatial differences which are required in any semiotic system (Saussure called language 'a series of differences of sound combined with a series of differences of ideas') *and* to temporal *deferment* (presence is always deferred by signifiers). *Positions*

contains an especially valuable summation of structuralism and
Derrida's critique of it.

Barbara Johnson, in a relatively small number of papers, has
established herself as the outstanding American exponent of
Derridean deconstruction. It is almost impossible to detach a
coherent extract from her elegant essay, but the first stage in her
deconstructive reading of Barthes demonstrates the hidden
motivation of Barthes' choice of study text in *S/Z* (see III,3,E).
She argues that the form of Barthes' critical theory is already
inscribed in the Balzac novella. The distinction between
'readerly' and 'writerly' corresponds to the crucial difference in
the novella between ideal woman and castrato. She points out
the instability of Barthes' moves. His praise of 'writerly' (plural,
disseminated) texts goes naturally with favouring 'castration'
(the castrato, like Barthes' own writerly book with its chopping
up of Balzac's text, is indeterminate and created by the knife),
but, in fact, he associates castration with the processes of the
readerly text, which cuts off meaning in its full flowering, and
imposes closure. This curious relation between Barthes' critical
method and the text he is studying illustrates the central post-
structuralist argument about 'metalanguages'. All masterful
discourses, such as criticism, which aim to explain other
discourses, are 'metalanguages'. Barthes and others frequently
argue that criticism can only interweave its discourse with the
text it addresses, and can never stand apart from it in the
position of knowledge. His own critique of Balzac, as Johnson
shows, confirms this view. Her reading also illustrates the
deconstructive concept of *aporia* (logical impasse). Writers think
they are establishing a meaning by negotiating apparently
determinate concepts, but in practice they find themselves in a
dizzying and aporetic recession from definite meaning.

Following Barthes and Derrida, Geoffrey Hartman rejects the
conventional boundary line between literature and criticism (see
Barthes, III,3,E). The 'indeterminacy' of writing affects criticism
as much as literature. His own critical writings (though not the
extract) are often as 'unreadable' and equivocal as any post-
modernist text. However, his appropriation of Derrida is
evidently accommodated to Anglo–American needs. His
suspicion of excessive abstraction and especially his humanistic
faith are attractive to even traditional readers. He transforms
indeterminacy into Keatsian 'negative capability' (see Keats,
III,4,A) and Wordsworthian innocent vision. Indeterminacy is

the condition of humanity: it describes our uncertainty and humility in the face of experience. Hartman's fanciful kind of deconstructive writing entirely lacks the philosophical rigour of Derrida and Johnson.

Background reading

Jonathan Arac *et al.*, *The Yale Critics: Deconstruction in America* (Minneapolis: Minnesota UP, 1983).

Jonathan Culler, 'Jacques Derrida', in *Structuralism and Since: from Lévi-Strauss to Derrida*, ed. John Sturrock (Oxford: Oxford UP, 1979).

Jonathan Culler, *On Deconstruction: Theory and Criticism after Structuralism* (Ithaca: Cornell UP, 1983).

Robert Con Davis and Ronald Schleifer (eds), *Rhetoric and Form: Deconstruction at Yale* (Norman: University of Oklahoma Press, 1985).

Vincent B. Leitch, *Deconstructive Criticism: An Advanced Introduction* (New York: Columbia UP, 1983).

Christopher Norris, *Deconstruction: Theory and Practice* (London: Methuen, 1982).

William Ray, *Literary Meaning: From Phenomenology to Deconstruction* (Oxford: Blackwell, 1984).

Richard Rorty, *Consequences of Pragmatism* (*Essays 1972–1980*) (Brighton: Harvester Press, 1982).

Michael Ryan, *Marxism and Deconstruction* (Baltimore: Johns Hopkins UP, 1982).

Robert Young (ed.), *Untying the Text: a Post-Structuralist Reader* (Boston, London and Henley: Routledge & Kegan Paul, 1981).

(A) FRIEDRICH NIETZSCHE

The Will to Power (1901)

481 (1883–1888)

Against positivism, which halts at phenomena – 'There are only *facts*' – I would say: No, facts is precisely what there is not, only interpretations. We cannot establish any fact 'in itself': perhaps it is folly to want to do such a thing.

'Everything is subjective,' you say; but even this is interpretation. The 'subject' is not something given, it is something added and invented and projected behind what there is. – Finally, is it necessary to posit an interpreter behind the interpretation? Even this is invention, hypothesis.

In so far as the word 'knowledge' has any meaning, the world is knowable; but it is *interpretable* otherwise, it has no meaning behind it, but countless meanings. – 'Perspectivism.'

It is our needs that interpret the world; our drives and their For and Against. Every drive is a kind of lust to rule; each one has its perspective that it would like to compel all the other drives to accept as a norm. [. . .]

600 (1885–1886)

No limit to the ways in which the world can be interpreted; every interpretation a symptom of growth or of decline.

Inertia needs unity (monism); plurality of interpretations a sign of strength. Not to desire to deprive the world of its disturbing and enigmatic character! [. . .]

604 (1885–1886)

'Interpretation,' the introduction of meaning – not 'explanation' (in most cases a new interpretation over an old interpretation that has become incomprehensible, that is now itself only a sign). There are no facts, everything is in flux, incomprehensible, elusive; what is relatively most enduring is – our opinions.

605 (SPRING–FALL 1887)

The ascertaining of 'truth' and 'untruth,' the ascertaining of facts in general, is fundamentally different from creative positing, from forming, shaping, overcoming, willing, such as is of the essence of philosophy. To introduce a meaning – this task still remains to be done, assuming there is no meaning yet. Thus it is with sounds, but also with the fate of peoples: they are capable of the most different interpretations and direction toward different goals.

On a yet higher level is to *posit a goal* and mold facts according to it; that is, active interpretation and not merely conceptual translation.

606 (1885–1886)

Ultimately, man finds in things nothing but what he himself has imported into them: the finding is called science, the importing –

art, religion, love, pride. Even if this should be a piece of childishness, one should carry on with both and be well disposed toward both – some should find; others – *we* others! – should import!

(Friedrich Nietzsche, *The Will to Power*, trans. Walter Kaufmann and R. J. Hollingdale (New York: Vintage Books, Knopf and Random House, 1968), pp. 267, 326, 327.)

(B) JACQUES DERRIDA

Of Grammatology (1967)

By a slow movement whose necessity is hardly perceptible, everything that for at least some twenty centuries tended toward and finally succeeded in being gathered under the name of language is beginning to let itself be transferred to, or at least summarized under, the name of writing. By a hardly perceptible necessity, it seems as though the concept of writing – no longer indicating a particular, derivative, auxiliary form of language in general (whether understood as communication, relation, expression, signification, constitution of meaning or thought, etc.), no longer designating the exterior surface, the insubstantial double of a major signifier, *the signifier of the signifier* – is beginning to go beyond the extension of language. In all senses of the word, writing thus *comprehends* language. Not that the word 'writing' has ceased to designate the signifier of the signifier, but it appears, strange as it may seem, that 'signifier of the signifier' no longer defines accidental doubling and fallen secondarity. 'Signifier of the signifier' describes on the contrary the movement of language: in its origin, to be sure, but one can already suspect that an origin whose structure can be expressed as 'signifier of the signifier' conceals and erases itself in its own production. There the signified always already functions as a signifier. The secondarity that it seemed possible to ascribe to writing alone affects all signifieds in general, affects them always already, the moment they *enter the game*. [. . .]

It is as if the Western concept of language (in terms of what, beyond its plurivocity and beyond the strict and problematic opposition of speech [*parole*] and language [*langue*], attaches it *in general* to phonematic or glossematic production, to language, to voice, to hearing, to sound and breadth, to speech) were revealed today as the guise or disguise of a primary writing: more fundamental than that which, before this conversion, passed for the simple 'supplement to the spoken word' (Rousseau). Either writing was never a simple 'supplement' or it is urgently necessary to construct a new logic of the 'supplement'. [. . .]

The notion of the sign always implies within itself the distinction between signifier and signified, even if, as Saussure argues, they are distinguished simply as the two faces of one and the same leaf. This notion remains therefore within the heritage of that logocentrism which is also a phonocentrism: absolute proximity of voice and being, of voice and the meaning of being, of voice and the ideality of meaning. [. . .]

We already have a foreboding that phonocentrism merges with the historical determination of the meaning of being in general as *presence*, with all the subdeterminations which depend on this general form and which organize within it their system and their historical sequence (presence of the thing to the sight as *eidos*, presence as substance/essence/existence [*ousia*], temporal presence as point [*stigmé*] of the now or of the moment [*nun*], the self-presence of the cogito, consciousness, subjectivity, the co-presence of the other and of the self, intersubjectivity as the intentional phenomenon of the ego, and so forth). Logocentrism would thus support the determination of the being of the entity as presence.

(Jacques Derrida, *Of Grammatology*, trans. Gayatri C. Spivak (Baltimore and London: Johns Hopkins UP, 1976).)

Positions (1972)

Kristeva: What is the *gram* as a 'new structure of nonpresence'? What is *writing* as *différance*? What rupture do these concepts introduce in relation to the key concepts of semiology – the (phonetic) *sign* and *structure*? How does the notion of *text* replace, in grammatology, the linguistic and semiological notion of what is *enounced*?

Derrida: The reduction of writing – as the reduction of the exteriority of the signifier – was part and parcel of phonologism and logocentrism. We know how Saussure, according to the traditional operation that was also Plato's, Aristotle's, Rousseau's, Hegel's, Husserl's, etc., excludes writing from the field of linguistics – from language and speech – as a phenomenon of exterior representation, both useless and dangerous. [. . .]

In effect, alphabetical writing seems to present speech, and at the same time to erase itself before speech. Actually, it could be shown, as I have attempted to do, that there is no purely phonetic writing, and that phonologism is less a consequence of the practice of the alphabet in a given culture than a certain ethical or axiological *experience* of this practice. Writing *should* erase itself before the plenitude of living speech, perfectly represented in the transparence of its notation, immediately present for the subject who speaks it, and for the subject who receives its meaning, content, value.

Now, if one ceases to limit oneself to the model of phonetic writing, which we privilege only by ethnocentrism, and if we draw all the consequences from the fact that there is no purely phonetic writing (by reason of the necessary spacing of signs, punctuation, intervals, the differences indispensable for the functioning of graphemes, etc.), then the entire phonologist or logocentrist logic becomes problematical. Its range of legitimacy becomes narrow and superficial. This delimitation, however, is indispensable if one wants to be able to account, with some coherence, for the principle of difference, such as Saussure himself recalls it. This principle compels us not only not to privilege one substance – here the phonic, so called temporal, substance – while excluding another – for example, the graphic, so called spatial, substance – but even to consider every process of signification as a formal play of differences. That is, of traces.

Why traces? And by what right do we reintroduce grammatics at the moment when we seem to have neutralized every substance, be it phonic, graphic, or otherwise? Of course it is not a question of resorting to the same concept of writing and of simply inverting the dissymmetry that now has become problematical. It is a question, rather, of producing a new concept of writing. This concept can be called *gram* or *différance*. The play of differences supposes, in effect, syntheses and referrals which forbid at any moment, or in any sense, that a simple element be *present* in and of itself, referring only to itself. Whether in the order of spoken or written discourse, no element can function as a sign without referring to another element which itself is not simply present. This interweaving results in each 'element' – phoneme or grapheme – being constituted on the basis of the trace within it of the other elements of the chain

or system. This interweaving, this textile, is the *text* produced
only in the transformation of another text. Nothing, neither
among the elements nor within the system, is anywhere ever
simply present or absent. There are only, everywhere, differences
and traces of traces. The gram, then, is the most general concept
of semiology – which thus becomes grammatology – and it
covers not only the field of writing in the restricted snse, but
also the field of linguistics. [. . .]

The gram as *différance*, then, is a structure and a movement no
longer conceivable on the basis of the opposition presence/absence.
Différance is the systematic play of differences, of the traces of
differences, of the *spacing* by means of which elements are related
to each other. This spacing is the simultaneously active and
passive (the *a* of *différance* indicates this indecision as concerns
activity and passivity, that which cannot be governed by or
distributed between the terms of this opposition) production of
the intervals without which the 'full' terms would not signify,
would not function. It is also the becoming-space of the spoken
chain – which has been called temporal or linear; a becoming-
space which makes possible both writing and every
correspondence between speech and writing, every passage from
one to the other.

The activity or productivity connoted by the *a* of *différance*
refers to the generative movement in the play of differences. The
latter are neither fallen from the sky nor inscribed once and for
all in a closed system, a static structure that a synchronic and
taxonomic operation could exhaust. Differences are the effects of
transformations, and from this vantage the theme of *différance* is
incompatible with the static, synchronic, taxonomic, ahistoric
motifs in the concept of *structure*. But it goes without saying that
this motif is not the only one that defines structure, and that the
production of differences, *différance*, is not astructural: it produces
systematic and regulated transformations which are able, at a
certain point, to leave room for a structural science. The concept
of *différance* even develops the most legitimate principled
exigencies of 'structuralism.'

Language, and in general every semiotic code – which
Saussure defines as 'classifications' – are therefore effects, but
their cause is not a subject, a substance, or a being somewhere
present and outside the movement of *différance*. Since there is no
presence before and outside semiological *différance*, one can
extend to the system of signs in general what Saussure says of
language: 'Language is necessary for speech to be intelligible

and to produce all its effects; but speech is necessary for language to be established; historically, the fact of speech always comes first.' There is a circle here, for if one rigorously distinguishes language and speech, code and message, schema and usage, etc., and if one wishes to do justice to the two postulates thus enunciated, one does not know where to begin, nor how something can begin in general, be it language or speech. Therefore, one has to admit, before any dissociation of language and speech, code and message, etc. (and everything that goes along with such a dissociation), a systematic production of differences, the *production* of a system of differences – a *différance* – within whose effects one eventually, by abstraction and according to determined motivations, will be able to demarcate a linguistics of language and a linguistics of speech, etc.

Nothing – no present and in-*different* being – thus precedes *différance* and spacing. There is no subject who is agent, author, and master of *différance*, who eventually and empirically would be overtaken by *différance*. Subjectivity – like objectivity – is an effect of *différance*, an effect inscribed in a system of *différance*. This is why the *a* of *différance* also recalls that spacing is temporization, the detour and postponement by means of which intuition, perception, consummation – in a word, the relationship to the present, the reference to a present reality, to a *being* – are always *deferred*. Deferred by virtue of the very principle of difference which holds that an element functions and signifies, takes on or conveys meaning, only by referring to another past or future element in an economy of traces. This economic aspect of *différance*, which brings into play a certain not conscious calculation in a field of forces, is inseparable from the more narrowly semiotic aspect of *différance*. It confirms that the subject, and first of all the conscious and speaking subject, depends upon the system of differences and the movement of *différance*, that the subject is constituted only in being divided from itself, in becoming space, in temporizing, in deferral; and it confirms that, as Saussure said, 'language [which consists only of differences] is not a function of the speaking subject.' At the point at which the concept of *différance*, and the chain attached to it, intervenes, all the conceptual oppositions of metaphysics (signifier/signified; sensible/intelligible; writing/speech; passivity/activity; etc.) – to the extent that they ultimately refer to the presence of something present (for example, in the form of the identity of the subject who is present for all his operations, present beneath every accident or event, self-present in its 'living speech,' in its enunciations, in the present objects and acts of its language, etc.) – become nonpertinent. They all amount, at one moment or another, to a subordination of the movement of *différance* in favor of the presence of a value or a *meaning* supposedly antecedent to *différance*, more original than it, exceeding and governing it in the last analysis. This is still the presence of what we called above the 'transcendental signified.'

(Jacques Derrida, *Positions*, trans. Alan Bass (London: Athlone Press, 1981; published by arrangement with University of Chicago Press), pp. 24–5, 25–7, 27–9. French original was published by Editions de Minuit (Paris, 1972).)

(C) PAUL DE MAN

'Semiology and Rhetoric' (1973)

One of the most striking characteristics of literary semiology as it is practiced today, in France and elsewhere, is the use of grammatical (especially syntactical) structures conjointly with rhetorical structures, without apparent awareness of a possible discrepancy between them. In their literary analyses, Barthes, Genette, Todorov, Greimas, and their disciples all simplify and regress from Jakobson in letting grammar and rhetoric function in perfect continuity, and in passing from grammatical to rhetorical structures without difficulty or interruption. Indeed, as the study of grammatical structures is refined in contemporary theories of generative, transformational, and distributive grammar, the study of tropes and of figures (which is how the term rhetoric is used throughout this essay, not in the derived sense of comment, eloquence, or persuasion) becomes a mere extension of grammatical models, a particular subset of syntactical relations. In the recent *Dictionnaire encyclopédique des sciences du langage*, Ducrot and Todorov write: '. . . rhetoric has always been satisfied with a paradigmatic view over words (words substituting for each other), without questioning their syntagmatic relationship (the contiguity of words to each other). There ought to be another perspective, complementary to the first, in which metaphor, for example, would not be defined as a substitution but as a particular type of combination. Research inspired by linguistics or, more narrowly, by syntactical studies, has begun to reveal this possibility – but it remains to be explored.' Todorov, who calls one of his books a *Grammar of the Decameron*, rightly thinks of his own work and that of his associates as first explorations in the elaboration of a systematic grammar of literary modes, genres, and also literary figures. Perhaps the most perceptive work to come out of this school, Genette's studies of figural modes, can be shown to be assimilations of rhetorical transformations or combinations to syntactical, grammatical patterns. Thus a recent study, now printed in *Figures III* and entitled 'Métonymie chez Proust,' shows the combined presence, in a wide and astute selection of passages, of paradigmatic, metaphorical figures with syntagmatic, metonymic structures. The combination of both is treated descriptively and nondialectically without suggesting the possibility of logical tensions.

One can ask whether this reduction of figure to grammar is legitimate. The existence of grammatical structures within and beyond the unit of the sentence in literary texts is undeniable, and their description and classification are indispensable. The question remains if and how figures of rhetoric can be included in such a taxonomy. This question is at the core of the debate going on, in a wide variety of apparently unrelated forms, in contemporary poetics; but I do not plan to make clear the connection between this 'real' problem and the countless pseudo-problems that agitate literary studies. The historical picture of contemporary criticism is too confused to make the mapping out of such a topography a useful exercise. Not only are these questions mixed in and mixed up within particular groups or local trends, but they are often co-present, without apparent contradiction, within the work of a single author.

Neither is the theory of the question suitable for quick expository treatment. To distinguish the epistemology of grammar from the epistemology of rhetoric is a redoubtable task. On an entirely naive level, we tend to conceive of grammatical systems as tending toward universality and as simply generative, that is, as capable of deriving an infinity of versions from a single model (that may govern transformations as well as derivations) without the intervention of another model that would upset the first. We therefore think of the relationship between grammar and logic, the passage from grammar to propositions, as being relatively unproblematic: no true propositions are conceivable in the absence of grammatical consistency or of controlled deviation from a system of consistency no matter how complex. Grammar and logic stand to each other in a dyadic relationship of unsubverted support. In a logic of acts rather than of statements, as in Austin's theory of speech acts, which has had such a strong influence on recent American work in literary semiology, it is also possible to move between speech acts and grammar without difficulty. The performance of what are called illocutionary acts, such as ordering, questioning, denying, and assuming, within the language is congruent with the grammatical structures of syntax in the corresponding imperative, interrogative, negative, and optative sentences. 'The rules for illocutionary acts,' writes Richard Ohmann in a recent paper, 'determine whether performance of a given act is well-executed, in just the same way as grammatical rules determine whether the product of a locutionary act – a sentence – is well formed. . . But whereas the rules of grammar concern the relationships among sound, syntax, and meaning, the rules of illocutionary acts concern relationships among people.' And since rhetoric is then conceived exclusively as persuasion, as actual action upon others (and not as an intralinguistic figure or trope), the continuity between the illocutionary realm of grammar and the perlocutionary realm of rhetoric is self-evident. It becomes the basis for a new rhetoric that, exactly as is the case for Todorov and Genette, would also be a new grammar. [. . .]

These remarks should indicate at least the existence and the difficulty of the question, a difficulty which puts its concise theoretical exposition beyond my powers. I must retreat therefore into a pragmatic discourse and try to illustrate the tension between grammar and rhetoric in a few specific textual examples. Let me begin by considering what is perhaps the most commonly known instance of an apparent symbiosis between a grammatical and a rhetorical structure, the so-called rhetorical question, in which the figure is conveyed directly by means of a syntactical device. I take the first example from the subliterature of the mass media: asked by his wife whether he wants to have his bowling shoes laced over or laced under, Archie Bunker answers with a question. He asks, 'What's the difference?' Being a reader of sublime simplicity, his wife replies by patiently explaining the difference between lacing over and lacing under, whatever this may be, but provokes only ire. 'What's the difference?' did not ask for difference but meant instead 'I don't give a damn what the difference is.' The same grammatical pattern engenders two meanings that are mutually exclusive: the literal meaning asks for the concept (difference) whose existence is denied by the figurative meaning. As long as we are talking about bowling shoes, the consequences are relatively trivial; Archie Bunker, who is a great believer in the authority of origins (as long, of course, as they are the right origins), muddles along in a world where literal and figurative meanings get in each other's way, though not without discomforts. But if a *de*-Bunker rather than a Bunker, a de-bunker of the *archē* (origin), an 'Archie Debunker' such as Nietzsche or Jacques Derrida, asks the question 'What is the Difference?' we cannot even tell from his grammar whether he 'really' wants to know 'what' difference is or is merely telling us that we should not even try to find out. Confronted with the question of the difference between grammar and rhetoric, grammar allows us to ask the question, but the sentence by means of which we ask it may deny the very possibility of asking. For what is the use of asking, I ask, when we cannot even authoritatively decide whether a question asks or doesn't ask?

The point is as follows. A perfectly clear syntactical paradigm (the question) engenders a sentence that has at least two meanings, one which asserts and the other which denies its own illocutionary mode. It is not that there are simply two meanings, one literal and the other figural, and that we have to decide which one of these meanings is the right one in this particular situation. The confusion can only be cleared up by the intervention of an extratextual intention, such as Archie Bunker setting his wife straight; but the very anger he displays is indicative of more than impatience: it reveals his despair when confronted with a structure of linguistic meaning that he cannot control and that holds the discouraging prospect of an infinity of similar future confusions, all of them potentially catastrophic in their consequences. Nor is this intervention really a part of the minitext constituted by the figure, which holds our attention only as long as it remains suspended and unresolved. I follow the usage of common speech in calling this semiological enigma 'rhetorical.' The grammatical model of the question becomes rhetorical not when we have, on the one hand, a literal meaning and, on the other hand, a figural meaning, but when it is impossible to decide by grammatical or other linguistic devices which of the two meanings (that can be entirely contradictory) prevails. Rhetoric radically suspends logic and opens up vertiginous possibilities of referential aberration. And although it would perhaps be somewhat more remote from common usage, I

would not hesitate to equate the rhetorical, figural potentiality of
language with literature itself. I could point to a great number
of antecedents to this equation of literature with figure; the most
recent reference would be to Monroe Beardsley's insistence in his
contribution to the essays in honor of William Wimsatt that
literary language is characterized by being 'distinctly above the
norm in ratio of implicit (or, I would say rhetorical) to explicit
meaning.'

(Paul de Man, 'Semiology and Rhetoric', *Textual Strategies: Perspectives
in Post-Structuralist Criticism*, ed. Josué Harari (London: Methuen, 1980),
pp. 124–7, 128–30.)

(D) GEOFFREY H. HARTMAN

Criticism in the Wilderness (1980)

'Indeterminacy' is a word with bad vibes. It evokes a picture of
the critic as Hamlet, 'sicklied o'er with the pale cast of thought.'
It is often said to involve an attack on the communicative or
edifying function of literature. A pseudoscientific or anti-
humanist bias is ascribed to critics when they do not replace
words by meanings quickly enough. We like to consume our
literature. We like to think of critics as service stations that keep
readers fueled for their more important business, refreshing them
and speeding them on.

Yet indeterminacy, though not an end to be pursued but
something disclosed by liberal and thoughtful reading, is more
like a traffic sign warning of an impasse. It suggests (1) that
where there is a conflict of interpretations or codes, that conflict
can be rehearsed or reordered but not always resolved, and
(2) that even where there is no such conflict we have no
certainty of controlling implications that may not be apparent or
articulable at any one point in time. This 'tacit component' will
be mentioned again. But two things should already be clear. The
referential function of words in ordinary situations, where the
context is easily determined, is not in question. At the same
time, all statements are potentially overdetermined and have a
circumference larger than their apparent reference. [. . .]
To methodize indeterminacy would be to forget the reason for
the concept. It does not doubt meaning, nor does it respond to
an economy of scarcity and try to make reading more

'productive' of meaning. Quite the contrary: it encourages a form of writing – of articulate interpretation – that is not subordinated naively to the search for ideas. From this perspective the apparently opposite demands for *objective interpretation* on the part of E. D. Hirsch and for *subjective criticism* on the part of Norman Holland ignore equally the resistance of art to the meanings it provokes. Reduction of multiple meaning, according to Hirsh, is achieved through the postulate of a determinate and determinable authorial intention. Holland places the reduction of meaning of the 'defensive mastery' of the artist and the defensive misery of the reader. Hirsch would regulate the understanding, so that it does not waste itself; Holland would deregulate it, since the problem is not subjectivity but our overreaction to it, an excess of social rules and psychic defences.

Though the issue of multiple meaning and its reduction is raised by both critics, they eventually leave art behind. Holland evangelizes the very difficulty of gaining an interpretation of art, suggesting that the interpretive work builds up, by way of the classroom, a community of readers who share this interpersonal, reflective experience; Hirsch seeks to rationalize literary studies by arguing that interpretation of art must abide by the rules of interpretation generally, that meanings are hypotheses subject to canons of verifiability. The concept of indeterminacy, however, explores the 'blind lawfulness' (Kant) of imagination, or how art allows the understanding to produce its own form of meaningfulness. 'As it must not, so genius cannot be lawless,' Coleridge wrote in his *Lectures on Shakespeare*, 'for it is even this that constitutes its genius – the power of acting creatively under laws of its own origination.'

I realize that reduction of meaning and the role of the principle of indeterminacy would need more exposition than I can offer here. May I emphasize the following: As a guiding concept, indeterminacy does not merely *delay* the determination of meaning, that is, suspend premature judgments and allow greater thoughtfulness. The delay is not heuristic alone, a device to slow the act of reading till we appreciate (I could think here of Stanley Fish) its complexity. The delay is intrinsic: from a certain point of view, it is thoughtfulness itself, Keats's 'negative capability,' a labor that aims not to overcome the negative or indeterminate but to stay within it as long as is necessary.

How long, though? That cannot be abstractly answered. Forms of closure will occur, precipitated by acts of writing or reading. But it is the *commentary process* that matters: the taking away, modification, elaboration, of previous meanings. 'All symbols are fluxional; all language is vehicular and transitive' (Emerson). As long as criticism is also commentary, the work of art that is its 'referent' is established as a constant variable, and its successive actualization (its 'history') must itself be studied, as in the reception theory of the School of Konstanz associated with Hans Robert Jauss and Wolfgang Iser.

To compile an inventory of meanings in their structural relations ('structuralism') or of the focusing and orientative acts of consciousness in *their* relations ('phenomenology'), seems rather distant from what we do as critics, even when unusually introspective. This is where the gap between the 'scientific' approach to literary studies and humanistic criticism is most apparent; and I have not been able to bridge it. The gap is like that between *langue* and *parole* in Saussure, or between grammar and the living language, or between a principle and its application. (In hermeneutics, as Hirsch reminds us, a difference was often discerned between subtlety of understanding and subtlety of explication – of articulating and applying one's understanding. Gadamer, however, thinks these are or can be fused.) On the whole, I favor moving 'indeterminacy' from the area of grammatical, semiotic, or phenomenological reduction to that of humanistic criticism itself: that is, we take back from science what is ours; we do not allow ourselves to depend on the physical or human sciences for the model of a *mechanism* that fascinates by its anonymous, compulsive, impersonal character. (So, for example, on the strange foundation of unconscious process the most elaborate structures, including art, are built up.) Through interpretive criticism we ascertain the kind of relation we have to that mechanism, as writing and reading disclose it. Wordsworth's 'dim and undetermined sense/Of unknown modes of being' is also what moved him to autobiography, and to define that which has no single, exclusively personal, locus. Yet the perspective disclosed may be, precisely, the absence of one and only one context from which to view the flux of time or the empirical world, of one and only one method that would destabilize all but itself, of one and only one language to rule understanding and prevent misunderstanding.

To put it another way: we read to understand, but to understand *what*? Is it the book, is it the object (in the world) revealed by the book, is it ourselves? Or some transcendental X? [. . .]

We read, as we write, to be understood; yet what we gain is

the undoing of a previous understanding. Indeterminacy, as a concept, resists formally the complicity with closure implied by the wish to be understood or the communication-compulsion associated with it. Criteria of correctness or correspondence (of *truth*) may be caught up in this complicity. Indeterminacy functions as a bar separating understanding and truth. Understanding is not disabled but is forced back on the conditions of its truth: for example, the legitimacy of its dependence on texts. If this seems too radical a perspective, there remains the puzzle that the reception of literary works is usually accompanied by an uneasiness about their reduction to meaning. Reduction *of* meaning, that is, may work against reduction *to* meaning. Reading itself becomes the project: we read to understand what is involved in reading as a form of life, rather than to resolve what is read into glossy ideas.

(Geoffrey H. Hartman, *Criticism in the Wilderness* (New Haven and London: Yale UP, 1980), pp. 265, 269–71, 271–2.)

(E) BARBARA JOHNSON

'The Critical Difference: Balzac's *Sarrasine* and Barthes's *S/Z*' (1978)

I shall begin by recalling the manner in which Barthes outlines his value system:

> Our evaluation can be linked only to a practice, and this practice is that of writing. On the one hand, there is what it is possible to write, and on the other, what it is no longer possible to write. . . What evaluation finds is precisely this value: what can be written (rewritten) today: the 'writerly' (le scriptible). Why is the writerly our value? Because the goal of literary work (of literature as work) is to make the reader no longer a consumer, but a producer of the text. . . Opposite the writerly text is its countervalue, its negative, reactive value: what can be read, but not written: the 'readerly' (le lisible). We call any readerly text a classic text (p. 4).

Here, then, is the major polarity which Barthes sets up as a tool for evaluating texts: the readerly versus the writerly. The readerly is defined as a product consumed by the reader; the writerly is a process of production in which the reader becomes a producer: it is 'ourselves writing'. The readerly is constrained by considerations of representation: it is irreversible, 'natural', decidable, continuous, totalisable, and unified into a coherent whole based on the signified. The writerly is infinitely plural and open to the free play of signifiers and of difference, unconstrained by representative considerations, and transgressive of any desire for decidable, unified, totalised meaning. [. . .] Barthes goes on to divide the story [Balzac's 'Sarrasine'] diachronically into 561 fragments called lexias and synchronically into five so-called voices or codes, thus transforming the text into a 'complex network' with 'multiple entrances and exits'.

The purpose of these cuts and codes is to pluralise the reader's intake, to effect a resistance to the reader's desire to restructure the text into large, ordered masses of meaning: 'If we want to remain attentive to the plural of a text . . ., we must renounce structuring this text in large masses, as was done by classical rhetoric and by secondary-school explication: no construction of the text' [pp. 11–12]. In leaving the text as heterogeneous and discontinuous as possible, in attempting to avoid the repressiveness of the attempt to dominate the message and force the text into a single ultimate meaning, Barthes thus works a maximum of disintegrative violence and a minimum of integrative violence.

Let us now turn to Balzac's 'Sarrasine' itself. The story is divided into two parts, the story of the telling and the telling of the story. In the first part, the narrator attempts to seduce a beautiful Marquise by telling her the second part; that is, he wants to exchange narrative knowledge for carnal knowledge. The lady wants to know the secret of the mysterious old man at the party, and the narrator wants to know the lady. Story-telling, as Barthes points out, is thus not an innocent, neutral activity, but rather part of a bargain, an act of seduction. But here the bargain is not kept; the deal backfires. The knowledge the lady has acquired, for from bringing about her surrender, prevents it. The last thing she says is precisely: 'No one will have *known* me.'

It is obvious that the key to this failure of the bargain lies in the content of the story used to fulfil it. That story is about the passion of the sculptor Sarrasine for the opera singer La Zambinella, and is based not on knowledge but on ignorance: the sculptor's ignorance of the Italian custom of using castrated men instead of women to play the soprano parts on the operatic stage. The sculptor, who had seen in La Zambinella the perfect female body for the first time united in one person, a veritable Pygmalion's statue come to life, thus finds out that this image of feminine perfection literally has been carved by a knife, not in stone but in the flesh itself. He who had proclaimed his willingness to die for his love ends up doing just that, killed by La Zambinella's protector.

How is it that the telling of this sordid little tale ends up subverting the very bargain it was intended to fulfil? Barthes's answer to this is clear: 'castration is contagious'; 'contaminated by the castration she has just been told about, [the Marquise] impels the narrator into it' (p. 36).

What is interesting about this story of seduction and castration is the way in which it unexpectedly reflects upon Barthes's own critical value system. For in announcing that 'the tutor text will ceaselessly be broken, interrupted without any regard for its natural divisions', is Barthes not implicitly privileging something like castration over what he calls 'the ideology of totality'? 'If the text is subject to some form,' he writes, 'this form is not unitary . . . finite; it is the fragment, the slice, the cut up or erased network' (p. 20; translation modified). Indeed, might it not be possible to read Balzac's opposition between the ideal woman and the castrato as metaphorically assimilable to Barthes's opposition between the readerly and the writerly? Like the readerly text, Sarrasine's deluded image of La Zambinella is a glorification of perfect unity and wholeness:

> At that instant he marvelled at the ideal beauty he had hitherto sought in life, seeking in one often unworthy model the roundness of a perfect leg; in another, the curve of a breast; in another, white shoulders: finally taking some girl's neck, some woman's hands, and some child's smooth knees, without ever having encountered under the cold Parisian sky the rich, sweet creations of ancient Greece. La Zambinella displayed to him, united, living, and delicate, those exquisite female forms he so ardently desired (pp. 237–8).

But like the writerly text, Zambinella is actually fragmented, unnatural, and sexually undecidable. Like the readerly, the soprano is a product to be 'devoured' ('With his eyes, Sarrasine devoured Pygmalion's statue, come down from its pedestal' [p. 238]), while, like the writerly, castration is a process of production, an active and violent indetermination. The soprano's appearance seems to embody the very essence of 'woman' as a signified ('This was woman herself' [p. 248]), while the castrato's reality, like the writerly text, is a mere play of signifiers, emptied of any ultimate signified, robbed of what the text calls a 'heart': 'I have no heart,' says Zambinella, 'the stage where you saw me . . . is my life, I have no other' (p. 247).

Here, then, is a first answer to the question of why Barthes might have chosen this text: it explicitly thematises the opposition between unity and fragmentation, between the idealised signified and the discontinuous empty play of signifiers, which underlies his opposition between the readerly and the writerly. The traditional value system which Barthes is attempting to reverse is thus already mapped out within the text he analyses.

(Barbara Johnson, 'The Critical Difference: Balzac's *Sarrasine* and Barthes's *S/Z*', in *Untying the Text: A Post-Structuralist Reader*, ed. Robert Young (Boston, London and Henley: Routledge & Kegan Paul, 1981), pp. 167, 168–70. Originally in *Diacritics*, vol. 8, no. 2 (1978).)

PART IV:

HISTORY AND SOCIETY

In Part 1 The discussion of 'mimesis' included theories about the representation of history in literature. Two further central historical questions which arise in literary study are: (1) is there a history of literature? and (2) what is literature's role in history? The first question asks if it is possible to isolate the 'literary system' and to trace its evolution. The second question implies that literature is part of history and cannot be separated from it without loss.

The terms 'tradition', 'influence', 'allusion' and 'topos' are often used by critics who are concerned with the continuities which link the stages in literary history. A great deal of scholarly editing and philological activity centres on problems of defining a work's literary antecedents ('sources and analogues'). Commentaries often cite passages from earlier writers either as influences, sources, or simply as parallels. It is sometimes difficult to determine whether a particular parallel is a source, or just one citation among many, of a commonplace idea whose source cannot be ultimately determined. Ernst Robert Curtius believed that the notion of the literary commonplace (the 'topos') was a more fruitful one than the rather positivistic 'influence'. T. S. Eliot also rejected the narrowly chronological conception of literary history. Claudio Guillén and Harold Bloom revised the idea of 'tradition' in the light of structuralism and Freudian theory. Finally, Julia Kristeva's term 'intertextuality' challenges all traditional notions of influence and tradition and suggests that all texts are made from multiple transpositions of other texts (literary and non-literary). 'Intertextuality' includes conscious 'borrowing' or allusion but also every conceivable unconscious citation.

You're reviewing me!

The task of relating literature and history is one of the most complex facing literary study. A major tradition of thought associated with the German philosopher Hegel produced an approach to the study of literature and its 'background' which has profoundly influenced twentieth-century studies. The Hegelian tradition and the 'determinist' ideas of Comte provided alternative founding concepts for the 'historicist' view of history. This view looks for *unifying* principles which can explain the multiplicity of historical events. Taine, Lovejoy and Tillyard have each provided critics with such unifying notions: the soul of the race, the unit idea, the world-picture. Each principle is a matrix of ideas which are expressed in literature. Raymond Williams questioned the separateness of the categories 'art' and 'society', and suggested that the whole entity ('culture' or 'society') is a total expression of a way of life. The so-called 'New Historicists' (Stephen Greenblatt, Jonathan Dollimore, Alan Sinfield, and others) have challenged the modern historicist tradition, and, in the case of the British critics, followed the historical approach of writers such as E. P. Thompson and the later Raymond Williams who conceive history not in terms of unity but of complex patterns of contradiction, dominant and subordinate currents, and declining and emergent energies.

The 'sociology' of literature is concerned largely with the ways in which social and economic changes modify, facilitate, or inhibit the writer's productive activity. The introduction of commodity production, the invention of printing, photography or the silicon chip, the waning of 'liberal' ideas, and changes in cultural milieu and the writer's relationship to production, are some of the historical conditions which radically affect the nature of art.

In Marxist criticism, literature and art are often considered as part of 'ideology'. We are essentially social beings, and therefore our ideas are conditioned by the dominant 'common sense' of the society into which we are born. 'Ideology' in this sense is not a set of political doctrines but an often unconsciously held image or picture of the world of social relations, which includes concepts which appear self-evident (such as 'freedom', 'the individual', 'choice', 'rights', 'the self'). Some Marxist critics treat literature as a special region within (or even adjacent to) ideology, possessing an ability to reflect upon or crystallize the ideological conflicts of its historical period. It would be possible within this tradition to talk about literature as having a 'relative autonomy'. Other Marxists regard this 'privileging' of literature as 'idealist', and as making the same mistakes as T. S. Eliot made in talking about tradition as an 'ideal order'. They (for example, Terry Eagleton and Tony Bennett) prefer to consider literary production as an integral if complex part of ideology in general.

CHAPTER 1

TRADITION AND
INTERTEXTUALITY

T. S. Eliot's concept of tradition was a revolutionary one in English criticism, partly because he brought into the mainstream of critical thought the legacy of 'idealist' philosophical thought which had discreetly run through English culture from Coleridge to Bernard Bosanquet and F. H. Bradley. Eliot's debt to Bradley is well documented and begins in his doctoral thesis (a study of Bradley). Using Bradley's theory of 'internal relations', Eliot was able to combine two apparently contradictory dimensions: system and innovation. Literary history had been understood as a linear sequence – atoms strung out on the thread of time – composed of a series of 'original' texts (see Young, II,2,D). Romanticism was oddly complicit with positivism in this linking of uniqueness and fact: the writer's originality is foregrounded in the context of a lifeless history of 'objects'. The standard histories of literature often combine these apparently disparate modes of thinking. Eliot, on the other hand, conceives of tradition not as dead remains but as a 'simultaneous order': the major texts of tradition coexist in the mind of the present. The 'new' literary work is not 'original' in the Romantic sense, because its newness is only definable in *relation* to the already existing order of tradition: the new work must both *change* and *conform to* tradition. Eliot's 'ideal order' is taken from Bosanquet and Bradley, who aimed (as had Plato) to reconcile the many and the one, the whole and the part. Similarly, Eliot sought to reconcile tradition and the individual talent in a formulation that remained *the* theory of modernism for decades.

Ernst Robert Curtius's 'timeless present' resembles Eliot's 'tradition', and Curtius also rejects history in the form of a 'catalogue-like knowledge of facts'. Modern culture, he argued, was both 'wholly new' and yet 'conditioned at every point by antique culture'. Both Eliot and Curtius had personal motives for wanting to preserve tradition. Curtius wanted to resist the barbarism of the Nazis and their repression of history. Unlike Eliot, he emphasizes the importance of close philological study of the transmission of classical culture, and, like Erich Auerbach (see III,5,C), he uses the classical theory of rhetoric as his instrument of inquiry. 'Topoi' are 'storehouses of trains of thought', some of which are historically determined, and others of which are 'timeless'. Claudio Guillén's *Literature as System* (see IV,2,F) follows Eliot in the belief that 'process and individuality require each other' (A. N. Whitehead's words), but considers that mere 'critics' are satisfied by a narrowly atomistic approach to literature; only the 'literary historian' brings process and individuality together.

Raymond Williams' *The Long Revolution* developed a materialist analysis of tradition in opposition to Eliot (and Leavis). He regards the notion of an 'ideal order' as unhistorical. There is no 'tradition', only specific selections of valued works. The selection of what is considered valuable can never be objectively verified or justified. The specific interests of classes and institutions work to preserve 'tradition' in a rigid and unchanging form. Interestingly, Williams, in this early study, seemed to encourage educational institutions to step back from this selective tendency and to embrace the role of 'preservation'. By preserving even an apparently worthless antiquity the academy may make possible a subsequent revaluation in the selective tradition. The radical aspect of Williams' argument has been taken up more recently in Marxist criticism. The 'selective tradition' is what is preserved as the culture of the dominant ideology, and involves the exclusion or marginalization of alternative practices. In his *Marxism and Literature* (1976), Williams formulated the historical transmission of culture as a process involving *residual*, *dominant* and *emergent* elements. This model conceived literary history as involving not only change, continuity and discontinuity, but also the effects of *power*.

Harold Bloom offers a novel version of poetic tradition in his studies *The Anxiety of Influence* (1973) and *A Map of Misreading* (1975). He combines Freudian psychology, the theory of tropes, and cabbalistic mysticism in his poetic 'history'. All great poets, he argues, suffer from a sense of 'belatedness': coming late in history they fear that their poetic 'fathers' will have already used up all the available poetic inspiration. They experience an Oedipal hatred of the father, a desperate desire to deny paternity, and to assert their own originality. This 'anxiety of influence' produces various defensive strategies and makes it

possible for them to discover a poetic space in which an
authentic inspiration can be expressed. Poetic sons find ways of
'swerving' from the strong poems of their fathers. The swerving
involves a creative 'misreading' of their precursors. Bloom's
somewhat idiosyncratic theory has some affinities with post-
structuralist ideas: Derrida, Foucault and others regard all
strong critical readings of texts as misreadings in the sense that
they ignore the pervasive 'play' of signification which always
disrupts every reading (see Derrida on 'différance', III,7,B).

Julia Kristeva's semiotic theory challenges the notions of
'tradition' and 'influence' from a more radical viewpoint. Her
concept of 'intertextuality' is part of a wider psychoanalytic
theory which questions the stability of the 'subject' (see
Kristeva, II,5,F). She defines intertextuality as *transposition* of
sign-systems, *not* in the 'banal' sense of the 'study of sources' but
as part of the semiotic process which goes beyond the sort of
rational control involved in 'making an allusion' or 'using a
source'. Notice also that 'transposition' can mean not only
transference from written system to written system but also from
non-literary and non-linguistic systems to a literary system. She
goes so far as to say that *every* signifying system is no less than
'a field of transpositions of various signifying systems'. This in
turn throws into question the unity and substantiality of the
subject who is the site of this play of systems (compare Barthes,
III,3,E). The problem in her approach for traditional literary
criticism is that few of the familiar categories of the discipline
survive: 'literary work', 'tradition', 'author', 'source', and so on.

Background reading

R. S. Crane, *Critical and Historical Principles of Literary History* (Chicago
    and London: University of Chicago Press, 1971).
Geoffey Green, *Literary Criticism and the Structures of History* (Lincoln,
    Nebraska: Nebraska UP, 1983).
Gregory S. Jay, *T. S. Eliot and the Poetics of Literary History* (Baton Rouge:
    Louisiana State UP, 1983).
Laurent Jenny, 'The Strategy of Form' (on intertextuality), in Todorov
    (ed.), *French Literary Theory* . . . (see III, 6).
J. P. Plottel and H. Charney (eds), *Intertextuality: New Perspectives in
    Criticism* (New York Literary Forum, 2, 1978).
Robert Weimann, *Structure and Society in Literary History* (London:
    Lawrence & Wishart, 1977), esp. ch. 2: 'The Concept of Tradition
    Reconsidered'.
Richard Wollheim, 'Eliot and F. H. Bradley', in *Eliot in Perspective, A
    Symposium*, ed. G. Martin (London: Macmillan, 1970).

(A) T. S. ELIOT

'Tradition and the Individual Talent' (1919)

We dwell with satisfaction upon the poet's difference from his predecessors, especially his immediate predecessors; we endeavour to find something that can be isolated in order to be enjoyed. Whereas if we approach a poet without this prejudice we shall often find that not only the best, but the most individual parts of his work may be those in which the dead poets, his ancestors, assert their immortality most vigorously. And I do not mean the impressionable period of adolescence, but the period of full maturity.

Yet if the only form of tradition, of handing down, consisted in following the ways of the immediate generation before us in a blind or timid adherence to its successes, 'tradition' should positively be discouraged. We have seen many such simple currents soon lost in the sand; and novelty is better than repetition. Tradition is a matter of much wider significance. It cannot be inherited, and if you want it you must obtain it by great labour. It involves, in the first place, the historical sense, which we may call nearly indispensable to anyone who would continue to be a poet beyond his twenty-fifth year; and the historical sense involves a perception, not only of the pastness of the past, but of its presence; the historical sense compels a man to write not merely with his own generation in his bones, but with a feeling that the whole of the literature of Europe from Homer and within it the whole of the literature of his own country has a simultaneous existence and composes a simultaneous order. This historical sense, which is a sense of the timeless as well as of the temporal and of the timeless and of the temporal together, is what makes a writer traditional. And it is at the same time what makes a writer most acutely conscious of his place in time, of his own contemporaneity.

No poet, no artist of any art, has his complete meaning alone. His significance, his appreciation is the appreciation of his relation to the dead poets and artists. You cannot value him alone; you must set him, for contrast and comparison, among the dead. I mean this as a principle of aesthetic, not merely historical, criticism. The necessity that he shall conform, that he shall cohere, is not onesided; what happens when a new work of art is created is something that happens simultaneously to all the works of art which preceded it. The existing monuments form an ideal order among themselves, which is modified by the introduction of the new (the really new) work of art among them. The existing order is complete before the new work arrives; for order to persist after the supervention of novelty, the *whole* existing order must be, if ever so slightly, altered; and so the relations, proportions, values of each work of art toward the whole are readjusted; and this is conformity between the old and the new. Whoever has approved this idea of order, of the form of European, of English literature will not find it preposterous that the past should be altered by the present as much as the present is directed by the past. And the poet who is aware of this will be aware of great difficulties and responsibilities.

In a peculiar sense he will be aware also that he must inevitably be judged by the standards of the past. I say judged, not amputated, by them; not judged to be as good as, or worse or better than, the dead; and certainly not judged by the canons of dead critics. It is a judgment, a comparison, in which two things are measured by each other. To conform merely would be for the new work not really to conform at all; it would not be new, and would therefore not be a work of art. And we do not quite say that the new is more valuable because it fits in; but its fitting in is a test of its value – a test, it is true, which can only be slowly and cautiously applied, for we are none of us infallible judges of conformity. We say: it appears to conform, and is perhaps individual, or it appears individual, and may conform; but we are hardly likely to find that it is one and not the other.

To proceed to a more intelligible exposition of the relation of the poet to the past: he can neither take the past as a lump, an indiscriminate bolus, nor can he form himself wholly on one or two private admirations, nor can he form himself wholly upon one preferred period. The first course is inadmissible, the second is an important experience of youth, and the third is a pleasant and highly desirable supplement. The poet must be very conscious of the main current, which does not at all flow invariably through the most distinguished reputations. He must be quite aware of the obvious fact that art never improves, but that the material of art is never quite the same. He must be aware that the mind of Europe – the mind of his own country – a mind which he learns in time to be much more important than his own private mind – is a mind which changes, and that this change is a development which abandons nothing *en route*, which does not superannuate either Shakespeare, or Homer, or the rock drawing of the Magdalenian draughtsmen. That this development, refinement perhaps, complication certainly, is not, from the point of view of the artist, any improvement. Perhaps not even an improvement from the point of view of the psychologist or not to the extent which we imagine; perhaps only in the end based upon a complication in economics and machinery. But the difference between the present and the past is that the conscious present is an awareness of the past in a way and to an extent which the past's awareness of itself cannot show.

(T. S. Eliot, 'Tradition and the Individual Talent', *Selected Essays*, 2nd edn (London: Faber & Faber, 1934), pp. 14–16.)

(B) E. R. CURTIUS

European Literature and the Latin Middle Ages (1948)

The 'timeless present' which is an essential characteristic of literature means that the literature of the past can always be active in that of the present. So Homer in Virgil, Virgil in Dante, Plutarch and Seneca in Shakespeare, Shakespeare in Goethe's *Götz von Berlichingen*, Euripides in Racine's *Iphigenia* and Goethe's. Or in our day: The *Thousand and One Nights* and Calderón in Hofmannsthal; the *Odyssey* in Joyce; Aeschylus, Petronius, Dante, Tristan Corbière, Spanish mysticism in T. S. Eliot. There is here an inexhaustible wealth of possible interrelations. Furthermore, there is the garden of literary forms – be they the genres (which Croce is forced by his philosophical system to declare unreal!) or metrical and stanzaic forms; be they set formulas or narrative motifs or linguistic devices. It is a boundless realm. Finally, there is the wealth of figures which literature has formed and which can forever pass into new bodies: Achilles, Oedipus, Semiramis, Faust, Don Juan. André Gide's last and ripest work is a *Theseus* (1946).

Just as European literature can only be seen as a whole, so the study of it can only proceed historically. Not in the form of literary history! A narrative and enumerative history never yields anything but a cataloguelike knowledge of facts. The material itself it leaves in whatever form it found it. But historical investigation has to unravel it and penetrate it. It has to develop analytical methods, that is, methods which will 'decompose' the material (after the fashion of chemistry with its reagents) and make its structures visible. The necessary point of view can only be gained from a comparative perusal of literatures, that is, can only be discovered empirically. Only a literary discipline which proceeds historically and philologically can do justice to the task. [. . .]

Today the relation between the antique and the modern world can no longer be conceived as 'survival,' 'continuation,' or 'legacy.' We adopt Ernst Troeltsch's universal-historical view. According to him, our European world is based 'not upon a reception of Antiquity nor upon a severance from it, but upon a thorough and at the same time conscious coalescence with it. The European world is composed of the antique and the modern, of the old world which has passed through all stages from primitivism to cultural overripeness and disintegration, and of the new world which begins with the Romanic-Germanic peoples in the time of Charlemagne and which also passes through its stages.' But at the same time 'these two worlds, so widely sundered in their mentality and their historical development, are so interwined, so coalescent in a conscious historical memory and continuity, that the modern world, despite the fact that it has a spirit which is wholly new and wholly its own, is intimately penetrated and conditioned at every point by antique culture, tradition, legal and political forms, language, philosophy, and art. It is this alone which gives the European world its depth, its fullness, its complexity, and its movement, as well as its bent toward historical thinking and historical self-analysis . . .' [. . .]

According to Toynbee, the Roman Empire is the universal-state end phase of the Hellenic civilization. This is followed, from 375 to 675, by an 'interregnum,' then by 'the Western civilization.' The latter stands to the Hellenic civilization in the relation of 'affiliation,' is its daughter civilization. In this way the facts established by Troeltsch are defined by a more precise chronology and terminology. The dependent relationship of 'affiliation' implies the same thing as Troeltsch's concept of 'thorough coalescence' and 'continuity.' Whether one is to distinguish 'renaissances' within the process is a question of expedience. They must be tested individually. What is fundamental is the concept that the substance of antique culture was never destroyed. The fallow period of decline which extended from 425 to 775 affected only the Frankish kingdom and was later made good. A new period of decline begins in the nineteenth century and reaches the dimensions of catastrophe in the twentieth. This is not the place to discuss its significance. [. . .]

In the antique system of rhetoric topics is the stockroom. There one found ideas of the most general sort – such as could be employed in every kind of oratory and writing. Every writer, for example, must try to put the reader in a favourable frame of mind. To this end, until the literary revolution of the eighteenth century, a modest first appearance was recommended. The author had next to lead the reader to the subject. Hence for the introduction (*exordium*) there was a special topics; and likewise for the conclusion. Formulas of modesty, introductory formulas, concluding formulas, then, are required everywhere. Other topoi can be used only for some particular species of oratory – for the judicial oration or the epideictic oration. An example!

1.   TOPICS OF CONSOLATORY ORATORY

A sub-species of epideictic oratory is the consolatory oration (λόγος παραμυθητικός, *consolatio*), or consolatory treatise, whose abbreviated form is the letter of condolence. This genre will serve to show us what topics is.

Achilles knows that he is destined to an early death. He accepts his lot, finds consolation in the thought (*Iliad*, XVIII, 117 f.): 'Not even the mighty Herakles escaped death, albeit most dear to Kronian Zeus the King.' At Archytas' grave Horace reflects upon the theme: all must die. Even the heroes (*Odes*, I, 28, 7 ff.):

> *Occidit et Pelopis genitor, conviva deorum,*
> *Tithonusque remotus in auras,*
> *Et Jovis arcanis Minos admissus; habentque*
> *Tartara Panthoiden . . .*

> (Gone too the sire of Pelops, guest of the gods,
> Tithonus too, snatched into air,
> And Minos who Jove's secrets knew; yea, Tartarus
> Holds Panthous' son . . .)

In an elegy on the death of Tibullus, Ovid argues that the greatest poets of the past also had to die (*Amores*, III, 9, 21 ff.). The imperial philosopher Marcus Aurelius points out that Hippocrates, who cured many sicknesses, himself fell sick and died. And Alexander, Pompey, Caesar, 'they who so often razed

whole cities to the very ground,' had to depart this life. Such
were the grounds of consolation found by the poets and sages of
Antiquity.

But in the Christian era people must certainly have found
other things to say? Yes, a great Christian like Augustine found
deeper consolation. He recalls the friend of his youth, Nebridius,
with the words: 'Now his ear hangs no longer on my mouth, but
the mouth of his soul lies at the eternal fount . . . and he is
blessed without end. Yet I believe not that he is so intoxicated
therewith as to forget me. For thou, Lord, whom he drinks,
rememberest us' (*Conf.*, IX, 3, 6). But the literati of the
Christian era cling to the well-tried grounds of consolation
supplied by pagan rhetoric. Only now they no longer enumerate
heroes or poets who had to die, but partriarchs. They were very
long-lived, to be sure, but . . . Fortunatus (ed. B. Leo, p. 205 f.)
names Adam, Seth, Noah, Melchizedek, and many others in
proof of the statement:

> *Qui satus ex homine est, et moriturus erit.*
> (Who comes of the seed of man, for him death waits.) [. . .]

2. HISTORICAL TOPICS

Not all topoi can be derived from rhetorical genres. Many stem
originally from poetry and then pass over into rhetoric. Since
Antiquity there has been a perpetual exchange between poetry
and prose. To poetic topics belongs the beauty of nature in the
widest sense – hence the ideal landscape with its typical
equipment. So do dreamlands and dream ages: Elysium (with
eternal spring without meteorological disturbances), the Earthly
Paradise, the Golden Age. So do the active principles in life:
love, friendship, transience. All these themes concern basic
relations of existence and hence are timeless – some more, others
less. Less: friendship, love. They reflect the sequence of
psychological periods. But in all poetical topoi the style of
expression is historically determined. Now there are also topoi
which are wanting throughout Antiquity down to the Augustan
Age. They appear at the beginning of late Antiquity and then
are suddenly everywhere. To this class belong the 'aged boy'
and the 'youthful old woman,' which we shall analyze. They
have a twofold interest. First, as regards literary biology, we can
observe in them the *genesis of new topoi*. Thus our knowledge of

the genetics of the formal elements of literature is widened.
Secondly, these topoi are indications of a changed psychological
state; indications which are comprehensible in no other way.
Thus our understanding of the psychological history of the West
is deepened, and we approach spheres that the psychology of
C. G. Jung has explored.

(Ernst Robert Curtius, *European Literature and the Latin Middle Ages*, trans.
Willard R. Trask (London: Routledge & Kegan Paul, 1953), pp. 15,
19–20, 79–80, 82. Original German was published by A. Francke
Verlag, Berne, 1948.)

(C) RAYMOND WILLIAMS

The Long Tradition (1961)

When it is no longer being lived, but in a narrower way survives
in its records, the culture of a period can be very carefully
studied, until we feel that we have reasonably clear ideas of its
cultural work, its social character, its general patterns of activity
and value, and in part of its structure of feeling. Yet the survival
is governed, not by the period itself, but by new periods, which
gradually compose a tradition. Even most specialists in a period
know only a part of even its records. One can say with
confidence, for example, that nobody really knows the
nineteenth-century novel; nobody has read, or could have read,
all its examples, over the whole range from printed volumes to
penny serials. The real specialist may know some hundreds; the
ordinary specialist somewhat less; educated readers a decreasing
number: though all will have clear ideas on the subject. A
selective process, of a quite drastic kind, is at once evident, and
this is true of every field of activity. Equally, of course, no
nineteenth-century reader would have read all the novels; no
individual in the society would have known more than a
selection of its facts. But everyone living in the period would
have had something which, I have argued, no later individual
can wholly recover: that sense of the life within which the novels
were written, and which we now approach through our selection
Theoretically, a period is recorded; in practice, this record is
absorbed into a selective tradition; and both are different from
the culture as lived. [. . .]

Within a given society, selection will be governed by many
kinds of special interest, including class interests. Just as the
actual social situation will largely govern contemporary selection,

so the development of the society, the process of historical change, will largely determine the selective tradition. The traditional culture of a society will always tend to correspond to its *contemporary* system of interests and values, for it is not an absolute body of work but a continual selection and interpretation. In theory, and to a limited extent in practice, those institutions which are formally concerned with keeping the tradition alive (in particular the institutions of education and scholarship) are committed to the tradition as a whole, and not to some selection from it according to contemporary interests. The importance of this commitment is very great, because we see again and again, in the workings of a selective tradition, reversals and re-discoveries, returns to work apparently abandoned as dead, and clearly this is only possible if there are institutions whose business it is to keep large areas of past culture, if not alive, at least available. It is natural and inevitable that the selective tradition should follow the lines of growth of a society, but because such growth is complex and continuous, the relevance of past work, in any future situation, is unforeseeable. There is a natural pressure on academic institutions to follow the lines of growth of a society, but a wise society, while ensuring this kind of relevance, will encourage the institutions to give sufficient resources to the ordinary work of preservation, and to resist the criticism, which any particular period may make with great confidence, that much of this activity is irrelevant and useless. It is often an obstacle to the growth of a society that so many academic institutions are, to an important extent, self-perpetuating and resistant to change. The changes have to be made, in new institutions if necessary, but if we properly understand the process of the selective tradition, and look at it over a sufficiently long period to get a real sense of historical change and fluctuation, the corresponding value of such perpetuation will be appreciated.

(Raymond Williams, *The Long Revolution* (1961; Harmondsworth: Penguin, 1965), pp. 66–7, 68–9.)

(D) HAROLD BLOOM

The Anxiety of Influence (1973)

Poetic Influence – when it involves two strong, authentic poets, – always proceeds by a misreading of the prior poet, an act of creative correction that is actually and necessarily a misinterpretation. The history of fruitful poetic influence, which is to say the main tradition of Western poetry since the Renaissance, is a history of anxiety and self-saving caricature, of distortion, of perverse, wilful revisionism without which modern poetry as such could not exist. [. . .]

If to imagine is to misinterpret, which makes all poems antithetical to their precursors, then to imagine after a poet is to learn his own metaphors for his acts of reading. Criticism then necessarily becomes antithetical also, a series of swerves after unique acts of creative misunderstanding.

The first swerve is to learn to read a great percursor poet as his greater descendants compelled themselves to read him.

The second is to read the descendants as if we were their disciples, and so compel ourselves to learn where we must revise them if we are to be found by our own work, and claimed by the living of our own lives.

Neither of these quests is yet Antithetical Criticism.

That begins when we measure the first *clinamen* against the second. Finding just what the accent of deviation is, we proceed to apply it as corrective to the reading of the first but not the second poet or group of poets. To practice Antithetical Criticism on the more recent poet or poets becomes possible only when they have found disciples not ourselves. But these can be critics, and not poets.

It can be objected against this theory that we never read a poet as poet, but only read one poet in another poet, or even into another poet. Our answer is manifold: we deny that there is, was or ever can be a poet as poet – to a reader. Just as we can never embrace (sexually or otherwise) a single person, but embrace the whole of her or his family romance, so we can never read a poet without reading the whole of his or her family romance as poet. The issue is reduction and how best to avoid it. Rhetorical, Aristotelian, phenomenological, and structuralist criticisms all reduce, whether to images, ideas, given things, or phonemes. Moral and other blatant philosophical or psychological criticisms all reduce to rival conceptualizations. We reduce – if at all – to another poem. The meaning of a poem can only be another poem. This is not a tautology, not even a deep tautology, since the two poems are not the same poem, any more than two lives can be the same life. The issue is true history or rather the true use of it, rather than the abuse of it, both in Nietzsche's sense. True poetic history is the story of how poets as poets have suffered other poets, just as any true biography is the story of how anyone suffered his own family – or his own displacement of family into lovers and friends.

Summary – Every poem is a misinterpretation of a parent poem. A poem is not an overcoming of anxiety, but is that anxiety. Poet's misinterpretations or poems are more drastic than critics' misinterpretations or criticism, but this is only a difference in degree and not at all in kind. There are no interpretations but only misinterpretations, and so all criticism is prose poetry.

Critics are more or less valuable than other critics only (precisely) as poets are more or less valuable than other poets. For just as a poet must be found by the opening in a precursor poet, so must the critic. The difference is that a critic has more parents. His precursors are poets and critics. But – in truth – so are a poet's precursors, often and more often as history lengthens.

Poetry is the anxiety of influence, is misprision, is a disciplined perversenss. Poetry is misunderstanding, misinterpretation, misalliance.

Poetry (Romance) is Family Romance. Poetry is the enchantment of incest disciplined by resistance to that enchantment. [. . .]

A poem is a poet's melancholy at his lack of priority. The failure to have begotten oneself is not the cause of the poem, for poems arise out of the illusion of freedom, out of a sense of priority being possible. But the poem – unlike the mind in creation – is a made thing, and as such is an achieved anxiety.

(Harold Bloom, *The Anxiety of Influence: A Theory of Poetry* (New York: Oxford University Press, 1973), pp. 30, 93–5, 96.)

(E) JULIA KRISTEVA

The Revolution in Poetic Language (1974)

As we know, Freud specifies two fundamental 'processes' in the work of the unconscious: *displacement* and *condensation*. Kruszewski and Jakobson introduced them, in a different way, during the early stages of structural linguistics, through the concepts of *metonymy* and *metaphor*, which have since been interpreted in the light of psychoanalysis.

To these we must add a third 'process' – the *passage from one sign-system to another*. To be sure, this process comes about through a combination of displacement and condensation, but this does not account for its total operation. It also involves an altering of the thetic *position* – the destruction of the old position and the formation of a new one. The new signifying system may be produced with the same signifying material; in language, for example, the passage may be made from narrative to text. Or it may be borrowed from different signifying materials: the transposition from a carnival scene to the written text, for instance. In this connection we examined the formation of a specific signifying system – the novel – as the result of a redistribution of several different sign-systems: carnival, courtly poetry, scholastic discourse. The term *intertextuality* denotes this transposition of one (or several) sign-system(s) into another; but since this term has often been understood in the banal sense of 'study of sources', we prefer the term *transposition* because it specifies that the passage from one signifying system to another demands a new articulation of the thetic – of enunciative and denotative positionality. If one grants that every signifying practice is a field of transpositions of various signifying systems (an intertextuality), one then understands that its 'place' of enunciation and its denoted 'object' are never single, complete and identical to themselves, but always plural, shattered, capable of being tabulated. In this way polysemy can also be seen as the result of a semiotic polyvalence – an adherence to different sign-systems.

(Julia Kristeva, *The Revolution in Poetic Language*, trans. Margaret Waller (New York: Columbia UP, 1984), pp. 59–60.)

CHAPTER 2

HISTORY

Literary critics have often declared that great literature is timeless, and that great writers transcend the particular outward forms of history because their works give us a universally valid account of human nature (see Dr Johnson, I,3,D). Before the nineteenth century critics worked with very limited notions of historical development. The neoclassical critics, for example, combined universalism with a view of literature as part of a general progress or decline of civilization. It was nineteenth-century continental thought that provided new scientific and philosophical foundations for the historical study of literature.

The philosopher Karl Popper (1902–) uses the term 'historicism' to describe any study of history which attempts to predict on the basis of 'laws', 'patterns', 'trends', and so on. The laws of history may be founded on God (Plato), the Spirit of Man (Hegel), or material forces of production (Marx). Popper use of the word 'historicism' tends to blur distinctions between different approaches. First, there is a positivistic historicism associated with the philosophy of Comte (1798–1857), who believed that the methods of the natural sciences were the only reliable ones for establishing knowledge, since only that which is observed can be said to exist. The ideal of a neutral 'value-free' science deeply affected historical study. Hippolyte Taine (1828–93) was the first to elaborate a strictly deterministic history of literature. His first assumption is that national histories can be explained by 'some very general disposition of mind and soul'. This elementary 'moral state' is conditioned by environmental factors – 'the race, the surroundings, and the epoch'. From the resulting disposition arises a certain 'ideal model of man' which is expressed pre-minently in literature.

The second sense of 'historicism', the dominant one, which

Popper included in his usage, arose from German Romanticism. Hegelian and neo-Hegelian historiography has deeply influenced the study of literature and history. Hegel saw history as the self-realization of the human spirit – the rational expression of human freedom. History is the development of 'Spirit' in time. Particular events and physical reality in general are part of a large 'absolute spirit of history'. Hegel's dialectical view of history emphasizes change and development. Each phase in human civilization is superseded by a higher one which includes what is negated in the former phase: 'each successive phase becomes in its turn a material, working on which it exalts itself to a new grade'. The new phase incorporates all earlier phases (cf. Eliot, IV,1,A). Literature is conceived as the 'ideal' (as opposed to 'real') activity of the spirit of a people.

On the whole English scepticism has prevented the general acceptance of continental historicism. Nevertheless a 'weak' version of it has influenced English cultural history. Literary history sometimes followed the positivist method of Comte or the 'Darwinian' theories of Spencer (John Morley, Sir Sidney Lee, Edward Dowden, and John Addington Symonds). According to Hegel all aspects of the national culture express a 'national spirit' which is a temporary form of the absolute spirit on its path through history. The notion of the *zeitgeist* (spirit of the age) shaped the thought of major cultural historians (Carlyle, Burkhart, Lovejoy). The Marxist term 'reification' may be used to describe a characteristic trait of historicist literary study. The observation of facts and events gives rise to period generalizations, which in turn become abstracted terms – the Elizabethan World Picture, the Age of Reason, and so on. Finally, the spiritual abstraction is treated as the *cause* of real events and actions (compare Blake, IV,4,A). The disorder of Elizabethan politics and society is the subject of Shakespeare's history plays. The concern for 'order' is expressed in these plays, in Shakespeare's plays in general, and finally in Elizabethan literature in general. E. M. W. Tillyard, whose views are here being summarized, concludes 'Now this idea of cosmic order was one of the genuine ruling ideas of the age'. Such 'notions about the world and man' were 'quite taken for granted by the ordinary educated Elizabethan'. The notion of order (or 'degree') is to be found in Hooker's *Ecclesiastical Polity* and in Shakespeare's *Troilus and Cressida*. For some reason Hooker is taken as typical of the 'age' rather than Marlowe or Montaigne. Tillyard's approach does not recognize the possibility that the idea of 'degree' in *Troilus* may not be an expression of a fundamental notion of the age, but a notion undergoing change and contestation. His model of history cannot accommodate competing world-views or the contest between dominant and emergent ideologies.

A. O. Lovejoy's concept of 'unit ideas' evidently influenced Tillyard. At first his approach appears more 'scientific' (even Comtian) in its rigour. However, the Hegelian strain predominates in his concern to show how unit ideas (nature, the chain of being, and so on) are diffused throughout the cultural life of a nation. He also anticipates Tillyard in supporting the view that dominant cultural ideas are more directly manifested in the writings of minor authors. Tillyard's best illustration of the unit idea of 'degree' is from Sir John Davies' *Orchestra* (1596; the poem was edited by Tillyard in 1945). In Davies a dominant world view is represented in a purely ideological form and appears as a self-evident truth. In *Troilus*, on the other hand, Ulysses' speech on degree is represented within a dramatic context as a *contested* view, and its validity as an 'idea' is suspended.

In *The Long Revolution* (1961) Raymond Williams acknowledges that literature is part of a larger social organization but denies that it could be regarded as merely *illustrating* the whole organization. Williams was not only rejecting Tillyard but also the then dominant British Marxist orthodoxies, which reduced literature to a mere 'epiphenemon' (mechanically produced surface effect). He redefines 'culture' as a 'whole way of life', which includes social, economic and political organization, as well as the creative arts. This model clearly contradicts the Marxist 'base and superstructure' model with its distinction between the socio-economic base and the cultural and ideological superstructure. Since 1968 the influx of continental Marxist thought has reduced the gap between Williams' work and the Marxist tradition. 'Western Marxism' does not treat culture as the mere product of social and economic processes.

Lucien Goldmann's and Claudio Guillén's approaches to literature and history were affected by structuralism (see III,6). Goldmann called his form of Marxist theory 'genetic structuralism'. He concentrated on 'consciousness' – that mental reality, including ideas and art, which is conditioned by but not absolutely determined by material existence. A major influence on his thinking was Georg Lukács' *History and Class Consciousness* (1922). Goldmann's notion of a 'world view' differs from

Tillyard's. It describes the comprehensive and far-reaching form of group consciousness which affects all kinds of relationships between people and between people and nature. He argued that a major writer creates an advanced version of a world view by increasing 'very considerably the degree of structural coherence which the collective consciousness itself has so far attained only in a rough and ready fashion'. Notice that it is the *structure* of the world view and not the content which is important. The structure concerns the principles or underlying categories by which it orders reality. The structure expresses an ultimate view of reality (which might be transcendental, 'tragic', or materialist, for example). The structure may be shared by cultural agencies and forms which appear to involve quite different contents. For example, *Le Dieu Caché* (1964) shows that Racine's pagan plays express the same world view as Jansenist theology, Pascal's philosophy, and a social group (the *noblesse de la robe*). The Jansenists' 'tragic' world view saw the individual as divided between a hopelessly sinful world and a God who is absent. The same ('homologous') structure with a different content appear in the other forms. This 'totalizing' strategy is typical of both the Hegelian and the Marxist forms of historicism. Later Marxist thinkers (especially Louis Althusser) challenged this Hegelian legacy in Marxism.

Guillén argues that literature forms a distinct system (an objective process rather than a series of works), which should not be reduced or subordinated to other contiguous systems. Only by seeing the literary system as one system alongside the economic, political and other systems is it possible to do justice to the complexity of the social totality. He suggests that the systems may be related in two ways: our 'ideal literary historian' must decide whether the interactions between systems are to be understood by using a 'domination' model or an 'interaction model'. Here Guillén puts his finger on the central issue facing all literary historians: do we regard certain systems as fundamental and determining, or do we treat them all as autonomous areas of human practice which interact in a free way? Vulgar Marxism accepts a 'domination' model, while liberal or humanistic historians prefer the (pluralistic) 'interaction' model. Within Marxism, Louis Althusser accepts that the literary system has some degree of 'specificity' and autonomy, even though 'in the last instance' the economic system determines the orientation of the social formation as a whole. His model involves both interaction and domination.

Background reading

Jonathan Dollimore and Alan Sinfield (eds), *Political Shakespeare* (Manchester: Manchester UP, 1985).
John Drakakis (ed.), *Alternative Shakespeares* (London: Methuen, 1985), Introduction.
Wilbur Sanders, *The Dramatist and the Received Idea* (Cambridge: Cambridge UP, 1968), ch. 1: 'Literature as History'.
René Wellek, 'English Literary Historiography during the Nineteenth Century', in *Discriminations: Further Concepts of Criticism* (New Haven and London: Yale UP, 1963).

(A) H. A. TAINE

History of English Literature (1864, 1886)

There is then a system in human sentiments and ideas; and this system has for its motive power certain general traits, certain marks of the intellect and the heart common to men of one race, age, or country. [. . .]

New elements become mingled with the old; great forces from without counteract the primitive. The race emigrates, like the Aryan, and the change of climate has altered in its case the whole economy, intelligence, and organisation of society. The people has been conquered, like the Saxon nation, and a new political structure has imposed on it customs, capacities, and inclinations which it had not. The nation has installed itself in the midst of a conquered people, downtrodden and threatening, like the ancient Spartans; and the necessity of living like troops in the field has violently distorted in a unique direction the whole moral and social constitution. In each case, the mechanism of human history is the same. One continually finds, as the original mainspring, some very general disposition of mind and soul, innate and appended by nature to the race, or acquired and produced by some circumstance acting upon the race. These mainsprings, once admitted, produce their effect gradually: I mean that after some centuries they bring the nation into a new condition, religious, literary, social, economic; a new condition which, combined with their renewed effort, produces another condition, sometimes good, sometimes bad, sometimes slowly, sometimes quickly, and so forth; so that we may regard the whole progress of each distinct civilisation as the effect of a permanent force which, at every stage varies its operation by modifying the circumstances of its action.

Three different sources contribute to produce this elementary moral state – the *race*, the *surroundings* and the *epoch*. [. . .]

Beside the permanent impulse and the given surroundings, there is the acquired momentum. When the national character and surrounding circumstances operate, it is not upon a *tabula rasa*, but on a ground on which marks are already impressed. According as one takes the ground at one moment or another, the imprint is different; and this is the cause that the total effect is different. [. . .]

And if now you consider no longer a brief epoch, as our own time, but one of those wide intervals which embrace one or more centuries, like the middle ages, or our last classic age, the conclusion will be similar. A certain dominant idea has had sway; men, for two, for five hundred years, have taken to themselves a certain ideal model of man: in the middle ages, the knight and the monk; in our classic age, the courtier, the man who speaks well. This creative and universal idea is displayed over the whole field of action and thought; and after covering the world with its works, involuntarily systematic, it has faded, it has died away, and lo, a new idea springs up, destined to a like domination, and the like number of creations. And here remember that the second depends in part upon the first, and that the first, uniting its effect with those of national genius and surrounding circumstances, imposes on each new creation its bent and direction. The great historical currents are formed after this law – the long dominations of one intellectual pattern, or a master idea, such as the period of spontaneous creations called the Renaissance, or the period of oratorical models called the Classical Age, or the series of mystical compositions called the Alexandrian and Christian eras, or the series of mythological efflorescences which we meet with in the infancy of the German people, of the Indian and the Greek. Here as elsewhere we have but a mechanical problem; the total effect is a result, depending entirely on the magnitude and direction of the producing causes. The only difference which separates these moral problems from physical ones is, that the magnitude and direction cannot be valued or computed in the first as in the second. If a need or a faculty is a quantity, capable of degrees, like a pressure or a weight, this quantity is not measurable like the pressure or the weight. We cannot define it in an exact or approximative formula; we cannot have more, or give more, in respect of it, than a literary impression; we are limited to marking and quoting the salient points by which it is manifested, and which indicate approximately and roughly the part of the scale which is its position. But though the means of notation are not the same in the moral and physical sciences, yet as in both the matter is the same, equally made up of forces, magnitudes, and directions, we may say that in both the final result is produced after the same method. It is great or small, as the fundamental forces are great or small and act more or less exactly in the same sense, according as the distinct effects of race, circumstance, and epoch combine to add the one to the other, or to annul one another. Thus are explained the long impotences and the brilliant triumphs which make their appearance irregularly and without visible cause in the life of a people; they are caused by internal concords or contrarieties. There was such a concord when in the seventeenth century the sociable character and the conversational aptitude, innate in France, encountered the drawing-room manners and the epoch of oratorical analysis; when in the nineteenth century the profound and elastic genius of Germany encountered the age of philosophical compositions and of cosmopolitan criticism. There was such a contrariety when in the seventeenth century the rude and lonely English genius tried blunderingly to adopt a novel politeness; when in the sixteenth century the lucid and prosaic French spirit tried vainly to cradle a living poetry. That hidden concord of creative forces produced the finished urbanity and the noble and regular literature under Louis XIV and Bossuet, the grand metaphysics and broad critical sympathy of Hegel and Goethe. That hidden contrariety of creative forces produced the imperfect literature, the scandalous comedy, the abortive drama under Dryden and Wycherley, the vile Greek importations, the groping elaborate efforts, the scant half-graces under Ronsard and the Pleiad. So much we can say with confidence, that the unknown creations towards which the current of the centuries conducts us, will be raised up and regulated altogether by the three primordial forces; that if these forces could be measured and computed, one might deduce from them as from a formula the specialties of future civilisation; and that if, in spite of the evident crudeness of our notations, and the fundamental inexactness of our measures, we try now to form some idea of our general destiny, it is upon an examination of these forces that we must ground our prophecy. For in enumerating them, we traverse the complete circle of the agencies; and when we have considered race, circumstance, and epoch, which are the internal mainsprings, the external pressure, and the acquired momentum, we have exhausted not only the whole of the actual causes, but also the whole of the possible causes of motion. [. . .]

The more a book represents important sentiments, the higher is its place in literature; for it is by representing the mode of being of a whole nation and a whole age, that a writer rallies round him the sympathies of an entire age and an entire nation. This is why, amid the writings which set before our eyes the sentiments of preceding generations, a literature, and notably a grand literature, is incomparably the best. It resembles that admirable apparatus of extraordinary sensibility, by which physicians disentangle and measure the most recondite and delicate changes of a body. Constitutions, religions, do not approach it in importance; the articles of a code and of a catechism only show us the spirit roughly and without delicacy. If there are any writings in which politics and dogma are full of life, it is in the eloquent discourses of the pulpit and the tribune, memoirs, unrestrained confessions; and all this belongs to literature: so that, in addition to itself, it has all the advantage of other works. It is then chiefly by the study of literatures that one may construct a moral history, and advance toward the knowledge of psychological laws, from which events spring.

(H. A. Taine, *History of English Literature*, trans. H. Van Laun (New York: Henry Holt, 1886), pp. 7, 9–10, 12, 13–14, 20.)

(B) ARTHUR O. LOVEJOY

The Great Chain of Being (1936)

By the history of ideas I mean something at once more specific and less restricted than the history of philosophy. It is differentiated primarily by the character of the units with which it concerns itself. Though it deals in great part with the same material as the other branches of the history of thought and depends greatly upon their prior labors, it divides that material in a special way, brings the parts of it into new groupings and relations, views it from the standpoint of a distinctive purpose. Its initial procedure may be said – though the parallel has its dangers – to be somewhat analogous to that of analytic chemistry. In dealing with the history of philosophical doctrines, for example, it cuts into the hard-and-fast individual systems and, for its own purposes, breaks them up into their component elements, into what may be called their unit-ideas. [. . .]

Of what sort, then, are the elements, the primary and persistent or recurrent dynamic units, of the history of thought, of which he is in quest? They are rather heterogeneous; I shall not attempt a formal definition, but merely mention some of the principal types.

There are, *first*, implicit or incompletely explicit *assumptions*, or more or less *unconscious mental habits*, operating in the thought of an individual or a generation. It is the beliefs which are so much a matter of course that they are rather tacitly presupposed than formally expressed and argued for, the ways of thinking which seem so natural and inevitable that they are not scrutinized with the eye of logical self-consciousness, that often are most decisive of the character of a philosopher's doctrine, and still oftener of the dominant intellectual tendencies of an age. [. . .]

Second, any unit-idea which the historian thus isolates he next seeks to trace through more than one – ultimately, indeed, through all – of the provinces of history in which it figures in any important degree, whether those provinces are called philosophy, science, literature, art, religion, or politics. The postulate of such a study is that the working of a given conception, of an explicit or tacit presupposition, of a type of mental habit, or of a specific thesis or argument, needs, if its nature and its historic rôle are to be fully understood, to be traced connectedly through all the phases of men's reflective life in which those workings manifest themselves, or through as many of them as the historian's resources permit. It is inspired by the belief that there *is* a great deal more that is common to more than one of these provinces than is usually recognized, that the same ideal often appears, sometimes considerably disguised, in the most diverse regions of the intellectual world. [. . .]

It is this [wide-ranging] characteristic of the study of the history of ideas in literature which often puzzles students – even advanced students – in the present-day literature departments in our universities. Some of them, at least, my colleagues in those departments often tell me, are repelled when called upon to study some writer whose work, *as* literature, is now dead – or at best, of extremely slight value, according to our present aesthetic and intellectual standards. Why not stick to the masterpieces, such students exclaim – or at least to these *plus* the minor classics – the things that can be still read with pleasure, or with a feeling of the significance for men of the present age of the ideas or the moods of feeling which they express? This is a natural enough state of mind, if you don't regard the study of literary history as including within its province the study of the ideas and feelings which other men in past times have been moved by, and of the processes by which what may be called literary and philosophical public opinion is formed. But if you *do* think the historian of literature ought to concern himself with these matters, your minor writer may be as important as – he may often, from this point of view, be more important than – the authors of what are now regarded as the masterpieces. Professor Palmer has said, with equal truth and felicity: 'The tendencies of an age appear more distinctly in its writers of inferior rank than in those of commanding genius. These latter tell of past and future as well as of the age in which they live. They are for all time. But on the sensitive responsive souls, of less creative power, current ideals record themselves with clearness.' And it is, of course, in any case true that a historical understanding even of the few great writers of an age is impossible without an acquaintance with their general background in the intellectual life and common moral and aesthetic valuations of that age; and that the character of this background has to be ascertained by actual historical inquiry into the nature and interrelations of the ideas then generally prevalent.

(Arthur O. Lovejoy, *The Great Chain of Being* (1936; New York: Harper & Row, 1960), pp. 3, 7, 15, 19–20.)

(C) E. M. W. TILLYARD

The Elizabethan World Picture (1943)

This small book has come out of an attempt to write a larger one on Shakespeare's Histories. In studying these I concluded that the pictures of civil war and disorder they present had no meaning apart from a background of order to judge them by. My first chapter set out to describe that background. When it was finished, I found that it applied to Shakespeare's Histories no more than to the rest of Shakespeare or indeed than to Elizabethan literature generally. I also found that the order I

was describing was much more than political order, or, if
political, was always a part of a larger cosmic order. I found,
further, that the Elizabethans saw this single order under three
aspects: a chain, a set of correspondences, and a dance. Here
then was a subject too big for a single chapter in a more
specialized book, a subject demanding separate treatment.

Now this idea of cosmic order was one of the genuine ruling
ideas of the age, and perhaps the most characteristic. Such
ideas, like our everyday manners, are the least disputed and the
least paraded in the creative literature of the time. The
Victorians believed in the virtue of self-help, yet we do not
associate the poems of Tennyson or the novels of George Eliot
with the belief. They take it too much for granted. Of course if
we read these works with the idea in our minds we shall find
abundant hints of it. And to be ignorant of it makes us less able
to understand these two authors. The province of this book is
some of the notions about the world and man which were quite
taken for granted by the ordinary educated Elizabethan; the
utter commonplaces too familiar for the poets to make detailed
use of except in explicitly didactic passages, but essential as
basic assumptions and invaluable at moments of high passion.
Shakespeare glances at one of these essential commonplaces
when, in *Julius Caesar*, he makes Brutus compare the state of
man to a little kingdom. The comparison of man to the state or
'body politic' was as fundamental to the Elizabethans as the
belief in self-help was to the Victorians. [. . .]

Those (and they are at present the majority) who take their
notion of the Elizabethan age principally from the drama will
find it difficult to agree that its world picture was ruled by a
general conception of order, for at first sight that drama is
anything but orderly. However, people are beginning to perceive
that this drama was highly stylized and conventional, that its
technical licences are of certain kinds and fall into a pattern,
that its extravagant sentiments are repetitions and not novelties;
that it may after all have its own, if queer, regulation. Actually
the case is such as I have described in my preface: the
conception of order is so taken for granted, so much part of the
collective mind of the people, that it is hardly mentioned except
in explicitly didactic passages. It is not absent from non-didactic
writing, for it appears in Spenser's *Hymn of Love* and in Ulysses'
speech on 'degree' in Shakespeare's *Troilus and Cressida*. It occurs
frequently in didactic prose: in Elyot's *Governor*, the Church
Homily *Of Obedience*, the first book of Hooker's *Laws of*

Ecclesiastical Polity, and the preface to Raleigh's *History of the World.* [. . .]

The conception of order described above must have been common to all Elizabethans of even modest intelligence. Hooker's elaborated account must have stated pretty fairly the preponderating conception among the educated. Hooker is not easy reading to a modern but would have been much less difficult to a contemporary used to his kind of prose. He writes not for the technical theologian but mediates theology to the general educated public of his day. He is master of the sort of summary which, though it avoids irksome and controversial detail, presents the general and the simplified with consummate force and freshness. He has the acutest sense of what the ordinary educated man can grasp and having grasped ratify. It is this tact that assures us that he speaks for the educated nucleus that dictated the current beliefs of the Elizabethan Age. He represents far more truly the background of Elizabethan literature than do the coneycatching pamphlets or the novel of low life.

Hooker's version is of course avowedly theological and it is more explicit, but the order it describes is Elyot's and Shakespeare's. His name for it is law, law in its general sense. Above all cosmic or earthly orders or laws there is Law in general, 'that Law which giveth life unto all the rest which are commendable, just and good, namely the Law whereby the Eternal himself doth work'. By a masterly ambiguity he avoids the great traditional dispute whether a thing is right because God wills it, or God wills it because it is right. God created his own law both because he willed it and because it was right. Though voluntary it was not arbitrary, but based on reason. That divine reason is beyond our understanding; yet we know it is there. God's law is eternal, 'being that order which God before all ages hath set down with himself, for himself to do all things by'. God chose to work in finitude in some sort to show his glory; and having so chosen he expressed the abundance of his glory in variety. The sense of full life given by Shakespeare's 'degree' speech is a close poetical parallel to this theological doctrine of variety. [. . .]

Hooker's first book comes to rest in a final summary, which includes the notion of law or order as harmony ('Take but degree away, untune that string, And hark what discord follows'):

> Wherefore that here we may briefly end: of law there can be no less acknowledged than that her seat is the bosom of God, her voice the harmony of the world: all things in heaven and earth do her homage, the very least as feeling her care and the greatest not exempted from her power; both angels and men and creatures of what condition soever, though each in different sort and manner yet all with uniform consent, admiring her as the mother of their peace and joy.

Though little enlarged on by the poets, cosmic order was yet one of the master-themes of Elizabethan poetry. It has its positive and its negative expressions. First there is an occasional full statement, as in Spenser's *Hymns*. Then there are the partial statements or the hints. Ulysses' 'degree' speech is a partial statement. The long scene between Malcolm and Macduff at the English court and the reference to the healing power of the English king draw their strength from the idea.

(E. M. W. Tillyard, *The Elizabethan World Picture* (London: Chatto & Windus, 1943), pp. v–vi, 7, 10–11, 11–12.)

(D) RAYMOND WILLIAMS

The Long Revolution (1961)

If we take a particular work of art, say the *Antigone* of Sophocles, we can analyse it in ideal terms – the discovery of certain absolute values, or in documentary terms – the communication of certain values by certain artistic means. Much will be gained from either analysis, for the first will point to the absolute value of reverence for the dead; the second will point to the expression of certain basic human tensions through the particular dramatic form of chorus and double *kommos*, and the specific intensity of the verse. Yet it is clear that neither analysis is complete. The reverence, as an absolute value, is limited in the play by the terms of a particular kinship system and its conventional obligations – Antigone would do this for a brother but not for a husband. Similarly, the dramatic form, the metres of the verse, not only have an artistic tradition behind them, the work of many men, but can be seen to have been shaped, not only by the demands of the experience, but by the particular social forms through which the dramatic tradition developed. We can accept such extensions of our original analysis, but we cannot go on to accept that, because of the extensions, the value of reverence, or the dramatic form and the specific verse, have meaning only in the contexts to which we have assigned them. The learning of reverence, through such intense examples, passes beyond its context into the general growth of human consciousness. The dramatic form passes beyond its context, and becomes an element in a major and general dramatic tradition, in quite different societies. The play itself, a specific communication, survives the society and the religion which helped to shape it, and can be re-created to speak directly to unimagined audiences. Thus, while we could not abstract the ideal value or the specific document, neither could we reduce these to explanation within the local terms of a particular culture. If we study real relations, in any actual analysis, we reach the point where we see that we are studying a general organization in a particular example, and in this general organization there is no element that we can abstract and separate from the rest. It was certainly an error to suppose that values or art-works could be adequately studied without reference to the particular society within which they were expressed, but it is equally an error to suppose that the social explanation is determining, or that the values and works are mere by-products. We have got into the habit, since we realized how deeply works or values could be determined by the whole situation in which they are expressed, of asking about these relationships in a standard form: 'what is the relation of this art to this society?' But 'society', in this question, is a specious whole. If the art is part of the society, there is no solid whole, outside it, to which, by the form of our question, we concede priority. The art is there, as an activity, with the production, the trading, the politics, the raising of families. To study the relations adequately we must study them actively, seeing all the activities as particular and contemporary forms of human energy. If we take any one of these activities, we can see how many of the others are reflected in it, in various ways according to the nature of the whole organization. It seems likely, also, that the very fact that we can distinguish any particular activity, as serving certain specific ends, suggests that without this activity the whole of the human organization at that place and time could not have been realized. Thus art, while clearly related to the other activities, can be seen as expressing certain elements in the organization which, within that organization's terms, could only have been expressed in this way. It is then not a question of relating the art to the society, but of studying all the activities and their interrelations, without any concession of priority to any one of them we may choose to abstract. If we find, as often, that a particular activity came radically to change the whole organization, we can still not say that it is to this activity that all the others must be related; we can only study the varying ways in which, within the changing organization, the particular activities and their interrelations were affected. Further, since the particular activities will be serving varying and sometimes conflicting ends, the sort of change we must look for will rarely be of a simple kind: elements of persistence, adjustment, unconscious assimilation, active resistance, alternative effort, will all normally be present, in particular activities and in the whole organization.

The analysis of culture, in the documentary sense, is of great importance because it can yield specific evidence about the whole organization within which it was expressed. We cannot say that we know a particular form or period of society, and that we will see how its art and theory relate to it, for until we know these, we cannot really claim to know the society. This is a problem of method, and is mentioned here because a good deal of history has in fact been written on the assumption that the bases of the society, its political, economic, and 'social' arrangements, form the central core of facts, after which the art and theory can be adduced, for marginal illustration or 'correlation'. There has been a neat reversal of this procedure in the histories of literature, art, science, and philosophy, when these are described as developing by their own laws, and then something called the 'background' (what in general history was the central core) is sketched in. Obviously it is necessary, in exposition, to select certain activities for emphasis, and it is entirely reasonable to trace particular lines of development in temporary isolation. But the history of a culture, slowly built up from such particular work, can only be written when the active relations are restored, and the activities seen in a genuine parity. Cultural history must be more than the sum of the particular histories, for it is with the relations between them, the particular forms of the whole organization, that it is especially concerned. I would then define the theory of culture as the study of relationships between elements in a whole way of life. The analysis of culture is the attempt to discover the nature of the organization which is the complex of these relationships.

Analysis of particular works or institutions is, in this context, analysis of their essential kind of organization, the relationships which works or institutions embody as parts of the organization as a whole. A key-word, in such analysis, is pattern: it is with the discovery of patterns of a characteristic kind that any useful cultural analysis begins, and it is with the relationships between these patterns, which sometimes reveal unexpected identities and correspondences in hitherto separately considered activities, sometimes again reveal discontinuities of an unexpected kind, that general cultural analysis is concerned.

(Raymond Williams, *The Long Revolution* (1961; Harmondsworth: Penguin, 1965), pp. 60–3.)

(E) LUCIEN GOLDMANN

Towards a Sociology of the Novel (1964)

These [collective] unities are no doubt merely complex networks of inter-individual relations, but the complexity of the psychology of individuals derives from the fact that each of them belongs to a fairly large number of different groups (familial, occupational, national, friends and acquaintances, social classes, etc.) and that each of these groups acts upon his consciousness thus helping to form a unique, complex, and relatively incoherent structure, whereas conversely, as soon as we study a sufficiently large number of individuals *belonging to one and the same social group*, the action of other different social groups to which each of them belongs and psychological elements due to this membership cancel each other out, and we are confronted with a much simpler, more coherent structure.

From this viewpoint, the relations between the truly important work and the social group, which – through the medium of the creator – *is, in the last resort, the true subject of creation*, are of the same order as relations between the elements of the work and the work as a whole. In either case, we are confronted by the relations between the elements of a comprehensive structure and the totality of this structure, relations of both a comprehensive and an explanatory kind. That is why, although it is not absolutely absurd to imagine that if the individual Racine had received a different education, or lived in a different environment, he might have been able to write plays like those of Corneille or Molière, it is, on the other hand, absolutely inconceivable that the seventeenth-century *noblesse de robe* should have developed an Epicurean or radically optimistic ideology. [. . .]

In reality, the relation between the creative group and the work generally appears according to the following model: the group constitutes a process of structuration that elaborates in the consciousness of its members affective, intellectual, and practical tendencies towards a coherent response to the problems presented by their relations with nature and their inter-human relations. With few exceptions these tendencies fall far short of effective coherence, in so far as they are, as I said earlier, counteracted in the consciousness of individuals by the fact that each of them belongs to a number of other social groups.

Furthermore, mental categories exist in the group only in the form of tendencies moving towards a coherence I have called a world-view, a view that the group does not therefore create, but whose constituent elements it elaborates (and it alone can elaborate) and the energy that makes it possible to bring them together. The great writer (or artist) is precisely the exceptional individual who succeeds in creating in a given domain, that of the literary (or pictorial, conceptual, musical, etc.) work, an imaginary, coherent, or almost strictly coherent world, whose structure corresponds to that towards which the whole of the group is tending; as for the work, it is, in relation to other works, more or less important as its structure moves away from or close to rigorous coherence.

One can see the considerable difference that separates the sociology of contents and structuralist sociology. The first sees in the work a *reflection* of the collective consciousness, the second sees it on the contrary as *one of the most important constituent elements* of this collective consciousness, that element that enables the members of the group to become aware of what they thought, felt, and did without realizing objectively its signification. One can understand why the sociology of contents proves more effective when dealing with works of average importance, whereas conversely genetic-structuralist literary sociology proves more effective when dealing with the masterpieces of world literature. [. . .]

[. . .] in concrete research, we must begin with the analysis of each of the writer's works, studying them as far as possible in the order in which they were written.

Such a study will enable us to make provisional groupings of writings on the basis of which we can seek in the intellectual, political, social, and economic life of the period, structured social groupings, in which one can integrate, as partial elements, the works being studied, by establishing between them and the whole intelligible relations and, hopefully, homologies.

The progress of a piece of genetic-structuralist research consists in the fact of delimiting groups of empirical data that constitute structures, relative totalities, in which they can later be inserted as elements in other larger, but similar structures, and so on.

This method has, among others, the double advantage first of conceiving of the whole set of human facts in a unitary manner and, then, of being both *comprehensive* and *explanatory*, for the elucidation of a significatory structure constitutes a process of *comprehension*, whereas its insertion into a larger structure is, in relation to it, a process of *explanation*. Let us take an example; to elucidate the tragic structure of Pascal's *Pensées* and Racine's tragedies is a process of comprehension; to insert them into extremist Jansenism by uncovering the structure of this school of thought is a process of comprehension in relation to the latter, but a process of explanation in relation to the writings of Pascal and Racine; to insert extremist Jansenism into the over-all history of Jansenism is to explain the first and to understand the second. To insert Jansenism, as a movement of ideological expression, into the history of the seventeenth-century *noblesse de robe* is to explain Jansenism and to understand the *noblesse de robe*. To insert the history of the *noblesse de robe* into the over-all history of French society is to explain it by understanding the latter, and so on. Explanation and understanding are not therefore *two* different intellectual processes, but one and the same process applied to two frames of reference.

The hypothesis formulated in the first study of this volume leads me to add a few reflections to the methodological writings concerning the sociology of culture that I have published so far and, particularly, to the present study.

It has proved, in effect, that the relation between the work and the social structure with which it is associated is much more complex in capitalist society, and notably in the case of the literary form that is most closely associated with the economic sector of this society, the novel, than in the other literary or cultural creations examined in my previous studies.

In these studies, my research led me to the hypothesis that the work is situated at the meeting-point between the highest forms of the tendencies to coherence proper to the collective consciousness and the highest forms of unity and coherence of the individual consciousness of the creator.

Important cultural works could no doubt have a critical, even oppositional, character in relation to the over-all society in so far as they are associated with a social group oriented towards such a critical and oppositional character in relation to society as a whole. Having said this, cultural creation was nonetheless always based upon a close coincidence between the structure and the values of the collective consciousness and the structures and values of the work.

However, this situation becomes much more complex in a market society, in capitalist society, where the existence and development of an economic sector has precisely as a consequence a tendency to the disappearance or, at least, a reduction in the status of the collective consciousness as mere reflection.

In this case, the literary work can no longer be based on the total or almost total coincidence with the collective consciousness and is situated in a rather different dialectical relationship with the class with which it is associated.

(Lucien Goldmann, 'The Genetic-Structuralist Method in the History of Literature', *Towards a Sociology of the Novel*, trans. Alan Sheridan (London: Tavistock Publications, 1975), pp. 158, 159–60, 162–3, 167.)

(F) MICHEL FOUCAULT

'Nietzsche, Genealogy, History' (1971)

From these observations, we can grasp the particular traits of historical meaning as Nietzsche understood it – the sense which opposes 'wirkliche Historie' to traditional history. The former transposes the relationship ordinarily established between the eruption of an event and necessary continuity. An entire historical tradition (theological or rationalistic) aims at dissolving the singular event into an ideal continuity – as a teleological movement or a natural process. 'Effective' history, however, deals with events in terms of their most unique characteristics, their most acute manifestations. An event, consequently, is not a decision, a treaty, a reign, or a battle, but the reversal of a relationship of forces, the usurpation of power, the appropriation of a vocabulary turned against those who had once used it, a

feeble domination that poisons itself as it grows lax, the entry of
a masked 'other'. The forces operating in history are not
controlled by destiny or regulative mechanisms, but respond to
haphazard conflicts. They do not manifest the successive forms
of a primordial intention and their attraction is not that of a
conclusion, for they always appear through the singular
randomness of events. The inverse of the Christian world, spun
entirely by a divine spider, and different from the world of the
Greeks, divided between the realm of will and the great cosmic
folly, the world of effective history knows only one kingdom,
without providence or final cause, where there is only 'the iron
hand of necessity shaking the dice-box of chance'. Chance is not
simply the drawing of lots, but raising the stakes in every
attempt to master chance through the will to power, and giving
rise to the risk of an even greater chance. The world we know is
not this ultimately simple configuration where events are reduced
to accentuate their essential traits, their final meaning, or their
initial and final value. On the contrary, it is a profusion of
entangled events. If it appears as a 'marvelous motley, profound
and totally meaningful', this is because it began and continues
its secret existence through a 'host of errors and phantasms'. We
want historians to confirm our belief that the present rests upon
profound intentions and immutable necessities. But the true
historical sense confirms our existence among countless lost
events, without a landmark or a point of reference.

(Michel Foucault, 'Nietzsche, Genealogy, History', *Language
Counter-Memory, Practice: Selected Essays and Interviews*, ed. and
trans. D. F. Bouchard, trans. S. Simon (Oxford: Blackwell, 1977),
pp. 154–5, 156–7.)

(G) CLAUDIO GUILLÉN

Literature as System (1971)

We saw earlier that the diachronic study of literature implied
two requirements: 'historicity' and 'specificity.' A third
requirement, then, would be 'structure,' or 'system,' or
'integration.' I shall soon return to these terms, with which the
linguist and the social scientist are familiar. Essentially, the
literary historian cannot be satisfied with an atomistic approach
to literature (though the critic may). Insofar as history demands

interpretation, and interpretation rests upon constructive principles, it is not sufficient to enumerate – to arrange a row of individual objects. This seems evident enough when the subject is European literature. But even if the topic were less ambitious, literary history would still presuppose the existence of extensive processes and configurations, rather than of merely partial or isolated events. In practice, this is what the better literary historians have achieved. In theory, there is much that remains to be done, and it is generally thought today that the most useful analogies can be drawn from linguistics and the social sciences – especially from the latter.

Louis Hjelmslev, in the essay titled 'An Introduction to Linguistics' (1937), discussed the differences between the broad view of linguistic systems and the regional study of linguistic change: the latter he called 'idiodiachrony,' as opposed to 'padiachrony.' Similarly, the concern of the historian of European literature is with 'pandiachronic' objects of study, such as movements and currents. At the same time, the peculiar 'complexity' of his task is such that the relationships between these different currents or processes, on the one hand, and between literary history and what I have been calling the other 'species' of history, on the other, are continuing problems. [. . .]

To be sure, it is absurd to conceive of the history of literature as a kind of separate 'current,' while social institutions and economic conditions run their own 'parallel' but distinct courses. The impact of the latter on the workings of the poetic imagination is constant as well as crucial. On the other hand, it is equally absurd to overlook the extraordinary continuity of literary forms – to assume that every year poetry is reborn, like the Phoenix, from its ashes. (This essential continuity, as I said earlier, is what a history of *new* works only, instead of systems, fails to render impressively enough.) A writer's response to his social experiences and origins, which I do not underestimate, but which I assume implies a contact between intelligible processes, may take the form of the revolutionary use of an inherited medium such as the novel, and thus be simultaneously (Robbe-Grillet is a good example) an answer to fresh social conditions and a link within the internal history of the literary system to which the novel belongs. As Madame de Staël suggested long ago, and Harry Levin has decisively shown for us, literature is an 'institution.' This does not mean that it should be confused with other institutions. The very opposite is intended – and left-wing critics can ill afford to forget that literature has been one of the most formidable, durable, and self-perpetuating of all historical institutions. [. . .]

'Integration,' or 'cultural integration,' is a characteristic term used by some anthropologists to designate the forces working for order and coherence in a culture otherwise based on a certain structural differentiation. It has the merit of implying the passage of time. Though 'pattern,' for example, is a merely structural term, integration has the added meaning of 'process behind structure.' These are instructive concepts for us, insofar as our task consists, I think, in retaining recent advances in the idea of structure while rewinding, so to speak, the clock of historical time. Our ideal literary historian, like the student of cultures, is a 'structural diachronicist.' This being said, the further and more arduous question arises of whether structural relations are, as it were, reciprocal; or as I suggested earlier, of whether we have in mind for literary history a 'domination model' or an 'interaction model.' Marxist literary critics, for example, who often are structural diachronicists, may postulate that all correlations between economic or technological structures and literary structures follow the same direction, and thus manifest a kind of instrumentality on the part of the verbal imagination. This is a pure instance of the domination model. On the other hand, Marxists are also interested in 'ideology', in the disparity between theory and practice, values and behavior. They show that these disparities can be acknowledged, 'healed,' or contradicted by the artist, so that a process of clarification or even of *liberation* may begin, through the constraints of artistic form. As a militant old liberal, Georg Brandes, said a century ago, 'a nation has a literature in order that its horizon may be widened and its theories of life confronted with life.'

(Claudio Guillén, *Literature as System* (Princeton NJ: Princeton UP, 1971), pp. 483–4, 505–6.)

CHAPTER 3

SOCIETY

Many different kinds of study lay claim to the title 'sociology of literature'. They include the following: (1) literary criticism which uses a social-historical perspective (e.g. Raymond Williams' *The Country and the City*, 1973, and Malcolm Bradbury's *The Social Context of Modern English Literature*, 1971); (2) the use of literature as social document (e.g. Lewis Coser's *Sociology through Literature*, 1963); (3) studies of the sociology of writers and of book production (e.g. Robert Escarpit, *Sociologie de la littérature*, 1958). The first category is the broadest and easiest to assimilate to critical practice. All the approaches criticize formalism for isolating writers and their works from the societies which provide the facilitating or limiting environment from which they emerge. The historical era into which writers are born will inevitably establish conditions which they cannot absolutely transcend, whatever myths of genius we may cultivate (see II,2). The development of book production and distribution, class structure, the formal and informal institutions for the dissemination of 'taste' or ideas, and prevailing social values, are just some of the 'social' conditions which will affect the viability of authors' careers.

Social criticism of literature in all periods often takes the form of comment upon shifts in cultural values following social change. After the Civil Wars following Julius Caesar's assassination the Roman poet Horace celebrated a new period of classicism, in which refinement and moral strictness were expressed in literary style. The crudities of Lucilian satire were replaced by the nuances of Horatian raillery. Similarly after the English Civil Wars the early Augustan poets celebrated the growing refinement which was associated with a court newly arrived from exile in France where 'eloquence' and 'conversation'

were cultivated. The vulgarity and moral earnestness of the
Puritans is replaced by a light-hearted and elegant 'good sense'.
John Dennis, in the early eighteenth century looks back with
nostalgia on these halcyon days of Charles II before middle-class
earnestness reasserted itself. He complains that the skills of satire
and comedy are lost in the new cultural desert of business and
politics.

Marx never formulated a sociology of art, but his incidental
discussions of literature and art concern a wide range of
aesthetic, political and economic issues. His study of commodity
production draws attention to the writer's insertion in the
capitalist economy. Great literature is not necessarily
'productive' from the capitalist point of view. An interesting
sidelight on his comments on Milton is the fact that the
professional writer was indeed slow to evolve within the
capitalist economy. The reliance on patronage continued well
into the eighteenth century. This aristocratic system continued
for a time alongside the new 'market' system. 'Grub Street'
symbolized the exploitative side of the capitalist book trade,
although many 'hacks' combined writing with another profession.

During the 1930s German Marxism was forced into complex
and 'aestheticized' responses to the Fascist takeover. The
Frankfurt School (especially Adorno, Marcuse and Horkheimer)
treated art and literature as a privileged region, the only one
resistant to totalitarianism. Adorno believed that serious art,
unlike popular art which tended to collude with prevailing
ideologies, was set apart from reality, and its detachment
allowed it to criticize reality not by direct reflection but by
providing a 'negative' image of the alienated and fragmented
condition of modern society. Walter Benjamin had a brief
association with Adorno, but his highly personal brand of
Marxism (especially his view of modern culture) contradicted the
Frankfurt School. In 'The Work of Art in the Age of Mechanical
Reproduction' he argues that modern technical innovations
(cinema, radio, and so on) have profoundly altered the status of
the 'work of art'. Once, artistic works had an 'aura' derived
from their uniqueness, but the new media shatter this quasi-
religious feeling about the arts. The technologies for reproducing
art objects encourage a more politically open arena for art. On
the other hand, he was aware that the new technology was only
potentially revolutionary. His outlook was nearer to Brecht than
to Adorno who saw modern media as producing merely a
cheapening and commercialization of art. Like Brecht, Benjamin

believed that it was necessary for artists to respond to their modern situation by revolutionizing the artistic forces of production (compare Brecht, I,2,E). This technical innovation arises, he argued, in direct response to a complex historical combination of social and technical changes. Paris, the anonymous great city of the Second Empire, was the subject of Baudelaire's and Poe's writings. Their technical innovations were a direct reaction to the asocial and fragmented conditions of urban existence. The petit-bourgeois citizens living under a 'satiated reactionary regime' find pleasure in haunting the arcades of the city. The arcades are microcosms of the world of commodity production, where the *flâneur* strolls in a mood of intoxication with the spirit of commodity capitalism. The literary product of this cultural cluster is the *feuilleton* – the modest paperbacked book of the market place.

Malcolm Bradbury attempts to provide a sociology of modern literature which does not yield to the harrowing pessimism of the Frankfurt School or the millenial vision of Benjamin. He reminds us that, on the one hand, the bourgeois humanism of Victorian society produced expansive and confident literature and that, on the other hand, the 'alienation' of modern artists is not necessarily a sign of their impotence in the face of social fragmentation but rather the inner condition of their creativity. Bradbury secretes into the myth of the alienated modern writer a version of the religious 'fortunate fall'; civilization's fall from human wholeness provides the writer with a '*fortunate* disability'. Alienation, like sin, is a foundation for good works. Bradbury recognizes that for some artists modern civilization projects an emptiness and nothingness, but it is evident that the liberal in Bradbury prefers the redemptive image of art.

Background reading

Elizabeth and Tom Burns (eds), *Sociology of Literature and Drama: Selected Readings* (Harmondsworth: Penguin Books, 1973).

Centre for Contemporary Cultural Studies (Birmingham University), *Working Papers in Cultural Studies* (Birmingham: CCCS, 1971–), esp. no. 6 (1974).

Robert Escarpit, *Sociology of Literature* (London: Frank Cass, 1971).

Stuart Hall, 'Cultural Studies: Two Paradigms', in *Culture, Ideology and Social Process*, ed. Tony Bennett *et al.* (London: Batsford, 1981).

Richard Hoggart, 'Contemporary Cultural Studies: An Approach to the Study of Literature and Society', in *Contemporary Criticism*, ed. Malcolm Bradbury and David Palmer (London: Arnold, 1970).

Martin Jay, *The Dialectical Imagination: A History of the Frankfurt School* (London: Heinemann, 1973), ch. 6: 'Aesthetic Theory and the Critique of Mass Culture'.

Jacques Leenhart, 'The Sociology of Literature: Some Stages in its History', *The International Social Science Journal*, 19 (1967).

(A) JOHN DENNIS

'A Large Account of the Taste in Poetry, and the Causes of the Degeneracy of It' (1702)

But now, as Parts, Education and Application are necessary to succeed in the writing Poetry, they are requisite in some degree for the forming a true judgment of it. No man can judge of a Beautiful imagination in another, without some degree of it in himself. And as for the judging rightly of any thing without Judgment, that is a contradiction in terms. And if Philosophy and a knowledge of the World are necessary to a Comic Poet, for his forming his Characters; if an acquaintance with the best Authors among the Ancients and Moderns, be requisite for the attaining the Vivacity and Grace of the Dialogue; why, then for the forming a true judgement of these, the same Learning and the same Experience are necessary. And lastly, if a Poet had need to have his mind free, that he may the more thoroughly enter into the concerns of the Theatre, and put on the Passions and Humours of his different Characters, so as to make them by turns his own; why the Spectator, that he may judge whether the Author does this or no, must enter into those Passions and Humours in some proportionable degree, and consequently ought to have his mind free from all avocations of Business, and from all real vexatious Passions.

Having premis'd all this, we shall now come to show: first, that in the Reign of King *Charles* the Second, a considerable part of an Audience had those Parts, that Education and that Application, which were requisite for the judging of Poetry, and that they who had not were influenced by the authority of those who had; and secondly, that in the present Reign very few in an Audience have the forementioned qualifications; and that those who have them not have not the advantage to be influenced by the authority of those who have.

First then, in the Reign of King *Charles* the Second, a considerable part of an Audience had those parts, which were requisite for the judging of Comedy. And we have shown above that those parts comprehend principally a fine Imagination and a sound Judgment. Well, but says an Objector, Are not the Imaginations and Judgements of Mankind the same that they were then, or is Humane Nature decay'd since the Reign of *Charles* the Second? To which I answer, that the capacity of imagining and of judging have been in all Ages equal in Mankind. But then this is certain, that the faculties of the Soul, like the parts of the Body, receive nourishment from use, and derive skill as well as they do force and vigour from exercise. Now I leave to any one to judge whether the imaginative faculty of the Soul must be more exercised in a Reign of Poetry and of Pleasure, or in a Reign of Politics and of Business. [. . .]

Secondly, then in the Reign of King *Charles* the Second, a considerable part of an Audience had such an Education as qualified them to judge of Comedy. That Reign was a Reign of Pleasure – even the entertainments of their Closet were all delightful. Poetry and Eloquence were then their Studies, and that human, gay, and sprightly Philosophy, which qualify'd them to relish the only reasonable pleasures which man can have in the World, and those are Conversation and Dramatic Poetry. In their Closets they cultivated at once their Imaginations and Judgements, to make themselves the fitter for conversation, which requires them both. And the Conversation of those times was so different from what it is now, that it let them as much into that particular knowledge of Mankind, which is requisite for the judging of Comedy, as the present Conversation removes us from it. The discourse, which now everywhere turns upon Interest, rolled then upon the Manners and Humours of Men. For let us take a little view of the state of the Nation, during the Reign of that Prince, from the year Sixty to Eighty. They were overjoy'd to find themselves delivered from the apprehensions of another Civil War, and not only in quiet, but as they thought, in profound security. They were at the same time free from Fears and Taxes, and by reason of that plenty which overflowed among them, they were in the happiest condition in the World, to attain to that knowledge of Mankind, which is requisite for the judging of Comedy. For while some were dissolv'd in the wantonness of ease, and grown careless how they exposed themselves, others were at leisure to observe their frailties; to watch the turns and counterturns of their Humours, and trace the windings of them up to their very springs. All the sheer Originals in Town were known, and in some measure copied.

But now the case is vastly different. For all those great and numerous Originals are reduced to one single Coxcomb, and that is the foolish false Politician. For from *Westminster* to *Wapping*, go where you will, the conversation turns upon Politics. Where-ever you go, you find Atheists and Rakes standing up for the Protestant Religion, Fellows who never saw a Groat in their Lives vehemently maintaining Property, and People that are in the *Fleet* and the *Kings Bench* upon execution for their Lives going together by the ears about the Liberty of the Subject.

(John Dennis, 'A Large Account of the Taste in Poetry, and the Causes of the Degeneracy of It', *The Comical Gallant* (London, 1702), sig. a2^v–a3^r, a3^r–a3^v.)

(B) KARL MARX

'Theories of Surplus Value' (1905)

These definitions [of labour] are therefore not derived from the material characteristics of labour (neither from the nature of its product nor from the particular character of the labour as concrete labour), but from the definite social form, the social relations of production, within which the labour is realised. An actor, for example, or even a clown, according to this definition, is a productive labourer if he works in the service of a capitalist (an entrepreneur) to whom he returns more labour than he receives from him in the form of wages; while a jobbing tailor who comes to the capitalist's house and patches his trousers for him, producing a mere use-value for him, is an unproductive labourer. The former's labour is exchanged with capital, the latter's with revenue. The former's labour produces a surplus-value; in the latter's, revenue is consumed.

Productive and unproductive labour in here throughout conceived from *the standpoint of the possessor of money, from the standpoint of the capitalist*, not from that of the *workman*; hence the nonsense written by Ganihl, etc., who have so little understanding of the matter that they raise the question whether the labour or service or function of the prostitute, flunkey, etc., brings in returns. A writer is a productive labourer not in so far as he produces ideas, but in so far as he enriches the publisher who publishes his works, or if he is a wage-labourer for a capitalist. [. . .]

The same kind of labour may be *productive* or *unproductive*.

For example Milton, who wrote *Paradise Lost* for five pounds, was an *unproductive labourer*. On the other hand, the writer who turns out stuff for his publisher in factory style, is a *productive labourer*. Milton produced *Paradise Lost* for the same reason that a silk worm produces silk. It was an activity of *his* nature. Later he sold the product for £5. But the literary proletarian of Leipzig, who fabricates books (for example, Compendia of Economics) under the direction of his publisher, is a *productive labourer*; for his product is from the outset subsumed under capital, and comes into being only for the purpose of increasing that capital. A singer who sells her song for her own account is an *unproductive labourer*. But the same singer commissioned by an entrepreneur to sing in order to make money for him is a *productive labourer*; for she produces capital.

(Karl Marx, 'Theories of Surplus Value' (1905), *On Literature and Art* (Moscow: Progress Publishers, 1976), pp. 143–4.)

(C) WALTER BENJAMIN

'The Flâneur', *Charles Baudelaire, A Lyric Poet in the Era of High Capitalism* (1969)

Once a writer had entered the marketplace, he looked around as in a diorama. A special literary genre has preserved his first attempts at orienting himself. It is a panorama literature. It was not by chance that *Le Livre des cent-et-un*, *Les Français peints par eux-mêmes*, *Le Diable à Paris*, *La Grande Ville* enjoyed the favour of the capital city at the same time as the dioramas. These books consist of individual sketches which, as it were, reproduce the plastic foreground of those panoramas with their anecdotal form and the extensive background of the panoramas with their store of information. Numerous authors contributed to these volumes. Thus these anthologies are products of the same belletristic collective work for which Girardin had procured an outlet in the *feuilleton*. They were the salon attire of a literature which fundamentally was designed to be sold in the streets. In this literature, the modest-looking, paperbound, pocket-size volumes called 'physiologies' had pride of place. They investigated types that might be encountered by a person taking a look at the marketplace. [. . .]

The leisurely quality of these descriptions fits the style of the *flâneur* who goes botanizing on the asphalt. But even in those days it was not possible to stroll about everywhere in the city. Before Haussmann wide pavements were rare, and the narrow ones afforded little protection from vehicles. Strolling could hardly have assumed the importance it did without the arcades. 'The arcades, a rather recent invention of industrial luxury,' so says an illustrated guide to Paris of 1852, 'are glass-covered, marble-panelled passageways through entire complexes of houses whose proprietors have combined for such speculations. Both sides of these passageways, which are lighted from above, are lined with the most elegant shops, so that such an arcade is a city, even a world, in miniature.' It is in this world that the *flâneur* is at home; he provides 'the favourite sojourn of the strollers and the smokers, the stamping ground of all sorts of little *métiers*', with its chronicler and its philosopher. As for himself, he obtains there the unfailing remedy for the kind of boredom that easily arises under the baleful eyes of a satiated reactionary regime. In the words of Guys as quoted by Baudelaire, 'Anyone who is capable of being bored in a crowd is a blockhead. I repeat: a blockhead, and a contemptible one.' The arcades were a cross between a street and an *intérieur*. If one can speak of an artistic device of the physiologies, it is the proven device of the *feuilleton*, namely, to turn a boulevard into an *intérieur*. The street becomes a dwelling for the *flâneur*; he is as much at home among the façades of houses as a citizen is in his four walls. To him the shiny, enamelled signs of businesses are at least as good a wall ornament as an oil painting is to a bourgeois in his salon. The walls are the desk against which he presses his notebooks; news-stands are his libraries and the terraces of cafés are the balconies from which he looks down on his household after his work is done. That life in all its variety and inexhaustible wealth of variations can thrive only among the grey cobblestones and against the grey background of despotism was the political secret on which the physiologies were based. [. . .]

On his peregrinations the man of the crowd lands at a late hour in a department store where there still are many customers. He moves about like someone who knows his way around the place. Were there multi-storied department stores in Poe's day? No matter; Poe lets the restless man spend an 'hour and a half, or thereabouts' in this bazaar. 'He entered shop after shop, priced nothing, spoke no word, and looked at all objects with a wild and vacant stare.' If the arcade is the classical form of the

intérieur, which is how the *flâneur* sees the street, the department
store is the form of the *intérieur*'s decay. The bazaar is the last
hangout of the *flâneur*. If in the beginning the street had become
an *intérieur* for him, now this *intérieur* turned into a street, and he
roamed through the labyrinth of merchandise as he had once
roamed through the labyrinth of the city. It is a magnificent
touch in Poe's story ['The Man of the Crowd'] that it includes
along with the earliest description of the *flâneur* the figuration of
his end.

Jules Laforgue said about Baudelaire that he was the first to
speak of Paris 'as someone condemned to live in the capital day
after day.' He might have said that he was the first to speak
also of the opiate that was available to give relief to men so
condemned, and only to them. The crowd is not only the newest
asylum of outlaws; it is also the latest narcotic for those
abandoned. The *flâneur* is someone abandoned in the crowd. In
this he shares the situation of the commodity. He is not aware of
this special situation, but this does not diminish its effect on him
and it permeates him blissfully like a narcotic that can
compensate him for many humiliations. The intoxication to
which the *flâneur* surrenders is the intoxication of the commodity
around which surges the stream of customers.

If the soul of the commodity which Marx occasionally
mentions in jest existed, it would be the most empathetic ever
encountered in the realm of souls, for it would have to see in
everyone the buyer in whose hand and house it wants to nestle.
Empathy is the nature of the intoxication to which the *flâneur*
abandons himself in the crowd.

(Walter Benjamin, *Charles Baudelaire: A Lyric Poet in the Era of High
Capitalism*, trans. by Harry Zohn (New Left Books, 1973), pp. 35, 36–7,
54–5. Original German was published by Suhrkamp Verlag, Frankfurt,
1969.)

'The Work of Art in the Age of Mechanical Reproduction' (1955)

The presence of the original is the prerequisite of the concept of
authenticity. Chemical analyses of the patina of a bronze can
help to establish this, as does the proof that a given manuscript
of the Middle Ages stems from an archive of the fifteenth
century. The whole sphere of authenticity is outside technical –
and, of course, not only technical – reproducibility [. . .]

The situations into which the product of mechanical reproduction can be brought may not touch the actual work of art, yet the quality of its presence is always depreciated. This holds not only for the art work but also, for instance, for a landscape which passes in review before the spectator in a movie. In the case of the art object, a most sensitive nucleus – namely, its authenticity – is interfered with whereas no natural object is vulnerable on that score. The authenticity of a thing is the essence of all that is transmissible from its beginning, ranging from its substantive duration to its testimony to the history which it has experienced. Since the historical testimony rests on the authenticity, the former, too, is jeopardized by reproduction when substantive duration ceases to matter. And what is really jeopardized when the historical testimony is affected is the authority of the object.

One might subsume the eliminated element in the term 'aura' and go on to say: that which withers in the age of mechanical reproduction is the aura of the work of art. This is a symptomatic process whose significance points beyond the realm of art. One might generalize by saying: the technique of reproduction detaches the reproduced object from the domain of tradition. By making many reproductions it substitutes a plurality of copies for a unique existence. And in permitting the reproduction to meet the beholder or listener in his own particular situation, it reactivates the object reproduced. These two processes lead to a tremendous shattering of tradition which is the obverse of the contemporary crisis and renewal of mankind. Both processes are intimately connected with the contemporary mass movements. Their most powerful agent is the film. Its social significance, particularly in its most positive form, is inconceivable without its destructive, cathartic aspect, that is, the liquidation of the traditional value of the cultural heritage. [. . .]

The concept of aura which was proposed above with reference to historical objects may usefully be illustrated with reference to the aura of natural ones. We define the aura of the latter as the unique phenomenon of a distance, however close it may be. If, while resting on a summer afternoon, you follow with your eyes a mountain range on the horizon or a branch which casts its shadow over you, you experience the aura of those mountains, of the branch. This image makes it easy to comprehend the social bases of the contemporary decay of the aura. It rests on two circumstances, both of which are related to the increasing significance of the masses in contemporary life. Namely, the desire of contemporary masses to bring things 'closer' spatially and humanly, which is just as ardent as their bent toward overcoming the uniqueness of every reality by accepting its reproduction. [. . .]

The uniqueness of a work of art is inseparable from its being imbedded in the fabric of tradition. This tradition itself is thoroughly alive and extremely changeable. An ancient statue of Venus, for example, stood in a different traditional context with the Greeks, who made it an object of veneration, than with the clerics of the Middle Ages, who viewed it as an ominous idol. Both of them, however, were equally confronted with its uniqueness, that is, its aura. Originally the contextual integration of art in tradition found its expression in the cult. We know that the earliest art works originated in the service of a ritual – first the magical, then the religious kind. It is significant that the existence of the work of art with reference to its aura is never entirely separated from its ritual function. In other words, the unique value of the 'authentic' work of art has its basis in ritual, the location of its original use value. This ritualistic basis, however remote, is still recognizable as secularized ritual even in the most profane forms of the cult of beauty. The secular cult of beauty, developed during the Renaissance and prevailing for three centuries, clearly showed that ritualistic basis in its decline and the first deep crisis which befell it. With the advent of the first truly revolutionary means of reproduction, photography, simultaneously with the rise of socialism, art sensed the approaching crisis which has become evident a century later. At the time, art reacted with the doctrine of *l'art pour l'art*, that is, with a theology of art. This gave rise to what might be called a negative theology in the form of the idea of 'pure' art, which not only denied any social function of art but also any categorizing by subject matter. (In poetry, Mallarmé was the first to take this position.)

An analysis of art in the age of mechanical reproduction must do justice to these relationships, for they lead us to an all-important insight: for the first time in world history, mechanical reproduction emancipates the work of art from its parasitical dependence on ritual. To an ever greater degree the work of art reproduced becomes the work of art designed for reproducibility. From a photographic negative, for example, one can make any number of prints; to ask for the 'authentic' print makes no sense. But the instant the criterion of authenticity ceases to be applicable to artistic production, the total function of art is reversed. Instead of being based on ritual, it begins to be based on another practice – politics.

(Walter Benjamin, 'The Work of Art in the Age of Mechanical Reproduction', *Illuminations*, trans. Harry Zohn (London: Jonathan Cape, 1970), pp. 222, 223, 224–5, 225–6. Original German published by Suhrkamp Verlag, Frankfurt, 1955.)

(D) MALCOLM BRADBURY

The Social Context of Modern English Literature (1971)

In liberal western society, then, the artist's role is recognized and respected but it is not institutionalized; it functions on a *laissez-faire* basis. If he can find the means to exist, in the economics of the market or by some form of patronage, he has great independence of creative action. He need not live in the same country as his audience or serve them in any other way than by impersonal publication. He can, through that market, make considerable profit and win considerable prestige. The situation has been one favourable to the production of a major art, expansive, varied, original, qualitatively and humanly dense and rich. The classically successful environment for the liberal artist is of course that of the nineteenth century: in that environment art became a centrally independent way of knowing, acquiring many of the functions formerly associated with religion and religious wisdom, enlightening men and alleviating their sorrows, advancing their comprehension and their sensibilities. To read any major study of the mid-Victorian literary scene – for instance, Gordon Haight's recent brilliant life of George Eliot – is to discover how a liberal exercise of the artistic function could produce writing consonant with the shared intellectual and emotional activity of a literate, intelligent and inquisitive middle class. That sort of expanding community between a freely placed writer and an audience themselves humanistically engaged with art obviously represents an ideal version of the liberal relationship between artist and society. But this humanist view of art – an art that contained and lived alongside man, enlarging his conduct and sympathies, testifying to his humanity, introducing him to sectors of the world of which he had no experience, serving as a secular and open-ended wisdom – now seems to us to have been thrown into doubt. A number of important modern writers have embodied it with a profound authority – E. M. Forster or George Orwell, for instance – but many have not.

Hence another aspect of our modern view of the arts. For, while we believe that art should and can be free, we also believe that we live in a time and society exceptionally difficult for the production of art – a view that has also played a big part in our expectation about writers and the work they give us. I have shown that there are sound enough reasons for this belief, just as there are for the conviction that the free writer has the profoundest significance for us. Now both of these two views – that writers are free, and that they live in profoundly unfortunate circumstances – reach back to the Romantic movement, in this country and even more in America, Russia or France. For the right to freedom was often held to involve a necessary quest into loneliness, and to involve a risky journey into the dangerous, Promethean dimensions of artistic knowledge. [. . .]

The 'liberal' situation of the artist in our century, then, has hardly been that of the liberal artist of the past. It is hardly surprising, therefore, that our tolerance sometimes has a bemused air to it, as our humanistic expectations are persistently baffled. Indeed it may be that we as readers have lost some of those humanistic expectations ourselves. [. . .]

Something of the broad change in temper I am trying to convey can be suggested by comparing the words which have had vogue for describing the sense of distance between the liberal writer and society. Matthew Arnold's word, which obviously represented a deep nineteenth-century value, was *disinterestedness*, and by it he meant to say that the writer was independent of particular class or sectarian interests in society, particular social needs and urgencies, and committed to the ideal realm of art and the wish to make it prevail in society. The modern word is more commonly *alienation*, a word so over-used, in political, psychological and religious connotations, as to be almost beyond definition. We may use it to suggest the emptiness and lack of resources of the modern writer, the deprivation of funds that he needs to create an adequate art; or we may mean it, much more honorifically, to suggest that internal independence and scepticism which enables him to *create* an adequate art. Then again we may refer to a detachment which is separate from society in wanting to rebuke it, reform it, and make it liberally whole again; or we may be speaking of a revolutionary alienation which seeks a totally different state of affairs in which liberalism has no place at all. So we may be speaking of the artist or intellectual who seeks to preserve a disinterested overview of society in order to maintain that kind of spirit and value that belongs to the inheritance of liberal art; or we may be referring to an absolute and thorough-going nihilism in artists for whom plight, degradation and despair are a *modus vivendi*. There have been innumerable accounts – some of them literary-historical, some psychological, some sociological; but what is striking about most of them is that they assume the state to be likely or inevitable. And though there is normally an assumption of neurosis or social dislocation, there is a tendency to associate this with the *fortunate* disability. Edmund Wilson, in his title-essay in *The Wound and the Bow*, cites the classical story of Philoctetes as a myth of the artist: isolated by his wound, he is redeemed by his skill with his bow – the power of artistic creativity. In short, we can take alienation as a force from outside, driving the writer away and into exile; or we can regard it as something internal and structural to the artistic condition in particular individuals or in artists generally, that quality Plato saw in the poet which made him a dangerous member of his ideal Republic.

(Malcolm Bradbury, *The Social Context of Modern English Literature* (Oxford: Blackwell, 1971) pp. 114–15, 118, 119–20.)

CHAPTER 4

IDEOLOGY

The concept of 'ideology' is one of the most contentious in modern thought. The Marxist tradition has evolved several senses of the term. At its simplest level ideology refers to the forms of social consciousness (political, religious, aesthetic, and so on) which both legitimate the ruling class and express their interests. These 'representations' (for example of the 'free individual', 'the welfare state', or 'the market') embody the roles and images which fix individuals to their social functions. According to Gramsci the ruling classes exercise a 'hegemony' over the other classes largely through an ideological domination which includes a mastery over the people's 'common sense'.

The question of the relations between literature and ideology has been long debated. One solution ('vulgar Marxism') is to see literature as merely the expression of dominant ideologies. Writers are unable to see the truth about their societies because they are caught up in the 'false consciousness' of ideology. Others (e.g. Eagleton) have argued that ideology is not such a simple 'screen' projecting the illusions of the bourgeoisie. Louis Althusser wrote that we are all the 'subjects' of ideology, which summons us to take our places in the social structure. This 'interpellation' works through the material 'State Apparatuses' in religion, education, the law, and so on. His theory of ideology 'in general' describes the way ideology is reproduced in all societies. He defines ideology as 'a representation of the imaginary relationship of individuals to their real conditions of existence'. This 'imaginary' consciousness helps us to make sense of the world, but also masks or represses our real relationship to it. The idea of 'freedom', for example, promotes the belief in the freedom of all men, including labourers, but it masks the 'real relations' of liberal capitalist economies. A dominant system of ideology is accepted as a common-sense view of things by the dominated classes and thus the interests of the dominant classes are secured. However, art is not simply an expression of ideology, according to Althusser.

Engels' well-known letter to Margaret Harkness argued that socialist novelists should avoid political tendentiousness. He added that even reactionary writers of realistic fiction appear to transcend their political commitments. It is as though 'realism' itself guarantees a certain detachment in the author and an ability to penetrate the structure of his or her society. Balzac, supporter of the Bourbon dynasty, is, in his fiction, 'compelled to go against his class sympathies'. Althusser accepts Engels' argument but transforms it by attributing this transcendence to art itself rather than to the writer. He refuses, in his 'Letter on Art', to treat great literature as mere ideology. He assigns it instead to a region somewhere between 'knowledge' and ideology. Art can achieve this, because it is able to effect a 'retreat' (a fictional 'distance') from the very ideology which feeds it.

Pierre Macherey's *A Theory of Literary Production* (1966) influenced Althusser's letter. According to Macherey, when that state of consciousness we call ideology enters the literary text it takes on a different form. Ideology is normally lived as if it were totally natural, as if its 'imaginary' discourse gives a perfect explanation of reality. However, once ideology is worked into a text all its contradictions and gaps are exposed. The critic must act like a psychoanalyst and attend to what the text is *not saying* – must read the text 'symptomatically' for its unconscious repressions. Macherey agrees with Althusser about literary texts' ability to go beyond the mere expression of an ideology: 'the text constructs a determinate image of the ideological, revealing it as an object rather than living it from within'. Art enables us to *see* ideology (which otherwise tends to remain invisible in its obviousness). Literature is able to achieve this distantiation through *literary form*.

Terry Eagleton's first theoretical work (*Criticism and Ideology*, 1976) rejects Althusser's and Macherey's 'privileging' of art, but nevertheless uses their general account of ideology. He argues that texts do not reflect historical reality but rather work upon ideology to produce the *effect* of the real. A novel appears to be free in its use of reality (it invents characters and events), but this is an illusion, since it is not free in its use of ideology. In taking ideology as its material (not 'reality') a novel reworks it ('produces' it, as a director 'produces' a play text) in an imaginative form. Thus the text works on reality at two removes. Literary criticism becomes the theory of 'the laws of the production of ideological discourses as literature'. It should be noted that more recently Eagleton has abandoned this Althusserian perspective for a less 'scientific' and a more 'political' form of Marxist criticism, following in the footsteps of Brecht and Benjamin.

Background reading

Steve Burniston and Chris Weedon, 'Ideology, Subjectivity and the Artistic Text', *Working Papers in Cultural Studies*, no. 10 (1977), 203–33.

Terry Eagleton, 'Pierre Macherey and the Theory of Literary Production', *The Minnesota Review*, no. 5 (1975), 134–44.

Terry Eagleton, *Criticism and Ideology* (London: New Left Books, 1976).

'Ideology and Literature', special issue of *New Literary History*, 4 (1973).

Colin Mercer, 'Culture and Ideology in Gramsci', *Red Letters*, no. 8 (1978), 19–40.

Michel Pêcheux, *Language, Semantics and Ideology*, trans. H. Nagpal (London: Macmillan, 1982).

(A) WILLIAM BLAKE

The Marriage of Heaven and Hell (1790)

The ancient Poets animated all sensible objects with Gods or Geniuses, calling them by the names and adorning them with the properties of woods, rivers, mountains, lakes, cities, nations, and whatever their enlarged & numerous senses could perceive.

And particularly they studied the genius of each city & country, placing it under its mental deity;

Till a system was formed, which some took advantage of, & enslav'd the vulgar by attempting to realize or abstract the mental deities from their objects: thus began Priesthood;

Choosing forms of worship from poetic tales.

And at length they pronounc'd that the Gods had order'd such things.

Thus men forgot that All deities reside in the human breast.

(William Blake, *The Marriage of Heaven and Hell* (1790).)

(B) FRIEDRICH ENGELS

Letter to Margaret Harkness, April 1888

If I have anything to criticise, it would be that perhaps, after all, the tale is not quite realistic enough. Realism, to my mind, implies, besides truth of detail, the truthful reproduction of typical characters under typical circumstances. Now your characters are typical enough, as far as they go; but the circumstances which surround them and make them act, are not perhaps equally so. In the *City Girl* the working class figures as a passive mass, unable to help itself and not even showing (making) any attempt at striving to help itself. All attempts to drag it out of its torpid misery come from without, from above. Now if this was a correct description about 1800 or 1810, in the days of Saint-Simon and Robert Owen, it cannot appear so in 1887 to a man who for nearly fifty years has had the honour of sharing in most of the fights of the militant proletariat. The rebellious reaction of the working class against the oppressive medium which surrounds them, their attempts – convulsive, half conscious or conscious – at recovering their status as human beings, belong to history and must therefore lay claim to a place in the domain of realism.

I am far from finding fault with your not having written a point-blank socialist novel, a 'Tendenzroman' [problem novel], as we Germans call it, to glorify the social and political views of the authors. That is not at all what I mean. The more the opinions of the author remain hidden, the better for the work of art. The realism I allude to may crop out even in spite of the author's opinions. Let me refer to an example. Balzac whom I consider a far greater master of realism than all the Zolas *passés, présents et à venir*, in *La Comédie humaine* gives us a most wonderfully realistic history of French 'Society', especially of '*le monde parisien*', describing, chronicle-fashion, almost year by year from 1816 to 1848 the progressive inroads of the rising bourgeoisie upon the society of nobles, that reconstituted itself after 1815 and that set up again, as far as it could, the standard of *la vieille politesse française*. He describes how the last remnants of this, to him, model society gradually succumbed before the intrusion of the vulgar moneyed upstart, or were corrupted by him; how the grande dame whose conjugal infidelities were but a mode of asserting herself in perfect accordance with the way she had been disposed of in marriage, gave way to the bourgeoisie, who horned her husband for cash or cashmere; and around this central picture he groups a complete history of French Society from which, even in economic details (for instance the re-arrangement of real and personal property after the Revolution) I have learned more than from all the professed historians, economists and statisticians of the period together. Well, Balzac was politically a Legitimist [supporter of the Bourbon dynasty]; his great work is a constant elegy on the irretrievable decay of good society, his sympathies are all with the class doomed to extinction. But for all that his satire is never keener, his irony never bitterer, than when he sets in motion the very men and women with whom he sympathises most deeply – the nobles. And the only men of whom he always speaks with undisguised admiration, are his bitterest political antagonists, the republican heroes of the Cloître Saint-Méry, the men, who at that.time (1830–36) were indeed the representatives of the popular masses. That Balzac thus was compelled to go against his own class sympathies and political prejudices, that he *saw* the necessity of the downfall of his favourite nobles, and described them as people deserving no better fate; and that he *saw* the real men of the future where, for the time being, they alone were to be found – that I consider one of the greatest triumphs of Realism, and one of the grandest features in old Balzac.

(Friedrich Engels, Letter to Margaret Harkness, April 1888, *On Art and Literature* (Moscow: Progress Publishers, 1976), pp. 90–2.)

(C) LOUIS ALTHUSSER

'A Letter on Art in Reply to André Daspre' (1966)

Art (I mean authentic art, not works of an average or mediocre level) does not give us a *knowledge* in the *strict sense*, it therefore does not replace knowledge (in the modern sense: scientific knowledge), but what it gives us does nevertheless maintain a certain *specific relationship* with knowledge. This relationship is not one of identity but one of difference. Let me explain. I believe that the peculiarity of art is to 'make us see' (*nous donner à voir*), 'make us perceive', 'make us feel' something which *alludes* to reality. If we take the case of the novel, Balzac or Solzhenitsyn, as you refer to them, they make us *see*, *perceive* (but not *know*) something which *alludes* to reality.

It is essential to take the words which make up this first provisional definition literally if we are to avoid lapsing into an identification of what art gives us and what science gives us. What art makes us *see*, and therefore gives to us in the form of '*seeing*', '*perceiving*' and '*feeling*' (which is not the form of *knowing*), is the *ideology* from which it is born, in which it bathes, from which it detaches itself as art, and to which it *alludes*. Macherey has shown this very clearly in the case of Tolstoy, by extending Lenin's analyses. Balzac and Solzhenitsyn give us a 'view' of the ideology to which their work alludes and with which it is constantly fed, a view which presupposes a *retreat*, an *internal distantiation* from the very ideology from which their novels emerged. They make us 'perceive' (but not know) in some sense *from the inside*, by an *internal distance*, the very ideology in which they are held.

(Louis Althusser, 'A Letter on Art in Reply to André Daspre' (1966), *Lenin and Philosophy and Other Essays*, trans. Ben Brewster (London: New Left Books, 1971), p. 204.)

'Ideology and Ideological State Apparatuses' (1969)

I say: the category of the subject is constitutive of all ideology, but at the same time and immediately I add that *the category of the subject is only constitutive of all ideology insofar as all ideology has the function (which defines it) of 'constituting' concrete individuals as subjects*. In the interaction of this double constitution exists the functioning of all ideology, ideology being nothing but its functioning in the material forms of existence of that functioning.

In order to grasp what follows, it is essential to realize that both he who is writing these lines and the reader who reads them are themselves subjects, and therefore ideological subjects (a tautological proposition), i.e. that the author and the reader of these lines both live 'spontaneously' or 'naturally' in ideology in the sense in which I have said that 'man is an ideological animal by nature'. [. . .]

To take a highly 'concrete' example, we all have friends who, when they knock on our door and we ask, through the door, the question 'Who's there?', answer (since 'it's obvious') 'It's me'. And we recognize that 'it is him', or 'her'. We open the door, and 'it's true, it really was she who was there'. To take another example, when we recognize somebody of our (previous) acquaintance ((*re*)-*connaissance*) in the street, we show him that we have recognized him (and have recognized that he has recognized us) by saying to him 'Hello, my friend', and shaking his hand (a material ritual practice of ideological recognition in everyday life – in France, at least; elsewhere, there are other rituals).

In this preliminary remark and these concrete illustrations, I only wish to point out that you and I are *always already* subjects, and as such constantly practise the rituals of ideological recognition, which guarantee for us that we are indeed concrete, individual, distinguishable and (naturally) irreplaceable subjects. The writing I am currently executing and the reading you are currently performing are also in this respect rituals of ideological recognition, including the 'obviousness' with which the 'truth' or 'error' of my reflections may impose itself on you.

But to recognize that we are subjects and that we function in the practical rituals of the most elementary everyday life (the hand-shake, the fact of calling you by your name, the fact of knowing, even if I do not know what it is, that you 'have' a name of your own, which means that you are recognized as a unique subject, etc.) – this recognition only gives us the 'consciousness' of our incessant (eternal) practice of ideological recognition – its consciousness, i.e its *recognition* – but in no sense does it give us the (scientific) *knowledge* of the mechanism of this recognition. Now it is this knowledge that we have to reach, if you will, while speaking in ideology, and from within ideology we have to outline a discourse which tries to break with ideology, in order to dare to be the beginning of a scientific (i.e. subjectless) discourse on ideology.

Thus in order to represent why the category of the 'subject' is constitutive of ideology, which only exists by constituting concrete subjects as subjects, I shall employ a special mode of exposition: 'concrete' enough to be recognized, but abstract enough to be thinkable and thought, giving rise to a knowledge.

As a first formulation I shall say: *all ideology hails or interpellates concrete individuals as concrete subjects*, by the functioning of the category of the subject.

This is a proposition which entails that we distinguish for the moment between concrete individuals on the one hand and concrete subjects on the other, although at this level concrete subjects only exist insofar as they are supported by a concrete individual.

I shall then suggest that ideology 'acts' or 'functions' in such a way that it 'recruits' subjects among the individuals (it recruits them all), or 'transforms' the individuals into subjects (it transforms them all) by that very precise operation which I have called *interpellation* or hailing, and which can be imagined along the lines of the most commonplace everyday police (or other) hailing: 'Hey, you there!' [. . .]

As the formal structure of all ideology is always the same, I shall restrict my analysis to a single example, one accessible to everyone, that of religious ideology, with the proviso that the same demonstration can be produced for ethical, legal, political, aesthetic ideology, etc.

Let us therefore consider the Christian religious ideology. I shall use a rhetorical figure and 'make it speak', i.e. collect into a fictional discourse what it 'says' not only in its two Testaments, its Theologians, Sermons, but also in its practices, its rituals, its ceremonies and its sacraments. The Christian religious ideology says something like this:

It says: I address myself to you, a human individual called Peter (every individual is called by his name, in the passive sense, it is never he who provides his own name), in order to tell you that God exists and that you are answerable to Him. It adds: God addresses himself to you through my voice (Scripture having collected the Word of God, Tradition having transmitted it, Papal Infallibility fixing it for ever on 'nice' points). It says: this is who you are: you are Peter! This is your origin, you were created by God for all eternity, although you were born in the 1920th year of Our Lord! This is your place in the world! This is what you must do! By these means, if you observe the 'law of love' you will be saved, you, Peter, and will become part of the Glorious Body of Christ! Etc. . . .

Now this is quite a familiar and banal discourse, but at the same time quite a surprising one.

Surprising because if we consider that religious ideology is indeed addressed to individuals, in order to 'transform them into subjects', by interpellating the individual, Peter, in order to make him a subject, free to obey or disobey the appeal, i.e. God's commandments; if it calls these individuals by their names, thus recognizing that they are always-already interpellated as subjects with a personal identity (to the extent that Pascal's Christ says: 'It is for you that I have shed this drop of my blood!'); if it interpellates them in such a way that the subject responds: '*Yes, it really is me!*' if it obtains from them the *recognition* that they really do occupy the place it designates for them as theirs in the world, a fixed residence: 'It really is me, I am here, a worker, a boss or a soldier!' in this vale of tears; if it obtains from them the recognition of a destination

(eternal life or damnation) according to the respect or contempt
they show to 'God's Commandments', Law become Love; – if
everything does happen in this way (in the practices of the well-
known rituals of baptism, confirmation, communion, confession
and extreme unction, etc. . . .), we should note that all this
'procedure' to set up Christian religious subjects is dominated by
a strange phenomenon: the fact that there can only be such a
multitude of possible religious subjects on the absolute condition
that there is a Unique, Absolute, *Other Subject*, i.e. God.

(Louis Althusser, 'Ideology and Ideological State Apparatuses' (1969),
ibid., pp. 160, 161–3, 165–6.)

(D) PIERRE MACHEREY

A Theory of Literary Production (1966)

The speech of the book comes from a certain silence, a matter
which it endows with form, a ground on which it traces a figure.
Thus, the book is not self-sufficient; it is necessarily accompanied
by a *certain absence*, without which it would not exist. A
knowledge of the book must include a consideration of this
absence.

This is why it seems useful and legitimate to ask of every
production what it tacitly implies, what it does not say. Either
all around or in its wake the explicit requires the implicit: for in
order to say anything, there are other things *which must not be
said*. Freud relegated this *absence of certain words* to a new place
which he was the first to explore, and which he paradoxically
named: the unconscious. To reach utterance, all speech envelops
itself in the unspoken. We must ask why it does not speak of
this interdict: can it be identified before one might wish to
acknowledge it? There is not even the slightest hint of the
absence of what it does not, perhaps cannot, say: the disavowal
(*dénégation*) extends even to the act that banished the forbidden
term; its absence is unacknowledged. [. . .]

It must then be possible to examine a work from an accurate
description which respects the specificity of this work, but which
is more than just a new exposition of its content, in the form of
a systematisation, for example. For as we quickly come to
realise, we can only describe, only remain within the work, if we
also decide to go beyond it: to bring out, for example, what the
work is *compelled* to say in order to say what it *wants* to say,

because not only would the work have wanted not to say it
(which is another question), but certainly the work did not want
to say it. Thus, it is not a question of introducing a historical
explanation which is stuck on to the work from the outside. On
the contrary, we must show a sort of splitting within the work:
this division is *its* unconscious, in so far as it possesses one – the
unconscious which is history, the play of history beyond its
edges, encroaching on those edges: this is why it is possible to
trace the path which leads from the haunted work to that which
haunts it. Once again it is not a question of redoubling the work
with an unconscious, but a question of revealing in the very
gestures of expression that which it is not. Then, the reverse side
of what is written will be history itself. [. . .]

'The expression of contradictory conditions', the work must
therefore 'reflect', independently of its fragmented reality (it is
dispersed in the multiplicity of its terms – terms which are
distinct, or at least analysable), the ensemble of the
contradictions which define the historical situation as an
insufficiency. This ensemble is not confused with this or that
specific contradiction (for example, with one of the
contradictions which Tolstoy describes directly) or with a simple
general contradiction which is the product of all the others. The
work is privileged in that it gives, in its own fashion, *a complete
view* of the historical complexity: its point of view is completely
significant. We have already seen that the work is defined by its
lack, its incompleteness. We are now stating that the work is
complete, that is to say, adequate to its meaning. These two
propositions do not annul each other. On the contrary, they are
an extension of each other: the work is not at fault in relation to
another work in which the absences would be made good, the
insufficiencies remedied; these absences make it exist, make it
irreplaceable. The mirror is expressive in what it does not reflect
as much as in what it does reflect. The absence of certain
reflections, expressions – these are the true object of criticism.
The mirror, in certain areas, is a blind mirror: but it is still a
mirror for all its blindness.

Because of the contradictory conditions in which it is
produced, the literary work is *simultaneously* (and it is this
conjunction which concerns us) a reflection and the absence of a
reflection: this is why it is itself contradictory. It would therefore
be incorrect to say that the contradictions of the work are the
reflection of historical contradictions: rather they are the
consequences of the absence of this reflection. Once again we see

that there can be no mechanical correspondence between the object and its 'image'. Expression does not mean a direct reproduction (or even knowledge), but an indirect figuration which arises from the deficiencies of the reproduction. Thus the work has a self-sufficient meaning which does not require to be completed; this meaning results from the disposition of partial reflections within the work and from a certain impossibility of reflecting. The function of criticism is to bring this to light. [. . .]

By definition, an ideology can sustain a contradictory debate, for ideology exists precisely in order to efface all trace of contradiction. Thus, an ideology, as such, breaks down only in the face of the real questions: but for that to come about, ideology must not be able to hear these questions; that is to say, ideology must not be able to translate them into its own language. In so far as ideology is the false resolution of a real debate, it is always adequate to itself *as a reply*. [. . .] Between the ideology and the book which expresses it, something has happened; the distance between them is not the product of some abstract decorum. Even though ideology itself always sounds solid, copious, it begins to speak of its *own absences* because of its presence in the novel, its visible and determinate form. By means of the text it becomes possible to escape from the domain of spontaneous ideology, to escape from the false consciousness of self, of history, and of time. The text constructs a determinate image of the ideological, revealing it as an object rather than living it from within as though it were an inner conscience; the text explores ideology (just as Balzac explores the Paris of the *Comédie humaine*, for instance), puts it to the test of the written word, the test of that watchful gaze in which all subjectivity is *captured*, crystallised in objective form. The spontaneous ideology in which men live (it is not produced spontaneously, although men believe that they acquire it spontaneously) is not simply reflected by the mirror of the book; ideology is broken, and turned inside out in so far as it is transformed in the text from being a state of consciousness. Art, or at least literature, because it naturally scorns the credulous view of the world, establishes myth and illusion as *visible objects*.

Tolstoy's work is engaged in a sterile social critique; but behind that futile generosity there figures a historical question which is placed within our grasp. Thus the work is certainly determined by its relation to ideology, but this relation is not one of analogy (as would be a reproduction): it is always more or less contradictory. A work is established against an ideology as much as it is from an ideology. Implicitly, the work contributes to an exposure of ideology, or at least to a definition of it; thus the absurdity of all attempts to 'demystify' literary works, which are defined precisely by their enterprise of demystification.

But it would not be correct to say that the book initiates a dialogue with ideology (which would be the worst possible way of becoming caught up in its game). On the contrary, its function is to present ideology in a non-ideological form. To take up the classical distinction between form and content – although the use of this distinction could not be generalised – it could be said that the work has an ideological content, but that it endows this content with a specific form. Even if this form is itself ideological there is an internal displacement of ideology by virtue of this *redoubling*; this is not ideology contemplating itself, but the mirror-effect which exposes its insufficiency, revealing differences and discordances, or a significant incongruity.

Thus we can gauge the distance which separates the work of art from true knowledge (a scientific knowledge) but which also unites them in their common distance from ideology. Science does away with ideology, obliterates it; literature challenges ideology by using it. If ideology is thought of as a non-systematic ensemble of significations, the work proposes a *reading* of these significations, by combining them as signs. Criticism teaches us to read these signs.

(Pierre Macherey, *A Theory of Literary Production*, trans. Geoffrey Wall (London, Henley and Boston: Routledge & Kegan Paul, 1978), pp. 85, 94, 128, 130–1, 132–3. Original French was *Pour une théorie de la production littéraire* (Paris: Maspero, 1966).)

(E) TERRY EAGLETON

Criticism and Ideology (1976)

In what sense is it correct to maintain that *ideology*, rather than *history*, is the object of the text? Or, to pose the question slightly differently: In what sense, if any, do elements of the historically 'real' enter the text? Georg Lukács, in his *Studies in European Realism*, argues that Balzac's greatness lies in the fact that the 'inexorable veracity' of his art drives him to transcend his reactionary ideology and perceive the real historical issues at stake. Ideology, here, clearly signifies a 'false consciousness' which blocks true historical perception, a screen interposed between men and their history. As such, it is a simplistic notion: it fails to grasp ideology as an inherently complex formation which, by inserting individuals into history in a variety of ways, allows of multiple kinds and degrees of access to that history. It fails, in fact, to grasp the truth that some ideologies, and levels of ideology, are more false than others. Ideology is not just the bad dream of the infrastructure: in *deformatively* 'producing' the real, it nevertheless carries elements of reality within itself. But it is not enough, therefore, to modify the image of 'screen' to that of 'filter', as though ideology were a mesh through which elements of the real could slip. Any such 'interventionist' model of ideology holds out the possibility of looking behind the obstruction to observe reality; but in the capitalist mode of production, what is there to be observed is certainly not the real. The real is by necessity empirically imperceptible, concealing itself in the phenomenal categories (commodity, wage-relation, exchange-value and so on) it offers spontaneously for inspection. Ideology, rather, so produces and constructs the real as to cast the shadow of its absence over the perception of its presence. It is not merely that certain aspects of the real are illuminated and others obscured; it is rather that the presence of the real is a presence constituted by its absences, and *vice versa*. [. . .]

History, then, certainly 'enters' the text, not least the 'historical' text; but it enters it precisely *as ideology*, as a presence determined and distorted by its measurable absences. This is not to say that real history is present in the text but in disguised form, so that the task of the critic is then to wrench the mask from its face. It is rather that history is 'present' in the text in the form of a *double-absence*. The text takes as its object, not the real, but certain significations by which the real lives itself – significations which are themselves the product of its partial abolition. Within the text itself, then, ideology becomes a dominant structure, determining the character and disposition of certain 'pseudo-real' constituents. This inversion, as it were, of the real historical process, whereby in the text itself ideology seems to determine the historically real rather than *vice versa*, is itself naturally determined in the last instance by history itself. History, one might say, is the *ultimate* signifier of literature, as it is the ultimate signified. For what else in the end could be the source and object of any signifying practice but the real social formation which provides its material matrix? [. . .]

The literary work appears free – self-producing and self-determining – because it is unconstrained by the necessity to reproduce any particular 'real'; but this freedom simply conceals its more fundamental determination by the constituents of its ideological matrix. If it seems true that at the level of the text's 'pseudo-real' – its imaginary figures and events – 'anything can happen', this is by no means true of its ideological organisation; and it is precisely because *that* is not true that the free-wheeling contingency of its pseudo-real is equally illusory. The pseudo-real of the literary text is the product of the ideologically saturated demands of its modes of representation.

History, then, operates upon the text by an ideological determination which within the text itself privileges ideology as a dominant structure determining its own imaginary or 'pseudo' history. This 'pseudo' or 'textual' real is not related to the historical real as an imaginary 'transposition' of it. Rather than 'imaginatively transposing' the real, the literary work is the production of certain produced representations of the real into an imaginary object. If it distantiates history, it is not because it transmutes it to fantasy, shifting from one ontological gear to another, but because the significations it works into fiction are already representations of reality rather than reality itself. The text is a tissue of meanings, perceptions and responses which inhere in the first place in that imaginary production of the real which is ideology. The 'textual real' is related to the historical real, not as an imaginary transposition of it, but as the product of certain signifying practices whose source and referent is, in the last instance, history itself.

(Terry Eagleton, *Criticism and Ideology* (London: New Left Books, 1976), pp. 69, 72, 74–5.)

PART V:

MORALITY, CLASS AND GENDER

What might be called the 'moral' tradition has always been the most anti-theoretical of the traditions of European criticism, and has been especially strong in Britain. If the best literature is that which fosters or embodies the best values, then criticism needs to be possessed of the same values it seeks to discover in literary texts. In this respect 'moral' critics try to rediscover their own image in the texts they read, and therefore they need to suppress the *difference* between literature and criticism. Theoretical self-consciousness will tend to *problematize* the critical activity, because theoretical discourses are evidently in competition, attempting rival conceptualizations of literary space. The moral critics cannot tolerate this rivalry, since their own positions must possess absoluteness to command moral authority. F. R. Leavis believed that literature invites us 'not to "think about" and judge but to "feel into" or "become" – to realise a complex experience that is given in the words'. This view supposes that the critic can become a delicate membrane, fully responsive to a work's moral complexity.

There is a large category of critical writing which regards literature as part of the general moral or political universe. Books, whether fact or fiction, which transgress the values of religion, morality or the state, are condemned as dangerous or deviant. Plato (in *The Republic*) and Dr Johnson went as far as to condemn stories for presenting ugly or immoral events, even if what they present is true. Sir Philip Sidney's *Apology* accepts the justice of such attacks on literature but argues that, in principle, literature has a high moral purpose. He anticipates Shelley's belief that the poet is a 'lawgiver' and 'seer'. The Romantic imagination (see I,1,C–E) transformed the notion of moral criticism. Shelley believed that the poet has no moral 'aim'. The imaginative faculty itself is 'the organ of the moral nature of man'. Ruskin's moral down-to-earth idealism treats art as if it serves 'life', and in this he returns by a circuitous route to the moralism of Plato. The Soviet Writers' Congress of 1934 marked the end of the revolutionary period of experiment in the arts. Zhdanov's keynote speech set the new tone of party dogmatism which required writers to be 'engineers of human souls'. Most Anglo–American moral criticism, in its reaction against this kind of Marxist moralism, shook off the Puritan temper present in much earlier English criticism. However, an extract from David Holbrook is included to show that serious writers are still capable of highly dogmatic and reductive moralism. 'The truths of psychiatry' are the source of his moral certainties.

There is another line of moral criticism which completely rejects the 'moralism' of the Puritan or Platonic traditions. It lacks completely the prescriptive attitude of the moralist. Matthew Arnold centres his criticism upon 'that great and inexhaustible world *life*'. Literature cannot grasp the fullness of 'life' by applying rules or by observing taboos and moral guidelines. Henry James and D. H. Lawrence actually attacked the moral prudishness of the English novel in their concern to give a 'direct impression of life'. Their aesthetic ideas were directed at conveying the fullness of the 'felt' quality of life. The moral critics from Matthew Arnold to F. R. Leavis all rejected a narrow moralism for a deep *seriousness*. In Arnold and Leavis especially there is a strong rejection of the dichotomy between form and content: beauty and truth go together. Shakespeare's creative and formal powers are inseparable from his 'moral' vision, in Leavis's view. A poetic richness actualizes a moral richness.

The covert moral certainties of Arnold and Leavis appear quite removed from the overt moral concern of socialist and feminist criticism. A class analysis of this critical difference might take the following form. The humanistic criticism of Arnold and Leavis was closely related to their class affiliations. Leavis rejected Arnold's 'high' seriousness and preferred a seriousness more akin to his lower-middle class origins. However, they both were able to claim a universality for their own class experience. The social origins of their aesthetic doctrines are masked as a broadly human discourse. This is not possible for working-class critics, because their perspective is marginalized by the dominant critical orthodoxies. Hoggart's *Uses of Literacy* was important mainly because it placed working-class culture on the map. Raymond Williams began as a Leavisite, but his working-class origins inevitably directed him towards a different understanding of culture. *Culture and Society* provides a new map of the development of English culture during the period of the rise of industrial society and the labour movement.

Some have argued that women have been the largest disadvantaged social class. Women's attempts at self-definition always start with gender. It would not occur to a man to say 'My problems start from my being a man.' The origins of sexual difference are hotly disputed. Among the causes which have been argued are: biology, women's experience, male domination of discourse, the unconscious, and social and economic conditions. Different arguments result in different theories. Elaine Showalter considers that women's writing has been neglected because of the difference of women's *experience* it expresses. Her book *A Literature of their Own* (1977) aims to recover 'the lost continent of the female tradition'. Hélène Cixous, a well-know French feminist critic, adopts the Lacanian psychoanalytic model (see II,5,E), and argues that women's writing is subversive, because the female body expresses a rejection of male, logical, 'phallocentric' discourse.

CHAPTER 1

MORALISM

I use the term 'moralism' to refer to approaches which require the writer to abide by an explicit value-system or social code. They refuse to allow literary texts any degree of freedom from the formal requirements of morality. Sidney and Shelley are partial exceptions in that they saw that literature establishes an imaginative distance from reality and therefore cannot be governed by the ordinary rules of morality.

Plato's view of art in *The Republic* is clearly determined by politics. The education of the 'guardians' requires the utmost vigilance, since the heroes they read about and the dramatic roles they play will have a shaping effect upon their characters. Modern readers are familiar with similar arguments for censorship of representations of 'sex and violence' in television and film. Plato believed that 'imitation' (dramatic role playing) of bad men could infect the soul of the imitator. Books in which the heroic characters (those likely to be the role-models for the guardians) are depicted behaving in unseemly ways are treated as dangerous. However, the guardians would not be inclined to be influenced by the bad behaviour of slaves and others of low class, since in them such behaviour would be appropriate!

The Renaissance in sixteenth-century England was soon followed by a strongly moralistic, Puritan reaction against the growth of literature and especially the secular drama. Roger Ascham's *Schoolmaster* (1570) attacked the fashionable 'Italianism' on moral grounds, while Stephen Gosson's *School of Abuse* (1579) ranted against 'poets, pipers, players, jesters, and suchlike caterpillars of the commonwealth' and called the poet 'father of lies'. Classical literature had often taught that literature is concerned with what is relevant to life (*utile*) as much as what is pleasing (*dulce*). Sir Philip Sidney accepted Gosson's low opinion of the actual English plays of his day, but used Plato's arguments in reverse to defend the dignity of classical and biblical poetry. Sidney did not accept Plato's arguments about illusionism. Poets are not the fathers of lies, because poetry and drama are fictive: they do not assert facts about anything, but work allegorically and figuratively to instruct. He follows Aristotle's view that poetry is more universal than history.

The rise of the novel in the eighteenth century posed a new problem for moralists. Plato had considered that Homer's version of myths (Cronus's mutilation of Uranus, and so on) were dangerous, but how much more potentially dangerous as models of the world were realistic novels. Dr Johnson believed that 'the power of example is so great as to take possession of the memory by a kind of violence and produce effects almost without the intervention of the will'. Johnson was influenced by eighteenth-century associationist psychology (see II,1,D) which made the association of ideas almost a tyrannical power. Since literature is a sort of rehearsal for life, novelists must make their selections from the indiscriminate chaos of experience according to the requirements of morality. When Johnson talks about fiction which inculcates a credible virtue, he is evidently thinking of the novels of Samuel Richardson which he much preferred to the morally liberal novels of Henry Fielding.

Like William Blake, Shelley believed that the moral customs of a particular era are the *result* of the imaginative vision of great men. What at one stage is a new and unorthodox understanding of human life later becomes the orthodoxy against which new minds struggle in the unending ethical development of human kind. Shelley identifies moral insight with the gift of imaginative insight into other states of being (compare Keats, III,4,A). The poet discovers the ideal aspects of other people which are not already embodied in existing moral codes. Homer's Achilles may appear unedifying but the 'planetary music' of the ideal world can be heard despite the barbarous and archaic form in which we receive the character. Shelley's thinking here is neoplatonic: the true imaginative world of the poets is inevitably cheapened by the vesture of time and mortality which they are compelled to use.

Ruskin emphasized the moral complexity of art, and tried to define its character without confusing it with the author's moral character. He saw that 'passionate' and immoral artists could write or paint works which possess moral vision. 'Morality' in this sense is a *contemplative* attribute. The high moral responsibility of the artist is to *reveal* the Beauty of Nature. Such a vision is not petty or concerned with the trivialities of life, but has a grandeur and nobility appropriate to the appreciation of the divinely appointed order (on grandeur cf. II,3). Ruskin also believed that the greatest art expressed a nation's 'social and political virtues', because no great art can be achieved in a corrupt society. This directly 'moral' emphasis made Ruskin unfashionable in the twentieth century, especially after the rise of a moral criticism informed by the linguistic sensitivity of New Criticism.

No less unfashionable after the 1930s were the very different moral exhortations of the Union of Soviet Writers whose Congress in 1934 formulated the doctrine of 'socialist realism' (see I,2,D), based on interpretations of Lenin's pre-revolutionary statements about art and literature. The innovative literary theory of the Formalists and the experimental art of the Futurists, film makers (Eisenstein and Pudovkin), Constructivists, and others, were allowed to flourish for a time after the Revolution of 1917, but gradually, as the economic situation came under control, doctrinaire voices prevailed and all experiment was suppressed. Zhdanov's call for a commitment to 'revolutionary romanticism' went completely against Engels' warnings to Maria Harkness (IV,4,B) against excessive 'tendentiousness'. Zhdanov saw nothing wrong in Soviet writers being utterly tendentious in their efforts to project 'a supreme spirit of heroic deeds and magnificent future prospects'.

Background reading

Graham Hough, *The Last Romantics* (London: Duckworth, 1947), ch. 1: Ruskin.

C. Vaughan James, *Soviet Socialist Realism: Origins and Theory* (London: Macmillan, 1973).

R. W. Matthewson, *The Positive Hero in Russian Literature* (Stanford, Cal.: Stanford UP, 1975).

F. G. Robinson, *The Shape of Things Known: Sidney's 'Apology' in Its Philosophical Tradition* (Cambridge, Mass.: Harvard UP, 1972).

R. B. Voitle, *Johnson the Moralist* (Cambridge, Mass.: Harvard UP, 1961).

(A) PLATO

The Republic

[BOOKS 2 AND 3]

And shall we just carelessly allow children to hear any casual tales which may be devised by casual persons, and to receive into their minds ideas for the most part the very opposite of those which we should wish them to have when they are grown up?

We cannot.

Then the first thing will be to establish a censorship of the writers of fiction, and let the censors receive any tale of fiction which is good, and reject the bad; and we will desire mothers and nurses to tell their children the authorised ones only. Let them fashion the mind with such tales, even more fondly than they mould the body with their hands; but most of those which are now in use must be discarded.

Of what tales are you speaking? he said.

You may find a model of the lesser in the greater, I said; for they are necessarily of the same type, and there is the same spirit in both of them.

Very likely, he replied; but I do not as yet know what you would term the greater.

Those, I said, which are narrated by Homer and Hesiod, and the rest of the poets, who have ever been the great storytellers of mankind.

But which stories do you mean, he said; and what fault do you find with them?

A fault which is most serious, I said; the fault of telling a lie, and, what is more, a bad lie.

But when is this fault committed?

Whenever an erroneous representation is made of the nature of gods and heroes, – as when a painter paints a portrait not having the shadow of a likeness to the original.

Yes, he said, that sort of thing is certainly very blameable; but what are the stories which you mean?

First of all, I said, there was that greatest of all lies in high places, which the poet told about Uranus, and which was a bad lie too, – I mean what Hesiod says that Uranus did, and how Cronus retaliated on him [Cronus mutilated his father]. The doings of Cronus, and the sufferings which in turn his son inflicted upon him, even if they were true, ought certainly not to be lightly told to young and thoughtless persons; if possible, they had better be buried in silence. But if there is an absolute necessity for their mention, a chosen few might hear them in a mystery, and they should sacrifice not a common [Eleusinian] pig, but some huge and unprocurable victim; and then the number of the hearers will be very few indeed. [. . .]

If then we adhere to our original notion and bear in mind that our guardians, setting aside every other business, are to dedicate themselves wholly to the maintenance of freedom in the State, making this their craft, and engaging in no work which does not bear on this end, they ought not to practise or imitate anything else; if they imitate at all, they should imitate from youth upward only those characters which are suitable to their profession – the courageous, temperate, holy, free, and the like; but they should not depict or be skilful at imitating any kind of illiberality or baseness, lest from imitation they should come to be what they imitate. Did you never observe how imitations, beginning in early youth and continuing far into life, at length grow into habits and become a second nature, affecting body, voice, and mind?

Yes, certainly, he said.

Then, I said, we will not allow those for whom we profess a care and of whom we say that they ought to be good men, to imitate a woman, whether young or old, quarrelling with her husband, or striving and vaunting against the gods in conceit of her happiness, or when she is in affliction, or sorrow, or weeping; and certainly not one who is in sickness, love, or labour.

Very right, he said.

Neither must they represent slaves, male or female, performing the offices of slaves?

They must not.

And surely not bad men, whether cowards or any others, who do the reverse of what we have just been prescribing, who scold or mock or revile one another in drink or out of drink, or who in any other manner sin against themselves and their neighbours in word or deed, as the manner of such is. Neither should they be trained to imitate the action or speech of men or women who are mad or bad; for madness, like vice, is to be known but not to be practised or imitated.

Very true, he replied.

(Plato, *The Republic*, from Books 2 and 3, trans. B. Jowett, 3rd edn (Oxford: Clarendon Press, 1888), pp. 59–60, 80.)

(B) SIR PHILIP SIDNEY

An Apology for Poetry (1595)

But it is that feigning notable images of virtues, vices, or what else, with that delightful teaching, which must be the right describing note to know a poet by, although indeed the Senate of Poets hath chosen verse as their fittest raiment, meaning, as in matter they passed all in all, so in manner to go beyond them – not speaking (table talk fashion or like men in a dream) words as they chanceably fall from the mouth, but peizing each syllable of each word by just proportion according to the dignity of the subject.

Now therefore it shall not be amiss first to weigh this latter sort of Poetry by his works, and then by his parts, and, if in neither of these anatomies he be condemnable, I hope we shall obtain a more favourable sentence. This purifying of wit, this enriching of memory, enabling of judgement, and enlarging of conceit, which commonly we call learning, under what name soever it come forth, or to what immediate end soever it be directed, the final end is to lead and draw us to as high a perfection as our degenerate souls, made worse by their clayey lodgings, can be capable of. [. . .]

The philosopher therefore and the historian are they which would win the goal, the one by precept, the other by example. But both, not having both, do both halt. For the philosopher, setting down with thorny argument the bare rule, is so hard of utterance, and so misty to be conceived, that one that hath no other guide but him shall wade in him till he be old before he shall find sufficient cause to be honest. For his knowledge standeth so upon the abstract and general, that happy is that man who may understand him, and more happy that can apply what he doth understand. On the other side, the historian, wanting the precept, is so tied, not to what should be but to what is, to the particular truth of things and not to the general reason of things, that his example draweth no necessary consequence, and therefore a less fruitful doctrine.

Now doth the peerless poet perform both: for whatsoever the philosopher saith should be done, he giveth a perfect picture of it in some one by whom he presupposeth it was done; so as he coupleth the general notion with the particular example. A perfect picture I say, for he yieldeth to the powers of the mind an image of that where of the philosopher bestoweth but a wordish description: which doth neither strike, pierce, nor possess the sight of the soul so much as that other doth. [. . .]

Now, to that which commonly is attributed to the praise of histories, in respect of the notable learning is gotten by marking the success, as though therein a man should see virtue exalted and vice punished – truly that commendation is peculiar to Poetry, and far off from History. For indeed Poetry ever setteth virtue so out in her best colours, making Fortune her well-waiting handmaid, that one must needs be enamoured of her. Well may you see Ulysses in a storm, and in other hard plights; but they are but exercises of patience and magnanimity, to make them shine the more in the near-following prosperity. And of the contrary part, if evil men come to the stage, they ever go out (as the tragedy writer answered to one that misliked the show of such persons) so manacled as they little animate folks to follow them. But the historian, being captived to the truth of a foolish world, is many times a terror from well doing, and an encouragement to unbridled wickedness. [. . .]

That imitation whereof Poetry is, hath the most conveniency to Nature of all other, insomuch that, as Aristotle saith, those things which in themselves are horrible, as cruel battles, unnatural monsters, are made in poetical imitation delightful. Truly, I have known men, that even with reading *Amadis de Gaule* (which God knoweth wanteth much of a perfect poesy) have found their hearts moved to the exercise of courtesy, liberality, and especially courage. Who readeth Aeneas carrying old Anchises on his back, that wisheth not it were his fortune to perform so excellent an act? [. . .]

Since then Poetry is of all human learning the most ancient and of most fatherly antiquity, as from whence other learnings have taken their beginnings; since it is so universal that no learned nation doth despise it, nor no barbarous nation is without it; since both Roman and Greek gave divine names unto it, the one of 'prophesying', the other of 'making', and that indeed that name of 'making' is fit for him, considering that whereas other Arts retain themselves within their subject, and receive, as it were, their being from it, the poet only bringeth his own stuff, and doth not learn a conceit out of a matter, but maketh matter for a conceit; since neither his description nor his end containeth any evil, the thing described cannot be evil, since his effects be so good as to teach goodness and to delight the learners; since therein (namely in moral doctrine, the chief of all knowledges) he doth not only far pass the historian, but, for instructing, is wellnigh comparable to the philosopher, and, for moving, leaves him behind him; since the Holy Scripture (wherein there is no uncleanness) hath whole parts in it poetical, and that even our Saviour Christ vouchsafed to use the flowers of it; since all his kinds are not only in their united forms but in their severed dissections fully commendable: I think (and think I think rightly) the laurel crown appointed for triumphing captains doth worthily (of all other learnings) honour the poet's triumph. [. . .]

Now then go we to the most important imputations laid to the poor poets. For aught I can yet learn, they are these. First, that there being many other more fruitful knowledges, a man might better spend his time in them than in this. Secondly, that it is the mother of lies. Thirdly, that it is the nurse of abuse, infecting us with many pestilent desires, with a siren's sweetness drawing the mind to the serpent's tale of sinful fancy, – and herein, especially, comedies give the largest field to ear (as Chaucer saith), – how both in other nations and in ours, before poets did soften us, we were full of courage, given to martial exercises, the pillars of manlike liberty, and not lulled asleep in shady idleness with poets' pastimes. And lastly, and chiefly, they cry out with an open mouth, as if they outshot Robin Hood, that Plato banished them out of his Commonwealth. Truly, this is much, if there be much truth in it. [. . .]

And certainly, though a man should grant their first assumption, it should follow (methinks) very unwillingly, that good is not good because better is better. But I still and utterly deny that there is sprung out of earth a more fruitful knowledge. To the second therefore, that they should be the principal liars, I answer paradoxically, but truly, I think truly, that of all writers under the sun the poet is the least liar, and, though he would, as a poet can scarcely be a liar. The astronomer, with his cousin the geometrician, can hardly escape, when they take upon them to measure the height of the stars. How often, think you, do the physicians lie, when they aver things good for sicknesses, which afterwards send Charon a great number of souls drowned in a potion before they come to his ferry? And no less of the rest, which take upon them to affirm. Now, for the poet, he nothing affirms, and therefore never lieth. For, as I take it, to lie is to affirm that to be true which is false; so as the other artists, and especially the historian, affirming many things, can, in the cloudy knowledge of mankind, hardly escape from many lies. But the poet (as I said before) never affirmeth. The

poet never maketh any circles about your imagination, to
conjure you to believe for true what he writes. He citeth not
authorities of other histories, but even for his entry calleth the
sweet Muses to inspire into him a good invention; in truth, not
labouring to tell you what is, or is not, but what should or
should not be. And therefore, though he recount things not true,
yet because he telleth them not for true, he lieth not, – without
we will say that Nathan lied in his speech, before alleged, to
David; which as a wicked man durst scarce say, so think I none
so simple would say that Aesop lied in the tales of his beasts: for
who thinks that Aesop writ it for actually true were well worthy
to have his name chronicled among the beasts he writeth of.
What child is there that, coming to a play, and seeing *Thebes*
written in great letters upon an old door, doth believe that it is
Thebes? If then a man can arrive, at that child's age, to know
that the poets' persons and doings are but pictures what should
be, and not stories what have been, they will never give the lie
to things not affirmatively but allegorically and figuratively
written. And therefore, as in History, looking for truth, they go
away full fraught with falsehood, so in Poesy, looking for fiction,
they shall use the narration but as an imaginative ground-plot of
a profitable invention.

(Sir Philip Sidney, *An Apology for Poetry* (1595), *Elizabethan Critical Essays*,
ed. G. Gregory Smith, 2 vols (London: Oxford UP, 1904), I. 160, 164,
169–70, 173, 180–1, 183–5.)

(C) SAMUEL JOHNSON

Rambler, no. 4 (31 March 1750)

The task of our present writers is very different; it requires
together with that learning which is to be gained from books,
that experience which can never be attained by solitary diligence
but must arise from general converse and accurate observation of
the living world. [. . .]

They are engaged in portraits of which everyone knows the
original and can detect any deviation from exactness of
resemblance. [. . .]

But the fear of not being approved as just copiers of human
manners is not the most important concern that an author of
this sort ought to have before him. These books are written
chiefly to the young, the ignorant, and the idle, to whom they

serve as lectures of conduct and introductions into life. They are the entertainment of minds unfurnished with ideas, and therefore easily susceptible of impressions; not fixed by principles, and therefore easily following the current of fancy; not informed by experience, and consequently open to every false suggestion and partial account.

That the highest degree of reverence should be paid to youth, and that nothing indecent should be suffered to approach their eyes or ears are precepts extorted by sense and virtue from an ancient writer by no means eminent for chastity of thought. The same kind, though not the same degree of caution, is required in everything which is laid before them, to secure them from unjust prejudices, perverse opinions, and incongruous combinations of images.

In the romances formerly written, every transaction and sentiment was so remote from all that passes among men that the reader was in very little danger of making any applications to himself. The virtues and crimes were equally beyond his sphere of activity; and he amused himself with heroes and with traitors, deliverers and persecutors, as with beings of another species, whose actions were regulated upon motives of their own, and who had neither faults nor excellencies in common with himself.

But when an adventurer is leveled with the rest of the world, and acts in such scenes of the universal drama as may be the lot of any other man, young spectators fix their eyes upon him with closer attention, and hope, by observing his behavior and success, to regulate their own practices when they shall be engaged in the like part.

For this reason these familiar histories may perhaps be made of greater use than the solemnities of professed morality, and convey the knowledge of vice and virtue with more efficacy than axioms and definitions. But if the power of example is so great as to take possession of the memory by a kind of violence, and produce effects almost without the intervention of the will, care ought to be taken that, when the choice is unrestrained, the best examples only should be exhibited, and that which is likely to operate so strongly should not be mischievous or uncertain in its effects. [. . .]

It is justly considered as the greatest excellency of art to imitate nature; but it is necessary to distinguish those parts of nature which are most proper for imitation. Greater care is still required in representing life, which is so often discolored by passion or deformed by wickedness. If the world be promiscuously described, I cannot see of what use it can be to read the account, or why it may not be as safe to turn the eye immediately upon mankind, as upon a mirror which shows all that presents itself without discrimination.

It is therefore not a sufficient vindication of a character that it is drawn as it appears, for many characters ought never to be drawn; nor of a narrative, that the train of events is agreeable to observation and experience, for that observation which is called knowledge of the world will be found much more frequently to make men cunning than good. The purpose of these writings is surely not only to show mankind, but to provide that they may be seen hereafter with less hazard; to teach the means of avoiding the snares which are laid by Treachery for Innocence, without infusing any wish for that superiority with which the betrayer flatters his vanity; to give the power of counteracting fraud, without the temptation to practice it; to initiate youth by mock encounters in the art of necessary defense; and to increase prudence without impairing virtue. [. . .]

In narratives where historical veracity has no place I cannot discover why there should not be exhibited the most perfect idea of virtue; of virtue not angelical, nor above probability, for what we cannot credit we shall never imitate, but the highest and purest that humanity can reach, which, exercised in such trials as the various revolutions of things shall bring upon it, may, by conquering some calamities and enduring others, teach us what we may hope and what we can perform. Vice, for vice is necessary to be shown, should always disgust; nor should the graces of gaiety or the dignity of courage be so united with it as to reconcile it to the mind. Wherever it appears, it should raise hatred by the malignity of its practices, and contempt by the meanness of its stratagems; for while it is supported by either parts or spirit, it will be seldom heartily abhorred.

(Samuel Johnson, *Rambler*, no. 4, *Works*, 12 vols (London, 1796), IV. 21–3, 23–4, 26.)

(D) PERCY BYSSHE SHELLEY

A Defence of Poetry (1821)

The whole objection, however, of the immorality of poetry rests upon a misconception of the manner in which poetry acts to

produce the moral improvement of man. Ethical science arranges
the elements which poetry has created, and propounds schemes
and proposes examples of civil and domestic life: nor is it for
want of admirable doctrines that men hate, and despise, and
censure, and deceive, and subjugate one another. But poetry acts
in another and diviner manner. It awakens and enlarges the
mind itself by rendering it the receptacle of a thousand
unapprehended combinations of thought. Poetry lifts the veil
from the hidden beauty of the world, and makes familiar objects
be as if they were not familiar; it reproduces all that it
represents, and the impersonations clothed in its Elysian light
stand thenceforward in the minds of those who have once
contemplated them, as memorials of that gentle and exalted
content which extends itself over all thoughts and actions with
which it coexists. The great secret of morals is love; or a going
out of our nature, and an identification of ourselves with the
beautiful which exists in thought, action, or person, not our own.
A man, to be greatly good, must imagine intensely and
comprehensively; he must put himself in the place of another
and of many others; the pains and pleasures of his species must
become his own. The great instrument of moral good is the
imagination; and poetry administers to the effect by acting upon
the cause. Poetry enlarges the circumference of the imagination
by replenishing it with thoughts of ever new delight, which have
the power of attracting and assimilating to their own nature all
other thoughts, and which form new intervals and interstices
whose void for ever craves fresh food. Poetry strengthens the
faculty which is the organ of the moral nature of man, in the
same manner as exercise strengthens a limb. A poet therefore
would do ill to embody his own conceptions of right and wrong,
which are usually those of his place and time, in his poetical
creations, which participate in neither. By this assumption of the
inferior office of interpreting the effect, in which perhaps after all
he might acquit himself but imperfectly, he would resign a glory
in a participation in the cause. There was little danger that
Homer, or any of the eternal poets, should have so far
misunderstood themselves as to have abdicated this throne of
their widest dominion. Those in whom the poetical faculty,
though great, is less intense, as Euripides, Lucan, Tasso,
Spenser, have frequently affected a moral aim, and the effect of
their poetry is diminished in exact proportion to the degree in
which they compel us to advert to this purpose.

(Percy Bysshe Shelley, *A Defence of Poetry* (1821), *The Prose Works*, ed.
R. H. Shepherd, 2 vols (London: Chatto & Windus, 1888), II. 11–12.)

(E) JOHN RUSKIN

Modern Painters (1856)

I come, after some embarrassment, to the conclusion, that poetry
is 'the suggestion, by the imagination, of noble grounds for the
noble emotions.' I mean, by the noble emotions, those four
principal sacred passions – Love, Veneration, Admiration, and
Joy (this latter especially, if unselfish); and their opposites –
Hatred, Indignation (or Scorn), Horror, and Grief, – this last,
when unselfish, becoming Compassion. These passions in their
various combinations constitute what is called 'poetical feeling,'
when they are felt on noble grounds, that is, on great and true
grounds. Indignation, for instance, is a poetical feeling, if excited
by serious injury; but it is not a poetical feeling if entertained on
being cheated out of a small sum of money. It is very possible
the manner of the cheat may have been such as to justify
considerable indignation; but the feeling is nevertheless not
poetical unless the grounds of it be large as well as just. In like
manner, energetic admiration may be excited in certain minds
by a display of fireworks, or a street of handsome shops; but the
feeling is not poetical, because the grounds of it are false, and
therefore ignoble. There is in reality nothing to deserve
admiration either in the firing of packets of gunpowder, or in the
display of the stocks of warehouses. But admiration excited by
the budding of a flower is a poetical feeling, because it is
impossible that this manifestation of spiritual power and vital
beauty can ever be enough admired. [. . .]
   And then, lastly, it is another infinite advantage possessed by
the picture, that in these various differences from reality it
becomes the expression of the power and intelligence of a
companionable human soul. In all this choice, arrangement,
penetrative sight, and kindly guidance, we recognize a
supernatural operation, and perceive, not merely the landscape
or incident as in a mirror; but, besides, the presence of what,
after all, may perhaps be the most wonderful piece of divine
work in the whole matter – the great human spirit through
which it is manifested to us. So that, although with respect to

many important scenes, it might, as we saw above, be one of the most precious gifts that could be given us to see them with *our own eyes*, yet also in many things it is more desirable to be permitted to see them with the eyes of others; and although, to the small, conceited, and affected painter displaying his narrow knowledge and tiny dexterities, our only word may be, 'Stand aside from between that nature and me:' yet to the great imaginative painter – greater a million times in every faculty of soul than we – our word may wisely be, 'Come between this nature and me – this nature which is too great and too wonderful for me; temper it for me, interpret it to me; let me see with your eyes, and hear with your ears, and have help and strength from your great spirit.'

All the noblest pictures have this character. They are true or inspired ideals, seen in a moment to *be* ideal; that is to say, the result of all the highest powers of the imagination, engaged in the discovery and apprehension of the purest truths, and having so arranged them as best to show their preciousness and exalt their clearness. They are always orderly, always one, ruled by one great purpose throughout, in the fulfilment of which every atom of the detail is called to help, and would be missed if removed; this peculiar oneness being the result, not of obedience to any teachable law, but of the magnificence of tone in the perfect mind, which accepts only what is good for its great purposes, rejects whatever is foreign or redundant, and instinctively and instantaneously ranges whatever it accepts, in sublime subordination and helpful brotherhood.

Then, this being the greatest art, the lowest art is the mimicry of it, – the subordination of nothing to nothing; the elaborate arrangement of sightlessness and emptiness: the order which has no object; the unity which has no life, and the law which has no love; the light which has nothing to illumine, and shadow which has nothing to relieve. [. . .]

The next character we have to note in the landscape-instinct (and on this much stress is to be laid), is its total inconsistency with all evil passions; its absolute contrariety (whether in the contest it were crushed or not), to all care, hatred, envy, anxiety, and moroseness. A feeling of this kind is assuredly not one to be lightly repressed, or treated with contempt.

But how, if it be so, the reader asks, can it be characteristic of passionate and unprincipled men, like Byron, Shelley, and such others, and not characteristic of the noblest and most highly principled men?

First, because it is itself a passion, and therefore likely to be characteristic of passionate men. Secondly, because it is wholly a separate thing from moral principle, and may or may not be joined to strength of will, or rectitude of purpose; only, this much is always observable in the men whom it characterizes, that, whatever their faults or failings, they always understand and love noble qualities of character: they can conceive (if not certain phases of piety), at all events, self-devotion of the highest kind; they delight in all that is good, gracious, and noble; and, though warped often to take delight also in what is dark or degraded, that delight is mixed with bitter self-reproach; or else is wanton, careless, or affected, while their delight in noble things is constant and sincere.

(John Ruskin, *Modern Painters*, 6 vols (1856; 2nd edn, Orpington and London: George Allen, 1892), III. 11, 144–6, 301–2.)

(F) A. A. ZHDANOV

'Soviet Literature' (1934)

Our Soviet literature is not afraid of the charge of being 'tendentious.' Yes, Soviet literature is tendentious, for in an epoch of class struggle there is not and cannot be a literature which is not class literature, not tendentious, allegedly non-political.

And I think that every one of our Soviet writers can say to any dull-witted bourgeois, to any philistine, to any bourgeois writer who may talk about our literature being tendentious: 'Yes, our Soviet literature is tendentious, and we are proud of this fact, because the aim of our tendency is to liberate the toilers, to free all mankind from the yoke of capitalist slavery.'

To be an engineer of human souls means standing with both feet firmly planted on the basis of real life. And this in its turn denotes a rupture with romanticism of the old type, which depicted a non-existent life and non-existent heroes, leading the reader away from the antagonisms and oppression of real life into a world of the impossible, into a world of utopian dreams. Our literature, which stands with both feet firmly planted on a materialist basis, cannot be hostile to romanticism, but it must be a romanticism of a new type, revolutionary romanticism. We say that socialist realism is the basic method of Soviet *belles lettres* and literary criticism, and this presupposes that revolutionary romanticism should enter into literary creation as a component part, for the whole life of our Party, the whole life of the working class and its struggle consist in a combination of the most stern and sober practical work with a supreme spirit of heroic deeds and magnificent future prospects. Our Party has always been strong by virtue of the fact that it has united and continues to unite a thoroughly business-like and practical spirit with broad vision, with a constant urge forward, with a struggle for the building of communist society. Soviet literature should be able to portray our heroes; it should be able to glimpse our tomorrow. This will be no utopian dream, for our tomorrow is already being prepared for today by dint of conscious planned work. [. . .]

Comrades, the proletariat, just as in other provinces of material and spiritual culture, is the sole heir of all that is best in the treasury of world literature. The bourgeoisie has squandered its literary heritage; it is our duty to gather it up carefully, to study it and, having critically assimilated it, to advance further.

To be engineers of human souls means to fight actively for the culture of language, for quality of production. Our literature does not as yet come up to the requirements of our era. The weaknesses of our literature are a reflection of the fact that people's consciousness lags behind economic life – a defect from which even our writers are not, of course, free. That is why untiring work directed towards self-education and towards improving their ideological equipment in the spirit of socialism represents an indispensable condition without which Soviet writers cannot remould the mentality of their readers and thereby become engineers of human souls.

(A. A. Zhdanov, 'Soviet Literature', in *Problems of Soviet Literature*, ed. H. G. Scott (London: Martin Lawrence Ltd, 1935), pp. 21–2, 22–3.)

(G) DAVID HOLBROOK

The Quest for Love (1964)

My purpose in writing this book is to urge that we are unlikely to have new writing of any consequence, minority or popular, unless the writer-as-artist makes his own positive quest for insight into such profound human truths as have to do with love and our dealings with reality, such as are being revealed by our increased insight into the mind, through recent psychoanalytical philosophy and practice. The question is not only one of writing: it has to do with our attitudes to life at large, our acceptance of possibilities of new growths in living power, based on hopefulness about the future, a belief in the continuity of life, creative attitudes, and positive values. There can be aims and values in our living, even in the absence of religious faith, if we listen to our deepest inward needs. The writer, teacher and critic who has to do with fiction, drama and poetry inevitably has to do with such aims and values, and such visions and concepts as we develop to help us to come at them. The writer is inevitably concerned with promoting (or obscuring) insight and understanding. There is no way of escaping this responsibility – one's literary work inevitably touches life thus. [. . .]

'The essential function of art is moral' – in the light of what we now know of the growth of human consciousness, this precept of D. H. Lawrence's needs to be upheld more than ever before. This sense of the relevance of art to actual living needs still to be exerted, in the face of mandarinism, in resistance to a new shrinking from moral energy and deep committed feeling among the literati. It is also most urgent for us to discriminate against the moral duplicity of the writer with one foot in the commercial worlds of advertising and mass journalism, and the other in sentimental cynicism and the exploitation of depressive attitudes. He weakens our reality sense, and he threatens our sanity by undermining our capacity for discrimination.

We do mould ourselves on others and are influenced by the character and quality of others, from childhood onwards, and our culture continues this process with effect on our moral choices. We do and can gain guiding concepts from our culture: the connection is as direct as that though it is never obvious. However complex its processes, it is only craven to deny that some real connection exists.

(David Holbrook, *The Quest for Love* (London: Methuen, 1964), pp. 14, 19.)

CHAPTER 2

LITERATURE AND 'LIFE'

Much of the best English criticism from Sidney to Leavis has concerned itself with the subtle connection between literature and 'life'. The aesthetic movement (see III,1) in England always seemed a rather shocking deviation from traditional concerns. Kant's description of aesthetic judgement as 'an entirely disinterested satisfaction' impressed a generation of critics between about 1890 and 1920, but there remained a strong distaste for the 'immoral' attitudes of the aesthetes. Baudelaire and Oscar Wilde were especially scornful of bourgeois morality:

> Poetry has no other end but itself . . . If a poet has
> followed a moral end, he has diminished his poetic force
> and
> is most likely to be bad. (Baudelaire)

> No artist has ethical sympathies. An ethical sympathy is an
> unpardonable mannerism of style. (Wilde)

However, it should not be forgotten that such 'decadent' attitudes have connections with modernist 'impersonality' (see III,4) and with formalistic types of criticism (III,2). Even the moral approaches represented in this section agree with the aesthetes in rejecting tendentiousness and moralizing. They all consider that major literature does not work by directly expressing ideas or attitudes, but by embodying an experience of life in a form and diction necessary to convey the experience. The 'poetic' element in poetry cannot be abstracted from the poem without destroying the 'moral' significance of the poem. Related to this view is Lionel Trilling's defence of 'great writers' who hold unacceptable political views. This was an especially embarrassing question for critics brought up on modernist poetry (Leavis was a leading advocate of Pound's, Eliot's and Yeats' poetry), since most of the great modernists were reactionary in

politics (Pound is the most notorious instance). Trilling argued
that, because of its grasp of present and past, their work was
always 'on the side of . . . generous impulses', and communicates
'energy' and 'fineness of life'. This argument has odd
resemblances to Engels' view of Balzac (see IV,4,B), except that
Trilling believes that important writers transcend not just their
own political outlooks but all political outlooks. However,
arguing from the opposite angle (in *A Gathering of Fugitives*, 1957)
he reminds the then fashionable New Critics (see III,2,E–H)
that questions of 'morality and truth' can never be excluded
from the criticism of literature.

Matthew Arnold thought that writers should be 'disinterested'
and should rise above the merely 'practical' level to a grander
contemplation of ideas. The greatest Greek literature possessed
this ability to express the 'permanent passions' of mankind. Like
many of his successors in the 'moral' tradition Arnold presents
certain social values as universal human values. This is
especially evident in *Culture and Anarchy* where he opposes the
ideal Hellenic attitude to life ('sweetness and light') to Hebraic
and Puritan attitudes ('fire and strength, strictness of
conscience'). Arnold regards the latter as narrow and fanatical,
while the Hellenic is 'the law of light, seeing things as they are'.
The term 'moral' is associated with the breadth and
completeness of Hellenism's spirit. In addition he requires 'high
seriousness' (Aristotle's *spoudaiotes*) in the current of ideas which
fosters great writers. Chaucer, according to this view, is not a
great writer, because his age lacked it.

Henry James' concept of 'point of view' (see III,5,E) requires
a 'reflector' whose quality of mind implies a certain *social*
refinement. The novel's point of view should express a
'consciousness . . . subject to fine intensification and wide
enlargement'. It is significant that James' novels are often set in
an upper-class milieu remote from the world of labour and
commerce. In sharp contrast to James (and Arnold) Lawrence is
an exponent of the 'mixed style' (see Auerbach, III,5,C): the
world of miners and gamekeepers is represented as of deep
moral significance.

Leavis' debt to Arnold is evident, but he dissociates himself
from Arnold's classical idiom: 'perhaps "high seriousness"
should be dismissed as a mere nuisance'. Leavis is rebelling
instinctively against a socially oriented value term. His own
norms are derived from a quite different tradition. His 'English
culture' is lower-middle class in its affiliations; it inscribes in its

tradition Cobbett, Jefferies, and Bunyan, and idealizes the
organic community of the English village (as depicted in George
Sturt's *Change in the Village*). Leavis defends George Eliot's
Puritan moral earnestness against the sneering denigration of the
aristocratic David Cecil. George Eliot's seriousness is 'profound'
rather than 'high'. It is interesting to note that Raymond
Williams rebels against some of Leavis' judgements on the
grounds of their social obtuseness. Just as Arnoldians cannot
appreciate the cultural values of the Puritan middle classes, so
Leavisites cannot grasp the culture of the industrial working
class. While Leavis admires the 'complete seriousness' of
Dickens' *Hard Times*, Williams declares that the novel was 'an
analysis of industrialism, rather than an experience of it'. The
point that I am making here is that *moral* criticism is often
covert social criticism, even though such critics are usually
deeply committed to a 'disinterested' and universal humanity.

One evident strength of the critics in this section is their
refusal to separate moral and aesthetic dimensions. Arnold's
'high seriousness' is inseparable from the 'grand style': 'superior
character of truth and seriousness' is inseparable from
'superiority of diction and movement'. James insisted that the
richness of a novel's representation of life will depend on the
writer's ability to burst the technical conventions of the genre.
Leavis always refused to define his criteria of moral value, and
believed that the standards of judgement involved in true
criticism were intuitive and interpersonal. An important poem
'realizes' human experience more *concretely* and with a greater
degree of actualization than an inferior poem. Its moral
greatness is inseparable from its poetic substance.

Leavis's social commitments (see above) are disguised as
disinterested judgements in his mature critical writing. His texts
are always densely woven readings of literature and other
criticism: he refuses to articulate a theory or intellectual point of
view, since the authenticity of criticism lies in its self-evident
quality and validity. Its essential form is summed up in the
question 'This is so, is it not?' The standards evoked by the
question are 'there' for the reader, provided that they have been
communicated by the organs of criticism. In this sense, *Scrutiny*,
the journal edited by Leavis (1932–53), served the 'function of
criticism' by promoting what its contributors saw as true
judgements. This was especially necessary in a period of 'mass
civilisation' (see *Culture and Environment*, 1933), which Leavis
thought particularly hostile to the cultivation of true standards of

judgement. He believed that the disappearance of the organic community of the English village had removed the only basis for a genuine 'national culture'. *Scrutiny* tried to supply the lack (see Mulhern, V,3,C).

Arnold's 'touchstone' approach to criticism resembles Leavis' 'practical criticism'. Arnold refuses to define abstractly what constitutes 'high quality' in poetry, preferring 'simply to have recourse to concrete examples'. The high qualities are expressed 'there'. Leavis prefers 'concrete analysis' to theoretical answers to the question of standards. His characteristic procedure is to adjudicate between examples. A Bronte poem is inferior to a Hardy poem because Hardy's possesses 'precisions of concrete realization, specificities, complexities', while Bronte's is 'declamatory' and lacks experiential concreteness. However, this judgement, which is finally a moral judgement, is established by a touchstone method: 'This is so, is it not?'

The term 'life' is central to the criticism of Matthew Arnold, Henry James and D. H. Lawrence. Arnold declared: 'A poetry of revolt against moral ideas is a poetry of revolt against life.' But, to define what is life-enhancing is not easy. James rejects the prescriptive approach of Besant. The value of a novel relates to the intensity of the impression of life it gives, but there can be no rule or guide to correctness: there must be freedom to explore 'life' in all its bewildering complexity. The dynamic flow of life can be grasped only if fiction gives us life 'without rearrangement'. The moral quality of a novel depends on its power to create the *illusion* of 'life'. D. H. Lawrence is even more radical in his demand for immediacy of life. James had recognized that much hidden artistry is required to create the illusion of life, but Lawrence wanted poetry to be '*direct utterance* from the instant, whole man'. Life itself has no 'finality, no finished crystalisation' and so free verse should be also 'instantaneous like plasm'. Lawrence was not conscious of the theoretical difficulties involved in his faith in 'representative form'. He appeared to believe that it is possible to find a verbal form which exactly corresponds to the form of 'life'. His own novels in their sprawling vitality pay witness to his moral theory of art.

Background reading

Perry Anderson, 'Components of a National Culture', in *Student Power* (Harmondsworth: Penguin Books, 1969), pp. 268–76 (on Leavis).

Chris Baldick, *The Social Mission of English Criticism 1848–1932* Oxford: Clarendon Press, 1983).

R. P. Bilan, *The Literary Criticism of F. R. Leavis* (Cambridge: Cambridge UP, 1979).

Robert Boyers, *Lionel Trilling: Negative Capability and the Wisdom of Avoidance* (Columbia and London: Univ. of Missouri Press, 1977).

Vincent Buckley, *Poetry and Morality* (London: Chatto & Windus, 1959).

William M. Chace, *Lionel Trilling: Criticism and Politics* (Standford, Cal.: Stanford UP, 1980).

D. J. Gordon, *D. H. Lawrence as a Literary Critic* (New Haven and London: Yale UP, 1966).

John Holloway, *The Victorian Sage* (London: Chatto & Windus, 1961).

Francis Mulhern, *The Moment of 'Scrutiny'* (London: New Left Books, 1979).

George Steiner, *Language and Silence* (London: Faber & Faber, 1967) pp. 37–45 (on Leavis).

Lionel Trilling, *The Liberal Imagination* (London: Secker & Warburg, 1951), 'Manners, Morals and the Novel'.

Lionel Trilling, *Matthew Arnold* (rev. 3rd edn, New York: 1963).

(A) MATTHEW ARNOLD

'The Function of Criticism at the Present Time' (1865)

It was not really books and reading that lacked to our poetry at this epoch; Shelley had plenty of reading, Coleridge had immense reading. Pindar and Sophocles – as we all say so glibly, and often with so little discernment of the real import of what we are saying – had not many books; Shakspeare was no deep reader. True; but in the Greece of Pindar and Sophocles, in the England of Shakspeare, the poet lived in a current of ideas in the highest degree animating and nourishing to the creative power; society was, in the fullest measure, permeated by fresh thought, intelligent and alive. And this state of things is the true basis for the creative power's exercise, in this it finds its data, its materials, truly ready for its hand; all the books and reading in the world are only valuable as they are helps to this [. . . .]

It is of the last importance that English criticism should clearly discern what rule for its course, in order to avail itself of the field now opening to it, and to produce fruit for the future, it ought to take. The rule may be summed up in one word, – *disinterestedness*. And how is criticism to show disinterestedness? By keeping aloof from what is called 'the practical view of things;' by resolutely following the law of its own nature, which is to be a free play of the mind on all subjects which it touches. By steadily refusing to lend itself to any of those ulterior, political, practical considerations about ideas, which plenty of people will be sure to attach to them, which perhaps ought often to be attached to them, which in this country at any rate are certain to be attached to them quite sufficiently, but which criticism has really nothing to do with. Its business is, as I have said, simply to know the best that is known and thought in the world, and by in its turn making this known, to create a current of true and fresh ideas. [. . .]

It is because criticism has so little kept in the pure intellectual sphere, has so little detached itself from practice, has been so directly polemical and controversial, that it has so ill accomplished, in this country, its best spiritual work; which is to keep man from a self-satisfaction which is retarding and vulgarising, to lead him towards perfection, by making his mind dwell upon what is excellent in itself, and the absolute beauty and fitness of things.

(Matthew Arnold, 'The Function of Criticism at the Present Time', *Essays in Criticism: First Series* (1865; London and New York: Macmillan, 1895), pp. 8, 18–19, 20–1.)

Preface to *Poems* (1853)

The poet, then, has in the first place to select an excellent action; and what actions are the most excellent? Those, certainly, which most powerfully appeal to the great primary human affections: to those elementary feelings which subsist permanently in the race, and which are independent of time. These feelings are permanent and the same; that which interests them is permanent and the same also. The modernness or antiquity of an action, therefore, has nothing to do with its fitness for poetical representation; this depends upon its inherent qualities. To the elementary part of our nature, to our passions, that which is great and passionate is eternally interesting; and interesting solely in proportion to its greatness and to its passion. A great human action of a thousand years ago is more interesting to it than a smaller human action of today, even though upon the representation of this last the most consummate skill may have been expended, and though it has the advantage of appealing by its modern language, familiar manners, and contemporary allusions, to all our transient feelings and interests.

These, however, have no right to demand of a poetical work that it shall satisfy them; their claims are to be directed elsewhere. Poetical works belong to the domain of our permanent passions; let them interest these, and the voice of all subordinate claims upon them is at once silenced. [. . .]

What, then, it will be asked, are the ancients to be our sole models? the ancients with their comparatively narrow range of experience, and their widely different circumstances? Not, certainly, that which is narrow in the ancients, nor that in which we can no longer sympathize. An action like the action of the *Antigone* of Sophocles, which turns upon the conflict between the heroine's duty to her brother's corpse and that to the laws of her country, is no longer one in which it is possible that we should feel a deep interest. I am speaking too, it will be remembered, not of the best sources of intellectual stimulus for the general reader, but of the best models of instruction for the individual writer. This last may certainly learn of the ancients, better than anywhere else, three things which it is vitally important for him to know: the all-importance of the choice of a subject; the necessity of accurate construction; and the subordinate character of expression. He will learn from them how unspeakably superior is the effect of the one moral impression left by a great action treated as a whole, to the effect produced by the most striking single thought or by the happiest image. As he penetrates into the spirit of the great classical works, as he becomes gradually aware of their intense significance, their noble simplicity, and their calm pathos, he will be convinced that it is this effect, unity and profoundness of moral impression, at which the ancient poets aimed; that it is this which constitutes the grandeur of their works, and which makes them immortal. He will desire to direct his own efforts towards producing the same effect. Above all, he will deliver himself from the jargon of modern criticism, and escape the danger of producing poetical works conceived in the spirit of the passing time, and which partake of its transitoriness.

(Matthew Arnold, Preface to *Poems*, 1853, in *English Critical Essays: Nineteenth Century*, ed. E. D. Jones (London: Oxford UP, 1916), pp. 307–8, 316–17.)

Culture and Anarchy (1869)

But men of culture and poetry [. . .] have often failed in morality, and morality is indispensable. And they have been punished for their failure, as the Puritan has been rewarded for his performance. They have been punished wherein they erred; but their ideal of beauty, of sweetness and light, and a human nature complete on all its sides, remains the true ideal of perfection still; just as the Puritan's ideal of perfection remains narrow and inadequate, although for what he did well he has been richly rewarded. Notwithstanding the mighty results of the Pilgrim Fathers' voyage, they and their standard of perfection are rightly judged when we figure to ourselves Shakespeare or Virgil – souls in whom sweetness and light, and all that in human nature is most humane, were eminent – accompanying them on their voyage, and think what intolerable company Shakespeare and Virgil would have found them! [. . .]

Sweetness and light evidently have to do with the bent or side in humanity which we call Hellenic. Greek intelligence has obviously for its essence the instinct for what Plato calls the true, firm, intelligible, law of things; the law of light, of seeing things as they are. Even in the natural sciences, where the Greeks had not time and means adequately to apply this instinct, and where we have gone a great deal further than they did, it is this instinct which is the root of the whole matter and the ground of all our success; and this instinct the world has mainly learnt of the Greeks, inasmuch as they are humanity's most signal manifestation of it. Greek art, again, Greek beauty, have their root in the same impulse to see things as they really are, inasmuch as Greek art and beauty rest on fidelity to nature – the *best* nature – and on a delicate discrimination of what this best nature is. To say we work for sweetness and light, then, is only another way of saying that we work for Hellenism. But, oh! cry many people, sweetness and light are not enough; you must put strength or energy along with them, and make a kind of trinity of strength, sweetness and light, and then, perhaps, you may do some good. That is to say, we are to join Hebraism, strictness of the moral conscience, and manful walking by the best light we have, together with Hellenism, inculcate both, and rehearse the praises of both.

Or, rather, we may praise both in conjunction, but we must be careful to praise Hebraism most. 'Culture,' says an acute, though somewhat rigid critic, Mr. Sidgwick, 'diffuses sweetness and light. I do not undervalue these blessings, but religion gives fire and strength, and the world wants fire and strength even more than sweetness and light.' By religion, let me explain, Mr. Sidgwick here means particularly that Puritanism on the insufficiency of which I have been commenting and to which he says I am unfair. Now, no doubt, it is possible to be a fanatical partisan of light and the instincts which push us to it, a fanatical enemy of strictness of moral conscience and the instincts which push us to it. A fanaticism of this sort deforms and vulgarizes the well-known work, in some respects so remarkable, of the late Mr. Buckle. Such a fanaticism carries its own mark with it, in lacking sweetness; and its own penalty, in that, lacking sweetness, it comes in the end to lack light too. And the Greeks – the great exponents of humanity's bent for sweetness and light united, of its perception that the truth of things must be at the same time beauty – singularly escaped the fanaticism which we moderns, whether we Hellenize or whether we Hebraize, are so apt to show. They arrived – though failing, as has been said, to give adequate practical satisfaction to the claims of man's moral side – at the idea of a comprehensive adjustment of the claims of both the sides in man, the moral as well as the intellectual, of a full estimate of both, and of a reconciliation of both; an idea which is philosophically of the greatest value, and the best of lessons for us moderns. So we ought to have no difficulty in conceding to Mr. Sidgwick that manful walking by the best light one has – fire and strength as he calls it – has its high value as well as culture, the endeavour to see things in their truth and beauty, the pursuit of sweetness and light. But whether at this or that time, and to this or that set of persons, one ought to insist most on the praises of fire and strength, or on the praises of sweetness and light, must depend, one would think, on the circumstances and needs of the particular time and those particular persons. And all that we have been saying, and indeed any glance at the world around us, shows that with us, with the most respectable and strongest part of us, the ruling force is now, and long has been, a Puritan force – the care for fire and strength, strictness of conscience, Hebraism, rather than the care for sweetness and light, spontaneity of consciousness, Hellenism.

(Matthew Arnold, *Culture and Anarchy* (1869; London: Smith, Elder, 1897), pp. 18–19, 106–8.)

Preface to Wordsworth's *Poems* (1879)

The question, *how to live*, is itself a moral idea; and it is the question which most interests every man, and with which, in some way or other, he is perpetually occupied. A large sense is of course to be given to the term *moral*. Whatever bears upon the question, 'how to live,' comes under it.

> Nor love thy life, nor hate; but, what thou liv'st,
> Live well; how long or short, permit to heaven.

In those fine lines Milton utters, as everyone at once perceives, a moral idea. Yes, but so too, when Keats consoles the forward-bending lover on the Grecian Urn, the lover arrested and presented in immortal relief by the sculptor's hand before he can kiss, with the line,

> Forever wilt thou love, and she be fair,

he utters a moral idea. When Shakespeare says that

> We are such stuff
> As dreams are made on, and our little life
> Is rounded with a sleep,

he utters a moral idea. [. . .]

If what distinguishes the greatest poets is their powerful and profound application of ideas to life, which surely no good critic will deny, then to prefix to the term ideas here the term moral makes hardly any difference, because human life itself is in so preponderating a degree moral.

It is important, therefore, to hold fast to this: that poetry is at bottom a criticism of life; that the greatness of a poet lies in his powerful and beautiful application of ideas to life – to the question: How to live. Morals are often treated in a narrow and false fashion; they are bound up with systems of thought and belief which have had their day; they are fallen into the hands of pedants and professional dealers; they grow tiresome to some of us. We find attraction, at times, even in a poetry of revolt against them; in a poetry which might take for its motto Omar Khayyám's words: 'Let us make up in the tavern for the time which we have wasted in the mosque.' Or we find attractions in a poetry indifferent to them: in a poetry where the contents may be what they will, but where the form is studied and exquisite. We delude ourselves in either case; and the best cure for our delusion is to let our minds rest upon that great and inexhaustible word *life*, until we learn to enter into its meaning. A poetry of revolt against moral ideas is a poetry of revolt against life; a poetry of indifference towards moral ideas is a poetry of indifference towards *life*.

(Matthew Arnold, 'Wordsworth', *Essays in Criticism: Second Series* (1888;
London: Macmillan, 1925), pp. 142–3, 143–4.)

'The Study of Poetry' (1880)

We should conceive of poetry worthily, and more highly than it
has been the custom to conceive of it. We should conceive of it
as capable of higher uses, and called to higher destinies, than
those which in general men have assigned to it hitherto. More
and more mankind will discover that we have to turn to poetry
to interpret life for us, to console us, to sustain us. Without
poetry, our science will appear incomplete; and most of what
now passes with us for religion and philosophy will be replaced
by poetry. Science, I say, will appear incomplete without it. For
finely and truly does Wordsworth call poetry 'the impassioned
expression which is in the countenance of all science'; and what
is a countenance without its expression? Again, Wordsworth
finely and truly calls poetry 'the breath and finer spirit of all
knowledge': our religion, parading evidences such as those on
which the popular mind relies now; our philosophy, pluming
itself on its reasonings about causation and finite and infinite
being; what are they but the shadows and dreams and false
shows of knowledge? The day will come when we shall wonder
at ourselves for having trusted to them, for having taken them
seriously; and the more we perceive their hollowness, the more
we shall prize 'the breath and finer spirit of knowledge' offered
to us by poetry. [. . .]

Critics give themselves great labour to draw out what in the
abstract constitutes the characters of a high quality of poetry. It
is much better simply to have recourse to concrete examples – to
take specimens of poetry of the high, the very highest quality,
and to say: The characters of a high quality of poetry are what
is expressed *there*. They are far better recognized by being felt in
the verse of the master, than by being perused in the prose of
the critic. Nevertheless if we are urgently pressed to give some
critical account of them, we may safely, perhaps, venture on
laying down, not indeed how and why the characters arise, but
where and in what they arise. They are in the matter and
substance of the poetry, and they are in its manner and style.
Both of these, the substance and matter on the one hand, the
style and manner on the other, have a mark, an accent, of high
beauty, worth, and power. But if we are asked to define this
mark and accent in the abstract, our answer must be: No, for

we should thereby be darkening the question, not clearing it. The mark and accent are as given by the substance and matter of that poetry, by the style and manner of that poetry, and of all other poetry which is akin to it in quality.

Only one thing we may add as to the substance and matter of poetry, guiding ourselves by Aristotle's profound observation that the superiority of poetry over history consists in its possessing a higher truth and a higher seriousness. [. . .] Let us add, therefore, to what we have said, this: that the substance and matter of the best poetry acquire their special character from possessing, in an eminent degree, truth and seriousness. We may add yet further, what is in itself evident, that to the style and manner of the best poetry their special character, their accent, is given by their diction, and, even yet more, by their movement. And though we distinguish between the two characters, the two accents, of superiority, yet they are nevertheless vitally connected one with the other. The superior character of truth and seriousness, in the matter and substance of the best poetry, is inseparable from the superiority of diction and movement marking its style and manner. The two superiorities are closely related, and are in steadfast proportion one to the other. So far as high poetic truth and seriousness are wanting to a poet's matter and substance, so far also, we may be sure, will a high poetic stamp of diction and movement be wanting to his style and manner. In proportion as this high stamp of diction and movement, again, is absent from a poet's style and manner, we shall find, also, that high poetic truth and seriousness are absent from his substance and matter.

(Matthew Arnold, 'The Study of Poetry', *Essays in Criticism: Second Series* (1888; London: Macmillan, 1925), pp. 2–3, 20–2.)

(B) HENRY JAMES

Preface to *The Portrait of a Lady* (1881)

There is, I think, no more nutritive or suggestive truth in this connexion [the novelist's choice of subject] than that of the perfect dependence of the 'moral' sense of a work of art on the amount of felt life concerned in producing it. The question comes back thus, obviously, to the kind and the degree of the artist's prime sensibility, which is the soil out of which his subject springs. The quality and capacity of that soil, its ability to 'grow' with due freshness and straightness any vision of life, represents, strongly or weakly, the projected morality. That element is but another name for the more or less close connexion of the subject with some mark made on the intelligence, with some sincere experience. By which, at the same time, of course, one is far from contending that this enveloping air of the artist's humanity – which gives the last touch to the worth of the work – is not a widely and wondrously varying element; being on one occasion a rich and magnificent medium and on another a comparatively poor and ungenerous one. Here we get exactly the high price of the novel as a literary form – its power not only, while preserving that form with closeness, to range through all the differences of the individual relation to its general subject-matter, all the varieties of outlook on life, of disposition to reflect and project, created by conditions that are never the same from man to man (or, so far as that goes, from man to woman), but positively to appear more true to its character in proportion as it strains, or tends to burst, with a latent extravagance, its mould.

(Henry James, Preface to *The Portrait of a Lady* (1881; London: Macmillan, 1921), 2 vols, I. xiv–xvi.)

Preface to *The Princess Casamassima*

The whole thing comes to depend [. . .] on the *quality* of bewilderment characteristic of one's creature, the quality involved in the given case or supplied by one's data. There are doubtless many such qualities, ranging from vague and crepuscular to sharpest and most critical; and we have but to imagine one of these latter to see how easily – from the moment it gets its head at all – it may insist on playing a part. There we have then at once a case of feeling, of ever so many possible feelings, stretched across the scene like an attached thread on which the pearls of interest are strung. There are threads shorter and less tense, and I am far from implying that the minor, the coarser and less fruitful forms and degrees of moral reaction, as we may conveniently call it, may not yield lively results. They have their subordinate, comparative, illustrative human value – that appeal of the witless which is often so penetrating. Verily even, I think, no 'story' is possible without its fools – as most of the fine painters of life, Shakespeare, Cervantes and Balzac, Fielding, Scott, Thackeray, Dickens, George Meredith, George

Eliot, Jane Austen, have abundantly felt. At the same time I confess I never see the *leading* interest of any human hazard but in a consciousness (on the part of the moved and moving creature) subject to fine intensification and wide enlargement. It is as mirrored in that consciousness that the gross fools, the headlong fools, the fatal fools play their part for us – they have much less to show us in themselves. The troubled life mostly at the centre of our subject – whatever our subject, for the artistic hour, happens to be – embraces them and deals with them for its amusement and its anguish: they are apt largely indeed, on a near view, to be all the cause of its trouble. This means, exactly, that the person capable of feeling in the given case more than another of what is to be felt for it, and so serving in the highest degree to *record* it dramatically and objectively, is the only sort of person on whom we can count not to betray, to cheapen or, as we say, give away, the value and beauty of the thing. By so much as the affair matters *for* some such individual, by so much do we get the best there is of it, and by so much as it falls within the scope of a denser and duller, a more vulgar and more shallow capacity, do we get a picture dim and meagre.

(Henry James, Preface to *The Princess Casamassima* (1886; London: Macmillan, 1921), 2 vols, I. xiv–xvi.)

'The Art of Fiction' (1884)

The only obligation to which in advance we may hold a novel, without incurring the accusation of being arbitrary, is that it be interesting. That general responsibility rests upon it, but it is the only one I can think of. The ways in which it is at liberty to accomplish this result (of interesting us) strike me as innumerable, and such as can only suffer from being marked out or fenced in by prescription. They are as various as the temperament of man, and they are successful in proportion as they reveal a particular mind, different from others. A novel is in its broadest definition a personal, a direct impression of life: that, to begin with, constitutes its value, which is greater or less according to the intensity of the impression. But there will be no intensity at all, and therefore no value, unless there is freedom to feel and say. The tracing of a line to be followed, of a tone to be taken, of a form to be filled out is a limitation of that freedom and a suppression of the very thing that we are most curious about. [. . .]

As people feel life, so they will feel the art that is most closely related to it. This closeness of relation is what we should never forget in talking of the effort of the novel. Many people speak of it as a factitious, artificial form, a product of ingenuity, the business of which is to alter and arrange the things that surround us, to translate them into conventional, traditional moulds. This, however, is a view of the matter which carries us but a very short way, condemns the art to an eternal repetition of a few familiar *clichés*, cuts short its development and leads us straight up to a dead wall. Catching the very note and trick, the strange irregular rhythm of life, that is the attempt whose strenuous force keeps Fiction upon her feet. In proportion as in what she offers us we see life *without* rearrangement do we feel that we are touching the truth; in proportion as we see it *with* arrangement do we feel that we are being put off with a substitute, a compromise and convention. [. . .]

He [the English novelist] is apt to be extremely shy, and the sign of his work, for the most part, is a cautious silence on certain subjects. In the English novel (by which of course I mean the American as well), more than in any other, there is a traditional difference between that which people know and that which they agree to admit that they know, that which they see and that which they speak of, that which they feel to be a part of life and that which they allow to enter into literature. There is the great difference, in short, between what they talk of in conversation and what they talk of in print. The essence of moral energy is to survey the whole field. [. . .] To what degree a purpose in a work of art is a source of corruption I shall not attempt to inquire; the one that seems to me least dangerous is the purpose of making a perfect work. As for our novel, I may say lastly on this score that as we find it in England to-day it strikes me as addressed in a large degree to 'young people', and that this in itself constitutes a presumption that it will be rather shy. There are certain things which it is generally agreed not to discuss, not even to mention, before young people. That is very well, but the absence of discussion is not a symptom of the moral passion. The purpose of the English novel – 'a truly admirable thing, and a great cause for congratulation' – strikes me therefore as rather negative.

There is one point at which the moral sense and the artistic sense lie very near together; that is in the light of the very obvious truth that the deepest quality of a work of art will always be the quality of the mind of the producer. In proportion as that intelligence is fine will the novel, the picture, the statue partake of the substance of beauty and truth. To be constituted of such elements is, to my vision, to have purpose enough. No good novel will ever proceed from a superficial mind; that seems to me an axiom which, for the artist in fiction, will cover all needful moral ground: if the youthful aspirant take it to heart it will illuminate for him many of the mysteries of 'purpose'.

(Henry James, 'The Art of Fiction' (1884), *Partial Portraits* (London: Macmillan, 1888), pp. 384, 397–8, 405–7.)

(C) D. H. LAWRENCE

Introduction to the American Edition of *New Poems* (1920)

But there is another kind of poetry: the poetry of that which is at hand: the immediate present. In the immediate present there is no perfection, no consummation, nothing finished. The strands are all flying, quivering, intermingling into the web, the waters are shaking the moon. There is no round, consummate moon on the face of running water, nor on the face of the unfinished tide. There are no gems of the living plasm. The living plasm vibrates unspeakably, it inhales the future, it exhales the past, it is the quick of both, and yet it is neither. There is no plasmic finality, nothing crystal, permanent. If we try to fix the living tissue, as the biologists fix it with formation, we have only a hardened bit of the past, the bygone life under our observation.

Life, the ever-present, knows no finality, no finished crystallisation. The perfect rose is only a running flame, emerging and flowing off, and never in any sense at rest, static, finished. Herein lies its transcendent loveliness. The whole tide of all life and all time suddenly heaves, and appears before us as an apparition, a revelation. We look at the very white quick of nascent creation. A water-lily heaves herself from the flood, looks around, gleams, and is gone. We have seen the incarnation, the quick of the ever-swirling flood. We have seen the invisible. We have seen, we have touched, we have partaken of the very substance of creative change, creative mutation. If you tell me about the lotus, tell me of nothing changeless or eternal. Tell me of the mystery of the inexhaustible, forever-unfolding creative spark. Tell me of the incarnate disclosure of the flux, mutation in blossom, laughter and decay perfectly open in their transit, nude in their movement before us. [. . .]

Much has been written about free verse. But all that can be said, first and last, is that free verse is, or should be, direct utterance from the instant, whole man. It is the soul and the mind and body surging at once, nothing left out. They speak all together. [. . .] We can be in ourselves spontaneous and flexible as flame, we can see that utterance rushes out without artificial form or artificial smoothness. But we cannot positively prescribe any motion, any rhythm. All the laws we invent or discover – it amounts to pretty much the same – will fail to apply to free verse. They will only apply to some form of restricted, limited unfree verse.

All we can say is that free verse does *not* have the same nature as restricted verse. It is not of the nature of reminiscence. It is not the past which we treasure in its perfection between our hands. Neither is it the crystal of the perfect future, into which we gaze. Its tide is neither the full, yearning flow of aspiration, nor the sweet, poignant ebb of remembrance and regret. The past and the future are the two great bournes of human emotion, the two great homes of the human days, the two eternities. They are both conclusive, final. Their beauty is the beauty of the goal, finished, perfected. Finished beauty and measured symmetry belong to the stable, unchanging eternities.

But in free verse we look for the insurgent naked throb of the instant moment. To break the lovely form of metrical verse, and to dish up the fragments as a new substance, called *vers libre*, this is what most of the free-versifiers accomplish. They do not know that free verse has its own *nature*, that it is neither star nor pearl, but instantaneous like plasm. It has no goal in either eternity. It has no finish. It has no satisfying stability, satisfying to those who like the immutable. None of this. It is the instant; the quick; the very jetting source of all will-be and has-been. The utterance is like a spasm, naked contact with all influences at once. It does not want to get anywhere. It just takes place.

(D. H. Lawrence, Introduction to *New Poems* (New York: B. W. Huebsch Inc., 1920), pp. ii–iv, vii, vii–ix.)

'Why the Novel Matters' (1936)

Now I absolutely flatly deny that I am a soul, or a body, or a mind, or an intelligence, or a brain, or a nervous system, or a bunch of glands, or any of the rest of these bits of me. The whole is greater than the part. And therefore, I, who am man alive, am greater than my soul, or spirit, or body, or mind, or consciousness, or anything else that is merely a part of me. I am a man, and alive. I am man alive, and as long as I can, I intend to go on being man alive.

For this reason I am a novelist. And being a novelist, I consider myself superior to the saint, the scientist, the philosopher, and the poet, who are all great masters of different bits of man alive, but never get the whole hog.

The novel is the one bright book of life. Books are not life. They are only tremulations on the ether. But the novel as a tremulation can make the whole man alive tremble. Which is more than poetry, philosophy, science, or any other book-tremulation can do.

The novel is the book of life. In this sense, the Bible is a great confused novel. You may say, it is about God. But it is really about man alive. Adam, Eve, Sarai, Abraham, Isaac, Jacob, Samuel, David, Bath-Sheba, Ruth, Esther, Solomon, Job, Isaiah, Jesus, Mark, Judas, Paul, Peter: what is it but man alive, from start to finish? Man alive, not mere bits. Even the Lord is another man alive, in a burning bush, throwing the tablets of stone at Moses's head.

(D. H. Lawrence, 'Why the Novel Matters', *Phoenix: the Posthumous Papers*, ed. Edward D. McDonald (London: Heinemann, 1936), p. 535.)

'Morality and the Novel' (1925)

If we think about it, we find that our life *consists in* this achieving of a pure relationship between ourselves and the living universe about us. This is how I 'save my soul' by accomplishing a pure relationship between me and another person, me and other people, me and a nation, me and a race of men, me and the animals, me and the trees or flowers, me and the earth, me and the skies and sun and stars, me and the moon; an infinity of pure relations, big and little, like the stars of the sky: that makes our eternity, for each one of us. Me and the timber I am sawing, the lines of force I follow, me and the dough I knead for bread, me and the very motion with which I write, me and the bit of gold I have got. This, if we knew it, is our life and our eternity: the subtle, perfected relation between me and my whole circumambient universe.

And morality is that delicate, for ever trembling and changing *balance* between me and my circumambient universe, which precedes and accompanies a true relatedness.

Now here we see the beauty and the great value of the novel. Philosophy, religion, science, they are all of them busy nailing things down, to get a stable equilibrium. Religion, with its nailed-down One God, who says *Thou Shalt*, *Thou shan't*, and hammers home every time; philosophy, with its fixed ideas; science with its 'laws'; they, all of them, all the time, want to nail us on to some tree or other.

But the novel, no! The novel is the highest complex of subtle inter-relatedness that man has discovered. Everything is true in its own time, place, circumstance, and untrue outside of its own place, time, circumstance. If you try to nail anything down in the novel, either it kills the novel, or the novel gets up and walks away with the nail.

Morality in the novel is the trembling instability of the balance. When the novelist puts his thumb in the scale, to pull down the balance to his own predilection, that is immorality.

The modern novel tends to become more and more immoral, as the novelist tends to press his thumb heavier and heavier in the pan: either on the side of love, pure love, or on the side of licentious 'freedom'.

The novel is not, as a rule, immoral because the novelist has any dominant *idea* or *purpose*. The immorality lies in the novelist's helpless, unconscious predilection. Love is a great emotion. But if you set out to write a novel, and you yourself are in the throes of the great predilection for love, love as the supreme, the only emotion worth living for, then you will write an immoral novel.

Because *no* emotion is supreme, or exclusively worth living for. *All* emotions go to the achieving of a living relationship between a human being and the other human being or creature or thing he becomes purely related to. All emotions, including love and hate, and rage and tenderness, go to the adjusting of the oscillating, inestablished balance between two people who amount to anything. If the novelist puts his thumb in the pan, for love, tenderness, sweetness, peace, then he commits an immoral act: he *prevents* the possibility of a pure relationship, a pure relatedness, the only thing that matters: and he makes inevitable the horrible reaction, when he lets his thumb go, towards hate and brutality, cruelty and destruction.

Life is so made that opposites sway about a trembling centre of balance. The sins of the fathers are visited on the children. If the fathers drag down the balance on the side of love, peace, and production, then in the third or fourth generation the balance will swing back violently to hate, rage, and destruction. We must balance as we go.

And of all the art forms, the novel most of all demands the trembling and oscillating of the balance. The 'sweet' novel is more falsified, and therefore more immoral, than the blood-and-thunder novel.

The same with the smart and smudgily cynical novel, which says it doesn't matter what you do, because one thing is as good as another, anyhow, and prostitution is just as much 'life' as anything else.

This misses the point entirely. A thing isn't life just because somebody does it. This the artist ought to know perfectly well. The ordinary bank clerk buying himself a new straw hat isn't 'life' at all: it is just existence, quite all right, like everyday dinners: but not 'life'.

By life, we mean something that gleams, that has the fourth-dimensional quality. If the bank clerk feels really piquant about his hat, if he establishes a lively relation with it, and goes out of the shop with the new straw on his head, a changed man, be-aureoled, then that is life.

The same with the prostitute. If a man establishes a living relation to her, if only for one moment, then it is life. But if it *doesn't:* if it is just money and function, then it is no life, but sordidness, and a betrayal of living.

(D. H. Lawrence, 'Morality and the Novel' (1925), *The Calendar of Modern Letters*, vol. 2, no. 10 (Dec. 1925), pp. 270–2.)

(D) F. R. LEAVIS

'Arnold as Critic' (1938)

The seriousness with which he conceived the function and the importance he ascribed to poetry are more legitimately expressed in the phrase, the best-known tag from the essay, 'criticism of life'. That it is not altogether satisfactory, the animadversion it has been the object of must perhaps be taken to prove: at best we must admit that the intention it expresses hasn't, to a great many readers, made itself satisfactorily clear. Nevertheless,

Arnold leaves us with little excuse for supposing – as some of his most eminent critics have appeared to suppose – that he is demanding doctrine or moral commentary on life or explicit criticism. Nor should it be necessary to point out that all censure passed on him for having, in calling poetry 'criticism of life', produced a bad definition is beside the mark. For it should be obvious to anyone who reads the phrase in its context that Arnold intends, not to define poetry, but, while insisting (a main concern of the essay) that there are different degrees of importance in poetry, to remind us of the nature of the criteria by which comparative judgments are made. [. . .]

In so far as Arnold ever attempts to explain the phrase, it is in such terms as those in which, in the essay on Wordsworth, he explains why it is that Wordsworth must be held to be a greater poet than the 'perfect' Gautier. But with no more explanation than is given in *The Study of Poetry* the intention seems to me plain enough for Arnold's purposes. To define the criteria he was concerned with, those by which we make the more serious kind of comparative judgment, was not necessary, and I cannot see that anything would have been gained by his attempting to define them. His business was to evoke them effectively (can we really hope for anything better?) and that, I think, he must be allowed to have done. We may, when, for example, he tells us why Chaucer is not among the very greatest poets, find him questionable and provoking, but the questions are profitable and the provocations stimulate us to get clear in our own minds. We understand well enough the nature of his approach; the grounds of his criticism are sufficiently present. Pressed for an account of the intention behind the famous phrase, we have to say something like this: we make (Arnold insists) our major judgments about poetry by bringing to bear the completest and profoundest sense of relative value that, aided by the work judged, we can focus from our total experience of life (which includes literature), and our judgment has intimate bearings on the most serious choices we have to make thereafter in our living. We don't ordinarily ask of the critic that he shall tell us anything like this, or shall attempt to define the criteria by which he makes his major judgments of value. But Arnold appears to challenge the demand and so earns reprobation for not satisfying it. By considering the age to which he was addressing himself we are able to do him justice; but if in this way he may be said to 'date,' it is not in any discreditable sense.

There is still to be met the pretty general suspicion to which Mr Eliot gives voice when he says that Arnold 'was apt to think of the greatness of poetry rather than of its genuineness'. It is a suspicion that is the harder to lay because, with a slight shift of accent, it turns into an unexceptionable observation: 'The best of Arnold's criticism is an illustration of his ethical views, and contributes to his discrimination of the values and relations of the components of the good life.' This very fairly accords due praise while suggesting limitations. We have, nevertheless, to insist that, but for Arnold's gifts as a literary critic, that criticism would not have had its excellence. And when the suspicion takes such form as the following, some answer must clearly be attempted:

> Yet he was so conscious of what, for him, poetry was *for*, that he could not altogether see it for what it is. And I am not sure that he was highly sensitive to the musical qualities of verse. His own occasional bad lapses arouse the suspicion; and so far as I can recollect he never emphasizes this virtue of poetic style, this fundamental, in his criticism.

Whatever degree of justice there may be in these suggestions, one point can be made at once: some pages of *The Study of Poetry* are explicitly devoted to considering 'genuineness' – the problem of how the critic makes those prior kinds of judgment, those initial recognitions of life and quality, which must precede, inform and control all profitable discussion of poetry and any evaluation of it as 'criticism of life'. Towards the close of the essay we read:

> 'To make a happy fireside clime
>   To weans and wife,
> That's the true pathos and sublime
>   Of human life.'

> There is criticism of life for you, the admirers of Burns will say to us; there is the application of ideas to life! There is undoubtedly.

And Arnold goes on to insist (in terms that would invite the charge of circularity if we were being offered a definition, as we are not) that the evaluation of poetry as 'criticism of life' is inseparable from its evaluation as poetry; that the moral judgment that concerns us as critics must be at the same time a delicately relevant response of sensibility; that, in short, we cannot separate the consideration of 'greatness' from the consideration of 'genuineness'. The test for 'genuineness' Arnold indicates in this way:

> Those laws [of poetic truth and poetic beauty] fix as an essential condition, in the poet's treatment of such matters as are here is question, high-seriousness – the high seriousness which comes from absolute sincerity. The accent of high seriousness, born of absolute sincerity, is what gives to such verse as
>
> 'In la sua volontade è nostra pace. . .'
>
> to such criticism of life as Dante's, its power. Is this accent felt in the passages which I have been quoting from Burns? Surely not; surely, if our sense is quick, we must perceive that we have not in those passages a voice from the very inmost soul of the genuine Burns; he is not speaking to us from these depths, he is more or less preaching.

This passage is old-fashioned in its idiom, and perhaps 'high seriousness' should be dismissed as a mere nuisance. But 'absolute sincerity', a quality belonging to the 'inmost soul' and manifested in an 'accent', an 'accent that we feel if our sense is quick' – this phrasing, in the context, seems to me suggestive in a wholly creditable and profitable way. And actually it has a force behind it that doesn't appear in the quotation: it is strengthened decisively by what has come earlier in the essay.

(F. R. Leavis, 'Arnold as Critic' (1938), *A Selection from Scrutiny*, compiled by F. R. Leavis, 2 vols (Cambridge UP, 1968), I. 261–2, 262–5.)

'"Thought" and Emotional Quality' (1945)

The poet, we can say, whose habitual mode – whose emotional habit – was represented by that poem ['Break, break, break'] would not only be very limited; we should expect to find him noticeably given to certain weaknesses and vices. Further, the reader who cannot see that Tennyson's poem, with all its distinction and refinement, yields a satisfaction inferior in kind to that represented by Wordsworth, cannot securely appreciate the highest poetic achievement at its true worth and is not very likely to be at all strong or sure in the kind of judgment that discriminates between *Break, break, break* and *Heraclitus*.

'Inferior in kind' – by what standards? Here we come to the point at which literary criticism, as it must, enters overtly into questions of emotional hygiene and moral value – more generally (there seems no other adequate phrase), of spiritual health. It seems best not to say anything further by way of immediate answer to the challenge. By the time we have closed the discussion of impersonality, a theme that will come up in explicit form again, a great deal more will have been said to elucidate, both directly and indirectly, the nature of the answer. The immediate business is to push on with the method of exploration by concrete analysis – analysis of judiciously assorted instances.

(F. R. Leavis, '"Thought" and Emotional Quality' (1945), *A Selection from Scrutiny*, compiled by F. R. Leavis, 2 vols (Cambridge UP, 1968), I. 213–14.)

'Mr Pryce-Jones, the British Council and British Culture' (1951)

When one read in Mr Noel Annan's *Leslie Stephen* (see chapter IX) an astonishing travesty of the idea and the practice of criticism as they are to be found in *Scrutiny* one reflected that the author's training had not been in the literary-critical field – though it was still disconcerting that the presumable qualifications to discuss Stephen's thought should be divorced from an elementary understanding of the nature of literary criticism. But where, one now has to ask, – where among the professionals in the literary-critical field – is such elementary understanding to be counted on? Mr Pryce-Jones [whose article on 'Literary Periodicals' Leavis is discussing] is reputed to occupy the editorial chair of an augustly institutional critical weekly; this passage (confirming the effect of what has been quoted above) gives the measure of his enlightenment about the function he has it in charge to promote: 'There is, in other words, no desirable life of which literary reviews are an essential component and in which fixed standards of criticism gain a kind of legal backing. . .'

'Fixed standards', 'impose accepted values', – no one .who knew what 'standards' are could talk about 'fixed standards' or 'imposing them' or providing them with a 'legal backing'. A judgment is a real judgment, or it is nothing. It must, that is, be a sincere personal judgment; but it aspires to be more than personal. Essentially it has the form: 'This is so, is it not?' But the agreement appealed for must be real, or it serves no critical purpose and can bring no satisfaction to the critic. What his activity of its very nature aims at, in fact, is a collaborative exchange or commerce. Without a many-sided real exchange – the collaboration by which the object, the poem (for example), in which the individual minds meet and at the same time the true judgments concerning it are established – the function of criticism cannot be said to be working. Without a wide coherent public, capable of making its response felt – capable, that is, of taking a more or less active part in that collaboration – there is, for the critic, no effective appeal to standards. For standards (which are not of the order of the measures in the Weights and Measures Office) are 'there' only in and by the collaborative process that criticism essentially is.

(F. R. Leavis, 'Mr Pryce-Jones, the British Council and British Culture' (1951), *A Selection from Scrutiny*, compiled by F. R. Leavis, 2 vols (Cambridge UP, 1968), I. 183.)

'Reality and Sincerity' (1952)

A difference in manner and tone between Hardy's poem ['After a Journey'] and the other two [Emily Brontë's 'Cold in the Earth' and Alexander Smith's 'Barbara'] will have been observed at once: unlike them it is not declamatory. The point should in justice lead on to a positive formulation, and this may not come as readily; certain stylistic characteristics that may at first strike the reader as oddities and clumsinesses tend to delay the recognition of the convincing intimate naturalness. It turns out, however, that the essential ethos of the manner is given in

Where you will next be there's no knowing.

This intimacy we are at first inclined to describe as 'conversational', only to replace that adjective by 'self-communing' when we have recognized that, even when Hardy (and it is significant that we say 'Hardy') addresses the 'ghost' he is still addressing himself. And it shouldn't take long to recognize that the marked idiosyncrasy of idiom and diction going with the intimacy of tone achieves some striking precisions and felicities. Consider, for instance, the verb in

Facing round about me everywhere. . .

There is nothing that strikes us as odd in that 'facing', but it is

a use created for the occasion, and when we look into its
unobtrusive naturalness it turns out to have a positive and
'inevitable' rightness the analysis of which involves a precise
account of the 'ghost's' status – which in its turn involves a
precise account of the highly specific situation defined by the
poem.

Then again, there is that noun in the fourth line which (I can
testify) has offended readers not incapable of recognizing its
felicity:

> And the unseen waters' ejaculations awe me.

'Ejaculations' gives with vivid precision that sound that 'awes'
Hardy: the slap of the waves on the rocky walls; the slap with
its prolonging reverberant syllables – the hollow voice, in fact,
that, in stanza three, 'seems to call out to me from forty years
ago' (and the hollowness rings significantly through the poem).

In fact, the difference first presenting itself as an absence of
declamatory manner and tone, examined, leads to the perception
of positive characteristics – precisions of concrete realization,
specificities, complexities – that justify the judgment I now
advance: Hardy's poem, put side by side with Emily Brontë's, is
seen to have a great advantage in *reality*. This term, of course,
has to be given its due force by the analysis yet to be done – the
analysis it sums up; but it provides the right pointer. And to
invoke another term, more inescapably one to which a critic
must try and give some useful force by appropriate and careful
use, if he can contrive that: to say that Hardy's poem has an
advantage in reality is to say (it will turn out) that is represents
a profounder and completer sincerity.

Emily Brontë's poem is a striking one, but when we go back
to it from Hardy's the contrast precipitates the judgment that, in
it, she is dramatizing herself in a situation such as she has
clearly not known in actual experience: what she offers is
betrayingly less real. We find that we have declamatory
generality – talking *about* – in contrast to Hardy's quiet
presentment of specific fact and concrete circumstance; in
contrast, that is, to detailed complexity evoking a total situation
that, as merely evoked, carries its power and meaning in itself.
Glancing back at Alexander Smith we can say that whereas in
postulating the situation of *Barbara* (he can hardly be said to
imagine it) he is seeking a licence for an emotional debauch,
Emily Brontë conceives a situation in order to have the
satisfaction of a disciplined imaginative exercise: the satisfaction

of dramatizing herself in a tragic role – an attitude, nobly impressive, of sternly controlled passionate desolation.

The marks of the imaginative self-projection that is insufficiently informed by experience are there in the poem, and (especially with the aid of the contrast with Hardy) a duly perceptive reader could discern and describe them, without knowing the biographical fact. They are there in the noble (and, given the intimate offer of the theme, paradoxical) declamation, and in the accompanying generality, the absence of any convincing concreteness of a presented situation that speaks for itself.

(F. R. Leavis, 'Reality and Sincerity' (1952), *A Selection from Scrutiny*, compiled by F. R. Leavis, 2 vols (Cambridge UP, 1968), I. 251–2.)

(E) LIONEL TRILLING

A Gathering of Fugitives (1957)

Not, it may be granted, by reason of the essence of literature but certainly by reason of prevailing accident, the judgment of literature is overtly and explicitly a moral and intellectual judgment. The cogency, the appositeness, the logicality, the *truth* of ideas must always be passed upon by literary criticism. Aestheticians, and some literary critics, are in a sweat to set limits upon this mode of judgment. They are committed to the idea that the aesthetic experience is characterized by its remoteness from considerations of practicality, and they tell us that literature is an art like any other, and that the right experience of it shares this general characteristic of the aesthetic experience, that considerations of practicality – morality and truth – are essentially irrelevant. Alas! literature seems always to be telling us the opposite. As against its own purely aesthetic elements, it is always mustering the reminders of the practical – of the mundane, the dirty, the ugly, the painful, the moral – and it does so very consciously: Jane Austen's objection to *Pride and Prejudice*, that it was too perfect, too unified and harmonious in its style, that its perfection needed to be ravished by the presence of something actual and dull and doctrinal, ought to be framed over the desk of every aesthetician and critic. Literature doesn't easily submit to the category of aesthetic contemplative

disinterestedness – so much of it insists '*De* TE *fabula* – this
means *you*,' and often goes on to say, 'And you'd better *do*
something about it quick.' Time and tradition diminish our
awareness of literature's nasty unaesthetic tendency to insist
upon some degree of immediate practicality, and the
aestheticians take all possible advantage of this effect of time and
tradition. But if human experience – human danger and pain –
is made the material of an artistic creation, the judgment that is
directed upon that creation will involve important considerations
of practicality and thus of cogency, relevance, appositeness,
logicality, and truth. Unless we get the clear signal from the
literary work itself that we are not to ask the question, we
inevitably do ask, 'Is this true, is this to be believed, is this to
shape our future judgments of experience?' And even when the
literary work does give us the clear signal that we are not to
apply this standard, we are sure to ask some such question as,
'What is being implied about logic and truth by this wilful
departure from logic and truth?'

(Lionel Trilling, *A Gathering of Fugitives* (London: Secker & Warburg,
1957), pp. 135–6.)

Beyond Culture (1965)

[S]ome great writers have in their work given utterance or
credence to conservative and even reactionary ideas,
and [. . .] some in their personal lives have maintained a settled
indifference to all political issues, or a disdain of them. No
reader is likely to derive political light from either the works or
the table talk of a modern literary genius, and some readers (of
weak mind) might even be led into bad political ways.

If these writers are to be brought to the bar of judgement,
anyone who speaks as their advocate is not, as Sir Charles
[Snow] says, defending the indefensible. The advocacy can be
conducted in honest and simple ways. It is not one of these
ways to say that literature is by its nature or by definition
innocent. Literature is powerful enough for us to suppose that it
has the capability of doing harm. But the ideational influence of
literature is by no means always as direct as, for polemical
purposes, people sometimes say it is. As against the dismay of
Sir Charles and the distinguished scientist at the reactionary
tendencies of modern literary genuises, there is the fact that the
English poets who learned their trade from Yeats and Eliot, or

even from Pound, have notably had no sympathy with the social ideas and attitudes of their poetical masters.

Every university teacher of literature will have observed the circumstance that young people who are of radical social and political opinion are virtually never troubled by the opposed views or the settled indifference of the great modern writers. This is not because the young exempt the writer from dealing with the serious problems of living, or because they see him through a mere aesthetic haze. It is because they know – and quite without instruction – that, in D. H. Lawrence's words, they are to trust the tale and not the teller of the tale. They perceive that the tale is always on the side of their own generous impulses. They know that, if the future is in the bones of anyone, it is in the bones of the literary genius, and exactly because the present is in his bones, exactly because the past is in his bones. They know that if a work of literature has any true artistic existence, it has value as a criticism of life; in whatever complex way it has chosen to speak, it is making a declaration about the qualities that life should have, about the qualities life does not have but should have. They feel, I think, that it is simply not possible for a work of literature that comes within the borders of greatness *not* to ask for more energy and fineness of life, and, by its own communication of awareness, bring those qualities into being. And if, in their experience of such a work, they happen upon an expression of contempt for some idea which they have connected with political virtue, they are not slow to understand that it is not the idea in its ideal form that is being despised, but the idea as it passes current in specious form, among certain and particular persons. I have yet to meet the student committed to an altruistic politics who is alienated from Stephen Daedalus by that young man's disgust with political idealism, just as I have yet to meet the student from the most disadvantaged background who feels debarred from what Yeats can give him by the poet's slurs upon shopkeepers or by anything else in his inexhaustible fund of snobbery.

(Lionel Trilling, 'The Leavis-Snow Controversy', *Beyond Culture* (1965; Harmondsworth: Penguin, 1967), pp. 150–1.)

CHAPTER 3

CLASS AND GENDER

Literature as an institution has tended to be an elitist preserve for obvious reasons. The level of literacy, economic independence and access to culture needed for someone to become a 'great writer' have been beyond the scope of most individuals until relatively recently. Historically, the system of education and the structure of communication have privileged certain classes. The middle classes did not emerge as significant in literary culture until the eighteenth century, when their economic and political power was expressed in the rise of the novel and an accompanying enormous growth in readership and book production and distribution. The rise of the labour movement in the late nineteenth and early twentieth centuries laid the foundation of a further development of literary production and readership. Leavis saw only a loss of tradition in these developments. Francis Mulhern argues that *Scrutiny's* strategy was to establish a cultural community which was above all class interests. Culture had fallen into the hands of a decadent, upper-class elite. The new elite would cut itself off from economic and social structures and cultivate through the study of literature a class-free intellectual life. After 1945, when grammar-school education became open to brighter working-class pupils a larger number of writers from lower-class backgrounds began to emerge. Raymond Williams and Richard Hoggart are the two best-known cultural critics to arise from humble backgrounds through the grammar-school system. However, Williams' own analysis of these processes is pessimistic: he considers that social institutions are too rigid to permit real change.

Richard Hoggart's celebrated *The Uses of Literacy* (1957) was for many the starting point in the study of a new continent – working-class culture as viewed from the inside. He reminds us

that many earlier literary representations of the working class
were either gross caricatures or patronizingly romantic. The
great Victorian novelists' attempts to convey working-class life
and politics were studied critically in Raymond Williams' *Culture
and Society* (1958). Hoggart is no less penetrating in his insight
into the way in which middle-class Marxists are often
patronizing or romantic about the working class. His own study
aims to give more than a merely factual or statistical account of
working-class culture, but rather to convey its inner rhythms and
to 'detect the differing pressures of emotion behind idiomatic
phrases and ritualistic observances'. Like Williams, Hoggart is
highly conscious of his own working-class origins and is inclined
to place a rather Leavisian emphasis upon the importance of
personal experience (cf. V,2,D). The interviewers in Raymond
Williams' *Politics and Letters* (1979) criticized him from this angle:
many social processes are simply not accessible through merely
'personal experience'. British empiricism (in its Leavisian form)
is not as naive as this suggests, but is nevertheless vulnerable to
the criticism. Despite (or perhaps because of) this theoretical
weakness, Williams and Hoggart were able to map out British
culture 'from below'.

Not all feminists are socialists, of course. Nevertheless, there is
an obvious parallel between the notions of class oppression and
gender oppression. Consciousness of these oppressions (race
would be a third focus) is a major source of revolutionary or
reformist ideologies in modern societies. Some feminists believe
that women's oppression can be understood only within a large
understanding of class oppression. Others reject this, arguing
that patriarchical societies predate class societies, and that
socialist societies are no less patriarchal than capitalist societies
(Kate Millett used the term 'patriarchy' to describe the cause of
women's oppression in *Sexual Politics*, 1970). Certainly, the
assumption of women's inferiority goes back a long way:
Aristotle declared that 'the female is female by virtue of a
certain lack of qualities'. One might see a continuity between
this and Freud's assumption that female sexuality is shaped by
'penis-envy'.

Feminists are understandably suspicious of 'theory', because
they see it as having masculine connotations. The power of the
natural sciences projects a daunting image of male structures
relentlessly pushing the human race towards destruction. Simone
de Beauvoir's *The Second Sex* (1949) established the principles of
modern feminism. When a woman tries to define herself, she

starts by saying 'I am a woman', revealing the fundamental
asymmetry between the terms 'masculine' and 'feminine'. 'Man'
defines the human, not woman. Woman is riveted into a
lopsided relationship with man: he is the One, she is the Other.
De Beauvoir shows with great erudition that man's dominance
has been secured through the ages by an ideological power:
legislators, priests, scientists and philosophers have all promoted
the idea of women's subordination. For feminists to break this
patriarchal power it is necessary to challenge men at the level of
theory, but without entering the theoretical domain on men's
terms. The psychoanalytic theories of Lacan and Kristeva (see
II,5,E–F) have suggested to some that female sexuality is
revolutionary, subversive and 'heterogeneous'. The female
principle is simply to remain outside male definitions of the
female. Hélène Cixous's 'The Laugh of the Medusa' is a
celebrated manifesto of women's writing which calls for women
to put their 'bodies' into their writing. She associates Kristeva's
'semiotic' system (see II,5,F) with female sexuality, which
transgresses the logic of male power systems. She believes that
feminist writing 'will always surpass the discourse that regulates
the phallocentric system'. Female sexuality is directly associated
with poetic productivity – with the psychosomatic drives which
disrupt the tyranny of unified and logocentric meaning. The
term 'phallogocentrism' wittily combines the feminist term
'phallocentrism' (determining meaning according to phallus-
power) and Derrida's 'logocentrism' (see III,7,B).

Tillie Olsen, Ellen Moers, Elaine Showalter, and others
building upon the work of Virginia Woolf, have developed
definitions of women's writing and established its lines and
traditions by encouraging printing houses to reissue 'lost' works.
Showalter examines British women novelists since the Brontës
from the point of view of women's experience. She defines the
tradition by establishing three phases: 'feminine', 'feminist' and
'female', each achieving a greater liberation than its predecessor
without losing its distinctiveness as women's writing. This field
of feminist activity has been called 'gynocriticism'. It deals with
the distinctive themes, structures and genres of women's writing,
the nature of female creativity and female language,and the
historical problems facing women as writers. Woolf believed that
women have always faced social and economic obstacles to their
literary ambitions. She was very conscious of the imposed
limitations of her own education. In 'Professions for Women' she
discussed the disabling nineteenth-century ideology of

womanhood. The ideal of 'the Angel in the House' called for
women to be sympathetic, unselfish, and pure. In order to make
space for writing a woman had to use 'wiles' and flattery. The
taboo of the expression of female passion was another serious
restriction. *A Room of One's Own* (1929) opens up the question of
female language and the nature of genres. Raymond Williams
argued, in *The Country and the City* (1976), that the pastoral genre
is a product of class ideology. In a similar way Woolf claims
that the genres were made by men for their own use. Only the
novel gives women a workable space, and even then the form
has to be reworked for its new purpose – expressing the female
body.

Background reading

[See *Working Papers in Cultural Studies*, IV. 3]
Elizabeth Abel (ed.), *Writing and Sexual Difference* (Brighton: Harvester,
    1982).
Michèle Barrett (ed.), *Virginia Woolf: Women and Writing* (London:
    Women's Press, 1979).
Josephine Donovan (ed.), *Feminist Literary Criticism: Explorations in Theory*
    (Lexington: Kentucky UP, 1975).
Mary Eagleton (ed.), *Feminist Literary Theory: A Reader* (Oxford:
    Blackwell, 1986).
Jane Gallop, *Feminism and Psychoanalysis: The Daughter's Seduction* (London:
    Macmillan, 1982).
Mary Jacobus (ed.), *Women Writing and Writing about Women* (London:
    Croom Helm, 1979).
Elaine Marks and Isabelle de Courtivron (eds), *New French Feminisms*
    (Brighton: Harvester Press, 1980).
Toril Moi, *Sexual/Textual Politics: Feminist Literary Theory* (London:
    Methuen, 1985).
K. K. Ruthven, *Feminist Literary Studies: An Introduction* (Cambridge:
    Cambridge UP, 1984).

(A) RICHARD HOGGART

The Uses of Literacy (1957)

It will be necessary to define rather more specifically what I
mean by 'the working- classes', but difficulties of definition are
less troublesome than are those of avoiding the romanticisms
which tempt anyone who discusses 'the workers' or 'the common
people', and these romanticisms deserve to be mentioned first.

For they increase the danger of over-stressing the admirable
qualities of earlier working-class culture and its debased
condition today. The two over-emphases tend to reinforce each
other, and so the contrast is often exaggerated. We may have
serious doubts about the quality of working-class life today, and
especially about the speed with which it may seem to
deteriorate. But some of the more debilitating invitations have
been successful only because they have been able to appeal to
established attitudes which were not wholly admirable; and
though the contemporary ills which particularly strike an
observer from outside certainly exist, their effects are not always
as consierable as a diagnosis from outside would suggest, if
only because working-class people still possess some older and
inner resistances.

No doubt such an over-emphasis is often inspired by a strong
admiration for the potentialities of working-class people and a
consequent pity for their situation. Related to it is a more
positive over-expectation which one frequently finds among
middle-class intellectuals with strong social consciences. Some
people of this kind have for a long time tended to see every
second working-class man as a Felix Holt or a Jude the
Obscure. Perhaps this is because most of the working-class
people they have known closely have been of an unusual and
self-selected kind, and in special circumstances, young men and
women at Summer Schools and the like, exceptional individuals
whom the chance of birth has deprived of their proper
intellectual inheritance, and who have made remarkable efforts
to gain it. Naturally, I do not intend in any way to limit their
importance as individuals. They are exceptional, in their nature
untypical of working-class people; their very presence at Summer
Schools, at meetings of learned societies and courses of lectures,
is the result of a moving-away from the landscape which the
majority of their fellows inhabit without much apparent strain.
They would be exceptional people in any class: they reveal less
about their class than about themselves.

From the pity – 'How fine they would be if only . . .', to the
praise – 'How fine they are simply because . . .': here we
encounter pastoral myths and 'Wife of Bath' admirations. The
working classes are at bottom in excellent health – so the
pastoral descriptions run – in better health than other classes;
rough and unpolished perhaps, but diamonds nevertheless;
rugged, but 'of sterling worth': not refined, not intellectual, but
with both feet on the ground; capable of a good belly-laugh,

charitable and forthright. They are, moreover, possessed of a
racy and salty speech, touched with wit, but always with its
hard grain of common sense. These over-emphases vary in
strength, from the slight over-stressing of the quaint aspects of
working-class life to be found in many major novelists to the
threadbare fancies of popular contemporary writers. How many
major English writers are there who do not, however slightly,
over-emphasise the salty features of working-class life? George
Eliot does so, unusually brilliant though her observation of
workers is; and the bias is more evident in Hardy. When we
come to our own much more consciously manipulative times, we
meet the popular novelists' patronisingly flattered little men with
their flat caps and flat vowels, their well-scrubbed wives with
well-scrubbed doorsteps; fine stock – and amusing too! Even a
writer as astringent and seemingly unromantic as George Orwell
never quite lost the habit of seeing the working classes through
the cosy fug of an Edwardian music-hall. There is a wide range
of similar attitudes running down to the folksy ballyhoo of the
Sunday columnists, the journalists who always remember to
quote with admiration the latest bon-mot of their pub-pal 'Alf'.
They have to be rejected more forcefully, I think, because there
is an element of truth in what they say and it is a pity to see it
inflated for display.

Again, one has sometimes to be cautious of the interpretations
given by historians of the working-class movement. The subject
is fascinating and moving; there is a vast amount of important
and inspiring material about working-class social and political
aspirations. But it is easy for a reader to be led into at least a
half-assumption that these are histories of the working classes
rather than, primarily, histories of the activities – and the
valuable consequences for almost every member of the working
classes – of a minority. Probably the authors would specifically
claim no more for them, and these aims are important enough.
But from such books I do sometimes bring away an impression
that their authors overrate the place of political activity in
working-class life, that they do not always have an adequate
sense of the grass-roots of that life.

A middle-class Marxist's view of the working classes often
includes something of each of the foregoing errors. He pities the
betrayed and debased worker, whose faults he sees as almost
entirely the result of the grinding system which controls him. He
admires the remnants of the noble savage, and has a nostalgia
for those 'best of all' kinds of art, rural folk-art or genuinely

popular urban art, and a special enthusiasm for such scraps of them as he thinks he can detect today. He pities and admires the Jude-the-Obscure aspect of working people. Usually, he succeeds in part-pitying and part-patronising working-class people beyond any semblance of reality.

It is some novels, after all, that may bring us really close to the quality of working-class life – such a novel as Lawrence's *Sons and Lovers*, at least, rather than more popular or more consciously proletarian fiction. And so, in their own way, do some of the detailed surveys of working-class life which sociologists have made during the last twenty years. These books convey powerfully the complex and claustrophobic impression which working-class life can make on an observer who tries to know it in all its concreteness. I mean the impression of being immersed in an endless forest, full of the most minute detail, all of it different and yet all of it similar; a great mass of faces and habits and actions, yet most of them apparently not very meaningful. The impression seems to me both right and wrong: right in that it indicates the sprawling and multitudinous and infinitely detailed character of working-class life, and the sense – often depressing to an outsider – of an immense uniformity, of always being part of a huge and seething crowd of people, all very similar even in the most important and individual matters. I think such an impression is wrong if it leads us to construct an image of working-class people only from adding together the variety of statistics given in some of these sociological works, from the numbers who do this or do not do that, from the percentage who said that they believe in God, or who thought free-love was 'alright in its way'. A sociological survey may or may not assist us here, but clearly we have to try to see beyond the habits to what the habits stand for, to see through the statements to what the statements really mean (which may be the opposite of the statements themselves), to detect the differing pressures of emotion behind idiomatic phrases and ritualistic observances.

A writer who is himself from the working-classes has his own temptations to error, somewhat different from but no less than those of a writer from another class. I am from the working classes and feel even now both close to them and apart from them. In afew more years this double relationship may not, I suppose, be so apparent to me; but it is bound to affect what I say. It may help me to come nearer to giving a felt sense of working-class life, to avoid some of an outsider's more obvious risks of misinterpretation. On the other hand, this very emotional involvement presents considerable dangers. Thus it seems to me that the changes described in the second half of this book are, so far, tending to cause the working classes to lose, culturally, much that was valuable and to gain less than their new situation should have allowed. To the extent that I can judge the matter objectively, that is my belief. Yet in writing I found myself constantly having to resist a strong inner pressure to make the old much more admirable than the new, and the new more to be condemned, than my conscious understanding of the material gave me grounds for. Presumably some kind of nostalgia was colouring the material in advance: I have done what I could to remove its effects.

In both halves of the book I discovered a tendency in myself, because the subject is so much part of my origins and growth, to be unwarrantedly sharp towards those features in working-class life of which I disapprove. Related to this is the urge to lay one's ghosts; at the worst, it can be a temptation to 'do down' one's class, out of a pressing ambiguity in one's attitudes to it. Conversely, I found a tendency to over-value those features in working-class life of which I approve, and this tempted me towards a sentimentality, a romanticising of my background, as though I were subconsciously saying to my present acquaintance – see, in spite of all, such a childhood is richer than yours.

(Richard Hoggart, *The Uses of Literacy* (London: Chatto & Windus, 1957), pp. 15–19.)

(B) RAYMOND WILLIAMS

The Long Revolution (1961)

There is no single relation between the nature of a society and the character of its literature, but there are significant and possibly significant relations which seem to vary with the actual history. Since social origins have been factually related, in varying ways, both to educational opportunity and to methods of life which affect a writer's following his vocation, it can be said that this complex is of permanent significance, and has visibly affected parts of our literary development. Yet the emphasis should not fall only on origins. The character of literature is also visibly affected, in varying ways, by the nature of the communication system and by the changing character of audiences. When we see the important emergence of writers from a new social group, we must look not only at them, but at the new institutions and forms created by the wider social group to which they belong. The Elizabethan theatre is an exceptionally complex example, since as an institution it was largely created by individual middle-class speculators, and was supplied with plays by writers from largely middle-class and trading and artisan families, yet in fact was steadily opposed by the commercial middle class and, though serving popular audiences, survived through the protection of the court and the nobility. This very protection, later, steadily narrowed both drama and audiences, until in the Restoration a very narrow class was setting the dominant tone. The formation in the eighteenth century of an organized middle-class audience can be seen as in part due to certain writers from the same social group, but also, and perhaps mainly, as an independent formation which then drew these writers to it and gave them their opportunity. The expansion and further organization of this middle-class audience can be seen to have continued until the late nineteenth century, drawing in new writers from varied social origins but giving them, through its majority institutions, a general homogeneity. This general situation has persisted, but already in the nineteenth century there were signs of a break, with individuals deviating from the majority patterns, and, by the end of the century, a distinct and organized minority deviation. The social situation of literature in the twentieth century has been largely the interaction of continuing majority patterns, with an increasingly standard route into them, and this marked dissenting minority, which has tended to support and value writers from outside the majority pattern, and to provide an alternative outlet and affiliation for dissenting members of the majority groups. If we compare the social basis of literature between 1850 and 1870 and that between 1919 and 1939 we find in both cases an organized middle-class reading public as the major element, but whereas in the earlier period the literature was comparatively homogeneous, with most of its creators drawn from the same social group as the actual public, in the later period there is evidence of two publics, a majority and a minority, the former continuing the earlier type of relationship, the latter, while attracting individual dissenters, finding its major figures from outside, either from another culture or from other social groups. A large part of important modern literature –

many novels, many plays, almost all poetry – has been communicated through the institutions of this minority public, in sharp contrast with the mid-Victorian situation, where the majority institutions were still closely related to the most important work of the time. The appearance of contributors from new social groups within the culture, which has attracted attention in recent years, has been normally through the institutions of this minority. Most of the new writers from the families of clerical and industrial workers are in fact being read not by the social groups from which they come, but by the dissident middle class. The expanding audience for novels and plays certainly includes members of new social groups, but in general they are simply being absorbed into the existing majority public. The danger of this situation is that the minority public may soon be the only identifiable group with an evident and particular social affiliation – defined largely through university education. There is some evidence that the separation of the majority public from its most creative members is leaving a cultural vacuum easily penetrated from outside. The rapid Americanization of most of the popular art-forms can be understood in these terms, at a time when so much of the best English art and thinking is closely related to an identifiable social minority which, with a limited educational system, most British people have no real chance of entering.

Thus the relations between literature and society can be seen to vary considerably, in changing historical situations. As a society changes, its literature changes, though often in unexpected ways, for it is a part of social growth and not simply its reflection. At times, a rising social group will create new institutions which, as it were, release its own writers. At other times, writers from new social groups will simply make their way into existing institutions, and work largely within their terms. This is the important theoretical context for the discussion of mobility, of which we have heard so much in our own generation. It is significant that mobility is now normally discussed primarily in individual terms and that the writer is so often taken as an example: he, like other artists, may be born anywhere, and can move, as an individual, very rapidly through the whole society. But in fact there are two major kinds of mobility: the individual career, which writers have often exemplified, and the rise of a whole social group, which creates new institutions and sometimes, as in the early eighteenth century, brings its writers with it. The problems of mobility can never be adequately discussed unless this distinction is made. Those affecting writers, in our own day, are primarily the result of a combination of individual mobility with the relative stability of institutions. This can be seen in the many literary works which take contemporary mobility as theme. At the end of the eighteenth century, Godwin, in *Caleb Williams*, produced an early example of such a career, with individual mobility very limited and with the institutions in relation to which it operated both powerful and harsh. Stendhal, in *Scarlet and Black*, took the same situation much further, ending with the individual being destroyed, first in character and then actually, instead of being merely hunted down to a compromise. The usual implication of Victorian treatments of this theme was (in default of one or other of the several magical solutions) that of control: the terms of origin must be basically respected, or the individual would degenerate. Hardy's protest, in *Jude the Obscure*, leaves the very effort hopeless. Lawrence introduced the new situation: the rapid if resentful rise, characteristically through art, into the dissident minority culture, but then, finally, into exile. In our own period, the characteristic pattern has been that of the more freely mobile individual mocking or raging at the institutions which are made available for him to join, or else, if he acquiesces, suffering rapid personal deterioration (cf. *Lucky Jim*, *Look Back in Anger*, *Room at the Top*). There is a continuing sense of deadlock, and much of the experience generated within it seems sterile. This is because the terms of mobility, thus conceived, are hopelessly limited. The combination of individual mobility with the stability of institutions and ways of thinking leads to this deadlock inevitably. And the experience of artists and intellectuals is then particularly misleading, for while such experience records particular local tensions, much of the real experience of mobility, in our is that of whole social groups moving into new ways of life: not only the individual rising, but the society changing. This latter experience is, however, very difficult to negotiate while the institutions towards which writers and thinkers are attracted retain their limited social reference, and while new groups have been relatively unsuccessful in creating their own cultural institutions. There is an obvious danger of the advantage of individual writers drawn from more varied social origins being limited or nullified by their absorption into pre-existing standard patterns (as obviously now in the system of higher education) or by their concentration on fighting these patterns, rather than finding or helping to create new patterns.

The problems of individual mobility have in fact been worked
through to the point where the definition of mobility in
individual terms can be plainly seen as inadequate. The whole
society is moving, and the most urgent issue is the creation of
new and relevant institutions.

(Raymond Williams, *The Long Revolution* (1961; Harmondsworth:
Penguin, 1965), pp. 265–9.)

(C) FRANCIS MULHERN

The Moment of 'Scrutiny' (1979)

The meaning that *Scrutiny* discerned in the social history of
modern England is by now a legend. The three hundred years
from the reign of Elizabeth to the present day saw an old
agrarian order governed by shared and settled custom driven
steadily towards dissolution. The crucial episode in this history
was the Industrial Revolution, which fatally disrupted an order
already shaken by the social effects of the Civil War and set the
country on a course of economic and social advance which, by
the early twentieth century, had flushed out the few remaining
enclaves of the old way of life. The essence of this process was
decline, from a homogeneous, naturally ordered and
psychologically whole community into an artificial, atomized and
psychologically splintered aggregate, from the 'coherent and self-
explanatory' life of Sturt's village into the urban-industrial
wasteland described and denounced in *Culture and Environment*; in
the terms made famous by the German sociologist Ferdinand
Tönnies, a fall from *Gemeinschaft* into *Gesellschaft*, in those of
Scrutiny, the calamitous loss of 'the organic community'. [. . .]
Whereas the old agrarian order had spontaneously reproduced
the values of 'culture' in society at large, the automatic tendency
of industrial 'civilization' was to negate them, and to marginalize
and disperse their representatives – the fate of 'culture' in the
modern epoch was personified in the isolated, mildly ridiculous
figure of 'the highbrow'. *Scrutiny's* strategic objective was
accordingly to *organize* the defenders of 'culture' as an effective
force. As the 'Manifesto' put it: 'the trouble is not that such
persons form a minority, but that they are scattered and
unorganized.' Its organizational model was of necessity that of
an *élite*. For if the industrial order was constitutionally inimical
to 'culture', it followed that none of its given classes or sub-

groups could provide a vehicle for 'continuity'. The 'minority' could only function as a compact, 'rootless' oppositional group formed and maintained against the natural bias of society, bearers of 'an autonomous culture, a culture independent of any economic, technical or social system as none has been before'. Its main area of activity was to be *literary criticism*. For in the degree that literature was the main surviving witness of an existential integrity that had disappeared from the social world, then, as Leavis argued, 'literary criticism . . . should be the best possible training for intelligence – for free, unspecialized, general intelligence, which there has never at any time been enough of, and which we are peculiarly in need of today.' [. . .]

The poet, as Leavis argued in *New Bearings*, was 'at the most conscious point of the race in his time'; poetry had the power to 'communicate the actual quality of experience with a subtlety and precision unapproachable by any other means'. But 'if the poetry and the intelligence of the age lose touch with each other', as a result, say, of the prevailing conception of the poetic, then 'poetry will cease to matter much, and the age will be lacking in finer awareness'. Although he did not press them on this occasion, the larger implications of Leavis's argument were clear. The progressive weakening of English poetic language had been set in train by the same historical process that had uprooted 'tradition'; the final exhaustion of the one would signal the death of the other, and, therewith, the extinction of the very memory of human community. A year or so later, introducing his selection from *The Calendar*, Leavis described this historical crux in more general and forthright terms: 'the fact that the other traditional continuities have . . . so completely disintegrated, makes the literary tradition correspondingly more important, since the continuity of consciousness, the conservation of the collective experience, is the more dependent on it: if the literary tradition is allowed to lapse, the gap is complete.'

The main task of a culturally responsible criticism was to recover and enforce the 'standards' on which the development of an authentically 'contemporary sensibility' depended; to combat those who obstructed the promulgation of authoritative 'standards'; to provide, through a rigorous assessment of literary history, an eligible past that could guide poetic practice in a detraditionalized society, and thus to avert that catastrophic 'lapse'.

(Francis Mulhern, *The Moment of 'Scrutiny'* (London: New Left Books, 1979), pp. 57–8, 76, 117.)

(D) VIRGINIA WOOLF

A Room of One's Own (1929)

The sentence that was current at the beginning of the nineteenth century ran something like this perhaps: 'The grandeur of their works was an argument with them, not to stop short, but to proceed. They could have no higher excitement or satisfaction than in the exercise of their art and endless generations of truth and beauty. Success prompts to exertion; and habit facilitates success.' That is a man's sentence; behind it one can see Johnson, Gibbon and the rest. It was a sentence that was unsuited for a woman's use. Charlotte Brontë, with all her splendid gift for prose, stumbled and fell with that clumsy weapon in her hands. George Eliot committed atrocities with it that beggar description. Jane Austen looked at it and laughed at it and devised a perfectly natural, shapely sentence proper for her own use and never departed from it. Thus, with less genius for writing than Charlotte Brontë, she got infinitely more said. Indeed, since freedom and fullness of expression are of the essence of the art, such a lack of tradition, such a scarcity and inadequacy of tools, must have told enormously upon the writing of women. Moreover, a book is not made of sentences laid end to end, but of sentences built, if an image helps, into arcades or domes. And this shape too has been made by men out of their own needs for their own uses. There is no reason to think that the form of the epic or of the poetic play suit a woman any more than the sentence suits her. But all the older forms of literature were hardened and set by the time she became a writer. The novel alone was young enough to be soft in her hands – another reason, perhaps, why she wrote novels. Yet who shall say that even now 'the novel' (I give it inverted commas to mark my sense of the word's inadequacy), who shall say that even this most pliable of all forms is rightly shaped for her use? No doubt we shall find her knocking that into shape for herself when she has the free use of her limbs; and providing some new vehicle, not necessarily in verse, for the poetry in her. For it is the poetry that is still denied outlet. And I went on to ponder how a woman nowadays would write a poetic tragedy in five acts. Would she use verse? – would she not use prose rather?

But these are difficult questions which lie in the twilight of the future. I must leave them, if only because they stimulate me to wander from my subject into trackless forests where I shall be lost and, very likely, devoured by wild beasts. I do not want,

and I am sure that you do not want me, to broach that very
dismal subject, the future of fiction, so that I will only pause
here one moment to draw your attention to the great part which
must be played in that future so far as women are concerned by
physical conditions. The book has somehow to be adapted to the
body, and at a venture one would say that women's books
should be shorter, more concentrated, than those of men, and
framed so that they do not need long hours of steady and
uninterrupted work. For interruptions there will always be.
Again, the nerves that feed the brain would seem to differ in
men and women, and if you are going to make them work their
best and hardest, you must find out what treatment suits them –
whether these hours of lectures, for instance, which the monks
devised, presumably, hundreds of years ago, suit them – what
alternations of work and rest they need, interpreting rest not as
doing nothing but as doing something but something that is
different; and what should that difference be? All this should be
discussed and discovered; all this is part of the question of
women and fiction

(Virginia Woolf, *A Room of One's Own* (London: Hogarth Press, 1929),
pp. 115–17.)

(E) SIMONE DE BEAUVOIR

The Second Sex (1949)

If her functioning as a female is not enough to define woman, if
we decline also to explain her through 'the eternal feminine',
and if nevertheless we admit, provisionally, that women do exist,
then we must face the question: what is a woman?

To state the question is, to me, to suggest, at once, a
preliminary answer. The fact that I ask it is in itself significant.
A man would never set out to write a book on the peculiar
situation of the human male. But if I wish to define myself, I
must first of all say: 'I am a woman'; on this truth must be
based all further discussion. A man never begins by presenting
himself as an individual of a certain sex; it goes without saying
that he is a man. The terms *masculine* and *feminine* are used
symmetrically only as a matter of form, as on legal papers. In
actuality the relation of the two sexes is not quite like that of
two electrical poles, for man represents both the positive and the
neutral, as is indicated by the common use of *man* to designate

human beings in general; whereas woman represents only the negative, defined by limiting criteria, without reciprocity. In the midst of an abstract discussion it is vexing to hear a man say: 'You think thus and so because you are a woman'; but I know that my only defence is to reply: 'I think thus and so because it is true,' thereby removing my subjective self from the argument. It would be out of the question to reply: 'And you think the contrary because you are a man', for it is understood that the fact of being a man is no peculiarity. A man is in the right in being a man; it is the woman who is in the wrong. It amounts to this: just as for the ancients there was an absolute vertical with reference to which the oblique was defined, so there is an absolute human type, the masculine. Woman has ovaries, a uterus: these peculiarities imprison her in her subjectivity, circumscribe her within the limits of her own nature. It is often said that she thinks with her glands. Man superbly ignores the fact that his anatomy also includes glands, such as the testicles, and that they secrete hormones. He thinks of his body as a direct and normal connection with the world, which he believes he apprehends objectively, whereas he regards the body of woman as a hindrance, a prison, weighed down by everything peculiar to it. 'The female is a female by virtue of a certain *lack* of qualities,' said Aristotle; 'we should regard the female nature as afflicted with a natural defectiveness.' And St Thomas for his part pronounced woman to be an 'imperfect man', an 'incidental' being. This is symbolized in Genesis where Eve is depicted as made from what Bossuet called 'a supernumerary bone' of Adam.

Thus humanity is male and man defines woman not in herself but as relative to him; she is not regarded as an autonomous being. Michelet writes: 'Woman, the relative being . . .' And Benda is most positive in his *Rapport d'Uriel*: 'The body of man makes sense in itself quite apart from that of woman, whereas the latter seems wanting in significance by itself . . . Man can think of himself without woman. She cannot think of herself without man.' And she is simply what man decrees; thus she is called 'the sex', by which is meant that she appears essentially to the male as a sexual being. For him she is sex – absolute sex, no less. She is defined and differentiated with reference to man and not he with reference to her; she is the incidental, the inessential as opposed to the essential. He is the Subject, he is the Absolute – she is the Other. [. . .]

But women do not say 'We', except at some congress of feminists or similar formal demonstration; men say 'women', and women use the same word in referring to themselves. They do not authentically assume a subjective attitude. The proletarians have accomplished the revolution in Russia, the Negroes in Haiti, the Indo-Chinese are battling for it in Indo-China; but the women's effort has never been anything more than a symbolic agitation. They have gained only what men have been willing to grant; they have taken nothing, they have only received.

The reason for this is that women lack concrete means for organizing themselves into a unit which can stand face to face with the correlative unit. They have no past, no history, no religion of their own; and they have no such solidarity of work and interest as that of the proletariat. They are not even promiscuously herded together in the way that creates community feeling among the American Negroes, the ghetto Jews, the workers of Saint-Denis, or the factory hands of Renault. They live dispersed among the males, attached through residence, housework, economic condition, and social standing to certain men – fathers or husbands – more firmly than they are to other women. If they belong to the bourgeoisie, they feel solidarity with men of that class, not with proletarian women; if they are white, their allegiance is to white men, not to Negro women. The proletariat can propose to massacre the ruling class, and a sufficiently fanatical Jew or Negro might dream of getting sole possession of the atomic bomb and making humanity wholly Jewish or black; but woman cannot even dream of exterminating the males. The bond that unites her to her oppressors is not comparable to any other. The division of the sexes is a biological fact, not an event in human history. [. . .]

Legislators, priests, philosophers, writers, and scientists have striven to show that the subordinate position of woman is willed in heaven and advantageous on earth. The religions invented by men reflect this wish for domination. In the legends of Eve and Pandora men have taken up arms against women. They have made use of philosophy and theology, as the quotations from Aristotle and St Thomas have shown. Since ancient times satirists and moralists have delighted in showing up the weaknesses of women. We are familiar with the savage indictments hurled against women throughout French literature. Montherlant, for example, follows the tradition of Jean de

Meung, though with less gusto. This hostility may at times be well founded, often it is gratuitous; but in truth it more or less successfully conceals a desire for self-justification. [. . .]

With still more reason we can count on the fingers of one hand the women who have traversed the given in search of its secret dimension: Emily Brontë has questioned death, Virginia Woolf life, and Katherine Mansfield – not very often – everyday contingence and suffering. No woman wrote *The Trial*, *Moby Dick*, *Ulysses*, or *Seven Pillars of Wisdom*. Women do not contest the human situation, because they have hardly begun to assume it. This explains why their works for the most part lack metaphysical resonances and also anger; they do not take the world incidentally, they do not ask it questions, they do not expose its contradictions: they take it as it is too seriously. It should be said that the majority of men have the same limitations; it is when we compare the woman of achievement with the few rare male artists who deserve to be called 'great men' that she seems mediocre. It is not a special destiny that limits her: we can readily comprehend why it has not been vouchsafed her – and may not be vouchsafed her for some time – to attain to the loftiest summits.

Art, literature, philosophy, are attempts to found the world anew on a human liberty: that of the individual creator; to entertain such a pretension, one must first unequivocally assume the status of a being who has liberty. The restrictions that education and custom impose on woman now limit her grasp on the universe; when the struggle to find one's place in this world is too arduous, there can be no question of getting away from it. Now, one must first emerge from it into a sovereign solitude if one wants to try to regain a grasp upon it: what woman needs first of all is to undertake, in anguish and pride, her apprenticeship in abandonment and transcendence: that is, in liberty.

> What I desire [writes Marie Bashkirtsev] is liberty to go walking alone, to come and go, to sit on the benches in the Tuileries Gardens. Without that liberty you cannot become a true artist. You believe you can profit by what you see when you are accompanied by someone, when you must wait for your companion, your family! . . . That is the liberty which is lacking and without which you cannot succeed seriously in being something. *Thought is shackled as a result of that stupid and continual constraint . . . That is enough to*

make your wings droop. It is one of the main reasons why
there are no women artists.

In truth, to become a creative artist it is not enough to be
cultivated – that is to say, to make exhibitions and bits of
information a part of one's life. Culture must be apprehended
through the free action of a transcendence; that is, the free spirit
with all its riches must project itself towards an empty heaven
that it is to populate; but if a thousand persistent bonds hold it
to earth, its surge is broken. [. . .]

Once again: in order to explain her limitations it is woman's
situation that must be invoked and not a mysterious essence;
thus the future remains largely open. Writers on the subject
have vied with one another in maintaining that women do not
have 'creative genius'; this is the thesis defended by Mme
Marthe Borély, a notorious anti-feminist; but one would say that
she sought to make her books a living proof of feminine
illogicality and silliness, so self-contradictory are they.
Furthermore, the concept of a creative 'instinct' must be
discarded, like that of the 'eternal feminine', from the old panel
of entities. Certain misogynists assert, a little more concretely,
that woman, being neurotic, could not create anything
worthwhile; but they are often the same men that pronounce
genius a neurosis. In any case, the example of Proust shows
clearly enough that psychophysiological disequilibrium signifies
neither lack of power nor mediocrity.

(Simone de Beauvoir, *The Second Sex*, trans. and ed. H. M. Parshley
(Harmondsworth: Penguin Books, 1972), pp. 15–16, 19, 22, 720–1, 723.
Originally published in French as *Le Deuxième Sexe* (1949).)

(F) ELAINE SHOWALTER

A Literature of their Own: British Women Novelists (1977, 1982)

There were three generations of nineteenth-century feminine
novelists. [. . .]

By the time the women of the first generation had entered
upon their careers, there was already a sense of what the
'feminine' novel meant in terms of genres. By the 1840s women
writers had adopted a variety of popular genres, and were

specializing in novels of fashionable life, education, religion, and community, which Vineta Colby subsumes under the heading 'domestic realism.' In all these novels, according to Inga-Stina Ewbank, 'the central preoccupation . . . is with the woman as an influence on others within her domestic and social circle. It was in this preoccupation that the typical woman novelist of the 1840s found her proper sphere: in using the novel to demonstrate (by assumption rather than exploration of standards of womanliness) *woman's* proper sphere.' A double standard of literary criticism had also developed, as I show in Chapter III, with a special set of terms and requirements for fiction by women.

There was a place for such fiction, but even the most conservative and devout women novelists, such as Charlotte Yonge and Dinah Craik, were aware that the 'feminine' novel also stood for feebleness, ignorance, prudery, refinement, propriety, and sentimentality, while the feminine novelist was portrayed as vain, publicity-seeking, and self-assertive. At the same time that Victorian reviewers assumed that women readers and women writers were dictating the content of fiction, they deplored the pettiness and narowness implied by a feminine value system. 'Surely it is very questionable,' wrote Fitzjames Stephen, 'whether it is desirable that no novels should be written except those fit for young ladies to read.'

Victorian feminine novelists thus found themselves in a double bind. They felt humiliated by the condescension of male critics and spoke intensely of their desire to avoid special treatment and achieve genuine excellence, but they were deeply anxious about the possibility of appearing unwomanly. Part of the conflict came from the fact that, rather than confronting the values of their society, these women novelists were competing for its rewards. For women, as for other subcultures, literature became a symbol of achievement.

In the face of this dilemma, women novelists developed several strategies, both personal and artistic. Among the personal reactions was a persistent self-deprecation of themselves as women, sometimes expressed as humility, sometimes as coy assurance-seeking, and sometimes as the purest self-hatred. In a letter to John Blackwood, Mrs. Oliphant expressed doubt about 'whether in your most manly and masculine of magazines a womanish story-teller like myself may not become wearisome.' The novelists publicly proclaimed, and sincerely believed their antifeminism. By working in the home, by preaching submission and self-sacrifice, and by denouncing female self-assertiveness, they worked to atone for their own will to write.

Vocation – the will to write – nonetheless required a genuine transcendence of female identity. Victorian women were not accustomed to *choosing* a vocation; womanhood was a vocation in itself. The evangelically inspired creed of work did affect women, even though it had not been primarily directed toward them. Like men, women were urged to 'bear their part in the *work* of life.' Yet for men, the gospel of work satisfied both self-interest and the public interest. In pursuing their ambitions, they fulfilled social expectations.

For women, however, work meant labor for *others*. Work, in the sense of self-development, was in direct conflict with the subordination and repression inherent in the feminine ideal. The self-centeredness implicit in the act of writing made this career an especially threatening one; it required an engagement with feeling and a cultivation of the ego rather than its negation. [. . .]

The literature of the last generation of Victorian women writers, born between 1880 and 1900, moved beyond feminism to a Female phase of courageous self-exploration, but it carried with it the double legacy of feminine self-hatred and feminist withdrawal. In their rejection of male society and masculine culture, feminist writers had retreated more and more toward a separatist literature of inner space. Psychologically rather than socially focussed, this literature sought refuge from the harsh realities and vicious practices of the male world. Its favorite symbol, the enclosed and secret room, had been a potent image in women's novels since *Jane Eyre*, but by the end of the century it came to be identified with the womb and with female conflict. In children's books, such as Mrs. Molesworth's *The Tapestry Room* (1879) and Dinah Craik's *The Little Lone Prince* (1875), women writers had explored and extended these fantasies of enclosure. After 1900, in dozens of novels from Frances Hodgson Burnett's *A Secret Garden* (1911) to May Sinclair's *The Tree of Heaven* (1917), the secret room, the attic hideaway, the suffragette cell came to stand for a separate world, a flight from men and from adult sexuality.

The fiction of Dorothy Richardson, Katherine Mansfield, and Virginia Woolf created a deliberate female aesthetic, which transformed the feminine code of self-sacrifice into an annihilation of the narrative self, and applied the cultural analysis of the feminists to words, sentences, and structures of language in the novel. Their version of modernism was a determined response to the material culture of male Edwardian novelists like Arnold Bennett and H. G. Wells, but, like D. H. Lawrence, the female aestheticists saw the world as mystically and totally polarized by sex. For them, female sensibility took on a sacred quality, and its exercise became a holy, exhausting, and ultimately self-destructive rite, since woman's receptivity led inevitably to suicidal vulnerability.

Paradoxically, the more female this literature became in the formal and theoretical sense, the farther it moved from exploring the physical experience of women. Sexuality hovers on the fringes of the aestheticists' novels and stories, disguised, veiled, and denied. Androgyny, the sexual ethic of Bloomsbury and an important concept of the period, provided an escape from the confrontation with the body. Erotically charged and drenched with sexual symbolism, female aestheticism is nonetheless oddly sexless in its content. Again, 'a room of one's own,' with its insistence on artistic autonomy and its implied disengagement from social and sexual involvement, was a favorite image.

In the 1960s the female novel entered a new and dynamic phase, which has been strongly influenced in the past ten years by the energy of the international women's movement. The contemporary women's novel observes the traditional forms of nineteenth-century realism, but it also operates in the contexts of twentieth-century Freudian and Marxist analysis. In the fiction of Iris Murdoch, Muriel Spark, and Doris Lessing, and the younger writers Margaret Drabble, A. S. Byatt, and Beryl Bainbridge, we are beginning to see a renaissance in women's writing that responds to the demands of Lewes and Mill for an authentically female literature, providing 'woman's view of life, woman's experience.' In drawing upon two centuries of the female tradition, these novelists have been able to incorporate many of the strengths of the past with a new range of language and experience. Like the feminine novelists, they are concerned with the conflicts between art and love, between self-fulfillment and duty. They have insisted upon the right to use vocabularies previously reserved for male writers and to describe formerly taboo areas of female experience. For the first time anger and sexuality are accepted not only as attributes of realistic characters but also, as in Murdoch's *The Severed Head*, Lessing's *The Golden Notebook*, and A. S. Byatt's *The Game*, as sources of female creative power. Like the feminist novelists, contemporary writers are aware of their place in a political system and their connectedness to other women. Like the novelists of the female aesthetic, women novelists today, Lessing and Drabble particularly, see themselves as trying to unify the fragments of female experience through artistic vision, and they are concerned with the definition of autonomy for the woman writer. As the women's movement takes on cohesive force, and as feminist critics examine their literary tradition, contemporary women novelists will have to face the problems that black, ethnic, and Marxist writers have faced in the past: whether to devote themselves to the forging of female mythologies and epics, or to move beyond the female tradition into a seamless participation in the literary mainstream that might be regarded either as equality or assimilation.

(Elaine Showalter, *A Literature of Their Own: British Women Novelists* . . . (1977; London: Virago, 1978, rev. edn, 1982), pp. 19, 20–2, 33–4, 34–6.)

(G) HÉLÈNE CIXOUS

'The Laugh of the Medusa' (1976)

I write this as a woman, toward women. When I say 'woman,' I'm speaking of woman in her inevitable struggle against conventional man; and of a universal woman subject who must bring women to their senses and to their meaning in history. But first it must be said that in spite of the enormity of the repression that has kept them in the 'dark' – that dark which people have been trying to make them accept as their attribute – there is, at this time, no general woman, no one typical woman. What they have *in common* I will say. But what strikes me is the infinite richness of their individual constitutions: you can't talk about *a* female sexuality, uniform, homogeneous, classifiable into codes – any more than you can talk about one unconscious resembling another. Women's imaginary is inexhaustible, like music, painting, writing: their stream of phantasms is incredible.

I have been amazed more than once by a description a woman gave me of a world all her own which she had been secretly haunting since early childhood. A world of searching, the elaboration of a knowledge, on the basis of a systematic experimentation with the bodily functions, a passionate and precise interrogation of her erotogeneity. This practice, extraordinarily rich and inventive, in particular as concerns masturbation, is prolonged or accompanied by a production of forms, a veritable aesthetic activity, each stage of rapture inscribing a resonant vision, a composition, something beautiful. Beauty will no longer be forbidden.

I wished that that woman would write and proclaim this unique empire so that other women, other unacknowledged sovereigns, might exclaim: I, too, overflow; my desires have invented new desires, my body knows unheard-of songs. Time and again I, too, have felt so full of luminous torrents that I could burst – burst with forms much more beautiful than those which are put up in frames and sold for a stinking fortune. And I, too, said nothing, showed nothing; I didn't open my mouth, I didn't repaint my half of the world. [. . .]

I write woman: woman must write woman. And man, man. So only an oblique consideration will be found here of man; it's up to him to say where his masculinity and femininity are at: this will concern us once men have opened their eyes and seen themselves clearly. [. . .]

Nearly the entire history of writing is confounded with the history of reason, of which it is at once the effect, the support, and one of the privileged alibis. It has been one with the phallocentric tradition. It is indeed that same self-admiring, self-stimulating, self-congratulatory phallocentrism.

With some exceptions, for there have been failures – and if it weren't for them, I wouldn't be writing (I-woman, escapee) – in that enormous machine that has been operating and turning out its 'truth' for centuries. There have been poets who would go to any lengths to slip something by at odds with tradition – men capable of loving love and hence capable of loving others and of wanting them, of imagining the woman who would hold out against oppression and constitute herself as a superb, equal, hence 'impossible' subject, untenable in a real social framework. Such a woman the poet could desire only by breaking the codes that negate her. Her appearance would necessarily bring on, if not revolution – for the bastion was supposed to be immutable – at least harrowing explosions. At times it is in the fissure caused by an earthquake, through that radical mutation of things brought on by a material upheaval when every structure is for a moment thrown off balance and an ephemeral wildness sweeps order away, that the poet slips something by, for a brief span, of woman. [. . .]

It is impossible to *define* a feminine practice of writing, and this is an impossibility that will remain, for this practice can never be theorized, enclosed, coded – which doesn't mean that it doesn't exist. But it will always surpass the discourse that regulates the phallocentric system; it does and will take place in areas other than those subordinated to philosophico-theoretical domination. It will be conceived of only by subjects who are breakers of automatisms, by peripheral figures that no authority can ever subjugate.

Almost everything is yet to be written by women about femininity: about their sexuality, that is, its infinite and mobile complexity, about their eroticization, sudden turn-ons of a certain miniscule-immense area of their bodies; not about destiny, but about the adventure of such and such a drive, about trips, crossings, trudges, abrupt and gradual awakenings, discoveries of a zone at one time timorous and soon to be forthright. A woman's body with its thousand and one thresholds of ardor – once, by smashing yokes and censors, she lets it articulate the profusion of meanings that run through it in every direction – will make the old single-grooved mother tongue reverberate with more than one language.

We've been turned away from our bodies, shamefully taught to ignore them, to strike them with that stupid sexual modesty; we've been made victims of the old fool's game: each one will love the other sex. I'll give you your body and you'll give me mine. But who are the men who give women the body that women blindly yield to them? Why so few texts? Because so few women have as yet won back their body. Women must write through their bodies, they must invent the impregnable language that will wreck partitions, classes, and rhetorics, regulations and codes, they must submerge, cut through, get beyond the ultimate reserve-discourse, including the one that laughs at the very idea of pronouncing the word 'silence,' the one that aiming for the impossible, stops short before the word 'impossible' and writes it as 'the end.'

Such is the strength of women that, sweeping away syntax, breaking that famous thread (just a tiny little thread, they say) which acts for men as a surrogate umbilical cord, assuring them – otherwise they couldn't come – that the old lady is always right behind them, watching them make phallus, women will go right up to the impossible.

(Hélène Cixous, 'The Laugh of the Medusa' (1976), *New French Feminisms*, ed. Elaine Marks and Isabelle de Courtivron (Brighton: Harvester Press, 1981), pp. 245–6, 247, 249, 253, 256.)

INDEX

*Note: page references to main author entries are printed in **bold** type. The title of novels, stories, plays and poems will be found under the appropriate author.*

Aarne, A., 353
Abel, Elizabeth, 522
Abrams, M. H., 6, 11, 80
absurd, the, 74
absence, 463–7
Adams, Hazard, 44
Addison, Joseph, 127
  Spectator, 126; No. 62, **133–5**;
    No. 160, **155–7**; No. 413,
    135–6; No. 416, **136–7**;
    No.417, **137–8**
Adolph, R., 98
Adorno, Theodor, 442
Aeschylus, 233, 410
  Agamemnon, 311
Aesop, 481
aesthetic (-ism), 36, 40–1, 63–4,
    71, 80, 166–7, 206, 208–11,
    244–67, 278, 281, 305, 490,
    516, 540
aesthetics, 10, 81, 126, 187
Albrecht, W. P., 152
Alcibiades, 49
Aldington, Richard, 307
alienation, 453
Alison, Archibald, 127
allegory, 113, 135, 289, 292–3,
    328, 474, 481
allusion, 401, 407
Althusser, Louis, 422, 455–7

'Ideology and ISAs', **460–3**;
    interpellation, 455, 461–3;
    'Letter on Art', 456,
    459–60
ambiguity, 270, 290, 295–7, 299
Amis, Kingsley,
  Lucky Jim, 529
Anacreon, 255
Anderson, Perry, 493
androgyny, 540
Anichkov, Professor, 276
Annan, Noel, 513
anthropology, 234
anti-humanism, 74–6
aporia, 382
Aquinas, St Thomas, 534–5
Arac, Jonathan, 383
archetype, *see* Bodkin and Frye
Aristotle, 5, 8, 41, 42–4, 66,
    78–80, 86, 88, 97, 99, 149,
    157, 174, 185, 186, 193, 195,
    225, 252, 275, 280, 345, 364,
    386, 416, 474, 479, 491, 501,
    520, 534–5, *see also* catharsis
  discoveries, 49, 350; peripeties,
    49, 350; *Poetics*, 3, 40, **45–51,**
    191, 243, 268, **271–3**, 343,
    350; unities, 78, 82
Arnold, Matthew, 453, 470,
    491–3, 509–12

criticism of life, 499, 510–11, 518; *Culture and Anarchy*, 491, **496–8**; 'The Function of Criticism, **494–5**; Hellenism and Hebraism, 497–8; high seriousness, 491–2, 501, 512; Preface to *Poems* (1853), **495–6**; Preface to *The Poems of Wordsworth*, **498–500**; 'The Study of Poetry', **500–1**, 510–11; sweetness and light, 497–8

Art for Art's Sake, 8, 11, 65, 244–6, 251, 253, 256, 451

Ascham, Roger
Schoolmaster, 473

Askoldov, S., 295

association (of ideas), 26, 126–8, 130–2, 134, 140–1, 144–5, 180–1, 249, 474

Atkins, J. W. H., 6

Auerbach, Erich, 41, 243, 292, 322, 406
figura, 58; *Mimesis*, 43, **56–9, 328–32**; mixed style, 329, 491; separation of styles 43, 329

Augustine, St
Confessions, 95, 413

Aurelius, Marcus
(Antoninus), 412

Austen, Jane, 503, 532
Pride and Prejudice, 516

Austin, J. L.
How to do Things with Words, **120–22**; speech acts (constative, performative, illocutionary, perlocutionary), 95–6, 120–2, 322–3, 333–5, 392–3

author, 303, 305, 315, 318–20, 323, 338–41, 365, 407

autonomy, 5, 246–7, 256–7, 270, 280, 402, 422

Babb, Howard S., 324

Bacon, Francis, 29, 97, 157
Advancement of Learning, 96, **101–3**; idols, 103–4; *Novum Organum*, **103–5**

Bainbridge, Beryl, 540

Bakhtin, Mikhail, 290–1
dialogic (polyphonic)/monologic, 291, 293–4, 304, 323; *Problems of Dostoevsky's Poetics*, **293–5**

Balzac, Honoré de, 57, 61, 71, 73, 366, 382, 456, 458–60, 466, 491, 502
Comédie Humaine, 60, 458, 465; *Cousine Bette*, 51; 'Sarrasine', 397–400

Bann, Stephen, 270

Barrett, Michèle, 522

Barthelme, Donald, 334

Barthes, Roland, 1, 76, 204, 323, 375, 390, 397–400, 407
already-written, the, 302, 305; codes, 291, 300–2, 398; 'The Death of the Author', 305, **318–20**; 'Introduction to the Structural Analysis of Narratives', **76–7**; readerly/writerly, 291, 382, 397–400; *S/Z*, 291, **299–302**, 382

Bashkirtsev, Marie, 536

Bate, Walter Jackson, 6, 81

Baudelaire, Charles Pierre, 65, 202, 245, 443, 447–9, 490
Paradis Artificiels, 319

Beardsley, Monroe, 394

beauty, 9, 10, 18–21, 25, 26, 28, 30, 32, 34, 64–5, 92, 136, 153–4, 169, 247–8, 251, 253–4, 271, 280, 286, 298, 306, 475, 484, 495, 497, 500, 506, 542

Becker, G. J., 44

Beckett, Samuel, 379
Watt, 334

Beerbohm, Max, 245

Bell, Clive, 246
Art, **259–61**; significant form, 245, 260

Bell, Ian F. A., 305

Benda, Julien, 534

Benjamin, Walter, 44, 442–3, 457
aura, 442, 450–2; 'The Flâneur', **447–9**; *flâneur*, the, 448–9; 'The Work of Art . . .', 442, **449–52**

Bennett, Arnold, 540
Bennett, Tony, 270, 403
Benveniste, Emile, 364–5
Bergson, Henri, 335
Berkeley, George, 27
Bernard, Claude, 42, 51–3
Besant, Walter, 493
Bible, the, 151, 155–6, 165, 289,
    292, 355, 359, 474, 480, 507,
    534
Bilan, R. P., 494
binary oppositions, 343–6, 381
Blackmore, R. D.
    Lorna Doone, 357
Blackwood, John, 538
Blake, William, 32, 230, 420, 474
    Marginalia, 80, **91–4**; *The
    Marriage of Heaven and Hell*,
    457; *Songs of Innocence and
    Experience*, 35; 'Ah! Sunflower',
    377–8
Bleich, David, 190
    resymbolization, 219–21;
    Subjective Criticism, 219
Blin, Georges, 365
Bloom, Harold, 401, 406–7
    The Anxiety of Influence, 406,
    415–17; *A Map of
    Misreading*, 406
Boccaccio, G.
    Decameron, 339
Bodkin, Maud, 224, 345
    *Archetypal Patterns in
    Poetry*, **231–5**
Boileau, Despréaux Nicolas, 151,
    174
    Epistles, 173
Booth, Wayne C., 40
    implied author, 323, 340–1;
    Rhetoric of Fiction, 323,
    337–42
Borges, J. L., 334
Borély, Marthe, 537
Bosanquet, Bernard, 405
Bossuet, J. B., 425, 534
Bowlt, John E., 270
Bowie, M., 224
Boyers, Robert, 494
Bradbury, Malcolm, 443
    *The Social Context of . . .
    Literature*, 441, **452–4**

Bradley, A. C., 11, 246
    'Poetry for Poetry's
    Sake', **256–9**; pure
    poetry, 258
Bradley, F. H., 405
Braine, John
    Room at the Top, 529
Brandes, G. M. C., 44, 440
Brecht, Bertholt, 42–4, 318,
    442–3, 457
    alienation effect, 43, 67–8, 70;
    'Alienation Effects in Chinese
    Acting', **66–70**, 269; gest, 67;
    'The Popular and the
    Realistic', **70–3**
Bromwich, David, 152
Brontë, Charlotte, 521, 532
    Jane Eyre, 539
Brontë, Emily, 493, 521, 536
    'Cold in the Earth', 514–16
Brooks, Cleanth, 6, 153, 290
    'Metaphor and the Tradition',
    285–6; *The Well Wrought Urn*,
    297–9
Buckle, H. T., 498
Buckley, Vincent, 494
Buffon, G. L. L., 264
Bunyan, John, 492
Burckhardt, Jacob, 420
Burnett, Frances Hodgson
    A Secret Garden, 539
Burniston, Steve, 457
Burns, Elizabeth and Tom, 443
Burns, Robert, 32, 143, 511–12
Butcher, S. H., 44
Byatt, A. S., 540
    The Game, 540
Byron, George Gordon, 293, 486

Calderón, 410
Capote, Truman, 41
Carlyle, Thomas, 420
carnival, 240, 418
Carroll, Lewis
    *Alice's Adventures in
    Wonderland*, 334
Casey, John, 98, 247
Cassirer, Ernst, 98, 219, 304
    Language and Myth, **111–13**
Castelvetro, L., 78

catharsis, 43, 149, 186, 191, 193–5, 225, 280
Cecil, David, 492
Cecilius, 168
Céline, L. F., 240
censorship, 476–7
Centre for Contemporary Cultural Studies, 443
Cervantes, Miguel de, 502
Cézanne, Paul, 355
Chaplin, Charlie, 371
character, 48–9, 60, 71, 90
Charlemagne, 411
Charles II, 192, 442, 444–5
Charney, H., 407
Chaucer, Geoffrey, 281, 480, 491, 510
Chicago School, 323
Chomsky, Noam, 347
Chrétien de Troyes
Perceval, 206
Cicero, 96, 100, 157, 321–2
Orator, 321, **324–7**
Cimarosa, D., 25
Cipriani, G., 26
Cixous, Hélène, 471
'The Laugh of the Medusa', 521, **541–3**
class, 60, 71–3, 230–2, 363–4, 406, 414, 441–2, 446, 452–3, 455–6, 458–9, 470–1, 488, 491–2, 519–20, 522–30, 535, 543
classicism, 4, 8, 43, 44, 56–7, 78–81, 97, 125–6, 146, 150, 152, 165, 209–10, 243, 289, 321–2, 355, 424, 473, 491
Clubbe, John, 11
Cobb, Samuel, 151
Cobbett, William, 492
Colby, Vineta, 538
Coleridge, S. T., 10–11, 81, 124, 126–8, 149, 152, 197, 205, 268, 279, 285, 306, 405, 494
'The Ancient Mariner', 233; *Biographia Literaria*, **142–5, 273–4**; Infinite I AM, 145; *Lectures on Shakespeare*, 395; *natura naturata*, 26; 'On Poesy or Art', **24–8**
Collingwood, R. G., 11, 206, 210

The Principles of Art, **35–6**
comedy, 45–7, 57–8, 84, 97, 171, 328, 330–2, 335, 349, 425, 444–5
Comte, Auguste, 402, 419–21
Conrad, Joseph, 358
Constructivism, 262, 475
Cooper, Lane, 44
Copernicus, Nicolas, 380
Corbière, Tristan, 410
Corneille, Pierre, 55, 83, 435
Coser, Lewis A., 441
Courtivron, Isabelle de, 522
Coward, Rosalind, 292
Cowley, Abraham, 135, 144, 284
Craik, Dinah, 538
The Little Lone Prince, 539
Crane, R. S., 279, 407
Critical Inquiry, 4
Croce, Benedetto, 39, 410
Aesthetic, **254–6**
Croll, Morris W., 98
Crosman, Inge, 190
Cubism, 31
Culler, Jonathan, 187, 383
literary competence, 347, 376, 378; *Structuralist Poetics*, 346, **375–9**
culture, 402, 405–6, 411, 421, 432–4, 436, 440, 442, 450, 489, 496–8, 522–31, 537, *see also* society
Curtius, E. R., 243, 322, 401, 405–6
European Literature . . ., 410

Daniel, Arnaut, 276
Dante Alighieri, 29, 37, 230, 289–90, 410, 512
Commedia, 56, 311; 'Letter to Can Grande', **292**
Davies, Sir John
Orchestra, 421
Davis, Robert Con, 224, 383
De Beauvoir, Simone
The Second Sex, 520, **533–7**
deconstruction, 1, 4, 291, 344, 381–3
decorum (propriety), 79, 81, 160, 321, 325–7

defamiliarization, 371, *see also*
    Shklovsky
Defoe, Daniel, 41, 341
De Man, Paul, 380–1
    'Semiology and
    Rhetoric', **390–4**
Demosthenes, 154
Denham, Robert D., 347
Dennis, John, 442
    Grounds of Criticism, 165; A
    Large Account of the Taste
    in Poetry . . .', **444–6**
De Quincey, Thomas, 319
Derrida, Jacques, 1, 3, 291,
    380–3, 393
    différance, 381, 386–90, 407;
    gram, 381, 387–8; *Of
    Grammatology*, **385–6**;
    logocentrism, 381, 386–7,
    521; phonocentrism,
    289, 381, 386;
    Positions, 381–2, **386–90**;
    presence, 7, 381, 386–7;
    spacing, 388–9; 'Structure,
    Sign and Play', 381;
    supplement, 381, 386;
    trace, 381, 387–8
Descartes, René, 97, 138
device, 281–2, 296, 393
diachronic, 440, *see also* Saussure
Diacritics, 4
Dickens, Charles, 502
    Bleak House, 346; *A Christmas
    Carol*, 372; *Hard Times*, 492
Diderot, Denis, 64, 199
difference, 344
Dilke, C. W., 306
Dilthey, Wilhelm, 198
Dionysius, 46
discourse, 335, 346, 364–6, 375–6,
    380
disinterestedness, 453, 490–2, 494,
    517
Dixon, Peter, 324
Dollimore, Jonathan, 423
Donato, Eugenio, 347
Donatus, 41
Donne, John, 173, 315–16
    'A Valediction Forbidding
    Mourning', 284
Donovan, Josephine, 522

Dostoevsky, F. M., 291, 293–5
Dowden, Edward, 420
Drabble, Margaret, 540–1
Drakakis, John, 423
Dryden, John, 135, 165, 187, 425
    *A Defence of an Essay of Dramatic
    Poesy*, 79, **84–5**; *Defence of
    the Epilogue*, **191–93**; *An
    Essay of Dramatic Poesy*, 78,
    81–4
Ducros, O., 390
Dumas, Alexandre (fils), 55

Eagleton, Mary, 522
Eagleton, Terry, 6, 243, 403, 455,
    457
    Criticism and Ideology, 456,
    466–8
ego, 214, *see also* subject
Ehrmann, Jacques, 347
Eisenstein, S. M., 371, 475
Eliot, George, 429, 452, 492, 503,
    523–4, 532
Eliot, T. S., 124, 128, 167, 287,
    297, 304, 315–16, 323, 379,
    401, 403, 405–6, 410, 420,
    490, 511, 517
    'Hamlet', **313–14**; 'Love Song
    of J. Alfred Prufrock', 315;
    objective correlative, 167,
    313; Tradition and the
    Individual Talent', **310–13,
    408–10**; unified
    sensibility, 270
Elledge, Scott, 81
Ellis, John, 292
Else, G. F., 44
Elyot, Sir Thomas, 430
    The Boke Named the Governour,
    429
Emerson, R. W., 396
emotion, 30, 32–4, 35–6, 71,
    74–5, 124, 146, 164–9,
    177–85, 195, 232, 260–1,
    277–8, 280, 304, 309, 311–13,
    317–18, 321, 324, 326, 485,
    508, *see also* feeling, passion
empathy, 65, 66, 195, 449
Empedocles, 46
Empson, William, 187, 270, 290

Seven Types of Ambiguity, **196–7,**
 295–7
Engels, Friedrich, 59, 63, 456,
 475, 491
 'Letter to Margaret
 Harkness', **458–9**
enunciation, 318–19, 386, 389,
 418
epic, 33, 35, 45–6, 62, 84, 133,
 171, 349
Epicurus, 192
Erlich, Victor, 270
Escarpit, Robert, 209, 443
 Sociologie de le littérature, 441
Essex, Robert Devereux, 2nd Earl
 of, 203–4
Euripedes, 410, 484
 Herakles, 330
Ewbank, Inga-Stina, 538
expression, 36, 254, 256, 316–17

fancy, 88, 125–28, 129–30, 132–3
 134, 137–8, 140, 142–6, 156,
 173, 181, 278, 482
feeling, 53, 67–8, 86–7, 142–3,
 161–2, 165–6, 175–82, 196,
 202, 279, 304–5, 311, *see also*
 emotion, passion
Fekete, John, 270
Felman, Shoshana, 224
feminism, 470–1, 520–2, 534, 537,
 539–40
Fielding, Henry, 337, 341, 474,
 502
 Tom Jones, 215
Fish, Stanley, 189, 395
Flaubert, Gustave, 55, 319, 337,
 339
 Madame Bovary, 338
Fleming, Ian L., 77
Fokkema, D. W., 6
Ford, Ford Madox, 341
foregrounding, 265
form, 25, 26, 27, 30, 32, 34, 62,
 64, 148, 162, 198, 246, 258,
 264–5, 276, 286, 298, 456,
 465–6
formalism, 73, 189, 441, 490, *see
 also* Russian Formalism
Forster, E. M., 453

Fortunatus, 413
Foucault, Michel, 366, 380, 407
 'Nietzsche, Genealogy, History',
 437–8
Frankfurt School, 442
free verse, 506
Freud, Sigmund, 75, 188, 212,
 222–7, 233, 235, 239–40, 290,
 303, 345, 401, 406, 417, 463,
 520, 540
 'Psychopathic Characters on the
 Stage', **225–7**
Frye, Northrop, 81, 224, 334, 335,
 345
 Anatomy of Criticism, **355–9**;
 archetypes, 355, 358–9
functions (narrative), 359–60, 362,
 see also Propp
Futurism, 475

Gadamer, Hans-Georg, 187,
 210–11, 396
 horizon of expectations, 187–8,
 213; *Truth and Method*, 210
Gallop, Jane, 522
Ganihl, Charles, 446
Gaunt, William, 247
Gautier, Théophile, 510
 Mademoiselle de Maupin, 245
gender, 470–1, 532–43
general/particular, 88–94, 110, *see
 also* universal
'general text', 291, 305, *see also*
 textuality
Genette, Gérard, 345–6, 390–2
 Figures III, 391; 'Frontiers of
 Narrative', **364–6**
Geneva School, 189
genius, 26–7, 124, 128, 140–1,
 142, 150–63, 251, 424, 428,
 441
genre, 359
George II, 187
Gerard, Alexander
 Essay on Genius, 127, **139–42**
gestalt psychology, 189
Gide, André
 Theseus, 410
Gibbon, Edward, 532
Gilbert, K. E., 6

Girardin, Emile, 447
Godwin, William
    Caleb Williams, 529
Goethe, J. W. von, 230, 425
    Faust, 231; Götz von
    Berlichingen, 410
Goldmann, Lucien, 421–2
    collective consciousness, 435,
    436–7; Le Dieu Caché, 422;
    genetic structuralism, 435–6;
    Towards a Sociology of the Novel,
    434–7; world view, 421
Goldstein, K., 368
Goncourt, Edmond de and Jules
    de, 55–6
    Henriette Maréchal, 56
Gordon, D. J., 494
Gosson, Stephen, 473–4
    School of Abuse, 473
Graff, Gerald, 270
grammar, 391–3, 396
Gramsci, Antonio, 455
Green, Geoffrey, 407
Greimas, A.-J., 345, 390
    actants, 359–63; Structural
    Semantics, 359–64
Griffith, D. W., 371
Guillén, Claudio, 401, 421–2
    Literature as System, 406,
    437–40
Guys, Constantin, 448
gynocriticism, 521

H. D., 307
Habermas, Jurgen, 212
Hagstrum, J. H., 81
Haight, Gordon, 452
Halsted, John B., 11
Hamilton, Paul, 12
Hardy, Thomas, 281, 315, 358,
    493, 523–4
    'After a Journey', 514–16; Jude
    the Obscure, 529
Harkness, Margaret, 456, 475
    City Girl, 458
Harrington, John
    The Rhetoric of Film, 372
Hartman, Geoffrey, 382–3
    Criticism in the Wilderness, 394–7
Hartley, David, 127, 144

Harvey, Gabriel
    Ciceronianus, 96
Hawkes, Terence, 347
Hawthorne, Nathaniel, 358
Hazlitt, William, 152
    'On Genius and Common
    Sense', 161–3
Hegel, G. W. F., 42, 59, 245–7,
    366, 386, 402, 419–22, 425
Hegemon of Thasos, 47
Heidegger, Martin, 188, 203, 213
Hemingway, Ernest M., 247,
    265–7, 337
    Green Hills of Africa, 266
Henn, T. R., 152
Heraclitus, 104
hermeneutics, 187–8, 203, 210,
    212–13, 217, 396
Herodotus, 49
Herrick, Robert, 278
Hervey, Sándor, 347
Hesiod, 476
heterogeneity, 197, 239–40, 268,
    521
Hewlett, M. H., 308
Hill, John Spencer, 129
Hipple, W. J., 152
Hippocrates, 412
Hirsch Jr., E. D., 395–6
    The Aims of Interpretation, 203–5;
    meaning/significance, 188,
    203–4, 289–90
historicism, 419–20, 422
history, (events, literary history,
    etc), 5, 49–50, 69–71, 88, 94,
    102, 187, 205–6, 213, 243,
    280, 320, 344, 363, 401–7,
    410–17, 419–40, 464–8,
    479–81
history of ideas, 426–31
Hjelmslev, Louis, 439
Hobbes, Thomas, 126–7
    Answer to Davenant, 125;
    Leviathan, 129–33
Hoffman, Frederick J., 224
Hofmannsthal, Hugo von, 410
Hoggart, Richard, 443, 519–20
    The Uses of Literacy, 470, 519,
    522–6
Holbrook, David, 470
    The Quest for Love, 488

Holland, Norman, 223, 395
  5 Readers Reading, **218–19**;
  identity theme, 190, 218–19
Hollander, R., 292
Holloway, John, 494
Holub, Robert C., 190
Homer, 15, 17, 22, 46–7, 80, 86,
  141, 154, 155–6, 159, 174,
  289, 322, 345, 408–9, 474,
  476, 484
  Iliad, 272, 348–9, 412;
  Odyssey, 165, 272, 348, 410
Hooker, Richard
  Laws of Ecclesiastical Polity, 420,
  429–30
Horace, 155, 156, 165, 174, 441
  Ars Poetica, 125; *Odes*, 412
Horkheimer, Max, 442
Hough, Graham, 475
House, A. H., 45
Housman, A. E., 164, 286
Howell, A. C., 98
Hoy, David Couzens, 190
Hugo, Victor, 250
Hulme, T. E., 11, 269
  Speculations, 146, **277–9**
humanism, 279, 394, 452–4
Hume, R. D., 81
Husserl, Edmund, 188, 216, 386
Hutcheson, Francis, 127
Huysmans, J. K.
  A Rebours, 245, **251–2**

ideas, 134–5, 137–8, 139–41, 162,
  see also Plato, Locke
ideology, 3, 5, 209, 212, 241, 247,
  291, 293, 303, 363, 402–3,
  406, 421, 435, 440, 455–68,
  488, 521
image, 308, 311
imaginary, 455–6, 468, 541, *see
  also* Lacan
imagination, 9–39, 54, 66, 80, 86,
  88, 93, 107, 109, 123–4,
  126–8, 129–30, 135–8, 140–1,
  142–6, 149, 152, 156, 160,
  163, 173, 178, 181, 222, 245,
  247–9, 257–8, 278, 304, 395,
  444–5, 470, 474, 481, 484–6,
  515–16

imitation (mimesis), 15, 20, 25,
  45–51, 56–7, 64–5, 77, 84–5,
  98, 99, 111–12, 152, 156, 191,
  193, 272, 335, 348–9, 401,
  473, 479, 482
imitation (of models), 155–7, 158–9
impersonality, 167, 304–5,
  310–13, 315, 336–7, 339, 342,
  490, 513, *see also* T. S. Eliot
indeterminacy, 5, 381–2, 394–5,
  397, 400
influence, 407, 415–17
Ingarden, Roman
  The Literary Work of Art, 189;
  schematized aspects, 189
intention, 204–5, 304, 315, 395,
  see also Wimsatt
intertextuality, 401, 407, 418
irony, 290, 299, 358
Iser, Wolfgang, 2, 189, 396
  The Act of Reading, **214–18**;
  implied reader, 189, 214–15;
  wandering viewpoint, 217

Jackson, J. R. de J., 12
Jacobus, Mary, 522
Jakobson, Roman, 1, 222, 272,
  390
  aphasia, 346, 367–9;
  literariness, 269; metaphor/
  metonymy, 369–71, 417;
  similarity/contiguity, 368–9;
  'Two Aspects of Language',
  367–71
Jakubinsky, Leo, 276
James, C. V., 475
James, Henry, 323, 338, 470,
  491–3
  'The Art of Fiction', **503–5**;
  'bewilderment', 336, 502;
  The Golden Bowl (Preface),
  336–7; *Portrait of a Lady*
  (Preface), **501–2**; *The Princess
  Casamassima* (Preface), **335–6**,
  502–3; 'showing'/'telling',
  323, 337–8
Jameson, Fredric, 45, 305, 347
  Marxism and Form, 247, **265–7**
Jansenism, 436
Jauss, H. R., 187–8, 396

horizon of expectations, 207–11,
    see also Gadamer; 'Literary
    History . . .', **205–11**
Jay, Gregory S., 407
Jay, Martin, 444
Jefferies, Richard, 492
Jefferson, Ann, 6
Jenny, Laurent, 407
Joad, C. E. M., 38
Johnson, Barbara, 382–3
    'The Critical Difference' (on
    Balzac and Barthes),
    397–400
Johnson, J. W., 6
Johnson, Robert V., 247
Johnson, Samuel, 3, 80, 419, 470,
    474, 532
    The History of Rasselas, **89**;
    Lives of the Poets, **90–1**;
    Preface to Shakespeare, **89–90**;
    Rambler, **481–3**
Jones, Ernest, 223
    Hamlet and Oedipus, **235–6**
Jones, John, 167
Jonson, Ben, 97, 192, 321–2
    The Alchemist, 335; *Timber, or
    Discoveries*, **99–101**
jouissance, 240
Joyce, James, 43, 410, 518
    Ulysses, 536
judgement, 100, 101, 125–6,
    132–4, 137, 142, 144, 158,
    173, 444–5
Jung, Carl, 222, 224, 231, 234,
    345, 414
    collective unconscious, 224,
    230–31; primordial experience,
    227–9, 231; *Psychology and
    Literature*, **227–31**

Kafka, Franz, 43
    The Trial, 536
Kallich, M., 129
Kant, Immanuel, 10, 98, 112,
    243, 246, 395, 490
    Critique of Judgement, 245,
    247–9; judgement of
    taste, 248
Keats, John, 233, 286, 303, 312,
    474, 499

egotistical sublime, 303, 307;
    Letters, **306–7**; negative
    capability, 303–4, 306, 382,
    395
Kennedy, George A., 324
Kinnaird, John, 152
Knights, L. C., 98
Kohn, H., 6
Krieger, Murray, 271, 305, 347
Kristeva, Julia, 223, 386, 521
    chora, 239; intertextuality, 401,
    407; *The Revolution in Poetic
    Language*, **417–18**;
    semiotic/symbolic, 223, 239–
    41; 521: 'The Speaking
    Subject', **238–41**
Kruszewski, 417
Kuhn, T. S., 220
Kunne-Ibsch, E., 6
Kurzweil, Edith, 224
Kyd, Thomas, 322

La Bruyère, Jean de, 173
Lacan, Jacques, 1, 3, 222, 223–4,
    471, 521
    'Desire . . . in *Hamlet*', 236;
    phallus, 224, 236–8
La Fayette, Comtesse de, 73
Laforgue, Jules, 449
Langer, Susanne, 219, 304
    Feeling and Form, 305;
    Philosophical Sketches, **316–18**;
    symbolic form, 98, 304–5, *see
    also* Cassirer
language, 35, 36, 39, 44, 45–7, 50,
    55–6, 77, 86–7, 95–122,
    166–7, 177, 184–5, 197–200,
    222–4, 238–9, 263, 266, 268,
    274–9, 287, 290–1, 296–7,
    300, 304–5, 308, 314, 318–19,
    326, 343–7, 351–79, 385–94,
    396, 417–18, 532, 543, *see also*
    style
langue/parole, 385–6, 388–9, *see also*
    Saussure
Lanser, Susan S., 324
Larkin, Philip, 373–5
    'Church Going', 374–5; 'The
    Whitsun Weddings',
    373–4

Lavers, Annette, 292
Lawrence, D. H., 223, 470, 489,
    491, 493, 518, 540
    life, 493, 507–9; 'Morality and
    the Novel', **507–9**; *New
    Poems*, (Introduction), **505–6**;
    Sons and Lovers, 525; 'Why the
    Novel Matters', **506–7**
Lawrence, T. E.
    The Seven Pillars of Wisdom, 536
Leavis, F. R., 3, 406, 469–70, 490,
    492–3, 519–20
    'Arnold as a Critic', **509–12**;
    Culture and Environment, 492;
    'Mr Pryce-Jones . ... and
    British Culture', **513–14**;
    New Bearings, 531; 'Reality
    and Sincerity', **514–16**;
    '"Thought" and Emotional
    Quality', **512–13**
Lee, Sidney, 420
Leenhart, Jacques, 444
Legrand, Michel, 361
Leitch, Vincent B., 383
Lenin, V. I., 63–4, 460, 475
Lentricchia, Frank, 12
Lesser, Simon, 225
Lessing, Doris, 540–1
    The Golden Notebook, 540
Lessing, G. E., 186
    'Letter to Nicolai', **194–5**
Levin, Harry, 439
Lévi-Strauss, Claude, 344
Lewes, G. H., 540
Lichtenstein, Heinz, 218
linguistics, 96, 113–15, 197–200,
    243–4, 281, 318, 346, 351–5,
    359–71, 388–90, 393, 417–18,
    439
Literature and History, 4
Locke, John, 80, 97–8, 133–4
    association of ideas, 108–9;
    *Essay Concerning Human
    Understanding*, **106–11**, 136;
    ideas (simple and complex),
    106–11; primary and
    secondary qualities, 126
Lodge, David
    The Modes of Modern Writing,
    346, **371–5**
Lodge, Rupert C., 12

Longinus, 124, 151–2, 164,
    171–2, 246
    On the Sublime, **153–4**, **167–9**
Louis XIV, 56, 425
Lovejoy, Arthur O., 420–1
    The Great Chain of Being, **426–8**;
    unit idea, 402, 421, 426–7
Lovell, Ernest J., 11
Lucan, 484
Lucilius, 441
Lukács, Georg, 40, 42–3
    'Art and Objective Truth',
    59–66; *History and Class
    Consciousness*, 421; partisanship
    of objectivity, 63;
    reflection, 60–6; *Studies in
    European Realism*, 466;
    totality, 61–2, 64–5
Lyly, John, 96

MacCabe, Colin, 225
MacCannell, Janet F., 225
McGann, Jerome J., 6
Macherey, Pierre, 460
    absence, 463–5; *A Theory of
    Literary Production*, 456, **463–6**
Macksey, Richard, 347
Mallarmé, Stéphane, 451
    'Salut', 376
Mansfield, Katherine, 536, 539
Marcuse, Herbert, 442
Marks, Elaine, 522
Marlowe, Christopher, 322, 420
Marvell, Andrew
    'Definition of Love', 286; 'To
    His Coy Mistress', 284, 316
Marx, Karl, 42, 188, 419, 442,
    449
    Theories of Surplus Value, **446–7**
Marxism, 5, 42, 44, 151, 212, 267,
    290, 303, 363, 402, 406,
    420–2, 434–7, 440, 442,
    455–68, 470, 520, 524, 540–1
Matthewson, R. W., 475
Mauron, Charles, 37
Medvedev, P., 291
Melville, Herman
    Moby Dick, 536
Mercer, Colin, 457
Meredith, George, 502

Merezhkovsky, D., 275
metalanguage, 382
metaphor, 32, 50, 105, 133–5, 146,
    156, 168, 211, 222, 283,
    285–6, 298, 317, 321, 325–6,
    328, 346, 356–8, 372–5, 380,
    390–1, *see also* Jakobson
metonymy, 222, 346, 371–3, 380,
    see also Jakobson
Meung, Jean de, 536
Michaud, Guy, 362
Michelangelo, 92
Michelet, Jules, 534
Mill, J. S., 166, 304, 540
    Autobiography, **178–9**; 'Two
        Kinds of Poetry', **180–2**;
        'What is Poetry', **179–80**
Miller, Owen, 190
Millett, Kate
    Sexual Politics, 520
Milton, John, 135, 144, 157, 164,
    173–4, 281, 321, 442, 499
    Comus, 174; *Paradise Lost*, 258,
        447
mimesis, *see* imitation
Minnis, A. J., 305
Mittenzwei, W., 45
modernism, 128, 285, 304–5, 323,
    405, 540
Moers, Ellen, 521
Moi, Toril, 522
Molesworth, Mary L.
    The Tapestry Room, 539
Molière, 55, 209, 435
Monk, S., 153
Montaigne, M. E. de, 330, 420
Montherlant, Henri de, 535
morality, 4, 5, 26, 34, 35, 80, 102,
    170, 173, 256, 260, 281–2,
    283, 289, 323, 416, 424–5,
    469–87, 492–518
Morawski, Stefan, 45
Morley, John, 420
Morris, Adelaide K., 12
Mowbray, Allan, 305
Mukařovský, Jan, 187, 246
    Aesthetic Function . . ., **261–4**
Mulhern, Francis, 493–4, 519
    The Moment of 'Scrutiny', **530–1**
Murdoch, Iris
    The Severed Head, 540

Murray, Gilbert, 232
myth, 112–13, 209, 224, 229–30,
    317, 345, 355–8, 361, 363,
    465, 474

narrative, 75, 77, 180, 323, 337,
    339, 344–6, 348–9, 359–66,
    483, 503
Nashe, Thomas, 32
naturalism 8, 41, 43, 53, 54–6, 74
naturalization, 378–9
nature, 25, 26, 27–8, 41, 51–4,
    78–94, 96–7, 99, 102, 103,
    136, 139, 142, 153, 158–9,
    161–2, 176, 249, 251–4, 479,
    482, 497
Needham, John, 167
neoclassicism, 4, 80, 151, 285,
    321, 380, 419
Nerval, Gérard de, 316
New Criticism, 1, 128, 167, 186–7,
    203, 243–4, 246, 268–70,
    290–1, 304, 323, 475, 491
New Historicism, 402
New Literary History, 4
Newton, Isaac, 220
Nicochares, 47
Nicolson, M., 153
Nietzsche, Friedrich, 230, 289,
    380, 393, 416
    The Will to Power, **383–5**
Norris, Christopher, 292, 383
Novalis, 250

Ohmann, Richard M., 322–3, 392
    'Speech, Action and Style', 322,
        333–5
Oliphant, Margaret, 538
Olsen, Tillie, 521
Olson, Elder, 190
Omar Khayyám, 499
omniscient author/narrator, 291,
    323
organic, 25, 34, 63, 66, 126–8,
    152, 159, 175, 268, 273, 279,
    310
originality, 71, 150–2, 157,
    158–63, 405–6, 444–5
Orsini, G. N. G., 12

Orwell, George, 453, 524
Osborne, John
  Look Back in Anger, 529
O'Shaughnessy, Arthur, 33
Otway, Thomas, 144
Ovid, 79, 289
  Amores, 412
Owen, Robert, 458
Owen, W. J. B., 81

Palmer, G. H., 428
paradox, 290, 297–9
Pascal, Blaise, 199, 422, 462
  Pensées, 436
passion, 23, 52, 74, 79, 81–4,
    86–8, 165, 169–72, 175–6,
    186, 250–1, 257, 320, 444,
    487, 495–6, 500, *see also*
    emotion, feeling
pastoral, 171, 328
Pater, Walter, 166, 244
  impressions, 249–50; *The
    Renaissance*, 196, 246,
    249–51
patriarchy, 520–1
Pauson, 46
Pavlov, I. P., 197
Pêcheux, Michel, 457
Pechter, E., 81
persona, 340
Petrarchism, 332
Petronius, 410
phallocentrism (phallogocentrism),
    471, 521, 542–3
Pheidias, 21
phenomenology, 123–4, 188–9,
    202, 396, 416
Phillips, William, 224, 225
philology, 406, 411
Picard, Raymond, 204
Pindar, 156–7, 494
Piscator, Erwin, 69, 72
Plato, 5, 8, 27, 41, 64, 151, 154,
    157, 278, 345, 381, 386, 405,
    419, 454, 470, 474, 480
  Ideas, 9, 14, 15–18, 64;
    Ion, 125, 150; *Republic*, 3, 9,
    12–18, 40, 56, **348–9**, 469,
    473, **476–7**; *Timaeus*, 239
pleasure, 83, 87, 126, 135, 138,

    169–71, 175–8, 191, 223,
    225–6, 247–8, 253, 273, 445,
    71–2, 280, 343, 350
Pleiad, the, 425
plot, 41, 45, 48–50, 55, 74, 81–4,
    191
Plotinus, 9–10
  Enneads, **18–21**; Ideal-
    Form, 18–19
Plottel, J. P., 407
plurality (of meaning), 187, 270,
    290–1, 299, 384–5, 395, 398,
    418
Plutarch, 99, 410
Poe, Edgar Allan, 358, 443, 448–9
poetics, 347, 391
point of view, 321, 323, 336–9,
    491
Polygnotus, 46, 49
polysemy, *see* plurality
Pope, Alexander, 27, 151, 165–6,
    174, 187
  Eloisa to Abelard, 173; *An Essay
    on Criticism*, 79, **85–6, 139,
    157–8**, 321; *The Rape of the
    Lock*, 173, 299
Popper, Karl, 419–20
post-modernism, 4
post-structuralism, 1, 5, 151,
    243–4, 268, 290–1, 305, 323,
    380, 407
Poulet, Georges, 189
  'Criticism and . . .
    Interiority', **200–2**
Pound, Ezra, 128, 223, 304, 356,
    490–1, 518
  'A Retrospect', **307–9**; 'The
    Serious Artist', **309–10**
Prague Linguistic Circle, 246, 265
Pratt, Mary Louise, 98
pre-romanticism, 8, 151
presence, 75–6, 303 , 467, *see also*
    Derrida
Propp, Vladimir, 359–62
  functions, 345, 354–5, 359–60,
    362; *Morphology of the
    Folktale*, **353–5**
Proust, Marcel, 43, 537
psychoanalysis, 5, 123, 128, 212,
    222–6, 244, 291, 304, 407,
    417, 489

Pudovkin, V., 475
Puttenham
    The Arte of English Poesie, 321,
        327-8

Rabelais, François, 197, 291
race, 423-6
Racine, Jean, 202, 204, 422, 434,
        436
    Iphigénie, 410
Raleigh, Sir Walter
    History of the World, 430
Raleigh, Sir Walter A.
        (critic), 246
Ransom, J. C., 129, 167, 284
    'Criticism Inc.', **279-83**; tissue
        of irrelevance, 282-3; *The
        World's Body*, 269
Raphael, 92
Rapin, René, 78, 186
    Reflections on Aristotle, **193-4**
Ray, William, 383
reader-response criticism, 123,
        127, 186-221, 291, 300, 346,
        396-7
realism, 8, 41-3, 57-66, 70-6,
        322, 346, 355-9, 456, 458-9,
        540
reception theory, *see* reader-
        response criticism
reflection, 435, 464-5, *see also*
        Lukács
Reid, Thomas, 127
Rembrandt, 161-2
representation, 4, 7-122, 243,
        248-9, 254, 260, 272, 332,
        345-6, 366, 401, 455, 476, *see
        also* realism
repression, 226, 234, 236, 240-1
Reynolds, Joshua, 80
rhetoric, 39, 80, 96, 125, 151, 165,
        321-28, 358, 380-1, 390-4,
        406, 412-13, 416
rhyme, 79, 84
Richards, I. A., 128, 129, 166,
        187, 196, 233, 246, 270, 298,
        304
    impulses, 128, 147-9, 183;
        Principles of Literary Criticism,
        147-9, 184-5, 195-6;

pseudo-statement, 183-4;
    Science and Poetry, **146-7,
        182-4**
Richardson, Dorothy, 539
Richardson, Samuel, 41, 474
Richelieu, Cardinal, 83
Ricoeur, Paul, 188
    Hermeneutics . . ., **211-14**
Riddel, Joseph N., 12
Rimbaud, Arthur, 201, 379
Rimmon-Kenan, S., 347
Robbe-Grillet, Alain, 43-4, 379,
        439
    'A Future for the Novel', **73-6**
Robey, David, 6, 271, 347
Robinson, F. G., 475
Robortello, F., 78
Roland, Alan, 225
Rollison, Philip, 292
romance, 136, 356-8, 417, 482
Romanticism, 1, 4, 8, 10, 11, 44,
        57, 76, 78, 80-1, 123-4, 128,
        150, 152, 164-7, 244, 246,
        268, 270, 278, 285, 303-5,
        380, 405, 420, 453, 469,
        487-8
Ronsard, Pierre de, 425
Rorty, Richard, 383
Rossetti, Dante Gabriel, 253
Rouseau, Jean Jacques, 386
rules, 27, 85-6, 125, 151, 155-6,
        158, 162, 174, 198, 339
Ruskin, John, 470, 474-5
    Modern Painters, **485-7**
Russell, D. A., 153, 324
Russian Formalism, 5, 238,
        243-4, 268-9, 290, 378
Ruthven, K. K., 522
Ryan, Michael, 383
Rymer, Thomas, 78

Saintsbury, George, 246
Saint-Simon, C. H., 458
Sanders, Wilbur, 423
Saussure, Ferdinand de, 96, 98,
        150, 222, 290-1, 343-6,
        387-9
    arbitrariness of signs, 114-15,
        344; *Course in General
        Linguistics*, **113-15, 351-3**;

langue/parole, 343–4, 346, 396;
signifier/signified, 352–3;
synchronic/diachronic, 343–4,
353
Schelling, F. W., 10, 64, 127
Schlegel, A. W., 10
Schlegel, F., 10
*Lectures on the History of
Literature*, **21–3**
Schleiermacher, F. E. D., 198–9,
212–13
Schleifer, Ronald, 383
Scholes, Robert, 347
Schopenhauer, Artur, 64
Schorer, Mark, 341
'Technique as Discovery',
286–8
Schulze, Earl J., 12
Scott, Walter, 502
Scrutiny, 492–3, 513, 519, 530
Selden, Raman, 6, 271
semiotics/semiology, 1, 4, 189,
239, 240, 344, 347, 351–2,
376, 381, 386–7, 390, 392–3,
396, 407, 418, *see also*
Kristeva
Seneca (tragedian), 329, 332, 410
Shaffer, Peter
Amadeus, 124
Shaftesbury, 3rd Earl of, 64
Shakespeare, William, 23, 32, 90,
144, 156, 176, 203–4, 233,
281, 307, 322, 328–32, 357,
409, 410, 428–31, 470, 494,
497, 499, 502
Cymbeline, 357; *Hamlet*, 223, 226,
235–8, 304, 313–14, 330–1,
335, 359; *Henry IV Part
2*, 328; *Julius Caesar*, 330–1,
429; *King Lear*, 331–2;
Macbeth, 313; *The Merchant of
Venice*, 330, 332; *A Midsummer
Night's Dream*, 321; *Much
Ado*, 357; *Othello*, 311, 330;
Richard II, 203; *Richard
III*, 331; *Romeo and Juliet*, 331;
The Tempest, 174; *Troilus and
Cressida*, 420–1, 429; *The
Winter's Tale*, 357
Shelley, Percy Bysshe, 469, 473–4,
486, 494

A Defence of Poetry, 11, **28–30,
483–4**
Shklovsky, Viktor, 11
'Art as Technique', **274–6**;
defamiliarization, 269, 274–5;
'Sterne's *Tristram Shandy*',
276–7
Shostakovich, D., 37
Showalter, Elaine, 521
A Literature of their Own, 471,
537–41
Sidgwick, Henry, 497–8
Sidney, Sir Philip, 469, 473–4,
490
An Apology for Poetry, **478–81**
signification, 75, 96, 108–11, 129,
222–4, 240, 351–3, 407, 418,
467, *see also* semiotics
signifier/signified, 114, 215, 222,
224, 237–9, 290, 300, 320,
344, 352–3, 385–6, 389–90,
398, 407, 467
Silverman, David, 292
Simpson, Lewis P., 271
Sinclair, May
The Tree of Heaven, 539
Smith, Adam, 127
Smith, Alexander
'Barbara', 514–15
Smith, Joseph H., 225
Smith, Logan Pearsal, 164
Snow, C.P., 517
Socialist Realism, 3, 42, 262, 470,
475, 487–8
society, 37, 51–3, 62, 65, 70–2,
261–4, 269, 320, 321, 334,
351, 402, 414–15, 422, 423,
431–7, 439–40, 443, 452–6,
475, 492–4, 518, 522–31
sociology, 37, 75, 525
sociology of literature, 210,
434–7, 441, 443, 452–4
Socrates, 46
Sollers, Phillipe, 366
Solzhenitsyn, Alexander
I., 459–60
Sophocles, 358, 494
Antigone, 431, 496; *Oedipus
Tyrannus*, 79, 191, 194, 350
Sophron, 46
Souriau, E., 360–2

Spark, Muriel, 540
Spencer, Herbert, 420
Spenser, Edmund, 135, 281, 321,
    357, 431, 484
    The Fairie Queene, 174, 359;
    Hymn of Love, 429
Spingarn, J. E., 6
spirit of the age, *zeitgeist*, 420
Spitteler, C., 228, 230
Spitzer, Leo
    Linguistics and Literary History,
    197–200; philological circle,
    198–200
Sprat, Thomas
    *History of the Royal
    Society*, **105–6**
Stael, Madame de, 439
Stanislavski, 68
Starkie, Enid M., 247
Steiner, George, 494
Steiner, Peter, 271
Stendhal, 57, 322
    Scarlet and Black, 529
Stephen, Fitzjames, 538
Stern, J. P., 45
Sterne, Laurence
    Tristram Shandy, 269, 276–7, 338
Stevens, Wallace, 11, 98
    The Necessary Angel, **36–9**;
    supreme fictions, 38
Stewart, Dugald, 127
Stoll, E. E., 314
Stone, P. W. K., 6
Strindberg, J. A., 43
structuralism, 1, 2, 7, 44, 77, 96,
    98, 128, 150, 239, 244, 291,
    301, 343–7, 351–79, 381–2,
    388, 396, 401, 416, 421–2,
    434–40
Sturt, George
    Change in the Village, 492
style, 43, 55, 57–8, 96, 99–102,
    105, 112, 139, 165, 168,
    265–7, 276, 315, 321–35, 340,
    370, 491–2, 500–1
subject, the, 211–12, 223, 239–41,
    290, 294, 300, 305, 318, 346,
    363, 383, 389, 407, 455,
    460–3, 534
subjectivism, 64–6
subjectivity, 4, 81, 123–241, 243,

248–9, 259, 262, 268, 305,
    364, 395, 465, 534
sublime, 57, 90, 92, 150–4, 164–5,
    167–9, 171–2, 270, 311,
    330–1, 496
Suleiman, Susan R., 190
Surrealism, 262, 371
Swift, Jonathan, 173
    Gulliver's Travels, 276
symbol, 112, 220–1, 229, 231,
    317–18
symbolic, *see* Cassirer, Langer,
    Kristeva
Symbolism, 31–5, 262, 285
Symonds, J. A., 420
Symons, Arthur
    *The Symbolist Movement in
    Literature*, 31

Tacitus, 309
Taine, Hippolyte A., 402, 419
    History of English Literature,
    423–6
Tasso, Torquato, 484
Tate, Allen, 167, 338–9
    extension/intension, 283–5;
    'Tension in Poetry', **283–5**
technique, 278, 286–8, 309, 338,
    341, *see also* device
tendentiousness, 63
Tennyson, Alfred, 34, 429
    'Break, break, break', 512
Terence, 41, 156
textuality, 243–4, 268, 300–2,
    319–20, 387–8, 468
Thackeray, W. M., 341, 502
Thibaudeau, Jean, 366
Thompson, E. M., 271
Thompson, E. P., 402
Thorpe, C. D., 129
Tibullus, 412
Tillotson, Kathleen, 339
Tillyard, E. M. W., 420–2
    *The Elizabethan World
    Picture*, **428–31**; world
    picture, 402, 429
Todorov, Tzvetan, 6, 347, 390–2
    Grammar of the Decameron, 391
Tolstoy, Leo N., 71, 275, 366,
    460, 464–5

Anna Karenina, 358, 370;
'Kholstomer', 275–6;
Resurrection, 359; *War and Peace*, 370
Tompkins, Jane P., 190
Tönnies, Fernand, 530
topoi (topics), 401, 406, 412–14
Torode, Brian, 292
Toynbee, Arnold, 411
tradition, 5, 211, 401, 405–17, 431–2, 450–1, 517, 531–2
tragi-comedy, 82
tragedy, 15, 17, 23, 40, 45–9, 57–8, 82–4, 149, 155, 171, 174, 191, 193–5, 232, 268, 271–2, 280, 321–2, 328, 330–2, 336, 349–50, 358
Trilling, Lionel, 490–1, 494
Beyond Culture, **517–18**; *A Gathering of Fugitives*, 491, **516–17**
Trimpi, Wesley, 98
Troeltsch, Ernst, 411
tropes, 100, 101, 105, 380, 390, 392, 406
Trotsky, Leon, 269
Tucker, Abraham, 127
type, 59, 80, 458

Ullman, S., 324
unconscious, 26, 222–41, 290, 396, 417, 427, 463–4
unities, *see* Aristotle
unity, 60, 62–3, 128, 145, 149, 181, 197, 268, 270, 271–4, 290, 295, 299, 378, 381, 384, 496
universal, 27, 29, 41, 50, 59, 62, 68, 80, 140, 143, 245, 248, 278, 282, 345, 411, 419, 474, 478, 496, *see also* general

Valdés, Mario J., 190
Verrocchio, Andrea del, 39
Vickers, Brian, 98
Virgil, 80, 86, 155, 157, 410, 497
Vivante, L., 233
Voitle, R. B., 475
Vološinov, V. N., 291

Waller, Edmund, 135
Warren, A. H., 167
Warren, Austin, 6, 129
Warton, Joseph, 165
An Essay on . . . Pope, **173–4**
Weedon, Chris, 457
Weimann, Robert, 407
Wellek, René, 6, 12, 45, 211, 247, 271, 423
Wells, H. G., 540
West, Jessamyn, 339
White, Hayden, 380
Whitehead, A. N., 406
Whitman, Walt, 121
Wilde, Oscar, 245, 490
The Decay of Lying, 246, **252–4**; *The Importance of Being Earnest*, 335
Willey, Basil, 98
Williams, Raymond, 6, 45, 402, 492, 519
The Country and the City, 441, 522; *Culture and Society*, 471, 520; key-word, 434; *The Long Revolution*, 406, **414–15**, 421, **431–4**, **526–30**; *Marxism and Literature*, 406; *Politics and Letters*, 520; selective tradition, 406, 415; structure of feeling, 414
Williams, William Carlos, 379
Williamson, George, 98
Wilson, Edmund, 247
The Wound and the Bow, 454
Wimsatt, W. K., 6, 153, 290, 305, 394
'The Affective Fallacy', 167; affective fallacy, the, 304; 'The Intentional Fallacy', **314–16**; intentional fallacy, the, 304
wit, 84, 85, 101, 132, 133, 135, 139, 173, 187, 192
Wittgenstein, Ludvig, 7, 98, 213
language games, 95, 115–19; *Philosophical Investigations*, 95, **115–19**; picture view of language, 95–6, 98; *Tractatus Logico-Philosophicus*, 116
Wolff, Janet, 305

Wollheim, Richard, 407
women's writing, 471, 532–43
Woolf, Virginia, 41, 322, 358,
    521–2, 536, 539
  A Room of One's Own, 522,
    532–3
Wordsworth, William, 3, 10,
    80–1, 124, 127, 142–4, 152,
    178–9, 182, 298, 303–4, 373,
    382, 396, 500, 510, 512
  'Intimations of Immortality',
    179; Preface to *Lyrical Ballads*,
    86–8, 175–8
world view, 422, *see also*
    Goldmann and Tillyard
Wright, Elizabeth, 225
Wycherley, William, 425

Xenarchus, 46
Xenophon, 168

Yale School, 381
Yeats, W. B., 11, 490, 517–18
  'The Symbolism of Poetry',
    31–5
Yonge, Charlotte, 538
Young, Edward, 405
  *Conjectures on Original
    Composition*, 151–2, **158–61**
Young, Robert, 383

Zeuxis, 49, 50
Zhdanov, A. A., 470, 475
  'Soviet Literature', **487–8**;
    revolutionary romanticism,
    487–8
Zola, Emile, 8, 40, 41–2, 458
  'The Experimental Novel',
    51–3; *Germinal*, 359;
    'Naturalism on the Stage',
    54–6